The Legal System of Scotland:
Cases and Materials

The Legal System of Scotland: Cases and Materials

A. A. PATERSON,
LL.B. (Edin.), D. Phil. (Oxon.), Solicitor

Professor of Law,
University of Strathclyde

&

T. St.J. N. BATES,
M.A., LL.M. (Cantab.)

Clerk of Tynwald,
Secretary of the House
of Keys and Counsel to the
Speaker, Isle of Man

Visiting Professor of Law,
University of Strathclyde

THIRD EDITION

EDINBURGH
W. GREEN/SWEET & MAXWELL
1993

First edition 1983
Second edition 1986
Third edition 1993

ISBN 0 414 01069 8

Printed in Great Britain by
M&A Thomson Litho Ltd.

To our families from whom the time was stolen

Alison and Jane

Christopher, Rachel, Michael, David and Helen

PREFACE

A legal system is the product of its time, yet it must draw on the past and prepare for the future. It thus behoves those concerned with the Scottish legal system not only to honour its past achievement but also to examine its present operation and respond to future needs. In this book emphasis is placed on a critical analysis of some of the contemporary aspects of the Scottish legal system and its future development.

That it has remained possible to maintain this approach is a measure of the continuing work of others. As this is essentially a cases and materials book, our primary debt is to those on whose work we have drawn, and to colleagues who have read and commented on selected drafts of earlier editions of the book. For their assistance with the third edition we are particularly grateful to Mrs. June Brown, Mr. Kenneth Christine, Dr. Eric Clive, Mrs. Caroline Dunn, Mr. Alistair Henry, Mr. Jim Murdoch, Ms. Caroline Murray, Mrs. Pam O'Connor, and the staff of the London and Manx Offices of Travers Smith Braithwaite.

We also wish to thank the following for permission to use copyright materials in the more extended extracts: Allen & Unwin Ltd., All Souls College Oxford, Basil Blackwell Ltd., Messrs. Butterworth & Co. Ltd., Castlemilk Law Centre, the Controller of Her Majesty's Stationery Office, Deborah Charles Publications, Edinburgh University Press, the Faculty of Advocates, Glasgow University Press, W. Green & Son Ltd., Justice, the Incorporated Council of Law Reporting for England and Wales, the Law Book Co. of Australia, the Law Centres' Federation, the Law Society of Scotland, the Legal Action Group, Levy & McRae, Martin Robertson & Co., Oceana Publications Inc., Octagon Books, the Office of Parliamentary Counsel, Oxford University Press, S.L.S. Legal Publications, Scottish Academic Press Ltd., the Scottish Association of Citizens' Advice Bureaux, the Scottish Council of Law Reporting, the Scottish Courts Administration, the Scottish Office, the Stair Society, Stevens & Sons Ltd., Sweet & Maxwell Ltd.; the publishers and editors of the *British Journal of Law and Society,* the *Journal of Social Policy,* the *Journal of Social Welfare Law,* the *Journal of the Society of Public Teachers of Law,* the *Law Quarterly Review, Legal Action,* the *Modern Law Review,* the *New Law Journal,* the *Liverpool Law Review,* the *Northern Ireland Law Quarterly, Public Law, SCOLAG Bulletin,* the *Statute Law Review;* Professor J.W.G. Blackie; Professor A.W. Bradley; the Hon. Lord Cameron; Professor C.M. Campbell; Lord Devlin; Professor T.C. Hartley; Mr. P. Lewis; Professor D.R. Miers; Mr. A.D. Miller; Professor W.L. Twining; Professor B. Schwartz; Mr. E. Sutherland; Professor H.W.R. Wade and Professor M. Zander.

The book is intended primarily for the undergraduate law student. In order to keep it within the means of the student, the tables of cases and

PREFACE

statutes include only those from which extracts have been taken and not all those cited, although in the absence of economic constraints complete tables would be preferable.

September 1993.   A. A. P.
                                                            T. St.J. N. B.

CONTENTS

EXCERPTS OF CASES

EXCERPTS OF LEGISLATION AND TREATIES

EXCERPTS OF BOOKS, ARTICLES etc.

CHAPTER 1

THE SHERIFF COURT

I. STRUCTURE AND ADMINISTRATION

Courts are normally classified according to their powers, their area of operation or the types of case they are permitted to handle. As the Grant Report observed (p. 7) the principal distinguishing features of the sheriff court are that it is local, it is presided over by professional judges and it has an extensive jurisdiction in both civil and criminal cases as well as possessing a wide range of administrative functions.

While the history of the court stems back to the 12th century its structure and administration in modern times is controlled by the Sheriff Courts (Scotland) Acts of 1907 and 1971. Thus, Scotland is now divided into six sheriffdoms which largely consist of groupings of local authority region or islands authorities. The sheriffdoms are (1) Grampian, Highland and Islands; (2) Tayside, Central and Fife; (3) Lothian and Borders; (4) Glasgow and Strathkelvin; (5) North Strathclyde; and (6) South Strathclyde, Dumfries and Galloway. The six sheriffdoms are subdivided into sheriff court districts of which there are currently 49, each of which has its own sheriff court building. Each sheriffdom has a sheriff principal who in addition to his judicial duties is under a duty "to secure the speedy and efficient disposal of business in the sheriff courts of that sheriffdom" (Sheriff Courts (Scotland) Act 1971, s. 15).

In addition to sheriffs principal there are 97 or so sheriffs who act as the judges at first instance in the sheriffdoms (although they are usually appointed to serve in a particular sheriff court district). Sheriffs, too, have wide-ranging administrative duties.

The Secretary of State for Scotland is responsible for the staffing, overall organisation and administration of the sheriff courts. In pursuance of this responsibility he may create or abolish sheriffdoms and sheriff court districts or alter their boundaries. He may also create temporary sheriffs and sheriffs principal or transfer sheriffs from one sheriffdom to another if this is required by illness, pressure of business or other like cause. In fact, since 1971 the functions of the Secretary of State in this area have been delegated to a civil service department known as Scottish Courts Administration. A further body, the Sheriff Courts Rules Council, which consists of sheriffs principal, sheriffs, sheriff clerks, practitioners in the sheriff court and consumer representatives is responsible for monitoring the operation of procedure and practice in civil proceedings in the court and for suggesting reforms.

1

II. CIVIL JURISDICTION

The civil jurisdiction of the sheriff court—those cases which it has the power to try and dispose of—is unusually wide for a local (or inferior) court.

H.M.S.O., *The Legal System of Scotland*, pp. 16–17

"3.10 At common law, the sheriff is 'judge ordinary of the bounds', that is to say, the judge of first instance having jurisdiction in all cases arising in his sheriffdom which are not allocated to other courts by express statutory provisions or common law rules. (By contrast, in England and Wales, the county court is a creature of statute exercising only jurisdiction conferred and defined by statute.) Partly for this reason the sheriff court's jurisdiction is very wide. Many different types of action may be brought there. The value of the subject matter which the court can deal with has, with very few exceptions, no upper limit, and a wide range of remedies may be granted."

For a civil court to have jurisdiction in a particular case it must (a) have authority over the defender, or the subjects in respect of which the remedy is sought, (b) have the power to grant the remedy sought, and (c) have the power to entertain the cause in question.

A. AUTHORITY OVER DEFENDER OR SUBJECT MATTER

This is primarily a geographical limitation on the courts' powers. The general rule is that a case must be raised in the forum of the defender. This is partly an equitable requirement and partly a pragmatic one. Scottish courts are reluctant to grant a decree which is unenforceable. (See *Ford* v. *Bell Chandler*, 1977 S.L.T. (Sh. Ct.) 90.)

Sheriff Courts (Scotland) Act 1907, s.4

"4. *Jurisdiction.*—The jurisdiction of the sheriffs, within their respective sheriffdoms, shall extend to and include all navigable rivers, ports, harbours, creeks, shores, and anchoring grounds in or adjoining such sheriffdoms. And the powers and jurisdictions formerly competent to the High Court of Admiralty in Scotland in all [civil] maritime causes and proceedings . . . including such as may apply to persons furth of Scotland, shall be competent to the sheriffs, provided the defender shall upon any legal ground of jurisdiction be amenable to the jurisdiction of the sheriff before whom such cause or proceeding may be raised . . . Provided always that where sheriffdoms are separated by a river, firth, or estuary, the sheriffs on either side shall have concurrent jurisdiction over the intervening space occupied by water."

Domicile and Matrimonial Proceedings Act 1973, s. 8(2)

"8.—(2) The court shall have jurisdiction to entertain an action for separation [or separation and aliment or divorce] if (and only if)—

(*a*) either party to the marriage in question—

(i) is domiciled in Scotland at the date when the action is begun, or

(ii) was habitually resident there throughout the period of one year ending with that date; and

(*b*) either party to the marriage—

(i) was resident in the sheriffdom for a period of forty days ending with that date, or

(ii) had been resident in the sheriffdom for a period of not less than forty days ending not more than forty days before the said date, and had no known residence in Scotland at that date."

[The sheriff court has jurisdiction in actions of declarator of death under the Presumption of Death (Scotland) Act 1977, s. 1(4), which contains provisions on the lines of s. 8(2).]

In other cases the position is governed by the Civil Jurisdiction and Judgments Acts 1982 and 1991. The former Act gives effect to the E.C. (Brussels) Conventions on jurisdiction and the enforcement of judgments in civil and commercial matters. The latter Act implements the closely paralleling Lugano Convention which extends essentially the same jurisdiction and enforcement rules to those E.F.T.A. countries which choose to ratify it. (The Conventions do not cover status, matrimonial property rights, succession, bankruptcy, liquidation, social security, arbitration, revenue or administrative cases.) Nowadays defenders are subject to four slightly different sets of rules on jurisdiction, although the basic rule that the case must follow the defender is still retained. Defenders domiciled in the territory of a contracting E.F.T.A. state whose cases fall within the Lugano Convention are governed by Schedule 1 to the 1991 Act. Defenders from other E.C. countries whose cases fall within the Brussels Conventions are governed by Schedule 1 of the 1982 Act, similarly placed defenders from other U.K. countries are governed by Schedule 4 to the 1982 Act and defenders in all other cases except those relating to status, capacity, custody, liquidation/sequestration, admiralty matters, commissary proceedings and appeals/review of tribunal decisions are governed by Schedule 7 to the 1982 Act.

In essence all defenders covered by the Acts may be sued in the courts for the place where they are resident and with which they have a substantial connection. In addition they may be sued in a particular sheriff court:

(1) if the case relates to a contract which is to be performed within the jurisdiction of that court;

(2) if the case relates to delict or quasi-delict and the harmful event took place within the jurisdiction of that court;

(3) if the case relates to a civil claim for damages arising from events which are the subject of criminal proceedings before that court:

(4) if the case relates to maintenance and the maintenance creditor is habitually resident within the jurisdiction of that court or if the matter is ancillary to proceedings relating to status and that court has jurisdiction under the Domicile and Matrimonial Proceedings Act 1973;

(5) if the case arises out of the operations of a branch, agency or other establishment located within the jurisdiction of that court;

(6) if there are a number of defenders and one of them is resident and has substantial ties with a place within the jurisdiction of that court;

(7) if the case is a counter claim arising from the same contract or facts which have given rise to a case which is pending before that court;

(8) if the case relates to the ownership or tenancy of immoveable property which is situated within the jurisdiction of that court;

(9) if the defenders have prorogated, *i.e.* accepted, the jurisdiction of that court by express agreement or by entering appearance before the court to oppose the action;

(10) if the case relates to a consumer contract completed in Scotland and the consumer or the defender resides in, and has substantial ties with a place within the jurisdiction of that court.

In cases where Schedule 7 applies defenders may also be sued in a particular sheriff court:

(1) if they have no fixed residence and they have been personally cited within the jurisdiction of that court;

(2) if they have no fixed residence in the United Kingdom and moveable property belonging to them has been arrested, or they own moveable property situated within the jurisdiction of that court;

(3) if the proceedings relate to moveable property situated within the jurisdiction of that court;

(4) if the proceedings are for interdict and it is alleged that the wrong is likely to be committed within the jurisdiction of that court;

(5) if the proceedings concern a debt secured over immoveable property situated within the jurisdiction of that court.

[For further details on the history and intention of the 1982 Act see the Report of the Scottish Committee on Jurisdiction and Enforcement (H.M.S.O.: 1980). For a further exposition of the provisions of the Acts see A.E. Anton, *Civil Jurisdiction in Scotland* (W. Green & Son: 1984) with a *Supplement* (with P. Beaumont) (1987) and P. Beaumont's annotations to the Current Law Statutes Annotated version of the Civil Jurisdiction and Judgments Act 1991.]

The geographical limitations contained within these provisions are not as restrictive as they may appear. Sheriffs acting under the Sheriff Courts (Scotland) Act 1907, Schedule 1, rule 20 may, upon sufficient cause, remit a case to be heard in another sheriffdom.

Wilson v. Hay
1977 S.L.T. (Sh. Ct.) 52

SHERIFF PRINCIPAL REID: "I respectfully adopt the view expressed in Fyfe in *Sheriff Court Practice*, para. 154: 'The theory of the transfer rules seems to be that the whole Sheriff Courts of Scotland are to be regarded practically as one system, that the hard and fast jurisdiction rules which have hitherto prevailed are to be relaxed, and that a Sheriff Court cause, in whatever district it is initiated, may be tried in that Sheriff Court which affords the maximum of convenience, at the minimum of expense, to all concerned.' . . . Rule 20 is expressed in terms sufficiently wide to enable causes to be transferred between courts having concurrent jurisdiction: or from a court having no jurisdiction to a court possessing jurisdiction; or vice versa (cf. Dobie, *Sheriff Court Practice*, p. 45). . . . It is hardly necessary to say that it is essential that either the transferring court or the court to which the cause is transferred should have jurisdiction over the defender. Otherwise, the matter is one for the sheriff's discretion."

B. POWER TO GRANT THE REMEDY

Sheriffs can grant a number of remedies. These include: petitory remedies (*e.g.* for payment, delivery or implement of a contract), actions of declarator (except declarators of marriage or nullity of marriage, and actions the direct or main object of which is to determine the personal status of individuals), actions for damages, possessory actions, suspensions and interdicts. (See the Sheriff Courts (Scotland) Act 1907, s. 5.)

C. POWER TO ENTERTAIN THE CAUSE

On policy grounds it is commonplace for the inferior courts in a country to be denied the more important cases. The sheriff court is unusual in this respect, since it has considerable breadth of jurisdiction. Some causes may only be heard in the sheriff court.

These are its privative or exclusive jurisdiction. Thus, under the Sheriff Courts (Scotland) Act 1907, s. 7 (as amended):

"All causes not exceeding one thousand five hundred pounds in value exclusive of interest and expenses competent in the sheriff court shall be brought and followed forth in the sheriff court only, and shall not be subject to review by the Court of Session."

[Privative Jurisdiction and Summary Cause Order 1988, S.I. No. 1993.]

Again, the sheriff court alone can entertain actions for summary removing (eviction from heritable property) and sequestration for non-payment of rent.

Duncan v. Lodijensky
(1904) 6 F. 408

LORD MCLAREN: "I never heard of an action of sequestration for rent being brought in the Court of Session. In the institutional writers reference is made to a class of actions in which the Judge Ordinary of the bounds has privative jurisdiction. It is hardly necessary to give instances, but there is a class of cases which are only competent in the Sheriff Court, and in which an action brought to the Court of Session would be dismissed as incompetent. The general character of such cases is that they relate to questions as to property within the sheriffdom in which there is a necessity for immediate decision, such, for example, as warrants for the sale of a pledge or for the sale of perishable articles when the right of possession is disputed. There can be no doubt that cases between the landlord and tenant of property situated within the Sheriff's territory have always been regarded as specially suited for decision in the Sheriff Court."

On the other hand there are remarkably few areas where the jurisdiction of the sheriff court is now excluded. The principal exclusion long related to actions affecting personal status. However, divorce actions (Divorce Jurisdiction, Court Fees and Legal Aid (Scotland) Act 1983) and declarator of death actions (Presumption of Death (Scotland) Act 1977) have become competent in the sheriff courts. Indeed, the great majority of divorce actions are now brought in the sheriff courts rather than the Court of Session (which formerly had exclusive jurisdiction in such cases). Thus in 1983 90% of family actions were heard in the Court of Session and only 10% in the sheriff court. By 1988 the ratio had been more than reversed with 7% in the Court of Session and 93% in the sheriff court. Somewhat anomalously there are still certain actions affecting personal status which are privative to the Court of Session.

Court of Session Act 1830, s. 33

"33. All actions of declarator of marriage, and of nullity of marriage, and all actions of declarator of legitimacy and of bastardy . . . shall be competent to be brought and insisted on only before the Court of Session."

Secondly, petitions for the liquidation of a limited company with a paid up share capital exceeding £120,000 can only be heard in the Court of Session (Companies Act 1985, s. 515).

The Grant Report, p. 24

"Also exclusive to the Court of Session are actions of reduction, actions for proving the tenor of lost documents, adjudications and inhibitions. There are also some actions which are exclusive to courts other than the Court of Session: thus, the Court of the Lord Lyon deals with questions of right to bear arms, the Lands Valuation Appeal Court with appeals against rateable valuations, and the Restrictive Practices Court with monopolistic practices."

These limitations apart, the sheriff court has a broad-ranging concurrent or overlapping jurisdiction with the Court of Session. Thus in contrast with the position in the English county court, there are no financial limits to the cases which a sheriff may hear. (With the sole exception of certain liquidation petitions, as we have seen.) Cases worth over a million pounds have been brought before the court. The Grant Committee considered whether such limits should be imposed but decided against the change. As the Committee noted, "the importance and difficulty of an action need not be directly related to the sum sued for." What was needed, they felt, was a flexible remit procedure between the sheriff court and the Court of Session.

The rules governing remits from the sheriff court to the Court of Session were eventually simplified under s. 16 of the Law Reform (Miscellaneous Provisions) (Scotland) Act 1980. This section permits a sheriff to remit a case on the motion of one of the parties "if he is of the opinion that the importance or difficulty of the cause make it appropriate to do so." [See *Mullan* v. *Anderson* 1993 S.L.T. 835.] Only if the action relates to custody or adoption may the sheriff remit the action of his own accord. Under section 44 of the Crown Proceedings Act 1947, proceedings raised against the Crown in the sheriff court must be remitted to the Court of Session if the Lord Advocate certifies that the proceedings may involve an important question of law, or may be decisive of other cases, or are for other reasons more fit for trial in the Court of Session.

It is unclear whether the flexibility which the Grant Report was seeking has been achieved. The reforms abolished the power of either party to insist that a case be remitted and restricted the freedom of sheriffs to remit a case of their own accord.

The provisions as to remits raise the longstanding question as to whether the division of labour between the sheriff court and the Court of Session is a rational one. This is not a question that appears to have received much attention in recent years in Scotland (with the exception of the legislative decision to restrict judicial review to the Court of Session) although the English county court has been the subject of numerous reviews. In each, the jurisdiction of the county court has been expanded—though it remains considerably narrower than that of the sheriff court. In the light of the most recent developments concerning status actions it must be questionable whether the sheriff court should not now have parallel jurisdiction with the Court of Session in all status actions.

In a series of cases in the last decade the Court of Session has made it clear that where actions are raised in that court which should, because of the size of the awards sought and the straightforwardness of the action, more appropriately have been raised in the sheriff court then the expenses awarded will be modified to the ordinary sheriff court scale. [See *Smith* v. *British Rail Engineering Ltd.*, 1985 S.L.T. 463, *McPherson* v. *British Railways Board*, 1985 S.L.T. 467, *Banks* v. *D.R.G. plc*, 1988 S.L.T. 825 and *McIntosh* v. *British Railways Board (No. 1)*, 1990 S.L.T. 637.]

III. PROCEDURE AND CASELOAD

A. ORDINARY CAUSE PROCEDURE

There are now two procedures in civil sheriff court cases, the ordinary and the summary cause. The great majority of actions which are competent within the sheriff court must be raised under the ordinary procedure. Such actions are heard by a sheriff sitting on his or her own or (occasionally) with an assessor. Civil jury trials are no longer competent in the sheriff court. The range of ordinary actions is considerable. It extends from actions for payment or delivery in excess of £1,500 to racial discrimination cases (outside the field of employment), from succession to copyright and from landlord and tenant (*e.g. Holiday Flat Co.* v. *Kuczera*, 1978 S.L.T. (Sh. Ct.) 47) to contravention of lawburrows. Lawburrows is a remedy akin to requiring caution for good behaviour. If a defender who has been ordained to find caution does any harm of the kind specified in the original application, a civil action of contravention of lawburrows can be raised against him. [See W. J. Stewart, "Lawburrows: Elegant Remedy or Absurd Form," 1988 S.L.T. (News) 181 and the case of *Morrow* v.

Neil, below.] Divorce actions must also be raised under the ordinary procedure, but where (1) the divorce is evidenced by separation (whether for two or five years), (2) there are no children of the marriage under 16 and (3) no financial claims, a simplified "do-it-yourself" procedure may be used.

TABLE 1

Ordinary Actions in 1991

Nature of Action	Initiated during Year	Disposed of					Pending at year end
		By final judgment		Remit to Court of Session	Taken out of court	Total	
		Unde-fended	De-fended				
Debt.	30,118	16,869	1,271	6	7,362	28,120	18,820
Delivery	1,032	582	40	—	303	994	806
Land or heritable estate	7,899	5,662	158	—	1,553	7,537	3,650
Personal injury .	1,072	76	85	—	508	968	1,407
Damages	653	68	28	—	370	594	886
Divorce	10,078	6,125	1,159	1	1,642	9,205	7,846
Furthcoming . .	132	77	8	—	25	112	98
Separation and aliment. . . .	87	28	12	—	50	102	124
Adherence and aliment. . . .	108	28	28	—	11	77	112
Custody and aliment. . . .	2,231	621	358	—	1,045	2,226	2,432
Variation of Court of Session decrees	131	50	34	—	44	139	131
Other actions . .	4,842	1,506	350	—	2,160	4,438	5,078
Grand total	58,383	31,692	3,531	7	15,073	54,512	41,390

[Source: Scottish Courts Administration.]

Table 1 reflects a pattern which has held true for many years, namely, that money claims, and debt actions in particular, predominate. There are, however, substantial numbers of divorce actions and landlord and tenant cases. In the last decade the number of ordinary actions raised in the sheriff courts has more than doubled, largely because of the transfer in divorce jurisdiction. The increase has led to a major reconsideration of the ordinary cause procedure designed to eliminate unnecessary delays, complexity and expense. It remains to be seen whether the introduction of the new rules will significantly alter the pattern of litigation in the ordinary cause. Thus, while 53% of personal injury actions in 1991 were defended at the time of the final judgment, only 37% of the aliment and 7% of the debt actions were so defended. This, taken together with the high proportion of ordinary debt actions which are unopposed reveals that even under the ordinary cause procedure debt actions are largely "administrative" (*i.e.* a rubber-stamp en route to diligence) rather than adversarial in character.

B. SUMMARY CAUSE PROCEDURE

Summary causes are regulated by the Sheriff Courts (Scotland) Act 1971, ss. 35–38 and by Act of Sederunt (Summary Cause Rules, Sheriff Court) 1976 (S.I. 1976 No. 476 (S. 44)) (as amended).

The Hughes Commission, p. 174

"11.11 The present summary cause procedure in the sheriff court was introduced in 1976 in the light of the recommendations of the Grant Committee. The main purpose of its introduction was to provide a procedure that was both efficient and cheap. The summary cause does not normally involve written pleadings and the lengthy procedure of adjustment that goes with the ordinary cause; there is no recording of evidence at the hearing itself. In most actions for the payment of money, the procedures can easily be carried through without the parties being required to appear in court—a considerable advantage in preventing loss of wages and travelling expenses. Appearance is required only when the action is defended, or when there is some dispute about the method of payment. Broadly speaking, the actions which may be brought by the summary cause procedure include most consumer claims, actions by corporate bodies for the recovery of debts, claims for the recovery of heritable property (for example repossession by commercial landlords or local authorities following non-payment of rent) and claims for damages where the sum involved does not exceed [£1,500]. The rules setting out the procedure and forms are complex and extend to some fifty pages."

Act of Sederunt (Summary Cause Rules, Sheriff Court) 1976, r. 17

"*Representation*

17.—(1) Except as hereinafter provided a party who does not elect to conduct his own cause shall be represented by an advocate or solicitor.

(2) A party shall be entitled to be represented by a person other than an advocate or solicitor at the first calling of a summary cause, and, unless the court at that calling otherwise directs, at any subsequent diet where the cause is not defended on the merits or on the amount of sum due:
Provided that the court in that cause is satisfied that the person is a suitable representative and is duly authorised to represent the party."

[Section 37 of the Sheriff Courts (Scotland) Act 1971 confers powers on sheriffs in certain circumstances to remit cases from the ordinary to the summary cause and vice versa.]

The limits on the type of case which can be raised under the summary cause procedure are such that the overwhelming majority of summary cause actions raised since its introduction in 1976 have been debt related. Most have been straightforward debt actions with almost a quarter relating to the non-payment of rent. Despite the provision for lay representation, in the great majority of summary cause actions the defender is unrepresented and no defence is entered. Unsurprisingly, over 90% of pursuers are public utilities or businesses with the great bulk of defenders being individuals. It follows that the summary cause procedure is even more administrative in character than the ordinary procedure.

Central Research Unit, "Debt Recovery," pp. 53–54

"6.11 . . . The court stage is largely an administrative procedure, and this is highlighted by the fact that in most cases the defender did not dispute the claim against him; only a small portion of cases went to proof (less than 1 per cent of summary cause payment actions) or were continued for several callings (4 per cent of summary cause payment actions continued at the first calling) thereby indicating an element of dispute about liability or delay in coming to an arrangement for payment for some reason or other. The majority of actions were undefended and only 3 per cent of defenders in summary cause payment actions were represented in court and only 8 per cent of pursuers.

6.12 . . . However, the court stage, from the delivery of the summons to the defender to the granting of decree, appears to play an important constructive role in the process of debt recovery as well as being the legal precursor of the doing of diligence. The court stage does this mainly by acting as a channel of, or spur to, communication between the debtor and creditor. The raising of court action itself may result in full settlement of the debt to the pursuer or may encourage the debtor to make an informal instalment arrangement for repayment; this is generally the background to the relatively large number of actions which were dismissed following receipt of the summons by the defender (30 per cent). It also may stimulate the resolution of disputes about, *e.g.* the amount owed, or defective goods and services."

The cheap and efficient procedure favoured by the Grant Committee simply transformed the sheriff court into a streamlined debt-collecting agency. This exactly replicated the experience in the United States.

Cavenagh and Sarat, "Thinking about Courts," p. 389

"In theory, small claims courts were courts for the 'ordinary person'; in theory, their informal procedures promoted access to justice for consumers, tenants, and others supposedly disadvantaged through market transactions.

In fact, many small claims courts were quickly recognized by creditors as the happy equivalent of state-subsidized debt collection agencies. The result: high volumes of debt actions in the state courts most conveniently available to creditors, typically resulting in default judgments for plaintiffs. 'In major cities, 75 per cent of all contract claims filed in courts of limited jurisdiction may end in default judgments' . . . Yngvesson and Hennessey (1975) . . . drew from a review of fourteen empirical studies of small claims courts a common theme: 'all of the studies point to the high number of business plaintiffs, the high number of non-business "individual" defendants (frequently identified as low-income consumers), and a high default rate.' "

The Hughes Commission, pp. 175–176

"11.15 The summary cause serves a useful purpose in disposing of routine cases of undisputed debt but it does not appear to encourage individuals to pursue claims—either individual claims for debt or consumer and other claims. There seems to be substantial public ignorance of the summary cause procedure. In our survey of legal needs some 99 per cent of respondents had no knowledge or only inaccurate knowledge of the summary cause procedure. This public ignorance is no doubt compounded by the uninformative name of the summary cause procedure. Another reason, however, appears to be the complexity of the procedure. . . . It is doubtful whether many people would be willing or competent to conduct their own cases in summary cause, even if they had heard of it or understood what it was. Indeed, the formalities make it impossible for the party litigant to conduct the whole case himself without professional assistance. A solicitor or sheriff officer must be employed to effect service and solicitors may not be willing to perform the task unless they are engaged for the whole case. It follows that where claims for small sums of money are at issue, the cost of legal representation is a significant disincentive to taking legal action. In addition, the expenses of a summary cause case which are borne by the losing party can be considerable, particularly where an action is defended. Indeed, in actions for small sums, expenses can exceed the value of the claim involved."

Economides, "Small Claims and Procedural Justice," p. 113

"At a very basic level, the problem can be viewed as the result of 'process costs' exceeding the amount in controversy and perceived gains. It is simply uneconomic, not only for individuals but also for society at large, for parties to involve themselves and others in the litigation, adjudication or arbitration of disputes over small amounts of money. The most common response then, is to avoid or endure the grievance which gives rise to the dispute."

Hunter, "The Courts and the Legal Profession," pp. 212–213

"It may be asked why consumers rarely bring actions against the suppliers? The main reason is probably that the game is not usually worth the candle. Economies of scale make it possible for the supplier to litigate even where each individual action is for a relatively small, to him even quite trivial, sum; but the citizen as a consumer is only rarely placed in a situation in which he might reasonably consider legal proceedings against a supplier. In addition, many citizens are not aware of their legal rights and are not in the habit of consulting legal advisers. The voice of the consumer is now heard quite loudly in Parliament but is hardly more than a whisper in the ordinary courts."

The complexity of the summary cause procedure which undoubtedly inhibits party litigants can be gauged from the fact that there are some 95 rules, many of which would be difficult for most laymen to comprehend. Rule 68A (contained in S.I. 1980 No. 445) is one such rule.

"Actions against Persons in Possession of Heritable Property without Right or Title

68A. In an action for recovery of possession of heritable property against a person in possession *vi clam aut precario* and without right or title to possess or occupy that property, the sheriff may in his discretion and subject to rule 81A, shorten or dispense with any period of time provided anywhere in these rules. An application by a party under this rule to shorten or dispense with any such period may be made verbally and the provisions in rule 93(1) and (2) shall not apply, but the sheriff clerk shall enter details of any such application in the Book of Incidental Applications."

Further evidence of the complexities of the summary cause procedure comes from another report produced by the Central Research Unit where it discussed summary cause contested proofs.

Central Research Unit,
"The Dundee Small Claims Experiment", paras. 6.12, 6.19
"The people who attended a proof found it to be complicated and even more formal than they had anticipated. People who were not legally represented had difficulties in putting questions to witnesses, and found it difficult to explain their case in a way which was acceptable to the Sheriff, although most people said that the Sheriff had tried to help them, and had himself asked the witnesses questions. Almost all of the people who had been required to give evidence in court said that they had found it difficult to answer the questions put to them by solicitors, and many people expressed the view that solicitors asking questions was an unnecessary complicated way of establishing straightforward facts" (para. 6.12).
. . . [I]n cases in which a contested adjudication took place more dissatisfaction was expressed by summary cause defenders and particularly personal defenders in actions brought by firms:
"The common view was that under summary cause it was presumed that the money claimed was owed, and that it was up to the defender to

prove that he did not owe the sum or that he had withheld payment for good reasons ('guilty till able to prove self innocent'). This was considered by them to be extremely unfair and to run contrary to everything which the courts were supposed to do. A few people said that they had not had an opportunity to explain their side of a disputed case to the Sheriff, and they considered this to be very unfair. Each of these people had lost the action, and was certain that if the Sheriff had heard both sides of the case the outcome would have been different. However they stressed that even if the outcome had not altered they would have been prepared to accept a decision made by the Sheriff" (para. 6.19).

The procedure's complexities have also ensured that, with the exception of a few eviction actions, the provision for lay representation has been little utilised.

C. SMALL CLAIMS

The deficiencies of the summary cause procedure stem from the fact that it retains most of the features of a fully adversarial procedure. Yet around the world there has been a near universal movement in the past 30 years away from adjudication in small claims and towards such alternatives as conciliation, mediation and arbitration. Scotland has now begun tentatively to follow this path but the crucial problem is to determine how far the relaxation in formalities should go.

Economides, "Small Claims and Procedural Justice," p. 118
"In deciding whether, and to what degree, a dispute is to be resolved by reference to legal norms it can be noted that legal informality in procedure possesses the advantage of being relatively cheap, accessible and simple, and hence easily understandable to the disputants. On the other hand, fundamental principles of procedural natural justice stand in danger of being eroded. Where safeguards derived from legal formality are absent, the weaker party may feel inclined to compromise or settle for something less than he would receive were he to rely on the full enforcement of his legal rights. Conversely, legal formality, although safeguarding these core principles, does so in only a limited number of cases because it is relatively expensive, complex and hence inaccessible. The most promising approach to finding a solution to the small claims problem would appear to lie in a synthesis of both formal and informal justice."

Some countries have opted for a modified adversary procedure in their small claims courts, with the judge adopting a semi-inquisitorial role. In England and in many states in the U.S.A. an arbitration model has been favoured, while in other parts of the U.S.A. neighbourhood justice centres have relied on mediation and conciliation to resolve small claims disputes. In Queensland

and New South Wales the referees who handle small claims are even enjoined not to give decisions according to the law but to make orders which are "fair and equitable to the parties to the proceedings concerning the dispute."

In 1978 the Scottish Consumer Council put forward proposals for an experimental small claims scheme which was subsequently introduced (though not in the form favoured by the Council) in Dundee Sheriff Court for the years 1979, 1980 and 1981. The adjudicators (sheriffs) were urged to make hearings "as relaxed and informal as possible." An inquisitorial approach was adopted by adjudicators and the strict rules of evidence were dispensed with—adjudicators were even permitted to accept evidence by telephone. Unlike the summary cause, the rules were few (14), short (3 pages) and simple.

Although defects in the nature of the experiment led to only 52 claims being lodged under it in the three years, it was accepted to be a success both by the consumer groups and the researchers evaluating the experiment ("A Research-Based Evaluation of the Dundee Small Claims Experiment" by Anne Connor with Barbara Doig, Central Research Unit, Edinburgh, 1983). The Government agreed and produced a Consultation Paper on *Summary Cause and Small Claims Procedures in Sheriff Courts* in 1984. After discussions with interested parties the Government's proposals were considerably modified. The skeletal form of the new procedure for small claims is contained in s. 18 of the Law Reform (Miscellaneous Provisions) (Scotland) Act 1985. The full details of the small claims procedure (which is technically a new form of summary cause procedure) are contained in the Small Claims (Scotland) Order 1988 (S.I. 1988 No. 1999) and the Act of Sederunt (Small Claims Rules) 1988 (S.I. 1988 No. 1976). Small claims are defined as actions for payment for £750 or less or actions for delivery or recovery of possession of moveable property or for the implement of an obligation (actions *ad factum praestandum*) where there is an alternative claim for less than £750. In 1989, the first full year of the new procedure, 73,946 small claims were raised in Scotland. More than 99% of them were payment actions.

1. WHAT SHOULD THE GROUNDRULES BE?

Joint research by the Central Research Unit of the Scottish Office and the law faculties of Strathclyde and Dundee Universities which was published in 1991, *Small Claims in the Sheriff Courts in Scotland*, monitored the operation of the new procedure in its first 18 months. In the six courts studied by the researchers 92% of claims were raised by large businesses or public utilities. In the

great majority of these cases there was no dispute that the money
was owing and decree was obtained without a hearing. At first
sight this might suggest that there would be merit in following the
lead provided in numerous states in America where business and
commercial organisations are barred from the small claims courts.
However, such a move would exclude "reverse consumer" cases
(*e.g.* where the consumer declines to meet the full cost of a
product on the grounds that it is defective).

The real areas of dispute in defining small claims have proved to
be whether it was correct to include personal injury cases and
whether the upper limit should be above £750. As to the former,
critics from widely different sectors of the legal profession have
argued that it was an error to include such potentially complex
cases in the procedure. They have been fortified in their argument
by the fact that cases which are included under the small claims
procedure are not eligible for legal aid. As to the proper upper
limit, the Scottish Consumer Council have suggested that it should
be higher than £750 (so that second hand cars and three piece
suites would be covered) but others have objected to any increase
in the upper limit since it would have the effect of excluding
significantly greater numbers of litigants from legal aid and thus
legal representation. [See D. O'Carroll and P. Brown, "Small
Claims" (1991) 181 SCOLAG 154.] To some extent the problems
caused by the cut-off level have been offset by s. 37 of the Sheriff
Courts (Scotland) Act 1971 (as amended) which permits small
claims to be remitted by the consent of both parties or by the
sheriff on his or her own accord if the case is complex, to the
summary or ordinary cause. Conversely, cases over the limit can
be treated as small claims if the parties so agree.

As to the format of small claims hearings, it was accepted by all
involved with the introduction of the procedure that it should be
informal and that the strict rules of evidence should not apply. The
1985 Act specifically provided that rules of law relating to
admissibility or corroboration of evidence were not to be binding
in small claims hearings. The Act and the Rules, however, are
silent as to whether sheriffs should adopt an inquisitorial approach
to hearings in small claims. As a result the research found that the
majority of sheriffs continued to wear their wigs and gowns and
made no attempt to adopt an inquisitorial approach.

2. PRELIMINARY HEARINGS

One of the major features of the English small claims procedure to
date has been the provision for a pre-trial review at which the
judge ascertains the nature of the dispute, advises the parties as to

evidence which may be required at the proof and occasionally acts as a conciliator. Ironically, just as preliminary hearings were being introduced as part of the Scots procedure to perform a very similar function, the English Civil Justice Review recommended that pre-trial review be dispensed with except in housing, personal injury and other particularly complex or difficult cases.

The report of the joint research project indicates that in practice, of actions raised by individuals, 59% were concluded without a hearing of any kind, 25% were concluded at the preliminary hearing stage with only 16% of cases going beyond a preliminary hearing. In cases which went no further than a preliminary hearing, the pursuer attended the hearing in person in only 20% of cases and represented him or herself in only 10%. Few problems were reported in relation to these largely uncontested preliminary hearings. However, in contested cases which went beyond a preliminary hearing there was widespread dissatisfaction with preliminary hearings amongst both litigants and advisers.

Small Claims in the Sheriff Court in Scotland, pp. 28–9, 43–4, 63

"In all but one of the sample courts, small claims preliminary hearings were scheduled for the same time and in the same courtroom as other civil business. In most courts, these other cases involved procedural matters for ordinary actions or first callings for summary causes which were frequently heard before small claims. This meant that parties to small claims had to sit around the court for a considerable period of time before their cases were called. No prior notification of this practice appeared to be given to small claims litigants in court correspondence nor was the order of precedence of court business explained to the parties when they arrived in court. Thus, on a number of occasions, party litigants were left to sit in the public benches without necessarily understanding what was going on and wondering when their cases would be called. . . .

So far as litigants were concerned, over half of those with experience of preliminary hearings were alienated or made nervous by their attendance at court, even although they were only required to speak a little. The time that litigants had to wait for their cases to be called and the presence of solicitors and members of the public in court all contributed towards this feeling. Further, party litigants often seemed to have difficulty in following the proceedings. This was not only a function of their lack of legal knowledge but often was because it was difficult to hear what was being said in court due to the acoustics of the courtroom, the noise made by solicitors and others entering or leaving the court and the tendency for sheriffs and solicitors to discuss issues in very soft voices as if they were having a private conversation. Some party litigants even appeared not to hear what was being said during the course of their own preliminary

hearing. This happened frequently when asides were made by the sheriff
to the sheriff clerk or a solicitor. Also, although sheriffs did make efforts
to avoid the use of legalistic language, it was clear that there were
occasions when party litigants were unable to understand what was being
said. This was most likely to arise when the other party was represented
by a solicitor. Despite these difficulties many party litigants commented
positively on the role of the sheriff when the time came for their case to
be called; they felt that the sheriff had tried to put them at their ease in a
basically alien environment. . . .

   The lay advisers' views on preliminary hearings were uniformly
unfavourable. Again and again they reiterated the same complaints about
formality, inaudibility and exclusivity:

   'The consumer doesn't have a chance to put their case properly. They
are left standing near the table not knowing what to do, while the
solicitors sit sniggering.'

   'The sheriffs have been helpful or think that they are, but it is still
terrifying. Sheriffs don't understand the difficulty for people not used to
it. It is like a closed shop. They do not understand the concept of user-
friendliness.' "

3. REPRESENTATION

There is a continuing debate as to whether legal representation
should be permitted in small claims hearings since lawyers tend to
add to the formality of proceedings. While most systems do permit
such representation it is usually discouraged by the limits that are
placed on the expenses that can be recovered from the other side and
the fact that legal aid is not available for representation in small
claims cases. The Law Societies of Scotland and England favour the
retention of the profession's right of audience in these cases, though
some reformers do not. Others have argued that banning legal
representation would not greatly affect business organisations but it
might disadvantage inarticulate party litigants. One solution to this
might be to encourage lay representation or, as the National Consumer Council has proposed, to permit legal representation if the
interests of justice require it because of the size and complexity of the
claim or the respective capacities of the parties.

   The Small Claims Rules permit representation by laypersons and
lawyers and provide for the service of the summons by the sheriff
clerk in small claims cases where the pursuer is not a partnership
or a body corporate or acting in a representative capacity. Only
31% of pursuers interviewed in the research project took advantage of this facility, the other 69% using a solicitor to serve the
summons. Indeed 56% of pursuers and defenders had a legal
representative at hearings (preliminary or full). Very few used a
lay representative. For the minority of individuals who were not

represented, the two most common reasons given for non-representation were that they thought it was unnecessary and because of the expense of using a solicitor. While figures of this magnitude are a little discouraging, it should be remembered that in England and Wales where small claims have been going for nearly 15 years longer than in Scotland 34% of plaintiffs and 21% of defendants are still legally represented in small claims hearings. Both the English and the Northern Irish experience suggest that the need for representation will decline over time.

4. EXPENSES

The Dundee experiment revealed that the fear of substantial and unpredictable expense was a major disincentive to individuals using the summary cause procedure. In most small claims schemes there are reasonable maximum limits to recoverable expenses. Thus it is normal for such litigants to have to meet their own lawyers' fees, though other expenses, *e.g.* court fees, witness expenses and travel costs may be awarded at the discretion of the adjudicator/arbiter. The 1985 Act and the Small Claims Rules provide that for cases below £200 no expenses will be recoverable. In other small claims expenses may be awarded up to £75. In cases where the debt is admitted, the rules limiting awards of expenses do not apply (1) where no defence is stated or (2) where one is stated but it is not proceeded with or (3) where one is stated and proceeded with but the defender is considered not to have acted in good faith as to the merits of the defence. Fears that these provisions might lead to sheriffs routinely awarding expenses beyond the set limits have proved to be groundless. The research report found very few cases where expenses had been awarded because of frivolous conduct by the defender. Indeed the research found that the expenses rules had worked well subject to two caveats. First, the fact that court dues are not refunded to successful pursuers in cases worth less than £200 was felt by many to be unfair. Secondly, there was some feeling that expert witnesses costs ought to be recoverable in whole or in part, in cases where such evidence was genuinely felt to be necessary.

5. RIGHT OF APPEAL

If small claims schemes provided an unrestricted right of appeal, defenders might simply appeal every case they lost. For this reason some schemes contain no right of appeal, while others permit appeal only on a point of law, or on certification by the adjudicator. The small claims procedure (s. 38 of the Sheriff Courts (Scotland) Act 1971 (as amended)) provides for appeal to the

sheriff principal on any point of law from the final judgment of the
sheriff. Fears that this relatively generous provision for appeal
might lead commercial defenders to appeal every case in which
they had lost have also proved to be groundless. Of the 73,946
small claims raised in Scotland in 1989, only 46 went to an appeal.
(There were 43 appeals in 1990 and only 40 in 1991.)

6. POSSIBLE REFORMS

The conclusion of the research report was that the small claims
procedure had been only partially successful. While it was generally thought to be cheap and relatively quick there was less
consensus as to its simplicity and informality, particularly in
contested cases. The full hearings were considered by consumers
and lay advisers to be almost as formal as the preliminary hearings
and not particularly simple for litigants who were unrepresented.
Although the court staff were of the opinion that sheriffs had made
an effort to make the procedure more informal than in other
procedures in the sheriff court, from the layperson's perspective
they have not gone far enough. The research establishes once
again how difficult it is for lawyers to appreciate that their daily
world is an alien one for most laypersons. Nevertheless it should
be stressed that a clear majority of the parties interviewed in the
research felt that they had been fairly treated by the sheriffs.

The research report and the consultation paper from the Scottish
Courts Administration which accompanied its publication raised a
number of issues for consideration as potential reforms. The
principal ones included:

(a) **Doing away with the requirement of a preliminary hearing in
all or many cases**.

As we have seen this proposal is in line with the recommendations of the English Civil Justice Review in 1988. It would remove
perhaps the most unsatisfactory feature of the procedure (except
in complex or difficult cases).

(b) **Holding full hearings at more convenient times for party
litigants, e.g. fixed appointments, or evenings or Saturday
mornings.**

Since the publication of the report there have been limited (but
successful) experiments designed to implement each of these
proposals in particular sheriff courts.

(c) **Endeavouring to achieve a more informal and less adversarial
approach to the hearing of small claims through a series of
practice notes.**

This proposal might lead to more sheriffs adopting an
inquisitorial approach and being willing to remove their wigs and

gowns and come down from the bench. Preliminary indications are that this proposal will not meet favour with a significant number of sheriffs. [For a depressing illustration of shrieval resistance to informality in small claims, see *Kulinski* v. *Hassell*, 1993 S.L.T. (Sh.Ct.) 23.]

(d) **Making provision for in-court lay advisers.**

The consumer movement are particularly supportive of this proposal which would provide advice and possibly representation by lay advisers based in courthouses. Such schemes exist in a number of courts in England and Wales though they are not without problems as to training, funding and mode of operation. [See further on small claims, C. Ervine, *Small Claims Handbook* (W. Green: 1992), Ervine, "Small Claims: A Progress Report," 1992 S.L.T. (News) 33 and C. Whelan (ed.) *Small Claims Courts: A Comparative Study* (Oxford University Press: 1990).]

IV. APPEALS

A. ORDINARY CAUSE

Sheriff Courts (Scotland) Act 1907, ss. 27–29

"27. *Appeal to sheriff principal*—Subject to the provisions of this Act an appeal to the sheriff principal shall be competent against all final judgments of the sheriff and also against interlocutors—

(*a*) Granting or refusing interdict, interim or final;

(*b*) Granting interim decree for payment of money other than a decree for expenses, or making an order *ad factum praestandum*;

(*c*) Sisting an action;

(*d*) Allowing or refusing or limiting the mode of proof;

(*e*) Refusing a reponing note; or

(*f*) Against which the sheriff either *ex proprio motu* or on the motion of any party grants leave to appeal."

[In addition to section 27 there is a general right of appeal to the sheriff principal against an interlocutor of the sheriff which is incompetent.]

"28. *Appeal to the Court of Session*—(1) Subject to the provisions of this Act, it shall be competent to appeal to the Court of Session against a judgment either of a sheriff principal or a sheriff if the interlocutor appealed against is a final judgment; or is an interlocutor—

(*a*) Granting interim decree for payment of money other than a decree for expenses; or

(*b*) Sisting an action; or

(*c*) Refusing a reponing note; or

(*d*) Against which the sheriff principal or sheriff, either *ex proprio motu* or on the motion of any party, grants leave to appeal."

[In addition, there is a general right in the Court of Session to intervene in respect of any incompetent or irregular proceedings in the sheriff court, or failure by a sheriff principal or sheriff to exercise jurisdiction, or excess of jurisdiction by the sheriff court.]

"29. *Effect of appeal*—An appeal shall be effectual to submit to review the whole of the interlocutors pronounced in the cause . . . "

These provisions create two alternative routes of appeal from a sheriff's decisions, one to the Inner House of the Court of Session direct, the other to the Inner House by way of the sheriff principal. There is a further appeal on points of law to the House of Lords.

TABLE 2
Appeal from Sheriffs in 1991

[For a recent example of an appeal from a sheriff reaching the House of Lords by way of a sheriff principal and the Inner House, see *R.H.M. Bakeries Ltd.* v. *Strathclyde Regional Council*, 1985 S.L.T. 214. See also *Laing* v. *Scottish Grain Distillers Ltd.*, 1992 S.L.T. 435.]

The Grant Report, pp. 104–105

"Appeals
347. No one denied that the appeal to the sheriff principal is cheap, quick and popular. Some, however, suggested that apparent advantages of the appeal are in fact defects. Cheapness may be achieved by the appeal being conducted by the solicitor who handled the case at first instance. Also, it was argued that the appeal is rather too convenient, and that there is something to be said for making an appeal difficult when judgment has been given by a competent court. The main objection we heard was that it is wrong in principle that an appeal should lie from a single judge to a single judge . . . We were also told that the appeal grew up by accident, that it

makes possible an undesirable multiplicity of appeals, and that by diverting appeals from the Court of Session it deprives the sheriff courts of guidance that they should receive from the Supreme Court. It was suggested that an appellate decision should have wider currency than that of the sheriff principal, which is valid only within the sheriffdom . . .

348. While recognising the theoretical defects of the appeal to the sheriff principal, we are of the opinion that it has worked well, is undeniably popular, and should if possible be retained. It is cheaper than an appeal to the Court of Session because it can be conducted by a solicitor, there is no necessity to print or duplicate papers, and travelling expenses to Edinburgh are avoided since the appeal is almost invariably heard locally. The time taken to dispose of an appeal in the sheriff court is somewhat shorter than in the Court of Session. The popularity of the appeal to the sheriff principal particularly in interlocutory matters, is self-evident; over ten times as many appeals are taken from sheriffs to sheriffs principal as from sheriffs to the Court of Session, and less than one-tenth of the appellate decisions of sheriffs principal are further appealed. We are impressed by the fact that almost all of our witnesses favoured the retention, in some form or other, of the appeal to the sheriff principal."

B. SUMMARY CAUSES

Sheriff Courts (Scotland) Act 1971, s. 38

"**38.** *Appeal in summary causes.* In the case of any summary cause an appeal shall lie—

(a) to the sheriff principal on any point of law from the final judgment of the sheriff, and

(b) to the Court of Session on any point of law from the final judgment of the sheriff principal, if the sheriff principal certifies the cause as suitable for such an appeal,

but save as aforesaid an interlocutor of the sheriff or the sheriff principal in any such cause shall not be subject to review."

Appellants request the sheriff to draft a stated case setting out his findings in fact and law. Where necessary he may add a narrative of the proceedings before him and a note stating the reasons for his decision in law. The stated case, which forms the basis of the appeal before the sheriff principal, also includes the question of law stated by each of the parties. In 1991 101 summary cause appeals to sheriffs principal were disposed of; most of them were unsuccessful.

V. MISCELLANEOUS AND ADMINISTRATIVE FUNCTIONS

Sheriffs also have not a few miscellaneous and administrative functions, some of considerable importance. Most of them take the form of summary applications as defined by s. 3 (*p*) of the Sheriff Courts (Scotland) Act 1907:

"(*p*) 'Summary application' means and includes all applications of a summary nature brought under the common law jurisdiction of the sheriff, and all applications, whether by appeal or otherwise, brought under any Act of Parliament which provides, or, according to any practice in the sheriff-court, which allows that the same shall be disposed of in a summary manner, but which does not more particularly define in what form the same shall be heard, tried, and determined."

TABLE 3

Miscellaneous and Administrative Applications in 1991

Nature of application	Number disposed of
Adoption of children	828
Bankruptcy	10,372
Bills of exchange	44
Caveats	3,638
Civil imprisonment	93
Conveyancing and Feudal Reform (Scotland) Act 1970	1,839
Diligence	11,006
Fatal accident inquiries	132
Civil Jurisdiction and Judgments Act 1982 (s.12, issue of certificates)	587
Judicial Factors—	
Appointment	220
Discharge	63
Maintenance Orders Act 1950/(Reciprocal Enforcement) Act 1972	282
Mental Health (Scotland) Act 1960, Part IV	698
Nuisances (Public Health (Scotland) Acts 1897 and 1968) . . .	40
Post mortem warrants	357
Presumption of Death (Scotland) Act 1977	5
Rates and taxes: Warrants to collect	4,622
Re-registration of births	7
Social Work (Scotland) Act 1968—	
Applications under section 16	82
Applications under section 42	3,128
Appeals under sections 49 and 50	304
Other business	6,511
Total	44,858

[Source: Scottish Courts Administration.]

Apart from the applications set out in Table 3 sheriffs also hear applications under the Heritable Securities (Scotland) Act 1894 (*Prestwick Investment Trust* v. *Jones*, 1981 S.L.T. (Sh. Ct.) 55) and the Fair Trading Act (*Director General of Fair Trading* v. *Boswell*, 1979 S.L.T. (Sh. Ct.) 9). Under the Licensing (Scotland) Act 1976 (as amended by the Law Reform (Miscellaneous Provisions) (Scotland) Act 1990, Part III) appeal lies to sheriffs from the decisions of licensing boards. Such appeals, of which there were 117 in 1991, are dealt with as summary applications. [It is not always entirely clear whether a sheriff is hearing an appeal in an administrative or a judicial capacity. Thus in *Rodenhurst* v. *Chief*

Constable, Grampian Police, 1992 S.L.T. 104 an Inner House of five judges had to be convened to overrule a 1958 case which had held that a sheriff in hearing an appeal against the revocation of a firearm certificate by a chief constable was exercising a judicial as opposed to an administrative function.]

Amongst the more unusual applications made to sheriffs are those which relate to lawburrows (*Morrow* v. *Neil*) and to burial grounds (*Sister Jarlath, Petitioner*).

Morrow v. Neil
1975 S.L.T. (Sh. Ct) 65

"A widow living in a tenement flat claimed that members of a family from a neighbouring flat had injured and threatened to injure her and her children and that she was afraid that they would commit further assaults upon her. She, accordingly, brought an action of lawburrows against these neighbours with the concurrence of the procurator-fiscal. The neighbours lodged defences and, after sundry procedure, a proof was heard. The sheriff considered, inter alia, the nature of the remedy sought, the procedure to be followed, what the pursuer had to prove in order to succeed, the standard of proof incumbent upon the pursuer, and the weight to be attached to corroboration.

Held (1) that the concurrence of the procurator-fiscal was unnecessary; (2) that defences should not have been lodged; (3) that the pursuer had to establish that she had reasonable cause to apprehend that the defenders would harm the person or property or herself or her family, tenants or servants, and that although she genuinely believed that the defenders were likely to harm her, her belief was not based on rational grounds; (4) that the standard of proof incumbent on the pursuer was proof on a balance of probabilities; and (5) that in the circumstances, where corroboration was available, the presence or absence of corroboration was an important consideration for the court in deciding whether or not a fact had been proved; and defenders *assoilized*."

Sister Jarlath, Petitioner
1980 S.L.T. (Sh. Ct.) 72

"A private burying place belonging to trustees for a religious order contained 46 bodies, the last of which had been interred in 1972. In order to carry out the reconstruction of their convent (which adjoined the said burying ground), the Mother Superior presented a petition to the sheriff principal for authority to disinter the 46 bodies and reinter them in a private cemetery elsewhere. Evidence was put before the sheriff principal to the effect that disintegration of all the bodies would be virtually complete.

Held that there was no reason in principle why the court should not grant the order sought in a suitable case; and prayer of the petition *granted*."

CHAPTER 2

THE COURT OF SESSION

I. STRUCTURE AND COMPOSITION

The Court of Session is the highest civil court based in Scotland. It is a central court, sitting only in Edinburgh.

Lord Cameron, "The Superior Courts," p. 23

"The Court of Session, which was established in 1532 by James V of Scotland and grew out of the King's Council, derives its name from the fact that when established it sat, and was required to sit, in one determined place—Edinburgh—thus obviating the necessity of litigants following the King's Council wherever it might move about the country. The Court itself sits in the Parliament House, Edinburgh, and with brief intermissions occasioned by civil convulsions has sat there continuously since at least the completion of the new Parliament House in 1640. It forms part of the College of Justice and members of the Court are still officially styled 'Senators of The College of Justice.' Within the College of Justice are included, Advocates, Clerks of Session, Writers to the Signet and certain others of the officers and officials of the court."

From 1532 until 1808 the whole court sat as one body. Understandably, counsel found it an unwieldy body to appear before; one contemporary newspaper editor referred to it as "a regular bear garden." [See also Henry Cockburn, *Memorials of His Time* (Black: 1856), pp. 245–246.]

During this period one of the 15 judges sat in the "Outer House" of the court to deal with preliminary issues in cases which would subsequently come before the whole court. In 1808 the court was divided into two Divisions, the First Division consisting of the Lord President and seven Ordinary Judges and the Second Division of the Lord Justice-Clerk and six Ordinary Judges. As before, one of the Ordinary Judges sat by rotation in the Outer House to handle preliminary issues.

The court as we know it today emerged from the Court of Session Act 1825. This provided that the seven junior Ordinary Judges of the court should normally sit as Lords Ordinary in the Outer House. The eight remaining members of the court formed the Inner House and sat in two Divisions. (The First and Second Divisions consisting respectively of the Lord President and the Lord Justice-Clerk each sitting with three senior Lords Ordinary.) Since that date the number of Senators of the College of Justice (known also as Lords of Council and Session) has been increased.

Under the Maximum Number of Judges (Scotland) Order (1991) (No. 2884) up to 25 Senators can be appointed. At present there are 25, one of whom (Lord Davidson) is the full-time Chairman of the Scottish Law Commission. Of the other 24, 16 are in the Outer House (and are primarily responsible for deciding cases at first instance), and eight are in the Inner House (the work of which is mainly appellate). In addition there are now eight temporary judges appointed in terms of s. 35(3) of the Law Reform (Miscellaneous Provisions) (Scotland) Act 1990.

Despite the hierarchical and divided structure of the court in modern times it is still collegiate in its essence. A number of consequences flow from this:

1. All decrees, though pronounced by a single judge are decrees of the Court of Session, and the judge who pronounces them only exercises a delegated jurisdiction. (*Purves* v. *Carswell* (1905) 8 F. 351 *per* Lord McLaren at p. 354.)

2. If necessary, an Outer House judge can be asked to sit in the Inner House to make up a Division. Equally, an Inner House judge can sit in the Outer House to relieve the pressure of business (*Purves* v. *Carswell*).

3. Where questions of difficulty or importance render it expedient, or the judges of a Division are equally divided, the judges may require a case to be reheard before such a larger court as is necessary to dispose of the case (Court of Session Act 1988, s. 36). This may be a Court of Seven (see *e.g. Reiley* v. *Kingslaw Riding School*, 1975 S.C. 28 and *Collie and Buyers*, 1981 S.L.T. 191) or, at least in theory, the Whole Court. The last reported case where this occurred was *Bell* v. *Bell*, 1940 S.C. 229. In it the judges split 7:6 with the deciding vote being that of the Lord Ordinary from whom the original reclaiming motion (appeal) came. In practice it is almost inconceivable that we will ever again see a decision of the Whole Court. This is because in any one week nowadays up to ten of the judges will be presiding in High Court trials. The combined pressure of the civil and criminal caseload would make a Whole Court hearing impractical and uneconomic.

Nevertheless there have been several small reforms to the Court which may, inadvertently, have begun to erode the collegiate nature of the Court. Thus it is no longer possible for a Lord Ordinary faced with a difficult question to refer a case to the Inner House for disposal or guidance nor for a Division of the Court to "seek the opinions" of the judges of the other Division or all the other judges of the Court on difficult or important points of law. Secondly, the senior judge in an Extra Division no longer automatically presides in an appeal—the Lord President directs who will preside. Again, promotion to the Inner House from the Outer House is no longer by seniority alone, now promotion is through selection by the Lord President and the Lord Justice-Clerk with the consent of the Secretary of State (see the Law Reform (Miscellaneous Provisions) (Scotland) Act 1990, s. 35(2) and Schedule 4, para. (4)). Finally, as we have seen there is now provision for temporary judges to sit who may well never become permanent members of the College of Justice.

II. JURISDICTION

A. AUTHORITY OVER DEFENDER OR SUBJECT MATTER
As in the sheriff court the general rule is that a case must be raised in the forum of the defender. The territorial jurisdiction of the Court of Session is the whole of Scotland and the territorial waters including parts of the Continental Shelf. [For further details, see W.A. Wilson, *Introductory Essays on Scots Law* (2nd ed.) (W. Green & Son: 1984) at pp. 32–35.]

Domicile and Matrimonial Proceedings Act 1973, s. 7(2), (3)
"(2) The Court shall have jurisdiction to entertain an action for divorce, separation or declarator of freedom and putting to silence if (and only if) either of the parties to the marriage in question—
    (a) is domiciled in Scotland on the date when the action is begun; or
    (b) was habitually resident in Scotland throughout the period of one year ending with that date.
(3) The Court shall have jurisdiction to entertain an action for declarator of marriage or declarator of nullity of marriage if (and only if) either of the parties to the marriage—
    (a) is domiciled in Scotland on the date when the action is begun; or
    (b) was habitually resident in Scotland throughout the period of one year ending with that date; or
    (c) died before that date and either—
        (i) was at death domiciled in Scotland, or
        (ii) had been habitually resident in Scotland throughout the period of one year ending with the date of death."

Presumption of Death (Scotland) Act 1977, s. 1(3)
"(3) The Court of Session shall have jurisdiction to entertain an action of declarator [of death] if and only if—
    (a) the missing person was domiciled in Scotland on the date on which he was last known to be alive or had been habitually resident there throughout the period of one year ending with that date; or
    (b) the pursuer in the action—

   (i) is the spouse of the missing person, and
   (ii) is domiciled in Scotland at the date of raising the action or
        was habitually resident there throughout the period of one
        year ending with that date."

[Note that in actions of status the forum of the pursuer can be used as well as the forum of the defender.]

In other cases the position is regulated by the Civil Jurisdiction and Judgments Acts 1982 and 1991. The jurisdiction of the court varies slightly depending whether the defender falls within the ambit of Schedule 1, Schedule 4 or Schedule 7 of the 1982 Act or Schedule 1 of the 1991 Act (see p. 3 above).

In essence all defenders covered by the Act may be sued in the courts for the place where they are resident and with which they have a substantial connection. In addition they may be sued in the Court of Session:

(1) if the case relates to a contract which is to be performed within the territorial jurisdiction of the court;

(2) if the case relates to delict or quasi-delict and the harmful event took place within the jurisdiction of the court;

(3) if the case is brought against them in their capacity as trusters, trustees or beneficiaries of a Scottish trust;

(4) if the case relates to maintenance and the maintenance creditor is habitually resident within the jurisdiction of the court or if the matter is ancillary to proceedings relating to status and the court has jurisdiction under the Domicile and Matrimonial Proceedings Act 1973;

(5) if the case arises out of the operations of a branch, agency or other establishment located within the jurisdiction of the court;

(6) if there are a number of defenders and one of them is resident and has substantial ties with a place within the jurisdiction of the court;

(7) if the case is a counter claim arising from the same contract or facts which have given rise to a case which is pending before the court;

(8) if the case relates to the ownership or tenancy of immoveable property which is situated within the jurisdiction of the court;

(9) if the proceedings are concerned with the validity of the constitution, the nullity or the dissolution of Scottish or Scottish controlled companies, partnerships or associations or the decisions of such bodies;

(10) if the defenders have prorogated, *i.e.* accepted, the jurisdiction of the court by express agreement or by entering appearance before the court to oppose the action;

(11) if the case relates to a consumer contract completed in Scotland and the consumer or the defender resides in, and has substantial ties with a place within the jurisdiction of the court.

In cases where Schedule 7 applies defenders may also be sued in the Court of Session:

(1) if they have no fixed residence and they have been personally cited within the jurisdiction of the court;

(2) if they have no fixed residence in the United Kingdom and moveable property belonging to them has been arrested, or they own immoveable property situated, within the jurisdiction of the court;

(3) if the proceedings relate to moveable property situated within the jurisdiction of the court;

(4) if the proceedings are for interdict and it is alleged that the wrong is likely to be committed within the jurisdiction of the court;

(5) if the proceedings concern a debt secured over immoveable property situated within the jurisdiction of the court;

(6) if the proceedings concern an arbitration which is conducted in Scotland or which is governed by Scots law;

(7) if the proceedings are principally concerned with the registration in the United Kingdom or the validity in the United Kingdom of patents, trade marks, designs or other intellectual property.

B. POWER TO GRANT THE REMEDY

Like the sheriff court, the Court of Session can grant a variety of possessory and petitory (payment, multiplepoinding, accounting; delivery and specific implement) remedies as well as declarator, damages, reduction, adjudication, suspension, interdict, petitions to the nobile officium and special cases.

C. POWER TO ENTERTAIN THE CAUSE

Generally the Court of Session has jurisdiction in all causes connected with Scotland unless excluded by statute. Its privative jurisdiction includes most actions of adjudication, reduction, proving the tenor, petitions for the liquidation of a limited company with a paid up share capital exceeding £120,000, petitions to the nobile officium, judicial review, special cases, summary trials (for which see, Court of Session Act 1988, s. 26) and certain actions of status (see also p. 7).

The Grant Report, pp. 38–39

"Reductions
119. Except for [some] very limited sheriff court powers . . . the Court of

Session has privative jurisdiction in reductions, in which the Court orders that a document, agreement, decision or court decree shall be of no effect. It may for instance reduce a will, contract or interlocutor, or the administrative decision of a public authority such as government department or local authority. Actions of reduction are rare, and a substantial proportion involve the reduction of sheriff court decrees, particularly where the decree was granted in error . . .

120. It was put to us that the sheriff court might have jurisdiction in all actions of reduction, but we do not feel able to endorse this proposal. A reduction is sometimes used as a kind of appeal against the decision of a sheriff court and we think it inappropriate that a sheriff court should have power to reduce its own decrees. As regards other reductions which are not now competent in the sheriff court, we consider that they frequently raise questions of great legal difficulty and importance which ought to be handled in the Court of Session . . .

Adjudications

121. The title 'adjudication' is applied to two types of actions. An adjudication in implement is an action in which a person who has paid for heritable property, but has not received a title, moves the court to grant him one. The second type, adjudication for debt, is a form of diligence in which heritable property is attached for debt. The decree of adjudication in this case vests the adjudged land in the creditor, subject to a right of redemption by the debtor within a period of ten years known as 'the legal'. Further action may become necessary after this period to exclude the debtor's right of redemption . . .

Actions for Proving the Tenor of Lost Documents

136. An action for proving the tenor of a lost document is at present privative to the Court of Session. No witness expressly suggested to us that actions for proving the tenor should be competent in the sheriff court, but we have considered whether this change might be made. The number of applications to the Court of Session for this purpose is, we understand, very small and they tend to raise difficult questions of fact and law. Having regard to the need for uniformity of decision in a very small field, and the unlikelihood of hardship or serious inconvenience to any number of litigants, we have concluded that actions for proving the tenor of lost documents should remain privative to the Court of Session."

[For a recent case on proving the tenor see *Crichton* v. *Wood*, 1981 S.L.T. (Notes) 66.]

In most other cases the Court of Session has concurrent jurisdiction with the sheriff court. [For details of the privative jurisdiction of the sheriff court see p. 6 above.] This raises the question as to why, when confronted with a choice of courts, some pursuers and their advisers prefer the sheriff court and some the Court of Session. In the absence of research, any answer to this question is necessarily speculative. Normally, the sheriff court will be more convenient, more accessible, cheaper and will often involve fewer delays than the Court of Session. Sometimes the choice will effectively be made by the Scottish Legal Aid Board, sometimes the perceived strengths and weaknesses of the local sheriff court will determine the pursuer's choice and sometimes potential problems of enforcement may tip the scales in the direction of the Court of Session. While some pursuers will be influenced by the simple and cheap appeal procedure available from the sheriff court others may be tempted to raise their actions in the Court of Session to avoid publicity or because of the higher levels of legal expenses awardable in that court. Pursuers who are minded to adopt the latter course in an attempt to put pressure on the defender to settle the action may find to their cost that they are only awarded expenses on the sheriff court scale. [See *Smith* v. *British Rail Engineering Ltd.*, 1985 S.L.T. 463 and *McPherson* v. *British Railways Board*, 1985 S.L.T. 467.] As in the sheriff court there is provision for an action raised in the Court of Session to be remitted by the Court at its own instance or on the application of one or both parties to the appropriate sheriff court (Law Reform (Miscellaneous Provisions) (Scotland) Act 1985, s. 14). [See *Gribb* v. *Gribb*, 1993 S.L.T. 178.]

III. PROCEDURE AND CASELOAD

A. THE OUTER HOUSE

The Outer House consists of 15 Lords Ordinary who sit singly (or occasionally with a civil jury of 12). The pressure of business today is such that it has become necessary to also call on the services of temporary judges.

Maxwell, *The Practice of the Court of Session,* p. 7
"The jurisdiction of a Lord Ordinary is both original and, to a limited extent, appellate. By virtue of his original jurisdiction, he is a judge of first instance in cases above [£1,500] in value, and in cases where the Court of Session has privative jurisdiction. His appellate jurisdiction includes jurisdiction to entertain at common law processes for the suspension and reduction of decrees of lower courts, and a statutory jurisdiction in causes arising under administrative law."

Cases are initiated in the Outer House in two ways; as actions and as petitions.

Civil Judicial Statistics 1983, p. 8

"The Court of Session
2.6 An action is initiated in the general department by the signeting of the summons (thus allowing it to be served on the defender) whereafter it is called in court not earlier than the fourteenth day after service. The defender has 14 days from calling to lodge defences, and failure to do so may result in a decree of absence (and expenses) for the pursuer. If defences are lodged the pursuer's representative draws up a consolidated record of claim and defence which is then adjusted by the representatives of both parties over about the following four months. The action then appears before the court to be disposed of. In defended consistorial (marriage, divorce and separation) actions the period between lodging defences and adjusting the record is shorter: in undefended actions, proof (the submission of evidence) may be made by affidavit. Petitions in the Court of Session specify parties affected by the cause: the process of adjustment of the petition (if answers are lodged) is, again, shorter than for actions initiated by summons."

1. ACTIONS
TABLE 1
Civil Actions completed in 1991

	Sheriff Court Ordinary	Outer House
Debt	28,120	1,289
Damages	1,562	1,657
Consistorial	9,384	483
Custody	2,226	0
Land	7,537	84

TABLE 2
Completed Outer House Actions 1991
Methods of Disposal

	Withdrawn	Final Jdt	No Proof NE/PAE*	Proof	Jury
Divorce	44	439	376	63	—
Declarator of Marriage/Nullity	2	8	8	—	—
Copyright, Trademark or Patent	4	2	2	—	—
Damages/Personal Injury	402	1,255	1,183	69	3
Debts	388	901	867	34	—
Land	31	53	50	3	—
Others	124	169	161	8	—
Total completed 3,822	995	2,827	2,647	177	3

*NE = No evidence led   PAE = Proof by affidavit evidence

[Source: Scottish Courts Administration.]

Tables 1 and 2 demonstrate that the Outer House, like the ordinary procedure in the sheriff court, is dominated by consistorial, debt and damages actions (though in different proportions).

(1) Adjudication: Non-consistorial Causes

It is worth stressing that Table 2 and its equivalent for the sheriff court (see p. 9 above) is only the tip of an iceberg. Many unpaid debts never reach a debt collection agency or a solicitor's office. Of those that do, many more are settled by correspondence without a writ being issued.

[See Scottish Office Central Research Unit paper, "Debt Recovery" 1981.]

Similarly the Pearson Commission (Cmnd. 7054, 1978) estimated that of 250,000 personal injury claims in the United Kingdom in a year, only 1% actually reach the courts.

What Table 2 shows is that of those non-consistorial causes where an action has been raised in court, only 2% get to a proof (trial).

TABLE 3

Completed Debt and Damages actions in the Outer House 1991

	1	2	3	4	
		Decree in absence	*Decree without*		
	Withdrawn	*of defences*	*evidence*	*Proof*	*Total*
Debts	388	712	155	34	1,289
Damages	402	59	1,124	72	1,657

[Source: Scottish Courts Administration.]

While there are clearly differences between debt and damages actions as Table 3 reveals (*e.g.* a far higher proportion of debt cases are undefended and thus decree is granted in absence), the overall picture is largely the same. The great majority of debt and damages cases where a writ has been served are disposed of by out of court settlement (column 1), by the court giving its stamp of approval to such a settlement (column 3) or by the court approving the pursuer's unopposed action without hearing evidence (column 2). In short, the role of the court in non-consistorial cases is mainly "administrative" in nature. [In fairness, it should be admitted that the figures in Table 2 do not contain reference to the motions and debates in defended cases (which relate to interim or incidental matters), which usually take the form of an adversarial contest.]

This conclusion prompts the question: why do so many cases settle? A partial answer is because a settlement ensures that a pursuer will get something, while if he goes to trial he may get nothing. Thus, a survey of Scottish personal injury cases conducted for the Pearson Commission in 1974 suggested that in almost 90% of cases which were disposed of without a proof (columns 1–3) some payment was made to the pursuer.

Phillips and Hawkins, "The settlement process," p. 497 *et seq.*
" 'A settlement,' Atiyah says, 'is a business bargain in which the plaintiff sells his claim . . . for what he can get and the buyer buys for as little as he has to pay.' One important consequence of the commercial nature of this transaction is that what is received in a claim in settlement is by no means what the courts would necessarily award. Moreover, claimants in minor cases of personal injury receive a much higher proportion of their losses than those involved in more serious cases . . .

There are two major reasons why the great majority of claims are settled rather than resolved by judgment of a court: the cost to the individual who wishes to pursue a claim for damages to its ultimate conclusion in the courts, and the risks involved in doing so.

Delay

One of the most important factors likely to affect a claimant's perception of the value of pursuing the case further is the delay likely to be involved. So far as the ordinary plaintiff is concerned, delay is costly since he receives no compensation until the case is settled (except sick pay or social security benefits or, occasionally, an interim payment where liability is not in dispute), while as a result of his injury his various expenses may be increased and his earning power possibly reduced. 'Even the most meritorious claims,' according to the Winn Committee, 'weaken in geometrical progression with the passage of time.' In contrast, the defendant's insurance company may not find it costly to delay settlement, depending on the rate of interest to be charged. [T]he existence of risk . . . encourages claimants to accept offers that are unfair in the actuarial sense. American insurance adjusters themselves openly exploit it, [and are taught to do so in their training] . . . 'In discussing the merits of a settlement the adjuster should always be specific and, if possible, pinpoint those areas that will most likely create doubt and uncertainty on the opposing side . . . Creating doubt . . . is the focal point of good claim negotiations'."

Paterson, "Judges: a political elite?" pp. 129–130
"[In] the Thalidomide case (*Att. Gen.* v. *Times Newspapers Ltd.* [1974] A.C. 273) . . . at first all the bargaining counters seemed to be on the side of Distillers. The parents were disunited and financially far weaker than the company. Their position in law was uncertain and counsel indicated that they were unlikely to win their case without being fought all the way to the House of Lords. This would involve delay and expense. Therefore efforts were made to settle the actions. However time was also against the parents since as the deformed children grew up the special equipment and

facilities which they required, imposed an increasing financial burden on the parents. Accordingly, the incentive to compromise for a lower figure than they might otherwise receive also increased. Distillers on the other hand were getting the interest on the money which they might eventually have to pay out, for as long as they could stave off a settlement. Therefore, there was little incentive for Distillers to settle. When they did make an offer to the parents in November 1971, they insisted that it was accepted by all the parents. Although this offer was a poor one judged by the standards of what the company finally offered, eventually all but five sets of parents were prepared (albeit reluctantly in many cases) to settle for the 1971 offer. When these five still held out one of the majority tried to have them removed as the representatives of the children on the grounds that they were being unreasonable.

It was only after this move had been defeated that the *Sunday Times* began its campaign on September 24th 1972. Yet when the *Sunday Times* was taken to the House of Lords over their right to publish an article in this campaign the Law Lords held if they did so they would be in contempt of court for bringing unfair influence on a litigant and thus perverting the course of justice. The point here is not that this decision was wrong, but that according to the . . . Law Lords, pressure placed on the parents by delay, anxiety, financial hardship, despair, disunity and the uncertainty of their legal rights, was not unfair but the exercise of their one effective weapon, newspaper publicity, was."

As these extracts suggest, although negotiation takes place in almost every contested case, as a method of resolving cases it can sometimes yield unfair results. This is not simply because negotiation may involve compromising legal rights but because the party with the stronger bargaining counters (including delay, anxiety and expense factors) can impose an unfair "settlement" on the other party and the adversarial system encourages the stronger party to do just that. (The cruel pressure exerted by a defence offer or "tender" of an inadequate but not totally derisory sum just before a proof, with its accompanying threat that the pursuer will have to meet all the expenses of the proof for both sides if he or she fails to "beat the tender", is but one case in point. See J. Robertson, "Learning to play the legal game of brinkmanship," *The Scotsman*, 28th September 1990.)

(2) Adjudication: Consistorial Causes

Almost exactly the same processes are at work in consistorial causes as in non-consistorial ones. The high "final judgment" figure is not an indication that negotiated settlements do not take place in divorce cases. It is simply that to obtain a divorce the court must grant a decree, and that decree cannot be granted without written or oral evidence from the pursuer. Approximately

60% of divorce cases are probably opposed at one stage or another, most commonly in relation to money (periodical allowance, capital sum and aliment) and to a lesser extent in relation to the custody of the children or the grounds of the divorce. These disputes are settled in a very similar fashion to personal injury cases.

Mnookin, "Bargaining in the shadow of the law," p. 76
"[There are] four factors that would seem to be important influences or determinants of the outcomes of bargaining . . . (1) the preferences of the divorcing parents; (2) the bargaining endowments created by legal rules that allow the imposition of a particular allocation if the parties fail to reach agreement; (3) the degree of uncertainty concerning the legal outcome if the parties go to court, and the parties' attitudes towards risk; (4) transaction costs, and the parties' respective abilities to bear these costs."

As an all-party group of M.P.s stated in 1980:

"All too often the courts are simply rubber-stamping arrangements made by the parents as part of the bargaining over financial and property matters in which the children are used as pawns."

Once the settlement is reached the cases go ahead undefended and the court grants approval to the settlement and the divorce usually on the basis of affidavit evidence (sworn documentary statements). The court is usually not concerned with the fairness or otherwise of the settlement nor to check the accuracy of the facts contained in the affidavit. As in the case of non-consistorial actions the work of the court is largely "administrative". [Again it has to be conceded that it is not unusual in consistorial cases for the court to be required to make rulings on incidental and interim matters following a contested hearing on an opposed motion.] Few cases remain defended to the last and in only a small minority of cases does the pursuer not get decree.

Negotiated settlements in consistorial causes, therefore, can suffer from similar flaws to those that can arise in non-consistorial causes. Furthermore, "defensive lawyering" and the adversarial approach of solicitors emphasises rather than reduces the area of conflict between the parties, thus leading to unnecessary suffering and bitterness. One answer to these problems would be to reduce the scope for bargaining. This may be done by exploring the possibilities for alternative dispute resolution (ADR) including: simplifying the grounds for divorce, by reducing the cost of divorce, or by encouraging conciliation.

Following the Report of the Working Party on Divorce Procedure (chaired by Lord Cowie) in 1980 a simplified and cheap "do-it-yourself" divorce procedure was introduced in January 1983. (The procedure is competent in both the Court of Session and the sheriff court.) Litigants who are eligible to raise their actions under this procedure do not require corroborated evidence (the evidence of a witness other than the pursuer). Having paid a fee of £40 (from which recipients of Income Support, Family Income Supplement or Legal Advice and Assistance are exempt) the pursuer simply sends in a completed form and a sworn statement (affidavit) to the court. Costing less than a tenth of the expense of a normal undefended divorce and having a simplicity which obviates the necessity of employing a solicitor (although over a third of applicants consult a solicitor in practice) the procedure has been well received by participants. [See Scottish Office Central Research Unit paper, "The Simplified Divorce Procedure" 1984.] While there is no doubting the popularity of the procedure (about a quarter of those seeking a divorce invoke the simplified procedure) its impact in reducing unnecessary conflict and bitterness is limited. This is because applicants are only eligible to use the procedure where the spouses have lived apart for at least two years (and both consent to the divorce) or for at least five years, there are no children of the marriage under 16 and neither spouse is seeking a financial award against the other from the court. (A recent working party chaired by Lord Cowie recommended that contrary to the practice in England and Wales, the simplified procedure should not be extended to other forms of divorce. It is perhaps unfortunate that there were no lay-persons on the working party.) In short, parties with children or who cannot agree on all financial matters or who have only recently separated cannot use the procedure. For them, conciliation schemes may be an answer.

Conciliation schemes have been one of the most successful forms of ADR operating in Canada, the United States of America and Australia for some years. England, too, has seen numerous conciliation schemes established in recent years. In Scotland there are now schemes providing a service in each sheriffdom but not in some of the remoter, rural districts. The oldest scheme, the Lothian Family Conciliation Service opened its doors in March 1984.

Wright, "Matrimonial Conciliation," p. 432

"Matrimonial conciliation . . . takes as its starting-point the recognition that the marriage has broken down, and then goes on to recognise that there is more to disputed divorce than can be dealt with by ordinary court proceedings between the spouses. The breakdown of the peculiarly close relationship of marriage often produces emotional upset, bitterness and distrust. While some of these features may arise in other disputes, a peculiar feature of divorce is that often a form of contact requires to be maintained after the proceedings are concluded. This is the situation, of course, where children, particularly children under sixteen, are involved. At a time when a party's own emotional problems have to be faced, the material and emotional needs of his or her children also need attention. Conciliation offers assistance in this situation, in two interrelated ways: first, by helping parties to understand and sort out their feelings; second, by helping parties to reach agreement on all or some of the issues about which they are in dispute.

Conciliation therefore involves both counselling and mediation. The conciliator requires a degree of experience in counselling in the area of personal interaction together with training in the art of mediation. It may well be suggested that a party's own lawyer can fulfil these functions, and indeed this often happens up to a point. But there are several reasons why lawyers are not able to achieve nearly as much along these lines as conciliators, and the experience of conciliation schemes bears this out. First, the individual lawyer is in an adversarial situation—as research shows, his client expects him to fight, not to be conciliatory (although, paradoxically, the same research also shows most clients acknowledging in general terms the need for a more conciliatory approach to the divorce process); second, in any case, the lawyer usually hears only one side of the case in person; third, the lawyer does not have all the necessary training and is not necessarily inclined towards a conciliatory approach; and, finally, the lawyer often does not have the time to spend on conciliation sessions. In many cases, it is understandably difficult for the solicitor to give priority considera- tion to the interests of the children of the marriage."

SAFCOS, "Family Conciliation Services," p. 187

"Update on family conciliation
Few tasks are less rewarding for a solicitor than dealing with disputes over custody and access. No matter how sensitively a solicitor handles the situation, his professional role is to try to win the case for his client; little can be done to meet the instinctive wish to reach the best outcome for the children. It is likely to be in the children's best interests to achieve a compromise outcome where both parents can accept, and for which they are both responsible. This also serves the client's best interest as he or she will be more likely to abide by an arrangement achieved through agreement. Experience shows clients are more satisfied when solicitors support conciliation.

Family conciliation is very effective at helping parents to settle arrange- ments together, especially access. The conciliator can reframe their opposing positions into common interests as the parties always share the common goal of wanting the best for the children. When this is openly acknowledged, although they may not agree on what *is* best, compromise can be achieved. By focusing on the children, on future arrangements rather than recriminations on the past, parties can move from their apparently entrenched positions. They can work out arrangements that meet the children's need to continue to have a loving relationship with each of their parents and their need for their parents to stop fighting.

There are now conciliation services available throughout Scotland, although not in every sheriff court district. Very many solicitors are already referring their clients to the services.

The importance of conciliation to the children of separating and divorcing parents and its value to the legal profession is recognised. The Society has agreed with the Scottish Association of Family Conciliation Services (SAFCOS) on a code of practice for conciliators and solicitors. A rule of court has been introduced to enable judges and sheriffs to refer parties to conciliation.

This article emphasises the importance of solicitors to the conciliation process, gives brief details of the code of practice and rule of court, describes the growth of conciliation services and the need for resources for further development.

The importance of the solicitor's role

The solicitor's role *vis-à-vis* conciliation is crucial. Research shows that where solicitors encourage their clients to attend conciliation there is a greater likelihood of agreement being reached.

Solicitors also have a vital role to play in referring their clients to conciliation at as early a stage as possible, before animosity escalates.

Solicitors have the opportunity to explain to their clients that conciliation is not to be confused with reconciliation, that it is not about getting couples back together again but proceeds on the basis that the relationship is over. People can be advised to contact the service for advice at any stage, even before they have actually separated if, for example, they want advice on how to tell the children they are going to separate. Solicitors can also explain that conciliation is not about counselling. If clients need long-term in-depth counselling then marriage guidance or other counselling agencies should be recommended, although it can be said that parties might come to the conciliation service later.

It can be explained by the solicitor that conciliation, in a relatively informal environment with an impartial third party, enables couples to discuss the practical arrangements for their children following separation or divorce. Parties will be encouraged by the conciliator to focus on their shared interest for the well-being of the children rather than on their disputes.

The main topic discussed in conciliation is usually access. Research shows that there is a very high success rate in reaching agreement on this issue in conciliation. Parents are motivated to work towards conciliation because they want the best for their children. Conciliation helps them to achieve their own solution rather than having one imposed on them by the court.

New rules of court—referral to family conciliation services

Judges and sheriffs have been convinced by the success of the family conciliation services in Scotland. On 9th April [1992] new rules were introduced into the Court of Session and sheriff court to allow the judiciary to refer parties to specified family conciliation services. Sheriffs will have the power to direct disputing couples to conciliation; judges in the Court of Session may do this if the parties agree.

A remit to the service will give parties an opportunity to be informed of the benefits to them and to their children of conciliation. They can then decide whether they wish to use the service or return to the court process. It is intended that the use of the rule will be educative rather than coercive. To force people to conciliate would be a contradiction in terms. We know from experience elsewhere, for example in Australia and California, that a high proportion of couples attending information sessions on conciliation subsequently go on to conciliate.

Solicitors are asked to recognise that the conciliation process may take a few weeks. Time is required to set up appointments and perhaps to try out various options before making a final decision on what seems to be the best arrangement for the family. This need not necessarily disadvantage say a father who has not seen his children for some time and who is trying to re-establish contact. The sheriff may award interim access at the same time as remitting to a conciliation service. Also the conciliation service may, for example, enable the couple to restart access during the conciliation process before final arrangements are made. Family conciliation can avoid delay in making access arrangements as it can take place while legal aid applications are processed.

Funding of conciliation services

The services in Scotland are already dealing with about 1,750 referrals a year from all over Scotland and the new rule of court will increase the workload. This will serve to highlight the present piecemeal and unsatisfactory funding of conciliation throughout Scotland. The national body, SAFCOS, is 75% funded by the Scottish Office; the services in Strathclyde and Central Regions are funded under the urban aid programme; and the other services receive very different amounts from their local authorities with grants ranging from a few hundred pounds in Dumfries and Galloway to approximately £49,000 in Lothian.

All services have (and Central Region will have later this year) a paid co-ordinator. This post is full-time only in Fife, Lothian, Strathclyde and Tayside. Conciliators are paid in areas where there is an adequate budget; in other areas conciliators are volunteers.

Standards of practice of conciliation are high in Scotland. All conciliators are carefully selected according to criteria laid down by SAFCOS and trained and/or accredited by SAFCOS.

In order that all sheriffs may fully use the rule of court conciliation should be locally available in every sheriff court district. To make this possible far greater resources than are at present made available to the

conciliation services would be required. SAFCOS would like to see some
sort of block grant system. At present, services have to spend a significant
proportion of their time in raising money to top up grants. The quality of
service provided throughout Scotland is recognised to be high, but there
cannot be a comprehensive spread of services until the funding is placed
on a regular basis.

Widespread support for conciliation
Many judges and sheriffs strongly support conciliation, seeing it as a
better way to reach a conclusion on what some of them say can be their
most agonising decisions. As one said: 'It is often surprising how the
bitterly irreconcilable can come to focus on the best interests of their
children, despite their personal antagonisms, when afforded the space,
understanding and objectivity which independent conciliation can provide. Agreements reached by parents are more likely to last and be in the
best interests of the children than any solution imposed by a court.'

An impressive list of organisations and individuals in the legal and
other professions supports conciliation and there is political support from
MPs in all parties. Support for conciliation comes from many solicitors
who refer clients, from those who have been and are directly involved in
steering groups to set up services and also from those who are on
management committees to run the services."

[For further discussions of conciliation in Scotland see J. Ross,
"The Challenge of Conciliation," 1987 J.L.S. 457; CRU, *Family
Conciliation in Scotland* (Scottish Office: 1990); A. Dick, "Court
or Conciliation: War and Peace?," 1991 S.L.T.(News) 209 and
Lord Ross, "Family Conciliation: The Child's View and Con-
fidentiality," 1991 J.L.S. 20. On divorce mediation see L. Parkin-
son, "Divorce Mediation—The Future," 1993 J.L.S. 85. On ADR
generally, see M. Upton, "ADR in Perspective," 1993 S.L.T.
(News) 75 and the "Modern Law Review Special Issue on Dispute
Resolution" (1993) 56 M.L.R. 277.]

(3) Jury Trials

Civil jury trials have become relatively scarce in modern times (in
the ten years to 1991 there have been an average of 4.5 jury trials
per annum in the Outer House). Such trials have once before
fallen into desuetude in Scotland, only to be re-introduced from
Westminster. How long they will continue to survive in the future
must be an open question. Although theoretically available in 16
types of action ranging from furiosity and idiotcy to life insurance
under the 1825 Court of Session Act, by the 1980s jury trials were
almost exclusively reserved for personal injury actions. Even in
these cases its efficacy as a means of deciding cases was coming
under attack. [For a rare case of a jury trial in a defamation case in
modern times see *Winter* v. *News Scotland Ltd.*, 1991 S.L.T. 828.]

Watt, "The News Reporter's Role," p. 495–496

"Jury Trial

Take . . . the diminution of the jury trial. In 1955 there was a total of 104 actions tried by that method. In 1960 the figure was up to 114. But five years later the total had dropped to 67, in 1970 it was 49, in 1975 18, and by 1978 it had dropped to a mere five cases.

This very remarkable change took place not as the direct result of any legislative intent affecting the rights of parties to civil actions to have their disputes determined by juries. It . . . occurred, as I see it, because juries were out of favour not only with the legal profession, or at least a majority of it, but also with insurance companies. It is this circumstance which has wrought another important but silent revolution in the conduct of reparation litigation in Scotland.

No statistics are available to establish the point, but it must be widely recognised that it is no longer judges and juries but insurance companies who determine in the majority of cases how much, if anything, an injured party should receive. Precedent has increasingly become available not from judicial opinion but from the tables kept in insurance offices. It is a development no doubt derived from the motive to save expense by avoiding a hearing in court, but it is a trend which causes some misgivings. I say so, not because it has necessarily had any deleterious effect on the doing of justice—I have no means of knowing that—but because it has been brought about without public consultation or any deliberate act of reform through the usual methods, and purely as a matter of expediency as seen from the viewpoint of practitioners in the fields of law and insurance."

In June 1988 the Scottish Courts Administration published a Consultation Paper on the Jury Trials in the Court of Session. Its tenor was to suggest that civil jury trials were no longer popular with litigants and would become increasingly inappropriate with the growth in admissibility of hearsay evidence following the introduction of the Civil Evidence (Scotland) Act 1988. Although the Lord President and a number of his colleagues favoured abolition of the civil jury (as did members of the Scottish Law Commission, the Sheriffs' Association and the Association of British Insurers) the majority of respondents (including the Law Society, several leading court firms and the consumer lobby) favoured retention. Rather to the surprise of the commentators the Lord Advocate subsequently announced that civil jury trials would be retained but suggested a number of possible reforms on which he invited comment: (1) Restriction of the right to jury trial to cases which do not raise difficult questions of law or factual issues of exceptional complexity; (2) The "right" to jury trial should become a privilege available only at the discretion of the court on special cause being shown; (3) Further guidance should be provided to the jury on appropriate levels of damages awards; (4) Reduction in the size of the civil jury to seven. (See 152 (1989) SCOLAG 66.) The Court of Session Act 1988, s. 11 did restrict civil jury trials to personal injury, defamation, delinquency and reduction cases. That apart, none of the proposed reforms have been implemented.

(4) Delay

One factor which plays a part in out-of-court negotiations as we have seen is the delays involved in litigation. Such delays are a perennial source of complaint. The Pearson Commission's study of personal injury cases in Scotland in 1974 cast some light on the problem.

TABLE 4

Delays in Personal Injury Cases

	Months
Average interval	
From injury to writ	26
From writ to fixing proof	12
From fixing of proof to disposal	6

[Source: Pearson Report Table 147.]

As can be seen the lengthiest delay occurs between the injury and the issuing of the writ. This is a product of Scottish legal rules and practice.

The Kincraig Committee on Personal Injuries Litigation, p. 8

"The present practice of having the issue on the merits and the issue on *quantum* decided at the same time and the rule that a pursuer can obtain no more than he concludes for, involve having to conclude for a specific sum as representing the maximum he can obtain. This can delay determination of the merits of a case because in many instances the medical condition of the claimant is not sufficiently static to enable reasonably accurate assessment of *quantum* to be made at an early stage."

The committee's findings (published in 1979) suggested that the delay between the signeting of the summons and the fixing of a proof (caused by the Scottish system of pleading) had been reduced since 1974. So too had the period between fixing a proof and the date of the trial. In the years following the Kincraig Committee, however, a rise in criminal work in the High Court led to greater calls on the Court of Session judiciary. This in turn led to the delay between fixing a proof and the actual hearing rising to 15 months by 1986. Indeed, it was partly on the strength of these delays that the government was persuaded to increase the number of judges in the Court of Session in 1985. Moreover, as the Kincraig Committee observed, the high incidence of settlements of actions in the week before and on the day of the trial (over one in two cases) causes a loss of judicial time which could otherwise be devoted to hearing cases which are not settled. [The Maxwell Report on the "Use of Judicial Time in the Superior Courts of Scotland" (1986) concluded that only 60% of the available judge time in the Court of Session was utilised—primarily because of the problems caused by late settlements.]

Although there are the occasional lengthy hearings (the evidence alone in *McColl* v. *Strathclyde Region* concerning the latter's proposal to add fluoride to the public water supply lasted for 143 days in 1981/82) the average personal injury case lasts less than two days. Delay at the hearing stage is therefore minimal.

The increases in delay in the mid-Eighties were compounded by a steady rise in the number of ordinary actions (excluding consistorial cases) and criminal cases at this time. Faced by a Government and a Treasury which was reluctant to expand the existing judicial complement to resolve the problem, a series of steps were initiated to confront the problem of delay head-on. In 1984 Rule of Court 89B was introduced which enables the court to grant a motion by the pursuer for "summary decree" if it is satisfied that the defences as lodged by the defender indicate that there is no defence to the action or any part of it. [See "Summary Decree in the Court of Session," 1987 S.L.T. (News) 93.] In the following year, in an endeavour to tackle the problem of delay in personal injury cases—particularly delays attributable to the Scottish system of pleading—an optional procedure was introduced in the Court of Session. Where the pursuer elects to adopt this procedure a streamlined and simplified form of pleadings is used and witness lists and documents are exchanged. The new procedure proved popular with pursuers as a means of putting pressure on defenders. (By 1988 the average duration of an optional procedure case was 8.5 months as compared with an average of 20 months for ordinary or jury trials. See SCA Consultation Paper on Jury Trials in the Court of Session, 1988.)

In September 1985 a Review body on the Use of Judicial Time in the Superior Courts was established under Lord Maxwell. Its Report in 1986 suggested guide times for the key intervals in civil litigation which were about a third of the then current intervals. (The average interval between the allowance of a hearing by way of proof or jury trial and the completion of the hearing was 15 months—Maxwell considered it should be between four and six months.) By careful overloading of the court rolls (listing many more cases for each day than the court could hear) on the assumption that most cases would be settled and by devising more accurate methods for assessing the likely length of hearings the court has managed to attain the Maxwell target figures. (See Lord Hope, "Judicial Business," 1991 J.L.S. 266.) With retired judges (Law Reform (Miscellaneous Provisions) (Scotland) Act 1985, s. 22) and temporary judges (Law Reform (Miscellaneous Provisions) (Scotland) Act 1990, s. 35(3)) the pace of litigation in the court is now such that the optional procedure has begun to lose some of its initial popularity.

The success of these measures has paralleled the success of another measure designed to streamline procedures within the Court. Following critical comments by Lord Fraser in the House of Lords in *Brown* v. *Hamilton District Council*, 1983 S.L.T. 397, Lord President Emslie set up a working party under Lord Dunpark to devise a simple and quick procedure for the Court of Session in cases alleging ultra vires action or failure to perform a statutory duty. The Act of Sederunt (1985 No. 500 (S. 48)) implementing (at least in part) the Dunpark Report recommendations provides petitioners with an expeditious form of judicial review. It provides for an accelerated first hearing, a panel of judges with expertise in the relevant branches of law and a limited scope for appeals. Research has shown that the new procedure has led to a substantial increase in applications for judicial review and that these applications have been dealt with extremely expeditiously—25% of petitions were disposed of in four weeks and 68% within two months. [See N. Drucker, "Research on the Scottish Courts" (1990) 164 SCOLAG 74. On judicial review generally see T. Mullen, *Guide to Judicial Review* (W. Green & Son: 1987), *West* v. *Secretary of State for Scotland*, 1992 S.L.T. 636 and W. Finnie, "Triangles as Touchstones of Review," 1993 S.L.T. (News) 51.]

Not the least interesting point about the comparative success of these recent initiatives in relation to delay in the Court of Session is the fact that the three procedures existing in the Court of Session prior to 1985 for expediting hearings have remained relatively unused. The first, summary trial (now governed by section 26 of the Court of Session Act 1988) permits parties to bring before the Lord Ordinary of their choice, for no extra payment, any actions competent in the Outer House except those relating to status. The hearing and the preliminary proceedings are expedited and the judge's decision is final. Secondly, under section 17 of the Law Reform (Miscellaneous Provisions) (Scotland) Act 1980 any Senator of the College of Justice can act as an arbiter or oversman in a commercial dispute when the state of business in the court warrants it. The third procedure is the special case before the Inner House (see p. 49 below).

The court returned to the problem of ensuring expeditious procedures in 1988 when a new Act of Sederunt for Commercial Actions was introduced in 1988. The procedure enables the pursuer to opt for a tailor-made, speedy approach to the commercial transactions of merchants and traders and deals in particular with the construction of commercial documents, export and import of merchandise and banking and insurance matters. The average commercial case under this procedure should take no longer than six months. In addition, a panel of three Lords Ordinary have been appointed as the specialist commercial court judges. It remains to be seen how successful this initiative will be.

2. PETITIONS

Causes initiated by petition are largely non-contentious. Where the petition is opposed, the respondent is almost invariably successful. There is a sense, therefore, in which it could be said that much of the petition work of the Outer House is also "administrative" in character.

TABLE 5

Outer House Petitions ended by Final Judgment 1991

Nature of petition	Number
For suspension, interdict and liberation.	49
In regard to factors, curators, etc.	153
Under the Companies Acts	145
For sequestration	125
Adoptions	3
Petitions under the Trust Acts . .	17
For custody and/or access to children	44
For admissions of solicitors	474
Other petitions	169
Administrative business	
Fiats issued (under the Debtors (Scotland) Act 1987).	36
Caveats	2,174
Other administrative business . . .	41
	3,430

[Source: Scottish Courts Aministration. Lodging a caveat prevents a certain course of action being taken without first informing the petitioner. Fiats simply prevent certain courses of action, for example the disposal of heritage by a debtor or the pledging of a husband's credit by a wife.]

B. THE INNER HOUSE

The Inner House, as we saw earlier, consists normally of two Divisions. The usual quorum is three and only occasionally is a full

Division of four judges convened. This enables the remaining judges to go on criminal circuit, to sit in the Outer House or to form an Extra Division (with the help of a Lord Ordinary) to assist with Inner House business. (In recent times an Extra Division has been sitting almost continuously, with the help of retired judges.) The Divisions are of equal authority and competence, though in some areas there is by custom a division of labour between them. Thus, the First Division hears most tax cases except capital transfer tax cases which are heard by the Second Division.

1. ACTIONS

The Inner House hears both actions and petitions. Its jurisdiction in respect of actions is overwhelmingly appellate. Although the appeal may sometimes be on fact as well as law, fresh evidence is rarely taken. The original transcript usually suffices. This nevertheless places the court hearing the appeal at a disadvantage as compared with the judge of first instance. As Lord Sumner observed in *Hontestroom* v. *Sagaporack* [1927] A.C. 37 at p. 47:

"Not to have seen the witnesses puts appellate judges in a permanent position of disadvantage as against the trial judge, and, unless it can be shown that he has failed to use or has palpably misused his advantage, the higher Court ought not to take the responsibility of reversing conclusions so arrived at, merely on the result of their own comparisons and criticisms of the witnesses and of their own view of the probabilities of the case."

TABLE 6

Inner House Actions disposed of in 1991

	Disposed of					
	By final judgment—originated in					
Nature of action	Inner House	Outer House	Sheriff Court	Elsewhere	Total	Taken out of Court
Debt		13	35		48	6
Delivery						
Succession						
Land or Heritable Estate . . .	1	3	8	3	15	5
Personal injury		21	14		35	4
Damages		9	5		14	7
Copyrights, etc						
Furthcoming		1			1	
Maritime						
Divorce		3	6		9	3
Other husband and wife . . .						
Parent and child						
Other actions of status						
Other actions	2	8	56	54	120	22
Total	3	58	124	57	242	47

[Source: Scottish Courts Administration.]

As the table shows, there are three main sources of appellate jurisdiction in the Inner House:

(1) By reclaiming motion from decisions taken in the Outer House. This is the biggest single source of appeals.

(2) Appeals from the sheriff court (usually direct from sheriffs, see p. 22 above).

(3) Appeals from administrative tribunals, the Land Court, and other courts of special jurisdiction, and also stated cases on a point of law in arbitrations (for which see, Administration of Justice (Scotland) Act 1972, s. 3. See, *e.g. John G. McGregor (Contractors) Ltd.* v. *Grampian Regional Council*, 1991 S.L.T. 365.).

The most celebrated source of original jurisdiction in actions is special cases on a point of law under the Court of Session Act 1988, s. 27:

"**Special cases**

27.—(1) Where any parties interested, whether personally or in some fiduciary or official capacity, in the decision of a question of law are agreed upon the facts, and are in dispute only on the law applicable to those facts, it shall be competent for them without raising any proceeding, or at any stage of any proceeding, to present to the Inner House a case (in this section referred to as a special case) signed by their counsel setting out the facts upon which they are so agreed and the question of law arising from those facts; and the parties may ask the Court either for its opinion or for its judgment on that question of law. . . .

(5) Any judgment pronounced by the Court by virtue of this section shall be liable to review by the House of Lords unless such review is excluded by consent of all the parties to the special case."

[See, *e.g. Carnegie Trustees* v. *University of St. Andrews*, 1968 S.C.(H.L.) 27 and *Spencer's Trustees* v. *Ruggles*, 1982 S.L.T. 165.]

2. PETITIONS

Very few Inner House petitions are opposed. The largest single type of petition—the appointment of notaries public—stems from the demand for notaries to hear the swearing of affidavits in divorce cases.

TABLE 7

Petitions ended by Final Judgment, 1991

Nature of petition	Inner House
In exercise of nobile officium . . .	19
Petitions by trustees for direction/ variation of trusts	12
Company petitions.	9
Reclaimed petitions	12
Appointments of notaries public. .	250
Other petitions	19
Total.	321

[Source: Scottish Courts Administration. For petitions on the Nobile Officium see Chap. 15 below.]

C. COURTS OF SPECIAL JURISDICTION

These include the Court of the Lord Lyon, the Court of Teinds, the Restrictive Practices Court, the Registration of Voters Appeal Court, the Election Petition Court, the Valuation Appeal Court, the Lands Tribunal for Scotland and the Scottish Land Court. Only the last three handle a sizeable caseload. It is the last which is perhaps the most interesting for reformers since it contains a number of innovative features. It is peripatetic, it consists of a legal chairman (having the status of a judge of the Court of Session) and four expert lay assessors including at least one Gaelic speaker, it encourages party litigants, its procedure is simplified and semi-inquisitorial and the formal rules of evidence are relaxed. The court deals primarily with agricultural and crofting tenancies.

TABLE 8

Cases Disposed of by the Scottish Land Court, 1981 to 1991

Nature of case	1981	1982	1983	1984	1985	1986	1987	1988	1989	1990	1991
Holdings revalued/fix fair rents, etc	447	563	255	175	397	196	30	57	63	15	13
Applications by landlords for resumption of part holdings . . .	222	203	221	209	201	220	'237	293	234	219	226
Applications under Crofting Reform (Scotland) Act 1976 (purchase of croft) . .	44	36	30	29	17	19	25	18	6	—	—
Other applications . . .	133	63	92	69	77	90	92	71	52	56	48
Total	846	865	598	482	692	525	384	439	355	290	287

[Source: Scottish Courts Administration.]

CHAPTER 3

THE HOUSE OF LORDS

I. JURISDICTION

The House of Lords has no original jurisdiction in Scots cases. It has appellate jurisdiction in fact and law in the case of final judgments of the Inner House of the Court of Session, except where appeal is excluded by statute. If the case originated in the sheriff court the appeal is limited to points of law. The House also has jurisdiction to entertain appeals against interlocutory judgments of the Inner House if the Division is not unanimous or if the Division itself grants leave to appeal.

A. CIVIL APPEALS

1. THE TREATY OF UNION 1707, ARTICLE XIX

"That the Court of Session or College of Justice do after the Union and notwithstanding thereof remain in all time coming with in Scotland as it is now constituted by the laws of that kingdom and with the same authority and privileges as before the Union subject nevertheless to such regulations for the better administration of justice as shall be made by the Parliament of Great Britain . . . And that no causes in Scotland be cognoscible by the Court of Chancery Queen's Bench Common Pleas or any other Court in Westminster Hall and that the said Courts or any other of the like nature after the Union shall have no power to cognosce review or alter the acts or sentences of the judicature within Scotland or stop the execution of the same . . . "

Since the House of Lords did not sit in Westminster Hall the Treaty of Union is silent on the question whether there were to be appeals to the British Parliament from the Court of Session after the Union.

Gibb, *Law from over the Border,* p. 3
"It is a historical mystery as yet unsolved what the Commissioners for negotiating the Union really intended to do about the right of appeal. Under Article XIX of the Treaty of Union it was agreed that no causes in Scotland should be 'cognoscible' by the Courts of Chancery, Queen's Bench, Common Pleas or any other Court in Westminster Hall. Language such as this of course leaves a loop-hole for the intrusion of the jurisdiction of the House of Lords and ingenious authors have suggested that the ambiguity of the article was not unintentional but was dictated by statesmanlike considerations. These learned authors state that if it had

51

been made plain to the people of Scotland that an appellate jurisdiction in the Lords was contemplated, the proposal would have inflamed the opposition of patriotic Scotsmen. A plan indeed was advanced by the English Commissioners for the erection, in Scotland, of a branch of the House of Lords, so to call it, composed of peers of Great Britain, but this came to nothing, as did a suggestion that the Scottish peers should be allowed to choose the court for the hearing of appeals from Scotland."

The Earl of Roseberie v. Inglis
House of Lords, 1708, *unreported*

Several months after the start of the Union the cause of *The Earl of Roseberie* v. *Sir John Inglis*, which had been decided by the Court of Session in 1695, was appealed to the House of Lords. The case is unreported. But Gibb in *Law from over the Border* describes the proceedings, as follows:

"In the year 1708 the Earl of Roseberie (*sic*) . . . decided to appeal against a decision of the Court of Session given before the Union in favour of Sir John Inglis. It would be interesting to have any record at all of what passed at the consultation of Lord Roseberie's advisers with their client before the launching of this appeal. It required a good deal of fortitude in an appellant to brave not only the obstacle of an adverse decision but that also of persuading a foreign tribunal that henceforth it was seised of a new jurisdiction, for which no statutory provision whatsoever had been made. It appears indeed that when the appeal was presented the officers of the House of Lords did not know what to do with it. The officers of the Court of Session, for their part, were unwilling to give the appellant copies and extracts for use in the House of Lords and had to be ordered to do so. On March 27, 1708, the Earl of Rochester reported 'that it was the opinion of the Committee that the respondents in this and all other cases of appeal from Scotland do put in their answers as respondents do in cases of appeal from the courts in England . . . and that the Clerk-Register and his deputies the principal clerks of session shall give authentic copies of the proofs and extracts of the proceedings' for the use at the Bar of the House. This appeal was finally dismissed for want of prosecution, but the ice was broken and a course of practice for handling Scots appeals was entered upon."

The first reported appeal from the Court of Session was *Greenshields* v. *Magistrates of Edinburgh* (1710–11) Rob. 12. The following extract is taken from the fuller English report in Colles 427 (1710).

"The appellant protested against the Lords of Session, and appealed to the Queen's Majesty, and the Lords; and . . . the Lords having declared by their order, that the prosecutors should be at liberty to argue in the first place, whether this appeal be regularly and properly before them or not, [the] respondents contended it was not, because . . . [*inter alia*] before the late Union of the two nations, it was never known that any appeal from the ecclesiastic judicatory of the Church, lay properly or regularly to the Parliament of *Scotland*; nor could any precedent be produced of such an appeal brought . . . After reading the extracts and transcripts of the orders and proceedings delivered, it was ordered by the Lords, that the petition and appeal be received . . . that [the] respondents answer before the first day of [the] session of Parliament, and that their counsel be at liberty to argue in the first place, whether this appeal be regularly and properly before this House or not. And, on 1st March, 1710, after hearing counsel to that point, it was resolved, that the petition and appeal [was] regularly and properly before the House."

[For a detailed account of contemporary events which shows that the Union commissioners did envisage that civil appeals would go from the Court of Session to the House of Lords and an explanation as to why the Articles of Union are silent on the point, see A.J. MacLean, "The 1707 Union" (1983) 4 Journal of Legal History 50.]

2. COURT OF SESSION ACT 1988, s. 40

"(1) Subject to the provisions of any other Act restricting or excluding an appeal to the House of Lords and of sections 27(5) and 32(5) of this Act, it shall be competent to appeal from the Inner House to the House of Lords—

(*a*) without the leave of the Inner House, against a judgment on the whole merits of the cause, or against an interlocutory judgment where there is a difference of opinion among the judges or where the interlocutory judgment is one sustaining a dilatory defence and dismissing the action;

(*b*) with the leave of the Inner House, against any interlocutory judgment other than one falling within paragraph (*a*) above.

(2) An interlocutor of the Court granting or refusing a new trial, on an application under section 29 of this Act, shall be appealable without the leave of the Court to the House of Lords; and on such an appeal the House of Lords shall have the same powers as the Court had on the application and in particular the powers specified in sections 29(3) and 30(3) of this Act.

(3) It shall be incompetent to appeal to the House of Lords against an interlocutor of a Lord Ordinary unless the interlocutor has been reviewed by the Inner House.

(4) On an appeal under this section all prior interlocutors in the cause shall be submitted to the review of the House of Lords."

Ross v. Ross
1927 S.C. (H.L.) 4

The defender's plea of no jurisdiction having been sustained by the

Lord Ordinary but repelled unanimously by the First Division on appeal, the defender endeavoured to appeal to the House of Lords. The Appeal Committee, applying s. 15 of the Court of Session Act 1808 [now s. 40 of the Court of Session Act 1988] dismissed the appeal as incompetent. In the course of his opinion (with which his colleagues concurred) Lord Dunedin set out the following four propositions:

"(1) The disability imposed on this House, which forbids the hearing of appeals against interlocutory judgments when there has been no difference of opinion in the Court below and no leave to appeal has been granted, is statutory, and cannot be got over either by the action of this House or by consent of parties. (2) The right to grant an appeal against an interlocutory judgment is confined to the Court of Session, and their discretion cannot be controlled by this House. (3) The right of appeal remains where the judgment, though interlocutory in form, is final in substance. (4) The test of finality in substance is to see whether the case would have been equally decided in substance whether the interlocutor under discussion had been pronounced as it was or had been pronounced to the opposite effect. Applying those propositions to the case in hand, it is a clear case for refusing the leave to appeal."

Since 1934 English civil appeals have only gone to the House of Lords with leave from the Court of Appeal or the Appeal Committee of the House. At first sight, therefore, it seems anomalous that Scottish civil appeals against final judgments still lie to the House as of right. In practice the emphasis on interlocutory matters which arises from the Scottish system of pleading, means that s. 40 of the 1988 Act acts as a substantial curb on appeals to the House.

3. APPEALS ORIGINATING IN THE SHERIFF COURT

Since the Court of Session Act 1825 appeals originating in the Sheriff Court which come to the House of Lords are restricted to matters of law only (see now the Court of Session Act 1988, s. 32(5)).

This seemingly clear position is subject to a number of caveats.

Sutherland v. Glasgow Corporation
1951 S.L.T. 185

LORD REID: "My Lords, as the proof in this case was led in the Sheriff Court section 40 of the Judicature Act, 1825, applies to the case and we are bound to accept the findings of fact set out in the interlocutor of the Second Division of 14th July 1949, which is now under appeal. But that is subject to two qualifications. In the first place, as explained by Lord Dunedin in *Owners of the 'Bogota'* v. *Owners of the 'Alconda'* . . . it is legitimate to go to the opinions of the Judges of the Division to explain any ambiguity there may be in the findings. And, secondly, if it appears that what purports to be a finding in law is really a finding in fact I think that it must be treated as a finding in fact. It has more than once been pointed out that if what purports to be a finding in fact is really a finding in law it should be treated as such: I need only refer to the speech of Lord Watson in *Gilroy Sons & Co.* v. *Price & Co.*, 20 R. (H.L.) 1. I think that the same principle must apply in the converse case."

Even where the House is entitled to hear appeals on a question of fact (which it always is, unless it is expressly excluded by statute) it will be slow to overturn the findings of fact in the lower courts.

As Lord Jauncey observed in *Higgins* v. *J. & M. Smith (Whiteinch) Ltd.*, 1990 S.L.T. 663 at p. 665:

"A lower appellate court will examine the transcript of evidence and reach its own conclusions as to the facts which have been established and the inferences which should be properly drawn therefrom. This review of the evidence is, however, subject to the important qualification that the appellate court will be slow to interfere with findings of primary fact based upon an assessment of credibility or reliability of witnesses. In this connection I draw no distinction between credibility in the narrow sense involving truth and untruth and reliability embracing quality of recollection and accuracy of description. The advantage possessed by the judge of first instance in relation to both these matters of seeing and hearing the witnesses is not to be lightly disregarded. Where there are concurrent findings of fact in the courts below, generally this House will interfere with those findings only where it can be shown that both courts were clearly wrong. It is nothing to the point that this House might on the evidence have reached a different conclusion which, as was said by Lord Chelmsford in *Gray* v. *Turnbull* at p. 54, was 'just as likely to be wrong' as was the conclusion of the lower courts. Lord Watson expressed a similar view in *The Owners of the 'P. Caland' and Freight* v. *Glamorgan Steamship Co. Ltd.* at p. 217. This is a salutary principle whose purpose is to prevent this House, as the ultimate court of appeal, from being flooded with cases which depend not upon important questions of law but upon pure questions of fact."

On the other hand, where the question at issue relates not to credibility or reliability but to inferences properly to be drawn from primary facts by the trial judge the House is less reticent about stepping in. [See Lord Keith, *Stair Memorial Encyclopaedia*, Vol. 6 at para. 830.]

B. CRIMINAL APPEALS

The House of Lords had no jurisdiction to hear criminal appeals from Scotland. There was no right of appeal from the Court of Justiciary to the Scottish Parliament prior to the Union and largely because of this the House of Lords in a series of cases in the eighteenth and nineteenth centuries steadfastly refused to entertain criminal appeals from the Court of Justiciary. In the last of these cases, *Mackintosh* v. *Lord Advocate* (1876) 3 R.(H.L.) 34, the Lord Chancellor (Cairns) stated at p. 36:

"Your Lordships have now the experience of upwards of one hundred and seventy years since the Union. Is there any instance produced of any appeal from an order of the Court of Justiciary during that time? No instance has been found, notwithstanding the diligence used by the learned counsel for the appellant. On the contrary, your Lordships have a most exhaustive and conclusive argument, delivered in this House by Lord Mansfield in Bywater's case, upon this very point. Lord Mansfield went through every case that was supposed to bear upon the question up to the time at which he spoke, and he shewed that there was no case of an appeal from an order of the Court of Justiciary, and that the one or two cases, the case of Mr Dempster and the earlier case of Elgin, which were supposed to bear an appearance to an appeal of that kind, really were no authorities whatever for holding that an appeal would lie. With regard to one of those cases, the case of Dempster, it appears to me to afford the strongest possible argument that an appeal would not lie, for that was a case in which, if this House could have exercised an appellate jurisdiction, it was obviously extremely well inclined to do so. But it found that it could not do so, and it therefore resorted to a very singular proceeding, which Lord Mansfield describes, and which was quite inconsistent with any assertion of an appellate right by this House.

From the time of Bywater's case down to the present day there is no instance of any appeal to this House from the Court of Justiciary, and it would be somewhat strange to imagine that during the period up to the Union, and during the period of nearly two centuries which have elapsed since the Union, down to the present time, there should during all that time have been slumbering a right to maintain an appeal from the Court of Justiciary, either to the Scottish Parliament in the first period, or to this House since the Union, and that right should never have been resorted to by any of the hundreds and thousands of those persons to whose interest it would have been to resort to it."

[For a fuller account of the history of the House's reluctance to hear Scottish criminal appeals see A.J. MacLean, "The House of Lords and Appeals from the High Court of Justiciary, 1707–1887," 1985 J.R. 192.]

This position was endorsed in the Criminal Procedure (Scotland) Act 1887 by s. 72, which provides that "all interlocutors and sentences pronounced by the High Court of Justiciary . . . shall be final and conclusive, and not subject to review by any court whatsoever."

[A similar provision relating to appeals from cases tried on indictment appears in s.17(1) of the Criminal Appeal (Scotland) Act 1926.]

It follows from the above that for most Scottish civil cases there is a two-tier appellate structure and that for some there can be three tiers: *e.g.* sheriff court (ordinary)—sheriff principal—Inner House—House of Lords. (In the period 1952–68, 15 per cent of Scottish appeals to the House of Lords originated in the sheriff courts: L. Blom-Cooper and G. Drewry, *Final Appeal* (1972) p. 379.) In England there has long been a body of opinion against even a second tier of appeal. Proponents of this view secured the abolition of appeals to the House of Lords in the 1870s only for the House's judicial functions to be restored at the eleventh hour. Part II of the Administration of Justice Act 1969 introduced a compromise which retained the two tiers of appeal but permitted certain categories of appeal to by-pass the Court of Appeal and "leapfrog" directly to the Lords. All parties to the case must consent to a "leapfrog" and both the trial judge and an Appeal Committee of the House must consider that the case involves a point of law of general public importance which is either wholly or mainly one of statutory construction, or one in respect of which the trial judge is bound by a decision of the Court of Appeal or of the House of Lords. A similar provision exists in New Zealand permitting appeals to "leapfrog" direct from the Supreme Court to the Privy Council, missing out the Court of Appeal. Such appeals are at the discretion of the Supreme Court alone and the consent of all the parties is not required. The court must, however, consider that the question involved is one which by reason of its "great general or public importance or of the magnitude of the interests affected or for any other reason," ought to be submitted to the Privy Council.

In practice the New Zealand provision has been little used and the forebodings that the 1969 Act might emasculate the Court of Appeal have proved groundless (the English "leapfrog" procedure has only been successfully invoked in five or so cases a year). As Gavin Drewry commented in "Leapfrogging" (1973) 89 L.Q.R. 260:

"[T]he appellate process tends to involve a sifting of a more or less complex body of fact, case-law and statutory construction, in varying proportions, and to be geared (at the highest level of 'general public importance' and legal complexity) to a two-stage process in which the Court of Appeal and the House of Lords play mutually complementary roles. One gains the clear impression that in many cases the Law Lords rely heavily upon the spadework done by the Court of Appeal, though it is difficult to estimate this quantitatively since it is seldom explicitly stated in the Lords' opinions (apart from a few instances where judgements below are expressly adopted)."

II. CASELOAD

Once established, the appellate jurisdiction of the House of Lords in Scottish cases soon attained a dominance which it was not to lose until the 1860s. Although the published statistics for eighteenth-century appeals are unreliable, it is clear from contemporary writings that Scottish litigants very quickly acquired a taste for appeals to the House—a development which was not welcomed by the Court of Session or by the commentators. By 1712 Fountainhall in his *Journal of Decisions* (Vol. 2, p. 734) was complaining that Scots appeals to the Lords "increased every year, to the great impoverishing and detriment of the Nation." In 1786 six times as many Scots appeals were presented as from England, and in the period 1794–1807 84 per cent (419 out of 501) of the appeals presented were Scots.

A number of explanations have been given for the prevalence of Scots appeals to the House in the eighteenth century. Most commonly, the English rule that an appeal to the House operated as a stay of execution of the judgment of the lower court, is blamed. This rule was applied by the House of Lords in Scots appeals from 1709 onwards. Since this was a reversal of the existing Scottish procedure, because appeals could take several years in the Lords and because it was possible to appeal directly from the interlocutory judgments of the Lords Ordinary it is very likely that the new ruling did encourage unsuccessful litigants in Scotland to appeal, simply as a delaying tactic. (It is not clear why this tactic was not equally popular in England.) Secondly, although in theory the House was sitting as a Scottish court when it heard Scots appeals, in reality such cases were usually argued by English counsel, using English law and terms of art, before lay peers and judges with no training or knowledge of Scots law. The forensic lottery thus produced (the House was more likely to reverse the Court of Session than to affirm it in the eighteenth century), coupled with the expense and inconvenience of appeals to the Lords must have "coerced" many respondents into settling even where they had a strong case. On the other hand the expenses incurred by an appellant who abandoned his appeal to the House even after a number of years, were minimal. Frivolous appeals were the order of the day.

Nevertheless, it was not until the Court of Session Act 1808 that Parliament responded to the Scottish appeals which were threatening to swamp the House of Lords. Section 15 provided (see p. 54 above) that in future appeals could only come from the First or Second Divisions and that interlocutory appeals from the Divisions would require leave (from the Divisions) except where the decisions were not unanimous. The Act also tackled the problem of the 1709 ruling by providing (s. 17) that the Divisions could give interim effect to their decrees pending the outcome of the appeal to the Lords. Despite these reforms the flood of Scots appeals continued unabated. Thus, of the 266 appeals pending before the House in 1811, 76 per cent were Scots. By 1827 the percentage of Scots appeals pending had only dropped to 64 per cent. It was not until the professionalisation of the House in the middle of the century (see Robert Stevens, *Law and Politics* (1979), Chap. 2), with the "abolition" of the lay peers' rights to vote on appeals and the elevation of several judges to the peerage, that the stature of the House as a court increased sufficiently to attract as many English appeals as Scottish ones. Only since the 1860s have the number of English appeals presented to the House consistently exceeded the number of Scottish appeals. (Even then there have been aberrant years, *e.g.* 1890 when 47 Scottish appeals were presented and only 30 English ones.)

Why Scottish appeals remained so numerous despite the reforms designed to curb them which were contained in the various Court of Session Acts of the first quarter of the nineteenth century, is still something of a mystery. Perhaps the habit had become engrained. Other, less charitable explanations have been put forward.

Gibb, *Law from over the Border*, p. 65
"Bethell, who later became Chancellor as Lord Westbury, was firmly persuaded of the litigiousness of the Scots. He spoke of their miserable ingenuity as soon as they became engaged in litigation when, so he said, there ensued an entire absence of prudence, sound sense and discretion."

The witnesses who gave evidence to the Select Committee on the Appellate Jurisdiction which reported in 1856 failed to agree on the matter.

Stevens, *Law and Politics*, p. 43
"On the question of why there were so many Scottish appeals, views varied. The Lord Advocate suggested that the Scots regarded appeals to the Lords as a lottery; Mr Anderson, Q.C. (Scotland), denied that the Scots were more litigious than the English, 'but when they go to law they are more persevering in their litigation'; and John Rolt, Q.C. (Scotland), claimed, 'It is the consistency of our character; having taken up a view, we maintain it'."

Whatever is the true explanation, a substantial flow of Scots appeals continued until the 1930s. Since then the number of Scots appeals has rarely exceeded ten a year—sometimes it has been much less.

TABLE 1

Appeals heard and disposed of in the House of Lords

Year	Scots Appeals	English Appeals
1860	18	27
1870	31	19
1880	12	22
1890	16	30
1900	8	56
1910	13	59
1920	23	45
1930	11	38
1939	4	41
1950	0	31
1960	9	29
1970	5	29
1980	4	69
1981	9	63
1982	7	72
1983	9	64
1984	3	56
1985	3	55
1986	5	46
1987	9	98
1988	3	67
1989	10	55
1990	3	48

[Sources: Judicial Statistics;
Final Appeal; Law and Politics.]

Although the introduction of legal aid for appeals to the House of Lords in 1960 led to a small increase in Scots appeals in the next ten years, since then they have dropped by a third. It seems probable that the high cost of such appeals even where legal aid is available will keep the House's Scottish caseload low. This might suggest that free legal aid should be available to facilitate appeals on important points of law. (The Hughes Commission seems to have favoured such a proposal. See R.8.30.)

III. COMPOSITION

Despite the overwhelming preponderance of Scottish appeals to the House of Lords in the 100 years following the Act of Union it was not until 1867 that the first judge with a training in Scots law began to sit consistently in the House. Understandably, legal scholars in recent times have attributed the anglicisation which took place in Scots law in the eighteenth and nineteenth centuries partly to the lack of Scots-trained judges in the Lords. Yet, curiously, the Scottish legal profession during this period was not as opposed to the absence of such judges as might have been anticipated. The quality of the Court of Session's decisions in the eighteenth century was not always of the highest (they were often given without reasons). The Scottish witnesses who gave evidence to the Select Committee on the Appellate Jurisdiction of the House of Lords in 1856, were convinced as to the value of retaining the "right" of appeal to the House in Scottish cases, but divided as to the merit of a proposal that a Scots-trained judge should be promoted to the House of Lords. The Lord Advocate, the Dean of Faculty, the majority of the Bar and the Writers to the Signet all appeared to favour such an appointment. But the Lord Justice-Clerk was but one of a number of dissenting voices.

"Opinions delivered before the Select Committee"
(1856)
2 Macq. at p. 664

"The Right Hon. LORD JUSTICE CLERK OF SCOTLAND: I always believed the suitors to be exceedingly unfavourable to any such notion as that of a Scotch Judge being placed upon the Court of Appeal. The present feeling, as far as my knowledge goes of the Faculty of Advocates, is quite new. I never heard the subject broached, during the eleven years I was Dean of Faculty; and I can speak from my positive knowledge that Lord Corehouse, Lord Moncrieff, Lord Murray, and others, who were seniors to me, thought that it was quite an essential feature of the Court of Appeal that there should be no Scotch lawyers, but that it should be composed entirely of English Judges. There are a great many benefits I think resulting from that."

The present-day provisions as to who may sit and vote in appeals to the House of Lords are contained in the Appellate Jurisdiction Act 1876, s. 5,

"An appeal shall not be heard and determined by the House of Lords unless there are present at such hearing and determination not less than three of the following persons, in this Act designated Lords of Appeal; that is to say,
(1) The Lord Chancellor of Great Britain for the time being; and
(2) The Lords of Appeal in Ordinary to be appointed as in this Act mentioned; and
(3) Such Peers of Parliament as are for the time being holding or have held any of the offices in this Act described as high judicial offices."

One of the first two Lords of Appeal in Ordinary to be appointed pursuant to the Act was Scots, thereafter there was always at least one Scottish Lord of Appeal and, since 1947, always at least two.

TABLE 2

Scots-trained Law Lords active from 1867–1993

Lords of Appeal		Judicial Peers
		Colonsay, 1867–74
Gordon, 1876–79		
Watson, 1880–99		Shand, 1892–1904
Robertson, 1899–1909		Kinnear, 1900, 1909–17
		Dunedin, 1905–09
Shaw, 1909–29	Dunedin, 1913–32	
Thankerton, 1929–48	Macmillan, 1930–39, 1941–47	Alness, 1934–37
Reid, 1948–75	Normand, 1947–53	
	Keith, 1953–61	
	Guest, 1961–71	
Fraser, 1975–85	Kilbrandon, 1971–77	Wheatley, 1975–88
	Keith, 1977–	Emslie, 1980–
Mackay, 1985–87		Mackay, 1987–
Jauncey, 1988–		

As can be seen from Table 2, although there have been several periods during this century when there have been three "active" Scots-trained Law Lords (indeed between 1930–32 three of the seven Lords of Appeal were Scots-trained), these periods have been the exception rather than the rule. Because Appellate Committees normally sit with five Law Lords, Scots-trained judges have rarely constituted a majority of those sitting in a particular case. In fact, there are still Scottish appeals where only one, or sometimes no, Scots-trained judge is sitting. Between 1952–68, 24% of the Scots appeals to the House were heard by an Appellate Committee including only one or no Scots-trained Law Lord (*Final Appeal*, p. 381). In 1975 the Lord Advocate, in response to a parliamentary question from Mrs. Winifred Ewing, stated:

"*The Lord Advocate*: Of the nine Lords of Appeal in Ordinary two are always appointed from the Scottish Bench or Bar.

Appeals are normally heard by five Lords of Appeal, and I understand that every effort is made to ensure that the two Scottish Lords of Appeal are present in the case of a Scottish appeal. Both Scottish Lords of Appeal sat in 15 of the 18 Scottish appeals heard during the period 1970–74; one sat in two of the remaining three, and in one case no Scottish Lord of Appeal was present"—893 H.C. Deb., col. 115 (W.A.), 10 June 1975.

When Halsbury was Lord Chancellor there is reason to believe that in at least one important Scottish appeal the "exclusion" of a Scots-trained judge was improperly motivated. Halsbury was not averse to "packing" the House where it suited him. This seems to have occurred in the *Free Church of Scotland* case ((1904) 7 F.(H.L.) 1).

Paterson, "Judges: A Political Elite?" p. 123

"This momentous Scots Appeal involved over £2 million and turned on a knowledge and understanding of Scottish ecclesiastical history and practice. It was decided unanimously in favour of the United Free church by the five Scottish judges in the Court of Session. In the House of Lords Halsbury favoured the Free Church but the six Law Lords split evenly. By tradition the Appeal should therefore have been dismissed but fortunately for Halsbury, one of his opponents (Shand) died before judgement could be delivered. Halsbury had the grace to order a re-hearing but despite press suggestions declined to invite Kinnear (the obvious Scottish Judge) to sit in the increased court, inviting two English judges instead. Halsbury's side won the rehearing but the political storm which resulted led the government to appoint a Committee chaired by Kinnear to reverse the impact of the decision. Two of the English judges admitted afterwards that had they had the guidance of a Scots judge familiar with the ecclesiastical position they would have voted the other way."

Nevertheless, even in Halsbury's time the exigencies of running an Appellate Committee in the House and a Judicial Committee in the Privy Council imposed limitations on the Lord Chancellor's room for manoeuvre in panel selection. In recent years the logistical problems have considerably increased.

Paterson, *The Law Lords*, pp. 87–89

"Selection for Appellate Committees although theoretically in the hands of the Lord Chancellor, is actually delegated to his Permanent Secretary who consults the Lord Chancellor in cases of difficulty. Lord Hailsham described the guidelines which operated in his first period as Lord Chancellor, in the following way,

'Obviously cases which have party political implications should normally be adjudicated by non-political judges. Also the composition of the panel must take account of the nature of the problems to be adjudicated upon, an expert in each of the relevant fields being made available where possible. A Scottish Law Lord should usually sit in all Scottish cases. These special considerations are, however, exceptional. The normal practice is to select the most convenient panel available.'

In practice the Permanent Secretary often has remarkably little room for manoeuvre. At the end of each legal term he meets with the Principal Clerk of the Judicial Office and the Judicial Clerk to the Privy Council. Together they compile a provisional list setting out the order for hearings of appeals in the following term in the House and in the Privy Council and the two Clerks brief the Permanent Secretary as to the talents needed in the various appeals. If there is a Chancery appeal in the Lords and a commercial case before the Privy Council then other things being equal the Chancery Law Lords will sit in the Lords. Equally, Chancery Law Lords tend not to sit on criminal appeals. When a Scots appeal comes to the Lords strong efforts are made to ensure that one, if not both, Scottish Law Lords will sit. But of course other things never are equal. If the Law Lord is Scottish he may be wanted to head a strong team in the Privy Council or to preside in an English appeal before a second Appellate Committee. A balance has to be struck to ensure that junior Law Lords are not relegated to the Privy Council for more than 50% of the year. Judges who have sat in an appeal in the Court of Appeal or in the Court of Session and since become Lords of Appeal, have to be excluded when that appeal comes before the Lords. On top of this, because of the difficulty in synchronising the hearing in the Appellate Committee and the Judicial Committee of the Privy Council, there is a tendency to keep the same or almost the same panel of Law Lords together for several appeals on end.

As if the logistical problems of organising suitable panels for the House and the Privy Council several weeks or months in advance were not enough, the Lord Chancellor's Office has to cope with subsequent developments—often at the last minute. A case may drastically overrun its estimate, a judge can fall ill, or decline to sit because of an interest in a case, he may want to attend a conference in a foreign country or be asked to serve as Chairman of a Royal Commission or a Public Inquiry. Such complications go a long way to ensuring that any present day Lord Chancellor would find it exceedingly difficult to 'pack the court' in cases of a particular type, even if he were minded to do so. They are also the explanation of the occasional 'freak' panel of Law Lords which is thrown up, *e.g.* one with five common law Lords of Appeal or one which contains no Scottish Law Lord in a Scots Appeal." [For a rare example of recusal and judicial disqualification on a significant scale in the House of Lords, see *In re Lonrho plc* [1990] 2 A.C. 154.]

Of the members of the Appellate Committee the presiding judge can exercise the most influence over the course and length of the argument presented to the court by counsel. Indeed, his leadership role in the exchanges between the Bench and counsel can often be greater in this phase of the decision-making process than in the drafting of the final decision. [See Paterson, *The Law Lords*, Chaps 4 and 5 and Paterson, "Scottish Lords of Appeal, 1876–1988" (1988) J.R. 235.] Possibly in recognition of the fact that experience is not synonymous with expertise when it comes to chairing Appellate and Appeal Committees, the rules on judicial precedence governing the right to preside at meetings of these Committees were changed in 1984. As Lord Hailsham announced to the House of Lords:

"As your Lordships know, the practice is that at sittings in the House itself, if present, the Lord Chancellor presides on the Woolsack. If he is not present . . . the Woolsack is taken by the senior Lord of Appeal present, seniority being reckoned from the date of first appointment. . . .

Nevertheless, the position is still not ideal, in that the duty of presiding is still governed by the order in appointment of the Lords of Appeal in Ordinary. . . . This has persuaded me that the time has now come to bring the arrangements in the House and in the Appeal and Appellate Committees into line with what is now the normal practice in other parts of the judicial system.

I have therefore advised Her Majesty that it would be appropriate for her in future to appoint the senior and second senior Law Lords who, between them, normally preside over two sittings of Committees, or of the House and the Judicial Committee of the Privy Council. . . . In the absence of either or both of them, precedence among the Lords of Appeal in Ordinary will thereafter continue to be governed as before, by the date of first appointment without regard to rank in the peerage."

LORD DIPLOCK: "My Lords . . . I hope that it will not be thought to be out of place if, as the longest serving, by many years, of the current Law Lords, I were to express my full support for the changes which my noble and learned friend upon the Woolsack proposes to make with regard to the office of presiding over the Appellate Committee and the Judicial Committee of the Privy Council.

Twenty-three years of sitting in appellate courts, both as a member and during the last nine years habitually as a presider, have taught me that the task of presiding over a plurality of judges in such a way as to promote an efficient and expeditious way of dealing with appeals is not the same as producing judgments which clarify and develop the law. The tasks call for different qualities. They may be combined in the same judge, but also they may not. To preside is a more taxing task, and increasing age may well render a judge less fit to undertake it, though still leave unimpaired his ability to produce judgments which clarify and develop the law.

For efficient administration of justice in the highest court in the United Kingdom seniority ought not to be the sole criterion to preside. No reflection is intended on any appellate judge that he should sit in a court presided over by one appointed later than himself."—453 H.L. Deb., col. 915–18, 27 June 1984. [The necessity for this change can be questioned, especially since its practical effect to date has been limited—other than to cause gratuitous offence north of the Border. See Paterson, "Scottish Lords of Appeal 1876–1988" (1988) J.R. 235 at p. 251.]

IV. DECISION-MAKING IN THE LORDS

Paterson, "Appellate Decision-Making in the Common Law World," pp. 1–3, 5–9
[This extract is derived from the author's interview-based research on the Law Lords.]
"It is a truth commonly neglected by scholars, that judicial decision making in the higher appellate courts in the Anglo-American world is typically a collective enterprise—a group activity rather than a multi-

ciplity of individual efforts. The size and content of the 'group' varies from court to court. Usually, it includes the counsel or the brief-writers as well as the sitting judges; sometimes, it extends to other judges or to law clerks; very occasionally, it includes legal academics or other 'outsiders.' Again, the form and nature of the exchanges between 'group-members' varies between courts. Thus, in the U.S. Supreme Court the bulk of the interchanges in the decision making process, whether between counsel and the Bench, Justice and law clerk or Justice and Justice, are in writing. In the House of Lords and the Privy Council they are mainly oral. Insignificant as such variations may seem, they entail that the role of the appellate judge in the Anglo-American world is far from homogeneous. . . .

In the House of Lords counsel and Law Lord alike consider that a predominantly oral approach, with the consequent flexibility which it gives to arguments, has advantages which cannot be matched in a written brief. Counsel can, and are expected to, respond to the thoughts expressed by the Court and to adjust their arguments accordingly. Lord Reid told me,

'[Counsel] have got to know their stuff and know it backwards and they have got to be a little bit, taking a hint, you know. A man who simply reads out his stuff from his notes and will not take a hint is not a good advocate.' Thus a case can change course in mid-stream as a result of a point thrown up in the debate. As another Law Lord remarked,

'I have known cases in which when the case started I was convinced that the appellant was either right or wrong and during the course of the case a point made either by me or by one of my colleagues has completely changed one's view.'

Moreover, oral argumentation, at least in the House of Lords and the Privy Council, both restricts the range of judicial creativity and exercises a persuasive influence on the decision ultimately reached, in a way that written briefs, at least in the U.S. Supreme Court, do not. As Lord Scarman recently observed,

'The judge, however wise, creative and imaginative he may be, is "cabin'd cribb'd, confined, bound in" not, as was Macbeth, to his "saucy doubts and fears" but by the evidence and arguments of the litigants. It is this limitation, inherent in the forensic process, which sets bounds to the scope of judicial law reform.'

Gillis Wetter in *The Styles of Appellate Judicial Opinions* concludes from this limitation that,

'the most notable effect of a court considering the primary function of its opinions to be the rendering of conclusive answers to the allegations of counsel . . . is that of shifting the responsibility for judicial law-making from the courts to the Bar . . . '

I think that Wetter is overstating his case, for the interchange between Bench and Bar is not all one way. It is a dialectic to which each side contributes. Each may borrow from the other. Nevertheless, it is clear that counsel's part in the decision making process in the Lords is a significant one even though it has been overlooked in much of the recent jurisprudential writing on judicial creativity. A scrutiny of *The Brethren*, of judicial diaries and other research, however, reveals that in the U.S. Supreme Court, despite occasional flattering references to counsel's arguments by Justices, the oral and written arguments of counsel contribute considerably less to the decision making process than is the case in the United Kingdom. This is in part due to the inflexibility of written briefs, in part to the lack of a specialist Supreme Court Bar and in part to the fact that Justices may (if they so desire) use their law clerks to assist them in researching the relevant law.

In the House of Lords or the Privy Council . . . there are constant discussions between the judges outside the Committee Rooms—at lunch, at the end of the day's hearing, in each other's rooms and in the mornings before the hearing resumes. Once the hearing comes to an end a formal conference is held. Thereafter, the presiding judge (in the Privy Council) assigns who is to write the opinion of the Court. In the House of Lords it is sometimes collectively agreed that a Law Lord will write the leading opinion but more often than not it is still unclear at the end of the conference who will write an opinion.

The Law Lords are divided as to the merits of the Privy Council practice of having a single majority judgment. One retired Law Lord commented,

'The people who were accustomed to being in the Privy Council got rather good at rendering one judgment that reflected the opinions of the others. There was a sort of tradition that you didn't take a strong line unless it was one which could be shared by the others.'

Other Law Lords were less enthusiastic. As one put it,

'We all know that in the Privy Council it gave quite a bit of weakness over the centuries to a Privy Council judgment that sentences were put in for the man who thought the appeal was doubtful as to whether it should succeed, and felt that it was more likely it should fail, as against the man who wrote it, who was certain it should succeed, and so he would put in the sentences. . . . You are getting a compromise judgment in a sense.'

Composite judgments of this sort are much rarer in the Lords, though there are some famous, not to say notorious, examples. As a result, the 'bargaining' over the content of the opinion of the court which is so prevalent in the U.S. Supreme Court is much less common in the House of Lords.

Yet, curiously, there are probably as many private discussions between individual Law Lords concerning an appeal as take place between Justices in the U.S. Supreme Court. This is largely due to two institutional factors. First, the Justices have their own chambers with several law clerks, secretaries and a messenger. Each functions as a small, independent law firm. The Justice relies on his law clerks for discussion in a case and collaborates with them while drafting his opinion. Thus he has less need to confer with his colleagues on difficult points than his transatlantic counterpart. Justice Powell has even gone so far as to assert that,

'The [Supreme] Court . . . is perhaps one of the last citadels of jealously preserved individualism. . . . The informal interchange between chambers is minimal, the most exchanges of views being by correspondence or memoranda. Indeed, a Justice may go through an entire term without being once in the chambers of all of the other eight members of the Court.'

Secondly, while the Justices frequently write comments on, or memoranda in response to, a colleague's circulated opinion, in the House of Lords this is practically never done. Either the Law Lord will comment orally to his colleagues on the opinion or he will simply adjust his speech to take account of the points made in the circulated opinion. As one Law Lord put it,

'At the stage where the opinions are circulated one's colleagues are very polite. If there is an obvious omission you draw attention to it, but you would seldom re-argue the merits.

Another commented,

'Generally you'd leave it alone unless it was a case where you'd agreed that only one judgment would be delivered or if you were going to follow a particular man you might go to him and say, "Look I'm, really almost in entire agreement with you so I just propose to say, 'I agree,' but I'm a bit stuck about this [phrase] . . . " You might do that.'

Of course, some judges participate in the exchanges which I have been describing, with greater effectiveness than others. Small group analysis of the U.S. Supreme Court has shown that both 'social leaders' (judges who endeavour to reduce tensions and to reconcile differences amongst their brethren) and 'task leaders' (judges who use their personality, intelligence, technical competence, esteem within the Court and persuasive ability to lead their brethren to a particular outcome in an appeal) exist on the Court. They are also to be found in the House of Lords and the Privy Council. The acid test for the 'group-orientated' Law Lord, however, is not how often he influences his colleagues. Some Law Lords have found to their cost that, if they 'lobby' their colleagues too persistently (particularly if they are not open to persuasion in return), they are very likely to have a negative influence on their colleagues. The acid test is whether he can influence a majority of his colleagues to share his point of view, particularly where this will result in a voting switch or even a reversal of the existing majority position. Such successes do occur but are remarkably hard to document. The final judgment cannot be taken at face value. A unanimous decision may emerge from a Court divided at the first conference. Equally, there have been 3: 2 decisions where none of the participants have ever felt any doubt. My researchers revealed that in the Lords most changes of mind take place at the hearing stage, but that they also occur between the first conference and the final judgment. In the U.S. Supreme Court, perhaps because of the pervasiveness of 'bargaining,' Justices frequently change their positions after the initial conference. Nevertheless, it is very difficult to establish that such changes in the House of Lords are the outcome of effective lobbying by 'group-orientated' Law Lords. What can be said is that the Law Lords with such an orientation have usually ended up on the majority side in cases in the past twenty years and where the House has been heavily divided."

The conclusion that appellate decision-making in the House of Lords is a collective activity has two implications. First, that the role of counsel in the decision-making process has hitherto been insufficiently recognised. Secondly, the traditional measure of success in an appellate judge, *i.e.* the long-term standing of his judgments, is incomplete. A judge who exercises "leadership" in his court may appear very little in the Law Reports, though profoundly influencing the outcome of the cases in which he sits.

Decision-making in the House of Lords has undergone a number of changes in the last 15 years largely as a result of reforms initiated by Lords Diplock and Wilberforce. First, the House has endeavoured to cut the cost of appeals to the Lords by introducing measures designed to curtail the length of the oral argument before the House.

M.V. Yorke Motors (a firm) v. Edwards
[1982] 1 All E.R. 1024

LORD DIPLOCK: "The length of time required for counsel's opening addresses at hearings of appeals to the House of Lords has been significantly reduced by the practice adopted over the last seven years under which all the members of the Appellate Committee who will be sitting on an appeal will have read in advance at least the judgments in the courts below and the written cases lodged by the parties. This practice of which the purpose is to reduce the length and consequently the cost of appeals to the House of Lords is one of which by now the Bar should be well aware. Signs are, however, now appearing that this awareness may be giving rise to a tendency to expand the written cases lodged by the parties so as to incorporate and develop in them detailed written arguments supported by lengthy citations from and references to numerous authorities, much on the same line as the written 'briefs' submitted by the parties in appeals to appellate courts in the United States which have resulted in oral argument playing a relatively insignificant role in the decision-making process adopted by appellate courts in that country.

The practice of this House whereby members of the Appellate Committee read in advance the judgments in the courts below and the parties' written cases is not intended to reduce the importance of the role played by oral argument in the decision-making process. Its purpose is to add to the cogency of the oral argument by eliminating the necessity for vocal exposition of facts already stated in the judgments below and the reading out of those judgments in extenso. Counsel are thus enabled from the outset to concentrate their arguments on what are the real issues in the appeal. A written case lodged by a party, which itself contains long and elaborate argument and citations from and references to numerous authorities, does nothing to serve this purpose that is not better done by a written case that follows the guidance contained in . . . the Directions as to Procedure applicable to Civil Appeals to the House of Lords . . . On the contrary, it defeats one of the principal objects of the practice by adding substantially to the costs of the appeal which the shortening of the oral hearing is designed to reduce. . . .

The case should set out the heads, but no more than the heads, of the argument on each of the issues which it is intended should be advanced by counsel for the party at the oral hearing to challenge or support, as the case may be, the decision on that issue of the court from which the appeal is brought. Detailed or elaborate argument added unnecessarily to the costs of preparing the case and is seldom helpful or time saving at the oral hearing. Reference to authorities relied on in support of the argument on any issue should be limited to key authorities (seldom numbering more than one or two on any one issue) which lay down the principle which it is contended is applicable, and the particular passage or passages in the judgments in which the principle is stated should be identified and, unless unduly lengthy, may helpfully be quoted verbatim. But references to numerous other cases in which that principle has been previously applied by courts to particular facts which it is claimed may be regarded as presenting some analogies to the facts of the case under appeal, are usually out of place in the written case and, I may add, more often than not turn out to be time wasting in oral argument also. Where, however, it is intended to rely, as persuasive authority, on cases decided by courts in other countries or legal writings such as the American Restatement, it is of assistance to their Lordships if specific reference is made to these in the written case."

Secondly, there has been a marked shift in the attitude of the House of Lords towards the issue of multiple judgments. Single judgments in the name of one Law Lord with concurrences from the other four Law Lords who have heard the appeal have become the norm rather than the exception, especially in cases involving statutory construction. [In 1974 25% of appeals to the Lords resulted in single judgments, by 1983 the figure had reached 68%. A. Bradney, "The Changing Face of the House of Lords" (1985) J.R. 178.]

Re Prestige Group plc
[1984] I.R.L. 166

LORD DIPLOCK: "[It] has become a frequent practice in this House when dealing with questions of statutory construction . . . [to have] only [one] reasoned speech; the other Law Lords [limiting] themselves to expressing their agreement with it. Because for historical reasons a decision of the House of Lords in the exercise of its judicial functions takes the form of a motion passed at the close of a debate between those Law Lords by whom the appeal was heard, the single reasoned speech (although of recent years it has not been read out viva voce but made available instead in written form) cannot accurately be termed 'the judgement of the court'. Nevertheless, lest there be any continuing misapprehension among litigants or their lawyers, it should be clearly understood that at the drafting stage what later emerges as a single reasoned speech has been the subject of prior consultations between all members of the appellate committee by whom the appeal was heard, which frequently result in the making of revisions that are incorporated in the final draft. Indeed, connoisseurs of judicial literary styles may find it possible in some cases to identify particular passages in the single speech of which the authorship is not that of the Law Lord by whom the first draft of the main body of the speech was prepared."

There are indications that already this shift towards single judgments has achieved the increased certainty within the legal community as to the meaning of decisions of the House, which was its aim. But critics of these developments would argue that the gain in certainty has been purchased at too great a price. Because the legal community tends to treat single judgments from the House of Lords as though they were statutes, the flexibility of the common law which has been its hallmark, is being curtailed. Single judgments freeze the development of the law—the incremental "trial and error" progress of the common law is being abandoned for the "stop-go" model of the log-jam. Future judges will find their room for manoeuvre has been much reduced by the actions of the present Law Lords. [For a powerful critique of single judgments in the Lords see F.A. Mann, "The Single Speech" (1991) 107 L.Q.R. 519.]

V. THE ROLE OF THE HOUSE OF LORDS

Drewry, "Leapfrogging," p. 263
"The role of the House of Lords as a final court of appeal . . . can be broken down into two closely related but ultimately quite different elements, review and supervision. The former is the process whereby mistakes at first instance are corrected and some kind of continuity and certainty maintained in the administration of justice. Supervision is the process of laying down fresh precedents and up-dating old ones for the guidance of lower courts in the hierarchy and of resolving that small percentage of cases embodying legal problems of a peculiarly high order both of difficulty and of public importance. These two functions cannot be separated if only because . . . points of law of general public

importance cannot be decided in the abstract but must arise in the course of litigation. But the emphasis is different: review is principally to do with achieving justice in the instant case while supervision has primarily to do with solving legal problems in the wider public interest."

Lord Reid (Interview, 1972)

"Well, the first . . . that comes to mind is that you've got to keep the laws of England and Scotland in line, and if you've got any United Kingdom statutes somebody's got to mediate and I think this is the best way of doing it. You can't have a sort of joint meeting at York. Then I think our function is twofold—(a) to clear up the messes, of which there are many, and (b) occasionally to be a bit bold and innovate a bit."

Stevens, *Law and Politics*, p. 627

"The future will lie in an acceptance of the element of discretion in the final appeal process, coupled with a responsibility to articulate the purposes and goals of different branches of the law. The courts in Britain are never likely to compete with the legislature; such a possibility runs counter to four hundred years of political and intellectual history. Complementarity with the legislature is, however, essential; and complementarity involves intelligent creativity. The next decade will show whether the appeal judges are capable of providing a rationale that will at a minimum make them an essential element in the British Constitution and, ideally, raise the issue of whether they might not appear as the junior partners of Parliament in the lawmaking process."

[See further on the role of the Lords, Lord Fraser of Tullybelton, "The House of Lords as Court of Last Resort for the United Kingdom" 1986 S.L.T. (News) 33.]

CHAPTER 4

CRIMINAL COURTS

In Scotland there are three levels of criminal court: the district court, the sheriff court, and the High Court of Justiciary. District courts handle primarily minor offences (mainly statutory) committed within their territorial jurisdiction (one of the local authority district or islands areas). Sheriff courts may deal with a wide range of offences (minor or serious) committed within the sheriffdom, including all those that can be raised in the district court and most that can be heard in the High Court. As in the district court, the sentencing powers of the sheriff court are limited. The High Court's jurisdiction extends throughout Scotland and sometimes beyond. Like the sheriff court its case jurisdiction is almost universal. It has exclusive jurisdiction with respect to certain grave offences and in practice all the most serious cases are tried in the High Court.

Criminal cases are conducted in two ways in Scotland. Under the solemn procedure serious crimes are tried by judge and jury either in the High Court or the sheriff court. The trial proceeds on the basis of charges contained in a document called an indictment and severe penalties are available on conviction. All other offences are dealt with under the summary procedure and trial is by a judge or judges without a jury, either in the sheriff or the district court. In summary trials the charges against an accused are set out in a document called a summary complaint.

I. THE PROSECUTION PROCESS

The prosecution of crime in Scotland is almost exclusively the prerogative of the Crown. The right to private prosecution though still extant is rarely invoked.

A. PUBLIC PROSECUTION

Sheehan, *Criminal Procedure in Scotland and France*, p. 109 *et seq.*

"The Public Prosecutor
132 Prior to 1587, most prosecutions were left in the hands of the injured party, although the King's Advocate, otherwise known as the Lord Advocate usually joined the prosecution for the King's interest partly in

73

order to preserve law and order, and partly out of financial interest as any fines went to the royal treasury. The instigation of criminal proceedings was however in the hands of the victim. In 1587, the Lord Advocate was empowered by an Act of Parliament to instigate criminal proceedings 'although the parties be silent or would otherwise privily agree'. This power of the Lord Advocate to prosecute without the concurrence of any private party made him the master of the instance, giving him an almost absolute right to decide who should be prosecuted, and, in the absence of legal provision to the contrary, in which court the case should be tried. The Lord Advocate is responsible for and directs all public prosecutions in Scotland. He is assisted by the Solicitor General for Scotland and [twelve] Advocate Deputes. The Lord Advocate and the Solicitor General are known as the Law Officers of the Crown, and the Advocate Deputes as Crown Counsel.

133 The Lord Advocate and the Solicitor General are appointed by the Queen on the recommendation of the Prime Minister. They are selected from among the leading senior counsel, and since they are political appointments, change office every time there is a change in government. The Advocate Deputes are advocates appointed . . . by the Lord Advocate . . . [on a part time basis but do not now demit office following a change in government. All prosecutions in the High Court are conducted by Advocate Deputes or occasionally, in cases of exceptional importance, by one of the Law Officers of the Crown.]

The Procurator Fiscal
135 The procurator fiscal is the prosecutor in the sheriff [and district] court, although his duties range much further. The office of procurator fiscal was known in the 16th century when he was an officer employed by the sheriff with the duty of collecting fines imposed by the court. Such fines were paid into a fund known as 'The Fisk', and the procurator fiscal appeared at the trial just before sentence was imposed. While the sheriff acted both as prosecutor and judge in his own court, the prosecuting duties were taken over by the procurator fiscal by the time of the 17th century . . . In 1927 the appointment of procurators fiscal was placed in the hands of the Lord Advocate and since then all procurators fiscal and their deputes have been whole-time civil servants. [Nowadays most of them are also solicitors. Such has been the increase in criminal work in the past decade that there are now over 250 procurators fiscal in Scotland and over 60 in Glasgow alone.] . . .

140 The procurator fiscal is subject to the direction of and control by the Lord Advocate, who issues general instructions in a Book of Regulations to all procurators fiscal concerning the conduct of their duties. In addition, from time to time the Lord Advocate issues instructions concerning specific matters by means of Crown Office circulars. The advantage of this system is that it promotes a high degree of uniformity of procedure and practice. The Lord Advocate may also issue instructions concerning the conduct of any particular case. Such instructions however do not derogate from the important functions of the procurator fiscal, who has been described as 'central to the criminal administration of Scotland'."

Procurators fiscal have a number of duties, including the investigation of all sudden or suspicious deaths, all deaths in the course of employment, all suicides, all anaesthetic and road traffic fatalities, and all serious fires and explosions occurring within their district. Their major functions, however, are the investigation of all crimes committed in their district, the prosecution of all cases taken to the district or sheriff court and the initial investigation and preparatory work for cases going to the High Court.

Gordon, "Criminal Proceedings in Scotland," pp. 253–254
"In practice much of the investigation is done by the police, who obviously have the organisation, training, experience and technical facilities which the procurator fiscal lacks, but once the fiscal is informed of an investigation he personally directs it, acting in frequent personal contact with the detective constables concerned, and giving instructions as to what enquiries are to be made and what information sought. In most cases the procurator fiscal may not know about the offence until the police have charged someone, but he is frequently consulted at an early stage, and he is called out personally to the locus of all suspected murders."

After conducting their investigations the procurators fiscal must decide whether or not a prosecution is warranted. In so doing they will take account of a number of factors.

Gordon, "Criminal Proceedings in Scotland," p. 274
"Perhaps the most important decision in the whole process is the decision whether to put on trial or not. Renton & Brown's *Criminal Procedure* gives some general principles to act as a guide to a prosecutor in making this decision. He should take account, of course [of whether the facts uncovered constitute a crime known to Scots law] . . . of whether there is sufficient evidence to justify proceedings—this is important in Scotland where a crime may clearly have been committed by someone but there may be no corroborative evidence and therefore no prospect of conviction; of whether the act is sufficiently important to be made the subject of criminal proceedings; of whether there is reason to suspect malice on the part of the informant . . . of whether there is sufficient excuse for the conduct of the accused to warrant abandonment of the proceedings; and of whether the case is more suitable for civil proceedings. The courts have also indicated that it is the prosecutor's duty not to enforce statutory regulations which are unrelated to modern conditions. These considera-

tions guide both the procurator fiscal in his initial decision and the Crown Office in issuing instructions in reported cases, but the Crown Office may also take account of wider questions of policy."

The guidelines contained in Renton and Brown were quoted with approval by the Crown Office in its evidence to the Hughes Commission, but not elaborated on. It is somewhat surprising in the era of the Justice Charter that we should still be in the dark as to whether Scottish prosecutors follow the English Director of Public Prosecution's approach to sufficiency of evidence if a prosecution is brought—is there a better than 50% chance of a conviction? Where there is sufficient evidence, the D.P.P. also asks himself whether it is in the public interest that a prosecution be brought. It seems likely the Crown Office expects Scottish prosecutors to ask themselves the same question.

It is at the stage of this initial decision of whether or not to prosecute that the significance of the Scottish system of independent prosecution is most clearly apparent. As one procurator fiscal has written:

Harris, "The Life of a Procurator Fiscal," p. 95
"Once the case is in the Procurator Fiscal's office, it is looked at by someone who has had no knowledge of the case until it lands up in front of him, and moreover by someone who has in no way been concerned with the police investigations into the case. Therefore preconceived notions of guilt or otherwise are less likely to affect that person's judgement. Because the police have charged a person with committing a crime, (this charge is contained in the police report) it does not mean the person will automatically be prosecuted by the Procurator Fiscal . . .

This highlights an important aspect of the work of the Procurator Fiscal—the separate identities of the police and the Procurator Fiscal. They are not, as is so often thought in league with each other against the criminals in an area. The duties of each are quite separate, and although in the majority of cases they take the same view of a case, their approach to a particular case will be from a different angle. . . . "

1. ALTERNATIVES TO PROSECUTION
One factor of increasing significance in relation to the decision as to whether to initiate a prosecution or not, is the range of options available to the fiscal other than prosecution in the courts. Over the last 15 years the number of recorded crimes has risen by over 70%. Inevitably, there has been a similar rise in the number of police reports to the fiscal service. Some commentators have gone so far as to say that the criminal justice system in Scotland is in crisis. Just as ADR is increasingly being talked of as a possible

solution to the problems of the civil justice system, so increasingly we find the prosecution service relying on non-court methods of disposal to tackle the growing caseload with which they are confronted. These include: no proceedings, warnings, conditional offers, fiscal fines and diversions. Thus in 1976, 93% of police reports resulted in a prosecution in court—the comparable figure for 1991 was only 53%.

Obviously, if the fiscal concludes that there is insufficient evidence to warrant a prosecution he or she may determine to mark the report as a "no pro" (no proceedings). But the decision to take no proceedings may also be taken if the case is a trivial one, one in which the fiscal considers that no useful purpose would be served by a prosecution or because of certain mitigating factors, *e.g.* the length of time which has passed since the offence was committed, age or other factors relating to the accused and the attitude of the victim.

Harris, "The Life of a Procurator Fiscal," p. 96
"It may be felt inappropriate to prosecute a person for a small theft if that person has already been punished—for example by losing his job, or by having to leave the neighbourhood and the likelihood of recurrence is small. Or, if a person feels so provoked by the behaviour of another over a period that he takes the law into his own hands, and commits a minor assault, without having instant provocation which would be recognised by the law, then prosecution of the person for assault would only aggravate an already raw situation, and the best thing that can be done is to let sleeping dogs lie. If a Procurator Fiscal decides to take no proceedings, then he need communicate that decision to no-one. It is not normal practice to send a formal intimation of this decision to the accused."

In 1986, "no pro-ing" was the most commonly used non-court option. However, thereafter it has taken second place behind conditional offers of fixed financial penalties—a trend that was accelerated as "no pro-ing" became more contentious following the publication of a report by the National Audit Office in 1989, *Prosecution of Crime in Scotland*, which, *inter alia*, highlighted the considerable variations between areas in terms of "no pro" percentages. (Not the least curious feature was that it was not always the busiest courts which had the highest percentages and vice versa. Thus a table published in 1990 shows that whilst the "no pro" rate in Glasgow was 23% the figures for Edinburgh and Aberdeen were 10% and 6% respectively. Equally while Stornoway had a rate of 2% Rothesay's was 16%. [See 1990 S.L.T. (News) 275].)

Alternatively, the fiscal may determine that the case requires some action short of prosecution or an administrative penalty and issue a formal warning to the accused either personally or by letter. Such warnings cannot be referred to in any subsequent court proceedings although it appears that lists of those who have been so warned are retained by fiscals. Warnings are most commonly used in shoplifting, speeding and breach of the peace cases. Easily the most commonly used alternative to court proceedings now are conditional offers of fixed financial penalties by fiscals to accused persons in a wide range of road traffic cases.

A majority of the Stewart Committee in their report, *Keeping Offenders Out of Court* (Cmnd. 8958: 1983) recommended that fiscals should be able to impose a fine of up to £50 on offenders, without reference to a court. However, there were powerful opponents to this proposal. Nevertheless, fiscal fines were introduced in 1988 under s. 56 of the Criminal Justice (Scotland) Act 1987 in relation to cases which could be prosecuted in the District Court (other than motoring offences). The fiscal offers the offender an opportunity of paying a fixed sum (currently £25) either as a lump sum or by instalment, to the court. If payment is made no prosecution is brought. Moreover payment is not a tacit admission of guilt and accepted fines are not recorded as convictions. [See K. Meechan, "Extrajudicial Punishment and Procurator Fiscal Fines," 1991 S.L.T. (News) 1.] It has now been suggested by the Scottish Office that the police should be able to offer "on the spot" fixed penalties to alleged road traffic offenders.

The Stewart Committee was united in its support for pre-trial diversion schemes in terms of which minor offenders in suitable cases are referred to agencies which can offer help to the offender. Social Work diversion is perhaps the best known and most successful of these. Following a pilot scheme in Ayr such schemes have been introduced throughout Scotland. Under them alleged offenders who are considered to be likely to respond positively to social work assistance and who agree to participate are referred to a social work department rather than prosecuted in court. [See I. Willock, "Diversion to Social Work Assistance" (1987) 131 SCOLAG 124.] Under pressure from Scottish Women's Aid it is being increasingly accepted that diversion schemes are inappropriate in domestic violence or child abuse cases. Diversion may also be to outside agencies like Councils on Alcoholism or to detoxification centres for persons arrested for being drunk in public. The labour intensiveness and thus the expense of such centres means that regrettably there are only two such centres in Scotland. [See S. Lloyd and A. Taylor, "Alternatives to Custody for Drunken

Offenders" (1985) 101 SCOLAG 24 and "Inverness gets new centre for drunken offenders" (1991) 179 SCOLAG 118.] Diversion may also take the form of Reparation and Mediation (recompensing the victim for the damage done) or a non-harassment agreement in neighbourhood disputes.

TABLE 1

Prosecutions in Scottish Sheriffdoms in 1990

Sheriffdom	Reports received	No Pros	Warning	Conditional Offers	Fiscal Fines	Diversions	Court Proceedings
N. Strath	43,973	8%	4%	26%	8%	0.2%	50%
S. Strath	64,284	8%	3%	27%	5%	0.2%	56%
Lothian	58,551	10%	3%	28%	2%	0.6%	49%
Glasgow	80,543	18%	5%	26%	3%	0.3%	41%
Grampian	46,090	8%	3%	27%	5%	0.7%	56%
Tayside	73,031	11%	4%	28%	5%	0.3%	50%

[Source: Parliamentary Answer reported in 1991 S.L.T. (News) 203.]

TABLE 2

Non-Court Disposals in Scotland

1990/91	%		1991/92	%
40,096	23	No Proceedings	35,434	20
13,788	8	Warnings	13,700	8
101,104	58	Conditional Offers	108,136	62
16,829	10	Fiscal Fines	15,028	9
1,381	1	Diversions	1,407	0.8
173,198		Overall Total	173,705	

[Source: The 1st Annual Report of the Crown Office and Procurator Fiscal Service 1991/92 (HMSO, 1992).]

As can be seen from these Tables there is a high degree of consistency between regions in the use of warnings and conditional offers but regional variations remain in the use of "no-proceedings" and Fiscal fines. In the absence of research the causes of these variations must remain a matter for conjecture.

2. PROSECUTION PROCEEDINGS

Once the procurator fiscal has decided that an offence has been committed and that a prosecution be initiated in respect of it, the next decisions to be made are by what procedure and in what court should the action be raised. It is the prosecution who make these choices and the defence have no say in them. Thus the accused cannot elect to be tried by a jury (solemn procedure) rather than by a judge alone (summary procedure). If the fiscal considers that the offence warrants trial on indictment he must make a report to the Crown Office. Crown counsel will then determine whether the case should proceed by indictment in the High Court or in the sheriff court or that the case be taken summarily or that no further proceedings should be taken. The usual test to be applied in determining whether to use the solemn or the summary procedure is whether, having regard to the gravity of the offence, an adequate sentence can be imposed by a summary court in the event of conviction.

[For further details concerning the operation of public prosecution today see the 1st Annual Report of the Crown Office and Procurator Fiscal Service 1991/1992.]

B. PRIVATE PROSECUTION

Apart from the Crown, summary prosecutions in Scotland can also be brought by certain public bodies for particular statutory offences (*e.g.* education authority actions against parents for permitting truancy), and by private landowners against daytime trespassers in pursuit of game (though actions of either sort are rare). Rarest of all are private prosecutions under the common law brought by victims of offences or their relatives. As we saw earlier, such private prosecutions were once the norm. By the nineteenth century they had become unusual and could only be brought with the concurrence of the Lord Advocate or the High Court. Until recently, the last successful attempt to raise such a prosecution was *J. & P. Coats Ltd.* v. *Brown* (1909) 6 Adam 19. There the Lord Advocate had refused to prosecute a coal exporter on a charge of fraud and the victims of the fraud were granted permission by the High Court to institute a prosecution in the High Court by way of criminal letters (the private equivalent of an indictment). After a number of unsuccessful attempts to invoke the procedure since then, it had been thought that it had become obsolete in all but name. However, in April 1982 the High Court granted a Bill for Criminal Letters at the instance of a woman who had been raped and severely slashed with a razor *H*. v. *Sweeney*, 1983 S.L.T. 48. The Lord Justice-General (Emslie) stated in the course of his opinion:

"The rights of a private prosecutor in our system of criminal jurisprudence have grown up alongside those of the Lord Advocate and indeed, historically, bulked larger in earlier times than those of the King's Advocate. These rights still exist and there seems to be no good reason in principle for saying that they should not be available in any case in which the Lord Advocate has, for any reason, declined to prosecute an offender to a conclusion."

The test applied by the High Court in this case was the test most clearly set out in *McBain* v. *Crichton*, 1961 J.C. 25. In that case a

Glasgow chartered accountant, who was a vice-president of a union of boys' clubs, an office which gave him a particular interest to prevent the corruption of youth, sought to prosecute a Glasgow bookseller for exposing for sale (and selling) *Lady Chatterley's Lover* by D.H. Lawrence, which he alleged was obscene. Lord Justice-General (Clyde) stated in his opinion (pp. 29–30):

"This Court can permit, and on rare occasions has permitted, a private prosecutor to proceed without the Lord Advocate's concurrence. But to entitle a private prosecutor to do so, he must be able to show some special personal interest in the matter which, notwithstanding the Lord Advocate's decision in the public interest, satisfies us that a private prosecution in respect of this special personal interest may proceed. Hume on Crimes, vol. ii, at p. 119, puts it thus: 'To support his instance the individual complainer must be able therefore to show some substantial and peculiar interest in the issue of the trial; an interest arising out of some injury which he, beyond others, has suffered on the occasion libelled, and at which he is entitled to feel more than the ordinary indignation, with which his fellow citizens will regard it. It is not therefore sufficient, that he has some feeble and remote concern in the issue, or one of a general nature, in common with a whole neighbourhood, or with all of the same order or class of society.'

But, in the present case, the wrong complained of, if it is a wrong . . . is of a quite general and public nature, committed against a whole neighbourhood or perhaps against the whole country, and, in its very nature, devoid of that personal and peculiar interest without which no private prosecution ever has been sustained in Scotland. [The complainer's interest to prevent the corruption of youth] . . . does not partake of that essential quality without which the prosecution could not proceed at the instance of a private party, because it does not show that the complainer personally and beyond all others has suffered owing to the wrong libelled. At the highest it would only invest him with an interest as protector of the morals of a class of persons in the community—namely the younger members of it. This is in its very nature a public and not a private or personal interest."

It remains a moot point whether the retention of private prosecution is justified or, as some have said, is an historical anachronism. [See further on private prosecution, *McDonald* v. *H.M. Advocate*, 1988 S.L.T. 713.]

C. REVIEW

The fact that prosecution in Scotland is almost exclusively in public hands raises the question whether a decision by a public prosecutor to prosecute or not to prosecute in a particular case is reviewable or one for which the prosecutor can be called to account. It appears that in the case of a decision by a procurator-fiscal not to prosecute, a complaint can be made to the Lord Advocate who may instruct the fiscal to make a report to him, after which the Lord Advocate will make the decision. Again, where a procurator fiscal has prosecuted summarily and the accused has been imprisoned and the sentence subsequently quashed, the fiscal may be found liable in damages to the accused if he can be shown to have acted with malice or without probable cause.

On the other hand, the Lord Advocate by constitutional convention is not required to give reasons to the courts or Parliament to justify any decision to prosecute or not to prosecute taken by him or by Crown counsel, though, as in the 1982 case, he will sometimes answer questions in Parliament and in the media in relation to such decisions. Nor can the Lord Advocate, Crown counsel or procurators fiscal in cases tried on indictment, be sued for their actings as public prosecutors. [See further, J. Edwards, *The Law Officers of the Crown* (Sweet & Maxwell: 1964) p. 177.]

McBain v. Crichton
1961 J.C. 25

LORD JUSTICE-GENERAL (Clyde): "The Lord Advocate . . . in this country is the recognised prosecutor in the public interest. It is for him, in the exercise of his responsible office, to decide whether he will prosecute in the public interest and at the public expense, and under our constitutional practice this decision is a matter for him, and for him alone. No one can compel him to give his reasons . . . the decision whether or not to prosecute is exclusively within his discretion."

[In *McDonald* v. *H.M. Advocate*, 1988 S.L.T. 713 the High Court observed that the Lord Advocate was criminally responsible for his own actings and he was not vicariously responsible for the actings of Crown Counsel, the Crown Office and procurators fiscal.]

II. COMPOSITION AND JURISDICTION OF THE COURTS

A. THE DISTRICT COURT

Since May 1975 there have been district courts (in all but one of the 56 local authority district and islands areas). Each consists of one or more justices of the peace (lay magistrates) sitting with a legal assessor (the clerk of the court—who must be legally qualified, District Courts (Scotland) Act 1975, s. 7) or, in four courts in Glasgow, a stipendiary magistrate (a judge of at least five years' standing as a solicitor or an advocate, District Courts (Scotland) Act 1975, s. 5).

The jurisdiction of criminal courts (the cases which they have the power to try and to dispose of) like that of their civil counterparts has three aspects, namely, limitations as to territory, power and competence. These aspects are governed by the place where the offence was committed and by the type of offence involved. In relation to the first aspect, for a district court to have jurisdiction the offence must have been committed within the district or islands area in which the court is situated. As to the second, in an effort to reduce congestion in the sheriff court the jurisdiction of the district court has been expanded to cover any statutory offence for which the maximum penalty does not exceed 60 days' imprisonment, a fine of £2,500 or both (Criminal Justice (Scotland) Act 1980, s. 7 as amended by the Criminal Justice Acts 1982 and 1991). These are the maximum penalties which can be imposed in the district court for common law or statutory offences unless a stipendiary magistrate is sitting when the maximum sentence becomes up to six months' imprisonment or a fine of £5,000 or both.

As to competence, the jurisdiction of the court includes breach of the peace, drunkenness, minor assaults, petty theft, offences under the Civic Government (Scotland) Act 1982 (*e.g.* soliciting, loitering and being a known thief) and certain minor statutory offences, *e.g.* parking fines. Again, in a bid to relieve pressure in the sheriff court section 7 of the Criminal Justice (Scotland) Act 1980, as amended, confers jurisdiction on the district court in cases of theft, reset, fraud, breach of trust or embezzlement where the amount does not exceed £2,500 and s. 48 of the Transport Act 1982 confers jurisdiction on the court in relation to endorsable road traffic offences provided their maximum penalty is within the district court limits.

Burns, "A Day in the Stipendiary Court," p. 14

"The system only works because everyone has confidence in the professionalism of the others. Of none is this more true than the stipendiary. If he knows his business and is consistent, many cases can be properly dealt with in a few sentences. It is almost a litany. The fiscal's eloquence may not extend beyond 'Usual thing, your Honour'. The defence may rest on 'He has a fixed address and money in his possession'. Almost as an aside from the bench comes 'Fined twenty pounds at two pounds a week'. Thus ends a saga that all began when he had come home, and, to let you understand, he had had a bit to drink, and when his mother-in-law said to him, and to let you understand . . .

It would be a mistake . . . to do down the importance of the district court. Quantitative judgments do not apply to law cases. The district court is the court that any citizen appearing in court is most likely to appear in. It is the first experience of court for people about to go off the rails. It has an overlap with social work to a greater extent than any other court. Without in any way wishing to diminish the importance of other courts, I have often thought that in human terms the determination of guilt or innocence of a middle-aged shoplifter carries at least equal weight with whether Slasher McGrew gets eight or ten years one hundred yards down the road at the High Court. The most unfortunate of society have their last lifeline, quite literally, in this court.

The miscellany of cases is astonishing. There is, of course, what the police officers call the 'heavy bevvy' brigade. In government circles, these are the 'male, single homeless', but the euphemism conceals the reality. To interview this lot calls for a stout stomach and preferably nasal catarrh of a robust sort. Mostly they are cheerful. Each has a face like an unshaved pound of mince with two poached eggs in the middle. They all appear to be on first-name terms with the stip and wish the compliments of the season to be extended to him. 'Ah plead guilty to havin' a drink, surr,' they usually say, as if letting one into a greatly guarded secret. Sometimes as they are called from the detention cell to the dock they will give a few bars of a song, or have difficulty with ragged trousers that are trying to fall down, or come to attention in the dock and endeavour a salute that pokes an eye. In the public benches the serried ranks of Tuscany can scarce forbear to cheer these performances. Even the stern demand for silence from the bench cannot still the smiles. Now and again what appears to be a party breaks out in the detention room and the police have to open the door and demand silence. An old-timer will come out of the room singing the HL1 song and stagger to attention in the dock with a cheery 'God bless ye, surr'. As the good Sheriff Ian Hamilton has remarked, it is not difficult to picture them hidden behind a hillock chucking boulders at Roman soldiers. The stips monitor their flock with a kindly firmness. Every so often a fine will do. Other times admonition is right. Sometimes prison is needed if only to save them. It is a great pity that the detoxification centres so bravely and piously legislated for in 1980 have vanished like the euphoria of the night before.

Sometimes prison seems the objective. 'The accused thereafter took a brick, your honour, and smashed the public house window. He stood around for some time, but nothing happened. Accordingly, he went to the nearest police station and reported what he had done. Officers came round with him to the pub where they found the brick and the damage and duly arrested him. Cautioned and charged he replied, 'I done it to get away from the wife' . . .

Unpaid fines are obviously a problem. A long and weary means-enquiry court is intertwined with quiet moments of the day's business. The excuses are all the same. 'Ah forgot.' 'The wean had measles.' Occasionally, 'Ah'd nae money', or, from women, 'The rent needed payin'.''

[See further on district courts Z. Bankowski, N. Hutton and J. McManus *Lay Justice* (T. & T. Clark: 1987).]

B. THE SHERIFF COURT

Although the district court caseloads are increasing as fiscals divert more and more cases from the sheriff court, the latter is without doubt the more important "inferior" criminal court both in terms of jurisdiction and of caseload (see Table 3 below). Criminal proceedings in the sheriff court are heard either before the sheriff principal or sheriff alone (summary proceedings) or together with a jury of 15 (solemn proceedings).

The territorial jurisdiction of the court in criminal cases is regulated by the Criminal Procedure (Scotland) Act 1975, s. 288(1):

". . . the jurisdiction of the sheriffs within their respective sheriffdoms shall extend to and include all navigable rivers, ports, creeks, shores and anchoring grounds in or adjoining such sheriffdoms and shall include all criminal maritime causes and proceedings (including such as may apply to persons furth of Scotland) provided the accused shall upon any legal ground of jurisdiction be subject to the jurisdiction of the sheriff before whom such cause or proceeding may be raised."

While sitting summarily the sheriff can impose a £5,000 fine or three months' imprisonment or both (Criminal Procedure (Scotland) Act 1975, s. 289 (as amended)) and six months' imprisonment in the case of certain re-offenders (section 290). On indictment the sheriff may impose a sentence of up to three years' imprisonment, an unlimited fine or both (Criminal Justice (Scotland) Act 1987, s. 58(1)). If the sheriff feels the case should be heard in a higher court he may remit it to the High Court at any stage (Criminal Procedure (Scotland) Act 1975, s. 286). In addition, if he feels that his sentencing powers in a solemn case are inadequate he can remit it to the High Court for sentence (s. 104).

In relation to competence the sheriff court has concurrent jurisdiction with district courts in its sheriffdom (Criminal Procedure (Scotland) Act 1975, s. 288(4)) and a wide concurrent jurisdiction with the High Court for offences committed within its sheriffdom. Its case jurisdiction, in fact, is almost universal, though a few serious crimes are within the exclusive jurisdiction of the High Court. The Thomson Committee considered a proposal that sheriff courts should be competent to try all cases except murder and treason but found little support for the suggestion (paras. 13.08–9).

C. THE HIGH COURT OF JUSTICIARY

Lord Cameron, "The Superior Courts," p. 30
"The High Court of Justiciary is the supreme criminal court in Scotland, taking its title from the ancient office of the Justiciar. Since 1887 the members of the court are the same as the members of the Court of Session, but instead of being officially designed as Senators of the College

of Justice, they are known as Commissioners of Justiciary . . . The head
of the court is the Lord Justice General, who also holds the office of Lord
President of the Court of Session, while the second senior judge is now
the Lord Justice Clerk."

Unlike the Court of Session, the High Court of Justiciary goes on
circuit (and has done since its constitution in the 17th century). At
present there are four circuits, Home (Edinburgh), West
(Glasgow, Stirling and Oban), North (Perth, Dundee, Aberdeen
and Inverness) and South (Ayr, Dumfries and Jedburgh). The
court is not restricted to these towns, however, and may sit
anywhere in Scotland. In practice there is an almost permanent
sitting of the court in Glasgow.

As a trial court the High Court normally consists of one Lord
Commissioner and a jury of 15. In cases of difficulty or importance
two or more judges in the court can sit with the jury (Criminal
Procedure (Scotland) Act 1975, s. 113(4)) but this happens only
infrequently (see, e.g. H.M. Advocate v. McKenzie, 1970 S.L.T.
81). A larger court can be convened to consider points of difficulty
if the presiding judge so requests (see, e.g. Hay v. H.M. Advocate,
1968 S.L.T. 334) and must be so convened when a petition to the
nobile officium is heard (Milne v. McNicol, 1944 J.C. 151).

The territorial jurisdiction of the High Court extends to crimes
committed anywhere in Scotland or in Scottish territorial waters. It
can also deal with certain crimes committed furth of Scotland, e.g.
murder or hi-jacking by a Scots person anywhere in the world or
piracy or offences against the Geneva Convention Act 1957
committed outside the United Kingdom. [For a full account of the
Extraterritorial Jurisdiction of the High Court see Renton and
Brown's Criminal Procedure, paras. 1.08–1.22.] The court can
impose the death sentence for treason and possesses unlimited
powers of imprisonment and fine in other cases.

Unless expressly excluded by statute the High Court's original
case jurisdiction is unlimited. It has exclusive jurisdiction regarding
certain crimes namely, treason, murder, attempted murder, rape,
incest, deforcement of messengers (interfering with officers of the
court in the exercise of their duties, now usually charged as assault
or breach of the peace), breach of duty by magistrates and offences
under the Official Secrets Acts. The High Court alone can remedy
extraordinary or unforeseen occurrences in criminal cases through
the exercise of its nobile officium (see Chapter 15 below).

III. CASES

In 1990 the number of persons proceeded against in solemn and
summary cases was 190,333 of whom 31% (59,368) were charged

with crimes and the remainder (130,965) with offences. Almost all offences (as opposed to crimes) were proceeded against summarily. In about 7% of cases (mostly summary ones) the charges are withdrawn or a plea of not guilty is accepted. This may be for a variety of reasons, *e.g.* because the fiscal has re-assessed the case, because a key witness is not available or fresh evidence becomes available which suggests that the accused is innocent, or because the accused has absconded or is unavailable for trial due to illness or some other reason. This is proportionately far fewer than the percentage of civil cases which are taken out of court. The difference is more apparent than real since withdrawals in criminal cases are equivalent only to civil actions which are abandoned by the pursuer. Criminal cases which are disposed of following negotiations are rarely withdrawn in the way that their civil counterparts are.

TABLE 3
Cases called for trial

	1980	1985	1990
High Court	576	1,036	950
Sheriff court (remits to High Court)	101	150	32
Sheriff court (solemn)	3,420	3,264	3,298
Total solemn	4,097	4,450	4,280
Sheriff court (summary)	172,403	108,628	93,677
District courts	72,839	78,681	80,686
Stipendiary magistrates	12,023	18,308	10,925
Total summary	257,265	205,617	185,288
Overall total	261,362	210,067	189,568

[This table demonstrates the significance of the sheriff court as an inferior court, and the growth in High Court cases in the past decade. The decline in summary cases must be set in a context where nearly half of the charge reports received by Fiscals are disposed of out of court.]

In general the more serious the charge the greater the likelihood that the accused person will plead "not guilty". On the other hand the greater the ease of proof, the more likely the accused will plead "guilty", *e.g.* speeding offences. Table 4 suggests that once proceedings have begun an accused's chances of escaping a conviction of some sort are low—particularly in the case of motor vehicle offences (95% chance of conviction). On the other hand if the case goes to trial (proof) the chances of an acquittal (not guilty or not proven) are dramatically higher (between 30 and 50%). The reason for the high conviction rate in Table 4 is the high number of cases in which the accused pleads guilty at or before trial. In 1982 75% of those accused of a crime pled guilty (and 84% of those charged with offences). By 1991 only 59% of those charged with a crime in the sheriff court (and 78% of those charged with offences) were pleading guilty. (See "Improving the Delivery of Justice: Review of Criminal Evidence and Criminal Procedure" (Scottish Office, 1993) at p. 8.) Why do so many accused persons plead guilty?

TABLE 4

Cases called for trial and disposed of in 1990

	% PNGA[1,2] or deserted	% Acquitted not guilty	% Acquitted not proven	% Charge proved
1. Non-sexual crimes of violence	9	13	5	73
2. Crimes of indecency	3	5	3	90
3. Crimes of dishonesty	11	5	1	83
4. Fire-raising, vandalism, etc.	6	6	1	86
5. Other crimes	11	5	1	83
Total crimes	10	6	2	83
6. Miscellaneous offences	6	5	2	87
7. Motor vehicle offences	4	1	0	95
Total offences	5	3	1	91
Total crimes and offences	7	4	1	89

1. Plea of not guilty accepted.
2. Includes cases where proceedings are dropped after a person has been called to court e.g. if witnesses cannot be traced.

[Source: Scottish Office Statistical Bulletin Criminal Justice Series, May 1992.]

A. WHY PLEAD GUILTY?

Part of the answer is that in many cases, particularly where a minor offence is involved, *e.g.* a parking violation or drunkenness, the accused does not deny the offence. This is equivalent to the many civil debt actions where decree in absence is taken because the defender does not deny the debt.

Secondly, it has been suggested that the high conviction rate in summary cases, particularly in the district court, discourages those who might otherwise plead not guilty. Thus McBarnet has attacked the simpler, cheaper procedures of summary courts for encouraging an "ideology of triviality" which ill accords with the media image of the "ideology of justice" derived from the higher courts where a jury determines issues of fact, a record of the proceedings is kept and the accused is almost always represented.

[See D. McBarnet, *Conviction* (Macmillan: 1981) and "Magistrates Courts and the Ideology of Justice" (1981) 8 *British Journal
of Law and Society* 181.]

The third, and perhaps the most significant reason for the high
level of guilty pleas is the widespread practice of "plea bargaining"
or plea negotiation. Just as in civil cases (see Chapter 2 above)
many criminal cases are "resolved" between the parties by negotiation prior to coming before the court for judgment. Nevertheless
the analogy is not complete because the outcome of the case, the
sentence, ultimately depends on the judge in a way that civil
settlements generally do not.

B. PLEA NEGOTIATION

The term plea negotiation covers a wide variety of informal and
formal processes which take place in many legal systems. In
Scotland it takes the form of plea adjustment, *i.e.* the reduction of
a charge, the dismissal of one or more charges where the accused is
charged on several counts or the exclusion of information about
the criminal incident or accused person in a charge, in return for
an admission of guilt by the accused. The parties involved include
the public prosecutor, the accused's legal adviser and the accused.
Judges are not involved in the process in Scotland and are not
permitted to be so in England, although they take part in plea
negotiations over sentences as a matter of course in the United
States. The process, however informal, usually involves two stages:
the discussion between the prosecutor and the legal representative
for the accused, and that between the legal representative and his
client.

The phenomenon of plea negotiation or plea adjustment, far
from being officially frowned on, has received approval in high
places. Chief Justice Burger of the United States Supreme Court in
1971 described it as "an essential element in the administration of
justice". In 1981 the Solicitor-General for Scotland in a written
answer in the House of Commons (14 H.C. Deb., col. 452, 10
Dec. 1981) commented:

"The practice of plea adjustment is set out in para. 21.02 of the second
report of the Thomson committee which was set up to examine criminal
procedure in Scotland. It reads:
'There is no statutory authority for plea adjustment but it is accepted as
proper practice for either the accused's legal adviser or the prosecutor to
approach the other and negotiate the acceptance of a partial plea.
Normally such an approach comes from the defence but it is perfectly
proper for the prosecutor to intimate to the defence that he would be
willing to accept a plea of guilty to some of the charges in an indictment

or complaint and drop the others or to accept a plea of guilty to less than the full extent on any particular charge. An offer of this sort, made by the prosecutor or the defence, cannot be founded upon by the other if not accepted.'

I approve of this practice which is confined to discussion between the defence and the prosecutor. The judge is not involved and therefore there can be no discussion as to the sentence to be imposed. All that is agreed is the plea which the defence will offer and which the prosecutor will accept.

If satisfactory pleas can be adjusted, valuable court time is freed to permit other cases to be heard. This creates speedier justice, which is in my opinion a very desirable aim."

It is impossible to gauge the frequency of plea adjustment from the published statistics. Crown Office statistics show that in a third of all solemn cases and a tenth of all summary cases the accused changes his original plea of not guilty to a guilty plea at a later stage. (The 1993 consultation paper on Criminal Evidence and Procedure suggested that the figures were even higher.) In many of these cases plea negotiations will have taken place. In many more, such negotiations will occur before any plea has been tendered. A study conducted by Susan Moody and Jacqueline Tombs (1982) has shown, however, that there are considerable regional variations and that prosecutors in the busy urban courts feel under more pressure to negotiate with the defence than their rural colleagues. Such variations are also attributable to the lack of Crown Office guidelines on the situations in which and the ways in which plea adjustment should take place.

1. WHY DO PLEA NEGOTIATIONS OCCUR?

A number of reasons have been put forward to explain why plea negotiation is as prevalent as it is.

Sheehan, *Criminal Procedure in Scotland and France*, p. 119
"The advantages to the prosecutor of a plea of guilty are that he need not proceed to trial, his onus of proof is discharged, and the accused will be convicted (of which there can be no guarantee if the matter goes to trial). The advantages to the defence are that they may obtain some concessions such as a reduced charge, the dropping of certain charges and the possibility of a lighter sentence (the accused being able to maintain in mitigation that he had never sought to deny his guilt and repented of his actions—an attitude which is more difficult to explain if the accused had denied his guilt by pleading not guilty)."

The position is rather more complicated than Sheehan makes out. The argument that a guilty plea and a contrite accused will

attract a lesser sentence is accepted by some defence agents—
particularly in indecency cases where it protects the victim from
the embarrassment and the tribulations of the witness box. Nevertheless the English practice of allowing an almost automatic
discount in sentence for those pleading guilty (which has been
approved in the Court of Appeal) has no Scottish counterpart.

Nicholson, *The Law and Practice of Sentencing in Scotland*, pp. 218–219
"There is no comparable, approved, practice in Scotland . . . In a legal
system which presumes innocence and which permits every accused
person to go to trial if he wishes, there can be nothing of a mitigating
nature in the fact that many people nonetheless plead guilty; and, of
course, it would be quite unacceptable that a person who was found guilty
after trial should be punished more severely simply because he had not
pled guilty . . . [The] reason . . . for not accepting a plea of guilty as
being a mitigating circumstance in itself is that, if there were a regular
practice to that effect, it might easily be seen as the court offering an
inducement to accused persons to plead guilty rather than go to trial."

This was just the criticism that the High Court did indeed launch
against the English practice in the case of *Strawhorn* v. *McLeod*,
1987 S.C.C.R. 413. Moreover, as the Court observed such a
practice might disable judges from exercising their discretion fully
and freely in a particular case. Some commentators have, nevertheless, been somewhat ambivalent about the possible breadth of
the ruling in the *Strawhorn* case.

Nicholson, *Sentencing Law and Practice in Scotland* (2nd ed.),
para. 9–36
"It is to be noted, however, that what the High Court described as
objectionable in the case of *Strawhorn* was a *practice* of giving a discount
for a plea of guilty. That does not, it is submitted, mean that a court must
never impose a lower sentence on account of a plea of guilty. Whether
that will be appropriate, however, will always depend on the circumstances of a particular case and, it is suggested, on the extent to which a
plea of guilty is itself a reflection of a mitigating circumstance, such as
genuine remorse, or has truly mitigating consequences, such as avoiding
the need for young children to give evidence in court."

[See also Sheriff Gordon's Commentary on the *Strawhorn* case in
1987 S.C.C.R. at p. 416 where he notes that by offering the Crown
a certain conviction, less inconvenience for witnesses and a saving
of court time and resources, accused persons are likely to feel that
they should at least have a hope of more lenient treatment in
suitable cases. Sheriff Gordon adds that if this is not the case then

guilty pleas might become rarer—an outcome "that would not necessarily be to the overall benefit of the criminal justice system."]

Sheehan is correct to point to the prosecutor's interest in a negotiated plea but as the Moody and Tombs study has shown the picture is again more complex than at first appears. First, prosecutors are not in general neutral as to whether a prosecution should succeed—the survey found that most fiscals considered that if proceedings have been instituted their implicit assumption was that the accused was guilty of some or all of the charges. The unpredictability of trials, particularly jury trials, and the defence's chances of acquittal (see Table 4 above) encourages the prosecutor to agree to a plea which will guarantee a conviction. As in civil cases a negotiated "settlement" ensures that the pursuer/prosecutor is at least partly successful. Secondly, prosecutors regard some cases, *e.g.* assaults on the police, as unsuitable for a negotiation, while in others the prosecutor considers that the accused would be sufficiently punished by a plea to a lesser charge and is therefore willing to accept the plea. The third and major factor is caseload pressures.

Moody and Tombs, "Plea Negotiations," pp. 120–121
"The major reason for negotiation of pleas offered by fiscals is to cut down on the number of trials, particularly at summary level. Neither the fiscal service nor the sheriff and district court personnel are equipped to deal with the volume of cases which would go to trial if pleas were not negotiated: 'it saves judicial time, fiscal time, defence time and very particularly it saves expense to the state in paying witnesses'; 'it is undoubtedly useful for the court and for the public . . . if every person who pled not guilty initially went to trial there would be a lot more folks coming into the court as witnesses—at vast expense to the Exchequer.'
. . . The feeling that they are bound by constraints on time and money which makes them more vulnerable to offers from the defence is strongly expressed by some fiscals: 'it was my intention not to appear to be a person who was prepared to negotiate pleas but the system beats me'; 'I think we have to concede quite often . . . although we are not supposed to. I am being honest about this, other fiscals might not acknowledge it. I am sure we all do it'; 'you should be taking every trial on its merits and negotiating any pleas in that trial on their merit but you cannot help but think of the other ten trials.' "

[Curiously studies have shown that there is no correlation in America between caseload pressure and the percentage of cases going to trial, and that in the 1930s plea bargaining existed when there was no overload in the courts. See the *Law and Society*

Review special issue on plea bargaining, Volume 13 (1979), pp. 189–582.]

For the accused a suitable plea can hopefully avoid the risk of a heavy sentence, the uncertainties of trial and minimise the economic loss caused by the delay in waiting for trial. For the accused's solicitor it can also be advantageous if a guilty plea is tendered rather than the case going to trial, for he too may be subject to intolerable pressures of work.

2. THE MERITS OF PLEA NEGOTIATION

At first glance plea negotiation seems to be in the interests of all the participants as well as the state. There are, however, some indicators to suggest that the process has its drawbacks. First, unlike judges in England, Scottish judges are bound to accept guilty pleas tendered by the defence and accepted by the prosecutor, since the Crown is the master of the instance. As in the civil cases therefore, the judges will accept the negotiated settlement without investigation of the circumstances to see if the settlement is a fair one. The significance of this is highlighted by the findings of the Moody and Tombs study. This study showed that some fiscals include extra charges which are unlikely to stand up in court because they are hoping for a plea to the lesser charge. Most fiscals disapproved of including charges as bargaining counters only but they not infrequently included charges which they could not prove, for evidential reasons or in an effort to show a course of conduct. The study also showed that many fiscals assert, and some defence agents accept, that the deletion of a few minor charges has very little effect on the sentence of the court. Thus in some cases an accused will have been persuaded to plead guilty in exchange for little in return from the prosecution.

The dangers of defence agents in England persuading their reluctant clients to make a guilty plea were the theme of John Baldwin and Michael McConville's *Negotiated Justice* (Martin Robertson: 1977). Ross Harper makes the same point in his booklet *My Client, My Lord* (Law Society of Scotland: 1981), but most of his chapter on plea negotiation relates to how to persuade a client to accept a guilty plea.

Harper, "Plea Negotiation," pp. 44–45

"You have a duty to relate to your client the likely consequences of his going to trial as against those of a well-adjusted plea. If you put forward options in a disinterested manner, nine times out of ten your client will decide, in those dreadful words, to 'give it a run'. You are entitled—

indeed you have a duty—to use reasonable persuasion without hectoring and forcefulness without threatening. Your client should be told the odds for and against conviction or acquittal and the likely result of conviction . . .

If a client pleads not guilty at the outset he is not likely to change his mind without good reason. After evidence is obtained, an interview in the office may lead to a plea. More often than not in the security of an office the client will persist in his denial.

The psychological time is on the morning of the court. Civil practitioners know well that a tender consistently refused may well be accepted in an action for damages on the morning of proof. The imminence of the case concentrates the mind wonderfully. As one moves towards the time of the trial the plea becomes that much more negotiable."

If these arguments suggest that plea negotiations do not always work to the benefit of the accused, Ross Harper's final paragraph hints at why plea negotiation has its drawbacks for the administration of justice. The Thomson Committee's main criticism of plea adjustment (para. 21.04) was the fact that so much of it occurs at the last minute. This was also a criticism made by the Sheriffs' Association in their evidence to the Hughes Commission, who pointed to the disruptions caused by such last-minute pleas to witnesses, jurors, prosecutors and judges. These issues lie at the heart of the 1993 Review of Criminal Evidence and Procedure which noted with alarm that about 80% of trials do not go ahead when programmed. Attempts by court administrators to tackle the problem of late pleas by setting down more summary trials for any one day than could possibly be heard, either exacerbate the problem by encouraging fiscals to "settle" cases by accepting a plea or lead to chaos when less than the anticipated 50% of trials go off. Such disruptions may be the price for avoiding the crippling overload if all cases went to trial but late changes of plea produce unnecessary delays for cases which are definitely going to trial.

However, the obvious solution of encouraging fiscals and defence agents to negotiate at an early stage (put forward by the Thomson Committee and endorsed by the Crown Office in a note published in 1980 S.L.T. (News) 42) is unlikely to work without some additional changes (the 1993 Review calls for mandatory intermediate and first diets, routine disclosure of prosecution witness statements to the defence and far greater efforts to agree uncontentious evidence). This is because, as the Moody and Tombs study showed, defence agents are in a much better bargaining position if they approach the harassed fiscal at the last minute. Without time for reflection, or to take advice and faced with an impracticable caseload on the date of trial fiscals are more prone to accept a negotiated plea. It is also easier for the agent to persuade his client to change his plea at this stage as Harper indicates.

It remains a matter for debate how defensible plea negotiation is. Those who object to the "behind the scenes" way in which it currently operates may be attracted by the argument recently aired in England and Wales by the Bar Council and the Director of Public Prosecutions and since endorsed by the English Royal Commission on Criminal Justice, 1993 (R.156) that plea agreements should be formalised and clear sentence discounts offered for early guilty pleas. To many Scots lawyers this will be anathema which may account for the greater caution of the 1993 Review on the topic. But how else might the practice be improved? Moreover it is unclear whether the prevalence of guilty pleas suggests that it is not in the interests of justice that all cases go to trial or that the ideal of the adversarial system cannot be achieved, or merely that society is not prepared to devote sufficient resources to enable it to be achieved. [See further on plea negotiation in Scotland A.V. Sheehan, *Criminal Procedure* (Butterworths: 1990 pp. 74ff.]

C. DELAY

It has been said that justice delayed is justice denied. In recognition of this, Scottish criminal procedure contains a number of devices designed to reduce delay. First, there is provision both in summary and in solemn cases for an accelerated guilty plea (if the prosecutor agrees). In solemn cases a letter signed by the accused intimating a complete or partial plea of guilty in terms of the Criminal Procedure (Scotland) Act 1975, s. 102 (as substituted) can lead to the case being disposed of by the sheriff or the High Court on remit within two weeks or so of the letter being received. [Ironically this can put pressure on the accused to plead guilty to get the case over quickly, as the Royal Commission on Criminal Procedure recognised (Cmnd. 8092: 1981, p. 185).]

Secondly, sections 331A and 101 of the Criminal Procedure (Scotland) Act 1975 provide that in summary and solemn cases where the accused is being held in custody, he must be brought to trial within 40 or 110 days respectively, otherwise he will normally be immune from prosecution for the offence, unless the delay was not the fault of the prosecution. Section 101 (as substituted) further provides that if a solemn trial has not been commenced within 12 months of the accused's first appearance on petition, he will normally be immune from prosecution for the offence, unless the delay was not the fault of the prosecution. (Contrast *McGinty* v. *H.M. Advocate*, 1985 S.L.T. 25 with *H.M. Advocate* v. *Swift*, 1985 S.L.T. 26.) The Thomson Committee proposed that a similar rule should be introduced in summary cases (the period being six months) but this has not so far been implemented. Nevertheless, if there has been "undue delay" by the Crown in raising proceedings in a summary case which results in "gross or grave prejudice" to the accused, then the complaint will be dismissed on the grounds of *mora* (delay). (See *Tudhope* v. *McCarthy*, 1985 S.L.T. 392.)

[See further on delay in criminal cases, the statistics contained in parliamentary answers reported in 1990 S.L.T. (News) 282 and 1991 S.L.T. (News) 205, and K. Miller *et al, Delay in Summary Criminal Proceedings* (CRU: 1989).]

IV. REPRESENTATION

The importance of representation in criminal cases seems now to be taken for granted. This development has been further reinforced by the rulings of the European Court of Human Rights in cases such as *Granger* v. *United Kingdom* (1990) 12 E.H.R.R. 469 (requiring that free legal aid be available in an appeal involving complexity and the liberty of the accused). The question posed by civil libertarians is not whether representation should be encouraged in the more important cases but whether it should be provided free of charge for every accused who wishes it, regardless of means. The problem facing the Treasury is how to pay for the existing provision far less any expansion. However, even more serious is the problem for the public that criminal legal aid expenditure is beginning to so dominate the overall legal aid bill that its continued rise is having destructive knock-on effects on non-criminal legal aid. The savage cuts in legal aid which were announced in the Autumn of 1992 will, in Scotland, impact almost entirely on the civil legal aid budget which has already fallen in real terms by 28% over the last five years. There seems a real risk that the activities of the European Court of Human Rights will encourage governments in the United Kingdom to protect criminal legal aid expenditure at the expense of persons of modest or moderate incomes with divorce, housing or employment cases.

Legal aid in Scotland is governed by the Legal Aid (Scotland) Act 1986 which created the Scottish Legal Aid Board ("the Board") as a non-departmental public body to be responsible for the administration of legal aid in Scotland (see Chapter 11 below). Legal aid is available to accused persons under three different headings: advice and assistance (for initial advice, and advice by way of representation following a guilty plea), the duty solicitor scheme which provides advice for those in custody or attending an identification parade and criminal legal aid which covers the preparation prior to trial, the trial itself and any appeal arising therefrom.

A. ASSISTANCE BY WAY OF REPRESENTATION

Assistance by way of Representation (ABWOR) was introduced as part of Advice and Assistance (see Chapter 11 below) in 1987 to simplify summary criminal legal aid procedure and to encourage earlier plea changes (from not guilty to guilty). Research has shown that it has largely succeeded in the first objective but failed in the second. [See F. Rutherdale, *The Impact of "Assistance by way of Representation"* (CRU: 1990).] ABWOR is available in summary criminal cases where an accused person, who is not in custody, has plead guilty or changed his or her plea to guilty within 14 days of the original "not guilty" plea. To be eligible for ABWOR the accused must meet the same financial tests as for Advice and Assistance. In addition the offence must be such that, if proved, would be likely to lead to a sentence involving loss of liberty or livelihood of the accused. Alternatively, ABWOR can be extended to accused persons who are financially eligible but who are unable to understand the proceedings or make a plea in mitigation because of age, inadequate knowledge of English, mental illness or other mental or physical disability or incapacity. The research suggested that although loss of liberty was the criterion most frequently cited by solicitors using the scheme (64%), in only 6% of cases in the research project was a custodial sentence imposed. Despite the recent furore in England and Wales over the introduction of fixed fees for some criminal legal aid work, the Scots solicitors interviewed in the research project approved of the standard block fee arrangement which already exists for ABWOR work in Scotland.

B. THE DUTY SOLICITOR SCHEME

Under this scheme (originally introduced in 1967) and now governed by the Legal Aid (Scotland) Act 1986, s. 22 (and accompanying regulations) in all sheriff and district courts a "duty solicitor" drawn from the solicitors undertaking criminal legal aid work in these courts is available on a rota basis, for every day of the year.

The Hughes Commission, p. 89

"8.11 When the duty solicitor is informed that a person has been taken into custody charged with murder, attempted murder or culpable homicide and that he wishes the duty solicitor's services, he is required to visit that person in custody and to advise him and act for him until he is brought to a sheriff court for his judicial examination. In all cases where the accused is in custody and is dealt with under solemn procedure (those tried with a jury), the duty solicitor is required to visit the accused before his judicial examination and represent him at that examination. In summary cases, the duty solicitor is required to interview any accused person in custody who wishes his services and to represent that accused up to the first diet at which he is called on to plead. If a plea of guilty is tendered, the duty solicitor will continue to act for the accused until the case is terminated. Typically, this will involve the presentation of a plea in mitigation."

The duty solicitor's services are also available to represent accused persons at identification parades. The services are provided free of charge and the solicitor is reimbursed out of state funds. In 1991/92 duty solicitors represented 17,066 accused persons in custody at their initial appearance in the sheriff court and 7,007 in the district court.

C. CRIMINAL LEGAL AID

Criminal legal aid since its inception has been granted by the court both in solemn and in summary cases—normally the court before which the accused makes his or her first appearance. In solemn cases all that the court requires to be satisfied is that the accused person's financial circumstances are such that the expenses of the case cannot be met without undue hardship to the accused or his or her dependants. (In Scotland, unlike England, accused persons who are granted legal aid are not required to pay a contribution.) In summary cases the same financial test was and is applied but in addition the judge had to determine whether it was in the interests of justice that legal aid be granted in the case. This criterion ensured that legal aid was not available for many minor cases heard before the sheriff and district courts. The "interests of justice" test was controversial for several reasons. First, it was felt by many observers that it was inappropriate that the same body that was determining the case should also decide beforehand where the interests of justice in the case might lie. Secondly, research established that there were widespread variations between courts in interpreting the eligibility criteria for legal aid in summary proceedings. This in turn led to substantial differences between courts in the success rate of applications for legal aid in summary cases (in 1984 the range extended from 60% to 99%). Certainly, when the Board was established it was given the responsibility for awarding legal aid in summary cases partly as a bid to ensure greater consistency in the application of the "interests of justice" test. To assist the Board the Legal Aid (Scotland) Act 1986, s. 24(3) lays down the factors to be taken into account by the Board in applying the "interests of justice" criterion:

"(a) the offence is such that if proved it is likely that the court would impose a sentence which would deprive the accused of his liberty or lead to loss of his livelihood;

(b) the determination of the case may involve consideration of a substantial question of law, or of evidence of a complex or difficult nature;

(c) the accused may be unable to understand the proceedings or to state his own case because of his age, inadequate knowledge of English, mental illness, other mental or physical disability or otherwise;

(d) it is in the interests of someone other than the accused that the accused be legally represented;

(e) the defence to be advanced by the accused does not appear to be frivolous;

(f) the accused has been remanded in custody pending trial."

[These have since been elaborated on by the Board in its newsletter "The Recorder," issue 9, Winter 1991/92.]

For the time being the courts have been left with the responsibility of awarding legal aid in solemn cases and in summary cases where the accused has been convicted and is facing a sentence of imprisonment or detention for the first time (Legal Aid (Scotland) Act 1986, s. 23). While there is no appeal against a court's decision not to award legal aid it is possible to apply to the Board in summary cases where legal aid has been refused to ask for a review. (Almost 50% of reviews result in a grant of legal aid.) Since 1990 in cases where legal aid has been refused by the Board for a criminal appeal and the appeal is ultimately successful it has been possible to recover the expenses of the action from the Board.

Consistently over the last decade about 99% of applications for legal aid in solemn cases have been granted. In 1989/90 86% of applications in sheriff court cases and 82% of applications in district court cases were granted. However, this leaves a misleading impression in that although almost all those who stand trial under solemn procedure do so with legal aid, only a minority of accused persons in summary cases are so aided (approximately 20%). It is not clear how many persons plead guilty in summary cases because they are refused legal aid or because they are convinced that they would not be granted legal aid in any case, and so do not apply. Certainly, very few accused persons in summary cases are unrepresented at trial. Nevertheless, a significant majority of persons accused of summary offences are not legally aided, fall outwith the scope of the duty solicitor scheme and plead guilty.

D. REFORM

Whether, in the light of the growing problems in funding legal aid, more resources should be made available in summary cases possibly at the expense of civil litigants is a question for debate. Criminal legal aid (including Advice and Assistance and ABWOR) has accounted for a sizeable majority of all net legal aid expenditure in the last decade (in 1991/92 it was 70%). In 1985 the Scottish Office issued a consultation paper on Legal Aid in Scotland proposing, *inter alia*, the establishment of the Scottish Legal Aid Board and clearer guidance over the "interests of justice" test. However, it also contained suggestions that legal aid should not be so easily available in solemn cases to persistent offenders or those who had received criminal legal aid on previous occasions. Further it was suggested that a grant of legal aid might be reviewed if, *e.g.* the line of defence is significantly different from that stated in the application for legal aid. These latter proposals caused a storm of protest from the legal profession and the consumer bodies since they were seen as a thinly veiled agenda for expenditure cuts.

Law Society Response to S.H.H.D. Consultation Paper
"Criminal Legal Aid

27.3 The Law Society is wholly opposed to the proposals that legal aid should not be available to persistent offenders and that regard should be paid to previous grants of criminal legal aid to the applicant or to his criminal record when considering applications for criminal legal aid. It may well be the case that a persistent offender is just the person who requires legal aid, his being a known offender having weighed against him in the fact of his arrest and the decision to prosecute. The criteria suggested proceed on a presumption of guilt on the part of the applicant for criminal legal aid, the more so if he is a known offender or has a previous record. Such criteria are repugnant to the Law Society and are contrary to human rights and natural justice.

27.4 Quite apart from that, they create practical difficulties of enormous proportions. It does not seem to be appreciated that access to legal advice eradicates a significant number of unnecessary trials. Under these proposals, there will be many more pleas of not guilty with many more and much longer trials imposing further strain on the administration of the Courts. Judges will require to guide and instruct unrepresented accused in their defence and valuable Court time will be expended on this exercise. Who will precognosce witnesses on behalf of the accused? Will it be the accused himself? How is he likely to fare when interviewing Crown witnesses including the police officers who arrested him? He may well be prevented from approaching witnesses by the operation of the Bail (Scotland) Act 1980. Will he have the knowledge or the ability to approach the Procurator Fiscal and negotiate an acceptable plea with him? Who will cite witnesses for the defence? Will it be the Crown or the

Sheriff Clerk for the accused? . . . What will the accused make of the Crown productions and will he be able to prepare and lodge his Special Defence? What about an accused person who is detained in custody? Is he going to be allowed out of prison to do so? What is his position to be? How is he going to be able to prepare his defence? Is he expected to know about and be able to make a submission of no case to answer? Is it appreciated that persistent offenders are more likely to be the subject of police attention, more likely to be on Petition, more likely to receive severe sentences if convicted? These proposals are quite insupportable and ignore totally the conclusion of the Royal Commission on Legal Services in Scotland that the grant of legal aid should not depend on the accused's criminal record (8.55).

27.5 Legal representation assists not only individuals but the Courts by the presentation of information in a concise, relevant and intelligible way. Such a presentation is beyond the capability of most accused persons. It is extremely unusual for an accused person defending himself to present a coherent case or to conduct a cross-examination, far less an expert cross-examination.

27.6 The European Convention on Human Rights and Fundamental Freedoms states in Article 6(3)(c) that 'everyone charged with a criminal offence has the right to defend himself in person or through legal assistance of his own choosing or, if he has not sufficient means for legal assistance, to be given it free when the interests of justice so require; and (b) to examine or have examined witnesses against him and to obtain the attendance and examination of witnesses on his behalf under the same conditions as witnesses against him'. Article 6(3)(c) guarantees the right to an effective defence either in person or through a lawyer and where the conditions of Article 6(3)(c) are fulfilled, a state *must* provide effective assistance (*Artico*-v-*Italy*, 1980, Series A, Number 37) . . . [See now *Granger* v. *U.K.* (1990) 12 E.H.R.R. 469.]

37.2 There may be a variety of good reasons why the line of defence presented at the trial is significantly different from that stated in the application for legal aid. At the time of application for legal aid, no opportunity has been given to investigate the circumstances of the offence and the solicitor requires to proceed on the applicant's version of events. It is only once the case has been fully investigated that a firm view can be taken on the line of defence to be pursued. Criminal trials are not set pieces where everyone knows his part and matters proceed smoothly to a denouement. Even the prosecutor may be taken by surprise by the evidence given by Crown witnesses and the turn the case takes.

37.3 A criminal prosecution is of necessity a fluid process requiring flexibility and adaptability on both sides. New evidence may come to light as the case proceeds or a change of emphasis may occur permitting a new line of defence to be examined. It is contrary to the interests of justice to suggest that a defence agent may not address himself to those developments and completely unacceptable that he should be penalised for doing so by having the legal aid certificate cancelled. Is it intended that similar restrictions will be placed on the Crown and if not, why not?"

In the event these particular proposals have not been implemented, to date, but since 1985 the growth in criminal legal aid expenditure has gone unchecked. Perhaps inhibited by the decisions of the European Court of Human Rights the Scottish Office has done nothing to rectify the growing imbalance in legal aid expenditure (although a review of eligibility for criminal legal aid is promised for 1993). It is perhaps worthy of note that the Royal Commission on Legal Services in Scotland (the Hughes Commission) considered that it would be too costly to extend criminal legal aid to all accused persons or even to all those accused of an offence for which a prison sentence might be imposed (although ABWOR has gone some way in that direction). However, the Commission were concerned that the duty scheme did not extend to individuals who are not held in custody and that many of the accused persons who do receive assistance from a duty solicitor feel that they are given insufficient time and facilities to brief the duty solicitor (three minutes is not uncommon). The Commission accordingly recommended that the duty scheme or an equivalent should be available to all accused persons before the initial hearing (r. 8.19) and that full details of an alleged offence should be given to the accused prior to receiving the initial advice (r. 8.24). The Commission also proposed the introduction of legal advice clinics in prisons (r. 8.26).

In the light of the ever rising cost of criminal legal aid it is perhaps not surprising that these proposals have not been taken up. However, the same justification cannot be put forward for the Scottish Office's failure to explore the possibilities of another Commission proposal—experimenting with public defenders (state-salaried lawyers who would act for accused persons) along the lines of schemes in Australia, Canada and the United States (r. 8.29). Such a scheme might well result in a net saving for the state— though opponents consider that it might also lead to a decline in quality of representation as the budget would be more easily pared than the present system. Certainly, we have now reached the situation where it will be necessary to demonstrate that society is getting value for money from its ever rising criminal legal aid bill. In England and Wales this has led to fixed fees in criminal cases and franchising (see Chapter 11 below) of legal aid firms which meet certain quality assurance standards. It is as yet unclear what proposals the Scottish Office has to parallel such developments although the Scottish Legal Aid Board is known (for good reason) to be sceptical as to the merits of introducing franchising (at least in its English format) to Scotland.

V. POWERS

Apart from the power to imprison or to fine, criminal courts have a wide variety of measures open to them where an accused is found guilty. A court may:

(a) discharge the offender absolutely (under summary procedure, no conviction is recorded);

(b) place the offender on probation (with or without a community service requirement) under the supervision of a social worker for one to three years (under summary procedure, no conviction is recorded);

(c) impose a community service order requiring the offender to undertake unpaid work;

(d) dismiss the offender with an admonition;

(e) defer sentence;

(f) sentence a young offender as follows:

(i) to a detention centre for between four weeks and four months (not available as a sentence in district courts);

(ii) to a young offenders' institution for a period not exceeding that of imprisonment which the court could have imposed on an adult;

(g) sentence a child to a period of detention in a place and on such conditions that the Secretary of State may direct;

(h) make a hospital or guardianship order if the accused is suffering from mental disorder (no conviction is recorded in summary procedure).

TABLE 5
Court Disposals in 1990

Persons proceeded against	190,333
Custodial sentences	12,458
Community Service Orders	4,449
Probation	3,873
Fine	132,213
Other	15,014
No charge proved	22,326

[Source: Scottish Office Statistical Bulletin
Criminal Justice Series, 1992.]

As Table 5 shows much the most common outcome in cases which are taken to trial is a fine. This is particularly true in the district court where 90% of penalties imposed are fines—the comparative figure for the sheriff court being 71%. In addition to the powers listed above the court has two other measures open to it. First, in fine default cases the court can now, with the consent of the offender, order him or her to undertake between ten and 60 hours Supervised

Attendance either of the community service type of activity or attendance at courses on topics such as on money management, first aid, alcohol or drugs. [Law Reform (Miscellaneous Provisions) (Scotland) Act 1990, s. 62. See also P. Morran, "Supervised Attendance Orders" (1992) 192 SCOLAG 137.]

Secondly, under the Criminal Justice (Scotland) Act 1980, s. 58, a court may make a compensation order requiring a convicted person to pay compensation for any personal injury, loss or damage caused by the acts which constituted the offence. The scope of the compensation is not limited to cases where a civil court could award damages, thus convictions obtained under consumer protection legislation, *e.g.* the Trades Description Act 1968 and the Fair Trading Act 1973 can now be of more tangible benefit to consumers. [See P. Duff, "Compensation Orders in the Sheriff Court," 1982 S.L.T. (News) 171. On the use of Compensation Orders in practice see G. Maher and C. Docherty, *Compensation Orders in the Scottish Courts* (CRU: 1989).]

It is worth stressing, however, that in Scotland, courts (except in private prosecutions) cannot make an award of expenses either against an accused who has been convicted or in favour of an accused who has been acquitted. The Thomson Committee (Chapter 61) recommended that this should continue to be the case.

VI. APPEALS

A person convicted under summary or solemn procedure may appeal against the conviction or the sentence or both. The prosecutor can only appeal against an acquittal or the sentence imposed in summary cases, and even then only on a point of law. All appeals in criminal cases go to the High Court of Justiciary sitting as an appeal court, composed of three or more Lords Commissioners of Justiciary. (See, *e.g. H.M. Advocate* v. *Kirkwood*, 1939 S.L.T. 209 and *Docherty* v. *H.M. Advocate*, 1987 S.L.T. 784 where 11 and 9 judges sat respectively.) In 1990 there were 423 solemn appeals, 1,457 summary appeals and 13 appeals by prosecutors. (For fuller details on trends in appeals, see *Appeals in the Scottish Criminal Courts* (Scottish Office, 1993).)

A. SUMMARY APPEALS

1. By Stated Case

Criminal Procedure (Scotland) Act 1975, s. 442

"442(1) . . .

(a) any person convicted in summary proceedings may appeal under this section to the High Court—

    (i) against such conviction;

    (ii) against the sentence passed on such conviction; or

    (iii) against both conviction and such sentence;

(b) the prosecutor in such proceedings may so appeal on a point of law—

    (i) against an acquittal in such proceedings; or

    (ii) against a sentence passed in such proceedings.

(2) By an appeal under subsection (1)(a) of this section or, as the case may be, against acquittal under subsection (1)(b) of this section, an appellant may bring under review of the High Court any alleged miscarriage of justice in the proceedings, including, in the case of an appeal under the said subsection (1)(a), any alleged miscarriage of justice on the basis of the existence and significance of additional evidence which was not heard at the trial and which was not available and could not reasonably have been made available at the trial."

[The above section was substituted by the Criminal Justice (Scotland) Act 1980, Sched. 3, para. 1. The provision for fresh evidence in summary appeals was totally new, and does not apply to prosecution appeals.]

In a stated case the judge in the inferior court prepares a statement of the facts found proved by him and formulates the questions of law (if any) which the accused or the prosecutor wishes to have answered. There is now provision for objections by the accused and his advisers to the form of the statement to be noted. For the first time, and contrary to the proposals of the Thomson Committee, the High Court has been given the power (Criminal Justice (Scotland) Act 1980, Sched. 3) to authorise a re-trial as an alternative to upholding or dismissing an appeal (Criminal Procedure (Scotland) Act 1975, s. 452A). The court may in certain circumstances increase the sentence imposed on the accused—but only if the accused has appealed against the sentence.

2. BY BILL OF SUSPENSION OR ADVOCATION

If an appeal by stated case would be inappropriate or incompetent the accused may appeal by bill of suspension against conviction or sentence and the prosecutor can appeal against acquittal by bill of advocation, on the ground of an alleged miscarriage of justice in the proceedings (Criminal Procedure (Scotland) Act 1975, s. 453A). Despite the efforts of the Thomson Committee and the passing of the Criminal Justice (Scotland) Act 1980 it is still not exactly clear when a bill of suspension should be used as opposed to a stated case. The best view seems to be that a bill of suspension is for reviewing procedural irregularities. Advocation is also used for review of irregularities usually in the preliminary stages of a case. Hitherto advocations have been rare and there is no reason to think that they are likely to increase in criminal proceedings.

3. NOTE OF APPEAL

Appeal against sentence by a convicted person is now normally dealt with by an accelerated "note of appeal" procedure (Criminal Procedure (Scotland) Act 1975, s. 442B). The court may increase the length of the sentence.

4. EXPENSES

In appeals from summary cases the High Court can award such expenses both in the High Court and in the inferior court as it may think fit. This seems to be intended as a sanction against frivolous appeals, although successful applicants can also benefit from the provision. See *Hamilton* v. *Friel*, 1992 S.L.T. 819.

B. SOLEMN APPEALS

As in summary cases there is now only one ground of appeal—miscarriage of justice. The accused (but not the prosecutor) can appeal against conviction on indictment, or sentence or both. He cannot appeal against any sentence fixed by law, *e.g.* life imprisonment for a conviction of murder (Criminal Procedure (Scotland) Act 1975, s. 228 (as substituted)). Leave to appeal from the trial judge is no longer required, and fresh evidence can, as in summary appeals, be heard. Again, as in summary appeals, the High Court can authorise a new prosecution for the same or any similar offence arising out of the same facts (Criminal Procedure (Scotland) Act 1975, s. 255 (as substituted)). See *Mackenzie* v. *H.M. Advocate*, 1983 S.L.T. 220 and *Cunningham* v. *H.M. Advocate*, 1984 S.C.C.R. 40. It is up to the Crown to decide whether or not a fresh prosecution (a re-trial) will take place. For a trenchant critique of the prosecutor's right to seek a re-trial see "Criminal Appeals, Retrials and Acquittals", 1984 S.L.T. (News) 341. The Appeal Court has used its re-trial powers sparingly—on only five occasions up to 1992 and only in one of them was a conviction attained.

Where the appeal is against sentence an accelerated, "note of appeal" procedure is used (s. 233 (as substituted)). The court may only increase the sentence if there has been an appeal against sentence. Expenses cannot be awarded in solemn appeals.

As a result of the Criminal Justice (Scotland) Act 1980, s. 35, advocation has now been extended to appeals from all solemn cases (Criminal Procedure (Scotland) Act 1975, s. 280A). Such appeals by the prosecutor in respect of alleged irregularities in the proceedings are unlikely to be very frequent.

C. LORD ADVOCATE'S REFERENCE

Where a person tried on indictment is acquitted of a charge the Lord Advocate may refer a point of law which has arisen in relation to that charge to the High Court for their opinion (Criminal Procedure (Scotland) Act 1975, s. 263A, inserted by the Criminal Justice (Scotland) Act 1980, s. 37). This is like an appeal on a point of law but has no effect on the acquittal in the trial. It was not thought that such references would occur frequently, and so it has transpired. Up to the end of 1992 there had only been three Lord Advocate's references. [These are reported in 1984 S.C.C.R. 62, 1986 J.C. 137 and 1992 S.L.T. 1010.]

CHAPTER 5

TRIBUNALS

Tribunals are an important element in the legal system of Scotland.
Many, but not all, tribunals are kept under review by a statutory
body, the Council on Tribunals. In 1991, the last year for which
reasonably complete figures are available, the tribunals under the
specific supervision of the Council's Scottish Committee disposed
of over 31,000 cases. In the same year, the tribunals under the
general supervision of the Council disposed of over 750,000 cases,
a significant proportion of which would be cases in Scotland.

I. THE DEVELOPMENT AND RATIONALE OF TRIBUNALS

There is a wide range of tribunals in Scotland with different
functions, composition and procedure. This diversity is a product
of the history of their development.

Wraith and Hutcheson, *Administrative Tribunals*, pp. 29–33
"Scottish legal history points to a much closer relationship between the
administration of justice and the conduct of government than a superficial
understanding of the separation of powers doctrine would admit. As in
England, there was a period before the modern differentiation of
legislative, executive and judicial institutions and functions had
developed. Distinct judicial institutions appeared later in Scotland than in
England, and the separation of functions occurred later still; indeed the
differentiation of functions was probably never complete so long as
Scotland was an independent kingdom. Three or four centuries ago, both
at national and local levels, the same governmental organs exercised
administrative, legislative and judicial functions. The growth of separate
arrangements for judicial work during the sixteenth century was as much
for reasons of practical convenience as for reasons of principle. The
College of Justice was formally constituted in 1532 to give a firm and
continuing basis to the Court of Session and the High Court of Justiciary
with criminal jurisdiction was established in 1672. Yet the King's Council
continued to exercise both civil and criminal jurisdiction and today it is
difficult to see why certain cases came to the Council rather than to the
Court of Session or the High Court of Justiciary.

Since its inception, the Court of Session had been able to exercise some
control over the jurisdiction of subordinate and inferior courts, a task
which during the sixteenth and seventeenth centuries was itself subject to
intervention from the Council. After the Union of 1707, the abolition of
the separate Privy Council for Scotland had repercussions for the role of

the central civil court similar to those arising from the disappearance of conciliar jurisdiction in England: it was thereafter the duty of the Court of Session to provide redress for citizens' grievances which formerly had gone properly to the Privy Council. By comparison with the common law courts in England, the supervisory control of the Court of Session was marked by a greater flexibility that must in part have been due to the fact that no separate court of equity developed in Scotland. Through the exercise of the 'nobile officium', the Court of Session had an ultimate right to provide an extraordinary equitable remedy in a situation in which the strict law provided none. The eighteenth-century Scottish law reports provide numerous examples of an extensive supervisory jurisdiction being exercised by the Court of Session over inferior courts and tribunals, and this jurisdiction was not ignored in legal scholarship.

For certain purposes, the Court of Session itself could take on a different form to exercise a specialized jurisdiction. By what the late Lord President Cooper called 'a remarkable anticipation of the modern *ad hoc* tribunal' the multifarious ecclesiastical business arising after the reformation and associated with parish churches, manses, stipends and teinds (or tithes) was vested first in statutory commissions and then transferred to the Court of Session itself, sitting as the 'Commission for the Plantation of Kirks and the Valuation of Teinds'. In this capacity between 1707 and 1925, the Court of Session performed a wide variety of administrative and judicial functions for the church, during a period when the church itself had major public responsibilities in the government of Scotland, for example in the poor law and in education. (Since 1925, what remains of this jurisdiction is undertaken by a judge sitting as Lord Ordinary on Teinds.) In a similar way today, senators of the College of Justice may sit to exercise a specialized statutory jurisdiction as the Lands Valuation Appeal Court, hearing appeals against rating assessments made by local Valuation Appeal Committees, and, less frequently, as the Registration of Voters Appeal Court and the Election Petition Court. In 1708, a Court of Exchequer for Scotland was reconstituted and equipped with procedures similar to those in the English Court of Exchequer but in 1856 its jurisdiction was transferred to the Court of Session, which still deals with revenue cases by procedures derived from English revenue practice . . . Many other inferior courts and tribunals, often exercising administrative functions, have existed in Scotland . . .

During the nineteenth century many specialized organs of central and local government were established, often with power to settle disputes arising out of the exercise of their administrative functions. [They were] superseded by government departments and local authorities."

From the early part of the twentieth century the development of the welfare state in particular led to the establishment of many tribunals. The use of tribunals was considered by the Donoughmore Committee on Ministers' Powers which reported in 1932 (Cmd. 4060) and was fully examined by the Franks Committee on Administrative Tribunals and Enquiries which reported in 1957.

Franks Committee, paras. 35–37

"At the time of the Donoughmore Committee (1929–32) there were few kinds of tribunal (although some of them, for example the Courts of Referees under the Unemployment Insurance Acts, dealt with important issues affecting large numbers of the population), and the Committee was able to regard tribunals as somewhat exceptional, to be resorted to only in special circumstances and requiring strict safeguards. The position today is different. The continuing extension of governmental activity and responsibility for the general well-being of the community has greatly multiplied the occasions on which an individual may be at issue with the administration, or with another citizen or body, as to his rights, and the post-war years have seen a substantial growth in the importance and activities of tribunals. In some cases new policies or regulating legislation have meant new tribunals . . . in other cases an earlier system has been adapted to wider purposes . . . in other cases tribunals now perform functions previously carried out by the courts . . .

Tribunals today vary widely in constitution, function and procedure . . . Most tribunals deal with cases in which an individual citizen is at issue with a Government Department or other public body concerning his rights or obligations under a statutory scheme. But a few . . . are concerned with disputes between citizens. Still others . . . have regulatory functions and are therefore just as much administrative bodies as they are adjudicating tribunals. Some tribunals, like the courts, have a detailed code of procedure, with testimony on oath and strict rules of evidence. Most have a simple procedure, usually without the oath and sometimes with a ban on legal representation. Finally, there are differences regarding appeals. Sometimes there is no appeal, and further redress can only be had by seeking a court order to set aside the decision. But in most cases there is an appeal—either to an appellate tribunal, a Minister or the courts.

Reflection on the general social and economic changes of recent decades convinces us that tribunals as a system for adjudication have come to stay. The tendency for issues arising from legislative schemes to be referred to special tribunals is likely to grow rather than to diminish . . . ''

Tribunals are concerned with an immense spectrum of administrative activity, ranging from some of the functions of the Director-General of Fair Trading to the Crofters Commission, from industrial tribunals to children's hearings, from the Immigration Appeal Tribunal to the Value Added Tax Tribunal for Scotland. The membership of tribunals, although commonly a chairman and two members, varies greatly. A civil servant may be classified as a tribunal for certain statutory purposes: National Insurance Commissioner's decision no. R(G)1/80; on the other hand, the Employment Appeal Tribunal, despite its name, is a superior court of record, which normally sits with a judge of the Court of Session and two or four lay members: Employment Protection (Consolidation) Act 1978, Sched. 11, paras. 12, 16. The jurisdiction of tribunals varies. Some, such as the Immigration Appeal Tribunal, have a U.K. jurisdiction; some have a Scottish jurisdiction, although paralleled by other tribunals elsewhere in the United Kingdom; some are peculiar to Scotland, for example the Crofters Commission and children's hearings. Although there is a degree of central monitoring, tribunal procedure also varies. Some are more formal than others; some, such as Social Security Appeal Tribunals, are inquisitorial and some, such as Immigration Adjudicators and Industrial Tribunals, are essentially adversarial in their procedure.

Their range and diversity have made tribunals difficult to classify and evaluate. Traditionally, they have been evaluated in institutional terms and in comparison with courts.

Franks Committee, paras. 38–45

"We agree with the Donoughmore Committee that tribunals have certain characteristics which often give them advantages over the courts. These are cheapness, accessibility, freedom from technicality, expedition and expert knowledge of their particular subject. It is no doubt because of these advantages that Parliament, once it has decided that certain decisions ought not to be made by normal executive or departmental processes, often entrusts them to tribunals rather than to the ordinary courts . . .

Moreover, if all decisions arising from new legislation were automatically vested in the ordinary courts the judiciary would by now have been grossly overburdened . . .

Tribunals are not ordinary courts, but neither are they appendages of Government Departments. Much of the official evidence, including that of the Joint Permanent Secretary to the Treasury, appeared to reflect the view that tribunals should properly be regarded as part of the machinery of administration, for which the Government must retain a close and continuing responsibility. Thus, for example, tribunals in the social service field would be regarded as adjuncts to the administration of the services themselves. We do not accept this view. We consider that tribunals should properly be regarded as machinery provided by Parliament for adjudication rather than as part of the machinery of administration. The essential point is that in all these cases Parliament has deliberately provided for a decision outside and independent of the Department concerned, either at first instance . . . or on appeal from a decision of a Minister or of an official in a special statutory position. . . . Although the relevant statutes do not in all cases expressly enact that tribunals are to consist entirely of persons outside the Government service, the use of the term 'tribunal' in legislation undoubtedly bears this

connotation, and the intention of Parliament to provide for the independence of tribunals is clear and unmistakable.

We have already expressed our belief that Parliament in deciding that
certain decisions should be reached only after a special procedure must
have intended that they should manifest three basic characteristics:
openness, fairness and impartiality. The choice of a tribunal rather than a
Minister as the deciding authority is itself a considerable step towards the
realisation of these objectives, particularly the third . . .

In the field of tribunals openness appears to us to require the publicity
of proceedings and knowledge of the essential reasoning underlying the
decisions; fairness to require the adoption of a clear procedure which
enables parties to know their rights, to present their case fully and to
know the case which they have to meet; and impartiality to require the
freedom of tribunals from the influence, real or apparent, of Departments
concerned with the subject matter of their decisions . . .

. . . This is particularly so when a Government Department is a
frequent party to proceedings before a tribunal . . . "

Describing tribunals by reference to the ideals adopted by the
Franks Committee has increasingly been considered, both in
factual and policy terms, as inadequate. So, for instance, it is
difficult to attribute to tribunals both the advantage of being better
able than courts to adjudicate in areas of law with a high policy
content, which in any event implies an assessment of the judiciary
which is perhaps less true than it once was, and the advantage of
having a high degree of independence from Government departments which effectively determine the policy.

Again, the cheapness of tribunals may be a limited economic
evaluation. There is contemporary criticism of the inadequate level
of Departmental resources devoted to initial assessment of social
security benefit claimants. If the resources devoted to assessment
are low this contributes to the volume of appeals to Social Security
Appeal Tribunals and, therefore, no doubt, to the trend of their
increasing delays in adjudicating appeals.

It may be true that as compared with courts many tribunals
avoid procedural technicality, but the law with which they are
concerned is frequently both technical and complex. This is
certainly the case with, say, employment law, social security law
and immigration law.

One response to this is to assert the value of courts within the
legal system, as the Franks Committee did, or even to propose the
institutional merger of tribunals and courts. Indeed, the supervision of the tribunal decision-making may be indirectly contributing to such a result.

Hughes Commission, p. 204

"We have had evidence, particularly from the Scottish Legal Action Group, suggesting that because of the expense, delay and formality of court procedures, there has been a 'flight' from the courts into alternative tribunals—statutory tribunals, statutory arbitrations or voluntary arbitrations. We think that there is an element of truth in this, though it can be exaggerated. It is not always the case that these alternatives are either quicker or cheaper (to the litigant or the State) than the civil courts; but cheapness, speed and informality are certainly characteristic of some of them. What we are not disposed to accept is the implication of some of the evidence that the civil courts have incurable defects and must always be looked upon as places of last resort; and accordingly that, wherever practicable, alternative tribunals should be made available. We certainly do not want to discourage arbitration or specialist tribunals for types of cases for which they are, for one reason or another, particularly suitable. We firmly believe, however, that the civil courts are, and should remain, the principal means for resolving civil disputes. We are anxious lest undue resort to remedies outwith the court may lead to the needed reform of court procedures being delayed and neglected. The aim should be to develop in the civil courts themselves those same qualities of cheapness, speed and informality in so far as these are compatible with fair and respected judicial procedures."

Abel-Smith and Stevens, *In Search of Justice*, pp. 227–228

"Courts are said to be administering rules of law while tribunals are thought to be administering both law and policy. We would maintain that no such clear line can or should be drawn. Indeed it was the evolution of this myth which helped establish the tribunal system by convincing the judges of the ordinary courts that they were concerned with legal but not with policy questions. But continued insistence on this unsatisfactory distinction makes it increasingly difficult to entrust new matters to the courts or to merge courts and tribunals. Properly understood, tribunals are a more modern form of court. In some cases they may have more discretion than the courts, and this is particularly true of the policy-oriented tribunals . . . Conversely the court-substitute tribunals are often as precedent-conscious as, and may even exercise a much narrower discretion than, the ordinary courts.

But we would reaffirm our position that there is no fundamental difference between courts and tribunals. We would argue, therefore, that every effort should be made to merge the two . . . "

However, one of the considerations which make tribunals an appropriate form of adjudication is that they can be an ideal mechanism for decentralised determination of legal issues raised by large numbers of people. They only become an ideal mechanism where the tribunals provide consistent and accurate adjudication. This is an issue which faces many jurisdictions and its general aspects have been influentially explored in J. Mashaw, *Bureaucratic Justice* (Yale U.P.: 1983).

In a Scottish and U.K. context there has been an increased awareness that the objective of providing consistent and accurate adjudication is paramount and that this objective may only with difficulty be reconciled with some of the attributes of tribunals identified by the Franks Committee, such as cheapness and lack of procedural technicality.

Sometimes the reconciliation may be attempted by reforming the structure and operation of tribunals, as was done with the former Supplementary Benefit Appeal Tribunals and National Insurance Local Tribunals in the 1980s.

Sainsbury, "Social Security Appeals: in Need of Review?" pp. 336–338
"Prior to the HASSASSA [Health and Social Services and Social Security Adjudication Act 1983] reforms there was a clear distinction between the administration and adjudication of supplementary benefit on the one hand and of national insurance benefits on the other. Decisions under the national insurance scheme lay with the statutorily independent insurance officer in the first instance, and with the National Insurance Local Tribunal (NILT) on appeal. Thence, there was a further right of appeal to the Social Security Commissioner. In contrast, initial decisions on the main means-tested benefit, supplementary benefit, were made by DHSS officials on behalf of the Supplementary Benefits Commission. Appeals were possible to Supplementary Benefit Appeals Tribunals (SBATs) but there was no right of appeal to the Social Security Commissioner. Under the industrial injuries scheme, 'disablement questions' were (until 1983) decided by a medical board of two doctors, from which an appeal was possible to a Medical Appeal Tribunal. Medical boards also heard appeals on mobility allowance on medical questions. Further appeal was allowed to the MAT, comprising a legally-qualified chairman and two doctors of consultant status.

Although NILTs were generally regarded as working satisfactorily, SBATs were subject to repeated criticisms in the 1970s. The strong current of dissatisfaction with SBATs led the DHSS to commission research by Professor Kathleen Bell of Newcastle University into their operation. Bell's research revealed numerous shortcomings in the SBAT system; tribunal chairmen, most of whom were not legally qualified, were found to have a limited knowledge and understanding of supplementary benefits; proceedings were unsystematic; there was an over-reliance on the clerk (an official seconded from the DHSS); decisions were not recorded satisfactorily; and discretion was not exercised in a disciplined or systematic way. Bell concluded that a comprehensive review was required as a matter of urgency and proposed a number of reforms to be achieved in three stages. Immediate improvements could be secured by providing training for chairmen and members; other changes would take longer to implement (such as the introduction of legally-qualified chairmen); whilst other changes were structural in nature, such as the provision of a further stage of appeal after the SBAT, and the merging of SBATs with NILTs.

Changes within the existing SBAT structure began to be implemented in 1977. More legally-qualified chairmen were appointed, training was instigated, a procedure manual produced, and a right of appeal from SBATs to the High Court in England and the Court of Session in Scotland was provided. Later, in the Social Security Act 1979, full-time senior chairmen were introduced, to have some responsibility for organising tribunals in addition to hearing cases.

Bell's structural reforms took longer to achieve. In 1980 the supplementary benefits scheme, which until then had been based largely on administrative discretion, was replaced by a scheme conferring legal entitlement to benefits. The case for merging SBATs and NILTs therefore became stronger, and the desirability of change was accepted by the government.

The culmination of the reforms which had begun in the late 1970s was HASSASSA, which in 1983 introduced a unified three-tier adjudication system comprised of adjudication officers (replacing insurance officers and supplementary benefit officers), a unified Social Security Appeal Tribunal (replacing SBATs and NILTs), and the Social Security Commissioner (whose jurisdiction now extended to supplementary benefit). Furthermore, the posts of Chief Insurance Officer and Chief Supplementary Benefits Officer (DHSS officials who had previously issued guidance to insurance officers and supplementary benefit officers respectively) were replaced by the statutorily independent Chief Adjudication Officer (whose primary tasks were to advise adjudication officers and to monitor the standards of their decision-making). Finally, the SSAT system was brought within a presidential organisation similar to that of other tribunals. The President is a barrister, advocate or solicitor of not less than ten years' standing appointed by the Lord Chancellor. As well as being responsible for the management of SSATs and MATs, the President also has a responsibility for training tribunal chairmen and members, and for ensuring that they have access to appropriate social security texts. To assist him, the President has seven Regional Chairmen of Tribunals to whom he can delegate appropriate duties. The rationale behind the presidential system is to remove any direct and obvious link between social security tribunals and the Department, and to concentrate experience and expertise relevant to both types of tribunal."

However, policy considerations may persuade the Government to pursue other alternatives. Sometimes it is necessary to recognise the autonomy of local authorities when providing a national social security benefit; housing benefit is a case in point. There it was eventually decided that allowing appeals to be determined by a national tribunal structure would undermine local authority autonomy because the decisions of such tribunals would have the capacity to overturn the decisions of publicly accountable local authorities. The statutory solution adopted was a system of initial internal administrative review by local authority officers, with the possibility of a further hearing before a review board of local authority councillors which would be subject to judicial review by the courts. [See Social Security and Housing Benefits Act 1982 and Social Security Administration Act 1992; Housing Benefit (General) Regulations 1987, S.I. 1987 No. 1971 (as amended); M. Partington & H. Bolderson, *Housing Benefit Review Procedures: A Preliminary Analysis* (Brunel University: 1984).]

On occasion, the Government has turned away from tribunals in areas where the number of claimants and the need for speedy determination of appeals would seem to make their continued use appropriate. One instance was the replacement of single payments under the supplementary benefit scheme by the social fund in 1988: see now Social Security Administration Act 1992, ss. 12, 64–66, 78, 167, 168. Despite institutional appearances to the contrary, the revised scheme for exercising and reviewing the discretionary decisions appears, on both official and academic assessment, to be providing speedy and independent determinations: *Annual Report of the Social Fund Commissioner for 1988–89* (HMSO: 1990); R. Drabble & T. Lynes, "Decision-making in Social Security: the Social Fund—Discretion or Control?" [1989] P.L. 317.

Sainsbury, "Social Security Appeals: in Need of Review?" p. 339
"The social fund replaced single payments under the supplementary benefit scheme in April 1988. The entitlement to payments for items such as furniture, cookers and refrigerators under regulations was replaced with a discretionary scheme of loans and grants which would be administered not by the statutory authorities, (i.e. the adjudication officer in the local office) but by social fund officers acting within the directions and guidance of the Secretary of State. Applicants dissatisfied with the decision of a social fund officer can obtain a review of the decision if they apply in writing giving the grounds for their request. The social fund officer who made the original decision will either grant the appeal in full or invite the claimant for an interview, at which the decision will be discussed. If the social fund officer is not prepared to change the decision, the case is passed on to a senior member of the local office management, who will again review the original decision. Claimants who are still dissatisfied may then request a further review by a social fund inspector. The inspectors have three possible courses of action. They can substitute their own decision, uphold the original decision or refer the decision back to the social fund officer. There is no right of appeal to the Social Security

Commissioner. The quality of decision-making by social fund inspectors is monitored by the Social Fund Commissioner who has a statutory responsibility to report annually to the Secretary of State. Reminiscent of the genesis of housing benefit review boards, the provision of a right of appeal to a social fund inspector was added to review by local office management only following the considerable opposition that the original proposals provoked."

In general terms, tribunals occupy a place within the legal system between (a) intra-Departmental determination and review, and (b) the courts. To maintain that place tribunals must offer decentralised, cheap and speedy adjudication, which is also consistent and fair, and must be capable of offering it to large numbers of people. This, in turn, depends on such factors as the selection, appointment and training of tribunal members, the procedures which tribunals adopt, the availability of representation and legal aid for those appearing before tribunals, and the nature and extent of judicial and non-judicial supervision and control of tribunals.

II. THE COMPOSITION OF TRIBUNALS

Wraith and Hutcheson, *Administrative Tribunals*, p. 93
"There are four distinguishable patterns [in the composition of tribunals]—first, where the tribunal is an individual sitting alone; second, where all members are entitled to be present, with provision for a quorum; third, where there is a single panel from which are normally selected a chairman and one or two other members; and fourth, where there is a chairman sitting with members of 'representative' panels."

Members of tribunals may be appointed by a variety of authorities. The Social Security Commissioners are appointed by the Crown; members of panels for children's hearings are appointed by the Secretary of State, to whom names of suitable applicants are submitted by a children's panel advisory committee in each regional and islands authority (Social Work (Scotland) Act 1968, Sched. 3); the panel of members of local valuation appeal committees is appointed by the sheriff (Local Government (Scotland) Act 1975, s. 4).

A common pattern is for members of a tribunal to be appointed directly by a government minister but for the chairman to be appointed by the Lord President of the Court of Session either directly or to a panel from which the selection is made by a government minister or by a president of tribunals. For example, the chairmen of industrial tribunals are selected by the President of Industrial Tribunals (Scotland) or his nominee, from a panel of chairmen appointed by the Lord President (the Industrial Tribunal

(Scotland) Regulations 1965 (reg. 5(2) (S.I. 1965 No. 1157)). The appointment of, amongst others, the chairmen of SSATs is governed by the Tribunals and Inquiries Act 1992, s. 6.

Tribunals and Inquiries Act 1992, s. 6(1), (2)

"(1) The chairman, or any person appointed to act as chairman, of any of the tribunals to which this subsection applies shall (without prejudice to any statutory provisions as to qualifications) be selected by the appropriate authority from a panel of persons appointed by the [Lord President of the Court of Session].

(2) Members of panels constituted under this section shall hold and vacate office under the terms of the instruments under which they are appointed, but may resign office by notice in writing to the [Lord President of the Court of Session]; and any such member who ceases to hold office shall be eligible for re-appointment."

Frequently, statutory requirements or informal arrangements seek to ensure that members of a tribunal are conversant with the circumstances of those who are likely to appear before them:

Social Security Administration Act 1992, ss. 40, 41(1)–(6)

"**40.**—(1) The President shall constitute for the whole of Great Britain, to act for such areas as he thinks fit and be composed of such persons as he thinks fit to appoint, panels of persons to act as members of social security appeal tribunals.

(2) The panel for an area shall be composed of persons appearing to the President to have knowledge or experience of conditions in the area and to be representative of persons living or working in the area.

(3) Before appointing members of a panel, the President shall take into consideration any recommendations from such organisations or persons as he considers appropriate.

(4) The members of the panels shall hold office for such period as the President may direct, but the President may at any time terminate the appointment of any member of a panel.

41.—(1) A social security appeal tribunal shall consist of a chairman and two other persons.

(2) The members other than the chairman shall be drawn from the appropriate panel constituted under section 40 above.

(3) The President shall nominate the chairman.

(4) The President may nominate as chairman—

(a) himself;

(b) one of the full-time chairmen appointed under section 51(1) below; or

(c) a person drawn from the panel appointed by the Lord Chancellor or, as the case may be, the Lord President of the Court of Session under section 6 of the Tribunals and Inquiries Act 1992.

(5) No person shall be appointed chairman of a tribunal under subsection (4)(c) above unless he has a 5 year general qualification or he is an advocate or solicitor in Scotland of at least 5 years' standing.

(6) If practicable, at least one of the members of the appeal tribunal hearing a case shall be of the same sex as the claimant."

[See also Schedule 2. The "President" is the President of social security appeal tribunals and other tribunals: s. 191; for the meaning of "5 year general qualification" see the Courts and Legal Services Act 1990, s. 71.]

The Industrial Tribunals (Scotland) Regulations 1965, reg. 5(3)

"For each hearing the two members of a tribunal other than the chairman shall be selected by the President (or by a member of the panel of chairmen for the time being nominated by the President for the purpose), as to one member from a panel of persons appointed by the Secretary of State after consultation with any organisation or association of organisations representative of employers, and as to the other members from a panel of persons appointed by the Secretary of State after consultation with any organisation or association of organisations representative of employed persons."

[The above paragraph was substituted by the Industrial Tribunals (Scotland) (Amendment) Regulations 1977 (S.I. 1977 No. 1474).]

Social Work (Scotland) Act 1968, s. 34(2)

"A children's hearing shall consist of a chairman and two other members and shall have both a man and a woman among the members."

Statutory requirements may create their own difficulties.

Cavenagh and Newton, "Administration tribunals: how people become members", p. 210

"Ambiguity about what lay members are supposed to contribute seems to have been the cause of practical problems in the Industrial Tribunal, where some lay members, particularly on the workers' side, appear to come on with the idea that they are there to 'represent' their own 'side' of industry; yet this conflicts fundamentally with the view of the previous Lord Chancellor [Lord Gardiner] as expressed in 1968 in a speech circulated to all members:

'One sometimes hears the members erroneously referred to as "the employers' representative" or "the employees' representative". They are not. They represent no one, except the interests of justice. Each is an entirely independent judicial officer, who decides a case upon its merits, upon the evidence and law applicable'.

But despite these words the problem persists and the misconception still seems quite widespread."

There is also the more general problem that, despite statutory requirements and informal arrangements, the membership of tribunals is not representative of society as a whole and may not provide a reasonable range of age and experience. These were, for example, legitimate criticisms of the former SBATs as Flockhart's research demonstrates, and Wikeley and Young suggest that the rather different structure of SSATs attracts similar criticism.

Flockhart, "Some Aspects of Tribunal Membership", pp. 99–100
"In the summer of 1971, a study of the membership of Supplementary Benefits Appeal Tribunals was carried out in Scotland . . .
[at that time SBAT members were drawn from three panels]:
(1) chairmen; . . .
(2) persons appointed by the Secretary of State from among persons appearing to him to represent work-people. In practice they are selected from lists of names submitted by local Trades Councils. They are referred to here as Trades Council members (TCMs); and
(3) other persons appointed by the Secretary of State, here referred to as Other members (OMs).
In terms of the Registrar General's Classification 78% of the chairmen and Other members, taken together, were from Social Classes I and II. The social class breakdown of [the tribunal members who responded to a questionnaire] is summarised in the table below:

Social Class	Chairmen	OM	TCM	All Members
I	4	4	0	8
II	15	35	14	64
III (Non-manual)	2	4	9	15
III (Manual)	1	0	38	39
IV	0	1	10	11
V	0	0	1	1
Unknown	4	4	2	10
Total	26	48	74	148

There is a case for arguing that a welfare tribunal should be composed of three 'ordinary people' drawn from the local community, sitting together as lay persons to assess the extent of social need. If so, it might be thought that these three lay persons should represent in themselves a reasonably varied and wide social experience. The membership of the tribunals in this study reflects a narrowing grouping of social class and age amongst the chairmen and Other members but is significantly less narrow in terms of social class among the Trades Council members. In addition, of the 148 members only sixteen were women, i.e. 11%. When asked to rate the importance of having at least one woman member on a tribunal 60% said it was unimportant."

Wikeley and Young, "The Marginalisation of Lay Members in Social
Security Appeal Tribunals," pp. 131–3

"Chairmen were generally rather younger than lay members. Nearly half
of the chairmen we interviewed were in their fifties; a quarter were under
50 and a further quarter aged 60 or more. By contrast the great majority
of members (63%) were over 60 years old. One quater of the chairmen
were female, indicating that there has been some success in appointing a
larger number of women to such posts (in 1982 the proportion was only
17%: Harris, 1983).

Earlier studies were critical of the unrepresentative nature of those
appointed to serve as lay members on tribunals (Lister, 1974, Fulbrook,
1978). The two lay members on each social security appeal tribunal, who
receive expenses but no fee, are now drawn from a single list of people
"appearing to the President to have knowledge or experience of conditions in the area and to be representative of persons living or working in
the area" (Social Security Act 1975, Sched. 10, para. 1(2)). Formerly
both of the old tribunals had employed a two panel system. In national
insurance local tribunals there were separate lists for employees and
employers, with the members nominated by Trades Councils and business
interests respectively to reflect the role of both sides of industry in
contributing to the national insurance fund. Supplementary benefit appeal
tribunals were constituted rather differently. One member, called the
Secretary of State's member, was meant to have knowledge or experience
of conditions in the area concerned and of the problems of people living
on low incomes. The other, the Trades Council member, was drawn from
a panel representing work people.

The Government's plan to abolish the two panel system, and with it the
automatic presence of at least one trade unionist on each tribunal, proved
to be so politically controversial that it was dropped to ensure the passage
of the HASSASSA Act 1983, before that year's General Election. The
proposal was subsequently reintroduced and enacted in the Health and
Social Security Act 1984. The rationale for the change, according to
Government spokesmen, was the need to provide a more broadly
representative base for tribunal membership. Critics feared that the
middle class bias in the tribunals' composition would only become more
pronounced (Wikeley, 1985).

In practice it seems that the creation of a single panel has made little
difference as yet to the make-up of tribunals. In our sample by far the
largest single group of members, some 37%, had been nominated by
trade unions, almost twice as many as fell into the next largest category,
those nominated by somebody within the tribunal system itself. These
trade union nominees were also amongst the longest serving members of
the tribunals, two thirds of them having been members for between five
and 15 years. As indicated above, members were on average older than
chairmen, although the proportion of women (38%) was higher than
amongst chairmen. Notwithstanding the continuing role of trade union
nominees, our findings suggest that the tribunal system has failed to build

up a broader base of lay membership to reflect in some measure the range of people that appear as appellants. Only one of the 97 members we interviewed described himself as unemployed. It is still the case that most appellants find themselves facing a row of white, rather elderly faces across the tribunal table."

[The figures are drawn from a study of 28 SSATs throughout Great Britain conducted in 1989/90; the full report of the research has been published: J. Baldwin, N. Wikeley and R. Young, *Judging Social Security* (OUP: 1992).]

Research suggests another problem is that in some tribunals, as compared with the chairmen, the other members (sometimes referred to as the "wing members") play a rather passive rôle. One reason for this can be the training and experience of the chairmen. The chairmen of some tribunals must be legally qualified; this is true of, for instance, industrial tribunals and of social security appeal tribunals. In such tribunals, where many of the issues to be considered may involve legal technicality, it might be expected that the legally qualified chairmen would play a dominant rôle. In any event, tribunal chairmen are likely to be more experienced than the other members and thus may be expected to be more influential.

The relative passivity of the members of tribunals is a concern. The appointment of members of tribunals is presumably intended to guard against bias in chairmen and to inject lay experience which may be relevant in considering certain aspects of claimants' cases. To some extent, the passivity of tribunal members may be corrected by training. Regional chairmen of SSATs, for instance, are responsible for providing training for the lay members. However, such training is limited and, in the view of some, is inadequate: C. Jones & M. Adler, *Can Anyone Get on These? A study of the systems of appointment and training of justices of the peace and members of social security appeal tribunals and children's panels in Scotland* (Scottish Consumer Council, Glasgow: 1990).

Wikeley and Young, "The Marginalisation of Lay Members in Social Security Appeal Tribunals," pp. 137–9

"Our observations of tribunal proceedings, based on a national sample, tend to confirm the view that the legalisation of the benefit system has made it more difficult for lay members to contribute (for a similar perspective on industrial tribunals, see Dickens *et al.*, 1985, p. 83). In the tribunal hearings which we observed few of the members played a major role. In part this is attributable to the widespread (but questionable) view amongst members that, in those cases where the appellant is not present at the hearing (around half of the total), there is nothing they can do other than rely on the submission of the presenting officer. Sometimes this is due to a sense of powerlessness in the face of tight statutory provisions which seem to admit of no exceptions. As one member commented:

"I'm a bit depressed on that score. It was far more interesting and our role was of far more value a few years ago, when there was an area of discretion. One was able to alter the result to fit the individual case. Now it is very rigid and sometimes I feel we are just rubber stamping a bad law." (Member, North Wales, Interview 121).

Even when appellants attend their appeal hearings, members generally fail to make their presence felt. In all, we found that less than a fifth of the members made anything more than a limited contribution to the proceedings that we observed. One of our most striking findings was that almost a half were entirely silent throughout the appeal hearing. These members did not ask a single question or make a single comment. By way of contrast, Jackson, Stewart and Bland (1987) found that members made no contribution at all in the public part of the hearing in something over one fifth of hearings. Even allowing for methodological differences, this suggests a marked diminution in the potential for members to play a positive part in hearings over the course of the last five years. The phasing out of lay chairmen, the growing experience of lawyer chairmen, the replacement of supplementary benefit by a much simpler system of income support, and the loss of discretion represented by the abolition of single payments, are all significant factors in this development. The issues raised in many social security appeals are too legal, too technical, and too complex to allow the average lay member much scope to make a significant contribution. This is not to imply that there was once a golden age of lay member participation—the Bell report (1975) on supplementary benefit appeal tribunals noted that it was only in a minority of hearings that both members played an active role. The problem of passive members seems, however, to have worsened considerably since Bell reported.

It is true that members may play a positive part in putting appellants at their ease even though they may not say a word—for example, by smiling, nodding or demonstrably paying close attention to the case. Yet about two thirds of those members who remained silent were entirely passive, and a few behaved in a distinctly off putting manner—such as by yawning or looking bored. One actually fell asleep during the hearing. Many of them can be said to have given the appearance of being seriously out of their depth.

It must be conceded that, with a few exceptions, we were only able to observe the public part of the tribunal proceedings. It should be noted that in terms of putting the appellant at ease and assisting in developing his or her case, this is the important stage of the hearing. Nevertheless, it might be argued that members who play only a limited role in the hearing may be more animated in the subsequent deliberations. A number of reasons lead us to doubt that this is the case. First, our interviews with chairmen and members themselves suggested that members often fail to participate actively in the deliberations following a hearing. Secondly, it was noteworthy that in 58% of the appeals observed, the deliberations took five minutes or less (in 21% of the cases in our sample there were no formal deliberations because the tribunal reached its decision in the course of the hearing). Thirdly, members rarely dissent from the decision considered correct by the chairman. In 331 cases out of our sample of 337, the decision was unanimous, and, in the six cases where there was disagreement, the chairman was in the majority. In other words, there was not a single case in which the chairman was outvoted by the lay members."

III. TRIBUNAL PROCEDURE

A. PROCEDURAL RULES

Wraith and Hutcheson, *Administrative Tribunals*, p. 131
"Given the diversity and range of formal and informal procedures, the dilemma is two-fold: on the one hand procedure should not be so technical and formal as to discourage legitimate applications, and on the other even the most informal of tribunals will need some guidelines if the proceedings are to be fair to both parties. This is a tightrope which not all tribunals have managed to walk successfully.

The point was put with great clarity by Lord Gardiner (then Lord Chancellor) in a speech at the opening of the Central Office of the Industrial Tribunals:

"Tribunals try to be free from technicality. A tribunal must have a framework of procedure within which to operate. Experience has shown that informality of atmosphere in hearings before tribunals can be positively inimical to orderly procedure. Within that framework of procedure, it is essential that there should be sufficient informality of atmosphere to put the lay litigant at his ease. Lawyers sometimes forget what an ordeal it is for the ordinary citizen to go to law. 80% of the cases coming before the Industrial Tribunals are claims for redundancy pay-ments. Many of the applicants, and a number of the respondents, are unsophisticated people caught up in a vast machine which they do not understand. They are frightened of what they imagine a court to be, and it is a major part of a tribunal's function to put them at their ease so that they present cases as well as possible. A tribunal must be tolerant and patient with the litigants before it, who are usually unrepresented, are often incapable of expressing themselves adequately, and are nearly always overwhelmed by the occasion. It is therefore essential that the proceedings should be kept as simple and as informal as possible within the framework of the procedure laid down by law.' "

Justice-All Souls Review, paras. 51–56
"The procedure of most tribunals differs markedly from that of the courts of law. Whereas the procedure in court is strongly adversarial that of

many tribunals combines the adversarial and the investigative. Thus, most tribunals can obtain their own evidence by calling witnesses, conduct examinations and inspect sites, and commission experts' reports. Even where there are no formal powers for these things tribunals often achieve them as a matter of practice.

There is a wide variety of procedures though, in the main, the order of proceedings in court is adopted but with much more latitude allowed to the applicant/appellant . . .

(a) Openness

With few exceptions the courts perform in public. In the case of tribunals there is much variation but private sessions are common (though this is scarcely noticed as in practice very few tribunal hearings are attended by members of the public or the press). Likewise judges have all the papers read to them in open court. Tribunal members, in order to save time, prepare for the hearings by reading the entire dossier in private.

(b) Evidence

Tribunals may rely on evidence that would be inadmissible in a court of law. The extent to which they do so varies according to the nature of the tribunal, and the nature of the case. Evidence is admitted if logically probative. Thus, hearsay is admissible. 'No doubt in admitting it, the tribunal must observe the rules of natural justice, but this does not mean that it must be tested by cross-examination. It only means that the . . . other side [must have] a fair opportunity of commenting on it and contradicting it', Lord Denning observed in *T.A. Miller Ltd.* v. *Minister of Housing and LG* [1968] 1 W.L.R. 992. Naturally tribunal members make considerable use of their own expertise in the subject matter.

(c) Standard of proof

The usual standard of proof, as in the civil courts, is the balance of probabilities, but there are some instances where the criminal standard ('beyond reasonable doubt') is adopted. The burden of proof is, as in the courts, on he who asserts, but there are a number of presumptions prescribed by statute that favour applicants/appellants in some tribunals.

(d) Rules of procedure.

Most tribunals have a general power to regulate their own proceedings, and they may adopt quite different rules. Franks found that there was 'general agreement on the broad essentials which the procedure (of tribunals) in this wider sense (of before and after as well as during the hearing) should contain'. They included the provision of notice of the right to apply to a tribunal, knowledge of the case to be met, a reasoned decision by the tribunal, and notice of any further right of appeal. Franks was not in favour either of a standard code of procedure or of a small number of codes (para. 63) but did envisage that the Council on Tribunals would have a statutory power to formulate rules of procedure. Neither this nor the . . . proposal that [there] should [be] a central supervisory drafting department was adopted. Regulations containing rules of procedure are drafted in the legal sections of the various departments. This accounts for much of their variety. The Council on Tribunals try to achieve a unifying effect through the process of consultation. Sometimes their advice is ignored."

[On the obligation to consult the Council on Tribunals on tribunal procedural rules see the Tribunals and Inquires Act 1992, s.8.]

Some aspects of tribunal procedure are governed by general statutory provisions. One of the most important is the:

Tribunal and Inquiries Act 1992, s.10(1)–(3), (6)

"**10.**—(1) Subject to the provisions of this section . . ., where—

(*a*) any tribunal specified in Schedule 1 gives any decision . . .

it shall be the duty of the tribunal . . . to furnish a statement, either written or oral, of the reasons for the decision if requested, on or before the giving or notification of the decision, to state the reasons.

(2) The statement referred to in subsection (1) may be refused, or the specification of the reasons restricted, on grounds of national security.

(3) A tribunal . . . may refuse to furnish a statement under subsection (1) to a person not primarily concerned with the decision if of the opinion that to furnish it would be contrary to the interests of any person primarily concerned . . .

(6) Any statement of the reasons for a decision referred to in paragraph (*a*) . . . of subsection (1), whether given in pursuance of that subsection or of any other statutory provision, shall be taken to form part of the decision and accordingly to be incorporated in the record . . ."

[S.10 applies to all tribunals under the jurisdiction of the Council on Tribunals. See also: *Crake* v. *Supplementary Benefits Commission; Butterworth* v. *Supplementary Benefits Commission* [1982] 1 All E.R. 498.].

B. APPEALS

From many tribunals an appeal lies to another tribunal on questions of law, or sometimes on questions of fact and law. In some cases there is no provision for further appeal, although tribunal decisions may be reviewed by the courts. So, for example, the Immigration Appeal Tribunal hears appeals from immigration adjudicators, but there is no provision for further appeal. In other cases, there is provision for appeal to the courts. For example, the Social Security Commissioners hear appeals from social security appeal tribunals (Social Security Administration Act 1992, ss.23, 24) and there is a further appeal to the Court of Session (*ibid.*, ss.24, 34).

Social Security Administration Act 1992, s.24(1), (2)

"(1) Subject to subsections (2) and (3) of this section, an appeal on a question of law shall lie to the appropriate court from any decision of a Commissioner.

(2) No appeal under this section shall lie from a decision except—

   (a) with the leave of the Commissioner who gave the decision or, in a prescribed case with the leave of a Commissioner selected in accordance with regulations; or

   (b) if he refuses leave, with the leave of the appropriate court."

See *Bland* v. *Chief Supplementary Benefit Officer* [1983] 1 All E.R. 557; see also *Burns* v. *Secretary of State for Social Services*, 1985 S.L.T. 351. Where the premises in which a tribunal normally exercises its functions are in Scotland, the appropriate court is the Court of Session; see also S.I. 1984 No. 451.]

In the case of certain tribunals there is provision for judicial review by the Court of Session by way of appeal or stated case. For example, the Tribunals and Inquiries Act 1992, s.11, applies to decisions of a number of other tribunals including most decisions of the Lands Tribunal for Scotland.

C. PRECEDENT

Justice-All Souls Review, para. 60

"Tribunals follow the precedents of the superior courts and, where appropriate, their own appellate tribunals. But they are not obliged to follow their own precedents and, indeed, are sometimes discouraged from doing so (e.g. *Merchandise Transport Ltd.* v. *British Transport Commission* [1962] 2 Q.B. 173). It is fundamental to any system of precedent that the existence of the precedents should be known, and the chairman and clerks of tribunals bear the chief responsibility for keeping abreast of them. The Franks Committee recommended that all final appellate tribunals should publish selected decisions and circulate them to any lower tribunals. It is plainly desirable that the precedents followed by tribunals should be made public but the extent to which they can be published is subject to limitations of cost."

The following decisions by National Insurance Commissioners (now Social Security Commissioners) demonstrate the use of precedent and reporting within a tribunal system.

R(1) 12/75
(Chief Commissioner) R.J.A. TEMPLE;
(Commissioners) J.S. WATSON, J.G. MONROE

"There have been nearly 60,000 Commissioners' decisions since 1948, and they fall into the following categories (a) unnumbered decisions (b) numbered decisions and (c) reported decisions.

(a) Unnumbered decisions which represent the vast majority of decided cases comprise those in which well established principles of law have been applied to the facts as found or in which the sole issues have been of fact. They were not thought by their authors to reflect any unusual circum-

stances or to contribute to the development of the law, save in some cases
to reinforce accepted lines of authority.

(b) Numbered decisions are those to which the Commissioner concerned has had a number allocated . . .

This ensures a limited distribution of the decision as being of interest
. . .

(c) Reported decisions are those selected for reporting. They are so
selected by the Chief Commissioner from numbered decisions and are
primarily so selected if he is satisfied that they deal with questions of legal
principle and that they command the assent of at least a majority of the
Commissioners . . .

In addition to single Commissioner's decisions, decisions may be given
by a Tribunal of three Commissioners nominated in accordance with what
is now section 116 of the Social Security Act 1975 to decide a question of
law of special difficulty. Such decisions are almost invariably reported.

Commissioners speak with equal authority. All their decisions whether
unnumbered, numbered or reported may be cited to Commissioners,
local tribunals and insurance officers. Where they decide questions of
legal principle they must be followed by insurance officers and local
tribunals in cases involving the application of that principle, unless they
can be distinguished . . .

If confronted with decisions which conflict, insurance officers and local
tribunals must prefer the decision of a Tribunal of Commissioners
(whether a unanimous or majority decision) to that of a single Commissioner. A reported decision, for the reasons given in paragraph 17(c),
should *prima facie* be given more weight than an unreported decision.
Subject to the foregoing insurance officers and local tribunals must
choose between conflicting decisions and there is no obligation on them
to prefer the earlier to the later or *vice versa*.

In so far as the Commissioners are concerned, on questions of legal
principle, a single Commissioner follows a decision of a Tribunal of
Commissioners unless there are compelling reasons why he should not,
as, for instance, a decision of superior Courts affecting the legal principles
involved. A single Commissioner in the interests of comity and to secure
certainty and avoid confusion on questions of legal principle normally
follows the decisions of other single Commissioners . . . It is recognised
however that a slavish adherence to this could lead to the perpetuation of
error and he is not bound to do so.

The insurance officer, local tribunals and Commissioners on questions
of legal principle are all bound to follow the decisions of the High Court
and Superior Courts."

[This decision was itself a decision of a Tribunal of three
Commissioners. The procedure indicated in this decision was
revised by a Practice Direction of the Chief Social Security
Commissioner of 28 October 1982. Commissioners now star deci-
sions which they consider may merit reporting and the Chief
Commissioner selects the decisions to be reported from these

starred decisions, after consulting the Commissioners and hearing any representations from those associated with particular cases.]

R (U) 8/80
(Commissioner) I.O. GRIFFITHS

"In Decision R(1) 12/75 a Tribunal of Commissioners held in relation to the Law of England that a Commissioner on questions of legal principle is bound to follow decisions of the High Court and Superior Courts, meaning the Court of Appeal and the House of Lords. So far as I can discover there is no decision as to binding (as opposed to persuasive) effect of Scottish decisions upon the question of legal principle. In cases such as this where the same legislation applies to both England and Scotland it is clearly desirable that the laws of both England and Scotland should be uniform. So far as the High Court is concerned there is a well settled practice in revenue and taxation matters where the same statutes apply that courts of first instance keep in line with the courts of Scotland. An English court follows a unanimous judgment of a higher Scottish court where the question involved is one which turns upon the construction of a statute which extends to Scotland, leaving it to be reviewed if thought fit by the Appeal Court see *Re Hartland*; *Banks* v. *Hartland* [1911] 1 Ch. 459 at page 466. The reason for this is the need to avoid interpretations which result in one meaning in one country and another in the other; *Commissioners for General Purposes of Income Tax for City of London* v. *Gibbs* [1942] A.C. 402 at 414. The position of a National Insurance Commissioner is different from that of a High Court Judge. All Commissioners are Commissioners for Great Britain. Commissioners who sit in Scotland are sometimes wrongly referred to as Scottish Commissioners. They are not—they are Commissioners sitting in Scotland. Moreover, the cases dealt with by Commissioners have no territorial connection. Cases occurring in Scotland are sometimes decided in London. Cases from the north of England are sometimes dealt with in Scotland particularly when oral hearings are concerned when it is easier for a claimant and his witnesses to travel to Edinburgh. It is quite obviously highly desirable that the same interpretation be applied on each side of the border.

In my judgment, I would apply to this case the same practice as is applied in the courts of first instance in the High Court in revenue and taxation cases, that is to say, I would follow the decision of a higher Scottish Court on a question of construction of the Social Security Act 1975."

IV. ADVICE, REPRESENTATION AND LEGAL AID IN TRIBUNALS

A. ADVICE AND REPRESENTATION

The importance of claimants and appellants seeking advice at an early stage is as great in areas of law which are largely subject to tribunal adjudication as it is to those primarily subject to judicial determination. The 1989 Genn report to the Lord Chancellor (which considered SSATs, industrial tribunals, immigration adjudicators and mental health review tribunals in England and Wales) emphasises the importance of such advice not only for individuals directly concerned but also for the working of the tribunals.

H. Genn and Y. Genn, *The Effectiveness of Representation at Tribunals*, p. 157

"The evidence presented in this chapter has established that the availability of advice about social security claims and immigration requests at an early stage, can improve the quality of claimants' applications to Departments. This may avoid adverse decisions which are incorreect, and thus reduce the number of occasions on which the appeals process is mobilised to perform an expensive, information-gathering function.

Advice following an adverse departmental decision or employment problem can filter out of the tribunal process unmeritorious cases, and contribute to the acceptability of that outcome by providing a comprehensive explanation of the legal basis for the Department's decision or employer's action.

Representatives can also reduce the number of tribunal hearings by conducting direct negotiations with Departments and employers in order to achieve the satisfactory resolution of claims before a tribunal hearing takes place.

Case preparation and the provision of evidence is fundamental to the outcome of hearings. Unrepresented appellants and applicants have difficulty in identifying the facts which are relevant to their case. They therefore have difficulty in producing the evidence necessary to prove the case. In these situations, it becomes the responsibility of the tribunal to elicit relevant information from those who appear at tribunal hearings, and even when this can be accomplished to the satisfaction of the tribunal, the necessary evidence may not be immediately available. This may lead to adjournments or decisions taken on inadequate evidence.

In all tribunals the average delay between the lodging of an appeal or application and the tribunal hearing was greatest in those cases that were ultimately successful. Advice and representation tends to increase the average delay in all tribunals, although in immigration hearings and industrial tribunal cases it can reduce average delay. The effect of representation on delay was greatest where solicitors represented social security appeals."

A consistent feature of some tribunals is how few of those appearing before them are represented. Previous research in Scotland has revealed such a pattern. In a 1974 survey of Edinburgh and East Fife, 41% were represented before NILTs and 30% before SBATs: M. Adler & A.W. Bradley, *Justice, Discretion and Poverty* (Professional Books Ltd.: 1976), pp. 109–127. A 1983 study of 80 appellants throughout Scotland revealed even lower percentages of representation before NILTs and SBATs: D. Kay, *Tackling Tribunals* (Scottish Consumer Council: 1984).

A low percentage of representation was also a finding of the 1989 Genn Report, which was based on a broader survey of tribunals in England and Wales. That report confirmed earlier findings, both in Scotland and elsewhere in the U.K., on the significance of representation on the outcome of tribunal adjudication, and again demonstrated that lawyers were not necessarily more successful than some other categories of representative when appearing before tribunals.

H. Genn and Y. Genn, *The Effectiveness of Representation at Tribunals,* pp. 77–78, 86–87, 99 and selected tables

Social Security Appeal Tribunals

Outcome of Social Security Appeal Tribunal Hearings by Presence of Appellant or Representative

	% Dismissed	% Allowed	% Total	% of Sample
Appellant not present	88	12	100	44
Appellant present alone	58	42	100	29
Appellant present with friend	53	47	100	7
Appellant present with representative	47	53	100	11
Total Weighted Cases = 1115				

Significant P<.00000

Social Security Appeals Tribunals Outcome of Hearing by Type of Representative

	% Dismissed	% Allowed	% Total	% of Sample
Welfare rights centre	33	67	100%	1
Law centre	34	66	100	*
Solicitor	44	56	100	1
Trade Union	46	54	100	1
CAB	48	52	100	4
Soc.Serv/Probation	49	51	100	1
Tribunal unit	53	47	100	1
Appellant unrepresented	56	44	100	37
Family/Friends	59	41	100	4
Other advice centre	65	35	100	2
Appellant absent	86	14	100	47
				100%
Total Weighted Cases = 1115 heard cases				

Significant P<.00001

Summary of Main Findings on Outcome of Hearings at Social Security Appeals Tribunals

1. Elderly appellants were less likely to succeed with appeals. Single parents were more likely to succeed with appeals.
2. Overpayment cases and disqualification from unemployment benefit cases were the most likely to succeed. Disqualification from supplementary benefit cases were the least likely to succeed.
3. Appeals decided in the absence of the appellant were the least likely to succeed.
4. Unrepresented appellants who attended their hearings were more likely to succeed if they had received some advice about their appeal.
5. All types of representation increased the likelihood of success. The overall success rate in social security appeals was 30%. Where the appellant was not present it was 12%. Where the appellant was present but unrepresented the success rate was 42%. Where the appellant was represented by someone other than a friend or relative it was 53%. Specialist advice and representation units had the most significant effect on success rates.
6. The presence of witnesses for the appellant increased the likelihood of success.
7. There were regional differences in success rates and large differences in success rates within regions between central urban hearing centres and outlying hearing centres.
8. There were significant differences in the rates at which appellants succeeded before different chairmen. Those chairmen who had the lowest success rates tended to sit at hearing centres with low representation rates.
9. A multiple regression analysis indicated that the identity of the chairman could reduce the chance of winning from 30% to 5%. It could also increase it to a maximum of 55%.
10. The multiple regression analysis indicated that holding constant factors such as characteristics of appellant, type of case, geographical location, type of chairman, etc., represented appellants are more likely to succeed with their appeals than unrepresented appellants. Specialist representation increases the probability that appellants will succeed with their appeal from about 30% to 48%.
11. The multiple regression analysis indicated that the main determinant of representation is advice, which is itself related to geographical location, and type of case. Those who live in urban areas are more likely, irrespective of case type and other factors, to obtain advice and representation at their hearing.

Hearings Before Immigration Adjudicators

Representation and Outcome of Hearings

Type of Representation	% Allowed or in Part	% of Representative Type in Sample
No representative	16%	8
UKIAS	31	49
Barrister	32	18
Solicitor	37	12
Specialist advice centre	40	2
Other advice centre	26	1
Law centre	24	4
JCWI	41	2
Relative/Friend	9	2
		100
Total % Allowed All Cases	30	

Total Weighted Heard Cases = 728 (Based on 770 unweighted cases)

SUMMARY OF MAIN FINDINGS ON OUTCOME OF HEARINGS BEFORE
IMMIGRATION ADJUDICATORS

1. Overall 22% of cases were allowed or allowed in part. Of those that went to a full hearing 30% were allowed or allowed in part. Where cases were decided on the papers 2% were allowed. There was regional variation in the rates at which appeals resulted in a full hearing. Leeds had the lowest rate of full appeals. This is related to the low advice rate identified in Chapter 2.

2. There were regional variations in success rate. Harmondsworth had the lowest success rate. Leeds the highest. There are, however, regional differences in type of appeal which might account for this.

3. Personal characteristics of appellants appeared to have little effect on success, although younger appellants were more likely to succeed and those with a previous immigration history were less likely to succeed with their appeals.

4. Political asylum, deportation cases, and visitors' extension cases were the least likely cases to succeed.

5. Unrepresented appellants were less likely to succeed with their appeals than represented appellants. All representatives, except friends and relatives, increased the likelihood of success.

6. A multiple regression analysis indicated that, holding other factors constant, the likelihood of success varied before certain adjudicators. The identity of the adjudicator could reduce the probability of success to 5% or increase it to 50% after controlling for other factors.

7. The multiple-regression analysis indicated that, holding all other factors constant, UKIAS has the highest rate of success among representatives, followed by solicitors and then other representatives. Over the sample as a whole, representation by counsel did not increase the likelihood of success more than representation by a solicitor or UKIAS. Representation by UKIAS would increase the probability of success from say 20% to approximately 38% after controlling for other factors.

Industrial Tribunals

Outcome of Industrial Tribunals in Relation to Applicants' Representation

	% Dismissed/ withdrawn	% Allowed	% Settled	% Total	% in Sample
Not represented	62	33	5	100	36
Solicitor	49	38	13	100	16
Barrister	47	30	22	100	12
Law centre	51	39	10	100	5
Trade Union	56	38	6	100	16
CAB/Other agency	67	27	5	100	7
Friend/Relative	67	29	4	100	

Total Weighted Heard Cases = 339 (Based on 550 cases)

SUMMARY OF MAIN FINDINGS RELATING TO OUTCOME OF INDUSTRIAL TRIBUNAL HEARINGS

1. Almost half of the applications to industrial tribunals were settled before a hearing. Applications were more likely to be settled where the applicant had obtained advice about his application.
2. The average amount of compensation received by applicants was, in general, higher if it was an award or settlement agreed after a hearing had commenced, than if it was agreed before a hearing.
3. Of the cases that resulted in a tribunal hearing, the applicants succeeded in 34% of cases. In 9% of cases a settlement was agreed after the hearing had commenced and a further 2% of applicants withdrew their applications after the hearing had commenced.
4. There was evidence that, as in social security appeals and immigration hearings, the identity of the tribunal chairman had an independent effect on the outcome of appeals.
5. The presence of witnesses for the applicant increased the likelihood that the applicant would succeed.
6. As far as representation is concerned, applicants can only improve their chances of success through representation when the respondent is not represented. Where the applicant is legally represented and the respondent is not represented the probability of the applicant succeeding is increased from 30% to 48%. Where the applicant has no representation and the respondent is legally represented the applicant's probability of success is reduced to 10%. Where the applicant is represented by a non-lawyer, and the respondent is represented by a lawyer the probability of the applicant succeeding is 18%. . . . "

B. LEGAL AID

The legal advice and assistance scheme extends to tribunal proceedings and there is also provision for making assistance by way of representation (Legal Aid (Scotland) Act 1986, Pt. II). (See Chapter 11.)

With the exceptions of the Lands Tribunal for Scotland and the Employment Appeal Tribunal, legal aid is not available in proceedings before tribunals in Scotland (*ibid.*, Sched. 1, para. 1; S.I. 1987 No. 381). However, it would be available in further court proceedings on a tribunal decision, and it is also available in certain court proceedings arising out of children's hearings (see further, C.N. Stoddart, *The Law and Practice of Legal Aid in Scotland* (3rd ed.) (W. Green & Son: 1990); (1989) 156 SCOLAG 142).

There are persuasive arguments, outlined in the extracts below, for a greater extension of the legal aid scheme to tribunals. An additional argument is that in rural areas, where there is limited access to advice and representation, solicitors may be the only available source of it. However, the financial implications of extending the legal aid scheme to tribunals would be considerable. There are those who view with caution such a development but would favour the financial encouragement of the provision of advice and representation by others.

Justice-All Souls Review, paras. 68–70

"The Lord Chancellor's Advisory Committee on Legal Aid considered the question of legal aid for tribunals in its Annual Report published in 1974 (HC20(1974–75)) and concluded that it was essential for applicants (a term it used to include appellants, claimants and, where appropriate, respondents) to have (i) access to competent advice as to their rights, the advisability of appealing and the consequences of doing so; (ii) frequently, assistance in gathering information and preparing the case; and (iii), in a limited number of cases, representation at the hearing (para. 31). 'There is a wide spectrum of need on the part of tribunal applicants, ranging from moral support and encouragement at one extreme to experienced legal advocacy on difficult issues of law at the other' (para. 33). The Committee found that there were many types of case that were too complex for the applicant to handle in which welfare organisations and trade unions had developed skills and expertise. It rejected the suggestion made to it that there should be a specialised body, decentralised in its administration throughout the country, for providing non-legal representation wherever that was needed, and preferred a system of financial support to those existing agencies that were providing non-legal help as part of their general service of advice and assistance (para. 34). The Committee did not consider that a tribunal could itself provide a satisfactory substitute for effective representation, especially where the other side was represented (para. 37).

The Committee recognised that the extension of legal aid to all tribunals did involve some risk of formalisation of the proceedings. It concluded that the issue to be considered was whether the advantages of informality outweighed those of representation: 'if they do, the right course, we suggest, will be to ban legal representation altogether; what cannot be justifiable is to restrict its benefits to those wealthy enough to afford it for themselves' (para. 38). The Committee also recognised that an extension of legal aid carried with it the danger of lengthening proceedings.

Having considered all the evidence it had received in response to a Working Paper it had published on the subject, the Committee, in 1974, concluded that legal aid should be extended to all statutory tribunals then within the supervision of the Council on Tribunals in which representation was permitted. However, since 1974 the Committee have modified their views somewhat in the face of limited resources."

Hughes Commission, pp. 72–73, 91–93

"We recommend in Chapter 8 an extension of legal aid to enable claimants to be represented before tribunals by a solicitor—but only in limited circumstances. We believe that the best way to meet the needs of claimants before many tribunals is to encourage the development of lay representation at tribunals. Although a number of organisations such as Citizens Advice Bureaux, trade unions and claimants rights groups do excellent work in representing tribunal claimants, there is considerable variation in the help and advice available to claimants appearing before tribunals. The availability of representation also varies with the subject matter of the particular tribunal. Most claimants making an application to a tribunal both lodge the application and appear before the tribunal without the benefit of any informed and independent advice. This is unsatisfactory.

We know that a number of projects to try to build up lay representation before tribunals have been encouraged in England. From our observations such projects have helped both to extend the amount of representation and advice before tribunals, and also to improve the quality of such representation and advice. There have, however, only been a few projects of this nature. Some projects have concentrated on the training of lay representatives while others have built up teams who could provide representation before particular tribunals. Yet another scheme was aimed at providing a 'duty representative' at National Insurance Tribunals, who could advise all claimants and appear on their behalf if necessary. The source of funding of the different projects varies and is often only guaranteed for a short period. The future of the existing tribunal representation units, given the present funding basis, appears to be very insecure. While the inquisitorial approach of a tribunal may mean that the quality of presentation of a claimant's case is less critical to the outcome of his case, there is considerable scope for developing the system of lay representation before tribunals, and we are strongly of the opinion that finance should be made available for this purpose. While we recognise that there are a variety of kinds of tribunal, we **recommend** that encouragement should be given to developing the provision of lay advice and representation before those tribunals in which lay participation is appropriate, and that adequate training should be provided for lay representatives . . .

Those who appear before tribunals do so to assert or protect rights and should, therefore, qualify for legal aid in terms of the principle we have enunciated. In support of this view, it can also be argued that where legal representation is allowed and one side can afford to use it, it is wrong to refuse legal aid to the other party. However, there is a difference between most tribunals and courts. Our courts traditionally rely on the adversarial procedure which generally demands a degree of skill and knowledge of the law on the part of the pleader. Tribunals of the kind we have in mind, such as the Industrial Tribunal, are accustomed to proceed by a more inquisitorial approach, which makes the quality of presentation less crucial to the outcome. We think that this form of procedure is well suited for tribunals of this type and should be encouraged. We had this in mind in recommending in Chapter 7 that lay representation at such tribunals should be developed by generalist advice agencies. We certainly would not prohibit the employment of lawyers for this purpose. No doubt there are cases where difficult questions of law arise in which the assistance of lawyers appearing for the parties is valuable to the tribunal in question, but we think that the use of lawyers ought not to be encouraged in the general run of these cases since they tend to introduce adversarial formality to which the proceedings are not well suited.

The Scottish Committee of the Council on Tribunals recommended to us that legal aid should only be available at tribunals in the absence of suitable lay representation. We endorse that approach, though we consider that a solicitor should be entitled to claim from the legal aid fund for undertaking representation if the tribunal certify that a substantial point of law was at issue. So that it might be widely known whether there is 'suitable lay representation' locally available, each tribunal should publish a list of agencies providing what is, in the view of the particular tribunal, suitable representation. However, though it is important to provide representation where needed, tribunal proceedings are intended to enable citizens to appear without a legal representative to conduct their case; and we do not wish to encourage representation where the person himself could, after receiving advice as to what was involved, adequately present his own case. Legal aid should, therefore, be made available for representation at tribunals only if the client would otherwise be unable to follow the proceedings, and then only where there is no lay representation locally available which is recognised by the tribunal as suitable.

Tribunal hearings can involve substantial points of law. In addition, therefore, where the chairman of the tribunal, on an application made before the hearing, considers that a substantial point of law is likely to arise it should be competent for the tribunal to grant legal aid. If a substantial point of law arises during the course of a hearing, the tribunal should be able to authorise legal aid and to adjourn the hearing to allow legal representation to be obtained. In many such cases, the individual may already be represented by a full-time trade union official or by a lay representative, and although persons with such alternative means of representation should not be granted legal aid in straightforward cases, in cases where a substantial question of law is likely to arise they should be treated as regards legal aid in the same way as others using the tribunal system. We do not expect that such cases will arise frequently, and experienced chairmen and clerks of tribunals will readily recognise the cases where substantial questions of law are likely to arise. In practice, this extension of legal aid to tribunals will best be made tribunal by tribunal. The Legal Aid Act 1979 makes provision for legal aid to be extended to tribunals by regulation. It is clear that such regulations will need to be preceded by an examination of tribunals individually to see which require (or allow) legal representation and before which the exclusion of legal aid might cause inequity. An examination should be undertaken to identify those tribunals at which a substantial point of law is most likely to arise. All such tribunals should include a legally qualified member.

To sum up as regards tribunals, we **recommend** that legal aid should be available for representation at a tribunal, but only if the client would otherwise be unable to follow the proceedings and if there is no lay representation available locally which is recognised by the tribunal as suitable. We **recommend** in addition that a tribunal should have power to grant legal aid where it considers that the matter before it gives rise, or is likely to give rise, to a substantial point of law."

V. A TRIBUNAL IN PRACTICE: THE CHILDREN'S HEARING

The reporter and the children's hearing are the most significant elements in the Scottish system of juvenile justice.

Reporters, of whom there are over 90, are employed by each of the regional and islands authorities. They have a substantial degree of independence once appointed, in that they cannot be removed from office nor be required to resign without the consent of the Secretary of State. The Secretary of State is empowered to prescribe their qualifications, but has not, as yet, done so. The reporters come from a variety of professional backgrounds; some are qualified in social work and some in law.

As indicated above each children's hearing is constituted from panels appointed by the Secretary of State in each regional and islands authority. For each children's hearing, three members of the panel sit, a chairman and two others. There must be both a man and a woman among the members sitting at each hearing.

Anyone may inform a reporter that he has reasonable cause to believe that, on one of a number of statutory grounds, a child "may be in need of compulsory measures of care." In practice, the vast majority of information received by reporters is from the police. Having received information, the reporter has a wide statutory discretion. He may refer the case to a children's hearing.

Before the hearing, the reporter arranges for social background reports and other appropriate reports, such as school and psychiatric reports, on the child.

Normally, the child, his parents, the reporter and a representative of the social work department attend the hearing. The child and his parents may also be represented. If the grounds of the referral are not accepted by the child or his parents, the children's hearing is required to instruct the reporter to make an application to the sheriff for a finding on whether the grounds are established, unless it is intended to discharge the case. Once the grounds are agreed or established, the children's hearing after considering the case may make a supervision requirement, which may include the child living in a residential establishment. An important element of the hearing process is that where a child is placed under a supervision requirement the case is kept under review.

Although a children's hearing is very informal in many respects, it has powers which may affect the right of children and their parents and is, therefore, subject to a range of procedural rules. The child or his parents may appeal against a decision of a children's hearing to the sheriff and a further appeal lies to the Court of Session on a point of law or procedural irregularity. In 1990, 27,427 cases were considered by children's hearings.

Martin et al., *Children out of Court*, pp. 102–107, 256

"FREQUENCY OF COMPLIANCE WITH CERTAIN PROCEDURAL REQUIREMENTS

	Per cent. of hearings
Formal rules	
Child identified by name and age	94
Purpose of hearing explained	63
Social background report referred to	35
School report referred to	60
Reasons for decision stated	58
Right to receive written reasons indicated	44
Right to appeal indicated	74
'Good practices'	
Right to legal aid indicated	6
Child asked if agrees/understands decision	37
Parent asked if agrees/understands decision	31
(N = 100%)	301

In 94 per cent of all cases, the child was identified by name and age (Act, s. 55) . . .

Surprisingly however there was a failure to explain the purpose of the hearing in slightly more than one-third of all the cases observed (Rules 17(1) and 19(2)). 'Failure' in the sense does not mean that an attempt to explain the purpose was judged to have been unsuccessful, but that no attempt was made. An explanation of the purpose of the hearing was given marginally less frequently when the case had been continued for reports (43 per cent) and when the child had been referred to a hearing on some previous occasion (41 per cent); but fully one-third of the children who were appearing before a hearing for the first time in their lives were offered no explanation of the hearing's purpose. Explanations were more often overlooked in truancy referrals and least often when the ground of referral was a fairly serious offence, but variations of this kind were not very striking . . .

The grounds of referral were put to the child and parent in exactly one-quarter of the hearings observed (Act, s. 42). What appears to be a quite serious level of omission is however attributable to the inclusion in the sample of 58 hearings that had been continued from a previous occasion, for reports or for some other reason, and 42 hearings that had previously been adjourned to go for proof. The grounds of referral were put in only a small minority of these cases (19 per cent and 29 per cent respectively of the two groups), but in those instances where the child was making his first appearance there was no failure to put the grounds of referral . . .

The chairman of the hearing is expected to disclose the essential features of any reports that have been made available to the panel members present unless he has reason to believe that disclosure would be detrimental to the interests of the child (Rules 17(3) and 19(4)). On the face of it, this obligation is overlooked fairly frequently. Social background reports were available in all but three of the hearings studied, and school reports in all but 34, yet there was no explicit reference to the former in two-thirds of all hearings and no explicit mention of the latter in two hearings in every five. No report was ever shown to the family, and a formal summary of the contents of a school report was given at only one hearing. A partial account of the contents of the social background report was given to the family at slightly more than 5 per cent of hearings, while an extract from the school report was conveyed about three times as frequently. Most of the references that were made to reports were in the nature of allusions: 'I can see the social worker says you're more settled at home'. The social background report was referred to in the same way at three hearings in every ten, and the school report at four in every ten hearings. Social background reports were mentioned more frequently in initial than in continued or adjourned hearings, more often in cases where the child had never previously appeared before a hearing, but in no category did the frequency of mention exceed 40 per cent. A similar pattern is found in the frequency with which school reports were mentioned, the proportion reaching as high as 70 per cent in the case of initial appearances . . .

When a hearing reaches a decision, the chairman has a duty to announce the nature of the decision, to give the family orally reasons for that decision, and to advise the family that they have a right to receive a written statement of reasons (Rule 17(4)). The obligation to formulate reasons at the conclusion of the hearing was overlooked in 42 per cent of the cases observed . . . Parents were notified of their right to receive a written statement of reasons at slightly less than one-half of all hearings . . . ; the more serious types of offence referral tended more often to elicit an indication that written reasons would be provided.

Appeals against the decisions of children's hearings are rare—perhaps twenty are raised every year—but it is essential for all families to be notified of their right to appeal. There was however a failure to adhere to this requirement at one hearing in every four . . . Even if a more lenient view is taken of this procedural failure when discharge was the outcome of the hearing, it is impossible to respond with any complacency to the neglect of Rule 17(4) in cases where a supervision order was imposed. Fortunately, these omissions occurred in only about one-seventh of such hearings, but anything that falls short of 100 per cent compliance must be taken extremely seriously.

ASPECTS OF AN IDEAL HEARING

	PERCENTAGE SELECTING GIVEN ATTRIBUTE	
	Panel members %	Social workers %
The full participation of the child and parents in the discussion.	85	94
The parents' and the child's understanding of *all* that takes place at hearings.	86	89
The hearing's impact on the child and parents as a serious event.	43	40
An atmosphere of communality and equality between family and other hearing members.	38	30
The difference between the hearing and the court.	19	22
The hearing as a body of authority with powers over the family.	13	9
The observance of all procedural requirements.	6	4
Conveying legal and technical information to the family	4	9
(N = 100%)		"

[This study was based on a representative sample of 3% of children's hearings in 1978–9 throughout Scotland (excluding Orkney, Shetland and the Western Isles). Questionnaires were sent to all children's panel members and to 300 Scottish local authority social workers. The extract refers to the Social Work (Scotland) Act 1968 and the Children's Hearings (Scotland) Rules, S.I. 1971 No. 492, but see now the Children's Hearings (Scotland) Rules 1986 (S.I. 1986 No. 2291). See also *Sloan* v. *B.*, 1991 S.L.T. 530 (and J.M. Thomson, 1991 S.L.T.(News) 421); *C.* v. *Kennedy*, 1991 S.L.T. 755.]

Would the broad social function of the children's hearings be inhibited by greater compliance with the procedural rules governing them?

VI. CONTROL OF TRIBUNALS

As tribunals determine the legal rights of the citizen it is important that they apply the law correctly and act with procedural propriety. In the case of some tribunals this may be ensured by appellate tribunals or by an appeal system which provides for the reference of a question of law to the ordinary courts. In addition to this, the ordinary courts may in certain circumstances exercise a more general supervision over tribunals, and the Council on Tribunals keeps under review the constitution and working of tribunals under its jurisdiction.

A. THE COURTS

The ordinary courts may review the decision of tribunals which have acted outside their jurisdiction and may quash decisions arrived at in breach of natural justice. Even following *West* v. *Secretary of State for Scotland*, 1992 S.L.T. 636, there is, however, doubt whether Scottish courts have a general power to review the decision of a tribunal which is within its jurisdiction but wrong in law. These matters raise questions of law which are somewhat outside the scope of this book [see further, *Remedies in Administrative Law* (Scottish Law Commission Memorandum No. 14, 1971); Court of Session Rules, Rule 260B (application for judicial review); W.J. Wolffe, "The Scope of Judicial Review in Scots Law" [1992] P.L. 625] but some of the issues are explored in the following extracts.

Watt v. Lord Advocate
1979 S.C. 120

LORD PRESIDENT (EMSLIE): "This case is not one in which the commissioner misconstrued certain statutory provisions in the course of attempting to answer the right question remitted for his decision. He misconstrued that very question itself and answered a different question as the result of his error. For these reasons I am persuaded that the pursuer is well founded in his contention that the decision of the commissioner was ultra vires . . . I feel bound to say that if, as I have held, the commissioner's decision proceeded upon an error of law, and if that error did not render his decision a nullity, I have the gravest doubt whether this court would have had power to review it . . . It seems clear that, however much of this is to be regretted, the Court of Session has never had power to correct an intra vires error of law made by a statutory tribunal or authority exercising statutory jurisdiction. As Lord Justice-Clerk Moncreiff said in *Lord Advocate* v. *Police Commissioners of Perth*, at p. 245: 'In the ordinary case it would now, I think, be held that where statutory powers are given, and a statutory jurisdiction is set up, all other jurisdictions are excluded . . . '. There is no indication in any subsequent authority that this view has been doubted or even questioned . . .

I cannot leave this case without expressing my regret that whereas it appears that the High Court in England still has, in spite of the provisions of s. 75(1) of the National Insurance Act 1965, jurisdiction in procedure by way of the prerogative writ of certiorari to correct errors of law by National Insurance Commissioners which appear on the face of the record, the Court of Session has no such power. It can hardly be suggested that it is in the best interests of statutory tribunals themselves that recourse to the appellate courts of the United Kingdom to determine difficult questions of law authoritatively should not be available in both of the great jurisdictions."

Reed, "Judicial Review of Errors of Law", pp. 241–244
"A distinction has traditionally been drawn between errors of law which go to jurisdiction and those which do not. In England, the latter have been reviewable only by way of certiorari and only if the error appears on the face of the record. In Scotland, errors of law within jurisdiction have not been reviewable at all, but it may be that the line between jurisdictional and non-jurisdictional errors would be so drawn as to permit review of decisions reviewable in England. In both jurisdictions it has become increasingly difficult to draw the line with much confidence, especially since the decision in *Anisminic* v. *Foreign Compensation Commission* [1969] 2 A.C. 147; . . .

The traditional distinction was well expressed by Lord Reid: 'If a magistrate or any other tribunal has jurisdiction to enter on the inquiry and to decide a particular issue, and there is no irregularity in the procedure, he does not destroy his jurisdiction by reaching a wrong decision. If he has jurisdiction to go right, he has jurisdiction to go wrong. Neither an error in fact nor an error in law will destroy his jurisdiction' (*R.* v. *Brixton Prison Governor, ex parte Armah* [1968] A.C. 192). However, as Lord Reid himself observed in *Anisminic*, this is true only if 'jurisdiction' is used in the narrow sense of the tribunal being entitled to enter on the inquiry in question. But 'jurisdiction' may also bear the wider sense of vires, as explained by Lord Pearce in *Anisminic*: 'Lack of jurisdiction may arise in various ways. There may be an absence of those formalities or things which are conditions precedent to the tribunal having any jurisdiction to embark on an inquiry. Or the tribunal may at the end make an order that it has no jurisdiction to make. Or in the intervening stage, while engaged on a proper inquiry, the tribunal may depart from the rules of natural justice; or it may ask itself the wrong questions; or it may take into account matters which it was not directed to take into account.'

The tribunal's jurisdiction is settled by the statute; so if it steps outside the statute at any stage in any of the ways listed by Lord Pearce, it exceeds its jurisdiction and its purported decision is a nullity. Lord Diplock has said extra-judicially that *Anisminic* 'renders obsolete the technical distinction between errors of law which go to "jurisdiction" and errors of law which do not' (33 C.L.J. 233, 243). However, all the judges in the House of Lords reaffirmed the traditional distinction. The clearest guidance was given by Lord Wilberforce: 'The extent of the interpretatory power conferred upon the tribunal may sometimes be difficult to ascertain . . . Sometimes it will be possible to form a conclusion from the form and subject-matter of the legislation. In one case it may be seen that the legislature, while stating general objectives, is prepared to concede a wide area to the authority it establishes: this will often be the case where the decision involves a degree of policy-making rather than fact-finding, especially if the authority is a department of government or the Minister at its head. I think that we have reached a stage in our administrative law when we can view this question quite objectively, without any necessary predisposition towards one that questions of law, or questions of construction, are necessarily for the courts.'

Thus the extent to which the courts will review errors of law—or, to put it another way, will substitute their interpretation of the statute for that of the tribunal—will vary according to the nature of the tribunal. Some are more or less judicial: the tribunal in *Anisminic*, for example, was charged with determining entitlement to compensation for sequestrated property, its decision turning on the interpretation of legal terms such as "successor in title" and "British national". Other tribunals may be set up to determine a great number of small claims requiring expertise and speed, or claims involving political or economic judgment rather than the application of fixed rules to facts discovered through the hearing of evidence.

Thus, although the English courts can intervene to correct even non-jurisdictional errors on the face of the record, this power has been sparingly exercised in respect of specialised tribunals such as those concerned with social security . . .

In Scots law the courts have no power to review a decision made intra vires, even if it involves an error of law. This is clearly established by the authorities (e.g. *Don Brothers, Buist & Co. Ltd.* v. *Scottish National Insurance Commissioners*, 1913 1 S.L.T. 221; *Smeaton* v. *Commissioners of Police of St Andrews* (1865) 3 M. 816), despite speculative arguments based on *Pryde* v. *Heritors and Kirk-Session of Ceres* (1843) 5 D. 552 (a decision whose ratio depends on the special nature of parochial boards, as explained by Lord Fullerton in *Edinburgh & Glasgow Railway Co.* v. *Meek* (1849) 12 D. 153).

Some examples of intervention may be given. In *Caledonian Railway Co.* v. *Glasgow Corporation* (1905) 7 F. 1020 the corporation was empowered to enter the width of streets on a register. Planning permission would not be granted without special consent where the building would reduce the width of the street. The corporation entered target widths greater than the actual widths. It was held to be doing something quite different from what the statute directed. In *Bennett* v. *Scottish Board of Health*, 1921 S.C. 772 the court was willing to determine whether a committee set up to hear complaints about "medical attendance and treatment" could hear a complaint about a doctor's abusive language during a visit: the committee's jurisdiction depended on the meaning of the statutory phrase. Finally, in *Hayman* v. *Lord Advocate*, 1952 S.L.T. 209 the approval of opticians depended (a) on their holding prescribed diplomas or being on an older approved list, and (b) on a finding by a committee that they had 'adequate, including recent experience'. Lord Cooper said that if the committee had investigated the pursuer's professional rectitude and the nature of his premises, instead of investigating whether he had recently utilised the prescribed qualifications so as to be a sufficiently experienced practitioner, then they had 'acted illegally by applying their minds to the wrong question and thus in effect acting *ultra fines compromissi*'. In these three cases the misinterpretation of the statutory language would have led the tribunal to do something quite different from what it was directed to do: to compile a quite different register from the one it was directed to compile, to hear a complaint it had no authority to hear, to make an inquiry into quite different matters from those it was supposed to investigate . . . [In the *Watt* case] Lord Emslie reaffirmed that the Court of Session had no power to correct an error of law within jurisdiction, and distinguished between cases in which the commissioner misconstrued statutory provisions in the course of answering the question remitted to him and cases where the question itself had been miscontrued so that a different question had been answered . . . any error of law, it appears, can be treated as jurisdictional by manipulating phraseology. In practice a distinction will be drawn; and one returns to Lord Wilberforce's dictum that it will be a functional distinction grounded in the nature of the tribunal's task."

Apart from the scope of judicial review, there are questions of the effect of judicial review on the tribunal system. Vigorous judicial assertion of the power to review may serve to undermine the tribunal system. So, *e.g.* the Court of Appeal in England, in *Chief Adjudication Officer* v. *Foster* [1991] 3 All E.R. 846, overruling previous decisions to the contrary, held that it was outside the jurisdiction of the Social Security Commissioners and of Social Security Appeal Tribunals to consider arguments that regulations were *ultra vires*. One consequence of the decision, although not in the instant case, may be that a claimant is obliged to raise some arguments by judicial review and others before a tribunal.

The relationship between the tribunal system and judicial review may also have more fundamental aspects. Despite the contemporary vigour of the remedy, judicial review is not well placed to provide the same degree of supervision over, often decentralised, administration as is a tribunal system. Certainly, as the following extract argues, it is undesirable to allow judicial review to compensate for a lack of a tribunal appellate structure (see also the address by the Rt. Hon. Lord Woolf on "Tribunals and the Courts" in the Annual Report of the Council on Tribunals 1991–92, App. E).

Annual Report of the Council on Tribunals 1991–92, paras. 2.2–2.5
"**2.2** In accordance with the recommendations of the Franks Report, we have always held the view that there should be a right of appeal on a point of law from tribunals to the courts. In some recent proposals for legislation we have noted a tendency to regard the machinery of judicial review as an adequate substitute. . . . In our view, judicial review is not apt for the purpose of providing a route of appeal from tribunal decisions. Still less does the existence of the machinery of judicial review relieve the policy maker from the need to consider the establishment of a new tribunal system or other form of appeal machinery to consider appeals against administrative decisions. . . .

2.3 Given the tendency to which we have referred, we think it right to emphasise here the distinction between a right of appeal and judicial review. The judicial review jurisdiction is fundamentally different from an appellate jurisdiction, not least in its discretionary element. An appeals procedure is a means by which a public body may be brought within the control of the courts when an issue of substantive law is at stake, whereas judicial review is a supervisory jurisdiction by which the courts may find the decision-making process of a variety of public bodies to be unlawful. Although it is true that an error of law may found both a successful appeal and a successful application for judicial review, the latter is not concerned with the question whether a decision was 'right' or 'wrong', it is concerned rather with the question whether something has gone so badly wrong with the decision-making process as to make it unlawful or an abuse of power.

2.4 In this connection, we draw attention to the comments of the House of Lords in *Regina* v. *Independent Television Commission, Ex parte TSW Broadcasting Ltd.* (*The Times*, 30th March 1992). Lord Templeman said in that case:
'Parliament may by statute confer powers and discretions and impose duties on a decision-maker who may be an individual, a body of persons or a corporation. Parliament may or may not provide machinery for an appeal against a decision. The appeal machinery may be concerned with fact or law or both. The appeal machinery may or may not involve the courts of law. For example, Parliament has provided that an appeal on fact or law shall lie from an Immigration Officer to an Immigration Tribunal. Parliament has

provided that an appeal on law only shall lie from the General or Special Commissioners of Income Tax to the High Court. Where Parliament has not provided for an appeal from a decision-maker the courts must not invent an appeal machinery. In the present case, Parliament has conferred powers and discretions and has imposed duties on the ITC. Parliament has not provided any appeal machinery. Even if the ITC makes mistakes of fact or of law, there is no appeal from their decision. The courts have invented the remedy of judicial review not to provide an appeal machinery but to ensure that the decision-maker does not exceed or abuse his powers'.

2.5 We trust that for the future departments will observe the distinction between a right of appeal and the discretionary remedy of judicial review, and not seek to rely on the existence of the latter in order to ignore the need for the former in appropriate cases."

B. THE COUNCIL ON TRIBUNALS

Following recommendations by the Franks Committee, a Council on Tribunals was established by the Tribunals and Inquiries Act 1958. The constitution of the Council and its powers are now embodied in the Tribunals and Inquiries Act 1992. Its principal powers with respect to tribunals are to keep under review the constitution and working of the tribunals listed in Schedule 1 to the Act, and to consider and report on matters referred to the Council by the Lord Chancellor and the Lord Advocate, concerning any tribunal other than an ordinary court of law, whether or not it is a scheduled tribunal (Tribunals and Inquiries Act 1992, s. 1). The Council also has powers to consider and report on the administrative procedures of statutory inquiries.

The Council has a statutory Scottish Committee which supervises certain specified tribunals in Scotland (*ibid.*, s. 2(2), Sched. 1, Pt. II). Before the Council reports on any of these tribunals, or on any matter referred to it by the Lord Advocate, it must consult the Scottish Committee (*ibid.*, s. 4). The Scottish Committee can also, in certain circumstances, report directly to the Lord Advocate, but it has not used this power. Some of the tribunals in Scotland, such as SSATs and the immigration adjudicators, are under the general supervision of the Council; others, such as industrial tribunals, rent tribunals and children's hearings, are under the particular supervision of the Scottish Committee. The Council makes an annual report to the Lord Chancellor and the Lord Advocate (*ibid.*, s. 4); these reports are laid before Parliament.

In addition to broader policy matters (see the extract above), much of the work of the Council on Tribunals involves (a) consultation with Government departments on primary legislation and on draft rules of procedure for tribunals and inquiries, and (b) monitoring the practice of tribunals within its supervisory jurisdiction.

The manner in which the Council is consulted on draft procedural rules for tribunals has, in the past, been a source of friction. In 1985, the Council indicated that it had received draft regulations from the DHSS only a week before the regulations were laid before Parliament and declared "such consultation verges on the farcical" (*Annual Report* 1984–85, H.C. 54, para. 2.4).

A code of practice on Government consultation with the Council was drawn up by the Council and circulated in 1982 by the Lord Chancellor and the Lord Advocate; revised codes of practice were circulated in 1986 and 1992 (for the text of the 1992 code, see *Annual Report of the Council on Tribunals* 1991–92, H.C. 316, Appendix I).

In the year ending July 31 1992, members of the Council and its Scottish Committee (and, in a few instances, their staff) paid 137 visits to 28 different types of tribunal. By means of such visits, the Council has the ability to provide long-term independent supervision of the work of a tribunal; so, for example, its annual reports reveal that every year since their inception, members of the Council or its Scottish Committee have visited a children's hearing. The extract below reflects other examples of the Scottish dimension of the supervisory role of the Council.

Not all the activities of the Council have a statutory basis. There is, for example, no statutory requirement for Government departments to consult the Council on primary legislation which may be within its terms of reference, and the Council has no specific statutory powers to investigate complaints concerning procedure at tribunals within its jurisdiction.

Annual Report of the Council on Tribunals 1991–92, paras. 2.43, 2.63
"**2.43** Last year we reported on the problems in Scotland arising from the lack of direct administrative support for immigration hearings, with cases handled by the Leeds office, no secretarial support and ad hoc accommodation for hearings. We hoped at that time that the problems would be quickly resolved since, following our representations, funding had been made available by the Lord Chancellor's Department to set up a new administration office in Glasgow. We can now report that the office is in operation with a Clerk and part-time assistant to deal with immigration cases in Scotland. While the improved administrative support should result in speedier and more efficient handling of cases, we are disappointed that the premises occupied by the staff are temporary and that what is

considered to be an unsuitable venue continues to be used for hearings in Glasgow. Securing acceptable premises is of particular importance since the Glasgow office became a centre for handling asylum cases in May of this year, covering the whole of Scotland. . . .

2.63 In Scotland, the Scottish Office Home and Health Department undertook a similar exercise to that carried out in England and Wales to consolidate and introduce a number of improvements to the National Health Service (Service Committees and Tribunal) (Scotland) Regulations 1974. The Scottish Committee welcomed the considerable improvements over the 1974 Regulations to the layout of the draft legislation and guidance literature. Following consideration of the drafts, the Department were notified of the Committee's continuing view that appellants should be able to have legal representation at hearings. The Committee recognised, however, that a reversal of policy on this issue was unlikely at this stage and asked for the Guidance Notes and Information Leaflets to include reference to the availability of legal advice and assistance for appellants requiring help in submitting a complaint. The Committee also asked for a specific provision to be included to give visiting members the right to observe the deliberations of Service Committees. The majority of the Scottish Committee's comments were adopted although, regrettably, the new Regulations continue to exclude legal representation for appellants. The Committee were concerned to note that the right for one of their members to sit in on deliberations had been omitted, even though such a right had been included in the similar Regulations governing Service Committees in England and Wales. The Department have apologised for what was an oversight and have undertaken to remedy the position pending a suitable opportunity to amend the regulations."

CHAPTER 6

THE EUROPEAN DIMENSION

European Community law and the European Convention on Human Rights create legal rights which are enforceable by Scottish litigants. These two distinct bodies of law each have a quite different status in Scotland. However, they have an important common feature. Their authoritative interpretation, and in some instances their enforcement, falls within the jurisdiction of bodies outside the United Kingdom. This is the European dimension of the Scottish legal system which is considered below.

I. EUROPEAN COMMUNITY LAW

A. INTRODUCTION

The United Kingdom became a member of the European Communities in 1973. There are, at present, 11 other Member States: France, Germany, Italy, Belgium, the Netherlands, Luxembourg, Denmark, Ireland, Greece, Spain and Portugal. The European Communities consist of three Communities, each established by a separate treaty, the European Coal and Steel Community (E.C.S.C.) which came into operation in 1952; the European Economic Community (E.E.C.) and the European Atomic Energy Community (EURATOM), both of which came into operation in 1958.

With its wide range of objectives, the E.E.C. is the most significant of these three. The E.E.C. Treaty provides for the creation of a common market and the harmonisation of economic policies within the Member States. This includes the elimination of customs duties and other barriers to trade between the Member States; the establishment of a common customs tariff; the establishment between Member States of the free movement of persons, goods, services and capital; the removal of various distortions of commercial competition; the creation of common policies in such matters as agriculture and transport, and such approximation of the domestic laws of Member States as is necessary to achieve the proper functioning of the Common Market.

The E.E.C. Treaty also seeks closer relations between Member States. This objective of a greater degree of integration and the institutional stresses of achieving the other objectives of the Treaty have led to significant contemporary attempts to achieve further institutional development: see the Single European Act 1986 (Cm

372) and the Treaty on European Union signed in Maastricht in 1992 ([1992] 1 C.M.L.R. 573) and Sir Leon Brittan, "Institutional Development of the European Community" [1992] P.L. 567.

Four principal institutions were established by the Community treaties. They serve all three Communities (see the Merger Treaty 1965, which entered into force in 1967), but their functions and powers differ somewhat with respect to each.

The *Commission* has a range of administrative functions. It formulates Community policies and, once they have been adopted, supervises their implementation. After extensive consultation, it initiates and drafts most Community legislative proposals and has a limited competence to enact legislation. It also has important duties, with corresponding powers, in monitoring compliance with Community law.

The Commission consists of 17 Commissioners, who are appointed by the governments of Member States for, at present, renewable four-year terms. Commissioners must be nationals of Member States, but no more than two may be nationals of the same state. Despite the method of appointment, Commissioners do not act as representatives of their states. They are required to carry out their functions independently and in the general interest of the Communities. Each Commissioner is given responsibility for specific areas of Community activity, but the Commission takes its decisions collectively.

The *Council of Ministers* is the principal political organ of the Communities; in many cases it acts by qualified majority. Supported by working parties of Commission officials and civil servants from the Member States, it makes the final decisions on Community policies and formally adopts most Community legislation of general application. Representatives of the governments of each Member State—normally government Ministers—sit on the Council; each Member State in turn takes the Presidency of the Council for a period of six months.

The *European Parliament* has 518 members who are directly elected from the Member States; it sits in Strasbourg in plenary session each month, except August, but a significant amount of its work is done in committees sitting in Brussels. When first established it was primarily an advisory body, but it has now acquired an increasingly significant role in the Community legislative and policy process (see E.E.C. Treaty, Art. 189; Single European Act, Art. 6). So, even at present more than 50% of its proposed amendments to Community legislation are adopted by the Council of Ministers.

The *Court of Justice* interprets, and ensures compliance with, Community law. Its composition, jurisdiction and procedure are considered below.

Other important Community institutions include the European Council, the Economic and Social Committee, which serves both the E.E.C. and EURATOM and has an advisory rôle in the Community legislative process, and the Court of Auditors, which was established in 1977 to examine the finances and financial management of the Community.

The principal sources of the law of the European Communities are (a) the treaties establishing the Communities and other related treaties, (b) legislation adopted by the Community institutions in the form of regulations, directives and decisions, (c) the case law of the Court of Justice. Community law has important characteristics. It prevails over inconsistent national law of the Member States (*e.g.* Case 6/64, *Costa* v. *ENEL* [1964] E.C.R. 585; *cf. Macarthys Ltd.* v. *Smith* [1979] 1 W.L.R. 1189), and much of it is directly effective, that is, it creates rights and duties which may be enforced in the courts and tribunals of Member States; and, even where it is not directly effective, an individual who is adversely affected by the failure of a Member State to implement Community legislation may be entitled to claim compensation from that state (Cases C–6 & 9/90 *Francovich and Bonifaci* v. *Italian State* [1992] I.R.L.R.84); see further J. Steiner, "From direct effect to *Francovich*: Shifting means of enforcement of Community law" (1993) 18 Eur.L.Rev. 3).

The status of European Community law in Scotland was established by the European Communities Act, which was passed by the U.K. Parliament in 1972. By virtue of that legislation, directly effective Community law was recognised as law in the United Kingdom and became enforceable before U.K. courts and tribunals (s. 2; for some of the difficulties which may arise from the provision see *Garden Cottage Foods Ltd.* v. *Milk Marketing Board* [1984] A.C. 130). The Act also recognised the jurisdiction of the Court of Justice of the Communities to interpret and enforce Community law, and its decisions became binding on U.K. courts and tribunals (ss. 2, 3).

B. THE COURT OF JUSTICE OF THE COMMUNITIES

1. COMPOSITION

The membership of the Court of Justice consists of 13 judges and six advocates-general (Art. 166, E.E.C. Treaty). The judges are chosen by common accord by the governments of Member States from "persons whose independence is beyond doubt and who possess the qualifications required for appointment to the highest judicial offices in their respective countries or who are jurisconsults of recognised competence" (*ibid.*, Art. 167). These qualifications have allowed not only judges and private practitioners to be appointed, but also lawyers who have pursued academic and political careers.

In practice, there is a judge appointed from each Member State. The appointments are for renewable six-year terms and there is no retirement age. The judges elect a President of the Court from amongst their number for a three-year renewable term.

While members of the Court of Justice, its judges are not permitted to hold any political or governmental appointments. They are not allowed to take any other employment unless an exemption is granted by the Council of Ministers, and after they cease to be members of the Court they must "behave with discretion" in accepting appointments (Art. 4, *Statute of the Court*). A judge may be dismissed if, in the unanimous opinion of the other judges and advocates-general, "he no longer fulfils the requisite conditions or meets the obligations arising from his office" (Art. 6, *ibid.*). No judge has been dismissed.

The advocates-general enjoy the same status as the judges, and the same provisions regarding appointment, qualifications, tenure and removal from office apply to them. The rôle of the advocate-general is to assist the Court by delivering impartial, independent and reasoned opinions on the cases coming before it. The opinion of the advocate-general is not binding on the Court, but it is carefully considered before the judgment is delivered and it is published with the judgment in the official report of the case.

The Single European Act established a Court of First Instance to relieve the volume of cases coming to the Court of Justice (E.E.C. Treaty, Art. 168A; Council Decision (E.C.S.C., E.E.C., Euratom) 88/591. It came into operation in September 1989.

The Court of First Instance has 12 judges who are appointed for renewable six-year terms by common accord of the governments of the Member States from "persons whose independence is beyond doubt and who possess the ability required for appointment to judicial office" (E.E.C. Treaty, Art. 168a(3); the *Statute of the Court of Justice* is applied to the appointments). The judges elect a President of the Court from their number for a renewable three-year term. The Court of First Instance sits in Chambers of three or five judges, but may sit as a full court. No advocates-general are allocated to the Court.

The jurisdiction of the Court of First Instance was initially limited to staff cases arising under the E.E.C. and Euratom

Treaties, actions brought under the E.C.S.C. Treaty against the Commission by undertakings in respect of levies, production, prices and competition (E.C.S.C. Treaty, Arts. 33, 35), and actions under E.E.C. Treaty, Arts. 173, 175 (in respect of competition rules) and 178 (these Articles are considered below) (Council Decision 88/591, Art. 3); however, from 1993, its jurisdiction extends to all direct actions (see below). Questions referred for a preliminary ruling under E.E.C. Treaty, Art. 177 (see below) are expressly excluded from the jurisdiction of the Court of First Instance (E.E.C. Treaty, Art. 168a(1)). There is a right of appeal, on points of law only, from the Court of First Instance to the Court of Justice (*ibid.*).

2. JURISDICTION

The jurisdiction of the Court rests primarily on the treaties establishing the three Communities. Most cases arise under the E.E.C. Treaty and the Court's jurisdiction under the treaty may be divided into: (a) references for preliminary rulings on questions of Community law from the courts and tribunals of Member States, and (b) direct actions.

(a) Preliminary Rulings

E.E.C. Treaty, Art. 177

"177—(1) The Court of Justice shall have jurisdiction to give preliminary rulings concerning:

(a) the interpretation of this Treaty;
(b) the validity and interpretation of acts of the institutions of the Community;
(c) the interpretation of the statutes of bodies established by an act of the Council, where those statutes so provide.

(2) Where such a question is raised before any court or tribunal of a Member State, that court or tribunal may, if it considers that a decision on the question is necessary to enable it to give judgment, request the Court of Justice to give a ruling thereon.

(3) Where any such question is raised in a case pending before a court or tribunal of a Member State, against whose decisions there is no judicial remedy under national law, that court or tribunal shall bring the matter before the Court of Justice."

Many rights and duties in Community law are determined by the courts and tribunals of Member States. Article 177 provides a mechanism for ensuring that Community law is interpreted in a uniform manner throughout the Community. It has also been used by the Court of Justice to develop important Community law principles such as the supremacy of Community law over national law and the direct effect of Community law.

In theory, and to a large extent in practice, the Court of Justice and the national court or tribunal have distinct rôles under Article 177. The national court or tribunal refers a question of Community law to the Court of Justice for a preliminary ruling; the Court of Justice gives the preliminary ruling which, subject to any subsequent ruling it may give, is binding on the national court or tribunal making the reference, and on other national courts or tribunals which have jurisdiction in the case (*e.g.* Case 29/68, *Milchkontor* v. *Hauptzollamt Saarbrücken* [1969] E.C.R. 165); the national court or tribunal then decides the case, applying the preliminary ruling on the question of Community law, to the extent that the question of Community law remains applicable to its determination. These distinct rôles permeate the jurisprudence of the Court of Justice on Article 177. The Court determines the scope of Article 177 and the limits of the discretion within it for national courts and tribunals, but largely avoids regulating the exercise of that discretion.

Article 177(1) sets out the instruments in respect of which the Court of Justice has jurisdiction to give rulings. Article 177(1)(b) clearly encompasses regulations, directives and decisions, but it has been liberally interpreted by the Court to include Association agreements between the Community and non-Member States (Case 181/73, *Haegeman* v. *Belgium* [1974] E.C.R. 449) and GATT (*e.g.* Cases 267–9/81, *SPI* [1983] E.C.R. 801), although other instruments have been excluded (Case 44/84, *Hurd* v. *Jones* [1986] E.C.R. 29).

The jurisdiction of the Court under Article 177(1)(b) extends to rulings on both the validity and interpretation of instruments. The Court has held that, while a national court or tribunal may seek a preliminary ruling on the validity of a Community instrument, the Court has exclusive jurisdiction over questions of validity and it is not competent for national courts or tribunals to hold Community instruments to be invalid: Case 314/85, *Firma Foto-Frost* v. *Hauptzollamt Lübeck-Ost* [1988] 3 C.M.L.R. 57. On questions of interpretation, the Court will normally avoid giving preliminary rulings on questions of national law or the compatibility of national law with Community law (*e.g.* Case 93/75, *Alderblum* [1975] E.C.R. 2147; Case 34/79, *R.* v. *Henn* and *Darby* [1979] 3795; *cf.* Case 244/78, *Union Laitière Normande* v. *French Dairy Farmers Ltd.* [1979] E.C.R. 2663). If the question referred to the Court would involve the interpretation of national law or a ruling on whether a national law or administrative act is contrary to Community law, the Court may well reformulate the question as an abstract question of Community law and give its preliminary ruling on the reformulated question (*e.g.* Case 28/70, *Otto Witt* [1970] E.C.R. 1021; Case 14/86, *Pretore di Salò* v. *X* [1987] E.C.R. 2545).

Article 177(2) empowers any national court or tribunal to refer questions of Community law for a preliminary ruling. Whether a body is a court or tribunal for the purposes of Article 177(2) is a matter of Community law, and the fact that it is not recognised as a court or tribunal in national law is not decisive (*e.g.* Case 61/65, *Vaasen* [1966] E.C.R. 261). For a body to be competent to refer a question under Article 177(2) the Court of Justice requires it to be one which exercises judicial functions, although these have not been closely defined (*e.g.* Case 36/73, *Nederlandse Spoorwegen* [1973] E.C.R. 1299; Case 65/77, *Razanatsimba* [1977] E.C.R. 2229; Case 246/80, *Broekmeulen* v. *Huisarts Registratie Commissie* [1981] E.C.R. 2311; *cf.* Case 138/80, *Borker* [1980] E.C.R. 1975).

Before a national court or tribunal makes a reference it must consider that a preliminary ruling on the question of Community law is "necessary to enable it to give judgment" (Art. 177(2) and, by implication, Art. 177(3)). This is a matter for the national court or tribunal and is not reviewable by the Court of Justice (*e.g.* Case 6/64, *Costa* v. *ENEL* [1964] E.C.R. 585; Case 13/68, *Salgoil SpA* v. *Italy* [1968] E.C.R. 453; Case 98/85, *Bertini* v. *Regione Lazio* [1986] E.C.R. 1885). However, the Court of Justice has refused to give preliminary rulings on questions which are manifestly irrelevant or hypothetical (*e.g.* Case 244/80, *Foglia* v. *Novello* (No. 2) [1981] E.C.R. 3045; *cf.* Case 232/82, *Baccini* v. *Office National De L'Emploi* [1983] E.C.R. 583), or which seek abstract advisory opinions (Case 149/82, *Robards* v. *Insurance Officer* [1983] E.C.R. 171).

Even where a national court or tribunal within Article 177(2) considers that a decision on a question of Community law is necessary to enable it to give judgment, it still has a discretion as to whether to refer the question to the Court of Justice for a preliminary ruling. However, here the distinction between the operation of the Community and national legal system is less clearly defined. In Community law any court or tribunal may refer a question to the Court of Justice, but national law may impose constraints on its power to do so. So, in Scots law an Article 177 ruling is binding not only on the national court or tribunal which made the reference and other courts and tribunals with jurisdiction in the case, but on all courts and tribunals (European Communities Act 1972, s. 3) (but see further below). Again, a decision to refer may be the subject of an appeal to a superior national court or tribunal. A Scottish illustration is *Wither* v. *Cowie*; *Wither* v. *Wood*, 1990 S.C.C.R. 741 where there was an appeal to the High

Court of Justiciary against the decision of a sheriff to seek an Article 177 preliminary ruling. In such circumstances, the Court of Justice may suspend consideration of the reference pending the outcome of the appeal (*e.g.* Case 31/68, *Chanel* v. *Cepeha* [1970] E.C.R. 403). However, the Court will give a ruling on the reference unless it is withdrawn by the court or tribunal which made it, or it is quashed on appeal by another national court or tribunal (Case 106/77, *Simmenthal* [1978] E.C.R. 629).

The operation of precedent is another area where national law may impose constraints on the discretion of a court or tribunal to refer a question of Community law for a preliminary ruling (see *Rheinmühlen-Düsseldorf*, below).

Despite these various considerations, Article 177 is widely used by national courts and tribunals falling within Article 177(2). In Scotland, there have been references for preliminary rulings from the Court of Session (Case 197/86, *Brown* v. *Secretary of State for Scotland* [1988] E.C.R. 5445) and the sheriff court (*Wither* v. *Cowie*, *Wither* v. *Wood*, 1990 S.C.C.R. 741; [1992] 2 C.M.L.R. 493). There have been over 70 judgments on references to the European Court from English courts within Article 177(2), ranging from the Court of Appeal to VAT tribunals and magistrates' courts.

National courts and tribunals falling within Article 177(3), unlike those within Article 177(2), are obliged to refer questions of Community law for a preliminary ruling by the Court of Justice. However, the obligation does not arise if the Community law question is not relevant to the case before the national court, or it involves a provision which has already been interpreted by the Court of Justice, or the correct application of Community law is obvious (Case 238/81, *C.I.L.F.I.T. Srl.* v. *Ministro della Santina* [1982] E.C.R. 3415). Within the Scottish legal system, the courts obliged to make a reference under Article 177(3) would include both the House of Lords and the High Court of Justiciary. For examples of Article 177 references by the High Court see Case No. 24/83, *Mehlich and Gewiese* v. *Mackenzie* [1984] E.C.R. 817, 1984 S.L.T. 449 (and 1985 S.L.T. (News) 53) and Case C–370/88, *Marshall* [1991] C.M.L.R. 419.

To some extent the obligation to refer depends on the nature of the judicial remedy available and the nature of the action itself. There may be an obligation to refer a question of Community law which arises before a court or tribunal where the remedy against its decision is merely discretionary.

On the other hand, the Court of Justice has held that where a question of Community law arises in interlocutory proceedings, in which the decision of the court is final, there is no obligation to refer if the point can be raised again in the main action (Case 107/76, *Hoffmann-La Roche* v. *Centrafarm* [1977] E.C.R. 957; Cases 35–36/82, *Elestina Morson & Sewradjie Jhanjan* v. *Netherlands* [1983] 2 C.M.L.R. 221; *cf. Portsmouth City Council* v. *Richards* [1989] 1 C.M.L.R. 673, C.A.).

Finally, a national court or tribunal may refer a question of Community law to the Court of Justice again where it has difficulty in understanding the initial preliminary ruling, or in applying it (*e.g.* Case 28/67, *Molkerei-Zentrale* [1968] E.C.R. 143), or when a new question of law arises or new factors have been submitted which might lead to a different ruling, but not merely for the purpose of challenging the initial ruling (Case 69/85, *Wünsche* v. *Germany* [1986] E.C.R. 947). The possibility of making a second reference would avoid most of the difficulties which might be created by the European Communities Act 1972, s. 3.

The importance of Article 177 for the uniform application of Community law is frequently emphasised by the Court of Justice. The Court did so in *Rheinmühlen-Düsseldorf*, where it also examined the effect of precedent on the capacity of a court or tribunal to make a reference.

Rheinmühlen-Düsseldorf
Cases 146, 166/73 [1974] E.C.R. 33, 139

[*Judgment of the Court of Justice*] "Article 177 is essential for the preservation of the Community character of the law established by the Treaty and has the object of ensuring that in all circumstances this law is the same in all States of the Community.

Whilst it thus aims to avoid divergences in the interpretation of Community law which the national courts have to apply, it likewise tends to ensure this application by making available to the national judge a means of eliminating difficulties which may be occasioned by the requirement of giving Community law its full effect within the framework of the judicial systems of the Member States.

Consequently any gap in the system so organised could undermine the effectiveness of the provisions of the Treaty and of the secondary Community law.

The provisions of Article 177, which enable every national court or tribunal without distinction to refer a case to the Court for a preliminary ruling when it considers that a decision on the question is necessary to enable it to give judgment, must be seen in this light.

The provisions of Article 177 are absolutely binding on the national judge and, in so far as the second paragraph is concerned, enable him to refer a case to the Court of Justice for a preliminary ruling on interpretation or validity.

This Article gives national courts the power and, where appropriate, imposes on them the obligation to refer a case for a preliminary ruling, as soon as the judge perceives either of his own motion or at the request of the parties that the litigation depends on a point referred to in the first paragraph of Article 177.

It follows that national courts have the widest discretion in referring matters to the Court of Justice if they consider that a case pending before them raises questions involving interpretation, or consideration of the validity, of provisions of Community law, necessitating a decision on their part.

It follows from these factors that a rule of national law whereby a court is bound on points of law by the rulings of a superior court cannot deprive the inferior courts of their power to refer to the Court questions of interpretation of Community law involving such rulings.

It would be otherwise if the questions put by the inferior court were substantially the same as questions already put by the superior court.

On the other hand the inferior court must be free, if it considers that the ruling on law made by the superior court could lead it to give a judgment contrary to Community law, to refer to the Court questions which concern it.

If inferior courts were bound without being able to refer matters to the Court, the jurisdiction of the latter to give preliminary rulings and the application of Community law at all levels of the judicial systems of the Member States would be compromised.

The reply must therefore be that the existence of a rule of domestic law whereby a court is bound on points of law by the rulings of the court superior to it cannot of itself take away the power provided for by Article 177 of referring cases to the Court."

Before a national court or tribunal makes a reference it must consider that a ruling on the question of Community law is "necessary to enable it to give judgment", and unless Article 177(3) applies, it must also decide whether to exercise its discretion to refer the question. In *Bulmer* v. *Bollinger*, Lord Denning offered "guide-lines" on these matters to English courts and tribunals.

H.P. Bulmer Ltd. v. J. Bollinger S.A.
[1974] Ch. 401

LORD DENNING, M.R.:

"(1) *Guidelines as to whether a decision is necessary*

(i) *The point must be conclusive.* The English court has to consider whether 'a decision of the question is *necessary* to enable it to give *judgment*'. That means judgment in the very case which is before the court. The judge must have got to the stage when he says to himself: 'This clause of the treaty is capable of two or more meanings. If it means *this*, I give judgment for the plaintiff. If it means *that*, I give judgment for the defendant.' In short, the point must be such that, whichever way the point is decided, it is conclusive of the case. Nothing more remains but to give judgment . . .

(ii) *Previous ruling*. In some cases, however, it may be found that the same point—or substantially the same point—has already been decided by the European Court in a previous case. In that event it is not necessary for the English court to decide it. It can follow the previous decision without troubling the European Court. But, as I have said, the European Court is *not* bound by its previous decisions. So if the English court thinks that a previous decision of the European Court may have been wrong—or if there are new factors which ought to be brought to the notice of the European Court—the English court may consider it *necessary* to re-submit the point to the European Court. In that event, the European Court will consider the point again . . .

(iii) *Acte claire*. In other cases the English court may consider the point is reasonably clear and free from doubt. In that event there is no need to interpret the treaty but only to apply it, and that is the task of the English court . . .

(iv) *Decide the facts first*. It is to be noticed, too, that the word is 'necessary'. This is much stronger than 'desirable' or 'convenient'. There are some cases where the point, if decided one way, would shorten the trial greatly. But, if decided the other way, it would mean that the trial would have to go its full length. In such a case it might be 'convenient' or 'desirable' to take it as a preliminary point because it might save much time and expense. But it would not be 'necessary' at that stage. When the facts were investigated, it might turn out to have been quite unnecessary. The case would be determined on another ground altogether. As a rule you cannot tell whether it is necessary to decide a point until all the facts are ascertained. So in general it is best to decide the facts first.

(2) *Guidelines as to the exercise of discretion*

Assuming that the condition about 'necessary' is fulfilled, there remains the matter of discretion . . . The English court has a discretion either to decide the point itself or to refer it to the European Court. The national courts of the various member countries have had to consider how to exercise this discretion. The cases show that they have taken into account such matters as the following.

(i) *The time to get a ruling*. The length of time which may elapse before a ruling can be obtained from the European court. This may take months and months. The lawyers have to prepare their briefs; the advocate-general has to prepare his submissions; the case has to be argued; the court has to give its decision. The average length of time at present seems to be between six and nine months. Meanwhile, the whole action in the English court is stayed until the ruling is obtained. This may be very unfortunate, especially in a case where an injunction is sought or there are other reasons for expedition. This was very much in the mind of the German Court of Appeal in Frankfurt in *Re Export of Oat Flakes*. It is said that it was important 'to prevent undue protraction of both the proceedings before the European Court and trial before the national courts'. On that ground it decided a point of interpretation itself, rather than submit it to the European Court.

(ii) *Do not overload the court.* The importance of not overwhelming the European Court by reference to it. If it were overloaded, it could not get through its work . . .

(iii) *Formulate the question clearly.* It must be a question of *interpretation only* of the treaty. It must not be mixed up with the facts. It is the task of the national courts to find the facts and apply the treaty. The European Court must not take that task on themselves. In fairness to them, it is desirable to find the facts and state them clearly before referring the question . . . In any case, the task of interpretation is better done with the facts in mind rather than in ignorance of them.

(iv) *Difficulty and importance.* Unless the point is really difficult and important, it would seem better for the English judge to decide it himself. For in so doing, much delay and expense will be saved. So far the English judges have not shirked their responsibilities . . .

(v) *Expense.* The expense to the parties of getting a ruling from the European Court . . . On a request for interpretation, the European Court does not as a rule award costs, and for a simple reason. It does not decide the case. It only gives advice on the meaning of the treaty. If either party wishes to get the costs of the reference, he must get it from the English court, when it eventually decides the case.

(vi) *Wishes of the parties.* If both parties want the point to be referred to the European Court, the English court should have regard to their wishes, but it should not give them undue weight. The English court should hesitate before making a reference against the wishes of one of the parties, seeing the expense and delay which it involves."

In a separate judgment, with which Stamp L.J. concurred, Stephenson L.J. refrained from adopting the detailed guidelines in Lord Denning's judgment. In any event, as we have seen, in Community law such guidelines are not binding on inferior courts and tribunals.

In the main, Lord Denning's guidelines tend to discourage Article 177 references. The House of Lords has adopted a more circumspect approach by indicating that courts and tribunals should be cautious in assuming no question of interpretation is raised by a Community legislative text and that a reference should not be made (*Henn and Darby* v. *D.P.P.* [1981] A.C. 850; see also the observation of Bingham J. in *Customs and Excise Commissioners* v. *ApS Samex* [1983] 1 All E.R. 1042, 1055). Certainly, English courts, including the Court of Appeal, have made substantial errors in assuming that a point of Community law is free from doubt (*e.g. Schorsch Meier* v. *Hennin* [1975] Q.B. 416; *cf. Miliangos* v. *George Frank (Textiles) Ltd.* [1976] A.C. 443, 465; *R.* v. *Secchi* [1975] 1 C.M.L.R. 383).

On the other hand, the delay in obtaining preliminary rulings from the Court of Justice, which presently may be up to two years, is an important consideration. In criminal cases it should normally, amongst other factors, discourage the making of a reference before the facts have been ascertained, so that the court is satisfied that the accused will not be acquitted on the facts or that the question of Community law is still relevant once the facts have been established (*Henn and Darby* v. *D.P.P.*, above; *R.* v. *Plymouth Justices, ex p. Rogers* [1982] Q.B. 863). On the other hand, where there is no serious dispute over the facts, particularly in large commercial cases, time and expense may be saved by making a reference at an early stage in the proceedings, and the same may be true when there is a challenge to the validity of a Community legislative instrument on which the proceedings will turn (see, *e.g.* *Polydor Ltd.* v. *Harlequin Records Shops Ltd.* [1980] 2 C.L.M.R. 413 (C.A.), Case 270/80, [1982] E.C.R. 329; *Lord Bethell* v. *Sabena* [1983] 3 C.M.L.R. 1).

The risk of overloading the Court of Justice is not, though, a factor which should greatly influence a court or tribunal in deciding whether to make a reference. Pennycuick V-C commented, "I doubt whether that is a legitimate consideration" (*Van Duyn* v. *Home Office* [1974] 1 W.L.R. 1107, 1116).

Although Lord Denning's guidelines may be criticised, some of them were adopted by Lord Cameron in the Court of Session.

Prince v. Secretary of State for Scotland
1985 S.L.T. 74

LORD CAMERON:

"I have no difficulty in appreciating the force of [the] argument that a reference to the European Court can competently be made when it appears that it may be necessary to do so at any appropriate stage of a litigation. Having regard however to our Scottish system of pleading, I would not normally be persuaded that such a necessity, with whatever degree of urgency that word be interpreted, should be held to arise until the pleadings have been adjusted and the real questions in dispute focussed on the pleadings. I am fortified in this view of the matter by reference to the judgment of Lord Denning in the case of *Bulmer* v. *Bollinger*. . . . In particular, I should find it difficult to make such a reference where preliminary issues of title, competency and relevancy remained unresolved. Neither this Court nor the European Court exists for the purpose of determining academic questions and, as both counsel pointed out, as the work-load of the European Court is both heavy and increasing, it is the more desirable that the Court should not be subjected to additions to its heavy burdens unless such addition is necessary. In the present case [counsel] for the defenders . . . indicated that he proposed to support all his preliminary pleas: I am in no position at this stage in the proceedings to assess the value or effect of these pleas when the arguments thereon have been fully deployed on adjusted pleadings. Thus, it may well be that neither occasion nor necessity for a reference will in this case ever arise. I certainly cannot prejudge the argument on these pleas. It is perhaps only right that I should add that in any event I would not accept or approve either of the questions proposed for reference as suitably drafted to raise the precise questions which the pursuers appear to wish to present."

In *Wither* v. *Cowrie*; *Wither* v. *Wood*, 1990 S.C.C.R. 741, the sheriff adopted Lord Denning's guidelines in deciding to make an Article 177 reference, and in the appeal against the decision to refer this approach was accepted by the High Court. In *Watt* v. *Secretary of State for Scotland* [1991] 3 C.M.L.R. 429, a decision by Lord Weir not to make an Article 177 reference also appears to have been derived from the guidelines. Lord Weir observed, "In my view when a challenge is made to the lawfulness of a matter of this kind based as it is on legislation by the Parliament of the United Kingdom, the grounds should appear to be cogent. In this case I am not satisfied that this test has been passed and indeed having regard to the decisions of the European Court to which I have been referred, I consider that the law of this subject is tolerably clear".

(b) Direct Actions

The four major categories of action which may be brought directly before the Court of Justice are (a) actions against Member States, (b) actions against Community institutions, (c) actions relating to the non-contractual liability of the Communities, and (d) staff cases. The volume of cases in some of these categories, particularly staff cases, coming before the Court of Justice has been significantly reduced as a result of the establishment of the Court of First Instance (see above).

The Commission (Art. 169) or another Member State (Art. 170) may bring a direct action against a Member State which fails to comply with Community law. Individuals and companies have no *locus standi* to bring such an action before the Court of Justice but, if the state is in breach of directly effective Community law, they would have a remedy before a national court. Before one Member State brings an action against another, the issue must first be referred to the Commission. Virtually all direct actions against Member States are brought by the Commission. The Commission initially indicates that there has been a breach of Community law and invites the Member State to submit its observations. If necessary, the Commission then delivers a reasoned opinion on the breach of Community law and requires the Member State to comply within a specified period. If the Member State fails to do so, the Commission may proceed to the Court of Justice. There the case is decided on the terms of the Commission's reasoned opinion and on the facts as they were at the time it was issued. Most of them do not proceed to judgment because the respondent state normally either complies with Community law or reaches a compromise with the Commission. Where the Court does find against a Member State, it must take the necessary measures to comply with the judgment (Art. 171). Most states do comply, but there are instances where they have been extremely dilatory in doing so.

Direct actions may be brought to challenge the legality of acts of the Council of Ministers and of the Commission (Art. 173); they are subject to a two-month limitation period. Any act which has legal effect may be challenged (*e.g.* Case 22/70, *Commission* v. *Council* [1971] E.C.R. 263), but on four grounds only: lack of competence, infringement of an essential procedural requirement, infringement of the E.E.C. Treaty or of any rule of law relating to its application, or misuse of powers. Where, contrary to the E.E.C. Treaty, the Council or Commission fail to act, this can also be challenged (Art. 175).

A Member State, the Council, the Commission and, for the purpose of protecting its powers, the European Parliament, may proceed under Article 173; a Member State or any Community institution may bring an action under Article 175. Individuals and companies may also bring actions under these Articles 173 and 175, but only in very limited circumstances which tend to be restrictively interpreted by the Court (*e.g.* Case 246/81, *Lord Bethell* v. *E.C. Commission* [1982] 3 C.M.L.R. 300). The legality of regulations adopted by the Council or the Commission may also be challenged indirectly. Any party, including an individual or a company, may challenge the applicability of a regulation which is in issue in proceedings before the Court (Art. 184). The regulation may only be challenged on the grounds specified in Article 173, but the limitation period laid down in that Article does not apply.

The Court also has jurisdiction in actions concerning the non-contractual liability of the Communities (*e.g.* E.E.C. Treaty, Art. 178). Relatively few such actions are brought and they are rarely successful. The Court imposes procedural requirements which tend to inhibit these actions. For example, before proceeding in the Court of Justice, a litigant may first have to seek a remedy in the courts of a Member State. The Court frequently requires this where the alleged liability arises out of a Community scheme which is jointly administered by a Community institution and a Member State (*e.g.* Cases 67–85/75, *Cotelle* v. *Commission* [1976] E.C.R. 391). The Court also adopts a restrictive approach to "the general principles common to the laws of Member States" (Art. 215) which is the basis of the law governing the non-contractual liability of the Communities. It has, for example, construed rather narrowly the liability of the Communities for the acts and omissions of its servants (*e.g.* Case 9/69, *Sayag* v. *Leduc* [1969] E.C.R. 329).

Finally, the Court has jurisdiction to hear actions brought against Community institutions by their employees in respect of their rights and status as laid down in staff regulations (*e.g.* Art. 179, E.E.C. Treaty). These "staff cases" represent a large proportion of the direct actions coming before the Court.

3. PROCEDURE

The Court of Justice sits either as a full court, for which the quorum is seven, or in Chambers of three or five judges. References for a preliminary ruling and the less difficult cases instituted by private litigants may be assigned to a Chamber of the Court. The full Court hears all actions brought by a Member State or a Community institution, and also certain other actions where the state or institution requests it to do so. A state or Community institution may, for example, request the full Court to hear a reference for a preliminary ruling where it has made a written submission on the reference.

Normally, parties must be legally represented before the Court (Art. 17, *Statute of the Court*). However, in a reference for a preliminary ruling, a party may appear in person if he is permitted to do so before the court or tribunal which made the reference. Community institutions and Member States are represented by an agent. On occasion they brief outside counsel as their agents, but often a member of the legal service of the institution or state is appointed. A lawyer representing an individual or company must be entitled to practise before a court of a Member State. In the case of Scotland, this would allow both solicitors and advocates to appear before the Court. In England, the Law Society and the Bar entered into an agreement in 1971 which restricted the right of solicitors to practise before the Court of Justice. The Law Society rescinded the agreement in 1981 and English solicitors can now appear in any direct action and have done so (*e.g.* Case 175/80, *Tither* v. *Commission* [1981] E.C.R. 2345). There has been no such agreement in Scotland.

Once proceedings are initiated before the Court an advocate-general is assigned to the case and a judge is appointed as rapporteur. Both play an important rôle in the determination of the case. At this time, one of the 10 official Community languages is designated as "the language of the case" (see Art. 29, *Rules of Procedure of the Court*). French is the working language of the Court and facilities for translation and interpretation into other Community languages are available, but the language of the case is authoritative for all purposes in the proceedings. Thus, strictly speaking, the authoritative judgment of the Court will be that in the language of the case, though the judgment will also be published in the other working languages of the Communities.

The principal stages in the conduct of a case before the Court are (a) the written proceedings, (b) the preliminary inquiry, (c) the oral proceedings, and (d) the judgment. The *written proceedings* are an extremely important element of the case. In preliminary rulings, proceedings are initiated by the reference from the national court or tribunal. The parties to the action in the national court, Member States, the Commission and, in some cases, the Council of Ministers, are all entitled to make written submissions on the reference. In direct actions proceedings are initiated by a written application to the Registrar of the Court. A defence is lodged, and this is usually followed by a written reply and a rejoinder. It is also normally at the stage of the written proceedings that questions of admissibility are considered by the Court.

In direct actions, the judge-rapporteur prepares a preliminary report after the written proceedings. On the basis of that report and the views of the advocate-general, the Court decides whether further evidence is required. The Court may obtain such evidence by conducting a *preliminary inquiry*. The inquiry, which may include the examination of witnesses, is inquisitorial rather than adversarial.

Before the *oral proceedings* the judge-rapporteur produces a report on the case which summarises the facts and the arguments in the written pleadings. This is made available to those making oral submissions. In a direct action, the parties may address the Court; in a reference for a preliminary ruling, those who have made written submissions may also make oral observations. The oral pleadings are not used to rehearse all the arguments in the written pleadings, but rather to emphasise the principal submissions and to comment on the report of the judge-rapporteur. Usually some two or three weeks after the oral submissions, the advocate-general presents his opinion on the case to the Court.

The *judgment* of the Court is always reserved, and a single judgment is delivered. The deliberations of the Court are based on a draft judgment prepared by the judge-rapporteur. This is considered in detail and where there is disagreement a vote is taken. Votes are cast in reverse order of seniority to avoid, it is said, the votes of senior and more experienced judges influencing their junior and less experienced colleagues. The deliberation of the judges takes place in private without the assistance of interpreters, and the working language is normally French. Some of the implications of this are considered in the extract below.

Hartley, *The Foundations of European Community Law,* pp. 71–72
"The choice of French as the working language of the Court means that the judges speak French when they discuss their judgment. All drafting is done in French and the final version approved by the Court is in French even if this is not the language of the case. The French text of the judgment is then translated into the language of the case and this text is signed by the judges and delivered in open Court. The result is that the text signed by the judges may be in a language which many of them do not understand. This throws a great deal of responsibility on those judges who are fluent in the language of the case to ensure that the translation truly reflects what was agreed on.

One drawback of the unilingual mode of operation of the Court is that it puts judges whose mother tongue is not French at a disadvantage. Most people feel less confident giving their opinions in a group discussion if they are not fully at home in the language spoken. French-speaking judges must therefore enjoy a subtle psychological advantage over their colleagues. The use of French in the deliberation room must, moreover, work to some extent in favour of French legal thinking: it is hard to draft a judgment in French without using French legal terminology, while concepts peculiar to other systems might be ignored simply because they cannot easily be expressed in French.

Another difficulty is that, although the official version of the judgment is in the language of the case, the French language version is the one actually agreed on by the Court and therefore might be said to represent the opinion of the Court more accurately than the former. One can imagine that if there is a discussion in the deliberation room as to exactly what was decided in a previous case, it is the French text which will be examined."

4. LEGAL AID

The Court of Justice may grant legal aid to parties in cases before it (Art. 76, *Rules of Procedure of the Court*; see also T. Kennedy, "Costs and Legal Aid Before the E.C.J", (1991) 36 J.L.S. 139). In direct actions, a decision on granting legal aid is taken by a Chamber of the Court during the initial stages of the written proceedings. In references for a preliminary ruling, the Court is also empowered to provide funds, in special circumstances, to assist the representation and attendance of a party.

Legal aid granted by the Court is in the form of a cash grant, which, in the case of direct actions, a recipient may be ordered to repay in whole or part if he loses the case. Legal aid granted for preliminary rulings is not repayable.

Civil legal aid (Legal Aid (Scotland) Act 1986, s. 13, Sched. 2, Pt. I) and criminal legal aid (*ibid.*, s. 21(1)) are available for references from Scottish courts for a preliminary ruling under Article 177 of the E.E.C. Treaty; no legal aid appears to be available for direct actions. Legal advice and assistance is available in Scotland on questions of Scots law (see Chapter 11). However, although European Community law is law in Scotland it is not, on one view, Scots law. In 1978, the Legal Aid Central Committee of the Law Society of Scotland took the view that the legal advice and assistance scheme is available in connection with proceedings in the Court of Justice "to a very limited extent, that is advising on jurisdiction and procedure" ((1978) 23 J.L.S. 143).

II. THE EUROPEAN CONVENTION ON HUMAN RIGHTS

A. INTRODUCTION

The European Convention on Human Rights is a treaty which provides for the protection and enforcement of certain basic rights of individuals. The United Kingdom was the first state to ratify the Convention; it came into force in 1953 and, by January 1993, it had been ratified by 27 states.

The ratifying states undertake to secure the rights in the Convention for everyone within their jurisdiction without discrimination (Arts. 1, 14). Where the rights are violated, they must provide an effective remedy before a national authority (Art. 13). In addition to this, the Convention established international enforcement procedures. An important feature of these procedures is that they are not only available to states party to the Convention but, in many cases, they may also be initiated by individuals.

The rights protected by the Convention include: the right to life (Art. 2); freedom from torture or inhuman or degrading treatment or punishment (Art. 3); freedom from slavery or forced labour (Art. 4); the right to liberty and security of the person, including procedural safeguards on arrest and detention (Art. 5); the right to a fair trial both when charged with a criminal offence and for the determination of civil law rights and obligations (Art. 6); the prohibition of retrospective criminal law (Art. 7); the right to respect for private and family life, home and correspondence (Art. 8); freedom of thought, conscience and religion (Art. 9); freedom of expression (Art. 10); freedom of peaceful assembly and association with others, including the right to join and form a trade union (Art. 11); and the right to marry and found a family (Art. 12).

The range of rights protected has been extended by a series of protocols to the Convention. The First Protocol provides that everyone is entitled to the peaceful enjoyment of their possessions (Art. 1); that no one shall be denied the right to education, and that states, in providing or controlling education, shall respect the right of parents to ensure that such education is in conformity with their religious and philosophical beliefs (Art. 2); it also requires states to hold free elections by secret ballot at reasonable intervals (Art. 3). The First Protocol entered into force in 1954 and has been ratified by the United Kingdom. However, the United Kingdom has not ratified the Fourth, Sixth and Seventh Protocols. The Fourth Protocol, *inter alia*, precludes a state from refusing to admit its own nationals, and under U.K. law not all citizens have the right to enter the United Kingdom. The Sixth Protocol provides for the abolition of the death penalty, except in respect of acts, specified in domestic law, which are committed in time of war or imminent threat of war; the death penalty still exists for limited purposes in the United Kingdom. The Seventh Protocol provides certain rights for aliens, the review of conventions for criminal offences, reparation for miscarriages of justice arising from convictions for criminal offences, protection against double jeopardy in criminal proceedings and equality of certain rights between spouses. Amongst the states which have ratified them, the Fourth Protocol has been in force since 1968, the Sixth Protocol since 1985 and the Seventh Protocol since 1988.

Many of the rights in the Convention are subject to qualifications and exceptions. When ratifying the Convention states may also limit their obligations by making reservations to specific provisions (Art. 64). The United Kingdom, for example, accepted the obligation to respect the right of parents under Article 2 of the first protocol "only so far as it is compatible with the provision of efficient instruction and training, and the avoidance of unreasonable public expenditure." Where it would not be inconsistent with their other international law obligations, states may also take measures derogating from their obligations under the Convention "in time of war or other public emergency threatening the life of the nation," but only "to the extent strictly required by the exigencies of the situation" (Art. 15). The United Kingdom has availed itself of this provision in respect of civil disturbances in Northern Ireland at various times since 1957, and most recently following the 1988 judgment in *Brogan* v. *U.K.* (E.C.H.R., Ser.A, No. 145). Although states are allowed a degree of discretion, the enforcement bodies established by the Convention are the final arbiters of whether there is an emergency within the meaning of Article 15 (*Lawless* v. *Ireland*, E.C.H.R., Ser. A, Nos. 1–3; *Ireland* v. *U.K.*, E.C.H.R., Ser. A, No. 25).

As we have seen, the United Kingdom is required to secure and enforce the rights in the Convention within its jurisdiction. However, the Convention has not been incorporated into domestic law by statute. Consequently, the rights in the Convention are not enforceable before courts in the United Kingdom. In England, some judges have been prepared to take provisions of the Convention into account, for example in the interpretation of statutes (*e.g. R.* v. *Home Secretary, ex p. Bhajan Singh* [1976] Q.B. 198; *R.* v. *Home Secretary, ex p. Phansophar* [1976] Q.B. 606; *Garland* v. *British Rail Engineering Ltd.* [1983] 2 A.C. 751; *R.* v. *Secretary of State for the Home Department, ex p. Brind* [1991] 1 A.C. 696; *cf. Malone* v. *Metropolitan Police Commissioner* [1979] Ch. 344). However, in Scotland this approach has not been accepted on constitutional grounds (*Surjit Kaur* v. *Lord Advocate*, below). However, it may be that the Convention standards could be used to determine reasonableness in the judicial review of executive action, as suggested by J.L. Murdoch in his consideration of the unreported Outer House decision in *Re Budh Singh* (July 13th 1988).

Murdoch, "The European Convention on Human Rights in Scots Law", pp. 49–51
" . . . Judicial review of executive action may, however, avoid certain of the constitutional issues which have troubled the Court of Session. Here, hostility to the Convention may be thawing. In *Re Budh Singh* in 1988, Lord Morison in the Outer House of the Court of Session was asked to consider whether the decision of an immigration official to deport Mr. Singh and his wife as illegal immigrants was unreasonable. There were two grounds of challenge. First, that had all the relevant facts been taken into account, no reasonable official could have come to such a decision. This, in the circumstances, was rejected. Secondly, that general immigration policy was unreasonable since the standard applied by the Home Office amounted to a breach of Article 8 of the Convention by failing to respect the pursuer's family life. On this point, Lord Morison remarked:
'I regard it as unnecessary for me to determine whether the Court is bound by the provisions of this Article: if the policy of the Home Office is one which ignores the obvious humanitarian principle of respect for family life, it would in my view be unreasonable and subject to the Court's review.'
Here was acceptance that executive action could be measured against the provisions of the Convention for certain purposes concerned with judicial

review. That is, the 'duty to act reasonably'—in terms of what is generally referred to as the *Wednesbury* principle—may be applied by considering the requirements of the treaty. Indeed, in view of the House of Lords' approach to irrationality in the *GCHQ* case, application of Lord Diplock's test of unreasonableness as 'a decision which is so outrageous in its defiance . . . of accepted moral standards' may lend itself to use of the Convention as a yardstick for examination of executive practice. (So far as procedural propriety is concerned, Convention guarantees may already provide such a test). In order to give substance to such an open-ended concept as respect for family life, Lord Morison was prepared to turn to the jurisprudence of the Strasbourg Court for assistance. British executive practice required, as Lord Morison summarised it, 'something out of the ordinary in regard to family circumstances to justify departure from the general practice of removing illegal entrants.' Neither in his opinion nor in that of the Strasbourg Court did this breach the humanitarian principle founded on by the pursuer. The Court had considered this matter in *Abdulaziz, Cabales and Balkandali* v. *United Kingdom* and decided that article 8 could not require state respect for choice of matrimonial residence. Lord Morison thus concluded that Home Office policy 'could not be described as one which involves a lack of respect for family life, unless there existed a general obligation such as the European Court rejected.'

This decision may go further than even recent English dicta. It opens up a potentially fruitful line of development in administrative law, avoiding much of the constitutional difficulty confronting Lord Ross, since it is the executive that has agreed to fetter its own action by accepting obligations to refrain from acting in certain ways. There are, to be sure, currently limits to any further development along these lines. Arguments of personal bar are restrained by issues of future fetter of executive discretion, and the English Court of Appeal has rejected any general suggestion of legitimate expectation advanced by litigants. More crucially, other judges may take a different stance. In *Leech* v. *Secretary of State for Scotland*, Lord Caplan in the Outer House disposed of submissions based on decisions of the European Commission and Court by noting that the Convention was not part of domestic law. This case concerned prisoners' correspondence, a particularly fruitful area of complaint to Strasbourg from Britain. Lord Caplan felt able to dispose of the issues by recourse only to domestic law. *Budh Singh* does, however, open up tentative use of the Convention in administrative law and with it jurisprudence of the European Court of Human Rights.

In the absence of legislation incorporating the Convention (or any similar provisions) and of constitutional arrangements permitting its policing by the judiciary, citizens of the United Kingdom are denied the same level of domestic protection of fundamental rights as are accorded other West Europeans. However, in England and Wales and in Northern Ireland, the courts permit discussion of Convention guarantees in the construction of statute and in the development of the common law. In this use, however, the judiciary exhibit caution and an awareness of the proper limit of judicial creativity.

In Scotland, on the other hand, little use has been made of the Convention, largely because of early dicta in two cases where the central issues of its potential use as a source of public policy to supplement formal legal sources were not considered. Both a more realistic analysis of the legislative process and a more sophisticated appreciation of the judicial function would overcome constitutional scruples as to the danger of introducing the Convention into legal arguments. A fruitful area for the Convention may be in administrative law, where more recently a willingness to consider arguments based on the treaty and on its interpretation by the Strasbourg Court has been expressed. Taking account of the Convention in such a manner may help to reduce the number of challenges disposed of in Strasbourg. . . . "

Surjit Kaur v. Lord Advocate
[1980] 3 C.M.L.R. 79

LORD ROSS: "With all respect to the distinguished judges in England who have said that the Courts should look to an International Convention such as the European Convention on Human Rights for the purpose of interpreting a United Kingdom statute, I find such a concept extremely difficult to comprehend. If the Convention does not form part of the municipal law, I do not see why the Court should have regard to it at all . . . Under our constitution, it is the Queen in Parliament who legislates and not Her Majesty's government . . . [To] use the Convention as an aid to construction is 'potentially dangerous,' because the Court is then challenging the well-settled principle that the Executive by itself cannot make law."

[See also *Moore* v. *Secretary of State for Scotland*, 1985 S.L.T. 38, 41; *Martin* v. *City of Edinburgh District Council*, 1988 S.L.T. 329, 330; *Ralston* v. *H.M. Advocate*, 1989 S.L.T. 474, 478.]

The Court of Justice of the European Communities has held the principles on which the European Convention is based must be taken into consideration in Community law; the European Convention effectively represents general principles of law which the Court of Justice will protect in enforcing Community law (*e.g.* Case 11/70, *Internationale Handelsgesellschaft* [1970] E.C.R. 1125; Case 4/73, *Nold* [1974] E.C.R. 491; Case 36/75, *Rutili* [1975] E.C.R. 1219; Case 63/83, *R.* v. *Kirk* [1984] E.C.R. 2689; Case 222/84, *Johnson* v. *Chief Constable, R.U.C.* [1986] E.C.R. 1651; Case C–159/90, *Society for the Protection of Unborn Children (Ireland) Ltd.* v. *Stephen Grogan and others* [1990] 1 C.M.L.R. 689; see generally H.G. Schermers, "The E.C. Bound by Fundamental Human Rights" (1990) C.M.L. Rev. 249; A. Clapham, "A Human Rights Policy for the E.C." (1990) E.L. 309; R.M. Dallen, "An Overview of the E.C. Protection of Human Rights" (1990)

C.M.L. Rev. 761; see also Single European Act 1986, preamble). However, the Court of Justice has not held that the European Convention is part of Community law (*cf.* Case 98/79, *Pecastaing* v. *Belgian State* [1980] E.C.R. 691, 716) and has declined to consider the compatibility of national legislation with the Convention (Cases 60, 61/84, *Cinéthèque S.A.* v. *F.N.C.F.* [1985] E.C.R. 2604; Case 12/86, *Demirel* v. *Stadt Schwäbisch Gmünd* [1987] E.C.R. 3719). Nevertheless, as we have seen, decisions of the Court of Justice on questions of Community law are binding on courts in Scotland; see further N. Grief, "The Domestic Impact of the European Convention on Human Rights as Mediated through Community Law" [1991] P.L. 555.

On the wider issue, many have argued that there should be some specific constitutional protection of human rights, or civil liberties, in the United Kingdom (see, *e.g.* Sir Leslie Scarman, *English Law—the New Dimension* (1974); M. Zander, *A Bill of Rights?* (1976); J. Jaconelli, *Enacting a Bill of Rights: The Legal Problems* (1980)). Although it is not free from legal difficulty one way of achieving this could be by incorporating the European Convention into domestic law by legislation: see A. Lester, "Fundamental Rights: the U.K. Isolated" [1984] P.L. 46; 524 H.L. Debs., col. 185, December 5th 1990. However, at present, individuals in the United Kingdom seeking to enforce their rights under the European Convention must rely largely on the enforcement procedures in the Convention itself.

B. ENFORCEMENT OF THE CONVENTION

1. THE INSTITUTIONS

Three institutions are concerned with the enforcement of the Convention. Two of them, the European Commission of Human Rights and the European Court of Human Rights, were established by the Convention. The third is the Committee of Ministers.

The European Commission of Human Rights: The number of members of the European Commission of Human Rights equals the number of states which have ratified the Convention; they are elected for a six-year renewable term by the Committee of Ministers (Arts. 20–22). No two members may be nationals of the same state (Art. 20), and, in practice, there is a member from each state which is a party to the Convention. However, members of the Commission sit in their individual capacity (Art. 23) rather than as representatives of their states. The appointments are part-time, and the Commission is greatly assisted in its work by a full-time secretariat; on the work of the Commission, see S. Naismith, "The European Commission of Human Rights" (1992) 37 J.L.S. 466.

The European Court of Human Rights: The number of judges on the European Court of Human Rights also equals the number of ratifying states (Art. 38). They must be qualified to hold high judicial office or be "jurisconsults of recognised competence" (Art. 39). They are elected by the Consultative Assembly of the Council of Europe (Arts. 39, 40). No two judges may be nationals of the same state (Art. 38), and normally there is a judge from each state which is a party to the Convention.

The Committee of Ministers of the Council of Europe: The Committee is comprised of the foreign ministers of the Member States of the Council of Europe. Most states appoint permanent representatives to the Council and they usually deputise for the foreign ministers at meetings of the Committee.

2. THE COMPLAINT BEFORE THE COMMISSION

The initial stages of the procedure are before the European Commission of Human Rights. The Commission receives the complaints of alleged violations of the Convention and determines whether they are admissible. The Commission also investigates each admissible complaint and tries to secure a friendly settlement of the dispute.

European Convention, Arts. 24, 25

"24. Any High Contracting Party may refer to the Commission, through the Secretary General of the Council of Europe, any alleged breach of the provisions of the Convention by another High Contracting Party.

25—(1.) The Commission may receive petitions addressed to the Secretary General of the Council of Europe from any person, non-governmental organisation or group of individuals claiming to be the victim of a violation by one of the High Contracting Parties of the rights set forth in this Convention, provided that the High Contracting Party against which the complaint has been lodged has declared that it recognises the competence of the Commission to receive such petitions. Those of the High Contracting Parties who have made such a declaration undertake not to hinder in any way the effective exercise of this right.

(2.) Such declarations may be made for a specific period . . . ''

A state which is a party to the Convention (a "High Contracting Party") may bring an alleged breach of its provisions before the Commission. Individuals and others may only petition the Commission when "claiming to be a victim of a violation of the rights" in the Convention (*e.g.* 436/58, *X* v. *Germany*, 2 Y.B. 386; *cf.* 4185/69, *X* v. *Germany*, 35 Coll 140) but this has been broadly construed by the European Court of Human Rights (*e.g. Klass*, E.C.H.R., Ser. A, No. 28; *Marckx*, E.C.H.R., Ser. A., No. 31; *de Jong, Baljet and van den Brink*, E.C.H.R., Ser. A., No. 77).

Furthermore, an individual may only submit a petition where the state which is the subject of the complaint has declared that it recognises the competence of the Commission to receive individual petitions. Although the United Kingdom has been a party to the Convention since 1953, it first made such a declaration in 1966. The declaration was initially only for three years, but it has been periodically renewed, most recently for a five-year period from January 1991.

European Convention, Arts. 26, 27

"26. The Commission may only deal with the matter after all domestic remedies have been exhausted, according to the generally recognised rules of international law, and within a period of six months from the date on which the final decision was taken.

27—(1.) The Commission shall not deal with any petition submitted under Article 25 which

(a) is anonymous, or

(b) is substantially the same as a matter which has already been examined by the Commission or has already been submitted to another procedure of international investigation or settlement and if it contains no relevant new information.

(2.) The Commission shall consider inadmissible any petition submitted under Article 25 which it considers incompatible with the provisions of the present Convention, manifestly ill-founded, or an abuse of the right of petition.

(3.) The Commission shall reject any petition referred to it which it considers inadmissible under Article 26."

To be admissible, a reference by a state must satisfy Article 26 (e.g. 788/60, *Austria* v. *Italy*, 6 Y.B. 796); an individual petition must satisfy both Articles 26 and 27.

Commission proceedings on the admissibility of a complaint are conducted in private. Before reaching a decision, the Commission usually assigns one of its members to prepare a preliminary report. To address the increasing number of petitions, the Commission has been empowered since 1990 to consider petitions which are viewed as clearly inadmissible in one of six Committees, each composed of three Commission members, and other petitions either sitting in plenary or in one of two Chambers, composed of either ten or 11 Commission members (Protocol 8). Further information may be sought from the parties to the dispute and the Commission will formally ask the state which is the subject of the complaint for its views on admissibility. There may also be written pleadings and oral hearings before the Commission; the state which is the subject of the complaint is entitled to an oral hearing if it requests it.

The Commission takes a decision on admissibility by majority vote. The decision is final and there is no appeal. However, if at a later stage the Commission establishes that an individual application does not comply with Article 27 it may, by unanimous vote, reject the application (Art. 29). Also, if the case proceeds to the European Court of Human Rights, the Court may differ from the Commission on the question of admissibility.

An individual petitioner may be granted free legal aid by the European Commission to pursue his case (*Addendum to Commission Rules of Procedure*, rr. 1–4). Normally, legal aid will not be granted until the respondent state's observations on the admissibility of the petition have been received. In some instances, the grant of legal aid is subject to a means test. The legal aid schemes in Scotland are not available to an individual wishing to petition the European Commission. However, the legal advice and assistance scheme may be available where Scots law is applicable to the petition, for example, where advice is sought on whether local remedies have been exhausted (see (1978) 23 J.L.S. 256, 259).

The vast majority of individual petitions are rejected as inadmissible by the Commission (see Table 1). They are most commonly rejected because either they are not submitted within the specified six-month period, or all domestic remedies have not been exhausted, or the petition is incompatible with the Convention. This is hardly surprising, for to satisfy these requirements the petitioner and his legal advisers must be thoroughly familiar with the jurisprudence of both the Commission and Court of Human rights and, in the case of Article 26, with the national law and legal system of the respondent state.

To satisfy Article 26, for example, the complaint must be pursued before all appropriate judicial and administrative authorities in the respondent state, to the highest instance available. However, the Commission has to be satisfied by the respondent state that a remedy is indeed available (*Alam and Khan* 10 Y.B. 478), and where a remedy is available it may be sufficient for the petitioner to have pursued the substance of the complaint (*Gazzardi*, E.C.H.R., Ser. A., No. 39). Thus, the Commission have decided that domestic remedies were not exhausted where a U.K. applicant, alleging unlawful arrest, had failed to bring a civil action against the police (5197/71, *X* v. *U.K.*, 42 C.D. 138), nor where a prisoner in England, alleging ill-treatment while in prison, failed to appeal to the competent prison authorities, including the Home Secretary (5282/71, *X* v. *U.K.*, 42 C.D. 99). However, the Commission does not require domestic remedies to be exhausted where they would have been likely to have been ineffective or to have provided insufficient redress. This may involve detailed consideration of the national law of the respondent state and an assessment of the reasonable likelihood of success if the petitioner had pursued a particular domestic remedy (*e.g.* 3505/68, *X* v. *U.K.*, 12 Y.B. 298; *Reed* v. *U.K.* (1979) 3 E.H.R.R. 136). It may also involve an appreciation of the prevailing military or political circumstances in the respondent state (*e.g.* 8007/77, *Cyprus* v. *Turkey*, 21 Y.B. 100; *cf.* 5577–83/72, *Donnelly et al.* v. *U.K.*, 19 Y.B. 84).

TABLE 1
Petitions from Individuals to the Commission
1955–1991

Petitions registered		21,077
Decisions on admissibility taken		18,820
(i) petitions declared admissible	1,227	
(ii) petitions declared inadmissible	18,809	
Admissible petitions later rejected during examination of merits		9

[Source: E.Comm. H.R. Survey of Activities and Statistics 1992; procedural factors create apparent statistical discrepancies.]

Once a petition is accepted as admissible, the Commission is required to establish the facts and secure a friendly settlement of the dispute (Art. 28). This is the responsibility of the full Commission, although supervision of the investigation and negotiation may be assigned to individual members. The examination of the facts of an admissible case, and in practice its legal merits, may involve the exchange of written pleadings, further oral argument and visits of inquiry by the Commission and its staff. This stage of the proceedings, which is conducted in private, frequently takes up to two years; in the more complex inter-state cases, somewhat longer.

In seeking a friendly settlement the Commission must ensure that there is not only an agreement between the petitioner and the respondent state but that the settlement is "on the basis of respect for human rights as defined [in the] Convention" (Art. 28). Where a friendly settlement is negotiated, the Commission submits a brief report on the terms of the settlement to the Committee of Ministers, and the report is published (Art. 30).

Where it is not possible to secure a friendly settlement, the Commission prepare a report on the facts and merits of the case, and proposals for subsequent action. The Commission report, which may include separate and dissenting opinions, is sent to the Committee of Ministers and the states concerned, but it is not published (Art. 31).

3. THE DECISION
(a) Committee or Court?

Within three months of the Commission report being transmitted to the Committee of Ministers, the case may be referred to the European 'Court of Human Rights. If no reference is made, it falls to the Committee of Ministers to decide whether there has been a violation of the Convention (Art. 32). The case may only be referred to the Court where the state or states concerned have recognised the compulsory jurisdiction of the Court or consent to the proceedings (Arts. 46, 48). The United Kingdom first recognised the compulsory jurisdiction of the Court in 1966, initially for three years. This has been periodically renewed most recently for a five-year period from January 1991.

A case may be referred to the Court by the Commission, the state whose national is alleged to be a victim of a violation of the Convention, the state which referred the case to the Commission, or the state against which the complaint has been lodged (Art. 48). An individual petitioner cannot refer a case to the Court.

By November 1992, 248 judgments of the Court, including one inter-state case, had been published. Most of these cases were referred by the Commission; some were referred jointly by the Commission and the respondent state.

Beddard, *Human Rights in Europe,* pp. 43–44
"There is nothing in the Convention or the Rules of Procedure of the Commission which gives any guidance as to when a case should go before the Court and when it should be left to the Committee of Ministers. Only in 11 cases has a State decided to go before the Court and in all but four of these cases the Commission too asked the Court for its views. One might consider that the Commission has a duty to transfer cases to the Court since the *travaux préparatoires* show that the Commission's role was introduced for those States unwilling to accept a Court. States themselves would presumably prefer the Committee of Ministers to the Court since, in the former, 14 votes are needed for an adverse decision, being the two-thirds majority required by the Convention, while in a Court of seven judges a simple majority of four adverse votes is all that is necessary to establish a violation of the Convention . . . It is difficult to discern any consistent practice in the cases so far. Generally, where the Commissioner's members unanimously or by a large majority believe that there has been no violation, the Committee of Ministers is chosen. Sometimes, however, even though the Commission feels strongly that there has been no violation, if it thinks that an important or complex legal decision is involved, it refers the case to the Court. Where the Commission is narrowly divided as to whether there is a violation, the present trend is to send the case to the Court."

(b) The Committee of Ministers

European Convention, Art. 32

"32—(1.) If the question is not referred to the Court in accordance with Article 48 of this Convention within a period of three months from the date of the transmission of the Report to the Committee of Ministers, the Committee of Ministers shall decide by a majority of two-thirds of the members entitled to sit on the Committee whether there has been a violation of the Convention.

(2.) In the affirmative case the Committee of Ministers shall prescribe a period during which the High Contracting Party concerned must take the measures required by the decision of the Committee of Ministers.

(3.) If the High Contracting Party concerned has not taken satisfactory measures within the prescribed period, the Committee of Ministers shall decide by the majority provided for in paragraph 1 about what effect shall be given to its original decision and shall publish the Report.

(4.) The High Contracting Parties undertake to regard as binding on them any decision which the Committee of Ministers may take in application of the preceding paragraphs."

The Committee of Ministers is not ideally suited to decide whether there has been a violation of the Convention. In practice, it does not rehear the case or take any further evidence, although its rules of procedure would allow it to delegate these matters to the Commission.

A decision that there has been a violation of the Convention requires a majority of two-thirds of the members entitled to sit on the Committee. Where a two-thirds majority is not reached, the case is not necessarily decided in favour of the state which was the subject of the complaint. The Committee has, on occasion, simply resolved to take no further action (*e.g. East African Asians* v. *U.K.*, 20 Y.B. 642; *Huber* v. *Austria*, 18 Y.B. 324).

Where a state is found to be in breach of the Convention and fails to comply with the measures required of it, the Committee may bring political pressure to bear and ultimately is empowered to suspend the state's membership of the Council of Europe (*Statute of the Council of Europe*, Art. 8).

(c) The European Court of Human Rights

The cases are normally heard by a Chamber of seven judges. A judge who is a national of any state which is a party to the case sits *ex officio*; the other judges are chosen by lot by the President of the Court (Art. 43). However, where a case raises an important question of interpretation, the Chamber of judges may refer the case to the full Court.

Except in inter-state cases, there are no parties to the cases before the Court. The proceedings are based on the report of the

Commission to the Committee of Ministers, and the Court is assisted in reaching its decision by written and oral pleadings by delegates for the Commission and agents for the state or states concerned. Thus, in cases arising from individual petitions, the Commission is assisting the Court in the interpretation of the Convention and not acting as an advocate for the individual petitioner. However, in practice, the Commission commonly sent its report on the case to the individual petitioner and included the petitioner's observations in its pleadings. Furthermore, the delegates of the Commission were assisted before the Court by the petitioner's lawyers, who were permitted to address the Court (see *Lawless* v. *Ireland*, E.C.H.R., Ser. A., Nos. 1–3; *de Wilde et al.* v. *Belgium*, E.C.H.R., Ser. A., Nos. 12, 14). After January 1983, petitioners were permitted to be directly represented before the Court by an advocate authorised to practise in any state party to the Convention, or by any other person approved by the President of the Court (Rules of the Court, rule 30(1)).

The judgment of the Court is final (Art. 52) and states parties to the Convention are under a duty to abide by the decision (Art. 53). The execution of the judgment is supervised by the Committee of Ministers (Art. 54). Where the Court decides that a state has acted contrary to the Convention, it has the power to include it in its judgment that "just satisfaction" be given to the complainant, in cases where the national law of the state does not provide for full reparation for a violation of the Convention (Art. 50).

4. AN EFFECTIVE PROCEDURE?

The enforcement procedure under the Convention has resulted in changes in the domestic law and practice in ratifying states. In the United Kingdom, for example, petitions by individuals eventually resulted in the introduction of immigration appeal tribunals and revised prison rules on access to lawyers. (See further, A.W. Bradley, "The United Kingdom before the Strasbourg Court" in Finnie, Himsworth & Walker (eds.), *Edinburgh Essays in Public Law* (1991); W. Finnie, "Jurisprudence of the European Court of Human Rights 1991" (1992) J.R. 287 (the first of projected annual surveys in the *Juridical Review*).

However, the procedure is too elaborate and lengthy to provide an adequate remedy to the individual whose rights have been violated. This is well illustrated by the case of *Campbell and Cosans*, E.C.H.R. Ser. A., No. 48, the first case from Scotland to reach the European Court of Human Rights.

Gordon Campbell attended a local authority primary school in Strathclyde, where corporal punishment was used for disciplinary purposes. The local education authority refused to give his mother an undertaking that her son would not be subjected to such punishment while at the school. Jeffrey Cosans was suspended from a local authority secondary school in Fife, after refusing, on his father's advice, to accept corporal punishment for attempting to take a prohibited short-cut through a cemetery on his way home from school. Although the local education authority was later willing to lift the suspension, the boy's parents would not allow him to return to school unless they received an undertaking that he would never be subjected to corporal punishment. The local education authority refused to give the undertaking and Jeffrey Cosans did not attend school from his suspension in September 1976 until he ceased to be of compulsory school age in May 1977.

Mrs Campbell and Mrs Cosans petitioned the Commission in, respectively, March and October 1976. Both alleged (a) that the use of corporal punishment in Scottish local authority schools constituted torture or inhuman or degrading treatment or punishment contrary to Article 3 of the Convention, and (b) that the United Kingdom had failed to respect their rights as parents to ensure that the education and teaching of their children was in conformity with their religious and philosophical convictions, contrary to Article 2 of the First Protocol to the Convention. Mrs Cosans also argued that, contrary to the same provision, the suspension of her son from school denied him the right to education.

The two petitions, which were joined by the Commission, were declared admissible in December 1977. In May 1978, the Commission reported to the Committee of Ministers. The case was referred to the Court both by the Commission and the United Kingdom government. In January 1982, the Court held unanimously that there had been no violation of Article 3 of the Convention; but, by six votes to one, it held that the United Kingdom had violated Article 2 of the First Protocol, as alleged. The judgment of the Court on the question of reparation was not delivered until March 1983; the claim for fees of Mrs Cosans' counsel was reduced by more than £3,000. Unlike many individual petitions, few of the facts in this case were in dispute and the exhaustion of domestic remedies was not really in issue. Nevertheless, the case was before the Commission and the Court for seven years. Furthermore, although the individual petitioners' cases were resolved, it was still necessary for the United Kingdom to bring its law and practice into conformity with the Convention. A number of education authorities altered their regulations to conform with Article 2 of the First Protocol and the U.K. Government eventually enacted legislation for the same purpose (the Education (No. 2) Act 1986, s. 48) which was brought into force in August 1987 (S.I. 1987 No. 344)—some 11 years after Mrs Campbell and Mrs Cosans petitioned the Commission.

Further procedural changes to address the problem of delay arising from increased use of the Convention await implementation or are being actively contemplated (see A.R. Mowbray, "Procedural Developments and the European Convention on Human Rights" [1991] P.L. 353). They are needed.

CHAPTER 7

THE JUDICIARY

While the Scottish judiciary numbers both legally qualified and lay individuals in its ranks, the bulk of criminal cases and all civil cases which proceed to an adjudication in Scotland are handled by legally qualified judges. (In England, by contrast, 98% of all criminal cases are dealt with by lay magistrates.) Nevertheless, all Scottish judges, lay and legal, possess considerable power—including the authority to deprive unsuccessful litigants of their funds, and in some cases, their liberty. The higher judiciary, moreover, can make, develop and restate the law (see Chaps. 13 and 14). In the light of these powers and of the virtual irremovability of the higher judiciary once appointed, it is clear that judicial selection is a matter of major public importance.

I. JUDICIAL SELECTION

Abraham, *The Judicial Process*, p. 23
"What principles should govern the selection of the men and women who dispense justice? To raise this question brings us face to face with moral, as well as political, questions of the greatest importance. However awe-inspiring their functions may be, our judges are still human beings. As such they make the ultimate decisions in the judicial process. In essence, there are just two basic methods of selection: *appointment* and *election*— no matter who does the actual appointing or electing—although . . . compromises between the two modes [have] been devised and [are] practised on certain levels of the judiciary in a good many jurisdictions. A collateral question is whether judges should be members of a career service as in France, chosen from a special group of lawyers as in England, or selected through appointments from the legal profession generally as in the United States. Practices of selection differ in large measure in accordance with the traditions and needs of the country concerned."

A. THE SUPERIOR COURTS

The nomination and appointment of Scottish judges in the superior courts is an inherent prerogative of the Crown. By constitutional convention Scottish appointments to the House of Lords and the offices of Lord President and Lord Justice-Clerk are by the Sovereign on the recommendation of the Prime Minister. Appointments to the Court of Session and the High Court of Justiciary are by the Sovereign on the recommendation of the Secretary of State for Scotland. Traditionally the Lord Advocate is consulted before any recommendations are made and in the past half century his advice has almost invariably been accepted.

The criteria for appointment to the House of Lords are set out in section 6 of the Appellate Jurisdiction Act 1876 (on such appointments see Chap. 3 above) and for appointments to the Court of Session and the High Court of Justiciary, in the Treaty of Union.

Treaty of Union 1707, Article XIX

"Hereafter none shall be named by Her Majesty or Her Royal Successors to be ordinary Lords of Session but such who have served in the Colledge of Justice as Advocates or Principal Clerks of Session for the Space of Five years or as Writers to the Signet for the Space of ten years with this provision that no Writer to the Signet be capable to be admitted a Lord of the Session unless he undergo a private and publick Tryal on the Civil Law before the Faculty of Advocates and be found by them qualified for the said Office two years before he be named to be a Lord of the Session yet so as the Qualifications made or to be made for capacitating persons to be named ordinary Lords of Session may be altered by the Parliament of Great Britain."

This provision has recently been extended through sections 35(1), 35(3) of and Schedule 4(1) to the Law Reform (Miscellaneous Provisions) (Scotland) Act 1990.

Schedule 4
Judicial Appointments
"Appointments of sheriffs principal, sheriffs and solicitors as judges of the Court of Session
1. The following categories of person shall, in accordance with this paragraph . . . be eligible to be appointed as judges of the Court of Session—
> (a) sheriffs principal and sheriffs who have held office as such for a continuous period of not less than five years; and
> (b) solicitors who, by virtue of section 25A (rights of audience) of the Solicitors (Scotland) Act 1980, have for a continuous period of not less than five years had a right of audience in both the Court of Session and the High Court of Justiciary."

Section 35(3) provides that any person qualified to become a judge of the Court of Session may be appointed by the Secretary of State (after consulting the Lord President) to act as temporary judges of the Court of Session.

At first blush the 1990 Act seems to have reduced the qualifying period for solicitors to become judges of the Court of Session from 10 years to five. In practice, however, no Writer to the Signet (solicitor) or Principal Clerk of Session has been appointed to sit in the Court of Session or the High Court of Justiciary in the past two centuries. The Lord Advocate, moreover, made it clear as the Bill proceeded through Parliament that the five-year period was selected simply to create a symmetry between the time period for advocates and solicitors. Judicial appointments to the higher courts in Scotland in modern times have invariably come from the senior ranks of the Scottish Bar (Queen's Counsel). In the same way it is highly unlikely that anyone will be appointed permanently under the new provisions until they have had many years of relevant experience.

The Scottish appointees to the House of Lords since 1876 include three Lord Presidents, four Lord Advocates, six former Lord Advocates, two from the Inner House and five from the Outer House. With the exception of Lord Mackay, all the Lord Presidents, Lord Advocates and former Lord Advocates were appointed before 1950 while those from the Inner and Outer Houses were appointed after that date. As the importance of political experience as an attribute declined so other factors have come into the reckoning. Thus of the eight Deans or former Deans, six were appointed after 1948. (See further on the Scottish Lords of Appeal, A. Paterson, "Scottish Lords of Appeal 1876–1988" (1988) J.R. 235).

Turning to the supreme courts in Scotland, of the 57 permanent higher judicial appointments in the last 40 years, all were Q.C.s, only five were of less than ten years' standing as Queen's Counsel while 17 had more than 15 years' standing. [The average standing was 14 years. The actual range of appointments was from seven years' standing to 19 years' standing.] Of the eight temporary judges appointed to the supreme courts by 1993, two were practising seniors and six were sheriffs. All of them were already Q.C.s or acquired that status immediately following on their appointment as temporary judges. Most noteworthy of all, one of them, Sheriff Hazel Aronson, thus became the first woman to sit as a supreme court judge.

PATHS TO THE BENCH

As Ian Willock argued in "Scottish judges scrutinised" (1969) 14 *Juridical Review* 193, Queens Counsel in the past whose careers have followed certain identifiable paths seem to have had an advantage in the pursuit of appointment to the higher judicial bench.

Since higher judicial appointments are made by the Executive there has always been a possibility that politics or party politics could play a part in such appointments. In its most obvious form this influence consisted of appointments as a reward for service to a political party (usually as an M.P.). Secondly, as in the case of appointments to the Federal judiciary in the United States, it has been manifested in attempts to place "right-thinking" appointees on the bench. In its weakest form it has led to candidates with political experience being favoured (irrespective of party) because of a belief that such experience is a useful attribute in a judge.

In England political factors, except occasionally in the last sense, now play little part in higher judicial appointments (less than 10 per cent of the higher judiciary in England have had political experience).

In Scotland the position now is broadly similar. Although a rather higher percentage of the supreme court judiciary has been active in politics (22%), the importance of political experience as a route to the bench is much less than it was only 20 years ago.

Thus in the 100 years prior to 1972 whenever the office of Lord President or Lord Justice-Clerk fell vacant it was filled by the Lord Advocate of the day or one of his predecessors. Lord Emslie's appointment as Lord President in 1972 was the first occasion in over 250 years when a vacancy in chair of the Court of Session had not been filled by the appointment of a Lord Advocate or former Lord Advocate. The break in tradition was maintained in 1989 when the Dean of Faculty, David Hope Q.C., replaced Lord Emslie as Lord President and Lord Justice-General. Nevertheless, 13 of the last 15 Lord Advocates to hold office have been elevated to the supreme courts (sometimes on their own recommendation). Of the 57 appointments to these courts in the last 40 years, 20 were advocates who had been active in politics. However, the political experience factor is clearly on the wane. Law officers hold office for longer than in the past and the political climate is less sympathetic to lawyer M.P.s becoming judges than once it was. Thus of the 25 Senators of the College of Justice in early 1993 only six were known to have had an involvement with politics and four of them were in the Inner House. Moreover it is now not uncommon for an appointee with political experience to come from another political party to that of the Lord Advocate. [See, further, on politics and judicial appointment, A. Paterson, "Judges: a political elite?" (1974) 1 *British Journal of Law and Society* 118 and S.C. Styles, "The Scottish Judiciary 1919–1986 " (1988) J.R. 41.]

The second route is by attaining the leadership of the Bar. The Scottish Bar (the Faculty of Advocates) elects its leader (the Dean) on merit, from the ranks of the successful Queen's Counsel.

Excluding the Dean and the Lord Advocate of the present day only four of the 25 holders of the office of Dean since 1900 have not been elevated to the higher court Bench. (Two of the four were thought to have disqualified themselves from judicial office by their handling of their business or private affairs.)

Appointment as a part-time sheriff principal was the third route. Since the office of sheriff principal became a full-time appointment in 1975, this route seems to have disappeared. However, other routes seem to be springing up to replace it. Senior advocates who have accepted appointment to the Presidency of Industrial Tribunals or to the Scottish Law Commission in recent years are thought to have been informed that acceptance of these posts would be likely to improve their chances of higher judicial appointment. Being chairman of a Medical Appeal Tribunal is also seen as useful experience. Again, with the expansion of criminal work in the High Court in the past ten years, counsel with aspirations to higher judicial office (but with little in the way of a criminal practice), have been led to believe that a period as advocate-depute will do their chances of eventual selection no harm.

It remains to be seen whether, as in the case of the sheriffs, appointment as a temporary judge will become an important stepping stone en route to a permanent post, an end point in itself, *e.g.* as an accolade in recognition of a distinguished career or a cheap expedient for the Treasury to supply judges for the High Court.

B. THE SHERIFF COURT

Sheriff Courts (Scotland) Act 1907, s. 11

"11. The right of appointing to the salaried offices of sheriff principal and salaried sheriff shall be vested in His Majesty, and shall be exercised on the recommendation of the Secretary of State."

Sheriff Courts (Scotland) Act 1971, s. 5

"5. *Qualification for offices of sheriff principal and sheriff.*—(1) A person shall not be appointed to the office of sheriff principal or sheriff unless he is, and has been for at least ten years, legally qualified.

For the purposes of this subsection, a person shall be legally qualified if he is an advocate or a solicitor."

Although solicitors have long been eligible for appointment to the shrieval bench, until the 1970s such appointments were largely restricted to former advocates. In 1967 there were 58 sheriffs of whom all but seven were former advocates. Following the Grant Report (which came out in favour of more solicitor appointments to the shrieval bench) the appointing authorities have been much more sympathetic to solicitors. Of the 109 permanent sheriffs appointed since 1967, 63 have been counsel and 46 solicitors (seven of whom were procurators fiscal). In the last decade there has been a rough parity between the numbers of former advocates and solicitors appointed as sheriffs. Some indication of the change can be seen from the fact that in 1967 12% of sheriffs were former solicitors, in 1985 it was 29% and by mid-1992 42% were former solicitors. In fact, in mid-1992 there were 97 permanent sheriffs of whom 12 had been Q.C.s, 44 junior advocates and 41 solicitors. Of the six sheriffs principal at that date five were originally Q.C.s but one had been a solicitor who was appointed first to be a sheriff and subsequently as a sheriff principal. Amongst those holding the post of temporary sheriff, however, the balance is reversed. Thus in mid-1992, of the 111 temporary sheriffs, 20 were Q.C.s, 21 were junior advocates and 70 were solicitors. In fairness it should be said that in general, advocates have tended to be appointed at a markedly younger age than solicitors and to the most sought-after shrieval posts. While several sheriffs have been promoted to sheriff principal, only one (Lord Caplan) has subsequently been elevated to the supreme court bench.

C. REFORM

The Scottish system of appointment to higher judicial office has been criticised for a number of reasons.

Campbell, "Judicial Selection," pp. 278–279

"First the Scottish system is open to attack in so far as it relies on executive appointment rather than on an independent committee. There is room for abuse and for political appointments . . .

Secondly the Scottish system is open to attack for its reliance on the knowledge and judgment of one man in selecting judges. Informal consultation and advising no doubt takes place—but is not *visible* or *open* . . .

Thirdly in relying almost exclusively on such a small 'pool' (the Faculty of Advocates) for judicial appointments, the Scottish system is open to attack on grounds of patronage, social class bias and narrowness of experience . . .

Fourthly in not regularly affording formal training to newly appointed judges the Scottish system is open to attack in so far as it does not fulfil its function of ensuring the judges are of the highest technical competence and that common standards are maintained.

In making each of these points, which together amount to total criticism of the Scottish system, the phrase 'open to attack' is used. Most of the attacks have been made by one critic or another. It is not necessary to agree or disagree with the criticisms, it is only necessary to recall that if the point at issue is *credibility* and *ostentatious impartiality* the Scottish system must be adjudged a failure. It fails to meet the rational requirements of a system that the public, the profession, legal scholars and other commentators may accept with any confidence."

[It is now 20 years since this critique was penned. At least in relation to the appointments to the supreme courts its message is just as pertinent today as it was then.]

1. THE APPOINTIVE MECHANISM

As we have seen, the Scottish system is primarily appointive, although when Deans of the Faculty are elevated to the Bench or local authority councillors sit *ex officio* in the district court elective elements have a part to play. David Pannick once argued ("Election of the judiciary" (1979) 129 New L.J. 1064) that judges in the House of Lords should be popularly elected from a short list of legally qualified candidates selected on merit (a proposal akin to "the Missouri plan" which operates with some success in about half of the United States in relation to State judicial appointments). This proposal attracted little support. Most other commentators favour an improved appointive system. Unlike the Lord Chancellor in England or the President of the United States (when appointing Federal judges) the Lord Advocate does not go through an elaborate semi-formal consultation process prior to making a nomination. [See G. Stott, "Lord Advocate's Diary" (Aberdeen University Press, 1991) *e.g.* at pp. 167, 172–173, 181, 184 and 188. On the procedures adopted by the Lord Chancellor, see A. Paterson, "Becoming a Judge" in R. Dingwall and P. Lewis (eds.) *The Sociology of the Professions* (Macmillan: 1983) and *The Judiciary* (Justice: 1992).] There is now a considerable body of opinion and commentary (particularly in England and Wales) to the effect that what is needed is an independent Judicial Commission of judges, lawyers and laypersons. Such judicial commissions have been experimented with in some Commonwealth countries, though it has been said that they tend to make "safe", unimaginative nominations. Nevertheless as the pool for judicial selection broadens on both sides of the border so the pressure is mounting to abandon the "old boy network" with its reliance on secret (and potentially prejudiced) references in favour of a more transparent process of selection on merit. Thus, in July 1993 Lord Mackay of Clashfern L.C., while rejecting the establishment of a judicial appointments commission, committed himself to a more open judicial appointment procedure. [See, *e.g.* Editorial "Shaking the

Foundations" (1990) 160 SCOLAG 2; D. Pannick *Judges* (Oxford University Press: 1987) at p. 68 and *The Judiciary* (Justice, 1992). *cf.* S. Nelson, "The Scottish Judiciary: A Case for Reform" (1992) 188 SCOLAG 71.]

2. QUALIFICATIONS FOR JUDICIAL APPOINTMENT

As we have seen the Law Reform (Miscellaneous Provisions) (Scotland) Act 1990 has, at least on paper, considerably broadened the pool from which appointments are made to the supreme courts. The present *de facto* stipulation that all appointees must be Queen's Counsel of sufficient standing has restricted selection to a pool of less than ten serious candidates (including the Law Officers and the Dean of Faculty). Allowing sheriffs principal and sheriffs to be considered more than doubles the pool. In practice, it is too early to tell whether we shall see sheriffs principal or sheriffs promoted to the higher courts with any regularity, even if they are appointed as temporary judges. As for solicitors with rights of audience, the first appointment from their ranks is likely to be more than a decade away.

There is also considerable pressure for more female judges to be appointed. To date no woman has been appointed permanently to the Court of Session Bench, (although in 1992 the first was appointed as a temporary supreme court judge), only one has become a sheriff principal and six (including one solicitor) have been appointed to the shrieval bench. The importance of this has been heightened by the unsatisfactory approach of some male judges to the handling of rape cases.

At one time the qualities required of a Court of Session judge were set out explicitly by statute. Thus an Act passed in 1592 stipulated that appointees must be God-fearing, well-read, practical in judgment, versed in the law, expeditious in the dispatch of business and possessed of independent means. Except perhaps in Northern Ireland, the first requirement is no longer seen as a relevant factor (nor are divorcees denied promotion to the Bench as once they were). Curiously, the long line of candidates who have refused judicial appointment on the grounds that they could not afford the drop in salary involved in leaving the Bar seems to indicate that the last requirement is not as irrelevant in modern times as might have been thought. One attribute which is missing from the statute is that the candidate should be in good health and possessed of a sound constitution. Both in England and Scotland appointing authorities in the past 30 years have seemed on occasion to turn a blind eye to the absence of this attribute in candidates appointed to the Bench.

3. TRIALS AND TRAINING

A common criticism of the British system of judicial appointment (as opposed to the Continental preference for a career judiciary) is that the qualities which make a successful advocate or court practitioner may not be those required to make a successful judge. Although little discussed in the literature, appointing authorities in Scotland and England have long sought to overcome this problem by appointing would-be judges on a part-time basis to see if they possess judicial qualities. English Q.C.s are encouraged to serve as recorders (part-time judges) and Scottish Q.C.s became part-time sheriffs principal until 1975 for the same reasons. Similarly, as we saw earlier, there are presently 111 temporary (part-time) sheriffs of whom 20 are Q.C.s. This partly makes up for the loss of part-time sheriffs principal as a way of giving Q.C.s a "trial run" as superior judges. It may be that appointment as a temporary judge in the supreme courts will be used in the same way. The problem is clearly a perennial one. In 1579 an Act was passed giving the Court of Session power to test the suitability of royal nominees to the Bench. Each nominee had to sit three days in the Outer House and one day in the Inner House and then be assessed on his handling of the cases he had heard. At least one nominee failed the test but in 1724 a further statute made it clear that the Crown could override the court's veto. These judicial examinations were only abolished in 1933, although they had become a formality many years earlier.

A closely related criticism is that British judges receive insufficient training before their appointment. Although in England there have for many years been one-day and one-week conferences for judges on damages, family law and sentencing, the Bridge Report on "Judicial Studies and Information" (H.M.S.O.: 1978) concluded that much more could and should be done. Following the report a Judicial Studies Board was established which is now chaired by a Lord Justice and its members include High Court and Circuit judges. In addition to introductory seminars for new judges appointed to the Crown Court it arranges visits to penal establishments, conducts sentencing exercises and runs refresher courses (every five years) for experienced judges sitting in the Crown Court. There is no Scottish equivalent to the Judicial Studies Board in part because of resource constraints and in part because opportunities for formal education and training increase with numbers.

Lord President Hope, "Judicial Business," 1991 J.L.S. 266
"Nevertheless, although we have no Judicial Studies Board of our own, there is already a considerable amount of activity in this field in Scotland.

The Sheriffs' Association in particular provides an introductory course each year for recently appointed sheriffs and temporary sheriffs as part of the scheme of introductory training which it organises for those appointed to these positions. The introductory course is a five-day residential course from Monday to Friday, usually in April, which is directed by members of the Council of the Association and has the support of SCA. It covers a wide range of topics in regard to both the criminal and civil jurisdictions of the sheriff court, with emphasis on procedural matters and various aspects of sentencing. It is compulsory for every new sheriff on appointment, whether he is a permanent or a temporary sheriff, and it is in addition to the receipt by every new sheriff of a minimum of five days' practical experience on the bench sitting alongside an experienced sheriff. In addition, the Sheriffs' Association holds a two-day judicial studies conference every two years for all permanent sheriffs and there have been a number of two-day judicial studies conferences organised at sheriffdom level, usually at weekends, by and for sheriffs within the sheriffdom. If you add to this the attendance by sheriffs at conferences, study days and seminars both here in Scotland and in other jurisdictions, and time spent by them on their own private studies—including such work as that done by Sheriffs Gordon and Johnston in their editorship of *Scottish Criminal Case Reports* and *Scottish Civil Law Reports*—you can see that a substantial amount of judicial studies are undertaken at present by sheriffs and I believe that they compare favourably with what is available in England and Wales under the direction of the Judicial Studies Board. A similar system for the training on appointment and continuing education of justices sitting in the district court is administered by the District Courts' Association.

In the case of Senators of the College of Justice there is, as you know, almost no formal training on appointment and there has been no attempt at devising any kind of formalised pattern for judicial studies in the course of a Senator's career. At one time a judge appointed to the Court of Session was required to undergo a formal trial as a Lord Probationer after receiving his commission under the Great Seal (Court of Session Act 1723, section 1). But that section has long been repealed and the practice abolished. In the past year I have instituted an induction programme for each new Senator on his appointment, in order to introduce him to various procedural and practical matters regarding his role as a judge in the Court of Session and in the High Court. In addition to this the Lord Justice-Clerk and I held a half-day seminar for the four judges who were appointed in 1990. But for various practical reasons it is not possible to deal with the matter otherwise than on an *ad hoc* basis as and when required. The number of appointments to the Supreme Court bench each year is very small in comparison to those appointed each year as sheriffs or temporary sheriffs, let alone as Crown Court judges or assistant recorders in England and Wales."

As the Lord President points out later in the article there may be a need for more formal training arrangements for temporary appointments to the supreme courts. He concludes, however, that the solution for judges appointed to the higher judiciary in Scotland will mainly consist of private study. Despite the Lord President's able apologetics there is still an argument that the Scots should have a Judicial Studies Board of their own. [On the need for more training for judges, see Sheriff Thomson, "From Sentences to Paragraphs," 1979 S.L.T. (News) 1, and Jessica Burns, "Judicial Education" (1989) 158 SCOLAG 171.]

D. THE DISTRICT COURT

District Courts (Scotland) Act 1975

Justices of the peace

"9.—(1) Subject to the provisions of this section, there shall, in Scotland, be a commission of the peace for each commission area; and the commission for any commission area shall be a commission under the Great Seal addressed generally, and not by name, to all such persons as may from time to time hold office as justices of the peace for the commission area.

(2) Justices of the peace for any commission area, other than stipendiary magistrates and ex officio justices, shall be appointed by name on behalf and in the name of Her Majesty by instrument under the hand of the Secretary of State, and a justice so appointed shall only be removed from office in like manner.

11.—(2) Each local authority may nominate up to one quarter of their members to serve as ex officio justices for their area, and any person so nominated shall hold office as ex officio justice from the date on which the local authority intimate their nomination to the Secretary of State and shall continue as such for the period during which he remains a member of the authority and continues to retain the authority's nomination.

14. The Secretary of State may make schemes and provide courses for the instruction of justices of the peace, and it shall be the duty of the justices' committee of a commission area to implement and administer any such schemes in accordance with arrangements approved by the Secretary of State."

In addition to *ex officio* justices, justices are appointed by the Secretary of State on the advice of the J.P. advisory committees appointed by him in each district and islands area. The committees advise both on the need for new appointments and as to the suitability of candidates for appointment. The Secretary of State (like the Lord Chancellor when considering appointments to the magistracy) takes the view that "commissions of the peace should be drawn from all social classes and be broadly representative of the community which they serve" (100 H.C.Deb., col. 435 (W.A.), March 13, 1981). Attempts are also made to attain a political balance between the main political parties on each commission, though not a religious balance, except in areas likely to be sensitive on the matter.

In mid-1992 there were 4,275 justices, 1,700 of whom were aged 70 or over and ineligible to sit. Of the remainder only a quarter were women. (In the year to April 1992 only 904 justices actually sat on the Bench.)

The low percentage of female justices suggests that the Secretary of State's efforts to appoint commissions which are "broadly representative of the community" have only been partially successful. It is likely that (as in England) the professional and managerial groups in the community are over-represented and that ethnic minorities as well as women are under-represented.

The existence of lay judges in Scotland (and *ex officio* justices in particular) has long been a source of discontent in legal circles. When local government was being reorganised in the 1970s there were strenuous efforts (not least by the legal profession) to abolish the lay judiciary altogether. Just when the battle seemed to have been won there was a change of government and lay justices were reprieved. The controversy was revived with a Scottish Office study in 1984 [now published as Z. Bankowski, N. Hutton and J. McManus, *Lay Justice* (T. & T. Clark, 1987)] concluding that the lay system works adequately and produces similar results to those which a professionalised system would. This study was fiercely criticised by the Law Society ("Professional Justice" (1985) 30 J.L.S. 13) who again called for the replacement of the lay justices by stipendiary magistrates' courts. Failing this the Society considered that a centralised training programme should be established to ensure the maintenance of standards throughout the country with compulsory refresher courses. Certainly, at present, although local training courses are run for justices on legal aid, procedure, evidence and sentencing (with visits to penal institutions) it is not entirely clear what their purpose is (presumably it is not to make them superficial lawyers) nor how effective they have been.

II. JUDICIAL INDEPENDENCE

A. JUDICIAL TENURE

The strongest safeguard of judicial independence in the United Kingdom is the security of tenure which judges possess. Tenure of high judicial office in Scotland is by custom and by Article 13 of the Claim of Right 1689, *ad vitam aut culpam, i.e.* during good behaviour. In the case of Law Lords section 6 of the Appellate Jurisdiction Act 1876, as amended, provides that:

"Every Lord of Appeal in Ordinary shall hold his office during good behaviour, . . . but he may be removed from such office on the address of both Houses of Parliament."

But the procedure for removing a judge from the Court of Session or the High Court is uncertain.

Esson, "Ad vitam aut culpam," pp. 64–65

Prior to the Union of the Parliaments in 1707 the Scottish Privy Council had a supervisory power over judges, and could remove the incompetent and corrupt ones; but this body was abolished in 1707. In a number of cases where complaints have been made about the exercise of judicial power this point has been discussed, and it would appear that the Address from both Houses of Parliament is the appropriate method . . . When counsel complained that Lord Hope had maliciously censured him whilst at the Bar, it was held that no action for damages would be competent against a judge of the Court of Session while acting in his judicial capacity: Lord Robertson said in that case [*Haggart's Trs.* v. *Hope* (1824) 2 Sh. App. 125]: 'If any judge, either judicially or not, should commit a wrong, God forbid there should be no remedy; but then the redress does not lie with us; it is by application to the King in Council or to Parliament.' One might well interpret the words 'King in Council' as Parliament in this instance since there can be no question of their judicial cognisance of such affairs. [In 1820 a petition was presented to the House of Commons charging Lord President Hope with malversation in his judicial capacity. The petition was rejected—but not on grounds of competency. In later cases judges have specifically stated that the appropriate procedure is an address moved in both Houses.]

Probably the most interesting case where this tenure was called in question was that of *Mackay and Esslemont* v. *Lord Advocate* [1937 S.C. 860]. Mackay and Esslemont were members of the Scottish Land Court, and so held judicial office; a clause in their commissions required them to retire at sixty-five or for ill-health. There was, however, nothing in the statute making this condition mandatory. Holding this clause to be *ultra vires*, Lord Robertson said, "Servants of the Crown who hold judicial offices, or offices of the nature of *munera publica* are not and (unless some statute provides otherwise) cannot be limited to a tenure at pleasure, but hold office *ad vitam aut culpam*. Any statutory interference with the life character of the appointment should be strictly construed."

The lack of a formal procedure for removing supreme court judges was graphically highlighted in 1990 with the resignation of a Court of Session judge. Even if the allegations concerning the judge had been established (which they were not) and even if they were inconsistent with holding high judicial office (again a moot point) it is far from clear what the authorities could have done if he had chosen not to resign.

Several statutes have imposed restrictions on the tenure of high judicial office. Amongst the earliest (and now, possibly, in desuetude) was the Land Purchase Act 1594, in terms of which Lords of Session who purchase land or property which is the subject of litigation risk forfeiture of their judicial office. Much later came section 2 of the Judicial Pensions Act 1959 under which all judges in the House of Lords and Senators of the College of Justice appointed since 1959 must retire on attaining the age of 75. Sheriffs principal and sheriffs, on the other hands, had to retire at 72 (Sheriffs' Pensions (Scotland) Act 1961, ss.6, 9). Following the passage of the Judicial Pensions and Retirement Act 1993 all Scottish judges appointed in the future will be required to retire at 70.

A rather different mechanism for terminating the appointment of a sheriff is contained in the Sheriff Courts (Scotland) Act 1971, s.12:

"12. *Removal from office, and suspension, of sheriff principal or sheriff.*— (1) The Lord President of the Court of Session and the Lord Justice Clerk may of their own accord and shall, if they are requested so to do by the Secretary of State, undertake jointly an investigation into the fitness for office of any sheriff principal or sheriff and, as soon as practicable after completing that investigation, shall report in writing to the Secretary of State either—
  (*a*) that the sheriff principal or sheriff is fit for office, or
  (*b*) that the sheriff principal or sheriff is unfit for office by reason of inability, neglect of duty or misbehaviour,
and shall in either case include in their report a statement of their reasons for so reporting.
  (2) The Secretary of State may, if a report is made to him under subsection (1) above to the effect that any sheriff principal or sheriff is unfit for office by reason of inability, neglect of duty or misbehaviour, make an order removing that sheriff principal or sheriff from office.
  (3) An order under subsection (2) above—
  (*a*) shall be made by statutory instrument, which shall be subject to annulment in pursuance of a resolution of either House of Parliament,
  (*b*) shall not be made so as to come into operation before the expiry, in relation to the order, of the period of forty days mentioned in section 5(1) of the Statutory Instruments Acts 1946."

Under section 15 of the District Courts (Scotland) Act 1975 justices of the peace can no longer sit after attaining the age of 70 and can be prevented from sitting by the Secretary of State on the grounds of infirmity, neglect of duty or failure to attend training courses.

Although temporary sheriffs may sometimes fail to have their appointment renewed (*e.g.* the one whose remarks in an under-age sex case had incensed the Asian community in 1982) only two permanent sheriffs have ever been removed through the use of the statutory procedure. The first occasion, in 1977, involved Sheriff Peter Thomson who was removed for "political activities incompatible with the holding of a judicial office." His offence consisted of associating himself (in his judicial capacity) too closely with a campaign for a Scottish plebiscite as a precursor to Scottish self-government. After a heated debate in the House of Commons an attempt to annul the Secretary of State's order was defeated by 170 votes to 52. (See 940 H.C.Deb., cols. 1288–1331, December 6, 1977.) The second, in 1992, involved Sheriff Ewen Stewart who was found by the Lord President and the Lord Justice-Clerk to be "unfit for office by reason of inability to perform the judicial functions which are expected of a sheriff . . . " Sheriff Stewart's downfall stemmed from one case too many in which he had interrupted incessantly (over 100 times) or made ill-advised and tactless remarks. Curiously, the senior judges did not make a finding of misbehaviour but one of inability. Sheriff Stewart claimed that inability was synonymous with physical and mental incapacity and threatened to raise an action of judicial review against the investigating team. He also took exception on natural justice grounds to aspects of the removal procedure, e.g. to not being shown the case against him, to the lack of a public hearing or an opportunity to cross-examine the witnesses on whose testimony the judges had relied.

Sheriff Stewart's observations raise the question as to whether we have got the procedures for the removal of lower court judges right. After all, if a judicial review was requested of how the procedures had been carried out, who would be found to preside? Several commentators, e.g. David Pannick in Judges (OUP: 1987) at pp. 96ff, the Chairman of the English Bar in 1992 and the recent report of Justice on The Judiciary (Justice: 1992) have called for the introduction of a Judicial Commission to set standards of conduct for judges and to monitor their performance through the provision of a complaints procedure and a disciplinary tribunal. The concerns of the commentators are perhaps even better founded in cases involving the higher judiciary because of the uncertainty as to the standards expected of them, as to the removal procedure and the lack of intermediate sanctions. As the original Justice sub-committee pointed out in 1972 in its report on The Judiciary (Stevens, 1972) the term "good behaviour" is imprecise and inadequate. Lord Hailsham endeavoured to explain them in an article entitled "The Lord Chancellor and Judicial Independence," 1980 Cambrian Law Review 40:

"It goes without saying that the misbehaviour complained of should be specified in the resolution and should be conduct of a culpable misuse of the judicial office or conduct calculated to bring the judicial office into disrepute. It would be contrary to every conception of fair play that it should not be specified (as was the case in a recent Commons resolution attacking Lord Denning) and it would be contrary to the terms of the judge's appointment . . . if conduct short of misbehaviour were relied on. At least in my view, misbehaviour means something much worse than a tendency to arrive at erroneous decisions or to make undesirable or ill considered remarks, and, so far as I know, the power of removal has seldom, if ever, been exercised."

The alleged inadequacy of the test stems from the fact that "good behaviour" does not expressly include the question of incapacity and incompetence. In England the Supreme Court Act 1981, s. 11, provides a mechanism for the removal of a judge of the Supreme Court who is "disabled by a permanent infirmity from the performance of the duties of his office and is for the time being incapacitated from resigning his office." There is no equivalent provision in Scotland and in neither country is there any machinery for tackling the unusual but relatively more frequent problem of judges who are unfit, as a result of physical or mental impairment, to carry out their duties but who are unwilling to resign. The Justice sub-committee concluded that judges should be removed for proven incapacity, mental or physical.

In practice the proposed reforms in the grounds and mechanism for the removal of the higher judiciary while desirable are likely to have little practical effect. No Scottish or English judge holding high judicial office has been removed by the formal address procedure since before 1707. This is not because there have not been any unfit or incapable judges during that time. The perceived importance of the separation of powers and the independence of the judiciary has been such that successive Lord Chancellors and Lord Presidents have preferred to put pressure—sometimes very strong pressure—on judges to resign rather than to invoke more formal measures. Since 1890 there have been at least 15 instances where judges of the superior courts in the United Kingdom have been the subject of strong pressures or inducements to resign, ostensibly on the grounds of ill-health which they were reluctant to face up to or were incapable of recognising.

The problem with such an approach is not just the secrecy with which it is pursued but that it provides no overt support for the democratic principle that public officials who are entrusted with considerable powers should be held accountable for the exercise of these powers. It may be that what is required is more effective intermediate sanctions.

At present if a judge abuses his or her power to convict of contempt of court (*Macara* v. *Macfarlane*, 1980 S.L.T. (Notes) 26), oppressively refuses an adjournment (*Tudhope* v. *Lawrie*, 1979 S.L.T. (Notes) 13; *McNaughton* v. *McPherson*, 1980 S.L.T. (Notes) 97), imposes his personal views on a jury (*McMillan* v. *H.M. Advocate*, 1979 S.L.T. (Notes) 68), appears to fall asleep on the bench (*R.* v. *Weston-super-Mare Justices, ex p. Taylor* [1981] Crim. L.R. 179), fails to give proper consideration to an application (*Rae, Petitioner*, 1982 S.L.T. 233), or refuses to disqualify himself from presiding at a trial because of views he had previously expressed (the striking miners' case, *Bradford* v. *McLeod*, 1986 S.L.T. 244), or fails to disqualify himself in a case in which the judge has been a dismissed employee of the accused (*Harper of Oban Ltd* v. *Iain Henderson*, 1988 S.C.C.R. 351) or appears to indicate a belief in the veracity of the Crown witnesses before the defence has been heard (*Hogg* v. *Normand*, 1992 S.C.C.R. 27) he or she can be publicly rebuked and/or reversed on appeal). [On disqualification generally, see I. Dickinson, "Disqualification of Judges on Account of Interest" (1984) 29 J.L.S. 446.] But an appeal is not always available (for example, the case where a rapist was merely fined because the judge held that the victim had been contributorily negligent in hitch-hiking), financially practicable or satisfactory (see *e.g. R.* v. *Langham and Langham* [1972] Crim. L.R. 457—another case where a judge appeared to be asleep). In these situations Scotland is potentially in a stronger position than England since it already possesses two intermediate mechanisms which are capable of development.

Justice, *The Judiciary*, pp. 50–51

"90. In Scotland, the Dean of Faculty has a duty to protect the interest of the Bar and all its members. In the past it was not unknown for him, if counsel were not being given a fair hearing, to intervene personally in order to remind the judge or judges of the rights and privileges of an advocate, and thereafter to remain in court seated beside the counsel appearing in the case, to make sure that the warning was heeded. Nowadays however such a complaint would be dealt with privately and after the event. The Dean investigates the complaint and, if he thinks it justified, he will have a word with the judge in question or possibly with the Lord President (who is expected to take it up with the judge). This procedure appears not to work as well as it should.

91. However, a more useful remedy is provided by the power of the Lord Advocate to investigate any matter connected with the administration of the law and law courts in Scotland. This is regularly invoked with reference to alleged misbehaviour by the lower judiciary, *e.g.* the sheriffs.

In each sheriff court district the Lord Advocate has a local official, the procurator-fiscal, who is responsible only to him and is independent of both police and judiciary. If anyone (lawyer, M.P., private citizen) complains to the Lord Advocate about a sheriff, his complaint will be remitted to the local procurator-fiscal for inquiry. The latter will interview any witness and investigate the complaint privately, and finally report back to the Crown Office (the Lord Advocate's department in Scotland). After considering the report the Lord Advocate may write personally to the sheriff about it, he may ask him to come to the Crown Office to discuss it or in an extreme case he may set in motion the machinery for removal of the sheriff.

92. The Lord Advocate's powers are not statutory but arise from his inherent common law right to inquire into anything which concerns the rights and interests of the public of Scotland . . . There is in principle no reason (even though it might give rise to a delicate situation) why this power should not be exercised in relation to a judge of the Court of Session; so far, however, this has never happened."

If the latter mechanism were to be extended to the Court of Session Bench and if a power of reprimand or censure were invested in the Lord President or a judicial commission, genuine grievances could be remedied without exposing the judiciary to a flood of unfounded and damaging accusations.

B. SALARIES

As a further protection to the independence of the judiciary the salaries of Senators of the College of Justice, sheriffs principal and sheriffs are paid out of the Consolidated Fund. [Administration of Justice Act 1973, s. 9; Sheriff Courts (Scotland) Act 1907, s. 14.] The salaries are therefore not subject to direct Parliamentary control. Further, while the size of the salaries can be increased by statutory order they cannot be reduced.

C. JUDICIAL IMMUNITIES

1. PARLIAMENTARY

The immunity from criticism of the judiciary in Parliament, except where a substantive motion has been tabled, is a custom of both Houses which has occasionally in recent times been honoured more in the breach than in the acceptance. Nevertheless, the following extract accurately summarises the general position.

Shetreet, *Judges on Trial*, p. 163
"The general rule is that the conduct of judges cannot be discussed in Parliament unless upon a substantive motion which admits of a distinct

vote of the House. Likewise, matters awaiting adjudication or pending before the courts cannot be brought before Parliament. As to motions for an inquiry into the conduct of a judge, the principle has been established that unless the *prima facie* case against the judge is strong and unless the charges, if proved, would justify an address for his removal, Parliament will not interfere. Given these principles, it seems that Parliament does not exercise any disciplinary function over judges short of removal by an address, and that it cannot pursue a course with the final aim not of an address for removal but of censure, criticism or condemnation of judicial conduct."

[See, however, the Speaker's ruling at 34 H.C.Deb., col. 285, Dec. 15, 1982.]

2. IMMUNITY FROM SUIT

Judges of the Court of Session and the High Court are absolutely immune from civil suit in respect of acts done and statements made in their judicial capacity, whether or not they are within their jurisdiction and irrespective of malice or improper motive. [*M'Creadie* v. *Thomson*, 1907 S.C. 1176.] The United States Supreme Court has ruled that the same rule holds true for judges of superior or general jurisdiction in America. [*Stump* v. *Sparkman* (1978) 435 U.S. 349.] In England it seems that the immunity ceases if the act done is outwith jurisdiction *and* motivated by malice. [*Sirros* v. *Moore* [1975] Q.B. 118.]

The position is less clear in relation to sheriffs and inferior judges, but John Mitchell has argued [*Constitutional Law* (2nd ed.), pp. 262–263] that sheriffs are as immune as Senators of the College of Justice, but that inferior judges are liable for acts outside their jurisdiction and probably for acts done within their jurisdiction where malice and want of probable cause can be shown.

Whatever the scope of a judge's immunity, commentators are agreed that some immunity is necessary to preserve the independence of the judiciary and to safeguard the administration of justice. [For further discussions of judicial immunities see D.L. Carey Miller, "Defamation by a judge? Fixing the limits?" 1980 J.R. 88 and M. Brazier, "Judicial immunity and the independence of the judiciary" [1976] P.L. 397.]

The problem with judicial independence is that almost every attempt to immunise the judiciary from undue pressure and influence has simultaneously the effect of making them less accountable to the society which they were appointed to serve. It is not clear how this impasse can be overcome. The best course seems to lie in trying to strike an appropriate balance between

independence and accountability. This would extend from the
procedures for judicial appointment to the setting and monitoring
of standards for judicial conduct. Thus, *e.g.* in relation to immunity from suit there may be a case, as Carey Miller has argued, for
restricting immunity from defamation suits to statements which are
reasonably relevant to the matters before the court.

CHAPTER 8

THE FACULTY OF ADVOCATES

Monopolies and Mergers Commission, "Advocates' Services," p. 3
"In essence and in origin the Faculty is an independent corporation consisting of those who have been admitted to practice as advocates before the Court of Session (the supreme civil court of Scotland). It has long been a common feature of courts in Western Europe that there is a defined and recognised group of lawyers admitted to practice as advocates before those courts and having sole right of audience apart (in some but not all cases) from party litigants. From a very early stage, those who were admitted to practice before particular courts formed themselves into independent corporations, which came to administer their own affairs and to regulate matters of professional discipline and conduct. The Faculty became a separate and identifiable corporate body during the late sixteenth or early seventeenth century.

Despite superficial resemblances, the Faculty is in certain basic respects unlike the Bar of England and Wales. Advocates form part of the College of Justice under a legal system which came into existence when Scotland was an independent nation and had close links with the continent. The Faculty has no written constitution but in origin, traditions and structure it can be compared with the Bars of most continental countries and their former colonies."

Faculty Evidence to the Hughes Commission, pp. 4–5
"It is a common feature of these independent corporations of advocates including the Faculty that they elect their own leader, known in some countries as the Dean and in others as the Batonnier. An important aspect of his function is to assert the rights of the corporation and its members vis-a-vis the court and government, to maintain high standards on the part of the members and to adjudicate upon questions of discipline and conduct. Other office-bearers are elected from amongst the general body of members, who have an equal right to speak and vote at meetings. Apart from the office-bearers there is usually a Council whose functions may be executive or merely consultative."

In 1992 the Faculty decided to constitute an elected Council to exercise most of the powers previously exercised by the whole Faculty in general meeting. These include the formulation of policy, making provision for the maintenance of the Library, regulating admission and professional conduct. The Council consists of the Faculty office-bearers and three members each from the ranks of senior counsel, senior juniors and junior juniors together with one elected from the ranks of non-practising members.

[On the history of the Faculty see J.M. Pinkerton's "Introduction" to *The Minute Book of the Faculty of Advocates*, Vol. I (The Stair Society: 1976), the essays contributed by G. Donaldson and N.T. Phillipson to N. MacCormick (ed.), *Lawyers in their Social Setting* (W. Green & Son: 1976) and paras. 499–1301 of Vol. 13 of the *Stair Memorial Encyclopaedia of the Laws of Scotland*.]

I. RECRUITMENT

Entry to the Faculty is regulated by the Faculty, not by legislation. Intrants require to pass professional examinations (though exemption from most of them can be obtained by taking the relevant subjects in a Scottish law degree) and hold a pass in the Diploma in Legal Practice from a Scottish University. They must also undergo a period of practical training (at least 12 months in a solicitor's office as a trainee followed by about 9 months' pupillage or "devilling" to a practising member of Faculty). Special provisions exist for the admission of candidates who are already barristers from England and Wales and Northern Ireland or legal practitioners from another member state of the European Community.

Faculty Evidence to the Hughes Commission, p. 5

"While it is the Court of Session which admits an Intrant to the public office of advocate, the Court since the latter part of the seventeenth century has left it to the Faculty to determine the conditions for admission and to determine whether an Intrant satisfies those conditions . . . The Court will not decline to admit to the Roll of Advocates a person who has been found duly qualified and admitted to membership of the Faculty."

The Hughes Commission, p. 263

"16.61 At present, the content of the devil's training is a matter entirely between him and his master. In practice, the content is constrained by the range of work the master does and many trainees will inevitably find that their work is unrepresentative of the work of the Bar as a whole. On the other hand, since many newly-qualified advocates may receive some of their work through late instructions when more senior advocates have had to call off in particular cases, we have had to consider whether there should be a minimum range of experience which each devil should acquire before he can be considered qualified. It would certainly seem desirable that all devils should gain experience in both civil and criminal work. We recognise, however, that the small size of the Faculty might make it impossible for all devils to acquire such a range of experience within the necessarily short period of devilling. Without imposing an absolute requirement, therefore, we **recommend** that the Faculty should strongly encourage all devils to obtain a wide range of experience. If necessary, this could be facilitated by changing devil masters during the period of devilling."

Pupils, even if they are experienced solicitor pleaders, are not permitted to speak in court. In an innovative move to overcome this problem and to provide free assistance to CAB clients the Faculty reached an agreement with Citizens' Advice Scotland in 1990 that a rota of pupils would be established to provide representation before tribunals for clients of individual bureaux with complex cases. The travelling expenses of the pupils are met by the Faculty. Although the number of clients assisted in any given year is relatively small, the scheme has otherwise been very successful.

[Since 1991, pupil masters are required to complete a report at the end of the period of pupillage confirming that the pupil has displayed sufficient diligence, competence and trustworthiness during his or her pupillage to make them suitable for admission to the Faculty.]

A. ADMISSION

Ultimately admission is determined by a resolution of the Faculty members gathered in public meeting, followed by the declaration of the oath of allegiance to the Sovereign, in open court.

[For an account of the pre-1966 procedure which involved the defence of a thesis in Latin (supposedly authored by the intrant) at public examination, see Pinkerton, "Introduction" (*supra*) and N. Wilson, "The Faculty of Advocates Today" *Acta Juridica* (1966) 227. For a fuller account of admission and pupillage today see paras. 1304–1314, Vol. 13, *Stair Memorial Encyclopaedia of the Laws of Scotland*.]

Professional qualifications aside, the Faculty imposes no formal restrictions on the numbers of candidates seeking admission to the Bar. Nor are Scottish intrants hampered, as English intrants are, by the need to obtain tenancies in chambers, which are in short supply. Nevertheless the cost of entry can still be high. The major outlay is simply living expenses to cover the two-year period from the start of pupillage when fees are not coming in. But there are many other items—the matriculation fee, entry money (payable in instalments), Faculty rates, Widows' and Orphans' Fund dues, indemnity insurance premiums, journal subscriptions, books, travelling expenses and the cost of wig, gown and other items of formal dress. The aspiring advocate requires either savings (over a quarter of recent intrants have practised as solicitors for a period for this reason), a working spouse, an understanding bank manager or private means. While some take the view that the initial outlays are merely the counterpart to the capital required to set up a business, others have expressed concern at the practical barriers which are imposed by the high cost of entry.

TABLE 1

Admissions

Year	Male	Female	All
1975	15	2	17
1976	11	2	13
1977	8	3	11
1978	15	—	15
1979	17	—	17
1980	13	2	15
1981	9	4	13
1982	10	2	12
1983	9	4	13
1984	9	—	9
1985	14	1	15
1986	14	2	16
1987	21	9	30
1988	15	4	19
1989	15	4	19
1990	25	5	30
1991	10	5	15
1992	27	5	32

The Hughes Commission, p. 265

"16.66 The period of unremunerated devilling is one of severe financial hardship, particularly as advocates frequently take a year to recover their fees and can thus have no effective income for about a year following their admission to the Bar. Even then, given that they are unlikely to receive a great deal of work in their first years, the total fees they receive are likely to be small. The financial barriers to entry to the advocate branch of the profession . . . undoubtedly affect the flow of intrants to the Bar, and it has been suggested that this leads to a bias in the class composition of the Bar in favour of those who can support themselves from private means during their period of devilling and for the first years after admission. For these reasons, and because supreme court judges and many sheriffs are recruited from the ranks of practising advocates, we think that the remuneration of devils is a matter of public interest, and [that consideration should be given to] the possibility of making grants available to devils from public funds . . . A further possibility would be for the Faculty to establish an arrangement with a financial institution to provide loans for devils. The Dean of Faculty already has a small loans fund at his disposal to help intrants who require assistance, but this is not

sufficiently large to accommodate those who may at present be discouraged from becoming advocates by the financial difficulties that exist
at the outset of a career at the Bar. We **recommend**, therefore, that the
Faculty should consider the possibility of arranging a wider loan scheme
for devils than is at present available, in view of the importance of
maintaining a representative flow of intrants to the Bar."

[In 1983 a scholarship fund was established from a bequest left by
Lord Reid which has provided about two scholarships a year. In
1992 the Faculty established its own scholarship programme.]

B. TAKING SILK

Scotland like England has a two-tier Bar divided between junior
and senior counsel. Elevation to the rank of senior or Queen's
Counsel is self-initiated, but premature application is discouraged
by the requirement that applicants must give notice of their
intention to apply for the right to wear a silk gown to all juniors
who were admitted to the Bar before them.

Monopolies and Mergers Commission, "Advocates' Services," p. 5
"The method of appointing Senior Counsel is as follows. When an
advocate feels that the time has come for him to take silk, he approaches
the Dean. If the Dean considers that the application is for any reason
undesirable he will say so. If the Dean approves, or if the applicant
insists, the Dean will discuss it with the Lord Justice General. The
applicant will then be told whether or not his application is likely to be
granted and, if not, why not. The formal application for silk is made by
letter to the Lord Justice General asking him to recommend the applicant
to Her Majesty, through the Secretary of State for Scotland, for appointment as one of Her Majesty's Counsel. In practice formal applications are
seldom made unless it is clear that they will be granted. A point to which
the Lord Justice General and the Dean have regard is that the number of
applications for silk granted should not be such as to result in excessive
depletion of the junior Bar. At present juniors are being given silk at
about age 40 after 10 to 15 years in junior practice. The number of Senior
Counsel is dictated by the needs of the work of the Bar."

[For further details on the status and function of senior counsel
and their historical origin in the late nineteenth century see para.
1317 of Vol. 13 of the *Stair Memorial Encyclopaedia of the Laws of
Scotland.*]

II. COMPOSITION

At any given time less than half of the Faculty will be in active
practice as advocates. This is because a member of the Faculty,
once admitted, remains a member even when he or she has ceased

to practise or has taken up an appointment that is incompatible with practice at the Bar. Thus in 1992 the Faculty included 98 judges, 12 academic lawyers, 18 working in central government or in industry, five Members of Parliament, 26 working furth of Scotland and over 280 practising advocates. In the past 30 years between a third and a quarter of practising advocates have been Queen's Counsel—a considerably higher proportion than has been the case in England.

TABLE 2
Size of the Faculty

Year	Nominal	Practising	(Q.C.s)
1710	250	170	
1832	442	?	
1860	300	115	
1876	337	130	
1962	281	106	
1967	285	114	
1975	322	128	(32)
1979	361	148	(36)
1982	387	173	(44)
1984	407	195	(50)
1985	417	202	(50)
1987	455	230	(49)
1990	490	250	(60)
1992	510	290	(75)

TABLE 3
Female Advocates in Practice

Year	Total	Year	Total
1974	3	1984	16
1975	4	1985	17
1976	5	1986	19
1977	6	1987	28
1978	8	1988	32
1979	8	1989	36
1980	8	1990	40
1981	13	1991	45
1982	13	1992	47
1983	16		

In the 20 years following the end of the second World War the practising Bar remained in the range of 100–115 advocates. As Tables 1, 2 and 3 reveal there has been a very considerable increase since then particularly in the past ten years. The same decade has witnessed the advent (for the first time in the Faculty's history) of women advocates practising at the Bar in sizeable numbers. A pilot study by Paxton as late as 1982 revealed that female advocates, although accepted by their male colleagues, were viewed by some with condescension. Only 60 or so women have ever been admitted to the Faculty and only seven have gone on to become Q.C.s., (three of whom were practising in 1992). Paxton found evidence of continuing sex discrimination in two related areas—in the attitude of some instructing solicitors and their clients and in the range of work which came to female advocates. One advocate reported how, when acting as junior counsel at a consultation, she was taken for a secretary by the client who said: "Now I want the wee lassie to tak' this down." Equally startling was another suggestion that: "Is it cos' I'm on legal aid that I've got to tak' a lassie?". Certainly, in 1982 there were some solicitors who would never instruct a woman. Times have changed in the last decade and any residual discrimination against female advocates is dying out as their numbers grow. Nevertheless, female advocates in Scotland have been fortunate that they have not had to overcome discrimination against them in the granting of tenancies in chambers, a problem which their English sisters have had to endure for many years. Moreover, a survey of both branches of the legal profession for *The Lawyer* in 1992 found that 52% of the female respondents complained of encountering discrimination in their work. [See H. Kennedy, "Women at the Bar" in R. Hazell (ed.), *The Bar on Trial* (Quartet Books: 1978), H. Kennedy, *Eve was Framed* (Chatto and Windus: 1992) and *The Lawyer* 8/12/92 at p. 6.]

III. ADVOCATES' SERVICES

Monopolies and Mergers Commission, "Advocates' Services," p. 4 "Advocates do not offer their services directly to the public; they accept instructions from solicitors. The professional services supplied by advocates . . . consist of services in relation to litigation, civil and criminal, in courts, tribunals and inquiries of all kinds, and of the giving of advice (including the drafting of documents) on legal matters."

[Since 1990 it has been competent for an advocate to accept instructions from a member of a recognised professional body without the need to use a solicitor. Over 20 such bodies have been recognised including associations of accountants, architects, actuaries, auctioneers, engineers and surveyors. For further details see para. 1348, Vol. 13, *Stair Memorial Encyclopaedia of the Laws of Scotland*.]

A. MONOPOLIES

For centuries advocates had the sole right of audience in the Court of Session and the High Court of Justiciary (if we exclude party litigants), a right they shared with other United Kingdom barristers before the House of Lords. These monopolies have been slightly eroded in recent years. Solicitors can appear to present unopposed motions in the Court of Session during the Vacations. Secondly, European Community lawyers now have certain rights of audience.

The European Communities (Services of Lawyers) Order 1978 (S.I. No. 1910), art. 5

"*Representation in legal proceedings*
5. No enactment or rule of law practice shall prevent an EEC lawyer from providing any service in relation to any proceedings, whether civil or criminal, before any court, tribunal or public authority (including appearing before and addressing the court, tribunal or public authority) by reason only that he is not an advocate, barrister or solicitor; provided that throughout he is instructed with, and acts in conjunction with, an advocate, barrister or solicitor who is entitled to practise before the court, tribunal or public authority concerned and who could properly provide the service in question."

[This Order implemented E.C. Council Directive No. 77/249/ E.E.C. For the definition of an E.E.C. lawyer see art. 2 of the Order.]

More recently still rights of audience in the supreme courts have been extended to certain solicitors following the passing of sections 24–27 of the Law Reform (Miscellaneous Provisions) (Scotland) Act 1990 (see pp. 215 below).

B. CONCURRENT RIGHTS

Practising advocates have concurrent rights of audience with solicitors before all the inferior courts and tribunals in which legal representation is permitted. In recent years they have frequently been instructed to appear at public inquiries. Advocates also share with solicitors the right to prepare writs for gain which relate to legal proceedings (see p. 237 below) but in practice it is the advocates who normally draft written pleadings in proceedings before the superior courts.

C. SENIOR AND JUNIOR COUNSEL

The division of labour between junior and senior counsel is now less clear cut than once was the case. In general, junior counsel are responsible for the written pleadings and the less onerous oral advocacy and advisory work. Senior counsel are usually instructed to conduct the more important types of litigation (usually with the assistance of junior counsel) and receive the more responsible advisory work.

The Hughes Commission, p. 227

"15.39 Following the report of the Monopolies and Mergers Commission on the supply of services by senior counsel, the so called 'two counsel rule' was suspended in 1977. The two counsel rule was a requirement in most civil proceedings that junior counsel had to be instructed whenever a senior was engaged; in criminal proceedings, on the other hand, it was possible for a senior counsel to be engaged on his own. Since 1977 there has no longer been any requirement to engage junior counsel when a senior counsel is instructed, although the senior has a right to insist that a junior must be instructed if he considers the case warrants it. The client has the reciprocal right to decline to instruct any particular advocate who so insists; and so far as we can judge from the relatively limited period of operation of the new arrangements they appear to be operating satisfactorily."

D. WORKING ARRANGEMENTS

Each advocate has a box in the main corridor of Parliament House in which instructions are placed and papers kept. His or her "place of work" during court hours is the Advocates' Library. For reasons of convenience and expense over two-thirds of the Bar now practise exclusively from Parliament House although some counsel (mainly seniors) retain "chambers" in the New Town for consultations with solicitors and clients after court hours.

In 1971 the Faculty set up a non-profitmaking company entitled Faculty Services Ltd. which employs the advocates' clerks, provides secretarial facilities and is responsible for the invoicing and collection of fees due to counsel. The 10 clerks each handle the work of a number of advocates colloquially known as their "stables." Each clerk is responsible for arranging his or her counsels' diaries, fixing consultations, suggesting replacement counsel and negotiating counsel's fee.

Monopolies and Mergers Commission, "Advocates' Services," p. 6

"25. Throughout his professional life, every advocate operates entirely on his own. The Faculty, or Faculty Services Limited, provides most facilities needed and any other sharing of facilities is purely in the nature of an *ad hoc* 'overhead-sharing' arrangement. There is no 'chambers' system such as exists in England. If an advocate cannot perform an item of work for which he has been instructed, he must (unless the matter is urgent) return the instructions to his clerk. The latter must seek fresh instructions from the solicitor before passing the work to another advocate, unless the matter is urgent or the clerk has a special arrangement with the solicitor. If the matter is urgent, the advocate passes the instructions to another advocate either directly or through the clerk. An advocate cannot employ another to help him nor is there any form of partnership."

It was suggested to the Hughes Commission that the ban on partnerships for advocates works against the interests of new advocates trying to get established or advocates who fall ill. The Faculty argued against any change stating that it would reduce the choice of counsel available to parties. The Hughes Commission concluded that the ban should continue.

Despite the Commission's conclusion on this point the Government in pursuit of its policy on deregulation and the elimination of restrictive practices included a provision in the Law Reform (Miscellaneous Provisions) (Scotland) Act 1990 on partnerships between advocates and between advocates and other professionals. Section 31 of the Act requires that any rule prohibiting such partnerships has to be approved by the Lord President and the Secretary of State (after consultation with the Director General of Fair Trading). The Director General's Report on the Faculty of Advocates' proposed rule which continued to outlaw such partnerships was published in June 1992. He concluded that a ban on partnerships between advocates or between advocates and other professionals would not significantly restrict or distort competition and would preserve a pool of independent advocates as well as maximising the range of choice for clients. The Director, perhaps influenced by media reports of substantial fees alleged to have been charged by counsel in the Orkney and Piper Alpha inquiries, nevertheless expressed concern as to the breadth of the choice available to clients in terms of advocates' fees.

One factor which contributes to the public's freedom of choice of counsel is the "cab rank rule."

The Hughes Commission, pp. 227–228

"15.40 The 'cab rank rule' is a professional rule applying to advocates and it is incorporated in a rule of court which states that:

'No advocate, without very good cause, shall refuse to act for any person tendering a reasonable fee, under pain of deprivation of his office of advocate.'

In practice, what this rule means is that an advocate cannot refuse to accept a case on the grounds that he does not like a client or his cause . . .

There are, of course, recognised circumstances which justify an advocate declining a case, the main ones being that he is already acting for a party with a conflicting interest; ill health; or that he has already been instructed in a case which would be likely to be called in court at or about the same time. We understand that one of the main benefits of the cab rank rule so far as the public interest is concerned is that there cannot be any occasion when a litigant would find himself without representation. If the advocate of the client's choice is for a good reason unable to take the case, the cab rank rule normally ensures that another suitable advocate is available."

As the Faculty pointed out in its evidence to the Hughes Commission, the cab rank rule prevents formal specialisation at the Scottish Bar, although individual advocates do come to acquire specialised practices to a greater or lesser extent.

E. REFORM

From time to time in the last 100 years, whenever litigation has decreased or concern over the cost of litigation has increased, dissident voices have been heard in Scotland as to the merits of the divided profession. The separation between counsel and solicitors it is said involves unnecessary expense and duplication of effort—in short that it acts as a restrictive practice which is not in the public interest. Inevitably this was a topic on which the Hughes Commission received considerable evidence—the bulk of it favouring the status quo.

The Hughes Commission, p. 231

"15.50 Our feeling after weighing the evidence is that we should be very hesitant to make any recommendation which could result in a diminution or restriction of the legal services which are available at the present time; and we are, on balance, more impressed by the arguments in favour of, than those against, the present divided profession. In particular, we see great value in having an independent advocate service which is available to all solicitors and, therefore, to all clients in Scotland. One of the strengths of the independent Faculty of Advocates based in Edinburgh is the concentration of facilities in the Advocates Library, in Parliament House, Edinburgh. This is a significant factor in keeping advocates' costs low and in making available to them adequate opportunities for research. While we appreciate that modern technological developments will in due course allow lawyers outwith Edinburgh to have equally good access to legal texts stored on electronic retrieval systems, we feel that the concentration of the Faculty in Edinburgh also allows opportunities for informal exchange of information and opinion which would not be as easy if the advocate branch of the profession were distributed up and down the country. Another benefit of the location of the separate advocates branch of the profession in Edinburgh is that it strengthens the control of discipline and the maintaining of high ethical standards and we have no doubt that for these reasons alone it is in the public interest. We **recommend,** therefore, that the legal profession in Scotland should continue to consist of two branches, namely solicitors and advocates."

[For further arguments on the unification of the profession, see **Hughes**, paras. 15.44–49 and S.S. Robertson, "Divided We Fall?" (1970) 15 J.L.S. 219.]

For a while in the late Eighties the topic of fusion attracted more serious consideration from both branches of the English legal profession. However, many members of both branches of the profession continued to be fiercely opposed to fusion. Interest began to shift to less radical options. Michael Zander suggested that the restrictive practices relating to litigation practice should be removed but that fusion should be a matter for individual practitioners to decide.

Zander, *Legal Services for the Community,* pp. 173–174
"The ideal would seem to be a situation where the rules permit the profession to organise itself in whatever way seems beneficial to *individual practitioners* in the light of their inclinations and the needs of their clients. There should, therefore, be no rule preventing lawyers from taking instructions only from other lawyers—but equally, legislation should prohibit any rule requiring it. Whilst most lawyers would . . . continue as before, some might experiment with new forms of organisation. Some solicitors would take cases in the higher courts . . . some barristers would take instructions from clients such as accountants, surveyors, banks and insurance companies, whilst others would be prepared to act directly for clients generally. (Barristers who held clients' moneys would, of course, have to be made subject to the same strict rules as now apply to solicitors.) Given the deep conservatism of the legal profession the probability is that change, if there were any, would be extremely slow. It would move at the speed at which lawyers themselves wanted to go. This at least should be permitted."

Zander's proposal is somewhat akin to the position favoured by the Law Society of Scotland known as the "New Zealand option". In New Zealand every intrant to the profession is admitted as both a barrister and a solicitor. The intrant then obtains a practising certificate to practise as a barrister, or a solicitor, or as a barrister and solicitor. In all three of these categories full rights of audience are enjoyed. However, those practising as barristers only, may not do so in partnership. This has ensured the survival of a separate Bar while offering full rights of audience to solicitors and barristers alike. However, the publication of the Scottish Office consultation paper, *The Practice of the Solicitor Profession in Scotland* (1987) contained only the proposals that rights of audience in the supreme courts be extended to suitably qualified solicitors and rights of audience generally should be extended to non-lawyers. The Law Society responded enthusiastically to the first whilst rejecting the second. The Faculty of Advocates rejected both.

In the event the Law Reform (Miscellaneous Provisions) (Scotland) Act 1990 contains both provisions. Section 24 (enacting a new section 25A to the Solicitors (Scotland) Act 1980) creates a framework by which solicitors can obtain the requisite extended rights of audience. It provides that solicitors seeking rights of audience in the Court of Session or House of Lords or the Judicial Committee of the Privy Council on the one hand or the High Court of Justiciary on the other must undergo a course of training in evidence and pleading in the supreme courts and demonstrate an adequate knowledge of relevant aspects of practice, procedure and issues of professional conduct. The Practice Rules relating to extended rights of audience for solicitors (Admission as a Solicitor with Extended Rights (Scotland) Rules 1992) were drawn up by the Law Society with the approval of the Lord President and the Secretary of State. They provide for a period of induction training covering the procedures and practices of the supreme courts, sitting-in in either the Court of Session or the High Court of Justiciary in Edinburgh, and examinations covering evidence, pleading, practice, procedure and professional conduct. While suitably experienced solicitors can be exempted from most of these requirements, they cannot be exempted from the examinations.

The Faculty of Advocates argued that solicitor advocates should be subject to the cab rank rule. This was opposed by the Law Society. Section 25A(6) contains a compromise. Solicitor advocates must give priority to their supreme court work and the Society has a collective obligation to find a solicitor advocate to represent any client with a case before the supreme courts who wishes representation by a solicitor advocate. Solicitor advocates, however, are not required to take every case that comes to them in their own field even if it is accompanied by a reasonable fee.

It remains to be seen how many solicitors will apply to become solicitor advocates with extended rights of audience in either the supreme civil or criminal courts (or both). Over 100 expressed interest in each but in the event only 32 solicitor advocates were admitted at the initial ceremonies. The crucial factor seems to relate to levels of remuneration. Advocates require little in the way of offices and back-up staff. As a result their overheads run at below 20% of their gross fees. Solicitors in even the most efficient firms are fortunate if only 60% of their gross fees go to overheads. Many firms operate with more adverse proportions than this. It follows that if solicitor advocates are paid the same rates as advocates they will not find it cost-effective to practise as solicitor advocates. While it appears fair that a solicitor advocate should be able to claim a fee for the solicitor's aspect of the work as well as the advocacy aspects, it appears that legal aid will only pay both sets of fees where two separate lawyers are involved (thus destroying most of the point of the reform). Even in private work the solicitor advocate will be at a disadvantage because of the overheads problem. Certainly on the civil side the notion of solicitor advocates being out of their offices for days on end while they attend a substantial proof seems a likely recipe for ruin. It follows that on the civil side solicitor advocates are most likely to appear during contested motions or short proofs where the counsel of their choice withdraws at the last minute and it is considered advisable that the proof be handled by a representative who is familiar with the case and the client.

Section 25 of the Law Reform (Miscellaneous Provisions) (Scotland) Act 1990 confers rights of audience on members of professional or other bodies whose applications have been accepted by the Lord President and the Secretary of State. This highly controversial provision only survived the Committee stage in the Commons by the casting vote of the chairman. Although applauded by the consumer bodies in Scotland as a move designed to increase client choice, the provision is strongly opposed by both branches of the legal profession. As yet there have been no moves to implement this part of the legislation.

IV. PROFESSIONAL PRACTICE, CONDUCT AND DISCIPLINE

A. COMPLAINTS AND DISCIPLINE

In contrast to the solicitors' branch of the profession, ultimate authority in determining what constitutes professional misconduct in an advocate lies in the Faculty and its elected office bearers, particularly the Dean. Unwritten standards of conduct governing the professional and private life of the advocate have existed for centuries, supplemented in specific areas by rulings issued from time to time by particular Deans. (The rulings of former Deans can be abrogated or modified by the current Dean.) The current Disciplinary Rules for the Faculty date from 1988. Any complaints against the conduct of advocates are addressed to the Dean who will either investigate them himself or arrange for their investigation. In determining the sanction to be imposed, if any, the Dean will frequently consult his Council. That year also saw the establishment of a Disciplinary Tribunal for the Faculty which can both adjudicate on complaints and serve as a sentencing body. However, any determination or disposal by the Tribunal is subject to review by the Dean who may modify or rescind it. To date the Tribunal has had very little to do, although a Q.C. was disciplined by the Tribunal in 1993 for breaching client confidentiality. Following the passing of the Law Reform (Miscellaneous Provisions) (Scotland) Act 1990 advocates can be found to have delivered inadequate professional services. As with solicitors, where complainants are dissatisfied with the way in which their complaint has been handled by the relevant professional body, they may write to the Scottish Legal Services Ombudsman (see p. 242 above). By 1993 only two or three such complaints had reached the Ombudsman.

The Hughes Commission commented adversely on the lack of a formal written code of conduct for advocates and recommended that one should be promulgated. Perhaps spurred on by the need to provide something for lawyers from E.E.C. countries the Faculty published a *Guide to the Professional Conduct of Advocates* in 1988.

B. PROFESSIONAL NEGLIGENCE

The scope of an advocate's liability for negligence is unclear. A century ago it was thought that an advocate could not be held liable for professional negligence. This was because he had no contract with his client, because of the discretion entrusted to and the judgment expected of counsel in the conduct of litigation and because at that time the law of delict provided no remedy for professional negligence.

Batchelor v. Pattison and Mackersy
(1876) 3 R. 914

LORD PRESIDENT (Inglis): "An advocate in undertaking the conduct of a cause in the Court enters into no contract with his client, but takes on himself an office in the performance of which he owes a duty, not to his client only, but also to the Court, to the members of his own profession, and to the public. From this it follows that he is not at liberty to decline, except in very special circumstances, to act for any litigant who applies for his advice and aid, and that he is bound in any cause that comes into Court to take the retainer of the party who first applies to him. It follows, also, that he cannot demand or recover by action any remuneration for his services, though in practice he receives *honoraria* in consideration of these services. Another result is, that while the client may get rid of his counsel whenever he pleases, and employ another, it is by no means easy for a counsel to get rid of his client. On the other hand, the nature of the advocate's office makes it clear that in the performance of his duty he must be entirely independent, and act according to his own discretion and judgment in the conduct of the cause for his client. His legal right is to conduct the cause without any regard to the wishes of his client, so long as his mandate is unrecalled, and what he does *bona fide* according to his own judgment will bind his client, and will not expose him to any action for what he has done, even if the client's interests are thereby prejudiced."

When the House of Lords ruled in *Hedley Byrne* v. *Heller* [1964] A.C. 465 that negligent advice could give rise to delictual liability even where there was no contractual relationship between the parties, one of the principal bases for counsel's immunity disappeared. This was confirmed by the House in *Rondel* v. *Worsley* [1969] 1 A.C. 191 but the House also concluded that sufficient public policy grounds existed to justify the continuation of counsel's immunity. These were (1) counsel's duties to the court (which he should not be inhibited from fulfilling by the fear of an action from his client), (2) the cab-rank rule, (3) the general immunity from civil liability which attaches to all persons participating in proceedings before a court of justice and (4) the undesirability of litigating again between counsel and client what has already been litigated between the client and the opponent.

Nevertheless it was established in *Rondel* v. *Worsley* that counsel's immunity was not a blanket one and that it only applied to such cases as fell within the area of public policy. This entailed that henceforth counsel must be treated as liable for professional negligence except in certain specified situations—but there was no consensus amongst the Law Lords as to exactly what these situations were. In *Saif Ali* v. *Sydney Mitchell & Co.* [1980] A.C. 198 the Law Lords had to decide more precisely where the dividing line between liability and immunity was to be drawn. The majority held that counsel's immunity from suit extended only to his conduct of a case in court and those matters of pre-trial work which were so intimately connected with the conduct of the case in court that they could fairly be said to be preliminary decisions affecting the way that case was conducted when it came to a hearing. The majority also held (*obiter*) that a solicitor acting as an advocate in court enjoys the same immunity as counsel. [Yet see *Murray* v. *Reilly*, 1963 S.L.T. (Notes) 49.]

Gamble, "Advocates' Liability," pp. 5–6
"The result of *Ali* is that counsel are now potentially liable (in addition to pure opinion cases) in all decisions connected with litigation, except the actual court-room appearances and other work necessarily and intimately connected with these, where they will continue to enjoy immunity. This latter category seems to include decisions on which witnesses are to be called or other evidence used, *e.g.* notes on the line or specifications of documents in Scots practice. It seems not to cover written pleadings or settlements or tendering in cases and advice thereon. The majority

speeches do not seek to particularise the test for immunity too much and there is certainly force in the minority view that its application will be difficult and may lead to uncertainty. It is submitted in general that it can be easily inferred from the thrust of the majority speeches that the test of intimate connection will be interpreted restrictively . . .

Now that the areas of liability and immunity have been delimited more precisely than formerly, what is important is to consider the circumstances where counsel can be liable for professional negligence in the post-*Ali* situation. It must be emphasised that removal of the former wide immunity does not mean automatic liability in every case of mistake or error of judgment. Counsel are now, over a large area of their work, subject to the same liability as other professional persons, no less but also no more. This liability is not excessively exacting. It is generally stated to be that no member of the relevant profession would have taken the course under attack or scrutiny if he had been acting with ordinary care and skill. This is familiar law as regards medical negligence, but it seems to represent a more general principle. In its application to counsel, it must be stressed that attacks on decisions involving judgment and discretion are unlikely to succeed and most matters where counsel are instructed include these very elements. This point is made in all the majority speeches in *Ali*. Thus the elements of discretion used in the nineteenth century cases to justify immunity for counsel reappear in *Ali* as the basic defences open to him. The practical result may well be the same in that it is submitted that the likelihood of an action succeeding against an advocate is relatively slight . . .

An important point requiring brief mention is whether *Ali* necessarily represents the law of Scotland. As an English decision, it is not strictly binding in Scotland, but as it is on a point of so-called "general jurisprudence" it is entitled to the highest respect and may be seen as perhaps almost binding. In particular, if the liability of counsel were to be litigated upon in Scotland, the Court of Session would, it seems, standing *Ali*, at least be entitled to over-rule earlier inconsistent Scots authorities."

Rodger, "At Risk," p. 465

"It seems unlikely that, if dealing with a Scottish appeal on the same point, the House of Lords would feel that they should not follow *Saif Ali* merely because it was an English case . . . None the less, the fact remains that *Saif Ali* is strictly speaking only highly persuasive and that the leading Scottish case is *Batchelor* v. *Pattison and Mackersy*, and that the reasoning at least in *Batchelor* is largely inconsistent with the approach in *Saif Ali*. . . . It would not, it is submitted, be sufficient under current notions of negligence, for an advocate to say that, however negligent his actings, they were done *bona fide* according to his judgement. If the exercise of judgement were shown to be negligent, then he would be liable. So one is forced to the conclusion that the reasoning in *Batchelor* no longer affords a safe guide to the reasoning which would be likely to find ultimate acceptance in a Scottish case today. . . .

So the Scots law position is rather unsatisfactory. We are left with a binding Inner House decision which looks unlikely to survive serious challenge either by reference to a larger court or by appeal to the House of Lords, but which still technically binds all courts lower than these. . . . It seems likely that lawyers and insurers will accept that *Saif Ali* represents the real position. There will scarcely be a rush on the part of the lawyers to clarify the position by means of litigation, so that *Batchelor* could well have a long, if sickly, life ahead of it."

[See further on the advocate's liability for negligence, para. 1380, Vol. 13, the *Stair Memorial Encyclopaedia of the Laws of Scotland*.]

The Faculty of Advocates certainly considers that the English cases might be followed in Scotland and since 1976 it has had a Compulsory Indemnity Insurance scheme. All practising advocates are required to have cover up to at least £100,000. To date there have been no claims against advocates under indemnity policies.

With the recent retreat by the House of Lords in the field of liability for negligent acts, it seems unlikely that we shall see much judicial threat to the advocate's (or solicitor advocate's) singular immunity from liability for professional negligence in the near future. Indeed, the Law Reform (Miscellaneous Provisions) (Scotland) Act 1990, s. 27 makes it clear that the immunity for liability for negligence will extend to non-lawyers who exercise rights of audience under the Act. This is unlikely to satisfy the critics of the immunity.

Wilson, "Carte Blanche for Counsel," pp. 211–212
"If advocates are held to be immune from liability for [negligence it leads to] the paradox . . . that lawyers . . . apply the rule 'ignorance of the law is no excuse' to all except the legal *élite*. Naturally no system which imposes liability for negligence on lawyers does so except in very clear cases—cases where no advocate of ordinary skill acting with ordinary care would have conducted himself as did the defender . . . The idea that the courts would be flooded with actions against advocates seems unrealistic. If they were, paradoxically the Bar as a whole would not lose. The professional solidarity which protects the medical man when sued would be even stronger if the defender was an advocate. As with the artist or the actor the difficulties of proving that an advocate was incompetent are formidable. Alleged negligence in cross-examination, for example, would seem to be no easier and no more difficult to prove than the surgeon's negligent handling of a scalpel in a very delicate operation or negligent treatment by a psychiatrist . . . If an advocate has been careless in the preparation and production of his case, or has failed in his duty to court and client and also perhaps to the public who finance legal aid, why should it be concluded that public policy must be invoked to protect him?

The surgeon and physician have not been spared the prospect of possible litigation by a vexatious and disgruntled patient . . . Other professions have comparable problems—yet the courts do not shield them from harassing actions on grounds of public policy. Professions other than the Bar may well enviously conclude that counsel . . . 'with the connivance of the judges, built for themselves an ivory tower and have lived in it ever since at the expense of their clients'."

The rationale for the immunity has been undermined by the judiciary itself. The argument from contract was abandoned in *Rondel* and that from the existence of the cab-rank rule had disappeared by the time of *Saif Ali*. Of the three remaining bases for the now limited immunity, the view that the immunity is required to encourage counsel to fulfil their obligations to the court seems suspect as Lord Diplock recognised in *Saif Ali* (at p. 220). In fact, as the Faculty of Advocates accepted in their evidence to the Hughes Commission the strongest argument for the retention of the immunity is because it is necessary that litigation should have a cut-off point.

Faculty Evidence to the Hughes Commission, pp. 24–25
"In a claim based upon alleged negligence in the conduct of a case in Court, there could be no way of investigating the question whether that negligence was the cause of any alleged loss without examining the whole facts and circumstances of the case . . . [*i.e.*] retrying the previous action . . . The fundamental reason why the conduct of a case in Court should not be scrutinised in later proceedings has nothing to do with the particular status requirements or deserts of Advocates as such or advocacy as a profession, but is an aspect of the public policy requirement that cases concluded by judicial decisions should not be reopened."

The obvious reply to this argument is why should the cut-off point be drawn where it is? If our legal system recognises the need for appeals (and it is not a ground for appeal that one's counsel has been negligent) and the occasional need for a retrial in civil and criminal cases, why should any investigation of professional negligence by a lawyer in a courtroom be prohibited? As the extracts from Gamble and Wilson suggest, there is no likelihood that if the immunity were removed it would lead to a flood of litigation. The Scottish Legal Aid Board scrutinises professional negligence applications carefully and would not support frivolous actions.

In the last analysis the question is, can the immunity from professional negligence for those conducting advocacy in court be justified when brain surgeons or heart transplant consultants are not so privileged? Do we really believe that litigation is more important than life?

CHAPTER 9

SOLICITORS

Solicitors (formerly known also as writers or law agents) constitute by far the larger sector of the legal profession in Scotland. The bulk of practising solicitors work in private practice (either on their own or in partnership) but in recent years an increasing proportion have been attracted into industry, public bodies and local or central government (see Table 6 below). Traditionally solicitors in private practice in Scotland have been seen as, and have seen themselves as general persons of business. However, in recent years it has become commonplace for solicitors (and those in larger firms in particular) to specialise. The professional body of Scottish solicitors is the Law Society of Scotland.

I. RECRUITMENT

Solicitors (Scotland) Act 1980, ss. 4, 5

"4. No person shall be qualified to practise as a solicitor unless—
    (*a*) he has been admitted as a solicitor; and
    (*b*) his name is on the roll; and
    (*c*) . . . he has in force a certificate issued by the Council of the Law society in accordance with the provisions of this [Act] authorising him to practise as a solicitor (referred to in this Act as a 'practising certificate').

5. (1) The Council may, with the concurrence of the Lord President, make regulations for—
    (*a*) practical training;
    (*b*) attendance at a course of legal education;
    (*c*) the passing of examinations . . . "

A. EDUCATION AND TRAINING

TABLE 1

Undergraduate Students in Law in Scotland

	1965–66	1970–71	1975–76	1980–81	1990–91
Aberdeen	124	212	352	380	450
Dundee	123	192	243	287	400
Edinburgh	430	443	508	512	560
Glasgow	357	299	391	447	510
Strathclyde	—	114	206	224	256
Total	1,034	1,260	1,700	1,850	2,176

[Sources: Report of the Royal Commission on Legal Services in Scotland (Cmnd 7846) (1980) (the Hughes Report); The Law Schools.]

Since 1825 admission to legal practice in Scotland has required a period of practical training (an apprenticeship or, more recently, a traineeship) coupled with the attainment of certain educational standards (the passing of examinations). Intrants have had the choice of taking the university examinations and degree (possession of which reduced the length of the practical training) or the examinations set by the professional bodies. In recent years the former has proved much the more popular route (since 1979 about 95% have taken this route). As Table 1 shows the number of undergraduate students taking a law degree in Scotland has more than doubled since 1965–66. Table 2 refines the picture by revealing that the number of Scottish law graduates peaked in 1979 and then dipped during the early 1980s but that towards the end of the decade numbers began to rise again.

TABLE 2
University graduates

Year	Law Graduates	Diploma Graduates	Year	Law Graduates	Diploma Graduates
1970	312	—	1981	542	230
1971	352	—	1982	483	407
1972	329	—	1983	486	425
1973	350	—	1984	529	454
1974	371	—	1985	468	464
1975	406	—	1986	464	415
1976	443	—	1987	468	400
1977	487	—	1988	511	383
1978	503	—	1989	536	415
1979	545	—	1990	509	408
1980	529	—			

[The Law Schools]

THE SOCIAL BACKGROUND OF LAW STUDENTS

Such evidence as we have suggests that law students in Scotland form a relatively homogeneous population. The social background of the students (judged by parental occupation) does not vary greatly between the law schools. In each, students from social classes I and II are heavily over-represented. Thus in Glasgow 77% of law students admitted from 1971–79 and in Edinburgh 70% of law students admitted from 1976–80 were from social classes I and II. The survey of students and apprentices carried out in 1978–79 on behalf of the Hughes Commission revealed a similar picture.

TABLE 3

Socio-economic group of fathers of law students and apprentices

		Students			Male household heads (GB 1976)
	Total	Intend solicitor training on graduation	Others	Apprentices	
Sample (unweighted)	595	350	245	419	
Socio-economic group of father	%	%	%	%	%
Professional	31	27	37	27	5
Employer/manager	30	32	27	25	17
Intermediate and junior non-manual	18	19	16	17	17
Skilled manual and own account workers	15	15	16	20	40
Semi-skilled and unskilled manual	2	3	1	4	21
Armed Forces/unclassifiable	3	3	3	7	*

[Source: Hughes Commission, Appendix 6, Table 1.3.]

In the Hughes survey 15 per cent of students and 21 per cent of apprentices stated that they had close relatives who were or had been lawyers in Scotland. Surveys carried out by the Law Society of Scotland (the latest in 1980) have shown that under 15 per cent of intrants in the last five years have had existing family connections with the profession. There is some evidence to suggest that the largest single parental occupational group from which law students are drawn is the teaching profession. There is also evidence that the intake of female students to Scottish law faculties has been increasing steadily. In 1970 less than 20% of law students in Scotland were female. Within 20 years they had reached parity with the males, a position which they still retain.

The Hughes Commission, pp. 244–5

Admission of law students
"16.8 In selecting among the candidates who present themselves, the universities rely to a very large extent on academic attainment at school. We have reviewed this practice because there is no guarantee that those with the best school results will make either the best law students or the best lawyers. Scottish Certificate of Education Higher and Ordinary grade marks have been criticised as being measures of a student's ability to learn and regurgitate material, rather than affording a measure of intellectual potential. Further, we think that a selection procedure which

depends so heavily on good school examination results is liable to produce a very homogeneous group of students, and thus limit the scope for a fruitful exchange of experience amongst them. An important unintended consequence of selecting those with the best school marks can often be the rejection of a disproportionate number of candidates from working class backgrounds and from the newer six-year secondary schools. Indeed, it has been alleged that this factor has contributed to the slowness of the profession to respond to people's need for legal assistance in the areas of personal rights, particularly those created by housing, social welfare and employment statutes in recent years.

16.9 We agree with the Ormrod Committee when they say 'the demands which the legal profession has to meet, and the roles which professional lawyers are called upon to play in society, are so varied, and require such different qualities, that the profession will always need to recruit men and women widely of different character, temperament and intellectual attainments'. We do not believe that any form of quota system for university admissions would be desirable; nor do we think that any explicit discrimination in favour of particular groups who are at present disadvantaged ('positive discrimination') would be practicable or acceptable. Nevertheless, we think that the present criteria for admission to university law faculties call for some adjustment, and we **recommend** that universities should use wider criteria than academic attainment at school when selecting law students for admission. In particular, we wish to see more account taken of the following considerations: firstly, each applicant's attitude for, and interest in, the study of law; secondly, the need for a student population more varied in age and socio-economic background so as to create a better educational environment; and thirdly, the need to ensure that all pupils of ability and potential, from whatever school background, have a real opportunity to study law at university if they so wish. To achieve this, the universities should continue to set a realistic minimum entry qualification based on academic attainment at school; that is a minimum level which indicates a high probability that the student will be able to fulfil the degree requirements. The three criteria outlined above should, however, come into play when the universities are deciding which candidates to admit of those who have the necessary minimum qualifications. We wish to emphasise that the minimum qualification should not be lowered for particular candidates; rather, once the minimum has been set, the selection should not favour exclusively those who have the best school marks."

[The Ormrod Committee reported on legal education in England and Wales in 1971; Cmnd. 4595]

Ultimately, it is a matter for debate whether the Hughes Commission's argument that a social imbalance in the population of law students is not in the interests of the public or the profession, has been made out. Nor is it clear whether the reform which the Commission favoured in this field can be achieved. What would happen if two applicants existed with similar academic records but one had a higher aptitude score than the other while the other ranked above the first in terms of social background desirability? Could such conflicts be resolved without in effect introducing a quota system or positive discrimination in some shape or form?

B. PRACTICAL TRAINING

Prior to 1980 intrants to the profession received their practical training by becoming indentured apprentices. Growing dissatisfaction in the 1970s with the apprenticeship as a form of training led to discussions between the Law Society, the Faculty of Advocates and the university law faculties. The outcome of the discussions was a proposal that a compulsory, one-year, full-time university-based postgraduate Diploma in Legal Practice should be introduced. The Diploma would provide the all-round practical training with a prescribed minimum standard of competence which was becoming increasingly difficult to attain in apprenticeships. The proposal was implemented and since October 1980, subject to transitional arrangements, all intrants to the profession must have obtained the Diploma. The Diploma is followed by a two-year "contract of training" with a solicitor.

TABLE 4
Apprenticeships 1935–1979 & Traineeships 1982–1992

Year	Apprentices/ Trainees	Year	Apprentices/ Trainees
1935	170	1972	278
1950	174	1973	315
1951	173	1974	314
1952	155	1975	328
1953	145	1976	354
1954	108	1977	385
1955	83	1978	390
1956	85	1979	430
1957	83	1982	392
1958	93	1983	399
1959	105	1984	393
1960	78	1985	420
1961	75	1986	360
1962	35	1987	365
1963	47	1988	384
1964	113	1989	453
1969	215	1990	431
1970	248	1991	403
1971	245	1992	395

[Source: The Law Society of Scotland.]

Table 4 shows that following a decline in apprenticeships during the early 1960s the demand for apprenticeships—fuelled by the ever increasing stream of LL.B. graduates (the full-time LL.B. degree was introduced in 1961)—grew steadily from 1964 to 1979 before levelling out in the 1980s. The figures suggest that approximately 80% of law graduates in the late 1970s were going on to the profession. One unexpected consequence of the introduction of the Diploma and traineeships was that the perennial student desire "to keep one's options open" led to 90% of graduates in the early 1980s wanting to take the Diploma. In 1985 the Government introduced a quota for Diploma grants which was lowered to 390 per annum in 1987—well below the demand for Diploma places (see Table 2). Perhaps because of this, by the early 1990s only 80% of law graduates were entering the Diploma. Nevertheless, the recession and a cut back in traineeship places available in the profession has ensured that the demand for traineeships and assistantships in the profession has begun to considerably exceed the supply. Even after the recession is over, the Government's commitment to the substantial expansion of higher education means that we are likely to move to a situation (which exists in many continental countries) where almost half of the Scottish law graduates by the year 2000 will be unable to find a job within the profession.

C. ADMISSION

Solicitors (Scotland) Act 1980, s. 6(1)

"Subject to the provisions of this section, no person shall be admitted as a solicitor in Scotland unless—
  (a) he is aged 21 years or over; and
  (b) he has satisfied the Council—
       (i) that he has complied with the provisions of any regulations made under section 5 that apply to him; and
       (ii) that he is a fit and proper person to be solicitor, and has obtained from the Council a certificate to that effect; and
  (c) he has paid such sum in respect of his admission as has been fixed by the Council with the approval of the Lord President."

TABLE 5

Solicitors admitted to the profession between 1949–1991

Year	Male	Female	All
1949	182	9	191
1952	113	12	125
1955	118	16	134
1958	74	7	81
1961	86	8	94
1964	65	4	69
1967	117	24	141
1970	102	10	112
1973	206	35	241
1976	224	59	283
1978	239	69	308
1980	265	132	397
1982	242	139	381
1984	256	171	427
1985	233	182	415
1986	223	186	419
1987	197	190	387
1988	207	175	382
1989	195	185	380
1990	203	194	397
1991	241	243	484

[Source: The Law Society of Scotland.]

Tables 4 and 5 reveal two trends. First, that from the mid-1960s onwards, the numbers entering the profession have been steadily rising until the late 1980s when numbers plateaued. Since 1990 the growth has begun again. Secondly, that the increase in female students has been reflected in the number of women entering the profession. (Over 55% of those admitted in 1992 as compared with 11% in 1975, were female.)

II. COMPOSITION

TABLE 6

Practising Solicitors

	1954	1992	% increase
Private Practice (Partners/Consultants)	2,420	3,678	52
Private Practice (Qualified Assistants)	445	2,116	376
Local Authorities	253	635	151
Central Government and Public Bodies	106	522	392
Industry/Commerce	48	241	402
Miscellaneous	34	299	779
	3,306	7,491	127%

[Source: Law Society Annual Reports.]

The trends in Tables 4 and 5 have had an effect on the composition of the profession. In the mid-1960s only 33% of the profession was aged under 40, by 1985 60% of the profession was under 40 and 27% under 30. (By 1992 the proportions had begun to drop again to 58% and 20% respectively). Again in 1975 only 9% of enrolled solicitors were female. By 1985 the figure had risen to 21% and in 1992 it was 31%. This does not necessarily mean that discrimination against women in the profession has been eliminated. A survey conducted by the Law Society of Scotland (at the suggestion of its Future of the Profession Committee) of its women members in 1984 revealed that many female solicitors consider the profession has not yet adapted to the needs of the increasing numbers of women entering the profession.

Law Society Report on Women in the Profession, pp. 2–3

"It is clear from the responses that the women members believe there is a need for change and do consider that they are discriminated against in many ways, both conscious and unconscious. The principal complaint is that the general attitude of men towards their women colleagues has not changed to meet the modern situation. In the view of many, there should be a much more general understanding by men of women's professional abilities and an acceptance that women can combine families and work and can and should be accepted as partners and in positions of responsibility. More effort should be made to overcome the disadvantages to women solicitors of male camaraderie arising out of social activities and business relationships and more encouragement given to women to take part in the work of the Society whose Council is at present dominated by men.

The one major practical step which the participants considered should be taken by the Society was to set up regular refresher courses. These would allow both men and women who had ceased practising for any reason to be brought up to date before returning to practice. It was suggested that such courses should be compulsory if anyone had been absent from practice for more than two years.

Coupled with a change in attitude towards women, the responses showed a need to alter working practices in order to utilise to the full the talents and skills of the women members and at the same time to meet their domestic commitments. . . . It was suggested that the introduction of part-time partnerships and assistantships, associate status and more flexible hours of working, holidays etc. should be considered and the view was strongly expressed that these changes should apply to both men and women to prevent those women enjoying these benefits from being categorised as second-class lawyers."

[See also W. Millar, "The Role of Women in the Profession" (1985) 30 J.L.S. 86.]

The available statistics afforded some empirical support for the survey results. Women are only gradually becoming principals in any significant numbers. In 1961 of the 1,209 principals (partners or sole practitioners) in Edinburgh and Glasgow, a mere five were women. In 1985 there were 1,530 principals in Scotland's two main cities of whom 86 (6%) were women despite the fact that 19% of all practising solicitors in the two cities were then women. Even by 1991 it is disappointing to note that of the 183 principals in Scotland's six largest firms, only 13 (7%) were women.

A. DISTRIBUTION

At the end of 1992 there were 1,095 solicitors' firms in Scotland with a total of 1,675 offices. (In England and Wales the comparative figures were 10,250 and 15,000). Table 7 reveals the geographical distribution of solicitor's offices in Scotland in 1992 at the regional level. It is clear that the great majority of legal offices in Scotland are to be found in the urban conurbations. Indeed, a 1989 survey commissioned by the Scottish Office indicated that 72% of solicitors' offices were in districts defined as urban (the remaining 28% being in rural districts). However, this distribution closely parallels that of the population as a whole, for the Table also shows that the population per outlet ratio is relatively uniform between the regions with a range of 18% below (Lothian) to 32% above (Fife) the national figure.

TABLE 7

Geographical distribution of solicitors' offices and population

Region	Population (Prelim Census 1991)	Total offices (1992)	Ratio Offices/Popln
Borders	102,649	39	1:2632
Central	267,964	69	1:3884
Dumfries & Galloway	147,064	55	1:2674
Fife	339,284	87	1:3900
Grampian	493,155	154	1:3202
Highland & Islands	279,995	79	1:3544
Lothian	723,678	297	1:2437
Strathclyde	2,218,229	761	1:2915
Tayside	385,271	134	1:2875
Scotland	4,957,289	1,675	1:2960

[Source: Law Society.]

The uniformity of the regional ratios masks two important factors. First, that the overall ratio is one that has changed substantially in the last decade. Thus in 1984 the population per outlet ratio for Scotland was considerably higher (1:4276). The change can be attributed to a slight fall in the population coinciding with a significant rise in the number of solicitors' offices (475) fuelled in part by the expansion in the profession noted in Table 6. For similar reasons the population per private practitioner ratio for Scotland rose from one private practitioner per 1,800 of the population in the 1970s to 1:1,066 in 1984 and 1:859 by 1992. Secondly, the relative uniformity at regional level hides considerable diversity at more local levels, as Tables 8 and 9 reveal.

TABLE 8

Private practitioners in the principal cities

Year	City	% Total Population	Solicitors	% Total Solicitors	Ratio Solicitor: Population
1911	Aberdeen	3.4	181	5	1: 905
	Dundee	3.5	122	3.4	1:1,352
	Edinburgh	9	952	27.0	1: 445
	Glasgow	16	733	21	1:1,070
1984	Aberdeen	3.7	303	6.3	1: 628
	Dundee	3.4	135	2.8	1:1,294
	Edinburgh	8.1	874	18.8	1: 480
	Glasgow	15	1,032	21	1: 739

[Source: Census returns, Almanacs and Directories.]

TABLE 9

Distribution of legal offices in Strathclyde Region in 1992

District	Population	Total offices	Ratio offices: population
Argyll & Bute	66,987	28	1:2392
Bearsden & Milngavie	39,522	9	1:4391
Clydebank	44,658	11	1:4060
Clydesdale	57,078	8	1:7135
Cumbernauld & Kilsyth	61,042	9	1:6782
Cumnock & Doon Valley	41,988	5	1:8398
Cunninghame	134,676	43	1:3132
Dumbarton	75,973	19	1:3999
East Kilbride	81,399	14	1:5814
Eastwood	58,322	7	1:8332
Hamilton	103,139	44	1:2344
Inverclyde	88,054	18	1:4892
Kilmarnock	78,558	25	1:3142
Kyle & Carrick	113,572	38	1:2989
Monklands	101,151	22	1:4598
Motherwell	140,320	30	1:4677
Renfrew	193,622	53	1:3653
Strathkelvin	83,616	13	1:6432
Total for Region outwith Glasgow	1,563,687	396	1:3949
Glasgow	654,542	365	1:1793
Total for Region	2,218,229	761	1:2915
Total for Scotland	4,957,289	1,675	1:2960

[Source: Paterson, *Unmet Legal Needs in Strathclyde*.]

Until the mid-1970s legal offices in Scotland were more concentrated in the urban areas and in the centre of cities than they are now. At that time all but nine of the 141 firms in Edinburgh, all but 11 of the 198 firms in Glasgow and all but three of the firms in Dundee were located in the city centres. Less than 10% of firms had branch offices and even fewer had branch offices in the suburbs. A pilot study, conducted in 1980 (Keatinge), however, revealed that solicitors' firms had been moving into industrial areas and in particular into new and developing towns in the previous ten to 15 years. The survey also revealed that there was an exponential growth in branch offices between 1975 and 1980. In that period 90 branch offices were opened in Scotland. Although the majority of them were located in the central belt, they were not, in the initial stages, situated in Glasgow or Edinburgh. Only three of the 29 opened between 1974 and 1976 as opposed to 22 of the 65 opened between 1977 and 1980 were located in Scotland's two principal cities. In fact, the spread of branch offices in the last 15 years has followed two paths. First, there has been a growth of linked offices across the country. Seven firms based in Edinburgh or Glasgow have branches in London. Eleven firms now have branches in Glasgow and Edinburgh. In addition over 70 firms in the two cities also have offices in towns and cities in other parts of Scotland.

Secondly, there has been a considerable increase in the number of branch offices in the suburbs. In 1970 there were only seven suburban branch offices in Glasgow and Edinburgh together, by 1980 there were over 40 and by 1985 Glasgow alone had 77 and Edinburgh 42—a seventeenfold increase in 15 years. The corresponding figures in Aberdeen were six and 15. In Edinburgh approximately half of the new offices have followed the pattern demonstrated in Birmingham by Bridges *et al.* [*Legal Services in Birmingham* (1975, Inst. of Judicial Administration, University of Birmingham)], by being located in major district shopping centres and presumably designed to attract property work. But the other half have been situated in local authority housing areas, usually at the instance of court firms in an endeavour to attract civil and criminal legal aid work. In Glasgow court firms have been even more active. In marked contrast to the picture in the early 1970s, by the end of 1992 there were over 200 head and branch offices in the suburbs of Glasgow and Edinburgh.

B. SIZE OF SOLICITORS' FIRMS

TABLE 10
Size of solicitors' firms

	Scotland		England	
	1977	1991	1979	1991
Sole practice firms	32%	38%	34%	38%
2–4 Partner firms	48%	42%	48%	43%
5–9 Partner firms	17%	15%	14%	14%
10 or more Partner firms	3%	5%	4%	5%

[Sources: Hughes Commission, Vol. I, p. 317; Law Society; Benson Commission, Vol. I, p. 187; Law Society.]

Table 10 reveals how similar the distribution of firms in terms of size has been in Scotland and England over the last 15 years. However, the somewhat static picture which emerges from the Table conceals the growth in large firm practice both in Scotland and in England in recent years. Thus in 1976 only two Scottish firms had more than 20 partners. By 1991, 15 firms had more than 20 partners and three had more than 30 partners. (Five had 100 or more fee-earners.) As might be expected there are many more large law firms in England and Wales. There 140 or so firms had more than 20 partners in 1992, including 77 with more than 100 fee earners. (The largest law firms in England and Wales are much larger than their Scottish counterparts. The largest of all—Clifford Chance—had 1,154 fee earners and 230 partners in 1992, making it more than eight times larger than its Scots equivalent.) Even these figures are misleading for the 5% of firms with more than ten partners in England contain 42% of all solicitors in private practice. In Scotland the concentration though not quite so high is still startling. Thus in late 1992 the 60 Scots firms with ten or more partners contained 33% of the private profession. This indicates that the importance of the large firm in the legal economy far exceeds its lowly status judged in terms of absolute numbers.

Large firm practice (sometimes known as "mega-lawyering") is even better established in the United States. In that country by 1991 more than ten firms had topped the 1,000 lawyer mark and over 50 firms had more than 300 lawyers. Nevertheless, mega-lawyering is far from the norm even in America—less than 10% of attorneys in private practice work in firms with more than 50 lawyers.

One contributing factor to the growth in large firm practice in Scotland has been that, in part as a response to the competitive pressure of the market, amalgamations between practices have become commonplace in Scotland over the past 20 years. This permits firms to offer a wide range of services and individual lawyers within these firms to specialise. Thus Campbell and Wilson found that nearly half the private practitioners in Scotland and 75% of those in large firms considered themselves to be specialists [C.M. Campbell and R.J. Wilson, *Public Attitudes to the Legal Profession in Scotland* (1972, Law Society of Scotland), pp. 105–106].

Along with the trend towards practice in larger units there has been over the past 50 years a substantial decline in the proportion of the profession who are in sole practice. In 1936 36% of English solicitors were sole practitioners, by 1992 only 8% of them were. Comparable data are not available in Scotland but Campbell and Wilson's study found that in 1971 13% of Scottish solicitors were in sole practice—a figure which had dropped to 10% in 1977 (Hughes, p. 317). By 1992 7% of all private practitioners were sole practitioners. Certainly, in the United States (where there are now more than 600,000 lawyers) 49% of those in private practice in 1980 were sole practitioners—a drop of only 1% since 1970.

Podmore, "The Sole Practitioner—A Declining Species," p. 356
"The causes of the decline in the proportion and number of sole practitioner solicitors are fairly obvious and involve both economic and administrative factors, including the rapidly increasing overheads which afflict all businesses in modern society but hit small firms particularly hard, the 'economies of scale' which only large units can enjoy, the problem of administration in the sole practice (for the sole practitioner is usually his own office manager) and, above all, the intense pressure of legal work on the 'man on his own.' The point is, of course, that in all matters 'the buck stops here' as far as the sole practitioner is concerned. In addition the sole practitioner faces the dilemma that he must choose between depth and breadth in the range of legal services which he performs. The ever-more complex nature of the law puts a premium on specialisation, but it is dangerous for all a solicitor's eggs to be in one basket. The successful practice in the modern world needs to offer both a degree of specialisation *and* a variety of services to clients, but the sole practitioner is not well suited to meet these apparently paradoxical demands. The advantages of the larger practice are manifest not only in areas such as specialist company and commercial work, but also in the more general work of the family solicitor . . .

Whether or not The Law Society by its policies encourages the growth of large practices, it seems inevitable that the sole practitioner solicitor will continue to be a declining species. Any 'man on his own' in modern society is something of an anomaly, existing in defiance of prevailing social and economic forces. Just as hypermarkets displace 'corner shop' grocers and large brewers devour small, so sole practitioner solicitors are likely to amalgamate and form larger, more viable, practices or perhaps cease to practise altogether. The disadvantages to the consumer of a situation where the number of firms is shrinking and those which remain are becoming larger lie in the restricted choice of solicitors' firms available, in the possible lack of easy access to a solicitor's office, and in the inevitable accompanying decline in the highly personal relationship which used to characterise (both in stereotype and, very often, in fact) the solicitor-client relationship. Several of the solicitors interviewed regretted this last trend. One observed, 'More and more one must be business-like. I regret this, because business efficiency can lead to a decline in professionalism. Business efficiency often means you must be ruthless, *e.g.* with a client who wastes your time . . . ' "

The stereotype of sole practice which has emerged from American research is of a graduate from a less prestigious law school whose work tends to be of a routine non-repeating nature for "one-shot" clients, *e.g.* criminal, family and personal injury work. As such, considerable disparities exist between the average income of sole practitioners and partners in the larger firms. Remuneration surveys in England and Wales have suggested that the latter, at least, also holds true on this side of the Atlantic. However, Hughes discovered relatively little discrepancy between the earnings of practitioners in different sizes of firm in Scotland.

In relation to Scotland the American stereotype seems rather wide of the mark. Sole practitioners do as much conveyancing work as other private practitioners, significantly less company work than those in large firms and rather more court work. (Hughes also found that sole practitioners on average earn 18% of their gross fees from legal aid—twice the average figure for other firms.) In fact, a pilot study conducted by Miller in 1981 suggested that sole practitioners in Scotland form neither a homogeneous nor a stable population.

Miller, "Sole Practice in Scotland," pp. 13–14
"Taking into account how long the practice has existed and how many employees it has, one may tentatively and rather impressionistically sketch in a typology of sole practitioners. Firstly, there are those who have been in sole practice for a long period, perhaps 15 years or more. They tend to have 2 or 3 employees. Their practice has stabilised at a level of moderate success. They work in only a very few fields of law . . .

Secondly, there are those who have been in sole practice for a period of 8 to 15 years or so. These may be subclassified into those whose practice is still gradually expanding towards a point where expansion is possible or necessary (a group which largely consists of practitioners who concentrate on conveyancing and wills, trusts and executries); those whose practice has already stabilised at a moderate level of success; and those who are still hanging on in very small practices against both the odds and the balance sheet.

Thirdly, there are those who have only been in sole practice for 6 or 7 years or less. Amongst these are many who will sooner or later move out of sole practice. Some practices expand rapidly, and quickly cease to be 'sole.' These solicitors perhaps receive their greatest reward from ambition-fulfilment rather than remuneration or pleasure at giving a good service. Of the rest of this group, a large number will be general practitioners who do a fair amount of legally-aided work. They have the greatest personal satisfaction from their work, but seem rarely to survive beyond 5 or 6 years as sole practitioners: either because the lure of mammon becomes too enticing, or because they, too, expand beyond sole practice."

C. THE WORK OF THE PROFESSION

Although we have no up-to-date information on the breakdown of fee income as between sole practitioners and others, the distribution of gross fee income in the profession as a whole and how it has changed in the last 15 years or so is set out in Table 11. While the growth in court and corporate work during this period are striking, it is equally noteworthy that domestic conveyancing is still the largest single source of income for the profession.

TABLE 11

Distribution of Gross Fee income of the Profession

	% gross fee income	
Field	1976	1991
Domestic Conveyancing	34	30
Court (Civil & Criminal)	16	24
Corporate (incl. Commercial Conveyancing)	12	23
Tax	—	1
Trust/Executry	21	10
Miscellaneous	17	14

[Sources: The Hughes Commission, Table 19.6; The Law Society.]

III. MONOPOLIES

Contrary to popular mythology (and the position in many other western democracies) solicitors in Scotland possess very few pure monopolies. Their rights of audience before the courts are shared with advocates and party litigants. Their monopoly in relation to applications for the confirmation of executors only extends to the making of such applications *for gain*. Even their conveyancing monopoly (which was not established until 1891: see A. Rodger, "Marching to an Alien Tune?" (1991) J.R. 1) is, strictly speaking, a misnomer, since it is shared with advocates and unqualified persons provided they do not draw or prepare the writ for gain (see the Solicitors (Scotland) Act 1980, s. 32).

The Hughes Commission, pp. 130–131

"9.22 Firstly, there is nothing in the monopoly which prevents a person doing his or her own conveyancing . . . Secondly . . . the statutory provisions prohibit a person who is not a solicitor or an advocate from preparing a writ relating to heritable or moveable property (with certain specific exceptions) only where such a writ is prepared for a fee, gain or reward, or the expectation of some reward. Thirdly, the monopoly has regard only to the drawing or preparing of a writ relating to heritable or moveable property . . . There is no monopoly with regard to negotiating the sale or purchase of a property, the exchange of missives, the making of searches in the Register of Sasines or the various other steps involved in the purchase or sale of a house. Having said this, however, we should say that it appears that solicitors have a virtual monopoly in all conveyancing work after the completion of the missives. The Keeper of the Registers has told us that it is very rare indeed for a writ to be presented for recording by anyone other than a solicitor. The difficulties and complexities of the legal procedures . . . and the requirement for personal undertakings to be given in letters of obligation, have all helped to maintain a monopoly for solicitors in conveyancing work which is in practice more extensive than that conferred by statute."

The Law Society in its evidence to the Hughes Commission argued that the conveyancing monopoly was in the public interest because (1) solicitors have to meet high standards of competence and discipline and (2) the guarantee fund and indemnity insurance (see below) protect the public in the event of fraud or negligence by solicitors. Hughes accepted the importance of competence, discipline and the protection of clients' financial interests but concluded that these could also be attained by other professional bodies.

Following the Hughes Report Mr. Austin Mitchell, M.P., introduced a private member's Bill in 1983 designed to end the solicitors' monopoly of conveyancing. The support he received persuaded the Government to undertake to introduce their own legislation in this field. The Government threat was sufficient to persuade both the Scottish and English Law Societies to relax their rules against the advertising of solicitors' services in 1985 (see Chapter 10 below). In Scotland the profession was also persuaded to abolish its recommended Table of Fees for conveyancing and executries. These developments have led to a more competitive market for legal services and reduced fees for conveyancing in certain parts of Scotland. [See Paterson and Stephen, *The Market for Conveyancing in Scotland* (CRU, 1990).]

Despite this it looked for several years as if the Law Society's efforts to persuade the Government to ignore the Hughes recommendation were bearing fruit. Thus when "licensed conveyancers" were created in England and the Building Societies Act 1986 was passed with provisions permitting institutional conveyancing south of the border, nothing was introduced in Scotland. The publication of two Scottish Office consultation papers, *The Practice of the Solicitor Profession in Scotland* (1987) and *The Legal Profession in Scotland* (1989) and a White Paper, *The Scottish Legal Profession* (1989) however contained a rude shock for the profession. The Government in its continuing efforts to remove what it regarded as anti-competitive restrictions on the supply of legal services had determined to abolish the solicitors' conveyancing and executry monopolies. Banks, building societies and insurance companies were to be given the opportunity to offer conveyancing and executry services. These provisions were included in the Bill but a rebellion by the Government's backbenchers forced the Scottish Office to withdraw its proposals for institutional conveyancing. The Scottish Conveyancing and Executry Services Board was established under the Law Reform (Miscellaneous Provisions) (Scotland) Act 1990, ss. 16–23 to regulate the training, admission and conduct of individual "qualified conveyancers" and "executry practitioners". However, in the light of the recession, the Board, and therefore the limited breaches to the conveyancing and executry monopolies contained in the Act, were suspended in 1992. Whether the profession will be able to stave off the continuing threats to these monopolies once the recession is over remains an open question.

IV. THE LAW SOCIETY OF SCOTLAND

The Law Society of Scotland was established by statute in 1949. Its objects are now set out in the Solicitors (Scotland) Act 1980.

Solicitors (Scotland) Act 1980, s. 1(2)
"The objects of the Society shall include the promotion of—
(a) the interests of the solicitors' profession in Scotland; and
(b) the interests of the public in relation to that profession."

All practising solicitors are required to be members of the Society and to obtain from the Society an annual practising certificate.

The business of the Society is carried out by the Council and by a large number of standing, ad hoc, and statutory committees, though the day-to-day work of the Society is done by the Society's full-time staff. The Society sets the educational, training and admission requirements for those wishing to enter the profession (see above). It is the Society which is responsible for the regulation of non-court work fees and which negotiates with the Lord President and the Scottish Office over court fees and legal aid remuneration rates respectively. In recent years it has come to play a valuable role in co-ordinating, recording and providing support services to groups of solicitors involved in multi-party court cases ranging from transport disasters to drug dependency suits. The Society safeguards the interests of the profession in relation to proposals for law reform both domestically and in Europe. (The Society established an outpost in Brussels in 1991.) It is also responsible for the regulation of professional standards, the investigation of complaints and the enforcement of professional discipline.

A. PROFESSIONAL PRACTICE, CONDUCT AND DISCIPLINE OF SOLICITORS

There are at least three different groups of standards governing the behaviour of Scottish solicitors. First, those relating to *professional conduct*. Second, those relating to the level of *competence* attained by the solicitor in performing legal tasks and thirdly the law of *negligence*. Analytically each set of standards is independent of the other and thus a solicitor can be guilty of misconduct without demonstrating a lack of competence or being negligent. On the other hand the standards are not mutually exclusive. Thus, the same conduct by a lawyer may constitute misconduct and negligence and provide an indication of deficiencies in competence.

In fact, improper professional conduct itself falls into three categories of seriousness. First, professional misconduct. Next unprofessional conduct, which is conduct which falls just short of misconduct but which may be punished by censure and/or an award of costs. Finally, there are breaches of etiquette or professional good manners. Until the last few years there was no formal code of ethics in Scotland although the American legal profession has had one since the early part of the twentieth century. Partly as a result of the activities of the CCBE (Conseil des Barreaux de la Communaute Europeenne) the Law Society of Scotland promulgated a brief Code of Conduct for Scottish Solicitors in 1989. (The

Faculty of Advocates published its Guide to the Professional Conduct of Advocates in 1988.) The Society also regularly introduces Practice Rules (which have been approved by the Lord President) under its delegated statutory powers.

Turning to standards of competence it seems clear that the services provided by solicitors range on a continuum of performance:

EXCELLENCE

COMPETENCE PLUS

THRESHOLD COMPETENCE

INADEQUATE PROFESSIONAL SERVICES

NON-PERFORMANCE

Increasingly, in the modern era, attention has begun to be placed on the quality of the service delivered to the client. With this has come the recognition that sometimes the performance of solicitors can fall below the standard of basic or threshold competence. Following the Solicitors (Scotland) Act 1988 the Law Society and the Scottish Solicitors Discipline Tribunal have been given powers to order the rectification of poor work and to compensate clients in instances where Inadequate Professional Services (IPS) have been delivered. Initially the Law Society took the view that the actings of solicitors could not be both IPS and professional misconduct or both IPS and negligence. Conceptually this was difficult to justify and it has now been recognised that a finding of IPS does not preclude a finding of misconduct or negligence.

1. THE COMPLAINTS PROCEDURE

The Law Society has the principal responsibility for investigating complaints against solicitors. When a complaint is received the secretariat endeavour to identify the gravamen of the problem and then write to the solicitor seeking his or her comments on the problem. If it is clear that the client has not spoken to his or her solicitor, the Society will send a copy of the client's letter to the solicitor and ask that the firm's complaints partner or senior partner meet with the client to discuss the complaint. If a meeting would not be useful or the meeting fails to bring agreement the Society will investigate the complaint. The complaints secretariat may handle the complaint administratively either by resolving to take no action on an unjustified claim or negotiating with both parties to see if a mutually acceptable reduction in fee or some other remedial action taken by the solicitor is possible. The great majority of complaints relate to delay or a failure to communicate with the client although "conduct unbecoming a solicitor" or "failure to adequately advise or to follow instructions" are also relatively frequent grounds. As such it is often possible to identify elements of IPS which the Society can persuade solicitors to remedy or compensate for after discussion with the client. Whilst such "service" complaints can also constitute conduct complaints which in the past frequently led to a finding of unprofessional conduct, there is evidence that findings of IPS are beginning to replace findings of unprofessional conduct in the Society's armoury. The secretariat, however, will not investigate complaints in respect of which the complainer has a legal remedy such as an action for professional negligence. If there are separable elements which relate to IPS or misconduct then action will be taken—otherwise the Society will limit itself to offering to put the complainer in touch with one of a panel of solicitors (colloquially known as "troubleshooters") recruited by the Society who are willing to act for complainants in cases of alleged solicitor negligence.

Complaints which the secretariat consider merit more detailed examination will be referred to one of three Complaints Committees (each has three laypersons to leaven a sizeable majority of solicitors). The Committees can dismiss the case or censure the solicitor but in a significant minority of cases (between a third and a quarter) they make a finding of misconduct which leads to a reprimand, the imposition of IPS sanctions or a prosecution before the Scottish Solicitors' Discipline Tribunal.

2. THE DISCIPLINE TRIBUNAL

The Scottish Solicitors' Discipline Tribunal consists of ten to 14 solicitors recommended by the Council of the Law Society and appointed by the Lord President, and four lay members appointed by the Lord President. Complaints can be brought before the Tribunal by a wide variety of individuals including the Lord Advocate, the Dean of the Faculty of Advocates, judges, court auditors and the Scottish Legal Aid Board. However, the great bulk of prosecutions are initiated by the Law Society who appoint a solicitor to act as fiscal in the case. The Tribunal has extensive powers and may strike solicitors off the roll, suspend them from practice for specified periods, fine them up to £10,000, censure them or suspend or revoke their rights of audience or investment business certificates. In the past the Tribunal had a discretion as to whether named publicity should be permitted in individual cases where a finding of professional misconduct was established. As a result of the Law Reform (Miscellaneous Provisions) (Scotland) Act 1990 decisions in all cases coming before the Tribunal must now be published (even those in which the prosecution fails).

The Tribunal also has wide powers in relation to Inadequate Professional Services and where this has been established can vary the fees and outlays charged by the solicitor to nil, can direct the solicitor to secure rectification of any error or omission at his or her own expense and direct the solicitor to pay compensation to the client of up to £1,000. [Appeals lie to the Court of Session— Solicitors (Scotland) Act 1980, s. 54.]

3. THE SCOTTISH LEGAL SERVICES OMBUDSMAN

In 1976 the office of the Lay Observer was created to examine allegations by members of the public that the Law Society had mishandled their complaints concerning the conduct of their solicitors. As such the Lay Observer could only act once the Society had completed its investigations into the original complaint. The Lay Observer could require the Law Society to produce their files on relevant cases and frequently submitted observations to the Society on their handling of the case. The Law Society, however, were not bound to follow any of the suggestions made by the Lay Observer.

In the Law Reform (Miscellaneous Provisions) (Scotland) Act 1990 the remit of the Observer was extended to cover complaints handling by the Faculty of Advocates and the Scottish Conveyancing and Executry Services Board. To mark the expanded role, the title of the office was changed to the Scottish Legal Services Ombudsman. By an unfortunate error the legislation contained no transitional provisions for the change in offices and a significant number of complaints which arose during the era of the Lay Observer could not be investigated by the Ombudsman. Perhaps the most significant power of the Ombudsman lies in his ability to take cases directly to the Scottish Solicitors Discipline Tribunal—as yet the power has not been exercised. The caseload of the Lay Observer and the Legal Ombudsman has been running at about 200–250 complaints a year of which about a third are ineligible for investigation. As Table 12 indicates a significant proportion of the Ombudsman's caseload are referrals from the Law Society.

TABLE 12
The Disposal of Complaints

Year	Complaints	Taken to discipline tribunal	Referred to trouble-shooters	Referred to lay observer
1974	759	13	—	—
1975	908	13	38	—
1976	956	12	15	15
1977	1,016	18	22	21
1978	1,005	11	38	14
1979	962	18	28	9
1980	839	32	37	17
1981	717	25	39	26
1982	633	21	26	33
1984	1,045	19	26	107
1985	888	35	33	86
1986	880	38	64	130
1987	873	36	48	116
1988	875	23	25	121
1989	1,178	46	36	125
1990	1,112	17	32	191
1991	1,224	23	43	—

[Sources: Law Society of Scotland Annual Reports,
the Journal of the Law Society of Scotland.]

4. PROFESSIONAL MISCONDUCT

Despite the promulgation of the Code of Conduct in 1989, the Practice Rules introduced by the Society at regular intervals and the publication (in recent times) of the decisions of the Discipline Tribunal it is not always easy to establish what does and does not constitute professional misconduct. There are some clear cases— misappropriation of clients' funds, submitting false legal aid claims, abuse of trust, breach of confidentiality or the breach of one of the Law Society's rules of professional practice, *e.g.* attracting business unfairly, sharing fees with unqualified persons or failing to keep proper accounts. In other areas the definition of professional misconduct is left very much to the Discipline Tribunal. If the Tribunal thinks a solicitor's behaviour constitutes misconduct, then it is misconduct. The Inner House has continually refused to offer clearer guidance in this area.

E. v. T.
1949 S.L.T. 411

LORD PRESIDENT (Cooper): "I shall not attempt to define professional misconduct. But if the statutory tribunal, composed as it always is of professional men of the highest repute and competence, stigmatise a course of professional conduct as misconduct, it seems to me that only strong grounds would justify this Court in condoning as innocent that which the Committee have condemned as guilty."

Sharp v. Council of the Law Society
1984 S.L.T. 313

"There are certain standards of conduct to be expected of competent and reputable solicitors. A departure from these standards which would be regarded by competent and reputable solicitors as serious and repehensible may properly be categorised as professional misconduct. Whether or not the conduct complained of is a breach of rules or some other actings or omissions the same question falls to be asked and answered and in every case it will be essential to consider the whole circumstances and the degree of culpability which ought properly to be attached to the individual against whom the complaint is made."

[It was established in *Council of the Law Society* v. *J.*, 1991 S.L.T. 662 that "the circumstances" could never include the fact that the solicitor was ignorant of a new practice rules which had only recently come into force. Somewhat surprisingly, however, the Court also ruled that the fact that the solicitor's breach of the practice rule involved no prejudice to the client might be relevant to establishing misconduct and not just a point which went to mitigation of sentence. This ruling seems at odds with the decisions of the Discipline Tribunal to the effect that ill health or substance addiction only go to mitigation and not to culpability.]

Report of the Clerk to the Discipline Tribunal 1979/80

"In considering any Complaint, the question is always whether there has been 'professional misconduct'. The phrase is not statutorily defined but in an early English case it was observed that 'if it is shown that a solicitor, in pursuit of his profession, has done something with regard to it which would reasonably be regarded as disgraceful or dishonourable by his professional brethren of good repute and competency, then it is open to the Disciplinary Committee to say that he had been guilty of professional misconduct'. This definition is not exhaustive but it is generally accepted as illustrating the required standard of proof."

Not only was it established in *E.* v. *T.* that professional negligence could amount to professional misconduct, since then the Tribunal has held in several decisions that gross carelessness, *e.g.* in the preparation of a case, in delaying the payment of an expert witness, or in carrying out a conveyancing transaction can also be misconduct. More often it will amount to IPS. Finally, it has also become clear from recent cases that the Tribunal and the Court will be prepared to find professional misconduct even in relation to behaviour which is entirely confined to the private life of the solicitor. [See, *e.g. United Bank of Kuwait* v. *Hammoud and Others* [1988] 3 All E.R. 418 at p. 430.]

5. THE GUARANTEE FUND

In addition to the protection given to clients by the Accounts Rules (which *inter alia* require solicitors to have at all times a sum at credit of their client bank account or client accounts not less than the total of the clients' money held by the solicitors) the solicitors' profession in Scotland and England maintain at their own expense funds (financed by annual or special levies on their members) which are used to recompense clients who have "suffered pecuniary loss by reason of dishonesty on the part of any solicitor." Although it is no longer unusual for an occupational group to underwrite its clients in this way against the defalcations of individual practitioners and although the funds do not cover loss due to professional negligence, they nevertheless afford protection to clients in the United Kingdom which lawyer's clients in many other countries have good reason to envy.

6. PROFESSIONAL NEGLIGENCE

The scope of professional negligence is not much clearer than that of professional misconduct. It is established that solicitors are liable for lack of due care and skill, judged by the standard of the reasonably competent practitioner. Thus a solicitor who, due to a conveyancing error, leaves his client with a defective title, or who delays so long that his client's action becomes time-barred or who fails to alert his client to the availability of legal aid will be liable for loss sustained by his client. But it is not clear whether this liability arises merely from contract or from contract and delict. It has been argued that the basis of liability of a solicitor to his own clients is contractual only and that he owes no duty in delict to his clients or to third parties, *Robertson* v. *Fleming* (1861) 4 Macq. 167.

In the light of radical developments in the law of delict in the past century, it is likely that Scottish courts would no longer accept this statement of the law. Nevertheless, the liability of Scottish solicitors to third parties remains uncertain, as does their liability for errors of judgment or when acting as advocates in the lower courts.

[For the position in England see *Ross* v. *Caunters* [1980] Ch. 297, *Saif Ali* v. *Sydney Mitchell & Co.* [1980] A.C. 198 and *Whitehouse* v. *Jordan* [1981] 1 W.L.R. 246. For a useful discussion of Scots law in this area see A. Gamble, "Solicitors and Claims by Third Parties" (1980) 25 J.L.S. 236.]

7. THE TROUBLESHOOTERS
"Complaints against solicitors," p. 179

"At one time a complainer . . . would be advised [that the Society has no powers to award financial compensation for any loss suffered through negligence] . . . and in some instances would be put in touch with a solicitor who was prepared to take on the case, or would be given a list of firms from which to select someone to act. Judging from the response from members of the public, this was totally inadequate and many complained that it was impossible to find a solicitor prepared to raise an action against a fellow-practitioner. With a view to combating this, the Society decided to set up a panel of solicitors in various parts of the country who would be prepared to advise complainers who felt they had grounds for a complaint based on negligence against their present solicitors.

In July 1974 the Professional Practice Committee decided to ask each member of the Council to suggest the name of a suitable solicitor within his constituency who would undertake this type of work . . .

[In 1975], a panel of twenty-four solicitors was set up . . . [By 1981 a team of 40 had been recruited.]

The scheme works in the following way. When a complaint is received from someone alleging negligence and there appears to be a *prima facie* case, or sometimes it is felt that the complainer is in need of separate legal advice, it may be decided to put him or her in touch with a 'troubleshooter' (as the members of the panel have come to be known). This is usually done when the complainer has indicated that he has been unable to obtain separate legal advice.

The Secretary dealing with complaints then gets in touch with one of the panel members and asks him if he would be prepared to undertake the case. If he is agreeable, a letter is written to him confirming that the case has been passed to him and a letter is written to the complainer advising him of the arrangement made. The onus is then on the complainer to get in touch with the solicitor and from that stage the normal solicitor/client relationship exists. The solicitor is not appointed by the Law Society and at the end of the day the client is responsible for the payment of fees in the normal manner . . . [An arrangement has been made with the Faculty of Advocates whereby troubleshooters can obtain counsel's opinion free of charge.]"

8. COMPULSORY PROFESSIONAL INDEMNITY INSURANCE
In 1977 the Law Society's Council after consulting the profession and several leading insurance brokers, resolved to invoke its powers under the Solicitors (Scotland) Act 1976 [now contained in the Solicitors (Scotland) Act 1980, s. 44] to introduce mandatory professional indemnity insurance through a single master policy held in the name of the Society. The step was taken because, following the withdrawal of several insurance companies from the market, solicitors were encountering increasing difficulties in

obtaining indemnity insurance cover; a quarter of the profession were thought to have no indemnity insurance. With a master policy the Society could bargain from a position of strength with the insurance companies over premiums and cover. From November 1, 1978, Scottish solicitors in terms of the policy have been covered for acts of professional negligence and for fraud or dishonesty on the part of their partners or staff. The limit for each and every claim by 1993 was £1 million irrespective of the size of the firm although additional cover can be purchased. There is an excess of £2,000 per principal up to a maximum of £20,000 on each and every claim. Fidelity claims (relating to the fraud or dishonesty of a partner or member of staff), have an excess which is double that of ordinary claims. Premiums can be weighted up to 250% in the event of a poor claims record. On the other hand there is a possibility of a "no claims bonus" of up to 30% of the premium. After a period in the late Eighties when the premiums/claims ratio was looking quite healthy, the claims ratio deteriorated in the early Nineties.

B. REFORM PROPOSALS

In recent years not a few of the reforms sought by consumer bodies and the Government in relation to the regulation of professional conduct and discipline have been implemented. IPS appears to be operating successfully and there is less overt criticism of the Law Society's complaints procedures. On the other hand, the need for an authoritative Guide to the Professional Conduct of Solicitors, along the lines of that produced by the Law Society for England is still strong. Furthermore, there are still those, e.g. the Scottish Consumer Council who are on record as favouring the establishment of an independent complaints body for lawyers. Despite this, and the fact that issues of competence are now being raised in relation to complaints and discipline, it must be doubted whether improved complaints procedure would do much to improve the competence of solicitors.

Zander, *Legal Services for the Community*, pp. 136–138
"But improved procedures for handling complaints and better remedies for aggrieved clients are unlikely to make any real impact on the quality of work done by lawyers. There are three main reasons. One is that hardly any clients have the energy or inclination to complain even if they feel there is something to complain about . . .
    Secondly, the failure to complain is often because the client is unaware of the fact that the work has been badly done. It is of the nature of many professional services that the client cannot evaluate what has been done for him and therefore cannot know its quality . . .

A third reason for reviewing complaints and disciplinary procedures as marginal to the problem of maintaining professional standards is that instances that are penalised are regarded by all concerned as exceptional. The presumption is that they are deviations from the norm, and the ordinary practitioner is, therefore, unlikely to be much influenced by reading or hearing that his colleague has been criticised for such failure . . .

The only way to meet this difficulty is to have some mechanism for conducting research into the way in which legal services of different kinds are *normally* provided."

Zander's solution is similar to a proposal of the Hughes Commission on competence—that the quality of professional work should be monitored (R. 16.35). This is now beginning to happen as firms come to recognise the importance of pursuing quality in order to gain an advantage over the competition. Firms that have registered for BS 5750 or begun to toy with Total Quality Management are already committed to "file inspections" on a regular basis by internal or external audit staff. Client satisfaction surveys are also becoming recognised as valuable marketing and client retention devices. In England the Law Society introduced a "client care" rule in 1991 requiring every firm to have an internal complaints procedure, to advise clients as to its existence and to keep them properly informed of the action being taken on their behalf. Scotland is still contemplating its reforms in this area but firms with three or more partners have been asked to appoint a complaints partner and to identify the same to the Society.

One reform which might help to raise professional standards is the proposal approved at the Society's AGM in 1993 that mandatory continuing legal education (or mandatory continuing professional development as the Scots have dubbed it) should be introduced here rather than on the lines of the English model. If finally approved, each member of the profession will be required to complete 20 hours of further education/training every year, partly through self study and partly through seminars and group training. A significant section of the curriculum would be devoted to management or skills training.

Finally, improved quality and efficiency may come from the increasing competition within the profession which has been engendered in recent years by the Government and to a lesser extent by the consumer movement. As we have seen several of the changes contained within the Law Reform (Miscellaneous Provisions) (Scotland) Act 1990 are designed to increase competition within the profession. However, the Conveyancing and Executry Board has been suspended (see p. 238 above) and the provisions for Multi-Disciplinary Partnerships (*e.g.* between solicitors and accountants) placed in abeyance until 1998 at the earliest. This leaves Multi-National Partnerships and extended rights of audience to bear the hopes of the reformers.

CHAPTER 10

UNMET LEGAL NEEDS

Since the 1960s "the unmet need for legal services" has been the subject of much discussion and research. It is argued that many people, through ignorance of the law or lack of financial resources, have an "unmet legal need." Those who are ignorant of the law do not enforce their legal rights, which simply go by default. This is said to be particularly so in areas such as consumer, housing, employment and social security law, where legislation has proliferated. Again, people with legal problems who cannot afford a lawyer may also be described as having an "unmet legal need." Egalitarian principles suggest that in such cases lawyers should be provided from public funds, if more affluent persons would employ a lawyer when faced with a similar legal problem. Such assertions are premised on a number of assumptions, for example as to the nature of legal problems, as to the assessment of legal needs and in relation to who should meet those needs.

I. THE NATURE OF LEGAL PROBLEMS

Zander, *Legal Services for the Community*, p. 273
"A legal problem may be defined to include any difficulty which can be solved by reference to law. Alternatively, it might be defined much more restrictively to mean problems that are in fact taken to lawyers. By this standard a social security problem would not qualify as a legal problem. Again, it may mean those matters that lawyers, or at least some lawyers, at any given time think *ought* to be taken to them for solution. Some lawyers would identify the social security problem as 'legal', others might not."

Lewis, "Unmet Legal Needs", pp. 78–79
"People often speak as if to say that someone has a legal problem is to make a statement of fact about his situation; once one has appreciated that situation, one can realize that it falls within the class of situations which raise a legal problem, and any lawyer can say what situations are contained in that class, just as he can say what the statute book has to say on some given point. A closely related way of speaking is to treat the judgment that someone has a legal problem as a judgment which is typically a clear one, admitting of no doubt; people either do or do not have a legal problem. It is this clarity which makes it possible to come to the judgment that people with a legal problem 'need' a lawyer, just as no-

one would suppose that an engineering problem could be solved by anyone else than an engineer.

This way of speaking should be suspect. Usually if we say simply that a person has a problem we mean that there is a difficulty about deciding what he should do or what should be done for him: that is what *makes* it a problem, not merely the presence of the circumstances which have to be coped with. If we define what kind of problem the person has or the circumstances present, if, say, we refer to an arithmetic problem, we are defining the kinds of solution seen as appropriate. Thus, to tell someone that the problem of measuring the height of a building is a trigonometrical problem is to suggest the methods that should be used to find out the answer . . .

It seems likely then that when someone says that a person has a legal problem or says that a particular problem under discussion is a legal one he is offering a suggestion about the action that the person should take or the method which should be adopted to solve the problem. The typical suggestion is that action should be taken before some court or similar institution or that the services of a lawyer should be employed. Very broadly, the point I should like to make in this paper is that if certain problems are spoken of as legal ones, and official support is given to legal methods of solving them, that is to take a particular attitude to problems of that kind, problems which may be capable of solution in some other way, and which may be seen by those most closely concerned as best solved in that other way. For instance, if a tenant in a flat has a leaking roof he may be regarded as having a legal problem; does his lease provide that the landlord should do the repairs, and is the mechanism of the courts adequate to ensure quick action? But he may choose to get a ladder and not a lawyer, and we can argue whether it is better that people should be made to fulfil their legal duties or that they should be encouraged to take practical steps to avoid material damage regardless of their legal responsibilities."

Arguments such as Lewis's have led some scholars to assert that there are no specifically legal problems only social ones which can be tackled by a variety of approaches only one or two of which may be specifically legal.

II. THE ASSESSMENT OF LEGAL NEED

Zander, *Legal Services for the Community*, pp. 274–275
"The need of the rich man to redress a legal wrong may be less than that of a poor man afflicted by the same problem. Perception of need will be influenced by the availability of resources . . . The more legal services are provided, the more the community may perceive the need for lawyers. (It has been found that if the number of hospital beds is increased, the average length of stay in hospital increases too.) Moreover, the concept

of need presumably ought to include some sense of a hierarchy of values. The need for a lawyer of a man who faces a charge carrying the death penalty is different from that of another whose kettle proves to be defective. Both can validly be said to need a lawyer, but the disparity between the extent of their needs is so gross as to require some stratification of levels of need. At the extremes this can be done without difficulty. But how is one to reach agreement as to the relative need of one man for reinstatement of his job, against another's claim for compensation for loss of the sense of smell, or a third man's protection against eviction?

One tenant faced with a notice to quit may throw it into the fire, believing (rightly) that he is fully protected by the Rent Acts. Another does so because he believes (wrongly) that he is legally protected, but comes to no harm because the landlord fails to follow through with proceedings for possession when the tenant sits tight. Did either have a 'need' for legal services? Or what of the tenant who leaves on receipt of the notice to quit because he believes (rightly) that he is not protected and he prefers to take the opportunity of reasonable alternative accommodation which has just presented itself rather than stay to fight a costly, losing battle? Should he first have seen a lawyer? From a certain point of view it would, of course, be reasonable to say that in any of these situations the tenant would have benefited from the additional peace of mind of having legal advice. Yet, there is room for differing views as to whether there was or was not a need for legal advice. The answer may be influenced both by one's capacity for empathy and by the value one places on the intervention of lawyers."

III. MEETING UNMET NEED

Zander, *Legal Services for the Community*, p. 275
"It cannot be assumed that a person with a legal problem has any need for legal services if by that is meant the services of lawyers. He may be best advised to take his problem, at no cost, to the local citizens' advice bureau, his trade union official, or a well-informed friend or relative. He may indeed be best served by doing nothing at all and allowing the problem to go unresolved, or to solve it by quite different means."

Lewis, "Unmet Legal Needs," pp. 87 and 95
"Discussions should not proceed on the basis of whether it would be generally agreed that a person should use a lawyer, but on whether his interests and temperament require an adviser, a negotiator, or a champion, and who in his particular situation can best fulfil this role. The answer might then be someone like his M.P., or one might want to set up new organizations or professions. [Alternatively] it might turn out on inquiry that the interests of individuals with problems might be best

served by referring them to solicitors, since to some extent they profess flexibility of role . . . It is said that if we give people rights we are acting in vain unless we give them the ability to enforce them. I sympathize with this, but representation by lawyers may not be the best way of doing it. If, for instance, we want to make consumers' rights against the sellers of unmerchantable goods effective, the best way may be to set up some kind of consumers' representative, or a small claims court where no lawyers are allowed. It may not be so; I only want to point out that giving legal aid for litigation is not the only possibility to be considered."

IV. STUDYING UNMET NEED

Despite the problems outlined above a number of surveys have been conducted in an endeavour to establish the existence of an "unmet legal need" in a particular geographical or legal area. Two strategies are used to get over the semantic hurdles. First, to study situations or areas where the "need" for legal assistance is so gross that the value judgment involved in asserting that there is a need for lawyers in that situation or area is one which would be widely accepted; *e.g.* studies of the number of accused persons who are unrepresented, of the number and success rate of unrepresented applicants appearing before tribunals or of the uneven distribution of solicitors in the country and the shortage of solicitors who are welfare specialists. The second strategy has been to go into the community to ask individuals about their "legal problems."

Zander, *Legal Services for the Community*, p. 277
"The most common technique of such studies is to take a check-list of 'legal problems' and ask members of the community which, if any, they have experienced, and, if so, what they did about them. It is obviously important in conducting such research not to alert the respondent to the fact that he is being asked about his response to legal problems. If he knew this it might slant his replies. He is, therefore, asked simply whether he has had, say, an accident, or has divorced his spouse, or has ever been threatened with eviction. It is then possible to evaluate the extent to which different members of the community do have problems that by one or another definition may be said to be 'legal'."

[Zander goes on to discuss a number of these studies.]

The difficulty in such research is in balancing the subjective and objective elements. Where the individual's subjective perception of need alone is relied on the researcher is not measuring unmet need for legal services but *perceived* unmet need for legal services which may depend on a number of factors including the individual's state of knowledge and even his psychological needs. Adopting such an approach makes it impossible for the researcher to say that an individual's perception that he has a need for legal services (no matter how trivial the problem) is erroneous, or for him to say that an individual has an unmet need for legal services but does not realise it. On the other hand where the researcher introduces objectivising factors, *e.g.* by stipulating the criteria which make a problem "serious," he risks substituting his own subjectivity and value judgments for those of the individuals whom he is studying.

Griffiths, "The Distribution of Legal Services in the Netherlands," p. 281

"The trouble is that legal services are a scarce good, in competition with other scarce goods, and it is a matter of personal judgment whether one's legal problems are, in relation to other things one could spend one's money for, 'serious' enough to justify such an expenditure. The question is never, is it 'serious'? but always, is it 'serious enough'?, and there is therefore no empirical criterion by which to measure the amount of legal services that anyone 'needs'. You want a divorce for £200, I prefer a colour T.V. Do I lack 'access' because I can't have both? Of course not— I decided I 'needed' a lawyer less than someone else might have: my legal problem was less 'serious' for me than yours was for you."

V. UNMET NEED: THE HUGHES APPROACH

The Hughes Commission, pp. 19–21

"*Legal services*

2.1 It is tempting to say that 'legal services are services provided by lawyers', but we reject this for two reasons. Firstly, not all work done by lawyers falls into the category of a legal service . . . Secondly, not all legal services are provided by lawyers. There are many sources of legal services outwith the legal profession. Other professional people, whether they be architects, accountants or social workers, give advice to their clients on the legal aspects of their services. Much of the work of organisations such as Citizens Advice Bureaux, consumer advice centres, trade unions and motoring organisations, consists of giving information and advice about the law. Such provision is as much a legal service as the same information and advice given by a lawyer . . . We also regard as a form of legal service the dissemination of information through notices, leaflets, advertisements and booklets which give the citizen information about his legal rights and responsibilities and how he may exercise or carry them out.

2.2 Accordingly, when we speak of legal services we mean advice, information or assistance involving a knowledge of rights and obligations conferred by law and of legal procedures, whether provided by a lawyer or otherwise. These services may include action taken on behalf of a client, or facilities used by a client (whether the client is an individual, a group or an organisation) . . .

Unmet Need

2.7 Ideally, the use made of legal services would express the total need for legal services. However, not all need results in use of legal services and in some cases the service provided may, by its inadequate quality or supply, fail to meet the whole need. The total need for legal services with which we must be concerned is the sum of actual use plus unmet needs. In broad terms the meaning of need for legal services and the nature of unmet need are clear enough. Certain causes of unmet need are clearly recognisable—shortages of lawyers in particular geographical localities and areas of the law, for example. There is, however, more to legal need than simply people having a legal problem and not being able to secure the services of an adviser. It is impossible to estimate how many legal problems there are, other than perhaps for research purposes in a small group under study. Many problems which could be resolved by legal means do not necessarily have to be. There are other non-legal solutions . . .

2.9 Where a citizen finds a non-legal solution which satisfies him, we would not be justified in claiming that he is deprived of legal services. That would depend on his awareness of his legal rights. In assessing the need for legal services we must therefore think in terms of two stages—firstly enabling the client to identify and, if he judges it appropriate, to choose a legal solution; and, secondly, enabling the client to pursue a chosen legal solution.

2.10 Accordingly, when we speak of a need for legal services in our Report we are speaking of a need for services—facilities, advice, assistance, information or action—to enable a citizen with a problem to assert or protect his rights in law by identifying and, if he so chooses, pursuing a legal solution, that is a solution which involves a knowledge of rights and obligations or of legal procedures. When we speak of 'unmet need' we are concerned about instances where a citizen is unaware that he has a legal right, or where he would prefer to assert or defend a right but fails to do so for want of legal services of adequate quality or supply."

Hughes recognises that "need" as in the "need for legal services" is a relative concept. In answer to the question, "when can an unmet need for legal services be said to exist?" Hughes resorts to stipulative definition—starting from the standpoint of the client and *the client's perception of need*. The implicit, if not explicit, assumption is that a need for legal services exists if a legal solution is available to a problem facing a person or group of persons, and *that person or group of persons* perceives that the legal solution is more convenient or satisfactory than the various non-legal solutions available.

Such an assumption is open to two challenges. First because the subjectively based concept of need which it enshrines posits a model of individuals as rational beings capable of making informed choices, when some litigants are anything but rational. This objection has little merit, indeed the model both avoids the trap of paternalism and accords with democratic theory. The second objection perhaps carries more credibility, namely, that the model ignores questions of cost. At a time when financial constraints on legal aid expenditure look like being with us for the foreseeable future it seems that the model should be adjusted to take account of issues such as value for money.

Hughes commissioned a public survey to discover how people attempted to solve problems of a relatively serious nature and to identify the extent of unmet need amongst them (as defined by Hughes). The Commission concluded (at pp. 51–52):

"5.16 Our evidence suggests that the unmet need for legal services in Scotland is not the result of people's dissatisfaction with the services they have obtained from lawyers. Those of our respondents who had consulted a solicitor were generally satisfied with the help they received. The problem is rather a considerable unwillingness on the part of the public to consult a solicitor in the first place—61 per cent of our respondents had never done so, although the proportion is smaller among younger people. It appears in particular that many people fail to take *independent* advice when faced with a comparatively worrying problem such as an accident or injury, a consumer complaint or a landlord/tenant dispute. Most judged these problems not appropriate for a solicitor. There are undoubtedly cases where the sum at issue is so small that it would be out of all proportion to incur the expense of employing a solicitor to recover it. If, as a result, people fail to assert their rights, this suggests that an alternative form of legal service may be needed. The small numbers taking legal advice . . . coupled with the level of dissatisfaction at the outcome . . . suggest strongly to us that significant numbers of people make decisions as to the value of legal advice on the basis of inadequate information.

5.18 From this analysis we can identify three major causes of unmet need for legal services. The first barrier the citizen has to overcome is one of information—he must know that he has a legal right. A further aspect of this barrier is that the citizen must know what sources of help are available to him, what order of costs might be involved, what financial assistance could be available, and in particular whether he is eligible for legal aid . . .

5.19 A second barrier between the citizen and legal services is ease of access. Not only must legal advisers be available in a convenient place at a convenient time, they must be seen as approachable . . .

5.20 A third barrier to use of legal services is cost."

A. THE PROBLEM OF IGNORANCE

The first stage in the Hughes approach to unmet legal need centres on the "need" of the citizen for information as to his legal rights, as to the legal and non-legal remedies available to him and as to the relative cost and viability of these remedies.

Kelly and Lorber, "The Medway: Unmet Need for
Legal Services," p. 10

"To a lawyer a specific situation may appear to be a legal problem, especially where apparent legal rights have been breached and legal remedies are available. However, an individual who actually experiences such situations may not perceive them as problem situations of a legal nature, or even problems at all. He may not apply the lawyer's definition of a social situation, and therefore will not bother to consult him. Although he may seek some social solution to his problem, he is effectively denied a legal solution, as he does not see the law as relevant to his circumstances. In many areas of the law, individuals with problems are completely ignorant of their legal rights and remedies."

Although the complexity and ever-changing nature of consumer, employment, housing and welfare legislation is such that it is highly unlikely that the average citizen has an accurate awareness of his legal rights in these areas, few studies have actually been carried out to test the legal awareness of the public.

The Hughes survey did not research this area either, though it did look into the public awareness of legal services. Table 1 summarises their findings.

TABLE 1

Proportion of respondents with no or very inaccurate information about
various schemes

	%
Legal aid	39
Legal aid symbol	48
Tribunal system	50
Small estates procedure	86
Legal advice and assistance	91
Summary cause procedure	99

N = 1,658 for each scheme

[Source: Hughes Commission, Appendix 4, Table 65]

[See also the National Audit Office Report on *The Administration of Legal Aid in England and Wales* (HMSO, London: 1992) at p. 50.]

Moreover the survey revealed that the lack of information amongst the public about legal services was not randomly distributed. Lack of knowledge was greatest amongst those in the lower socio-economic categories. This was particularly so in relation to knowledge of the legal aid system, with those categories of respondent who would be most likely to qualify for legal aid being least knowledgeable about it, *i.e.* manual workers or those over 65.

TABLE 2

Knowledge of legal aid and legal aid symbol, by socio-economic status

Socio-economic status	Proportion (%) of respondents in each group having no or very inaccurate knowledge about:	
	Legal Aid	Legal Aid Symbol
Higher professional/managerial	19	47
Lower professional/managerial	24	42
Other non-manual	31	40
Skilled manual	39	48
Semi- and unskilled manual	47	53
Other	55	64
All non-manual	28	41
All manual	43	50

[Source: Hughes Commission, Appendix 4, Table 66.]

[This last finding has been replicated in several Scottish studies. See, *e.g.* Myers, "CABx and Knowledge of Legal Services" (1976) 4 SCOLAG Bul. 46; S.C.C. Evidence to the Royal Commission on Legal Services in Scotland; "Awareness of Legal Services in Aberdeen" (1979) 31 SCOLAG Bul. 62.]

Hughes' strategy in relation to the problem of public ignorance of legal rights and remedies was to tackle it at source—at the level of the citizen. Accordingly the Hughes' recommendations included:

(1) the provision of teaching on law and legal services at school (R. 6.1);
(2) the advertisement by the Government of major changes in the law in the media (R. 6.4);
(3) the use of the media for the provision of public information on legal rights and legal services (Para. 6.13);
(4) the encouragement of CABx and law centres to devote a significant portion of their energies to community education (R. 6.6);
(5) the creation of a network of generalist advice agencies as information providers, for example as to the potential cost or viability of a legal solution to a client's problem (R. 7.1).

[The fifth recommendation is also relevant to the problem of access.]

B. *THE PROBLEM OF ACCESS TO LEGAL SERVICES*

The Royal Commission on Legal Services in England and Wales (Benson) laid less emphasis on the value of attempting to raise the general legal awareness of the public. Benson treated the problem of ignorance as a variant of the problem of access—defined by Benson as the problem of getting the potential client to the professional adviser who has the knowledge and expertise. Accordingly the Benson recommendations are designed to encourage direct access to solicitors, *e.g.* by permitting solicitors to advertise their specialisms, by subsidising private practitioners to move into deprived areas and by introducing a half-hour interview free of charge for all clients, irrespective of their means, when they consult a solicitor who undertakes legal aid work, paid for from the legal aid fund.

Hughes' definition of the problem of access was different. Hughes recognised the need for "initial advice to allow a citizen to identify and, if he judges it appropriate, to choose a legal solution to his problem" but was impressed by the record of lay advice agencies in this field.

The Hughes Commission, p. 39

"To recognise a potential legal solution to a problem, the citizen must have some knowledge of the legal rights and responsibilities involved. In many cases, people are aware only of the problem and have little awareness of its relationship to the complex and ever-increasing volume of legislation surrounding their daily lives. Further, many problems are not, at least to the person who suffers from them, clear-cut single issues. Before seeking any solution it is helpful, indeed often necessary, to discuss the problem in order to identify its various aspects and discover what is really at issue. The potential client therefore requires initial advice which will help to clarify the problem and to identify the possible solutions, including potential legal solutions. Many people are reluctant to enter a solicitor's office unless they are sure they have a real and important legal problem; but they are less reluctant to approach more informal advice agencies."

Some evidence of the reluctance of individuals to consult solicitors emerged from a pilot study of people's "Awareness of Legal Services in Aberdeen" (1979) 31 SCOLAG Bul. 62. When confronted with hypothetical consumer, housing, employment and social security problems and asked whom they would go to for help in relation to them, few respondents mentioned solicitors. The respondents' explanations for this included: "But it would be more bother than it was worth"; "But he'd just refer me to someone else"; "The advice people have their own solicitors"; "I've got through life without needing solicitors" (from a retired Post Office worker); "The small fee might not be all that small"; "Solicitors wouldn't be bothered with things like that"; "The Citizens Advice

Bureau do a better job—they handle more cases like that"; "It's better if you can sort things out for yourself"; "The CAB people put one on to a solicitor"; "I've never needed anything like that"; "They would be too busy"; 'It's simpler to go to the CAB"; "But that would just confuse me further"; "But they're not really questions for a solicitor".

VI. CITIZENS ADVICE BUREAUX SERVICES IN SCOTLAND

Allen, "CABx and Legal Services in Scotland," pp. 41–42
"A Citizens Advice Bureau is an information and advice centre which depends largely on local authority funding but remains firmly outside the statutory set-up. A bureau is run by an independent management committee drawn from local people. Its members may also include one or two councillors, and representatives of Social Work, Consumer Protection, and Housing Departments as well as perhaps a lawyer, teacher, community workers and others active in the community.

The bureau staff in Scotland are almost entirely volunteers, but a bureau aims by careful recruitment, selection and training policies to ensure a high standard of service combined with commitment and local knowledge. Administratively the key figure in a bureau is the organiser, who is now increasingly salaried, though improvements in the provision of salaries by local authorities have been hit by local government's financial problems.

A bureau has to satisfy certain conditions in its methods of operation and premises before it can register as a member of Citizens Advice Scotland. In exchange for registration, it receives regular updated information from CAS's Edinburgh offices and other back-up services such as training advice.

A Citizens Advice Bureau aims to provide a service of information and advice which is both geographically accessible and does not inhibit anyone who needs help. It steers away from formal reception desks or other trappings that might associate it with the official aspects of statutory departments and imposes no restrictions on the types of problems or enquiries that can be brought to it. One of the misgivings we have about the proliferation of advice-giving services is that the man-in-the-street is not always clear as to which, if any, single category his problem belongs to.

The Citizens Advice Bureau aspires to be the well-informed general practitioner of advice services, 'combining the roles of prevention, diagnosis and referral to the specialist consultant'. A bureau is therefore not a mere signpost. Many people, of course, come for simple information or to get the address of another agency and others are identified by the bureau as needing help from a lawyer or social worker. But the key criterion when deciding whether to advise a client to go elsewhere for help or to seek to help him at least initially within the bureau is what is felt to be in the client's interests. Increasingly clients come to bureaux with problems, rather than enquiries. They bring them to the bureau either because they have not liked to go to more official services or because other offices have not had the time to sort out their problems or have felt that they were not within their remit. They may be tired of being shunted from one office to another or they may have had to summon extra resources of courage to consult anyone at all about their problem. To take the easy way out, and give these people another address to go to, may not be what they are needing, nor will the information necessarily be used.

There is a growing consciousness amongst bureaux too that even in giving simple information, they are also passing on advice and that there is no easily defined point beyond which a bureau can say it does not act. If there is no boundary between information and advice, so there is none between advice and speaking on behalf of the client and even acting on his behalf. If there is someone else more able to do this job and acceptable to the client, then of course the bureau will refer. Most bureaux err on the side of diffidence rather than taking on too much, almost overwilling to defer to the 'professionals', whether they are lawyers, social workers or local government officials."

In 1991/92 the 67 CABx and three outreach bureaux in Scotland handled just over 600,000 initial and repeat inquiries. The majority of inquiries concerned money matters (primarily debt) followed by employment, consumer, housing and family matters.

TABLE 3

Inquiries handled by CABx

Category	1983/84		1991/2		Overall Change %
	No.	%	No.	%	
Family and Personal	34,362	9.6	52,023	8.2	+ 51.4
Housing	45,007	12.6	55,144	8.7	+ 22.5
Employment	44,911	12.5	81,003	12.9	+ 80.4
Goods and Services	56,086	15.6	69,699	11.1	+ 24.3
Money	93,203	26.0	279,916	44.5	+200.3
Maladministration	3,848	1.1	4,793	0.8	+ 24.6
Compensation for Injury/Damage	8,996	2.5	15,995	2.5	+ 77.8
Foreign Travel/Nationality	2,221	0.6	4,265	0.7	+ 92.0
Administration of Justice	4,529	1.3	5,573	0.9	+ 23.1
Miscellaneous	65,490	18.2	60,151	9.6	− 8.2
Total	358,653	100.0	628,562	100.0	+ 75.2

[Source: CAS Annual Reports.]

VII. CABx AS A PART OF LEGAL SERVICES

S.A.C.A.B. Annual Report 1981/82

"Much of the work of Citizens Advice Bureaux consists of giving information and advice about the law and more than [50%] of the enquiries made to bureaux have a legal dimension. The CAB service is a necessary and valuable complement to the legal profession. It attracts people who may need but would otherwise not seek legal advice. It provides the basic advice which can help a client to make an informed approach to the legal profession. It deals with areas of the law that the profession does not adequately cover and it acts as a sieve identifying cases which require the professional attention of solicitors . . . "

Allen, "CABx and Legal Services in Scotland," pp. 43–44

"1. Whilst bureaux handle many enquiries which have a legal element within them they are *not* setting themselves up to be lawyers and for the most part are most careful to refer a client to a lawyer as soon as it becomes apparent that he requires professional help. Skill at referring is increased the more dialogue there is between local lawyers and the CAB. It also depends on there being lawyers available to send the client to and on the client being willing to keep his appointment . . .

2. A matter of deep concern to us therefore is the uneven spread of the profession in Scotland. It is all too often the same areas which have neither a Citizens Advice Bureau nor a local lawyer. The two extreme situations for particular concern are the vast, sparsely-populated areas of the north of Scotland and the high-density, low-amenity housing estates of Edinburgh and Glasgow.

3. Lawyers need to be both better dispersed and more accessible to people. They need to be willing and interested in handling the less popular areas of law such as housing, consumer and welfare rights.

Legal sessions in the bureau

1. A better spread of lawyers' firms and more information about what work they will do will only help the client who has identified or had identified his problem as needing a lawyer. There are still those who do not want to go to a lawyer's office, at least initially. And there are those who have a problem with several facets, of which only one requires legal advice. Traditionally bureaux have relied on informal contact with a lawyer over the phone. This is not really as satisfactory as the client seeing a lawyer, and a standard development for bureaux is to invite local lawyers to run legal clinics on a voluntary basis within the bureau, usually one evening a week or fortnight.

2. [In 1993, 23 bureaux were operating legal sessions in Scotland.] . . . There is a steady flow of clients who visit the bureau during the day and return in the evening to seek the lawyer's advice (few fail to keep their appointments, which have the benefit of being in familiar surroundings).

The standard type of problem is the more complicated case of consumer redress, some aspect of a matrimonial problem, or a landlord or tenant seeking information about his rights. The system of sifting cases through the bureau ensures that the lawyer's time is used to the best advantage. Bureaux staff tend also to save up queries they have had themselves over the past week on aspects of the law. Solicitors seem also to enjoy the work; they often find it an interesting and challenging change from the normal run of business in a legal firm. There is no doubt too that in towns where the CAB runs legal sessions, there is a closer relationship between the legal profession and the CAB: each has a better understanding of the work of the other."

One problem with legal sessions was that the volunteer lawyers were not permitted by the ethical rules of the profession to take clients back to their office if they required further professional legal help. To overcome this it was agreed between the CAB service and the Law Societies in the U.K. that solicitors would be permitted to take any case requiring further professional help back to their own office, if this is what the client wishes, provided a rota scheme has been established. Under the scheme every solicitor in the area served by a particular bureau must be invited to participate in the legal sessions on a rota basis. Most of the Scottish bureaux with legal sessions currently operate a rota scheme but the time may be ripe to consider whether these should be modified. The ethical rule which necessitated the creation of rota schemes (the unfair attraction of business rule) has been greatly narrowed. As a result it might be considered that the bureaux should be permitted to select their volunteer advisers on the basis of expertise rather than being required to accept any solicitor however inexpert in social welfare law.

VIII. OTHER ADVICE CENTRES

Although CAS is undoubtedly the largest network of advice centres in Scotland there are many other agencies which are called on to give legal advice, *e.g.* neighbourhood information centres, consumer advice centres, citizens' rights offices, unemployed workers' centres, Women's Aid, Shelter, housing advice centres, and planning aid services. In addition, there are legal advice centres situated in the main conurbations of Scotland. These centres are usually staffed by practising solicitors or academic lawyers and normally operate once a week, either on a weekday evening or on a Saturday morning. While some centres will write letters for clients and even represent them at tribunals, others refer a high percentage of their inquiries to private solicitors.

IX. HUGHES AND THE PROBLEM OF ACCESS

The Hughes Commission, p. 69

"7.3 . . . an important part of the demand for legal services can be effectively and economically met by agencies providing general advice, initially through laymen, but with suitable back-up facilities (including referral to legal firms) to provide necessary further advice and assistance. These agencies can be particularly effective in helping clients to define the nature of their problems, which will often be complex and without a clearly identifiable 'legal' component; in providing a service in a convenient and familiar location; in assisting those with misgivings about the costs of legal help; and in reassuring clients who may not know their legal rights, or may have inhibitions about consulting solicitors."

Accordingly Hughes' primary solution to the problem of access was the introduction of a network of generalist advice agencies (R. 7.1). Hughes implicitly rejected the introduction of measures designed to encourage clients to go directly to the profession. They did not propose that clients should have a free, half-hour, diagnostic interview. Hughes considered it "wasteful to use a solicitor's skill to carry out tasks which a trained layman can perform effectively" (para. 7.4). Instead Hughes recommended that improved access to legal services should be promoted by the development of a network of generalist advice agencies which could "in appropriate cases provide the first access point to the machinery of legal services." These advice agencies would be based very much on the CAB model and would, the Commission hastened to add, be complementary to the services provided by solicitors. They would normally be staffed by trained volunteers and a paid organiser but with ready access to a range of specialist advisers. Such specialists would include lawyers who would normally be volunteer helpers or those taking part in a rota scheme or acting on a referral, although some salaried lawyers would be employed. While Benson was opposed to CABx building up teams of lawyers on their staff to act as legal advisers to clients (Benson had no objection to their being used as an information source for the staff of a CAB or a group of CABx), Hughes did not consider that salaried lawyers attached to generalist advice agencies should be limited in this way. Unfortunately Hughes devoted less than a quarter of a page to the problem of the link between the generalist advice agencies and the private practitioner—an area which has caused many problems in the past.

Nevertheless, overall it would appear that, not for the first time, the Hughes Commission demonstrated the more realistic approach to the problems of ignorance and access.

X. SOLICITOR ACCESSIBILITY

Advice centres are not intended to be, and, indeed, fall far short of being, the complete answer to the problem of access. Many clients will choose to employ a solicitor in private practice to solve their problems. Such clients face the problem of solicitor accessibility. Thus, a would-be client wishes to find a solicitor whose office is within a reasonable distance of the client's home or work and who is willing and competent to handle and, if possible, expert in handling his type of case. He should also be willing to do it at a reasonable price. There is reason to believe that solicitors with experience and expertise in legal aid work, or in social security, employment, education, consumer and local authority housing matters are in short supply and even less well-distributed than solicitors in general (see Paterson, "Unmet Legal Needs in Strath-clyde Region" unpublished report for Strathclyde Region, 1984). Even if the problems of distribution can be eased, for example, by grants or interest-free loans to encourage solicitors to set up offices in deprived or under-provided areas (Benson R. 16.5, Hughes R. 7.10), that is only the first hurdle. How are the other elements in the problem of solicitor accessibility to be overcome?

A number of surveys have been published which suggest that at present individuals choose their solicitors in the same ways as they select their doctors or dentists—mainly through acquaintances or on the recommendation of a relative or friend. These methods only overcome some of the problems of access. In the first place, many individuals, particularly those from the lower income sector of the population, do not have a "family solicitor" or a friend who is a solicitor. Secondly, assessing the competence of a solicitor is perhaps more difficult for a layman than assessing a doctor or dentist. Various solutions to the information needs of would-be clients have been put forward, ranging from individual advertising and solicitor directories to the certification of competence or expertise.

A. INDIVIDUAL ADVERTISING

The "Salisbury and Winchester Journal," December 6, 1779

CONVEYANCES made as cheap as by London
Attornies by JAMES MOXHAM, of Fordingbridge,
affifted by an eminent practitioner of the Law in London.

The "Daily Record and Mail" August 14, 1909

LAW, &c.

LAW Advice, 1s. Wills. Courts attended. Experienced Law Agents.—William Jarvie & Co., Writers, 50 Wellington Street, off Argyle Street. 9-8.30.

MARRIAGES Privately Completed, 10s; particulars sent free; experienced Law Agents.—William Jarvie & Co., Writers, 50 Wellington Street, off Argyle Street (convenient to all Stations). 9-8.30.

LAW Advice; Courts Attended; Marriages Privately Completed, 10s; particulars sent free.—John Younger, Writer, 19 Howard Street, off Jamaica St. 9 till 8.

As these advertisements show the prohibition on advertising by individual practitioners which many have regarded as one of the hallmarks of a profession is of comparatively recent origin, dating back only to the early twentieth century. When, in the 1970s, it was suggested that advertising should once more be permitted, proponents of the prohibition argued that individual advertising would undermine the relationship of trust between solicitor and client; it would be incompatible with the solicitor's duty to the wider community; it would be inherently misleading to the layman; and it would entail expenses which would have to be passed on to clients. Further, it was said that it would give larger firms an advantage in the market as compared with small firms which could not afford to advertise. Lastly, if price advertising was to be permitted it was alleged that it might encourage some solicitors to cut corners and thus lead to a reduction in the quality of legal services. Lying behind these objections seemed to be the feeling that advertising and competition were undignified and commercial, incompatible with the status of a profession.

Those who favoured the relaxation in the rule restricting individual advertising riposted that advertising would increase demand, innovation and competition; it would lower the price for routine legal services as a result of increased competition; it would enable consumers to make more informed choices as to which lawyer to approach with their problems; and it would make it easier for new lawyers to establish viable practices.

In *Bates* v. *State Bar of Arizona* (1976) 433 U.S. 350, the U.S. Supreme Court held, by a majority, that it was unconstitutional to prevent lawyers advertising the availability and cost of routine legal services, and in the succeeding years the Law Societies in Scotland and England came under considerable pressure to relax the prohibition in advertising. In 1976 the Monopolies and Mergers Commission pronounced itself in favour of individual advertising by solicitors in Scotland and England.

Monopolies and Mergers Commission,
Services of Solicitors in Scotland, pp. 31–33

"We [consider] . . . that the existing restrictions on the advertising of solicitors' services (i) prevent the public and potential new entrants to the profession being given information about the services offered by individual solicitors or firms of solicitors . . . (ii) are likely to have disadvantageous effects on the competitiveness and efficiency of the profession generally, on the introduction of innovatory methods and services and on the setting up of new practices . . .

125. We consider that . . . [the] general prohibition on advertising and soliciting business, should be terminated and replaced by a rule which would permit any solicitor in Scotland to use, whenever he thinks fit, such methods of publicity as he thinks fit, provided that:

(1) No advertisement, circular or other form of publicity used by a solicitor should claim for his practice superiority in any respect over any or all other solicitors' practices.

(2) Such publicity should not contain any inaccuracies or misleading statements.

(3) While advertisements, circulars and other publicity or methods of soliciting may make clear the intention of the solicitor to seek custom, they should not be of a character that could reasonably be regarded as likely to bring the profession into disrepute."

[For a further discussion of the competing arguments relating to solicitor advertising see Paterson, "Advertising by Lawyers; The American Experience" (1984) 29 J.L.S. 125, Macaulay, "Lawyer Advertising: 'Yes, but . . . ' " (Paper on Price Information and Public Controls, Consumer and Market Performance, presented to the Fourth European Workshop on Consumer Law, Brussels 1985).]

Despite the fact that both the Benson and Hughes Commissions endorsed the proposals of the Monopolies Commission, the profession continued to drag its feet. However, in 1983 the Government accepted that the practice rules of the profession required to be relaxed in an effort to permit more competition within the profession. Under Government pressure the English and Scottish Law Societies introduced revised practice rules permitting more individual advertising by solicitors (from 1 October 1984 and 1 March 1985 respectively).

The Scots adopted a minimalist approach. The only advertising that would be permitted was that specifically allowed under the Practice Rules. While relatively liberal in relation to the permitted media (television was allowed, cinema and bus posters were not) the provisions as to content were highly restrictive. The only significant advance on the pre-existing rule was the ability of a solicitor to advertise "any services provided by him in areas of practice in which he has experience". Yet this was strictly construed, thus excluding reference to specialisms or expertise, work done for particular clients, line drawings, photographs, chatty dialogue, blurb or offers to give a free or fixed fee interview to new clients. Advertisements which encouraged readers to telephone a solicitor were struck at as solicitation. Once it became clear that advertising did not herald the end of the profession or even professionalism as some critics had feared, a much less restrictive set of rules were introduced in 1987.

Thereafter solicitor advertising in Scotland became commonplace. A survey conducted in 1989 found that 57% of Scots firms had advertised in the previous six months—a higher figure than in the United States. (In fairness, however, the number of repeat or frequent advertisers was lower, perhaps much lower, than in the United States.) Predictably radio, television and cinematic advertising were pursued by less than 4% of firms but over 40% had experimented with an advertisement in a newspaper or freesheet. Price advertising, however, was very rare (less than 0.5%). As in the United States, Yellow Pages were seen by solicitors as a particularly effective form of advertising and over 40% of firms had advertised in them. Other promotional devices such as novelties, brochures and sponsorship had been used by about 25% of firms. Perhaps ominously, only 23% of firms reported that their promotional activities were part of a long-term plan. (This confirms the impression of observers that the majority of Scottish solicitor advertising to date has been tactical and ad hoc rather than strategic in nature.) [For fuller details on the survey, see Paterson and Stephen, *The Market for Conveyancing in Scotland* (Scottish Office, 1990), pp. 16–21.] The popularity of solicitor advertising and its non-problematic nature led in 1991 to the introduction of an even less restrictive set of rules on advertising.

Solicitors (Scotland) (Advertising and Promotion) Practice Rules 1991, rr. 4–8, 2(1)

"**4.** Subject to rules 5 and 8 hereof a solicitor shall be entitled to promote his services in any way he thinks fit.

5. A solicitor shall not make a direct or indirect approach whether verbal or written to any person whom he knows or ought reasonably to know to be the client of another solicitor with the intention to solicit business from that person.

6. Rule 5 shall not preclude the general circulation by a solicitor of material promoting that solicitor's services whether or not the persons to whom it is directed are established clients.

7. A solicitor shall not be in breach of these rules by reason only of his claim to be a *specialist in any particular field of law or legal practice; provided that:—

   (*a*) the onus of proof that any such claim is justified shall be on the solicitor making it; and

   (*b*) an advertisement of or by a solicitor or other material issued by or on behalf of a solicitor making any such claim shall conform otherwise to the requirements of rule 8.

8. An advertisement of or by a solicitor or promotional material issued by or on behalf of a solicitor or any promotional activity by or on behalf of a solicitor shall be decent and shall not:—

   (1) claim superiority for his services or practice over those of or offered by another solicitor; or

   (2) compare his fees with those of any other solicitor; or

   (3) contain any inaccuracy or misleading statement; or

   (4) be of such nature or character or be issued or done by such means as may reasonably be regarded as bringing the profession of solicitors into disrepute; or

   (5) identify any client or item of his business without the prior written consent of the client; or

   (6) be defamatory or illegal.

2.—(1)
   *'specialist' means an individual solicitor who possesses knowledge of and expertise in a particular branch or area of law or legal practice significantly greater than that which might reasonably be expected to be possessed by a solicitor who is not a specialist in that branch or area of law or legal practice."

As can be seen, the new rules are very close to the proposals of the Monopolies and Mergers Commission. Almost all restrictions on the media in which advertising can appear have been removed. As for content, anything can be published which is not specifically banned. A solicitor can even claim to be a specialist provided he or she can justify such a claim. Since being a "specialist" might mean only having experience in a particular field as opposed to expertise, the rules stipulate that a specialist must have knowledge and expertise in a particular area of law which is significantly greater than might be expected of a non-specialist. Finally, solicitors can now issue general mail-shots promoting their services provided

they do not target specific recipients for the circular (unless they know that the recipient has no existing solicitor or could not reasonably be expected to know that the recipient had a solicitor.) This is a bizarre restriction, requiring as it does that mail-shots be used inefficiently rather than aimed at those who are known to require the services of a solicitor. Targeted advertisements, on the other hand, are permitted as can be seen from the advertisement opposite which appeared in the *Shetland Times* following the oil tanker disaster in January 1993.

B. ALTERNATIVES TO INDIVIDUAL ADVERTISING

The Law Society preferred alternatives to individual advertising were institutional advertising of the services offered by the profession (which meets even fewer of the information needs of potential clients) and solicitor directories. It is not without irony that it was only in 1990, well after individual advertising had become successfully established, that the Law Society launched its largest and most sustained institutional advertising campaign, "It's never too early to consult a solicitor". The Society itself publishes the Directory of General Services provided by solicitors. The General Directory contains information about legal firms, individual solicitors and the areas of work which they normally handle (see Fig. 1).

EAST KILBRIDE DISTRICT

†Civil Legal Aid
‡Criminal Legal Aid
*Legal Advice and Assistance
§A.B.W.O.R.
H Home Visits

EAST KILBRIDE

BALLANTYNE & COPLAND
6 Princes Mall
(38649) (9-5.15 M-Fri or by appointment)
(† ‡ * § H)
Hugh J. Warden — 1977
Raymond Farrell
Stroma E. Spence — 1980

AUSTIN J. LAFFERTY & CO.
213 Edinburgh House, Princes Square
G74 1LJ
(63777/8) (9-5 M-Fri) († ‡ * § H)
Austin J. Lafferty — 1981

MACAULAY AND COMPANY
24–28 Calderwood Square G74 3BQ
(21092) (9.15-12.30; 1.45-5 M-Fri)
Margaret M. Macaulay — 1956

STRATHAVEN

ELDER & CRAIGMYLE
3 Bridge Street ML10 6AN
(22959) (9-5 M-Fri; 9.30-12 Sat) († ‡ * § H)
John Douglas Elder — 1979
Elizabeth White Craigmyle — 1980

Directories have advantages over individual advertising because they provide standardised information on the bulk of the profession, which enables comparisons to be made by consumers. Nevertheless, they still have a number of weaknesses in relation to coverage, distribution, content and compilation. The *General Directory* contains entries from only two-thirds of the profession and it is no longer updated on an annual basis. It is distributed to advice agencies, public libraries, social work departments and numerous other outlets, but too few are situated in places where individual members of the public can consult them directly. In the future the Directory would benefit from inclusion on television information systems such as Prestel and Oracle. The problem with content is that it does not contain information on fees or charging rates (though solicitors who will give the initial interview for £5 are identified), or on the expertise of practitioners or the time devoted by them to the problem categories in the Directory. There are directories in other countries, particularly in the United States, but also England and Wales which contain some of this information, but the Law Society of Scotland has hitherto been reluctant to publish such information in the Directory. The problem of content is linked to the problem of compilation—for the Directory is compiled by self-report. Some solicitors will tick every box—which is of little assistance to consumers. Even if solicitors were permitted to identify areas in which they specialise or work extensively this would not be a guarantee of expertise or even competence.

This problem was considered by the Royal Commissions. Benson concluded that some system of certification of specialisms should be introduced in England and Wales. In California, such a system, based on examinations and peer review, has been in operation since 1971.

The Benson Commission, p. 366

"*Eligibility for designation as a specialist*
27.21 We suggest that the following criteria should be satisfied.
(a) Designation should be granted to an individual and not to a firm. The solicitor concerned should have held a full practising certificate for at least five years immediately preceding his application.
(b) The solicitor should have devoted at least one-quarter of his time to the subject in question during each of the last five years.
(c) No solicitor should be designated as a specialist in more than two subjects at any one time.
(d) The claim to be designated as a specialist should be by written application to the Law Society which should satisfy itself that the

work carried out by the applicant has been such as to justify the designation of specialist. The names of referees should be provided if requested by the Law Society.

(e) The applicant should be interviewed by a panel of three experienced practitioners who should investigate in confidence the professional record and work of the applicant in order to determine whether the designation of specialist would be justified.

27.22 Applicants satisfying these criteria would be entitled to describe themselves as specialists in the appropriate category of work on their firm's writing paper, in the Solicitors' Directory, in the legal aid solicitors lists and other referral lists and in advertisements. A solicitor who has been recognised as a specialist should certify on every successive application for an annual practising certificate that he has devoted at least one-quarter of his normal working time to his specialism. A solicitor who ceases to meet this requirement should no longer be entitled to claim to specialise in it. In the event of a complaint being upheld against a solicitor's conduct or competence in his specialism, his designation as a specialist should be reviewed."

[See further, A.A. Paterson, "Specialisation and the Profession: Lessons from the United States," (1986) 31 J.L.S. 8.]

Hughes, on the other hand, was not convinced that such a system was worthwhile, preferring instead the introduction of a semi-formal system for monitoring the competence of the profession with reports from the Keeper of the Registers, court officials, judges and clients. Nevertheless, the extent of de facto specialisation (more than 70% of the profession in Scotland and England regard themselves as specialists) led the Scots and the English Law Societies in the 1980s to establish groups to investigate specialisation. As in the United States the choice lay between self-designation schemes and objective certification. In England panels for mental health review tribunals, child care and insolvency practitioners were established on the basis of interviews, course attendance and objective work experience tests in 1984 and 1985. The pressure grew on the profession to proceed with more panels fuelled by the endorsement of formal certification by the Civil Justice Review. Both Societies came out in favour of objective certification for panels using peer review and oral examination/ interviews. But even as these proposals emerged, a majority of the English Council of the Law Society in 1990, perhaps fearing a fragmentation of the profession into different sub-professions, forced through a change in the publicity code for solicitors. The reform allowed any solicitor to design themselves as a specialist provided they could justify their claim if challenged. This, of course, was simply self-designation in its crudest form. The Scots performed a similar volte face leaving the United Kingdom with a laxer approach to the publication of specialisation than any other country in the western world.

More recently, the relevant groups within the Societies have tried to revive the cause of certified specialists. In England panels of specialist personal injury solicitors and medical negligence specialists are being seriously considered. In Scotland an Employment Law panel was established in 1991 (to date only 20 solicitors have been recognised as accredited specialists and two of them are no longer in active practice). The Council has now approved the establishment of panels in Pensions Law, Agricultural Law, Commercial Leasing, Construction Law, Crofting Law, Child Law, Medical Negligence and Liquor Licensing and are considering further panels on Insolvency and Environmental Law. Certification will be based on peer review, considerable experience in the field, references and possibly a fixed minimum proportion of chargeable time in recent years. However, the scarcity of applicants to become registered Insolvency practitioners or certified Employment Law specialists suggests that the best vehicle for identifying specialist solicitors for Scottish clients has yet to be developed. One promising development, however, was the announcement in February 1993 that the Society had agreed to establish a panel of accredited mediators in the family law field whose membership is expected to be substantial.

CHAPTER 11

PAYING FOR LEGAL SERVICES

The third barrier between citizens and legal services identified by Hughes was cost. Hughes did not fall into the error of asserting that the poor use lawyers less often than other sectors of the community. Modern studies in the United States and in Australia and indeed the Benson Commission's user survey all show that *save in property related matters*, the public consults lawyers infrequently and that their use of lawyers is largely unrelated to class or income. However, the costs of professional services and of litigation in particular are now of such an order that all sectors of the community, except perhaps the most wealthy or those in commercial circles, are inhibited (though in varying degrees) from resorting to law. In response to the problem of cost a system of legal aid has evolved.

I. THE BACKGROUND TO LEGAL AID

The Hughes Commission, pp. 83–84

"8.2 Civil legal aid in more or less its present form was introduced in Scotland in 1950. Prior to that date, however, the Scottish legal profession had long accepted the representation of the poor without fee as a professional duty. An Act of 1424 made provision for the court to appoint an 'advocate' in civil cases for 'onie pure creature, for faulte of cunning, or expenses, that cannot, nor may not follow his cause'. In 1535, two advocates for the poor were appointed and received a stipend from the Treasury; but the system was probably rudimentary until the seventeenth century when there developed the practice of appointing members of the Society of Writers to the Signet as agents for the poor in the Court of Session. An Act of Sederunt of 10 August 1784, which probably for the first time formalised the procedure for admission to the poor's roll, required the Faculty of Advocates to appoint six advocates and the Writers to the Signet and the other agents practising in the Court of Session each to nominate four of their members to act for the poor in civil cases in the Court of Session. The applicant was required to produce a certificate of indigence from the minister and two elders of his parish and a report on the merits of the case by lawyers appointed for this purpose. This was, accordingly, the beginning of a system where the means of an applicant and the merits of his case are first examined before legal aid may be granted. From at least the 16th century, the legal profession accepted as a public duty the defence of poor persons on criminal charges. The statutory basis is uncertain, but two Acts of the Scottish Parliament in 1587 are thought to have regulated the provision of this service. Formal provision for the appointment of poor's agents in civil and criminal cases in the sheriff courts was made by the Act of Sederunt of 12 November 1825. Local schemes for providing representation for the poor were modified from time to time in the years after 1825, but the 'Poor's Roll' remained substantially in the same form until 1950. At an earlier stage, however, there had been recognition that radical reform was necessary, and a committee under the chairmanship of Sheriff Morton was appointed in 1936 to review the facilities available to poor persons as parties before the civil courts and as accused persons before the criminal courts. Before action could be taken on the Morton Report, the second world war intervened. In 1945, the Cameron Committee reviewed the need for legal aid in Scotland following a report on this subject which had been made by the Rushcliffe Committee relative to England and Wales. After considerable debate there emerged the Legal Aid (Scotland) Act 1949, which envisaged a system whereby persons of limited means could receive civil and criminal legal aid and advice. However, because of economic considerations at the time, civil legal aid alone was introduced in 1950. It was not until 1964 that criminal legal aid was introduced following a further review, this time by the Guthrie Committee. In 1972, legal advice and assistance (providing for limited advice and assistance short of representation in court) was added to the system."

II. LEGAL AID TODAY

A. ADMINISTRATION

There was always a latent conflict of interest between the Law Society acting as the governing body of solicitors and as the supervisor of the payment of substantial sums of public money to its members. For this reason the Hughes Commission (para. 8.73) recommended that legal aid in Scotland should be administered by an independent authority (a Legal Services Commission) to continuously review the scheme, to scrutinise accounts for payment and to experiment with new forms of delivering legal aid. In part in response to this recommendation the Government in the Legal Aid (Scotland) Act 1986 vested the administration of legal aid in the hands of a new non-departmental public body—the Scottish Legal Aid Board. (It consists of 11 individuals appointed by the Secretary of State, of which at least four must be lawyers.) However the remit of the Board is somewhat different to that suggested for the Legal Services Commission—its general functions consisting of administering the legal aid fund and securing that legal aid and advice and assistance are available in accordance with the 1986 Act. Unlike its predecessor, the Board was also given the responsibility for the assessment of applicants' resources in civil legal aid and for the granting of criminal legal aid in summary cases.

B. LEGAL AID IN CIVIL COURT PROCEEDINGS

Legal aid as it operates in Scotland and England today, consists of three basic schemes: Legal Aid in Civil Proceedings, Advice and Assistance and Criminal Legal Aid. (For further details on Criminal Legal Aid, see chapter 4 above.) Civil Legal Aid, which is governed by section 13 of the Legal Aid (Scotland) Act 1986 provides legal representation in virtually all proceedings before the more important and the most commonly used Scottish courts.

The proceedings in which legal aid is not available (described as the "excepted proceedings" in the Act) are those in respect of defamation or verbal injury (except in respect of certain counterclaims: Schedule 2, Part II, para. 2 of the Act); simplified divorce applications; election petitions; small claims at first instance; and proceedings under the Debtors (Scotland) Act 1987 other than proceedings under section 1(1) or 3(1). It would appear that any doubts as to whether legal aid was available for summary causes or proceedings for summary removing in which the liability for the debt and its amount were admitted have been removed by the passing of the 1986 Act (Stoddart, *Legal Aid in Scotland*, W. Green, 3rd ed, 1990, para. 7–18 and 7–19.) Legal aid is not available for any proceedings in the Court of the Lord Lyon, the Court of Teinds, the Registration of Voters Appeal Court, the Election Petition Court, the courts of the Church of Scotland and the military courts-martial. Perhaps most significant of all, legal aid is not available for proceedings before tribunals, with the exception of the Lands Tribunal for Scotland (Schedule 2, Part 1, para. 1 of 1986 Act) and the Employment Appeal Tribunal (Schedule 2, Part 1, para. 1 of 1986 Act), which is a superior court of record.

To qualify for civil legal aid the applicant must satisfy the Board as to the merits of his or her case as well as being financially eligible.

1. LEGAL CRITERIA

Legal Aid (Scotland) Act 1986, s.14(1)
" . . . civil legal aid shall be available to a person if, on an application made to the Board—
  (a) the Board is satisfied that he has a *probabilis causa litigandi*; and
  (b) it appears to the Board that it is reasonable in the particular circumstances of the case that he should receive legal aid."

This twofold legal eligibility test is commonplace in the western world although in some jurisdictions the two are subsumed under a single "reasonableness" test. Only the Netherlands are significantly out of line by merely requiring that the action be not "wholly unfounded" or unjustified in terms of the likely cost of the action.

2. Financial Criteria

Legal aid is available in civil cases to all persons:

(a) who do not have rights or facilities making it unnecessary for them to have legal aid (*e.g.* when a trade union will pay for the case as one of the benefits of membership or where the applicant is covered by a legal expenses insurance policy);

(b) whose "disposable" income (*i.e.* net wage under deduction of allowances for expenditure such as rent, hire purchase commitment and allowances for dependants) does not exceed the limit from time to time prescribed by the Secretary of State. The current upper limit is £6,800 or, in cases where the subject of the action is damages for personal injury or death, £7,500. Where the applicant's "disposable" income lies between the upper limit and £2,293 (the non-contributory limit) he or she will have to make a contribution towards the cost of the case. This will not exceed one third of the excess of the disposable income over £2,293;

(c) where the applicant has "disposable" capital (*i.e.* capital under certain deductions and disregarding the value of any house, furniture, personal clothing and tools of his trade) of more than £6,750, or £8,560 in damages for personal injury or death cases, he or she may be refused legal aid if it appears that they can afford to proceed without it. Where the disposable capital lies between these upper limits and £3,000 (the non-contributory limit) then applicants are required to contribute towards the cost of their litigation. This will be not more than the amount by which the applicant's disposable capital exceeds £3,000.

The Board calculates the maximum contribution of applicants by the simple process of totalling their capital and income contributions. However, if the likely cost of the action is below this sum an "actual" contribution will be fixed based on the Board's estimate of what the case will cost. Contributions from capital are usually paid in a lump sum but income contributions are normally payable by instalments over ten months. Where the assisted party is successful in his or her action but the expenses of the litigation are not recovered in full from the other side the Board will look to the assisted party to meet any shortfall from their contributions or any property recovered as a result of the action. [Section 17(5) Legal Aid (Scotland) Act 1986.] This is known as the "statutory clawback."

3. LIABILITY FOR EXPENSES

Mellick, "Legal Aid in Scotland," p. 188

"In the event of the legally assisted person failing in his action or defence and/or having an award of expenses made against him, then it is the duty of the solicitor to ask the court to modify the award or the sum payable thereunder to the opponent having regard to the means of the legally assisted person. Unless there has been any change in circumstances since the application for Legal Aid was made, this information is usually obtained from the Legal Aid application and from the Legal Aid Certificate . . . Alternatively up to date information must be supplied to the court. It is not uncommon for the court to limit any award of expenses against a legally assisted person to payment of an amount equal to the legally assisted person's original contribution: but the matter is entirely in the discretion of the court. A legally assisted person is very seldom ordered to pay the full amount of any award of expenses made against him. This is a safeguard to the legally assisted person against the possibility of insolvency or bankruptcy in the event of his otherwise engaging in litigation . . .

Provision is also made for the case where a legally aided person sues a non-legally aided person and fails in his action and has an award of expenses made against him. Presumably on the theory that public funds having financed the litigation of the legally assisted person, the court can where hardship can be shown on the part of the non-legal aid defender through his inability to recover expenses from the legally assisted person, make an order that the expenses of the non-legal aid defender be paid out of the Legal Aid Fund."

C. ADVICE AND ASSISTANCE

Advice and Assistance is a form of legal aid which enables persons of limited means to obtain advice on practically any matter involving an issue of Scots law. The main exclusion relates to steps in the institution or conduct of any proceedings before a court or tribunal. Even this restriction has been modified in recent times by the introduction of ABWOR (assistance by way of representation) as part of Advice and Assistance to cover representation in certain criminal proceedings and appeals under the Mental Health (Scotland) Act 1984. Unlike civil legal aid there are no merits tests. Advice and Assistance has the additional advantage of flexibility in that:

(1) The person seeking the advice need not go to the solicitor, provided that there is a good reason for not doing so. The advice may be obtained by telephone or mail or even through an adult intermediary who attends on the applicant's behalf.
(2) The solicitor need not give the advice and assistance at his or her office. It may be given outside the office *e.g.* in the home

of a disabled or infirm client, in hospital, in prison, in a police station or in the precincts of a court.

(3) The person giving advice need not be a solicitor—the task can be delegated to a competent and responsible representative employed in his or her office.

The statutory clawback operates in relation to Advice and Assistance as well, although, contrary to the position in civil legal aid actions, the Board has a discretion to allow the whole sum recovered to be paid over to the client without deduction of expenses where to do otherwise would cause grave hardship to the client or could only be effected with unreasonable difficulty.

D. STRENGTHS AND WEAKNESSES

A study of other legal systems reveals that legal aid can be provided in a wide variety of different forms. [See Paterson, "Legal Aid at the Crossroads" (1991) 11 *Civil Justice Quarterly* 124.] Principally these consist of the charitable model (provided by volunteer members of the profession on a gratuitous basis), judicare (provided by the private profession funded by the state), the salaried model (provided by state salaried lawyers) and the mixed model (provided by a mixture of private practitioners and state salaried lawyers). Legal aid in Scotland today (like the rest of the United Kingdom) primarily takes the form of the judicare model.

It is generally considered that its principal strengths relate to the fact that it is state funded, independently administered, broad in its scope, provides a wide choice of lawyer and risk protection if the action is lost. In all these respects the Scots model is superior to the charitable model. Although, as we shall see, eligibility for legal aid is declining in Scotland the proportion of the population covered is still greater than most other countries except the Netherlands. Indeed the per capita expenditure on all forms of legal aid in the United Kingdom exceeds any other country. [See E. Blankenburg, "Comparing Legal Aid Schemes in Europe" (1992) 12 *Civil Justice Quarterly* 106 and Legal Action Group, *A Strategy for Justice* (London, LAG, 1982).] Similarly, although there are significant omissions in the coverage of legal aid in Scotland the overall breadth of potential cover bears comparison with most other countries. In the eyes of the profession and perhaps also of the public the fact that any qualified lawyer can provide legal aid is seen as a significant advantage in that it maximises access. However, legal aid policy makers and others have begun to question whether this feature is always as beneficial as it appears, since it fails to address issues such as economies of scale, the benefits of specialisation and the cost-effectiveness of state salaried lawyers. Such doubts are strengthened by the fact that it appears that about 25% of solicitors in the United Kingdom do 75% of legal aid work. (In Quebec, by contrast less than 20% of the private profession undertakes any legal aid at all.) Finally, under the United Kingdom model of legal aid, the Legal Aid Fund bears the bulk of the risk of loss if assisted parties are unsuccessful in their actions since losing assisted parties will usually have their liability to pay the other sides' expenses severely modified by the court. In most European jurisdictions there is no such protection for assisted parties who are unsuccessful in their litigation.

Despite these advantages, the Scottish judicare model shares the drawbacks of its English counterpart. Indeed, viewed from the perspective of the state, of the profession and the consumer there are a number of weaknesses in the model.

The State's Perspective

The principal concern of western governments is that the cost of providing legal aid through the private profession is rising expo-nentionally—frequently well in excess of inflation. Thus in Scotland between 1987/88 and 1991/92 payments from the Legal Aid Fund rose from £48 million to £80 million and are projected to exceed £100 million in 1993. (In England and Wales between 1985/86 and 1990/91 average legal aid bills were rising at more than twice the rate in increase in the retail price index—NAO Report on *The Administration of Legal Aid in England and Wales* (H.M.S.O., London, 1992) at p. 12.) The rise is in part due to an increased throughput of cases but also to an increase in the unit cost of each case.

The Profession's Perspective

To the profession the deficiencies of the United Kingdom model of judicare are threefold. First, that bureaucratic hurdles are increasing, necessitating delays, abandonment or the option of doing work for nothing. Secondly, that there is no effective payment mechanism which supplies the necessary working capital to support firms through cash-flow problems. (Cases may take months or years to complete before a legal aid account can be rendered by the lawyers, who in the meantime may be out of pocket for considerable levels of incidental expenses, not to mention fees. In the Netherlands, by contrast, lawyers can receive lump sum payments in advance which reflect the level of legal aid work undertaken by them in the previous year.) Thirdly, the profession considers that the level of remuneration for legal aid work is inadequate since legal aid rates are now significantly below the private rates set by the profession and the court.

The Consumer's Perspective

Consumers, on the other hand, are more concerned that legal aid has still not been extended to cover proceedings before most tribunals despite the fact that tribunals now deal with many issues that are vital to the welfare of the ordinary citizen (see Chap. 5 above). Equally, the repeated failure to permit pursuers in defamation actions to obtain legal aid, effectively denies the bulk of the population the opportunity to defend their reputations against public vilification. The exclusion of small claims cases has been justified on the basis that the procedure is designed to be used without the assistance of qualified lawyers. While this may be acceptable where small sums are concerned, critics point to proposals that the financial limit for small claims be raised substantially as posing a threat to inarticulate litigants who would no longer be eligible for legal aid. [See D. O'Carroll and P. Brown, "Small Claims" (1991) 181 *SCOLAG* 154.] The strength of this critique, however, must be tempered by the fact that for many consumers with small claims or personal injury actions the operation of the statutory clawback can deprive them of much of the benefit of legal aid if they win their cases but are unable to recover costs from their opponent.

There is also concern that a declining proportion of the population is now eligible for legal aid. When civil legal aid was introduced in 1950, 80% of the population was eligible on income grounds. By 1978 the figure had fallen to 40%. Measures were introduced to bring the coverage up to 70% (in terms of income) but again the failure to keep pace with inflation meant that only about half the population were eligible by 1990. The position had not improved by early 1993 when the government announced their proposals for draconian cuts in eligibility for civil legal aid. [See M. Murphy, "Civil Legal Aid Eligibility," 1989 *Legal Action* October, p. 7 and LAG, *A Strategy for Justice* (Appendix 1) 1992.]

A third problem for consumers comes from the fact that the structure of legal aid in the United Kingdom presupposes that the problems of applicants are best tackled on an individual basis. Bodies of persons are ineligible for legal aid.

Myers, "The future of Legal Aid in Scotland," p. 316.
"Legal aid—as is the case with legal practice—has always emphasised the protection of individual rights. In modern society, more and more disputes affect groups. These disputes have been particularly significant in planning and development matters . . . [Yet] there has been an almost complete lack of legal assistance available for poorer communities faced with large-scale redevelopment or a loss of basic amenities.

The legal aid scheme provides a 'curative' service, offering legal assistance to pursue legal rights. It ought to be devoting more time and money to the provision of a 'preventive' service, educating groups in the community about law and legal rights."

Of course, one member of a group could raise an action as a test case and be granted legal aid, as Mrs McColl was in her action against Strathclyde Region's plans to add fluoride to the water supply. However, unless the Board consider that the applicant's individual interest is significant, it may well decide that it would not "be reasonable in the particular circumstances" to grant the application. This is all the more likely to be the case after the remarks by Lord Jauncey in *McColl* v. *Strathclyde Regional Council*, 1983 S.L.T. 616 criticising the award of legal aid to Mrs McColl. The considerable growth in disaster or multi-party litigation in Scotland in the last ten years however, has led the Board to adopt a collective approach (dovetailing with a parallel approach of the Law Society which endeavours to bring together solicitors in multi-party cases). The Board's strategy is for applicants in such cases to be covered by generous advice and assistance extensions (in some cases in excess of £2,000) and/or given a legal aid certificate limited to raising the action and then sisting it until one case—the "test" or lead case—is determined in the courts. In England the Board has introduced a form of tendering by firms wishing to undertake multi-party litigation funded by legal aid.

[Further drawbacks with the Scots model of legal aid include a lack of public awareness as to its scope and existence (see p. 258 above, chapter 10) and a lack of knowledge in many practitioners in relation to aspects of legal aid. See Paterson, "Legal Aid" (1985) 106 SCOLAG 103.]

III. HOW LEGAL AID IS USED

TABLE 1

Civil legal aid certificates issued in Scotland 1991/92

Divorce	39%
(all matrimonial)	(59%)
Custody/Adoption	15%
(all parent and child)	(23%)
Reparation	7%
Miscellaneous	11%

[Source: Annual Report Scottish Legal Aid Board 1991/92.]

TABLE 2
Advice and Assistance Bills paid 1991/92

	Scotland	England
Family/Matrimonial	22%	35%
Criminal	49%	21%
Reparation	6%	6%
Housing	3%	8%
Debt	5%	7%
Immigration	—	2%
Consumer	—	2%
Employer	1.3%	2%
Welfare Benefit/ Tribunal	1.5%	6%
Other	12.2%	11%

[Source: Annual Reports Scottish and English
Legal Aid Boards 1991/92.]

The picture of legal aid usage revealed in Table 1 is one that has remained relatively constant over the past 15 years. Civil Legal Aid in Scotland is overwhelmingly used to support litigation between husbands and wives. As Table 2 shows, the over-emphasis on traditional areas of law remains depressingly true of applications for Advice and Assistance. Yet, 60 per cent of the workload of the publicly funded law centres in England and Wales concerns housing, welfare, employment and immigration law. Legal advice centres in Scotland and England in addition handle many consumer cases. In part such discrepancies between the public and private sectors can be attributed to the limitations imposed on the work which law centres may undertake (see Chapter 12) but probably more significant is the operation of the statutory clawback and the lack of publicity given to the Legal Aid schemes.

IV. LEGAL AID: THE WAY FORWARD

1. THE PURPOSE OF LEGAL AID

Paterson, "The Purpose of Legal Aid," pp. 232–34

"The rationale for legal aid
There is no universally accepted rationale or justification for the provision of state subsidised legal services . . . Although it has occasionally been argued that legal aid is a form of wealth redistribution or that the redistribution of legal services can lead to desirable social change, neither argument has attracted many supporters. The two principal justifications for legal aid which are put forward today are: (1) a utilitarian argument that more widespread use of legal services is a public

good and that in a time of scarce resources the development of legal services should follow lines which would generate the greatest benefit for the greatest number of recipients; and (2) an argument that more widespread use of legal services is required in the interests of justice. Under this view the integrity of the adversary system (particularly where prosecutors are publicly funded) requires an equality in the distribution of legal services since its efficacy is predicated on both sides being competently represented.

One of the best expositions of this second line of thought is contained in the 25th Legal Aid Annual Report of the English Law Society (1975, para. 1): 'Legal aid is increasingly being thought of as a social service and part of the welfare ideal; its fundamental importance however, has not been sufficiently recognised in that its function is to ensure that justice—the first of all social services—is made available to all and is not confined to those able to bear the cost of protecting their lawful rights. The help afforded to those of limited means and the disadvantaged must be seen in the broad context of the role of the law itself, which provides the only foundation upon which the whole edifice of social welfare depends. In so far as the law is not made effective in the lives of all citizens it must fail in its social purpose and weaken all other social measures. Only through a truly comprehensive legal aid scheme can laws enacted to benefit those in need fully serve their intention. Legal aid is not an independent social instrument; it is an essential ingredient in the administration of justice without which the law must remain partial and socially discriminative.' Some exponents of this view have been prepared to go further and to argue that the receipt of legal services is a 'civil right' (34th Legal Aid Annual Report, para. 58). Such an assertion has problematic elements in the United Kingdom context since the entitlement to legal aid is hedged around with discretionary judgments. . . .

Civil legal aid

The [legal aid] consultation paper [issued by the Scottish Home and Health Department in 1985], however, asserted that: 'There are many misconceptions about the purpose of legal aid. In civil cases the aim is that legal aid should permit those of insufficient means that same opportunity to pursue their rights as is available to those of moderate rather than abundant means. It should in general not be available in a case which would not be pursued by a person of moderate means' (para. 4)."

If this statement is an assertion that persons of moderate means are and have always been ineligible for legal aid then it is incorrect, as we have seen. If it means that legal aid is designed to put a poor person in the same position as a person of moderate means then not only is it historically inaccurate but it also represents a major erosion in the availability of legal aid. The aim of legal aid has not been to put poor persons in the position of those of moderate means who are ineligible for legal aid. Its aim has been to enable persons of low or moderate income who meet the legal and financial tests for legal aid to raise or defend an action unhampered by their lack of resources or a fear of having to pay crippling expenses should they lose.

2. THE SCOPE OF LEGAL AID

Paterson, "Legal Services for All?" p. 327.

"In relation to legal aid [the Hughes Commission] looked first at the proposal of the Scottish Legal Action Group (which coincided with a proposal of the English L.A.G.) that the constraints on available funds are such that we should readjust our priorities in legal aid. In the first place certain services should be regarded as so essential, for example legal procedures relating to (a) the deprivation of liberty by custodial sentence or (b) the preservation of jobs, homes or welfare benefits, that they should normally be provided to everyone free of charge—at least up to the point of the first judgment of disposal. Secondly, S.L.A.G. proposed that certain desirable but non-essential legal services, for example help in making a will, obtaining a divorce, adoptions, minor criminal proceedings and the like, should be obtainable on payment of a flat rate contribution. Thirdly, services which would produce some gain for clients, for example house purchase and sale or forming companies or trusts, should be charged at a fair fee."

The Hughes Commission, pp. 90–91

"The scope of legal aid

8.16 The Scottish Legal Action Group proposal contains a number of points. For example, it does away with the principle of contribution on the basis of means. We know that many people find means testing abhorrent; but we believe that it is only fair that those who are able should make some contribution to the cost of the legal services they use. Some form of assessment of means will thus continue to be essential . . .

8.17 The Scottish Legal Action Group proposal also involves what might be called 'needs testing': a categorisation of kinds of case some of which would attract free legal aid; some of which would attract legal aid subject to a flat rate contribution; and some of which would attract no legal aid at all. In the way in which this was presented to us we were not convinced that the proposal was sound; and we thought it could lead to injustice. As regards civil matters we do not think it desirable for us, the legislature, or anyone else, to attempt to define in general terms for others what types of case are 'important' to them. Unless the category for which unlimited or generous legal aid is to be available were drawn so widely as to make this proposal meaningless, we think it inevitable that the proposal would result in legal aid being granted in cases of relative triviality and being withheld in cases where hardship cries out for it to be available. Nevertheless, we believe that there should be a limit, in principle, to the scope of legal aid. In civil matters, as we have already said, we believe it is right that the State should help a citizen to take legal action to assert or protect his rights; but we do not think it justifiable that public funds should be expended to assist individuals in arranging their affairs for the benefit of themselves or for others."

34th Legal Aid Annual Report 1983–84

"290. The Hughes Report . . . argument has some force, but it does not in our view constitute the decisive objection of principle to the ['needs testing'] proposal. In the context of legal aid, there is no reason why taxpayers generally should provide a 100% subsidy for people who can afford to contribute substantially towards the cost of their cases, however important are the particular rights those people wish to defend. We would not welcome a situation in which people of considerable means were able to litigate entirely at public expense. We adhere to the general principle that people should pay towards the cost of the legal services they require what they can reasonably afford. Insofar as it is necessary to ensure that people are not deterred from defending their fundamental rights, that objective can best be attained by maintaining the value of the legal aid limits generally.

291. Even were it to be agreed that there were areas of law involving fundamental civil rights, it is doubtful how far agreement would be reached over precisely what those areas were. And even if there were a consensus as to the types of cases that should be singled out, it is doubtful whether they would be easily defined in terms of categories of proceedings."

The Hughes proposal that legal aid should only be available to help citizens to assert or protect their rights, and not to assist them in arranging their affairs for the benefit of themselves or others, is based on a value judgment no less questionable than that contained in the proposals of the Scottish and English Legal Action Groups. Under the Hughes' scheme conveyancing, and the making of wills and contracts would be excluded but defence in any criminal proceedings and the pursuit and defence of civil proceedings would almost always be included. The Commission elsewhere decries "do it yourself" will forms, and lays heavy stress on the need for individuals to make wills having taken the appropriate professional advice. Yet in relation to legal aid the Commission argues that public funds should not be expended to help people make proper wills, rather they should be spent in assisting dependants fight over their succession rights which are not clear because the deceased person did not make a proper will. Similarly the

Commission's arguments may lead to public funds being spent on battles between taxpayers and the Inland Revenue or between trustees and beneficiaries.

3. ELIGIBILTY

The Hughes Commission and the Legal Aid Eligibility Review [SOHHD, *Review of Financial Conditions for Legal Aid: Eligibility for Civil Legal Aid in Scotland*, 1992] both floated the additional possibility of removing the upper eligibility limit of disposable income coupled with a sharply rising scale of contributions (ensuring that better off assisted parties would in effect pay near to 100% of the cost of their litigation). This proposal would remove the current anomaly whereby applicants just within the financial limits can afford to litigate and those with a few more pounds of disposable income, cannot. Although the fiscal implications of such a step are, perhaps surprisingly, not significant it seems unlikely that in times of economic restraint the government will go down this path.

Ostensibly, the Eligibility Review was an attempt to tackle anomalies caused by fixed eligibility limits. However, its principal proposal, the "safety net", appeared to be as much focussed on the growing Treasury concern with the spiralling cost of legal aid— particularly in England and Wales.

Paterson, "Financing Legal Services" p. 160
"In brief, the review proposed that contributions should be increased and made to last throughout a case while assessment of means should be made less expensive by adopting a more broad brush, not to say crude, approach. In a purported attempt to tackle the problems of those outwith the legal eligibility limits it was suggested that a safety-net should be introduced. Under this system the applicant would spend up to £2,500 of his or her own money (the spending limit) before becoming eligible for legal aid. While this proposal offered assistance to some better off litigants, the paper hinted that the scheme might also be applied to poorer applicants currently eligible for legal aid but with a contribution (*i.e.* those above the free legal aid threshold). For them the safety net would be more akin to a tripwire. The Government claimed that the proposal would encourage responsible litigation and settlements. In reality, however, there is no evidence of assisted parties behaving irresponsibly by pursuing their actions. Even those who fall below the free legal aid limit have an interest to be prudent in litigating because of the mechanism of the statutory charge. To suggest that the spending limit would encourage litigants to exercise greater control over their lawyers overlooks the fact that it is very difficult for lay clients to assess the quality of the work being done for them by their lawyer."

The Eligibility Review was heavily criticised by almost all of the respondents but worse was to follow. The Treasury, alarmed by the spiralling costs of legal aid in England and Wales which were being further driven up by the recession, called a halt, forcing the Lord Chancellor and his Scottish counterpart to introduce draconian cuts in civil legal aid in early 1993. These include the reduction of the free limit for civil legal aid from £3,060 to £2,293 per annum, freezing the upper eligibility limit, reducing dependants' allowances and increasing the contributions paid by assisted parties (from a quarter of the sum by which their disposable income exceeds the free limit, to a third). In addition, in future only applicants with a disposable income of £61 per week would receive advice and assistance free with the maximum level for eligibility being set at £147 with a contribution of £86.

The cuts are particularly unpalatable in Scotland for a number of reasons. First, they represent a fundamental departure from the purpose of legal aid as it has operated to date (see p. 285 above). Instead of access to justice being a citizenship right for a majority of the population, in future it will be a welfare benefit. Secondly, the cuts will only effectively reduce expenditure in relation to civil legal aid. Yet in this area real expenditure (taking into account inflation) fell by 28% between 1987/88 and 1991/92. Although it has risen substantially since then, this largely reflects increased demands from the public due to the recession, quicker submission of accounts by practitioners for the same reason and a much faster payment of accounts by the Legal Aid Board. The problem area of growth is criminal legal aid which has increased by 60% in real terms since 1987/88 and is taking over a greater and greater share of Advice and Assistance (37% in 1991/92) and of the total legal aid bill (70% of the total in 1992). The cuts will do nothing to remedy this situation, indeed they will exacerbate it, since criminal legal aid is non-contributory. In short they appear to be an English solution to an English problem applied North of the Border which may cause very severe damage to civil legal aid in Scotland in the future. All for the sake of an estimated saving of £2–£3 million per annum.

4. VALUE FOR MONEY

Whatever the merits of the cuts and the Eligibility Review it is clear that the United Kingdom, like most other jurisdictions with sophisticated legal aid programmes, is determined to improve the cost-effectiveness and quality of the services provided under legal aid. In these countries, *e.g.* the United Kingdom, Australia, Norway, and the Netherlands very similar proposals are being considered. These include fixed fees, vouchers, contracts and quality assurance. Germany and the Netherlands have long had fixed fees and found them to be an invaluable instrument in keeping expenditure in check. However, attempts to introduce them in England and Wales have been greeted with considerable hostility by the profession, who regard them as an open invitation to shoddy work. Proposals that eligible applicants for legal aid should be supplied with a voucher providing legal aid which could be cashed in with either salaried or private practitioners have been floated in the United States and Australia. There is no evidence to date that such schemes can provide effective quality controls.

Contracting out legal aid work to private lawyers on a bulk basis is an idea which has been examined in several countries, *e.g.* Norway, the Netherlands, Australia and the United States. In relation to duty lawyer schemes contracts are thought to have had some success in Australia but not in the United States. However, perhaps the most advanced plan for ensuring value for money from legal aid suppliers through the use of contracts is the English Legal Aid Board's supplier development strategy which has evolved from the Franchising project.

Paterson, "Financing Legal Services" pp. 163–164
"The [Franchising] project is confined to firms and advice agencies in parts of Birmingham who are prepared to implement certain quality systems. In return for putting these systems in place and operating them franchise firms receive certain advantages from the Legal Aid Board. Originally it was proposed that all decisions on advice and assistance, ABWOR and emergency applications would be delegated to the fran-chisees and that in addition firms would receive monthly payments in advance representing a twelfth of the firm's earnings from all types of legal aid over the past twelve months. After last minute negotiations with the Law Society it was agreed that the firms would get four new early payment systems: up to £250 on account for each self-granted emergency certificate, up to £150 on account of each self-certified ABWOR case, the right to be paid at least two hours' worth of costs each time an advice and assistance extension is granted in-house and 75% on account of costs incurred once a civil legal aid certificate has run for nine months.

The concept of franchising was chosen in preference to tendering or contracting-out since it offered more access to the public with a better guarantee of quality. Originally the Board wanted to pursue economies of scale and suggested that franchise firms should have a turnover of £40,000 a year in legal aid fees and employ supervisors who would not be permitted to supervise more than three categories of work or seven people doing that work. After extensive discussions with the profession and the consumer bodies these requirements were dropped for the purposes of the experiment. However it is probable that both the Board and the Lord Chancellor's Department presently envisage that the supplier development strategy which is emerging from the franchising experiment will hinge around firms prepared to specialise in and to undertake substantial amounts of legal aid work ("preferred suppliers"). If this line is pursued it may produce considerable problems of access, particularly in the rural areas.

Largely for these reasons the case for franchising in Scotland has hitherto seemed to be less attractive to Scottish policy makers. It may be therefore that the current proposals of the Ministry of Justice in the Netherlands on this issue will prove more attractive. These include the registration of legal aid practitioners. Registration would be subject to a number of conditions:

—a minimum (about ten) and a maximum number of cases that a lawyer can accept during one year;

—specialisation, restricting registration to a limited number of legal areas;

—good office procedures with adequate back-up cover;

—annual reports to the legal aid authorities.

Exceptionally, where there is good reason clients will be permitted to instruct private practitioners who are not registered. Registration will be refused if the conditions cannot be met, if the lawyer is over 70 or if the lawyer works much less efficiently than other members of the profession (judged by a series of performance indicators)."

V. ALTERNATIVES TO LEGAL AID

The ever increasing cost of legal aid to the Treasury has already prompted numerous proposals for curbing legal aid expenditure, as we have seen. It has also led reformers to consider alternatives to legal aid which might address the problem of the cost of legal services.

A. CONTINGENT FEES

Paterson, "Paying for Legal Services," pp. 237–238

"There are several variants on this theme. Straightforward contingent fees (arrangements whereby a lawyer takes a case on the basis that if he loses there will be no fee and if he wins he will obtain a percentage of the court's award) are unlawful and contrary to professional ethics in England, and prohibited at common law as *pacta de quota litis* in Scotland. Under the Land Purchase Act 1594 *c.* 220 it is also unlawful for any member of the College of Justice or any inferior court (including advocates, solicitors and clerks) to purchase pleas where litigation is pending. (The penalty under the Act is not nullity but deprivation of office for the offender!) It is not, however, illegal for debt collection agencies or claims assessors to purchase pleas or to undertake litigation for a fee which is a percentage of the sum in dispute or the sum recovered. On the other hand, solicitors who take a percentage fee on claims which they are instructed to litigate, might well be acting unlawfully if they habitually waive fees where no recovery is made.

It is not the taking of a proportion of the subject of the litigation on its own which is objectionable. It is always open for clients to enter into a special charging agreement with their lawyers. Moreover, the fees for extra-judicial settlements of claims for damages or reparation in cases where no proceedings in court have been initiated are calculated as a percentage of the sum settled for. Nor is it the agreement to act on the speculative basis that no fees will be payable unless the action is successful, which is objectionable. In X Insurance Co. v. A and B [1936 S.C. 225, 239] Lord President Normand remarked:

> 'It has long been recognised by our Courts that this is a perfectly legitimate basis on which to carry on litigation and a reasonable indulgence to people who . . . are . . . unable to finance a costly litigation.'

It is only where the percentage fee is combined with a speculative action that the agreement is struck at as a contingent fee. Yet, where a solicitor in Scotland has undertaken a speculative action for damages and subsequently settles it extrajudicially he is in effect receiving a contingent fee which is very unlikely to be declared *pactum de quota litis*."

[The acceptability of speculative fees was endorsed in the Law Reform (Miscellaneous Provisions) (Scotland) Act 1990, s. 36 which provides that solicitors and advocates can not only charge speculative fees but a percentage increase in the fee to a limit laid down by the court.]

Paterson, "Contingent Fees and their Rivals" pp.81–83
"In the United States of America, contingent fees are most frequently used in personal injury actions, though they are by no means confined to such cases. Indeed their usage ranges from product liability to debt collection cases and from employment discrimination to anti-trust actions. In certain areas of law, however, the courts and ethical codes prohibit the use of contingent fees on public policy grounds. These are criminal cases, family cases and in some states, legislative lobbying. Contingent fees may be calculated as a percentage rate, as a fixed fee, or on an hourly basis. In practice, percentage rates are the most common: a typical contingent fee agreement in the United States of America may provide that the lawyer's reward will be 25 per cent of any settlement prior to a writ being issued, a third of any settlement or award made after the writ is issued, and 40 per cent or more if either side appeals. For this, the expenses of the case (such as court dues, experts' reports and witness fees) are usually advanced by the lawyer.

The first, and strongest, argument in favour of contingent fees is that they permit poor clients who are unable to pay lawyers' fees to bring their cases to court. 'One shot' litigants, who engage in litigation very rarely, are often in a poor position to bear the financial risks of going to court. The American system allows these risks to be shifted to the lawyers, who can spread the risks over many cases, and are therefore in a better position to bear them. Again, contingent fees can be viewed as 'productivity bonuses' or as an unusual form of venture capitalism which encourages the commitment of the lawyer to the client's case.

On the other hand, contingent fees are frequently blamed for two ills which are said to beset the legal system in the United States: excessive awards and a litigation explosion. Critics point to the rise in the number of substantial jury awards in civil cases: in 1984, for example, there were 401 awards of over $1 million, compared with 27 in 1975. This is attributed to the juries' wish to ensure that the victim remains fully compensated after the contingent fee has been met. Nevertheless, it should be remembered that most damages awards are for small amounts. There are many other reasons why civil juries may make an occasional very large award—to show public indignation against the tortfeasor, for example, or as a result of inadequate directions from the judge, and it has not been proved that contingent fees are to blame.

The existence and extent of a litigation explosion is the subject of some debate amongst academics in the United States. Even if there has been a substantial increase in litigation, it is by no means established that this is undesirable or that contingent fees are responsible for it. Contingent fees have been used in the United States of America for over 80 years, and it is unlikely that they alone have effected an increase in litigation in the last 10 or 20 years.

The second, and more telling, argument against contingent fees is that they create a conflict of interest between the lawyer and the client. It is argued that lawyers will wish to avoid the heavy expense of preparing for trial and of the trial itself, when this will not add proportionately to the award. Thus they may encourage settlements when this is not in the client's best interests. For example, a lawyer may decide that the true worth of the claim is $33,000, but this will require 100 hours of work to obtain. At an early stage, after just five hours work, the insurance company offers $15,000. The lawyer who successfully urges acceptance gains an hourly rate of $3,000, compared with a rate of $330 if the case goes the full distance.

There have been two research studies to test whether this occurs in practice. The first, based on a non-random sample of 59 personal injury cases in New York found some evidence to support the theory that contingent fee lawyers invest less time than hourly paid lawyers in a given case (D. Rosenthal, *Lawyer and Client*, 1974). The second, more recent, study had a considerably larger sample drawn from 12 courts around the United States of America (Kritzer et al., 'The Impact of Fee Arrangements on Lawyer Effort' 19 *Law and Society Review* 251, 1985). The authors found that in comparison with hourly paid lawyers, contingent fee lawyers invested 20 per cent less time in the cases involving sums of around $6,000. But they devoted more time than their hourly paid counterparts to cases worth over $10,000. There was no clear evidence that the difference in hours allocated made any systematic difference to the damages awarded. As the authors themselves state, the results are not easy to interpret and it may be that the effects of fee arrangements on lawyers' behaviour are indirect rather than direct. In short, the case against contingent fees on the grounds of conflict of interest is not proven. All fee arrangements have their problems. Fixed fees are if anything more likely to cause lawyers to settle early, while hourly fees can encourage lawyers to 'run up the meter' by over preparing.

Thirdly, it is argued that contingent fees lead to excessive fees since lawyers have superior knowledge of the risks and costs involved, and they can use their superior knowledge to charge an unreasonable percentage. On the other hand many American states have taken action to control excessive fees and at least 17 states have enacted laws limiting the size of contingent fees. While controls can be placed on fees which are clearly excessive, it is much more difficult to ensure that fees are fair in every case. In practice, American lawyers tend to charge very similar contingent rates. This means that it is difficult for clients to shop around. Although a third may be fair in some cases, it will be very high in other cases where damages are high and the risk of failure is low. These clients are effectively subsidising those with weaker cases.

The final argument against contingent fees is that they encourage lawyers to use unethical tactics in the way they conduct cases. This argument carried considerable weight with both the Benson commission (1979) and the Hughes commission (1980), but there is little hard evidence to support it. Moreover, it appears to take an exceedingly pessimistic view of the ethical probity of the profession. Lawyers have a natural desire to win their cases, and it is not clear that a different basis for charging will by itself transform an honest lawyer into a dishonest one.

Should contingent fees be introduced in the United Kingdom?
The evidence suggests that in principle the arguments against contingent fees are not insurmountable provided certain safeguards are introduced, for example, maximum fee limits, judicial supervision, taxation and fee arrangements in writing. This does not necessarily mean that contingent fees are the best way forward in the United Kingdom. In the first place, the existence of the 'costs with the event rule' reduces the attractiveness of such fees to United Kingdom litigants since they are only protected from paying their own lawyers' costs if they lose—they will still have to pay the other side's costs. Moreover the practices of tendering or payments into court (which do not exist in the United States) may well encourage insurance companies to tender a poor settlement early in order to drive a wedge between the lawyer and the client. Alternatively, as Dr Carey Miller has argued ('A Case for Considering the Contingent Fee' (1987) 32 J.L.S. 461) the costs rule might be an advantage viewed from

an objective perspective since it might inject 'a desirable restraint upon legal action where the merit of the claim was questionable'. Unfortunately, in those situations where the costs with the event rule does not apply, for example, small claims and tribunals hearings, the level of award is usually too small to leave much over to pay the contingent fee.

Secondly, while they might be attractive to claimants with a substantial legal aid contribution, those outwith the legal aid limits, or those ineligible for legal aid, they would seem to offer little to the 80 per cent to 90 per cent of assisted parties who have no contribution to pay (unless there was a strong risk of the statutory clawback eating up much of the award). Thirdly, contingent fees would provide no assistance in cases where no financial claim was being made, for example, interdicts, declarators or petitions for judicial review. Even in personal injury cases their use could be limited since several studies have shown that 85 per cent to 90 per cent of English personal injury cases result in a payment to the plaintiff. Where the risk of loss is as small as this, the need for contingent fees is not evident. Nevertheless, there is abundant evidence that many, possibly a majority, of individuals with valid personal injury claims take no action because of the fear of costs. For them, contingent fees might be beneficial."

B. A CONTINGENT LEGAL AID FUND

Paterson, Financing Legal Services, pp. 167–169
"In 1966 (and again in 1978 and 1992) Justice put forward a proposal, which has since attracted considerable support, that a Contingency Legal Aid Fund (CLAF) be set up to underwrite the litigation costs of persons who fall outwith the ambit of the legal aid schemes. This proposal has now been floated by the Lord Chancellor's Department and the Scottish Office Home and Health in their consultation papers on eligibility for civil legal aid. The CLAF would initially be funded from a government grant, but subsequently from a proportion of the winnings of claimants whose cases had been supported by CLAF. Where claimants were unsuccessful, their costs and those of their opponents would be met by the Fund. The administrative costs of the Fund would be met from a non-returnable registration fee. This scheme, it is argued, would overcome the main disadvantages of contingent fees without losing many of their advantages. (Because the claimants' lawyers would be paid a normal fee, win or lose, there would be no conflict of interest and no possibility of excessive fees.)

Successful claimants would also pay less than under a normal contingent fee arrangement (20% was Justice's suggested figure, however the LCD suggest that 25–30% of a damages award would be needed for the Fund to be self-financing). While claimants would not be subject to a means test (though large corporations would be excluded) they would have to show (as in legal aid cases) that their claims had a reasonable prospect of success. Justice thought that the scheme should not be available to defendants nor would it apply where a reasonable sum of money was not at issue (the figure proposed was £500) since otherwise the returns to the Fund would be inadequate. However the LCD considers that a combination of high non-returnable fixed fees and subsidisation from reparation actions would enable the CLAF to be used even where damages were not in issue. The attraction of such a scheme to governments is that it is, in effect, an insurance which spreads the risk of loss to other litigants rather than the legal aid fund. The attraction to clients would be that it would cover areas, as well as people, presently excluded from legal aid.

To date only one jurisdiction has any substantial experience of a CLAF—Hong Kong. In 1984 Hong Kong introduced such a scheme as an adjunct to their legal aid scheme for those whose means were just outwith the legal aid limits but who were nonetheless unable to afford the services of private practitioners. The Supplementary Legal Aid Scheme (SLAS) is restricted to substantial (over $60,000) claims for death or personal injury. The scheme is administered by the Legal Aid Department, the usual merits test is applied and a more generous means test. Instead of legal aid contributions the applicants are required to pay fees of $1000 (about £80) which are returnable if they are successful. They must also agree to a deduction of between 10% and 12% of any damages recovered (though the deductions can be reduced by up to 50% if the claim is settled at an early stage). Up to November 1990 there had been 297 successful applications to the scheme, representing 67% of all decided applications. It was three or four years before income under the scheme consistently exceeded expenditure. In Hong Kong the start-up costs were met by an interest free loan of up to $1,000,000 from the State Lotteries Fund. This has now been repaid.

Similar proposals in Western Australia (also backed by the Lotteries Commission) led to the setting up of a 'Litigation Assistance Fund' in 1991. New South Wales and South Australia are also considering such Funds. The English Law Society is optimistic that taking advantage of the lessons to be learned from the Hong Kong experience it will be possible for a CLAF to become self-financing in a shorter period in the United Kingdom. One way to achieve this would be to make speedier cases eligible. The National Consumer Council is also supportive of such a development especially in class actions or test cases.

Nevertheless, the critics remain unconvinced. Carey Miller argues that a CLAF scheme involves unnecessary bureaucratic controls and administrative costs. The Benson Commission in a critique subsequently endorsed by the Legal Action Group argued that a CLAF scheme would be inequitable because poor successful claimants might be subsidising unsuccessful individuals or even companies. Furthermore, those who have suffered most in personal injury cases—and therefore have the largest claims, would have to pay the most, despite the fact that such claimants tend to be undercompensated as it is. The critics have also claimed that a CLAF would be vulnerable to adverse selection. Thus the success of the scheme would depend on a reasonable take-up. Yet claimants with good chances of success, it is said, would be reluctant to take part in the scheme and those who would be attracted to the scheme would have the weaker cases. Since litigants are rarely so claims-conscious as to know the strength of their own cases, and risk-averse claimants would be attracted by the immunity from paying costs offered by a CLAF, it is likely that this argument is overstated. Nevertheless, as we have seen, most personal injury pursuers/plaintiffs obtain an award of some sort and frequently solicitors will advise clients with strong cases to bypass legal aid in order to avoid delays. If CLAFs are to be set up in different parts of the world, lawyers will be torn between advising clients with strong cases to proceed without cover from the CLAF or legal aid on the one hand or suggesting that they apply to the CLAF because they know that the success of the scheme depends on a reasonable take-up by claimants."

C. GROUP LEGAL SERVICES

Paterson, "Paying for Legal Services," pp. 238–239
"One feature of contingent fees is that they spread the risk of loss among all pursuers. Prepaid legal services endeavour to reduce further the expense of going to law by spreading the risk of loss among an even larger sector of the community. There are two principal forms—group legal services and legal expenses insurance—which are in theory ana-lytically discrete, even if in practice most prepaid legal service schemes are hybrids lying at different intervals on a continuum between the two polar forms.

Group legal services are joint ventures between the legal profession and the public designed to provide routine and non-routine legal services for the individual members of a group at reduced or subsidised rates. The exponential growth of such schemes in the United States in recent years is partly attributable to their appeal to certain sectors of the profession because they provide a constant supply of legal work . . . and their appeal to group members because they usually offer easy access to specialist lawyers at a cheaper price than that available on the open market. Groups who have sponsored such schemes include, *inter alia*, trade unions, employers' organisations, trade associations, professional associa-tions, social clubs, automobile clubs and consumer groups.

The services offered under these schemes vary quite considerably, but the majority place a stress on preventive law. Most of them seem designed to encourage subscribers to undergo routine legal check-ups although few, if any, have specifically provided for this in the terms of the scheme. Consultations to cover routine legal services, *e.g.* house pur-chase, leases, preparation of wills, the completion of tax returns and company returns are comparatively inexpensive and efficient uses of legal expertise, and as such are strongly favoured by the schemes. Representation in court is highly expensive and accordingly less freely available. Typically, in return for an annual fee (which may be included in one's professional dues or as a fringe benefit offered by an employer) the group member and his family will be entitled to a stipulated number of hours of advice or back up or representation work from a lawyer, either free or at a reduced rate of charge . . . Claims which are considered by the lawyer to be frivolous, spiteful or very unlikely to be successful [will] usually be excluded . . . The schemes may be 'open' or 'closed' or somewhere in between. 'Open' schemes are those where the member may select any lawyer he chooses to provide the legal services offered in the scheme. 'Closed' schemes are those where the claimant is given little or no choice in the selection of the lawyer who will provide the services. Most group schemes are of the closed variety because by insisting that the legal services be provided by the staff lawyers of the group or by a restricted panel of private lawyers, the scheme organisers can take advantage of the economies of scale. The volume of cases enables greater specialisation and expertise to be built up among the lawyers and improved research facilities and machinery to be provided, while at the same time enabling fees to be kept down and the quality of the work monitored. It has been estimated that the average cost of a divorce in America under a closed scheme is approximately one-sixth the average cost of one under an open scheme. On the other hand, closed schemes largely remove the clients' freedom to choose their own lawyers and are liable to provoke accusations of unfair attraction of business from lawyers excluded from the schemes. Nor are they of assistance where the client's dispute is against the organisers of the scheme, *e.g.* a worker's dispute with his trade union.

In the United Kingdom group legal services are a well-established, although little discussed, phenomenon. Some employers offer legal services to their management staff as fringe benefits. The Automobile Association organises and funds certain legal services for its members as do the Medical Defence Union and the Medical Protection Society. But it is trade unions who have really developed such schemes on a large scale . . . Trade unions view legal services for their members as an important service and it is one of the strong 'selling' points of union membership. Unlike legal aid, the pursuer has no contribution to pay and if the case is lost the union pays all the expenses. Indeed, there is some evidence that in an attempt to boost the attractions of union membership, certain unions apply only a minimal merit test and will fund litigation which would have very little chance of success in court and which would be refused legal aid for lack of *probabilis causa*. It is clear that a considerable proportion of personal injuries cases in the United Kingdom are funded by trade unions and the structure of the legal aid schemes contributes to this, for applicants can be refused legal aid if they have access to other facilities or sources of financial assistance. The most common alternative sources of such assistance are trade unions. Although most group schemes in the United Kingdom are closed ones, both the Law Societies have declared that such schemes do not involve any unfair attraction of business. However, clients who resent the curtailment of their freedom of choice of lawyer under such schemes have to convince a legal aid committee that their objection is a reasonable one if they wish to avail themselves of the greater freedom of choice afforded by our legal aid schemes.

Unlike the United States, most group schemes in the United Kingdom restrict the legal services offered to areas relevant to the activities of the group and the emphasis is put on meeting the clients' non-routine and more serious legal needs, *e.g.* for representation in court. As such, the schemes are in many ways equivalent to legal expenses insurance."

D. LEGAL EXPENSES INSURANCE

Paterson, "Financing Legal Services" pp. 171–172

"Legal Expenses Insurance policies for individuals first appeared in mainland Europe in the 1920s but their significance in the legal services market dates from the 1960s. It is the dominant form of LEI in Europe (although in Sweden and in Italy trade unions are important providers of legal aid). It is estimated that at least 50% of all households in Germany have some kind of LEI and 80% in Sweden, though the figure is lower in other European countries. Predictably, the available evidence suggests that higher income individuals are disproportionately likely to take out LEI. In contrast to the evolution of group legal services in the U.S.A., individual LEI in Europe has developed along commercial lines. Its aim, like other forms of insurance is to spread the risk of loss consequent on the happening of an uncertain event. As a result the typical coverage of individual policies in Europe is restricted in a variety of ways—not least in excluding many of the routine legal expenses which are the primary focus of group legal services. Thus in Germany the drafting of wills and other documents, negotiations, representation in divorce and succession actions are usually excluded. Similar exceptions exist in Sweden. In fact, in most European countries the coverage of individual policies is closely aligned to more general areas of insurance. There is, however, little evidence available as to types of claims experienced by LEI companies. One of the few studies in this area was conducted in Germany and found that 39% of claims related to traffic violations, another 30% to other car related matters, and 31% to other areas (principally, consumer, labour law, and landlord and tenant cases).

The United Kingdom

In the United Kingdom individual LEI policies, whether free standing or 'add-ons' to car or home contents insurance policies, have only been available since 1974. Most policies provide a free legal advice telephone line, a free choice of lawyer and, most important in this context, they usually offer European-wide coverage. For individuals or firms ineligible for legal aid LEI clearly has much to offer, but there are a number of drawbacks. The policies tend to be expensive for the cover offered and the cover offered is limited—most have a financial ceiling on cover and most exclude matrimonial disputes, defamation, tax matters, building disputes and defence of criminal prosecutions involving violence. However, the importance of LEI as a factor for UK based litigants deciding to litigate abroad is most severely limited by its very restricted penetration of the market. Most people in the UK simply do not have an LEI policy. (A recent survey by the Consumers' Association and the Law Society, *Legal Expenses Insurance in the UK* (London: Consumer's Association/The Law Society, 1991) suggested that only 7% of respondents had any form of LEI.) Moreover, its relatively low penetration makes it at risk of 'adverse selection' thus undermining the viability of the market. For these reasons even the Eligibility Review felt unable to recommend it as a replacement for legal aid in the UK—at least for the time being."

While legal expenses insurance undoubtedly has its attractions for business organisations (who are ineligible for legal aid) a number of problems remain. First, marketing private schemes through lawyers in private practice has proved ineffective both in the United Kingdom and the United States. As in the case of health insurance, it may be easier to reach individuals by selling the package to employers or trade unions. Secondly, should the scheme be open or closed (see p. 298 above)? Thirdly, legal expenses insurance, unlike group legal services, is not suitable for routine legal expenses. Indeed it has been argued that to introduce comprehensive cover for legal expenses would be to contradict the basic philosophy behind insurance, *viz.* spreading the risk of an uncertain loss. Many legal needs are just the reverse—routine, foreseeable and within the control of the client. Comprehensive cover would encourage frequent use of the benefit and increase the possibility of adverse selection thus creating a situation where the great majority of subscribers would be high-risk individuals. Where all subscribers claim benefit, the premiums become uneconomic for there are no non-beneficiaries among whom to spread the loss. The beneficiaries would in effect have to bear the full cost of the legal services *and* the administrative costs of the middle man—the insurance company. Despite the hopes of some reformers in America, it would appear, therefore, that legal insurance cannot meet the routine unmet legal needs of the public and remain economically viable. It may provide a useful service for those ineligible for legal aid, but it is group legal services which in the long run are likely to make the greater impression on both the profession and the public.

E. CLASS ACTIONS

Reducing cost by spreading the risk of loss could also be achieved by introducing a form of action which aggregates claims, namely, the class action. This procedural innovation would enable a group of individuals who have similar complaints against a common defender (for example, a multiple accident claim, persons affected by a common pollutant, or consumers with the same defective product), to join together in one action to pursue their claims. A working party of the Scottish Consumer Council recommended in 1982 that class actions should be introduced in Scotland. One major obstacle to such a reform is the problem of financing class actions if contingency fees are not permitted. Both these issues are currently being investigated by the Scottish Law Commission.

[See, on class actions, M. Burns, "How to Benefit the Many" (1988) 139 *SCOLAG* 53.]

F. SELF HELP

Another way to reduce the expense of going to law is to do without legal representation. Following the Litigants in Person (Costs and Expenses) Act 1975 and the Acts of Sederunt (Expenses of Party Litigants) (S.I. 1976 No. 1606; S.I. 1983 No. 1438), party litigants can now recover expenses and outlays reasonably incurred (if awarded), though the remuneration rates are well below those of solicitors. The simplified "do-it-yourself" divorce procedure has proved popular. However, self representation has made less progress in relation to the new small claims procedure. As we saw in Chapter 2 less than a third of individual or small business parties in a small claim chose to represent themselves. [See CRU/Strathclyde and Dundee Universities, *Small Claims in the Sheriff Court* (Scottish Office, Edinburgh, 1991) at p. 23.] In the non-litigation spheres of conveyancing, wills and executries the "do-it-yourself" movement has again progressed further in England than in Scotland, although Scotland has a "small estates procedure" which makes it easier for laymen to handle small executries without the aid of a solicitor.

G. LAY REPRESENTATION AND ASSISTANCE

It was established by the Court of Appeal in *McKenzie* v. *McKenzie* [1971] P. 33 (and by implication by the House of Lords in the Scottish appeal of *Malloch* v. *Aberdeen Corporation (No. 2)*, 1973 S.L.T. (Notes) 5) that a lay person or a solicitor can attend court proceedings and sit beside a party litigant in order to assist him or her by prompting, taking notes and quietly giving advice. Such "McKenzie friends" have enjoyed some currency in squatting cases and latterly cases relating to the poll tax. Attempts to extend the tactic to lay advocacy before the courts have not always been well received. [See *Mercy* v. *Persons Unknown, The Times*, June 5, 1974; *E.M.A.* v. *A.C.A.S. (No. 1)* [1979] 3 All E.R. 223 and *R.* v. *Leicester City Justices* [1991] 3 W.L.R. 368.] (It is worthy of note that sections 25–29 of the Law Reform (Miscellaneous Provisions) (Scotland) Act 1990 and sections 27 & 28 of the Courts and Legal Services Act 1990 contain provisions for non-lawyers to be given rights of audience by the courts.)

The status of the "McKenzie friend" came under attack in *R.* v. *Leicester City Justices* [1991] 3 W.L.R. 368 when the Divisional Court upheld a decision of the Leicester City Justices to ban a "McKenzie friend" from sitting with, and providing advice and assistance to, two party litigants in a case relating to arrears of the community charge. In the event, the right of party litigants in civil cases to have the assistance of a "McKenzie friend" to give advice and to take notes was re-affirmed, on appeal, by the Court of Appeal. Nevertheless, the Court muddied the waters in a gesture which appears to owe much to symbolic politics, by indicating that the title and status of the "McKenzie friend" should be abandoned. However, in a more recent case, *Peggy Wood* v. *Law Society of England & Wales* (unreported, 1993), a High Court judge permitted a "McKenzie friend" to address the court on behalf of a physically infirm litigant.

In Scotland "McKenzie friends" have been even less common, and the right to lay representation before the Scottish courts is procedurally and practically limited (see, *e.g.* Sheriff Courts (Scotland) Act 1971, s. 36(1) (as amended) and Small Claims Rules 1988, r. 30). However, lay representation before tribunals is commonplace.

CHAPTER 12

THE FUTURE OF LEGAL SERVICES

The future of legal services is now more difficult to predict than at any time in the last decade. The scale and duration of the cuts in legal aid and legal services expenditure which have now begun, are unknown quantities. Undoubtedly, the most significant development in the last 20 years was the emergence and development of neighbourhood law centres. Yet, in the face of continuing financial stringency and the lack of a coherent Government strategy on funding, it is far from clear what the future holds for the law centre movement.

I. LAW CENTRES

There is no universally accepted definition of such centres but the Law Centres' Federation (the association of law centres) defines them as projects which:
(1) employ at least two full-time lawyers,
(2) provide legal services for a deprived community within a defined geographical area,
(3) are non-profit-making and funded at least 50 per cent by a public or charitable source, and
(4) have a constitution and management committee which is independent of any funding agency, local authority and the government.

On this definition there were about 57 such centres in the United Kingdom at the outset of 1993. Only one, Castlemilk, was located in Scotland, however, another (at Dumbarton) was established in the autumn of 1993. Moreover, there are another four projects in Scotland which are usually also described as law centres. Three are specialist centres focusing on housing law, child law and the interests of ethnic minorities respectively. The fourth (also in Glasgow) is located in Drumchapel housing estate. Most recently, in the summer of 1993, the Scottish Office provided Shelter with funds for a national law centre specialising in housing law. This will bring the total number of law centres in Scotland to seven.

Zander, *Legal Services for the Community*, pp. 78–80
"Law centres are different in a variety of ways from private firms of solicitors. On the most obvious level, they look different. Instead of the formality and staid dignity of the typical solicitor's office, law centres go

out of their way to present an informal, casual atmosphere. They are normally at street level in main shopping centres. Instead of the usual discreet nameplate, they have a large sign in the window, 'LAW CENTRE'. Their shop fronts and interiors are plastered with posters and notices about legal rights, campaigns for racial equality, meetings of the local tenants' association, and information as to what to do about bad housing, wife-battering, or harassment from landlords. They have large, open-plan offices with desks in every corner. The furniture is usually somewhat dilapidated. Lawyers, secretaries, receptionists, all tend to wear jeans and unconventional hair styles. Volunteer workers mill about. In several centres lawyers take their share of filing, receptionist and telephone-operator work and even typing. Law centres commonly have evening and Saturday sessions. Many have a 24-hour telephone emergency service, used mainly in criminal and harassment cases. Their services are free and they are permitted to advertise.

But the centres are different not only in the way they will provide their services, but also in the services they actually provide. One difference is the nature of the work they do. Most private firms of solicitors depend for the bulk of their income on conveyancing and probate work. Law centres typically devote the largest proportion of their time to landlord-tenant disputes and other housing problems. In a survey of the first fifteen law centres, housing problems accounted for 40 per cent or more of the total work-load in ten of the centres. Employment, social security and consumer problems played a larger part in the work of the centres than for most firms of solicitors.

Another difference is the type of client. Solicitors in private practice tend naturally to work for individual clients who instruct and pay them. Law centres place great emphasis on the value of helping groups and the community more generally. By concentrating on problems that affect large numbers of people rather than just individuals the law centres believe they are getting the best value out of their own scarce and over-stretched resources. Group and community work are increasingly the dominant mode of service provided by law centres. There are innumerable examples: forming and servicing tenants' associations; running campaigns on how to get rents or rates reduced; writing and distribution of leaflets, posters, pamphlets and even newspapers about aspects of the law; lecturing in schools, old people's homes, prisons, hostels; running surveys; performing in street theatre entertainment on legal rights.

Many centres have concentrated on particular local problems—bad landlords, breaches of the fire regulations, redevelopment plans of the local authority, relations between the police and the coloured community. Law centres commonly identify a problem and then go out of their way to try to cope with it. A centre may swamp the local county court with cases of illegal evictions as a means of sensitising the judge to the problem, and of alerting bad local landlords that evictions will be effectively resisted. In another area the centre may decide that too many elderly people are failing to get their heating allowance, or that immigrant workers are being exploited by a particular employer or that the harassment office of the local authority requires to be pressured to prosecute landlords who harass their tenants. One centre became aware that the fuel allowance in supplementary benefit payments was inadequate to meet the costs of tenants on a particular estate. It conducted a number of successful appeals, but a report it commissioned under the Legal Advice scheme from a consulting engineer showed the problem to be common to the estate generally. As a result, it started negotiations with the Supplementary Benefits Commission to get the rate of benefit raised for everyone living on the estate.

Law centres have used test cases in the traditional sense of cases that seek to establish a point of law in the courts. But they interpret the concept more broadly to include any form of legal action that involves community gain. It may be conducted purely at the local level and achieve no more publicity than is available from the local press. Yet if the conduct of one landlord, or employer, or builder, or local authority, is altered as a result, the action may have had its desired effect. Sometimes it is not necessary to achieve *any* publicity. The fact that the action has been started may be enough to achieve a settlement not merely for one person but for a whole group similarly situated. A law centre provides expertise in the special legal problems of the poor. It can take a long view and set priorities for action. It has a means of keeping the community informed of developments and of receiving the views of the community through its management committee and its network of local contacts."

The work of the first three law centres in Scotland is described in the following article:

Smith, "North of the Border", pp. 11

Castlemilk Law Centre
"Castlemilk is one of four major estates on Glasgow's periphery, housing about 25,000 people. The law centre occupies the ground floor of a small block of flats. Right opposite there is a run-down shopping centre, where Castlemilk Advice Centre, with which the law centre shared premises from its start in 1978 until 1984, is to be found. Two firms of solicitors also have offices in shop premises in the centre, with one—Ross Harper and Murphy—providing the smartest frontage in the complex. Most of the surrounding housing consists of low-rise blocks of flats, their uniform drabness relieved only by a small section of more colourful, recently rehabilitated stock. . . .

The law centre's largest area of work—about 40 per cent of its cases and 50 per cent in terms of time expended—concerns housing. Until recently, almost all the surrounding housing was owned by the local authority. (About a tenth of the Castlemilk estate has now been transferred to Scottish Homes, the equivalent of the English Housing Corporation. In addition, four housing associations have acquired houses.) Most of the housing work has involved repair claims—mainly relating to damp and condensation—against the local authority. The law centre has pursued a number of related cases of claims both for compensation while repairs were being done and for home loss payments.

During its many years as Scotland's only law centre, Castlemilk regarded disseminating its experience as a central task and, from early on, became involved in training, conferences and publications. Recent training sessions have covered fuel debts, cohabitation, sex discrimination and court debt orders, while over 150 people attended a conference on how to deal with dampness. The law centre's range of leaflets covers housing, police, family, drugs and debt. . . .

Legal Services Agency
The Legal Services Agency (LSA) is an interesting variant on the law centre concept. Reflecting the changing nature of the times, it describes itself as a 'community business', albeit within a charitable framework. It was developed by Glasgow's Technical Services Agency, a community-controlled architectural aid centre which has been very involved with dampness and condensation.

Unlike Castlemilk Law Centre, the LSA aims to serve the whole of the city and beyond into the Strathclyde region. Initial funding has come from the Federation of Strathclyde Community Business and Glasgow district council, though the aim is to raise core funding from fees for training and legal aid work. Its management committee is made up of representatives of its funders and community organisations throughout Strathclyde, which are among its 100 or so members.

Senior solicitor Paul Brown says that the idea is to be 'more research and developmentally minded then Castlemilk, which is a local law centre with the strong populist element of being orientated towards its community. Its approach is not possible for an agency based in a city centre.' Much of the LSA's early work has been related to housing—this, says Paul Brown, has been in response to demand. Now the LSA is getting to the stage where it can begin to choose priorities.

In common with all three law centres, the LSA has a creditable list of leaflets and booklets. These include rights guides like *Right to a Decent House* (co-published with Shelter) and an action pack on backdating benefits.

It has also published material on aspects of personal injuries, such as an introduction to post-traumatic stress disorder and a study of quantification of damages in head injury cases, based on papers produced for its courses.

Scottish Child Law Centre
The Scottish Child Law Centre is the one avowedly national law centre of the three. In 1988/89, for instance, it undertook training in all but one of the nine regions into which mainland Scotland is divided—from Inverness in the north to Dumfries in the south. Its location in Glasgow means,

however, that most of its work is concentrated in the Strathclyde region, in recognition of which it receives a limited amount of funding—£9,000 in 1990/91—from the regional council.

The centre is the equivalent of the Children's Legal Centre in London and, like it, grew out of the International Year of the Child in 1979. A group of professionals formed themselves the following year into the Scottish Child Law Group and began campaigning for more resources. A particular problem was the simple fact that no commercial publisher would produce a textbook equivalent to HK Bevan's *Child Law* for the small Scottish Market. So, there was no definitive collation of Scottish law on the subject. Funding was eventually obtained from the Scottish Office—first for a collection of legal material and then for the law centre.
. . .

The centre has focused particularly on the need for information—to the extent that it has not yet undertaken any continuing casework. It has embarked on an ambitious project, in conjunction with the Highland regional council, to bring together relevant child law cases in a database which will then be regularly updated. The plan is to produce the information on disc, hence the project's name—ChilDBase. Two of the centre's management committee members have worked on this project which will, when complete, have about 850 entries.

In addition, the centre has produced a number of publications, ranging from a single page of notes on leaving children unattended to a booklet on compensation for abused children under the Criminal Injuries Compensation Scheme (all three law centres collaborated on its content). The centre has organised a number of conferences, aimed largely at a professional audience, on subjects like child sexual abuse and access. It is also working on a pilot scheme, likely to start soon in the Lothian region, for lay spokespeople for children involved in children's hearings. Kathleen Marshall [the Director] says: 'We have an important function in being a voice for children and in letting professionals know what can be done to link children with the law.' "

Since its inception, the law centre movement in the United Kingdom has been dogged by three principal problems: independence, management and control; work style; and funding.

A. INDEPENDENCE, MANAGEMENT AND CONTROL

I. INDEPENDENCE

In order to offer free legal services and to advertise their existence law centres have needed a waiver from the Law Society of the ethical rule against the unfair attraction of business. In 1977 an agreed basis for waivers was reached in England:

"(i) 'Apart from initial advice and assistance . . . salaried solicitors will not normally act in cases where the professional business of the client involves:

(I) conveyancing; (II) commercial matters; (III) divorce proceedings; (IV) probate matters (save for personal applications in small estate(s)); (V) personal injury claims where the damages, as initially and approximately quantified exceed scale 2 of the county court costs band, or (VI) in criminal matters where the accused is aged 21 or over."

Like its English counterpart the Law Society of Scotland saw its power to grant waivers as a way of controlling the work which law centres should be permitted to undertake. The Hughes Commission recognising the difficulties that this had caused in relation to the setting up of Scotland's first law centre in Castlemilk, Glasgow, recommended (para. 7.15) that in future:

"Law Centres should concentrate their work on whatever areas of law are not adequately catered for locally by solicitors. There should be no prohibition on their doing other work, however, as long as they do not neglect the areas of need."

The Castlemilk management committee following this proposal renegotiated the scope of their centre's "statement of intent."

Castlemilk Law Centre's Statement of Intent, 1981

"The purpose of the Neighbourhood Law Centre is to provide advice, assistance and representation to clients from the Castlemilk area. Apart from initial advice and assistance and except in cases of emergency, the Centre's solicitors will not normally undertake (but will refer to private practitioners in accordance with the principles laid down in the guidelines on the use of referral lists) conveyancing, commercial matters, reparation, (other than non-personal injury cases not exceeding the maximum financial limit permissible under the Summary Cause procedure in the Sheriff Court and in respect of personal injury cases where the award would not exceed £400), matrimonial proceedings (and proceedings relating to the custody of children), testate and intestate succession (other than the preparation of wills and the administration of Small Estates as defined in the Confirmation of Small Estates (Scotland) Act 1979), and criminal matters (except in a court of summary jurisdiction for the purposes of offering pleas in mitigation, in cases where the accused is already a client of the centre, and the Director considers that legal aid is unlikely to be granted for the plea in mitigation and the accused cannot afford to instruct a solicitor in private practice). The Centre's activities will be directed primarily to Community Matters, Representation at Children's Panels and Appeals therefrom, Adoptions, Welfare Law, Housing, Consumer Protection, Immigration and Representation at Boards and Tribunals not covered by Legal Aid. Although the Centre will operate both the Legal Advice and Assistance and the Civil Legal Aid Scheme in appropriate cases, it will not take part in the Criminal Legal Aid Scheme. Only in cases where the Director alone considers there would be hardship will the Centre represent in any court a client who is outwith the financial limits of the Legal Aid Scheme subject to the foregoing."

In the early days the interpretation of this statement caused considerable friction between the Law Society and the Castlemilk management committee. So too did the Law Society's threat to put at risk the practising certificates of centre solicitors who stepped outside the Society's interpretation of the statement. (In England the Law Society has always accepted that the appropriate penalty for such "offenders" is withdrawal of the centre's waiver, rather than action against the individual solicitors involved.) However, today such differences have long since disappeared. Moreover, the locus for the Law Society to insist on adherence to statement of intent has largely been removed by the relaxation in the rules against advertising by solicitors and the reform of the practice rule against fee sharing with unqualified persons. It follows that the main constraints on the type of work a law centre can now undertake are those imposed by resources or the policy of the management committee. This, of course is the position that the Hughes Commission had recommended. This raises the possibility that law centres in Scotland could begin to emulate their counterparts in Sweden, Quebec and the Netherlands by competing with the private profession for staple legal aid work such as criminal or family law. However, given the paucity of publicly funded salaried legal services in Scotland serious questions must be raised as to the value to the wider society of such a development—particularly in areas which are adequately catered for by the private profession.

2. MANAGEMENT AND CONTROL

Law Centres' Federation, "The role of management committees"
"One of the fundamental principles of Law Centres is that they should be independently managed by representatives of their local community who are committed to the work of the Law Centre. It is only by having an active management committee of local people controlling the policy and organisation of the Law Centre that it can ensure that the service which is provided is appropriate and that the Law Centre is accessible to the people it is serving . . . Experience has shown that it is not easy to reflect in a management committee the various elements of a community. Clearly there will be limitations on how comprehensively it is able to represent the consumers of a service as a whole but a successful management committee will be composed of a majority of representatives of organisations which actually use and benefit from the centre and which reflect as far as possible the main areas of work of the law centre— tenants' associations, trades councils, women's groups and youth groups."

Law Centres' Working Group, "Evidence to the Benson Commission,"
pp. 46–47

"The most common shorthand description of the role of the Management
Committee is that they decide the policy of Law Centres. Policy means
choosing the most effective application of the resources in the community. That means the determination of priorities and, consequently,
the selection of the appropriate combination of work-methods, which is
to say how much effort will be put into each task. In order to perform this
central function, the Management Committee must be wholly free from
any interference which will prevent the execution of that task from being
one that is performed exclusively by way of representation of the
community. [There is] the possibility of conflict of interest between
funding agency and Law Centre but such external influences could also
come from other sources: Law Society, other professional representation,
central or local government if one or other is not the actual funding agent
. . . The truly effective Management Committee serves as a constant
check that the Law Centre is remaining responsive to local need and not
getting bogged down in rigid work-structures as professionals left to their
own devices have an inclination to do. By imposing upon the lawyers a
demand for constant explanation in terms that are comprehensible by a
lay Management Committee, they fulfil the additional valuable function
of preventing the lawyer from drifting back into a professional distance
from the community and hiding in the shadows of professional or
technical language and ideas. Again, only the truly local community
representative is in a position to judge the extent to which the Law
Centre is remaining properly accessible."

Cooper, "Structure and Management of Law Centres," p. 194

"In Brent, the management committee structure is carefully organised, in
such a way that it is democratically representative of certain selected
groups of the community. In Manchester, it is predominantly reflective of
statutory and professional agencies. In Adamsdown, . . . management
tends to be interested, local individuals from the community.

It is clearly important to establish the extent to which the management
committee members *really* direct policy rather than follow the policy
suggested by the staff. Random conversations with law centre staff in
centres in the United Kingdom throw up very different attitudes to the
problem. The theory of 'community control' is supported by all. But
many individuals acknowledge that this really means selective control by
those groups whose . . . perspective on the role of the centre is in line
with their own."

As Cooper's extract suggests the concept of community control
remains highly problematic. This is due to a number of factors.
There may, for example, be no single community but a multiplicity
of minority groupings whose interests clash, in the geographic area
which is a centre's catchment area. Secondly, even if a definable

community exists, how can representative members of it be identified? Can a committee composed largely of statutory representatives, *i.e.* representatives of the region, the district, the local law society, the national law society, the funding agency, be fairly described as community control? How can the demand of law centres for independence be reconciled with the argument that they ought to be accountable for their use of public funds? Do management committees actually control the work of the centre's staff?

These problems are not confined to the United Kingdom as the following extract about the work of the Redfern Legal Centre in Sydney reveals:

Smith, "Redfern Legal Centre," p. 9
"The district of Redfern has been subject to the problems usual in an inner area and the centre has been active in a variety of campaigns. It has, for instance, undertaken rent surveys and helped to establish a domestic violence project.

The centre works with some discrimination in relation to the 'community' which it serves: 'We recognise that there are many different groups of people within the geographical area often referred to as "our community". The interests of these groups can conflict. A recent example is the conflict between residents (and business people) who support the gentrification of the area, and the aboriginal community over proposals to create alcohol-free zones within the municipality. These happened to coincide with locations frequented by aboriginal people. The centre consulted the aboriginal community on this issue and prepared a submission.' This argued that the proposals would not stop public drunkenness but would exacerbate race relations.

Its management structure allows the centre to take an independent view of a local situation, as in this case. It is not under even notional community control. Issues are effectively decided by a management committee with an unashamedly volunteer and staff bias. Of its 15 members, five are staff, two are volunteer lawyers and four are volunteer students. Only one of the four other members must be from a local community organisation.

This management structure would render Redfern ineligible for membership of our Law Centres Federation. The lack of community control and domination of workers has attracted internal criticism."

The Benson Commission's solution to these problems was to argue that a central agency should be set up independent of central and local government which would be responsible both for financing and managing law centres, though local committees would remain to act in an advisory capacity and to sensitise the law centres to local circumstances (para. 8.25–27). The Law Centres'

Federation was aghast at this proposal which rejected community control out of hand. The Federation was far more sympathetic to the Hughes Commission proposal that law centres should be centrally funded (by a Legal Services Commission) but locally managed (para. 7.15):

"Law Centres should be managed by local committees representing the community on the widest possible non-partisan basis. Their independence of special interests should be written into their constitution, which will need to be approved and monitored by the Legal Services Commission from which their funds should come."

B. WORK STYLE

Typically, law centres concentrate their efforts on casework, groupwork, community education and, to a lesser extent, law reform. The balance between these activities varies between centres and over time, but the overall trend is for centres to move away from individual casework towards groupwork and community education.

Campbell, *Law Centres and Legal Services*, pp. 45–46
"6.2 The initial law centres . . . were of the open door variety. Briefly this meant that the centres sought to be as accessible as possible to their 'public client body', and they catered, without discrimination, to suppli-cant clients provided they were of moderate means. The primary tasks of the law centre staff were to provide advice and assistance on legal issues. In time deficiencies and weaknesses in such an orientation were noticed. Typically the law centres became submerged with work and could not cope with their backlog of cases. Some law centres in London indeed simply shut their doors (regularly or sporadically) for the days needed to allow staff to catch up on outstanding matters. Apart from pressure of business, however, the repetitive nature of much of the work came to be regarded as a striking feature. An analogy used was that law centre staff were behaving like doctors in setting and splinting a series of broken legs incurred when clients had fallen over an uncovered manhole . . . when a more constructive contribution to the community at large might have been to ensure the manhole was covered and safe. Surely it was wasteful to use professional skills treating problems on an entirely repetitive basis if the cause of the problem was not tackled? Thus if it became known that the unlawful practices of large landlords were the source of the stream of clients seeking advice about tenancy agreements, might it not be better to seek to persuade the landlord to alter or modify his practices? On this basis the undiscriminating policy of maintaining an open door was questioned, and the desirability of law centres selecting cases that deserved particular attention was appreciated.
6.3 In analogous ways the purely 'reactive' stance of the initial law centres was queried, and a 'proactive' orientation was recommended. It was

suggested that while general publicity about law centres was useful, in fact the ignorance, diffidence and suspicion of some members of the community were so deep rooted that more positive efforts to assist them must be made. Law Centre staff, it was thought, might 'go out to the people'. Educating members of the locality in their rights, about the availability of the law centre, about Citizens Advice Bureaux and the Legal Aid scheme, should be recognized as a priority.

6.4 Disseminating knowledge to individuals and groups would allow attention to be given to the *preventive* role of the law centre as well as its *curative* role. The total number of inquiries might be lessened if people gained some education in the law that affected their lives. A different, more group-orientated version of this perspective, was also developed. If law centres went out into a locality and spoke to groups they might encourage self-help and build up self-reliance in communities. Further their contacts would aid 'diagnosis' of the legal problems typically affecting residents of the community, and expertise would be enhanced as patterns of predominating difficulties were identified.

6.5 A further demand on law centres to rethink their philosophy, came with the call that test cases should be undertaken. The experience in the United States had indicated that test cases could be successfully pursued by neighbourhood law firms . . . Here the notion was to fight for changes in the law, or interpretations of the law, on behalf of the centre's constituency."

Stephens, "Law Centres and Citizenship: The Way Forward," pp. 108–109, 116

"Reactivity and proactivity may be viewed as opposite ends of a continuum, and individual law centres may be identified as exhibiting an operational philosophy tending towards one pole or the other. A reactive tendency or orientation within a law centre is based largely on a system of self-referral by clients of referrals from outside agencies. Once the client has decided to seek advice at the law centre the relationship with the lawyer is likely to be passive, the lawyer typically taking important decisions about the legal viability, processing, and eventual disposition of the case. Informed consent is low and many problems are handled or referred routinely, thus not allowing clients to develop their own legal and civil competences. The emphasis in such centres is on law and legal strategies, with few resources effectively devoted towards group work and educational projects in the community . . .

A more proactive approach seeks ways to transcend the individualizing process of the traditional lawyer-client relationship. It demands that law centres reach out into their respective communities in order to encourage collective and concerted action by neighbourhood groups. This requires that law centres act as a resource for such groups and that lawyers and non-lawyers within the centres co-operate to promote legal and non-legal solutions to commonly experienced problems. Expertise is shared with local people under a proactive orientation, and clients are encouraged to take an active role in the disposition of their case. The attempt is made to develop competence and to strengthen the capacity of clients to realize their rights through group formation. Despite difficulties in overcoming some of the problems caused by the adoption of an overly reactive approach, in the majority of British law centres the operational trend is towards proactivity.

Processing individual grievances in reactive law centres is unlikely to make any impact on the wider problems of poor housing standards, meagre welfare entitlements or rising unemployment. While it is true that proactive law centre policies will not provide 'ultimate' solutions, nonetheless more significant inroads can be made in respect of local solutions to such problems with the adoption of a proactive approach. The adoption of particular examples of groupwork and community campaigns in pursuit of solutions to commonly experienced local problems is the expression of community needs and demands; it is not the result of decisions unilaterally taken by law centre staff and imposed on the community."

Groupwork involves a number of strategies ranging from providing legal advice to local groups and associations (for example, tenants' associations, claimants' unions, environmental groups, women's groups, pensioners and single-parent groups) to undertaking broadly defined test cases. Nevertheless, successful groupwork not infrequently leads to an increased demand for law centres to take on individual cases. The experience of Castlemilk law centre is but one illustration of this phenomenon.

Castlemilk Law Centre

"In Castlemilk during the past few years the emphasis has been towards taking legal services to the community in forms of groups. The undernoted are some examples of the provision of that type of service:—

— The Law Centre acting as Legal Advisors to the Glasgow Tenants' Associations in their negotiations with Glasgow District Council on the drafting of the new Lease to be sent to all tenants under the Tenants' Rights, etc. (Scotland) Act 1980;

— arising from that the preparation of materials to explain the contents of the substantially amended Lease;

— preparation of materials on particular issues, *e.g.* eviction, dampness, flooding, employment and criminal injury to increase awareness of legal rights, such materials being distributed through community groups within Castlemilk;

— progressing test cases in Employment, Housing and Welfare Law;

— involvement with and speaking to community groups and schools to increase awareness of legal rights;

— assisting specific campaign groups, *e.g.* dampness action groups on the Law in relation to that subject.

This type of involvement which is very important and essential in the operations of a Law Centre, nevertheless creates a demand for legal representation on an *individual* basis. Where a solicitor from a Law Centre is involved in such community legal activities there does arise a demand by individuals for assistance with particular problems as a consequence of that involvement. Individuals who might otherwise have been reluctant to mention their own problems having seen a solicitor with whom they can identify and with whom they are familiar will then seek assistance. The assistance may be on any number of issues and in many instances will be unrelated to the matter which was the subject of the community legal process. This is in addition to those who will approach the Law Centre either through the knowledge of its existence or by recommendation from other clients who have been satisfied with the service received. The essential point being made is that any legal representation provision must embrace facilities for representing individuals in addition to acting for community groups or merely taking cases arising from the groups' activities."

Groupwork and educational work highlight the importance of having informed members of the community on the management committees of law centres in order to decide the priorities in the allocation of the centres' resources. Critics who object to the selectivity involved in such decisions ignore the fact that every reactive open-door law centre to date has sooner or later been forced into selectivity in relation to its clients because demand comes to outstrip resources. In the words of S. Wexler, "Practicing Law for Poor People," (1969–70) Yale L.R. 1049, 1055:

"A seemingly neutral policy of 'first-come, first served' cuts against the least informed, the least mobile and the most oppressed. Some sieve is inevitably applied to the work a poverty lawyer does; that sieve can be one he chooses consciously in order to serve a particular end, or it can be one he chooses without thinking, and with no aim at all."

The Benson Commission expressed disquiet at some of the group and community work (particularly local campaigns) undertaken by law centres, considering such activities to be too political or partisan in nature. Law centres, it thought, should confine themselves to providing legal advice to individuals and groups. Again, the Hughes Commission seemed more aware of the value of group and educational work. It argued that (para. 7.15) "law centres should play an active educational role in the community, ensuring that groups and individuals know the legal resources available to them." Hughes recognised the danger of law centres getting involved in community politics but believed that groups should continue to receive advice and representation from law centres.

C. FUNDING

Law centres in the United Kingdom have been funded from three main sources: central government (Community Development Projects, the Urban Aid Programme, the Lord Chancellor's Fund—now replaced by the Legal Aid Board—and Legal Aid), local government and charitable foundations. Today there is a growing tendency for centres to receive funding from a mix of these sources. Even the centres which are directly funded by the Legal Aid Board are gradually being moved over to joint funding with local authorities. [Legal Aid Board Annual Reports 1991–92, para. 6.28.] This seems a wiser policy than the proposal from the Benson and Hughes Commissions—also endorsed by Society of Conservative Lawyers [Prior, *Law Centres* (1984), p. 6]—that there should be a central funding agency with a long-term commitment to law centres. The vulnerability of such agencies has been graphically demonstrated by the repeated attacks on the budget of the U.S. Legal Services Commission by the Reagan and Bush administrations.

However, the recession and financial constraints on local authority spending caused by the non-payment of the community charge have put law centres under increasing financial pressure. One solution would be to expand the amount of legal aid work that such centres can undertake, unhampered by statements of intent. Since the statement of intent is predicated on two ethical rules which have largely disappeared (the ban on touting and fee sharing with unqualified persons) this proposal seems superficially attractive. The fact remains, however, that it is hardly a cost-effective use of public funds to finance law centres to undertake routine undefended divorces when there are many private firms which are perfectly capable of doing the work. Another solution—again favoured by the Royal Commissions—would be to permit law centres to charge clients for their services. This too would involve the removal of the restrictions on the work which law centres can undertake. It would also deprive law centres of much of their uniqueness and would be deeply unpopular with the law centre movement.

II. THE WAY FORWARD: PUBLIC OR PRIVATE?

A. WHAT IS NEEDED?

As the Lord Chancellor's Advisory Committee noted in their 34th Annual Report [1983–84] (p. 341) law centres aim to fill gaps in legal service provision by the private profession. Twenty years on these gaps remain unfilled. There is still a glaring shortage of private practitioners who are skilled in the fields of Child Law, Consumer Law, Welfare Law, Employment Law and Housing Law. These shortages cannot be made up by the heroic efforts of legal advice centre volunteer staff. Moreover, in many of these areas advice without the possibility of representation is a worthless commodity. [On the advantages of being represented before tribunals see chapter 4.] In the absence of any Tribunal Assistance Units in Scotland the burden of representation falls on welfare rights workers, voluntary advice workers and on law centre staff.

The deficiencies of the private profession in welfare and consumer law areas have long led other jurisdictions with developed legal aid programmes to try to adjust the balance between their public and private programmes. In England and Wales the Legal Aid Board Annual Report for 1990/91 indicated that less than a third of 1% of net expenditure on legal aid went to law centres. Research also suggests that advice agencies and law centres account for less than 2% of advice and assistance work. However, in the Netherlands 15% of legal aid expenditure goes to salaried lawyers in Buros, while in New South Wales and Quebec the comparable figures are 42% and 71% respectively. These figures clearly point to the fact that these countries have achieved significantly more success in introducing a mixed model of legal services provision than presently pertains in the United Kingdom.

B. COST EFFECTIVENESS

In the face of continued economic restraint and financial stringencies it is more imperative than ever that we should look at the relative cost effectiveness of various forms of publicly funded legal service. This is another reason why the balance between the public and private programmes of legal aid needs to be re-examined in the United Kingdom. From such a study a national policy could then emerge. The strong decentralisation of the law centre movement entails that there is a lack of uniform standards as to staffing, work methods, management recruitment and the quality of legal services provided. This makes it exceedingly difficult to say if the public funding of law centres is being as well directed as it could be or how such funds should be deployed in the future. The same problem exists even more acutely in relation to legal aid, which accounts for 98 per cent of the public funds expended on legal services in the United Kingdom. Do we get value for money from legal aid? The bulk of legal aid work is done by a relatively small number of firms in Scotland and England—is this more cost effective than all firms doing a little legal aid work? Would it be a more effective and economical strategy to develop more salaried legal services (such as law centres) rather than to continue to pay the private profession on a case-by-case basis under the present legal aid schemes? Questions such as these have hardly begun to be considered in the United Kingdom, although one pilot study has been completed in England which compared the delivery of legal services in private and public practice.

Sherr and Domberger, "Measuring Legal Work," pp. 80–82
"We compared the work of one law centre lawyer and one private solicitor practitioner in their handling, on behalf of complainants, of some 30 unfair dismissal cases divided equally between them. The particular subject area of unfair dismissals was chosen because it is one of the few in which both law centres and private practitioners operate, and the lawyers' work involves a smaller degree of procedural choice so that differences in the handling of cases would be more likely to result from differences between the two modes of operation, or between the lawyers themselves, than extraneous reasons related to the particulars of individual cases or individual approaches . . .

The lawyers' performance was assessed by measuring both inputs and outputs. On the input side measurement was in terms of hours spent by each lawyer over a case; . . .

On the output side two measures were used, one quantitative and one qualitative. Figures on success/failure and on gross compensation received are an obvious measure of output, but have to be treated with caution. This is because the award of compensation by the tribunal depends on a number of specific client characteristics, *i.e.* age, wage and length of employment, all of which must be taken into account when making comparisons . . . We . . . set out to identify any systematic differences in size of awards obtained by the private practitioner and the law centre, whilst being sure that these other factors did not obscure those differences by using a system of statistical analysis able to normalise for these different variables.

Some compensation figures alone leave out certain important qualitative aspects of legal performance. In order to capture these . . . we undertook a questionnaire survey of the clients in the sample in order to identify any marked differences in the degrees of clients' satisfaction with their cases. The clients were asked to rank their level of satisfaction in relation to questions such as the outcome of the case, the way in which it was handled, and the lawyer's explanation of the legal position and of the necessary legal steps to be taken.

Analysis and Summary of Results
In summary . . . the results of the study showed that on average the law centre devoted . . . less than a third of the time to its cases than was spent by the private practitioner. We would therefore have expected the latter to have better over-all results in terms of compensation obtained

for the client. Although the size of award obtained by the private practitioner was slightly higher, this difference did not reach statistical significance and could have been due to chance.

The results are consistent with the law centre having to exercise tighter control over the legal resources allocated to each case than the private practitioner. What is surprising is that differences in input levels are not reflected in significantly greater financial benefits for the private practitioner's clients. It would appear that the law centre, more independent from its individual clients, is in a better position to restrict its own input to a reasonable level for expected outcome. The private practitioner, however, for reasons of image, personal satisfaction, or client pressure spends more time in an illusory attempt to obtain larger gross benefits for his clients. Our calculations do not take into account the private practitioner's cost to his client for the extra work put in, and the slightly larger compensation received by them may be easily dissipated in their extra outlay for solicitors' fees. On the other hand the perceived slightly larger gross benefits may well give the clients a satisfaction that will not be removed by the lawyer's bill.

As regards client's satisfaction we did not find any significant differences between the two legal modes, although over-all the private practitioner's clients were a little more satisfied and he tended to provide them with more information concerning the legal position and the steps involved in the case than did the law centre. This tendency may well be a direct result of the pressure of caseload in a law centre, and the far less time spent on a case. It is an interesting counter-intuitive result since it is contrary to the image of the law centre, bringing law to the people by demystifying it for them with full explanations . . .

Conclusions

It would be tempting to draw policy implications from these findings, that public funds should be allocated to what seems to be the more economically 'efficient' mode of provision of legal service, the law centre, rather than through legal aid to the private practitioner.

Such temptation must be resisted, since the small size of the sample of cases and the fact that we only investigated one private practitioner and one law centre renders our findings suggestive at most.''

As the authors rightly point out, it would be dangerous to draw firm conclusions from such a limited pilot study. At first blush it might appear that salaried programmes must inevitably prove more cost effective than the private sector since they almost invariably pay lower salaries, take on a higher caseload, rely more on volunteers and para-legals and frequently undertake groupwork. Those with a high community education profile are arguably even more cost-effective because of their preventative approach. However, there are countervailing arguments. The start up costs of salaried lawyers are usually higher since they cannot be defrayed

from private earnings. Moreover, although salaried lawyers specialise in the poverty law areas they also tend to be younger and
less experienced than judicare lawyers. The pressure of heavy
caseloads tends to lead to staff "burnout" and salaried lawyers
tend to move on after a few years. Moreover, most judicare
programmes pay private practitioners considerably below the going
rate for private work and increasingly judicare work is being
delegated to less qualified and experienced staff. This may perhaps
account for the fact that the surveys in North America and
Australia comparing the relative cost-effectiveness of the private
and salaried approaches have been somewhat inconclusive. [See
National Legal Aid Advisory Committee, *Funding, Providing and
Supplying Legal Aid Services* (Commonwealth of Australia, 1989)
and NLAAC, *Legal Aid for the Australian Community* (Commonwealth of Australia, 1990).] The most comprehensive survey, The
Legal Services Corporation's *Delivery Systems Study* (1980), found
that there was little to choose between the judicare (legal aid) and
staff attorney (law centres) models in terms of cost, quality and
client satisfaction but that the staff-attorney programmes had a
greater impact on the "poverty community". Most of the studies
have concluded that it would be desirable to experiment with
mixed models. This would shift the debate away from the somewhat sterile and stereotyped debate as to which model is better, to
a more constructive inquiry as to the conditions under which each
model can be deployed to its best advantage or as to the appropriate division of labour between the two models in any given
environment. Such an approach would dovetail with the increasing
emphasis on quality assurance and specialist providers of legal
services for the poverty community by policymakers. [See the
discussion of Franchising in the previous chapter.]

There is clearly a need for research into these questions and for
a central body to be responsible for long-term policy and for
practical experiments in the provision of legal services. It is to the
credit of the Hughes Commission that it recognised this.

The Hughes Commission, pp. 353–354
"20.10 We [recommend] that a Legal Services Commission . . . should be
responsible for:
— the provision of public information as to legal rights and services in
   Scotland (R6.7);
— developing lay advice and representation at tribunals and training for
   lay representatives (R7.3);
— studying and experimenting with the best use of Law Centres in
   Scotland (R7.4);

— grants to advice centres and Law Centres, the conduct of research, experimenting with ways to provide services, and the setting of standards (R7.7);

— providing financial assistance to firms of solicitors to establish themselves in under-provided areas (R7.10);

— administering legal aid (R8.27);

— developing money management counselling in Scotland (R12.1);

— publishing advice on how to leave one's affairs in good order (R13.8);

In exercising all of the foregoing responsibilities, we consider that the fundamental principle guiding the Legal Services Commission should be to secure in the provision of legal services the best possible value for money consistent with justice."

The Hughes Commission's call for a Legal Services Commission has recently been reiterated by the Legal Action Group in a major policy report, *A Strategy for Justice* (LAG: 1992). This report was the product of a wide-ranging research study into legal aid programmes in Canada, Australia, the Netherlands and the United Kingdom. Its final chapter contains a detailed plan for the development of a genuinely planned and balanced mixed model of legal services provision.

LAG, *A Strategy for Justice* pp. 134–44

"LAG believes that services should be provided by the most effective and coherent means; but this must, of course, take existing provision into account. We envisage a mixed model of services, whereby private practitioners and other types of providers combine to ensure an overall pattern of comprehensive cover. This raises the controversial issue of salaried services.

The large-scale replacement of private practitioners by a salaried national legal service has been recently proposed by the Law Centres Federation. It argues that there should be 'a salaried service comprising independent generalist front-line advice and legal casework agencies, strategic services and specialist centres. All elements would be co-ordinated regionally and nationally.' The implications of the LCF proposal are unclear. Its salaried service could be seen as ultimately taking over the role of private practitioners, even in such traditional areas of legally aided practice as matrimonial law and crime; alternatively, it could remain as an additional and supplementary provision.

LAG considers that much more use could be made of salaried services—directly employed or indirectly resourced by the funding authority—which offer various advantages, including flexibility and cost-effectiveness. However, we recognise certain pragmatic limitations to major change. First, current providers have their areas of expertise. Law centres and advice agencies have concentrated on social welfare law, while private practitioners have a wealth of experience in traditional legally aided work, particularly in the fields of crime, matrimonial and personal injury. Second, the fact that salaried services, by their very nature, offer an easy target for a government that wishes to restrict costs cannot be ignored. Their widespread introduction allows for the possibility of capping the legal services budget, moving away from the advantages, despite the present unsatisfactory eligibility levels, of the current demand-led system of legal aid expenditure. Advice agencies and law centres already face funding problems. . . .

LAG's proposals are, therefore, expressly tempered by a concern to be realistic. While wishing to maximise services, we do not intend to put forward plans which provide government with the opportunity for cuts in provision. This makes us cautious about supporting any major extension of salaried services. However some restructuring is necessary, with greater priority given to the funding of advice agencies and the 'community legal centres' . . .

Advice services

A national policy on advice agencies is long overdue . . . [Earlier we] . . . argued for changes in central government funding of the national organisations representing the advice sector. Although the initiative reflected in the diversity of existing advice agencies has been a positive by-product of local funding, another, less welcome, consequence has been patchy provision. There needs to be some way of combining national standards of provision with locally determined forms.

Accordingly, there should be a statutory responsibility on local authorities to provide an adequate level of independent advice for those living and working within their areas; how such advice is best provided should be determined locally. The legal services commission, taking over an expanded role from the Legal Aid Board, should advise on a minimum acceptable level of provision, based on objective indices of need (such as local housing conditions and numbers of people on benefit), to prevent national standards being set so low that some authorities act opportunistically to cut their own existing provision. Subsidy from central government should be forthcoming for this minimum level.

More secure funding and greater national involvement in local provision raises the question of identifying and maintaining performance criteria. Adherence to such criteria, which should be linked to the needs of a particular area, not just based on a crude count of enquiries, would be a condition of funding.

Community Legal Services

A planned national network of community legal centres should be phased in gradually. This would avoid too great an initial expenditure, while also ensuring that centres are established only where adequate preparatory work has been done. . . .

Each community legal centre should employ at least three lawyers, two non-lawyer practitioners and two support staff. Volunteer legal advisers have played a vital role in assisting law centres, particularly in evening advice sessions. This tradition, which has not only provided a source of free labour but has also involved private practitioners in the voluntary sector, should continue, as should training and use of volunteer lay advisers. The exact range of services provided by each community legal centre, (which will depend, in part, on what is already available in the area) will have to be negotiated through the kind of local planning process that Belfast Law Centre has already experimented with in Northern Ireland. The overall objective is, however, quite clear: advice agencies and the community legal centre in an area should, between them, provide a comprehensive range of services within social welfare law.

The community legal centres should receive core funding to provide specified minimum levels of service, not only in relation to advice, assistance and representation, but also in the field of legal education and appropriate law reform activity. The presence of a central funding authority in the planning of this process would introduce a new dimension to the existing position, in which the majority of law centres are accountable only at a local level.

Core funding should be sufficient for the community legal centres to follow the voluntary advice sector tradition of acting without charge for all clients, thus providing the free element in essential legal services. Furthermore, the centres should be the vehicle by which representation is extended before tribunals. With a mix of lay and legally qualified practitioners, they will have the ability to provide the appropriate levels of representation in any case. Such a system would clearly be more economic than a wholesale extension of legal aid. However, at least one firm of private practitioners should also be encouraged, by franchise or other means, to provide a service in this area. As well as giving clients an element of choice, this would provide some measure of competition and comparison; it would also provide a safeguard against community legal centre staff becoming overworked, to the detriment of clients.

Community legal centre lawyers should be able to claim legal aid on a case-by-case basis for cases falling within their general areas of competence but outside the tribunal system, though they should be under a general injunction not to take such cases simply to raise finance.

Eventually, a network of community legal centres should cover the whole country. As a first step, a sufficient number should be established both to test and refine the idea. A reasonable target might be for the Legal Aid Board to fund 90 community legal centres, phased in over three years. A centre of the minimum size envisaged above would cost about £330,000 per year on current rates. So, in crude terms, establishing 30 in each of the next three years would require expenditure of £10 million in the first year, £20 million in the second and £30 million in the third. To start with, centres should be situated in poorer areas not currently covered by private practitioners doing social welfare law work. In some cases, rather than start a centre from scratch, an existing law centre may wish to transfer to the new regime. The law centre movement should not, however, be expected to transfer wholesale. . . .

Funding should also be made available for specialist law centres to provide back-up services such as information for advisers, nationally co-ordinated educational campaigns, law reform activity, specialist advice, and a resource for helping with, or taking over, the more complex and time-consuming cases. Such centres stimulate the quality of the work of all practitioners in their fields, as has been shown in Ontario and Australia, . . .

Private practitioners should continue as the main providers of services in the field of matrimonial and family work, crime and personal injury, as well as having some involvement in other areas of law. . . .

. . . Services in some areas of the country may be improved if legal aid were channelled through a smaller number of higher quality providers: one example is criminal work in certain inner city areas. However, some mechanism must remain whereby new practices can break into the market.

In looking for greater control over where and how legal services are provided, the [Legal Aid] Board's starting point should be to ask whether the existing pattern of services provides acceptable access to legal services. In support of its own definition of what is acceptable, it should draw up criteria setting minimum levels of provision. . . .

. . . If sufficient legal aid outlets do not exist, it must create them. It could do this through a range of measures, including grant aid towards the establishment costs of private practices, enhanced rates of legal aid remuneration or the setting up of a branch office with salaried lawyers or some form of mobile community legal centre."

CHAPTER 13

LEGISLATION

I. LEGISLATORS AND INTERPRETERS

Many activities and relationships are regulated by legislation, and the volume of legislation enacted is considerable. Each year, the Council of Ministers of the European Communities adopts some 5,000 regulations and directives which are drafted by lawyers in the Commission of the Communities. (On the Community legislative process, see T.St.J.N. Bates, "The Drafting of Community Legislation" [1983] Stat.L.R. 24; D. Gordon-Smith, "The Drafting Process in the European Community" [1989] Stat.L.R. 56.) In addition to other legislation, the United Kingdom Parliament enacts public general statutes. Most of this type of legislation is introduced by the Government and the remainder, private members' Bills, is introduced by members of either House who are not in the Government. It was estimated that, in 1974, some 3,480 such statutes were still in force, in whole or in part (349 H.C. Deb., col. 940) and those in force in 1965 ran to some 33,000 pages (*The Preparation of Legislation*, Cmnd. 6053 (1975), para. 7.2).

The volume of primary legislation is steadily increasing. The public general acts passed in 1901 totalled 247 pages; those passed in 1991 covered 2,222 pages. These statistics only suggest general trends and have to be qualified by such factors as changes in page size; neither, of course, is the length of statute necessarily indicative of its social or legal significance. (See generally *Making the Law* (Hansard Society: 1993) App. 7.) Nevertheless, the increasing volume of legislation remains a parliamentary concern: see, *e.g.* 514 H.L. Deb., col. 1157 (Jan. 24th 1990); 515 H.L. Deb., col. 382 (Jan. 31st 1990).

Public general Bills introduced by the Government are drafted, on the instructions of the relevant Government department, by legally qualified parliamentary drafters employed by the Government in the Lord Advocate's Department, the Office of Parliamentary Counsel and in Northern Ireland. Private members' Bills are normally drafted outside Government, although the Government may extend the assistance of parliamentary drafters to their sponsors.

Delegated legislation is made, usually by Government ministers, under statutory authority; it is almost always drafted by lawyers in the appropriate Government department (79 H.C. Deb., col. 313 (W.A.) (May 20th 1985); for the rôle of the departmental lawyer in respect of both primary and delegated legislation see A. Graham, "Well in on the Act—A Government Lawyer's View of Legislation" [1988] Stat. L.R. 4. Like primary legislation, and subject to the same qualifications, there has been a significant growth in the volume of delegated legislation. The number of general delegated instruments made in 1901 was 156; the number made in 1991 was 2,945 (*Making the Law* (Hansard Society: 1993), App. 7).

In addition, there are many rules of legal significance which are not contained in statutes or delegated legislation (*e.g.* immigration rules and codes of practice: see Immigration Act 1977, s. 3(2); *Alexander* v. *Immigration Appeal Tribunal* [1982] 2 All E.R. 768, 770; W. A. Wilson, "Knowing the Law and Other Things" (1982) J.R. 259; Lord Campbell of Alloway, "Codes of Practice as an Alternative to Legislation" [1985] Stat. L.R. 127; 469 H.L. Deb., cols. 1075–1104, (January 15th 1986); A. Samuels, "Codes of Practice and Legislation" [1986] Stat. L.R. 29, T.St.J.N. Bates, "Parliament, Policy and Delegated Power", *ibid.*, 114; W.A. Wilson, "Studying Statutes", (1992) J.R. 213, 218–219). Occasionally legislation may recognise a rule but not enact it (*Palatine Graphic Arts Co. Ltd.* v. *Liverpool City Council* [1986] 1 Q.B. 335).

Inevitably, much of the time of courts is occupied by interpreting legislation. In 1980, Lord Hailsham estimated that "nine cases out of ten which come before the House of Lords depend in the end upon the interpretation of a statute" (405 H.L. Deb., col. 302).

The importance of legislation as a source of law depends partly on the range of matters which it regulates, partly on its volume, but principally on the relationship between those who make it and those who apply and interpret it. It is with this relationship, and its uncertainties, that this chapter is primarily concerned. For a witty and erudite survey of such uncertainties, see W. A. Wilson, "Studying Statutes" (1992) J.R. 213.

U.K. legislation is criticised for its style, its language and its typography. Certainly U.K. primary legislation, as compared with some continental European legislation, is detailed. However, some argue that even with legislation which is detailed there could be stylistic improvements. So, for example, Sir William Dale, an experienced drafter, argues for a more relaxed style and shorter sentences.

Dale, "The European Legislative Scene," pp. 91–92
"As an Anglo-Saxon I wish my conclusions to be practical. They will relate to the style of legislation. Roger Scruton, Professor of Aesthetics at

London University, says, 'Style is the search for simplicity and natural-ness, for the phrase which not only says what you mean but also embodies within itself all the nuances.' He was talking philosophically; but his words both give to the draftsman a definition of style, and set an ambition before him. Simplicity, naturalness, and nuances are what we want—and nuances are what we get from statements of principle rather than rules. .

I conclude with two specific points. First, we ought to relax the strenuousness, the laboriousness, the narrowness, of the United Kingdom style, and aim at something freer, easier, and broader. It should not be difficult to achieve this. . . .

Secondly, one of the cardinal differences between civil law and common law styles of drafting is the length of the section. I am in favour of the short section for two reasons. The first reason is that it can be an aid to drafting. I have previously given examples taken from copyright legislation. There the draftsman had various categories of work to be treated, the rules to be in some respects the same for all categories, in other respects different. He dealt with the categories separately, in long, cumbersome sections, and was forced to repeat material. If he had drafted in short sections, there would have been no difficulty, each section laying down the appropriate rule for the category or categories the section covered. Short sentences can of course be grouped together, under a cross-heading.

The second reason is that to *think* in short sections and sentences will encourage more concise thoughts. We do not pay sufficient attention to the effect that form and verbal style may have on thought. To take an illustration so near the bone that it has appeared in these pages before. If Wordsworth had set out to describe what he saw from Westminster Bridge in a lyric or an epic poem rather than in a sonnet, he would have had thoughts greatly differing from those he expressed in his famous fourteen lines; thoughts not so telling, or so memorable.''

Again, as Sir William Dale argues below, even complex legisla-tion would be easier to interpret and apply if it contained state-ments of principle or "objects" sections, although this may not always be possible.

Dale, "Principles, Purposes and Rules," pp. 15, 24–26
"All legislation presumably has a purpose; it may, or it may not, state a principle; it will contain rules, if that is the right word. My chief object is to consider statements of principle, but all three topics are closely connected. I shall consider them separately, and then try to draw them together by suggesting a few practical conclusions. . . .

What are the practical conclusions to be drawn from all this? I suggest the following:

1. Parliament wishes its legislation to be effective. Its impact will be the greater if some principle is stated at 'each new step in a statute.' An

enunciation of principle gives to a statute a firm and intelligible structure. It helps to clear the mind of the legislator, provides guidance to the Executive, explains the legislation to the public, and assists the courts when in doubt about the application of some specific provision. But by a 'principle' we do not, on the one hand, mean a vague, jurisprudential generality, or maxim; nor, on the other hand, do we mean merely a particular provision broadly drafted: we mean a statement in general terms, showing on its face, so far as may be, the moral, social, or economic basis on which the statement itself, and the particular provisions which follow it, rest, and which is itself law-making.

2. But we should recognise that many statutes do not lend themselves to a statement of principle of that kind: minor amending Acts, for example, most penal statutes, Acts dealing with matters of administration, Consolidation Acts. I have particularly looked at chapters 1–40 of our Statute book for 1984 and see that the larger part of them fall within these four categories. We must find other ways of making the purport of a statute clear—an informative long title, for instance, or an objects clause. There is a trend in some Commonwealth countries to replace the long title by an objects clause. Looking again at chapters 1–40, we find long titles that are nicely informative to the Telecommunications Act, the Foreign Limitation Periods Act and the Rates Act. None of the Acts contains an objects clause, unless one counts section 1(1) of the Registered Homes Act, which almost manages an objects clause, a principle and 'rules' in one sentence—all the more meritorious in a Consolidation Act. But I have doubts about the indiscriminate use of objects clauses. I suggest they should be used if there is a particular legislative end to be achieved, as in the example from Barbados I have cited, or for some other specific purpose as recommended by the Renton Committee.

3. Yet that will still leave us with statutes that ought to signal their purport at the outset, and do not do so. Take the Prevention of Terrorism (Temporary Provisions) Act 1984 as an example. Of course one knows from the short title that the Act aims to prevent terrorism. But what sort of all the terrorism related in our newspapers is it directed to preventing? One has to go through the whole of the Act, which has five Parts, 19 sections and three Schedules, and runs to 20 pages, most meticulously, to find out. Stowed away in subsection (4) of section 1 and Schedule 1, subsection (6) of section 3, and subsection (5) of section 10 is the information that, so far, the Act is concerned with Northern Ireland. But then in section 12(3) there suddenly comes:

(3) The acts of terrorism to which this Part of this Act applies are—

    (a) acts of terrorism connected with the affairs of Northern Ireland; and

    (b) acts of terrorism of any other description except acts connected solely with the affairs of the United Kingdom or any part of the United Kingdom other than Northern Ireland.

It is the sort of drafting that numbs the mind. But my point is to suggest that the Act might perhaps have begun with something like this:

> This Act is directed to preventing terrorism in relation to Northern Ireland by means of the proscribing of organisations (Part I), the making of exclusion orders (Part II), and the prescribing of various offences (Part III). Powers of arrest and other powers conferred by Part IV extend also to international terrorism.

That is neither a statement of principle, nor is it an objects clause, though it resembles one. It is a descriptive clause. It might be given the marginal note 'Description of Act.'

4. The Prevention of Terrorism Act had been preceded by earlier Acts, and parts of it must have been difficult to draft. Still, it is a typical product of our legislative style, a true spider's web; and it is this legislative style that I maintain should be our main concern. The debate about principle versus detail, which has grown tiresome, deflects attention from the main problem of securing clarity of drafting throughout an Act. The two sides intend different things by 'principle,' and rarely does either side vouchsafe to us an example of what it does intend. Those arguing for drafting 'in terms of principle' really mean drafting the 'detail' in broader terms, whereas the other side attacks the concept as if its proponents mean drafting the 'detail' in terms of general statements of a jurispruden- tial nature. No conclusion is reached. Let us be clear that by a 'principle' we mean 'a first position'—first in place in the statute as well as in logic— 'from which others are deduced,' the 'others,' so far as they are not implied, being expressed in the remaining provisions of the statute, or the Part, as the case may be. The question we ought to be dwelling on is how to secure in these remaining provisions sufficiency of particularity without undue prolixity and complexity. This must be what the Prime Minister had in mind when, speaking of the 'thicket of detail,' she said that we ought to 'mount a rule of law, and not to make a multiplicity of regulations.' It is too easy to say that, as things stand, our Acts are much like regulations and our regulations much like Acts. We should be able to recognise a greater difference than that the Acts are bound in red, the Regulations in blue."

The need to express often complex matters with great precision may make it difficult for the parliamentary drafter to adopt a more relaxed style and to use, as is sometimes proposed, simpler language.

The Preparation of Legislation, paras. 11.2–11.5

"11.2 The most important technique, if the least tangible, is simplicity of vocabulary and syntax. Varying degrees of emphasis have been placed by witnesses on the need for this. Lord Simon of Glaisdale formulated the ideal in the following terms: 'Desirably the language of legislation should be as near to ordinary speech as precision permits'. But he recognised that 'most ordinary terminology contains ambiguity'. Another formula- tion (by Mr Ian Percival QC MP) is that 'wherever possible, what is intended should be set out in the simplest terms, in the language nearest to that which would be used by those affected by it'. The Statute Law Society suggest that 'clarity of expression, of grammar and construction should be a primary consideration'. According to the Faculty of Advocates 'The solution here must . . . lie in a compromise between the precision of technical language and the ready comprehensibility of the ordinary use of words . . . The words used should be reasonably simple . . . the sentences should be reasonably short'. A number of other witnesses have expressed a preference for simpler language than is to be found in most statutes at present. Many witnesses recognise, however, that it may be difficult or even impracticable to achieve it in some kinds of legislation, notably in fiscal statutes.

11.3 In paragraphs 6.3 and 6.4 we quoted criticisms of current drafting style by the Statute Law Society and other witnesses, and referred to the examples in Appendix B of particular statutory provisions that had caused difficulties of interpretation in the courts. On the other side of the scales should be placed the following tribute by Professor Driedger:

> 'With a new British statute, where I understand the subject matter and the social background, I really have no problems and no difficulty in reading and understanding the statute. Of course, if it is a statute dealing with your building societies, or your rent regulations, I would not understand it because I do not understand your practices, but an ordinary statute that deals with a familiar subject, or with a legal subject, I really have no difficulty in understanding. I think on the whole they are well written and well organised, and can be understood by anyone who is familiar with the subject matter of the statute and the circumstances that give rise to it.'

We would, moreover, mention here that Parliament does not always take kindly to the homely phrase. In a recent Bill the expression 'the owner has tried his best to let the building' was not well received in the House of Commons, which preferred the more orotund 'used his best endeavours'.

11.4 In the 1940s and 1950s, when those who are now senior draftsmen were learning the craft, there was still a general belief that the language, or rather the style, must be formalised, on mere grounds of decorum; and that the precision needed to attain immediate certainty overrode every other consideration. In both respects the belief has since weakened. Language is increasingly informal. As to certainty, the need for it remains amply recognised (as it must be); but certainty is obtainable at two different levels. One is where the draftsman deliberately words his clause so that at no point can it possibly be challenged for ambiguity, even by a reader (or legal practitioner) so perverse, or having such a professional interest in finding a way round the law, that he is resolved to find an ambiguity which to any ordinary reader is invisible. At this level of certainty, language becomes by gradations more and more convoluted, and the legislative proposition obscured. At the other level, sufficient certainty is obtained for a fair-minded and reasonable reader to be in no doubt what is intended, it being assumed that no one would take entirely perverse points against the draft, or that such points would be brushed aside by the court. Most of us are satisfied that there has been a substantial and desirable retreat from the first level, with resultant simplification and abbreviation of language.

11.5 On the other hand, the draftsman must never be forced to sacrifice certainty for simplicity, since the result may be to frustrate the legislative intention. An unfortunate subject may be driven to litigation because the meaning of an Act was obscure which could, by use of a few extra words, have been made plain. The courts may hold, or a Government department be driven to conclude, that the Act which was intended to mean one thing does not mean that thing, but something else. Where this occurs, the draftsman's discomfort is considerable, and he will instinctively guard against its happening to him a second time."

The Committee on the Preparation of Legislation, chaired by the Rt. Hon. Sir David (now Lord) Renton, did not suggest that drafting in a simpler style and language was an unrealistic aspiration. Indeed, success has been achieved in this regard in other Commonwealth countries: see, for example, I.M.L. Turnbull, "Clear Legislative Drafting: New Approaches in Australia" [1990] Stat. L.R. 161; P.E. Johnson, "Legislative Drafting Practices and other Factors affecting the Clarity of Canada's Laws" [1991] Stat. L.R. 1; W. Isles, "Legislative Drafting Practices in New Zealand", *ibid.*, 16. Recommendations that, without sacrificing legal certainty, a simpler drafting style should be considered in the U.K. are to be found in the Hansard Society Commission on the Legislative Process, "Making the Law", (Hansard Society: 1993), Chap. 4.

However, maintaining legal certainty while adopting a simpler drafting style is not always easy. Martin Cutts redrafted the Timeshare Act 1992 in a simpler style and language with a modern layout and typography (the "Clearer Timeshare Act 1993"). The new layout and typography was a distinct improvement, but the simpler language sometimes resulted in a loss of legal clarity. This is illustrated by a brief extract of the 1992 Act and the parallel provision from the 1993 redraft, followed by an extract of a letter to Mr Cutts from Mr Euan Sutherland, who drafted the 1992 Act.

Cutts, "Unspeakable Acts?"

"Timeshare Act 1992, s. 12(4)
'This Act shall have effect in relation to any timeshare agreement or timeshare credit agreement notwithstanding any agreement or notice.' "

"Clearer Timeshare Act 1993, s. 1.3
'The parties may not prevent this Act applying to an agreement.' "

Sutherland letter to Cutts

" . . . The clarity for the lay reader at which your draft aims has led, I think, in certain places to the danger described in that recommendation [i.e. the recommendation at para. 11.5 of *The Preparation of Legislation* quoted above]. For example, section 12(4) of the Act says that the Act has effect 'in relation to any timeshare agreement or timeshare credit agreement notwithstanding any agreement or notice'. Your section 1.3 says 'the parties may not prevent this Act applying to an agreement'. Certainly your formulation seems more straightforward. But what does it mean?

Imagine that an agreement is being made between a tourist and a British salesman abroad and the tourist asks that the contract be made subject to English law. If the salesman refuses, he is by doing so preventing the Act from applying to the agreement. Does section 1.3 prohibit that? Read simply, perhaps it does; and if it does, what is the effect of the prohibition? Does the Act apply anyway, or has the salesman merely committed a wrong for which no penalty is given? . . . "

[The words in square brackets have been added to clarify the context.]

Other factors, apart from statutory style and language, may contribute to the uncertainties which surround the relationship between the legislator and the interpreter. First, words are an imprecise way of conveying meaning and this may be accentuated in legislation. For example, legislation is normally drafted to regulate future events. As it is difficult to anticipate all such events broad terms are often used, and they may raise questions of interpretation. So, when legislation prohibits "fishing" does it include the act of pumping fish from nets into a boat after the fish have been caught (*Alexander* v. *Tonkin* [1979] 1 W.L.R. 629)? Is a person "driving" a car when grabbing the steering wheel from the driver while sitting in the front passenger seat (*Jones* v. *Pratt* [1983] R.T.R. 54), or when pushing a car with one hand on the steering wheel (*McArthur* v. *Valentine*, 1990 J.C. 146)? Do the words "without reasonable excuse" apply to the child or to the parent, where the parent is charged with "failing without reasonable excuse to secure the regular attendance" of a child at school (*MacIntyre* v. *Annan*, 1991 S.C.C.R. 465)? Is the cost of a headstone a reasonable expense incurred "in connection with the deceased's funeral" (*Prentice* v. *Chalmers*, 1985 S.L.T. 168)? Is a building with an annex 12 yards away which contains sleeping accommodation for travellers a "hotel" (*Chief Constable, Northern Constabulary* v. *Lochaber District Licensing Board*, 1985 S.L.T. 410)?

Secondly, the drafters may make mistakes. They may draft imprecisely. They may fail to provide for situations which the legislation would be presumed to encompass, or they may misunderstand the law on which the legislation is based. For example, the Official Secrets Act 1920 made it a specific offence to cause an obstruction "in the vicinity of" any prohibited place but not actually in it (*Adler* v. *George* [1964] 2 Q.B. 7), and in the Natal Ordinance No. 1 of 1856, the drafter misunderstood the relevant private international law (*Salmon* v. *Duncombe* (1886) 11 App. Cas. 627). See also A. Samuels, "Errors in Bills and Acts" [1982] Stat. L.R. 94.

Thirdly, legislative ambiguity may arise out of political expediency. For instance, an important consideration for a Government is that a Bill should be drafted to attract as little opposition as possible during its passage through parliament. Lord Thring, an early parliamentary drafter, wrote, "Bills are made to pass, as razors are made to sell" ((1874) 136 L.Q.R. 66). Mr Moran, of the Lord Advocate's Department, indicated that such political considerations still constrain the modern parliamentary drafter.

Moran, "The Parliamentary Draftsman," p. 36
"It has often seemed to me, in more jaded moods, that many of the critics of the parliamentary draftsman—particularly (let me whisper it) on the Bench—are under the impression that the object of their censure inhabits some secure and peaceful haven—a haven where he can draft his Bills untroubled by the ebb and flow of tides and currents or by the squalls which disturb the sea outside—a haven, above all, where time stands still. Were this the case, the draftsman's lapses would indeed merit little leniency. And is it true? It is not true. No such retreat exists for the draftsman. He is abroad on that sea—a political and parliamentary sea which is at best treacherous, and which can on occasion be cruel indeed. 'Oh, yes,' one is told, 'your clause is clear and accurate, but we can't have it presented that way: our back-benchers would vote against it.' Or: 'Yes, we accept that there is doubt here and we agree that the amendment which you have suggested would remove it. But if we put it down it will reopen the whole question of cruelty to animals (or gambling or police powers) and that will add at least two days to the Committee Stage, which the Whips say we can't afford.' Or, again: 'The Minister says the amendments must go down tonight. Yes, we know this is only a first draft of them and they're worth a week's thought anyway, but there it is.'

There it is indeed. You might be surprised how many statutes owe much of their shape and content not to the conscious wish of the parliamentary draftsman but to political or parliamentary accident entirely outwith his control."

[See also D. Johnstone, "Role of the Administrator in the Preparation of United Kingdom Legislation" [1980] Stat. L.R. 67;

G. Engle, "Bills are made to pass as razors are made to sell: practical constraints in the preparation of legislation" [1983] Stat. L.R. 7.]

Such political and parliamentary constraints may be particularly acute for those drafting Scottish legislation. (See J. Rankin, "Scottish Business at Westminster" (1988) 33 J.L.S. 423.) Governments are not generous in providing parliamentary time for purely Scottish legislation. As it is easier to find parliamentary time for one Bill rather than three or four, it is not uncommon for a Scottish statute to encompass a range of disparate provisions. So, for example the Law Reform (Miscellaneous Provisions) (Scotland) Act 1990 not only enacted a miscellany of law reform in Part IV but also provided for the supervision of charities in Scotland (Part I), made important reforms of the Scottish legal profession (Part II) and extensive amendment of the Licensing (Scotland) Act 1976 (Part III). Accommodating Scots law within a Bill which will apply to Great Britain or the United Kingdom, and which has been structured on the basis of English law, also creates a whole range of problems. See further, Lord Mackay of Clashfern, "The Drafting of Government Bills Affecting the Law of Scotland" [1983] Stat. L.R. 68.

Law reform and the rationalisation of existing legislation can be considered in a more detached and systematic manner. They may be considered by official bodies which are not as closely associated with the day-to-day concerns of ministers and civil servants in Government departments and the parliamentary draftsmen they instruct. Two such bodies are the Law Commission (which has English law as its principal concern) and the Scottish Law Commission.

Law Commission Act 1965, ss. 2, 3

"2.—(1) For the purpose of promoting the reform of the law of Scotland, there shall be constituted in accordance with this section a body of Commissioners, to be known as the Scottish Law Commission, consisting of a Chairman and not more than four other Commissioners appointed by the Lord Advocate.

(2) The persons appointed to be Commissioners shall be persons appearing to the Lord Advocate to be suitably qualified by the holding of judicial office or by experience as an advocate or solicitor or as a teacher of law in a university. . . .

3.—(1) It shall be the duty of each of the Commissions to take and keep under review all the law with which they are respectively concerned with a view to its systematic development and reform, including in particular the codification of such law, the elimination of anomalies, the repeal of obsolete and unnecessary enactments, the reduction of the number of separate enactments and generally the simplification and modernisation of the law, and for that purpose—

  (*a*) to receive and consider any proposals for the reform of the law which may be made or referred to them;

  (*b*) to prepare and submit to the [Lord Advocate] from time to time programmes for the examination of different branches of the law with a view to reform, including recommendations as to the agency (whether the Commission or another body) by which any such examination should be carried out;

  (*c*) to undertake, pursuant to any such recommendations approved by the [Lord Advocate], the examination of particular branches of the law and the formulation, by means of draft Bills or otherwise, of proposals for reform therein;

  (*d*) to prepare from time to time at the request of the [Lord Advocate] comprehensive programmes of consolidation and statute law revision, and to undertake the preparation of draft Bills pursuant to any such programme approved by the [Lord Advocate];

  (*e*) to provide advice and information to government departments and other authorities or bodies concerned at the instance of the Government with proposals for the reform or amendment of any branch of the law;

  (*f*) to obtain such information as to the legal systems of other countries as appears to the Commissioners likely to facilitate the performance of any of their functions.

(2) The [Lord Advocate] shall lay before Parliament any programmes prepared by the Commission and approved by him and any proposals for reform formulated by the Commission pursuant to such programmes.

(3) Each of the Commissions shall make an annual report to the [Lord Advocate] on their proceedings, and the [Lord Advocate] shall lay the report before Parliament with such comments (if any) as he thinks fit.

(4) In the exercise of their functions under this Act the Commissions shall act in consultation with each other."

[As amended by S.I. 1972 No. 2002.]

The Chairman of the Scottish Law Commission is a Senator of the College of Justice; of the other four members of the Commission, two are full-time and two part-time. The Commission has a small legal staff. In 1992, it comprised one full-time and two part-time parliamentary drafters (who prepare the draft legislation referred to in s. 3 above), the Secretary of the Commission and eight other lawyers; the Commission also has the assistance of a seconded depute procurator fiscal. During the summer, the Commission has for some years employed senior law students or recent graduates as research assistants; in 1990, five honours graduates in law were so employed.

The most significant duties of the Scottish Law Commission are proposing reforms in the law and preparing consolidation and statute law revision Bills (on the latter see Lord Simon of Glaisdale and J. Webb, "Consolidation and Statute Law Revision" [1975] P.L. 285; Sir Michael Kerr, "Law Reform in Changing Times" (1980) L.Q.R. 515). Opinions differ on how successful the Scottish Law Commission has been in carrying out its statutory duties: see D.M. Walker, "The Scottish Law Commission under Review" [1987] Stat. L.R. 115; *cf.* Lord Hunter, "Law Reform: the Scottish Law Commission" (1988) J.R. 158.

Much of the law reform undertaken by the Scottish Law Commission is within programmes drawn up by the Commission and approved by the Lord Advocate (ss. 3(1)(*b*), 3(2)) or at the request of Government departments (s. 3(1)(*e*)). However, proposed areas of law reform may also be submitted to the Commission from other sources. The Commission's Consultative Memorandum No. 60 on the law of mobbing and rioting was the product of a proposal from the Crown Agent and, in 1986, the Commission has considered computer crime at the instance of the Law Society of Scotland.

The Commission consults widely before recommending reforms of the law. This is done primarily by issuing consultative memoranda or, in recent years, discussion papers, on which comment is invited; other forms of consultation are also used, such as holding public meetings. Following consultation, the Commission publishes a report with its recommendations; the report often includes draft legislation based on the recommendations. The Scottish Law Commission had, by June 1992, published 135 reports and 94 consultative memoranda or discussion papers, some jointly with the (English) Law Commission; it had also published research papers and documents with a restricted circulation. Not all this work relates directly to domestic law. The Scottish Law Commission is sometimes invited to consider European Community law and international treaties; in 1976 it was asked to consider a White Paper containing proposals for devolution to Scotland and Wales, and it published a memorandum on the subject.

Although the Scottish Law Commission may present detached and carefully considered proposals for law reform it is dependent on the availability of parliamentary time if they are to be implemented. (Accelerated parliamentary legislative procedures apply to consolidation and statute law revision bills, so there the issue is less acute.) Successive governments have been slow in introducing as Government Bills those Commission law reform proposals which they have accepted; some Commission proposals have been introduced as Private Members' Bills. Various procedural solutions have been explored but, as the extract below indicates, finding parliamentary time for the legislative implementation of law reform proposals from the Scottish Law Commission, as indeed for Scottish legislation generally, remains a difficulty.

Scottish Law Commission: Annual Report 1991–92, paras. 1.5, 1.6

"1.5 In recent reports we have expressed concern over the slow rate of implementation of our recommendations for law reforms. During the year under review the Carriage of Goods by Sea Bill 1992, which gave effect to the joint report of the two Commissions on *Rights of Suit in Respect of Carriage of Goods by Sea*, was presented to Parliament, but fell on the calling of the General Election. It was, however, reintroduced in the present Parliament, made swift progress through both Houses, and received the Royal Assent in July. In addition, the Damages (Scotland) Bill 1992, which implements our report entitled *The Effect of Death on Damages*, has been introduced in the House of Lords by Lord Macaulay of Bragar. When this report was published in March 1992 it met with immediate approval from Government which expressed the wish that the recommendations be given effect in legislation at an early date. In view of the urgent and tragic plight of asbestosis victims whose dependents will benefit from implementation of this proposed reform, we trust that the Bill will not be subjected to avoidable delays or obstacles during its passage through Parliament.

1.6 In March 1992 the Law Society of Scotland generously devoted a whole session of its Annual Conference at Gleneagles to consideration of the question 'Law reform—who cares?'. The speakers at the session were Lord Morton of Shuna, Lord Fraser of Carmyllie and our Chairman. The following points emerged from the discussion. Lack of time on the floor of the House of Commons was identified as being the root cause of delays, and it was noted that this lack has held up implementation of recommendations from both Law Commissions. The Law Commissions have welcomed the experimental step proposed by the Select Committee on the Committee work of the House of Lords whereby special Standing Committee procedure would be applied to additional Government Bills, such as those arising from certain recommendations of the Law Commissions. Consideration could also be given to Lord Morton's suggestion that law reform Bills which fail to complete all their stages during one session of Parliament should be carried forward automatically into the next session. Even if these suggested reforms are brought about, they are unlikely to accelerate progress on the five substantial reports listed in our last report which still await parliamentary consideration. One of the causes of delay is that these reports contain controversial recommendations. Although they are the product of detailed research and, as a result of extensive consultation, have met with a measure of public approval, they nevertheless require and deserve critical and informed examination on the floor of each House of Parliament. It is to be hoped that the impetus for swifter implementation given by the Law Society at their

Conference and the reactivation of the Scottish Select Committee in the current Parliament will lead to an early increase in the number of Scottish law reform measures introduced in the House of Commons."

The rôle of the interpreter also contributes to the uncertain relationship between those who make law and those who apply and interpret it. At a fundamental level, legislation as a source of law depends on the recognition of the authority of the legislator. So, for example, judges in the United Kingdom recognise the supremacy of the U.K. Parliament as a legislative body (*e.g. Mortensen* v. *Peters* (1906) 8 F.(J.) 93), although in certain circumstances Community law (*e.g. Macarthys Ltd.* v. *Smith* [1979] 3 All E.R. 325) and possibly the Treaty and Acts of Union 1707 (*e.g. MacCormick* v. *Lord Advocate*, 1953 S.C. 396; *Murray* v. *Rogers* 1992 S.L.T. 221; and see N. Walker & C.M.G. Himsworth (1991) J.R. 45) may be recognised as prevailing over conflicting parliamentary legislation. To some extent interpretation is governed by statutory provisions and precedent, although the former may themselves be interpreted and the latter distinguished. Beyond that there is a wide measure of discretion left to the judiciary in the interpretation of legislation. There are, for example, a number of principles which judges may read into legislation unless the legislation expressly excludes them. Again, when faced with a legislative ambiguity, judges may choose to apply a variety of rules to resolve the ambiguity. The way in which this judicial discretion is exercised depends to some extent on the judge's perception of his constitutional rôle. Compare, for example, the views of Denning L.J., for which he was subsequently rebuked in the House of Lords ([1952] A.C. 189, at p. 191), with those of Lord Simon of Glaisdale.

Magor and St. Mellons R.D.C. v. Newport Corporation
[1950] 2 All E.R. 1226

DENNING L.J.: "I have no patience with an ultra-legalistic interpretation . . . We do not sit here to pull the language of Parliament and of Ministers to pieces and make nonsense of it. That is an easy thing to do, and it is a thing to which lawyers are too often prone. We sit here to find out the intention of Parliament and of Ministers and carry it out, and we do this better by filling in the gaps and making sense of the enactment than by opening it up to destructive analysis."

Stock v. Frank Jones (Tipton) Ltd.
[1978] 1 W.L.R. 231

LORD SIMON OF GLAISDALE: "The final task of construction is still, as always, to ascertain the meaning of what the draftsman has said, rather than to ascertain what the draftsman meant to say. But if the draftmanship is correct these should coincide. So if the words are capable of more than one meaning it is a perfectly legitimate intermediate step in construction to choose between potential meanings by various tests (statutory, objective, anomaly, etc.) which throw light on what the draftsman meant to say.

It is idle to debate whether, in so acting, the court is making law. As has been cogently observed, it depends on what you mean by 'make' and 'law' in this context. What is incontestable is that the court is a mediating influence between the executive and the legislature, on the one hand, and the citizen on the other. Nevertheless, it is essential to the proper judicial function in the constitution to bear in mind: (1) modern legislation is a difficult and complicated process, in which, even before a bill is introduced in a House of Parliament, successive drafts are considered and their possible repercussions on all envisageable situations are weighed by people bringing to bear a very wide range of experience: the judge cannot match such experience or envisage all such repercussions, either by training or by specific forensic aid; (2) the bill is liable to be modified in a Parliament dominated by a House of Commons whose members are answerable to the citizens who will be affected by the legislation: an English judge is not so answerable; (3) in a society living under the rule of law citizens are entitled to regulate their conduct according to what a statute has said, rather than by what it was meant to say or by what it would have otherwise said if a newly considered situation had been envisaged; . . . (5) Parliament may well be prepared to tolerate some anomaly in the interest of an overriding objective; (6) what strikes the lawyer as an injustice may well have seemed to the legislature as no more than the correction of a now unjustifiable privilege or as a particular misfortune necessarily or acceptably involved in the vindication of some supervening general social benefit; (7) the parliamentary draftsman knows what objective the legislative promoter wishes to attain, and he will normally and desirably try to achieve that objective by using language of the appropriate register in its natural, ordinary and primary sense: to reject such an approach on the grounds that it gives rise to an anomaly is liable to encourage complication and anfractuosity in drafting; (8) Parliament is nowadays in continuous session, so that an unlooked-for and unsupportable injustice or anomaly can be readily rectified by legislation: this is far preferable to judicial contortion of the law to meet apparently hard cases with the result that ordinary citizens and their advisers hardly know where they stand.

All this is not to advocate judicial supineness: it is merely respectfully to commend a self-knowledge of judicial limitations, both personal and constitutional."

II. THE LAW OF INTERPRETATION

A. EUROPEAN COMMUNITY LAW

European Communities Act 1972, s. 3(1), (2)

"3.—(1) For the purposes of all legal proceedings any question as to the meaning or effect of any of the Treaties, or as to the validity, meaning or effect of any Community instrument, shall be treated as a question of law (and, if not referred to the European Court, be for determination as such in accordance with the principles laid down by and any relevant decision of the European Court [or any court attached thereto.]).

(2) Judicial notice shall be taken . . . of any decision of, or expression of opinion by the European Court [or any court attached thereto] on any such question as aforesaid."

[For the definitions of "Treaties" and "Community Instrument" see section 1 and Schedule 1; the "European Court" means the Court of Justice of the European Communities: *ibid.*; the words in square brackets were added by the European Communities (Amendment) Act 1986, s. 2, in anticipation of the establishment of the Court of First Instance.]

Section 3 of the European Communities Act 1972, which reflects the Community obligations of the U.K. as a Member State, provides that decisions of, and principles laid down by, the Court of Justice of the European Communities, (the "Court of Justice"), or the Court of First Instance, on the interpretation and effect of Community treaties and Community legislation are binding on all courts in the United Kingdom. As indicated below, this status accorded to the jurisprudence of the Court of Justice has important implications for the manner in which U.K. courts interpret both Community law and domestic legislation.

However, before turning to those implications, there are complicating factors in establishing the principles of interpretation laid down by, and evaluating the decisions of, the Court of Justice and the Court of First Instance. The Court of Justice may sit as a full court, but it also sits for some purposes in Chambers of three or five judges; the Court of First Instance, which has a limited jurisdiction, may also sit as a full court or in Chambers of three or five judges. Thus it is possible that, in each Court, one Chamber may fail to follow the previous decision of another; this may be of somewhat less practical significance with respect to the Court of First Instance, which does not hear Article 177 references (see below). Secondly, advocates-general who, although not judges, are members of the European Court, submit opinions on cases before the Court; a similar arrangement exists in the Court of First

Instance. The opinions of the advocates-general are commonly more fully argued than the judgments; they are frequently adopted in the judgments, but sometimes they are not: *e.g.* Cases C–6 and 9/90, *Francovich and Bonifaci* v. *Italian Republic* [1992] I.R.L.R. 84 (retrospectivity of a state's liability to an individual for breaches of Community law). Finally, the Court of Justice does not regard itself as bound by its previous decisions (*e.g.* Case 48/72, *de Haecht (No. 2)*) [1973] E.C.R. 77; *cf.* Case 43/69, *Bilger* v. *Jehle* [1970] E.C.R. 127 and Case 10/69, *Portelange* [1969] E.C.R. 309), although it does prefer to follow them (*e.g.* Case 35/75, *Matisa* [1975] E.C.R. 1205, 1210).

Section 3(1) refers to principles laid down by the Court of Justice. Some of the more significant of these principles have obvious implications for the interpretation of national legislation which is implementing Community law, for example directives. They include such principles as the supremacy of Community law over inconsistent national law (*e.g.* Case 6/64, *Costa* v. *ENEL* [1964] E.C.R. 585; Case 11/70, *Internationale Handelsgesellschaft* [1970] E.C.R. 1125; Case 106/77, *Simmenthal* [1978] E.C.R. 629), and the circumstances in which Community legislation has direct effect and gives individuals rights which are enforceable in national courts (*e.g.* Case 149/77, *Defrenne* v. *Sabena* [1978] E.C.R. 1365; Case 93/71, *Leonesio* [1972] E.C.R. 287; Case 41/47, *Van Duyn* [1974] E.C.R. 1337; Case 148/78, *Ratti* [1979] E.C.R. 1629; Case 9/70, *Grad* [1970] E.C.R. 825).

In addition there are decisions of the Court of Justice which bear on the interpretation and effect to be given to national legislation in order to give effect to Community obligations. In *Von Colson* (Case 14/83, [1984] E.C.R. 1891), the Court of Justice held that a national court should interpret national legislation adopted to implement a directive in the light of the wording and purpose of the directive, so as to be in conformity with Community law (see also Case 222/84, *Johnston* v. *Chief Constable, R.U.C.* [1986] E.C.R. 1651, 1690; [1987] Q.B. 129, 153). In *Marleasing* (Case C–106/89, [1990] E.C.R. I–4135), the Court of Justice developed the duty placed on national courts requiring them to interpret national legislation in the light of Community law, so that national law conforms "so far as possible" with Community law. *Marleasing* suggests that this is not limited to national legislation implementing a Community obligation, but extends to the construction of all national legislation. Sometimes essentially procedural decisions of the Court of Justice determine the effect which national courts give to national legislation. So, in a preliminary ruling on a reference from the House of Lords, the Court of Justice held that where interim relief in a case concerning Community law could not be granted solely because of national legislation, a national court should suspend operation of the national legislation, in this case the Merchant Shipping Act 1988: *R.* v. *Secretary of State for Transport, ex p. Factortame Ltd.* [1990] 3 W.L.R. 818 (E.C.J.).

The response of Scottish and other U.K. courts to this jurisprudence of the Court of Justice is tempered by aspects of public law which, in their detail, fall outside the scope of this book. U.K. courts have, for instance, held that Community law prevails over inconsistent domestic law, unless in the case of primary legislation that legislation clearly demonstrates an intention to prevail over a Community obligation: see European Communities Act 1972, s. 2; *Macarthys Ltd.* v. *Smith* [1979] 3 All E.R. 325; *cf. Prince* v. *Secretary of State for Scotland*, 1985 S.L.T. 74.

What appears to be the more specific contemporary response of the U.K. courts is illustrated by the House of Lords, on a Scottish appeal, in *Litster* v. *Forth Dry Dock and Engineering Co. Ltd.*

Litster v. Forth Dry Dock and Engineering Co. Ltd.
[1990] 1 A.C. 546

The appellants were employees of Forth Dry Dock and Engineering Co. Ltd., which was one of a group of companies which became insolvent and went into receivership. The receiver agreed to sell the assets of the company to Forth Estuary Engineering Ltd. An hour before the assets were transferred, the receivers dismissed the employees with immediate effect.

LORD KEITH OF KINKEL: "My Lords, I agree with the speeches of my noble and learned friends Lord Oliver and Lord Templeman, which I have had the opportunity of reading in draft, and will add only a few observations of my own.

In *Pickstone* v. *Freemans plc* [1989] A.C. 66 there had been laid before Parliament under para. 2(2) of Sch. 2 to the European Communities Act 1972 the draft of certain regulations designed, and presented by the responsible ministers as designed, to fill a lacuna in the equal pay legislation of the United Kingdom which had been identified by a decision of the Court of Justice of the European Communities. On a literal reading the regulation particularly relevant did not succeed in completely filling the lacuna. Your Lordships' House, however, held that in order that the manifest purpose of the regulations might be achieved and effect given to the clear but inadequately expressed intention of Parliament certain words must be read in by necessary implication.

In the present case the Transfer of Undertakings (Protection of Employment) Regulations 1981, S.I. 1981/1794, were similarly laid before Parliament in draft and approved by resolutions of both Houses. They were so laid as designed to give effect to E.C. Council Directive 77/187 dated 14 February 1977. It is plain that if the words in reg. 5(3) of the 1981 Regulations 'a person so employed immediately before the transfer' are read literally, as contended for by the second respondents, Forth Estuary Engineering Ltd., the provisions of reg. 5(1) will be capable of ready evasion through the transferee arranging with the transferor for the latter to dismiss its employees a short time before the transfer becomes operative. In the event that the transferor is insolvent, a situation commonly forming the occasion for the transfer of an undertaking, the employees would be left with worthless claims for unfair dismissal against the transferor. In any event, whether or not the transferor is insolvent, the employees would be deprived of the remedy of reinstatement or re-engagement. The transferee would be under no liability towards the employees and a coach and four would have been driven through the provisions of reg. 5(1).

A number of decisions of the European Court, in particular *P. Bork International A/S (in liq.)* v. *Foreningen af Arbejdsledere i Danmark* Case 101/87 [1989] I.R.L.R. 41, have had the result that where employees have been dismissed by the transferor for a reason connected with the transfer, at a time before the transfer takes effect, then for purposes of art. 3(1) of E.C. Council Directive 77/187 (which corresponds to reg. 5(1)) the employees are to be treated as still employed by the undertaking at the time of the transfer.

In these circumstances it is the duty of the court to give to reg. 5 a construction which accords with the decisions of the European Court on the corresponding provisions of the directive to which the regulation was intended by Parliament to give effect. The precedent established by *Pickstone* v. *Freemans plc* indicates that this is to be done by implying the words necessary to achieve that result. So there must be implied in reg. 5(3) words indicating that where a person has been unfairly dismissed in the circumstances described in reg. 8(1) he is to be deemed to have been employed in the undertaking immediately before the transfer or any of a series of transactions whereby it was effected.

My Lords, I would allow the appeal."

LORD TEMPLEMAN: " . . . In *von Colson* v. *Land Nordrhein-Westfalen* Case 14/83 [1984] E.C.R. 1891 at 1909 (para. 26) the European Court, dealing with E.C. Council Directive 76/207 forbidding discrimination on grounds of sex regarding access to employment, ruled:

' . . . the Member States' obligation arising from a directive to achieve the result envisaged by the directive and their duty under Article 5 of the Treaty to take all appropriate measures, whether general or particular, to ensure the fulfilment of that obligation, is binding on all the authorities of Member States including, for matters within their jurisdiction, the courts. It follows that, in applying the national law and in particular the provisions of a national law specifically introduced in order to implement Directive No. 76/207, national courts are required to interpret their national law in the light of the wording and the purpose of the directive in order to achieve the result referred to in the third paragraph of Article 189.'

Thus the courts of the United Kingdom are under a duty to follow the practice of the European Court by giving a purposive construction to directives and to regulations issued for the purpose of complying with directives. In *Pickstone* v. *Freemans plc* [1989] A.C. 66 this House implied words in a regulation designed to give effect to E.C. Council Directive 75/117 dealing with equal pay for women doing work of equal value. If this House had not been able to make the necessary implication the Equal Pay (Amendment) Regulations 1983, S.I. 1983/1794, would have failed in their object and the United Kingdom would have been in breach of its treaty obligations to give effect to directives. In the present case, in the light of E.C. Council Directive 77/187 and in the light of the ruling of the European Court in *Bork's* case [1989] I.R.L.R. 41, it seems to me, following the suggestion of my noble and learned friend Lord Keith, that reg. 5(3) of the 1981 Regulations was not intended and ought not to be construed so as to limit the operation of reg. 5 to persons employed immediately before the transfer in point of time. Regulation 5(3) must be construed on the footing that it applies to a person employed immediately before the transfer or who would have been so employed if he had not been unfairly dismissed before the transfer for a reason connected with the transfer . . . "

LORD OLIVER: " . . . It will be seen that, as is to be expected, the scope and purpose of both the directive and the regulations are the same, that is to ensure that on any transfer of an undertaking or part of an undertaking, the employment of the existing workers in the undertaking is preserved or, if their employment terminates solely by reason of the transfer, that their rights arising out of that determination are effectively safeguarded. It may, I think, be assumed that those who drafted both the directive and the regulations were sufficiently acquainted with the realities of life to appreciate that a frequent, indeed, possibly the most frequent, occasion on which a business or part of a business is transferred is when the original employer is insolvent, so that an employee whose employment is terminated on the transfer will have no effective remedy for unfair dismissal unless it is capable of being exerted against the transferee. It can hardly have been contemplated that, where the only reason for determination of the employment is the transfer of the undertaking or the relevant part of it, the parties to the transfer would be at liberty to avoid the manifest purpose of the directive by the simple expedient of wrongfully dismissing the workforce a few minutes before the completion of the transfer. The European Court has expressed, in the clearest terms, the opinion that so transparent a device would not avoid the operation of the directive, and if the effect of the regulations is that under the law of the United Kingdom it has that effect, then your Lordships are compelled to conclude that the regulations are gravely defective and the government of the United Kingdom has failed to comply with its mandatory obligations under the directive. If your

Lordships are in fact compelled to that conclusion, so be it; but it is not, I venture to think, a conclusion which any of your Lordships would willingly embrace in the absence of the most compulsive context rendering any other conclusion impossible. . . . ''

[See also *Pickstone* v. *Freemans plc* [1989] A.C. 66; *cf. Duke* v. *G.E.C. Reliance Ltd.* [1988] A.C. 618, *Finnegan* v. *Clowney Youth Training Programme* [1990] 2 All E.R. 546 (H.L.); *R.* v. *D.H.S.S., ex p. Organon Laboratories* [1990] 1 C.M.L.R. 49, (C.A.); and J.D.N. Bates, "The Impact of Directives on Statutory Interpretation: Using the Euro-meaning?" [1986] Stat. L.R. 174.]

Litster shows that U.K. courts, following *Von Colson*, are capable of taking a robust approach in interpreting domestic legislation, enacted to implement Community obligations, to ensure compliance with Community law. Reference may be made to the Community obligation, and to decisions of the Court of Justice which interpret it, to ensure the compliance of national legislation with Community law and not merely for the purpose of resolving an ambiguity in the national legislation, at least where the national legislation has been enacted for the purpose of implementing the Community obligation. Following *Marleasing*, the role of national courts in construing national legislation to comply with Community law may be further enlarged.

The decision of the Court of Justice in *Bork*, to which reference is made in the Opinions in *Litster*, demonstrates that in the interpretation of Community law the Court of Justice places greater emphasis on the purpose of the legislation, and on its underlying policy, than on literal interpretation. Placing emphasis on purpose and policy obviously has greater utility where, as in the case of articles of Community treaties and many directives, legislation is drafted in terms of economic and social objectives and words and phrases are not closely defined. Also, the value of literal interpretation is limited where there are authoritative texts of legislation in different languages (*e.g.* Case 9/79, *Wörsdorfer* [1979] E.C.R. 2717; Case 80/76, *N. Kerry Milk Products Ltd.* [1977] E.C.R. 425; Case 150/80, *Elefanten Schuh* v. *Jacqmain* [1981] E.C.R. 1671; Case 13/83, *European Parliament* v. *European Council* [1986] 1 C.M.L.R. 138).

In considering the purpose and policy of legislation, the Court of Justice makes greater use of *travaux préparatoires* than U.K. courts. In Case 71/76, *Thieffry* [1977] E.C.R. 765, as an aid to interpretation the Court referred to a programme of proposals for eliminating discrimination which had been adopted by the Council of Ministers; and it frequently refers to explanatory notes of nomenclature in cases concerning the interpretation of the Community common customs tariff (*e.g.* Case 22/76, *Import Gadgets* [1976] E.C.R. 1371). However, the Court will not normally consider debates in the European Parliament as an aid to interpretation of Community legislation (Case 136/79, *National Panasonic (U.K.) Ltd.* v. *E.C. Commission* [1980] E.C.R. 2033 at pp. 2066–2067 *per* Adv.-Gen. Warner; *cf.* Case 29/69, *Stauder* v. *City of Ulm* [1969] E.C.R. 419, although it has referred to debates in the national parliaments of Member States when interpreting Community treaties (*e.g.* Case 6/60, *Humblet* [1960] E.C.R. 559). The Court has also refused to consider a subsequent legislative proposal from the European Commission in interpreting Community legislation (Case 113/83, *Re Road Haulage Licences: E.C. Commission* v. *Italy* [1985] 3 C.M.L.R. 407, 422). Nor for purposes of interpretation will it rely on minuted reservations of a Member State in its negotiations on a directive or domestic rules of interpretation in a Member State (Case 143/83, *Re Equal Pay Concepts: E.C. Commission* v. *Denmark* [1986] 1 C.M.L.R. 44). On the interpretation of Community legislation, see also T. Millett, "Rules of Interpretation of E.E.C. Legislation" [1989] Stat. L.R. 163.

Arguably on the basis of the European Communities Act 1972, s. 3, in the U.K., the emphasis on schematic and teleological interpretation adopted by the Court of Justice must be adopted in the construction of Community legislation (*e.g. H.P. Bulmer Ltd.* v. *J. Bollinger S.A.* [1974] Ch. 401; *R.* v. *Henn* [1981] A.C. 901; *Customs & Excise Commissioners* v. *Ap.S. Samex* [1983] 1 All E.R. 1042) and of domestic legislation implementing Community legislation (*e.g. Litster* v. *Forth Dry Dock and Engineering Co. Ltd.*; *Pickstone* v. *Freemans plc*; both cited above), in preference to domestic rules of statutory interpretation. This may involve departure from accepted domestic rules on recourse to non-legislative materials in the interpretation of Community legislation. So, for example, in *O'Brien* v. *Sim-Chem Ltd.* [1980] 1 W.L.R. 734, a background report issued by the Commission of the European Communities was considered in England to establish the legal effect of a directive.

B. STATUTORY RULES OF INTERPRETATION

Interpretation Act 1978, ss. 6–11

"**6.** In any Act, unless the contrary intention appears,—

    (*a*) words importing the masculine gender include the feminine;

    (*b*) words importing the feminine gender include the masculine;

    (*c*) words in the singular include the plural and words in the plural include the singular.

7. Where an Act authorises or requires any document to be served by post (whether the expression 'serve' or the expression 'give' or 'send' or any other expression is used) then, unless the contrary intention appears, the service is deemed to be effected by properly addressing, pre-paying and posting a letter containing the document and, unless the contrary is proved, to have been effected at the time at which the letter would be delivered in the ordinary course of post.

8. In the measurement of any distance for the purpose of an Act, that distance shall, unless the contrary intention appears, be measured in a straight line on a horizontal plane.

9. Subject to section 3 of the Summer Time Act 1972 (construction of reference to points of time during the period of summer time), whenever an expression of time occurs in an Act, the time referred to shall, unless it is otherwise specifically stated, be held to be Greenwich mean time.

10. In any Act a reference to the Sovereign reigning at the time of the passing of the Act is to be construed, unless the contrary intention appears, as a reference to the Sovereign for the time being.

11. Where an Act confers power to make subordinate legislation, expressions used in that legislation have, unless the contrary intention appears, the meaning which they bear in the Act."

[For examples of the use of these provisions see *Skinner* v. *Patience*, 1982 S.L.T. (Sh.Ct.) 81, *Adam* v. *Secretary of State for Scotland*, 1988 S.L.T. 300 (O.H.). For their application to legislation enacted before the 1978 Act came into force, see Sched. 2, Pt. I. The provisions also apply to the interpretation of subordinate legislation made after 1978 (s. 23(1)), except s. 9 which applies to subordinate legislation whenever made (Sched. 2).]

The Interpretation Act 1978 makes provision for the enactment and operation of legislation. As the extract illustrates, it also contains some general rules applicable in Great Britain for the interpretation of legislation enacted by the U.K. Parliament. However, these rules are not broad principles of statutory interpretation and the Act does not provide a comprehensive code for the interpretation of legislation.

In general, the rules that are in the Act only apply where no "contrary intention appears" in the legislation to be interpreted: *e.g. R.* v. *Brentwood Justices, ex p. Nicholls* [1992] 1 A.C. 1. The courts may, in practice, infer a contrary intention if the rules do not resolve the problem of interpretation. In *Prior* v. *Sovereign Chicken Ltd.* [1984] 1 W.L.R. 921, 928, Oliver L.J. observed, "I cannot for my part make sense of the provisions of the two sections . . . if . . . the provisions of section 6 of the Interpretation Act 1978 are applied to them".

The rules may also be too limited in scope to assist interpretation. Section 7 applies to service of documents by post, but has been held not to apply where a statute does not refer to *posting* documents: *House* v. *Emerson Electric Industrial Controls* [1980] I.C.R. 795. Sometimes the Act is ignored by courts when assistance might have been derived from the rules it contains, *e.g. Aikman* v. *White*, 1985 S.L.T. 535.

In 1969 the Law Commissions recommended a broad approach to interpretation, and included in their report draft legislation which, following the practice of some Commonwealth countries, would have put the major principles of interpretation on a statutory basis (Law Com. No. 21; Scot. Law Com. No. 11 (H.C. 256, 1968/69)). In 1975, the views of the Law Commissions received the support of the Renton Committee on the Preparation of Legislation (Cmnd. 6053). In 1980 and 1981, private members' Bills based on the Law Commissions' proposals were introduced by Lord Scarman but were not enacted. (See 405 H.L.Deb., cols. 276–306 (Feb. 13, 1980); 418 H.L.Deb., cols. 64–83, 1341–7; 419 H.L.Deb., cols. 518, 796–7 (Mar. 9 and 26, Apr. 7 and 13, 1981)).

C. STATUTORY DEFINITIONS

A word or phrase may be defined by statute (for an excellent survey see W.A. Wilson, "The Complexity of Statutes" (1974) 37 M.L.R. 497). A statutory definition may extend the ordinary meaning of a word: " 'horse' includes ass or mule" (Animal Health Act 1981, s. 89(1)). On the other hand, it may restrict ordinary meaning: " 'animal' does not include bird or fish" (Food Act 1984, s. 132(1)). The definition may give a word or phrase a precise meaning or illustrate it by examples. It may be generally applicable or have a limited applicability.

Interpretation Act 1978, s. 5 and Sched. 1

"**5.** In any Act, unless the contrary intention appears, words and expressions listed in Schedule 1 to this Act are to be construed according to that Schedule.

. . .

SCHEDULE 1

. . .

'Month' means calendar month. [1850] . . .

'Registered medical practitioner' means a fully registered person within the meaning of the Medical Act 1983. [1st January 1979] . . .

'Secretary of State' means one of Her Majesty's Principal Secretaries of State.

'Sheriff' in relation to Scotland, includes sheriff principal. [1889] . . .

'Writing' includes typing, printing, lithography, photography and other modes of representing or reproducing words in a visible form, and expressions referring to writing are construed accordingly."

[These definitions apply to statutes passed after the date or year specified and where no year or date is specified, to all statutes (Sched. 2, para. 4(1); in the absence of contrary intention, they also apply in the same way to subordinate legislation made after 1978 (s. 23(1)).]

Zoo Licensing Act 1981, ss. 1, 21

"1. . . . (2) In this Act 'zoo' means an establishment where wild animals (as defined by section 21) are kept for exhibition to the public otherwise than for purposes of a circus (as so defined) and otherwise than in a pet shop (as so defined); and this Act applies to any zoo to which members of the public have access, with or without charge for admission, on more than seven days in any period of 12 consecutive months . . .

21.—(1). In this Act—

> 'animals' means animals of the classes Mammalia, Aves, Reptilia, Amphibia, Pisces and Insecta and other multicellular organism that is not a plant or a fungus and 'wild animals' means animals not normally domesticated in Great Britain;
>
> 'circus' means a place where animals are kept or introduced wholly or mainly for the purpose of performing tricks or manoeuvres at that place; . . .
>
> 'pet shop' means premises for whose keeping as a pet shop a licence is in force, or is required, under the Pet Animals Act 1951 . . . ''

A statutory definition is normally binding, unless its application would be contrary to the purpose of the legislation (*Strathern* v. *Padden*, 1926 J.C. 9; *cf. Savoy Hotel Co.* v. *L.C.C.* [1900] 1 Q.B. 665).

Definitions of limited application are usually contained in one or more interpretation sections, but they may be elsewhere in the statute (*e.g.* Zoo Licensing Act 1981), and authoritative definitions may be included in a glossary of expressions (*e.g.* Social Security Act 1975, s. 168(1), Sched. 20).

A word or phrase may sometimes be defined in different ways in different parts of the same statute: see, for example, the definitions of "intestate estate" in the Succession (Scotland) Act 1964, ss. 1(2), 9(6)(*a*), 36(1) and (2), 37(1)(*a*) and (*b*), and of "container" in the Weights and Measures Act 1985, ss. 68(1), 94(1). In the Child Abduction and Custody Act 1985 the word "convention" refers to two different treaties in different parts of the Act: ss. 1(1), 12(1).

A definition in one statute may be incorporated by reference into another (*e.g.* the definition of "pet shop," above).

In addition to authoritative definitions, legislation may also provide examples and non-authoritative descriptions, as an aid to the user, which are not binding on the courts in interpreting the legislation (*e.g.* Consumer Credit Act 1974, s. 188 and Sched. 2; Wildlife and Countryside Act 1981, Scheds. 2–6).

D. PRECEDENT

The interpretation of a word or phrase in legislation enacted in the United Kingdom is governed by precedent (see Chap. 14), and generally courts are reluctant to overrule their own previous decisions on questions of interpretation.

Walker v. Dick Engineering Co. (Coatbridge) Ltd.
1985 S.L.T. 465

The pursuer averred that while cutting a piece of metal on a lathe, sharp cuttings from the metal emerged at speed and injured his hand. The Factories Act 1961, s. 14(1), provides that "every dangerous part of any machinery . . . shall be securely fenced . . . "

LORD DAVIDSON: ". . . the pursuer has averred a contravention by the defenders of s. 14(1) of the Factories Act 1961 . . . Counsel for the defenders presented two main arguments. In the first place he noted that . . . [I]t was well settled by the decisions cited that s. 14(1) of the Factories Act 1961 requires a distinction to be observed between the dangerous parts of a machine and the materials which are worked in that machine. In the present case the defect in the pursuer's pleadings was elementary, because plainly he was injured not by any part of the machine but by cuttings given off from the material worked on.

The second argument advanced by counsel for the defenders was that the dangers against which the fencing legislation was designed to protect the operator were limited. In particular, the decisions previously referred to laid down that there was no obligation to fence part of a machine in order to prevent material emerging or being ejected by it so as to cause injury. In the present case the pursuer did not aver that his body made contact with any part of the machine. His complaint was that he was injured by a piece of material which projected from the machine. Accordingly, on that separate ground, his case was irrelevant.

In my opinion the submissions made by counsel for the defenders are well founded in law. In *Johnson* v. *F.E. Callow (Engineers) Ltd.* [1971] A.C. at p. 343, after reviewing the main authorities relating to the protection afforded by s. 14 of the Factories Act 1961, Lord Hailsham L.C. said this: 'No-one contemplating the situation set up by this series of decisions can wholly avoid the conclusion reached by Holroyd Pearce, L.J., . . . that the gap in the protection afforded by the statute is one "which neither logic nor common sense appears to justify". It is however too late for the courts to close the gap. The gap can only be closed by legislation or to some extent by the use of the regulatory powers of the minister. It has, however, to be said that I for one would be slow to enlarge the gap or to extend the ambit of the criticised decisions beyond the limits required by the fact of the cases concerned and the reasoning of the judgments in them.' Counsel for the pursuer maintained that the pursuer's pleadings in the present case fall on the right side of the gap. I do not agree."

[See also *R.* v. *National Insurance Commissioner, ex p. Hudson* [1972] A.C. 944; *Carter* v. *Bradbeer* [1975] 1 W.L.R. 1204, 1206–1207, but see pp. 382–390.]

However, a decision on interpretation in one statute is merely persuasive where the same word or phrase falls to be interpreted in another statute (*Carter* v. *Bradbeer*, above; *Royal Court Derby Porcelain Co. Ltd.* v. *Raymond Russell* [1949] 2 K.B. 417). This is so even where a statute re-enacts a word or phrase which was judicially interpreted in earlier legislation (*Kelly* v. *MacKinnon*, 1982 S.C.C.R. 205, 211–212; *R.* v. *Chard* [1984] A.C. 279, 291, 294, 295).

The operation of the doctrine of precedent in questions of interpretation depends on the jurisdiction of the court and on the nature of the legislation. Thus, a decision on a question of interpretation by the House of Lords in a Scottish appeal is binding on courts in Scotland. Such a decision in an English civil appeal is similarly binding where the legislation applies in both Scotland and England (*Dalgleish* v. *Glasgow Corporation*, 1976 S.C. 32; see Chap. 14). However, other decisions by courts elsewhere in the United Kingdom, including decisions of the House of Lords in English criminal appeals, are only persuasive in Scotland (*Dalgleish* v. *Glasgow Corporation*, above). This is so, even where the decisions concern the interpretation of legislation which also applies in Scotland or which is legislation parallel to that applying in Scotland (*cf. Viewpoint Housing Association* v. *Lothian Regional Council, The Scotsman*, Nov. 6th 1991 (O.H.) and *Forest Hills Trossachs Club* v. *Assessor for Central Region*, 1991 S.L.T. (Lands Tr.) 42). So, for example, criminal legislation applying to both Scotland and England may receive divergent interpretation in the two jurisdictions (*e.g. Kelly* v. *MacKinnon*, 1982 S.C.C.R. 205; *cf. R.* v. *Freeman* [1970] 1 W.L.R. 788); this is clearly undesirable and, where it does arise, judges seek to rectify it (*e.g. Allan* v. *Patterson*, 1980 J.C. 57; *R.* v. *Murphy* [1980] Q.B. 434; *R.* v. *Lawrence* [1982] A.C. 510; *Keane* v. *Gallacher*, 1980 J.C. 77; *R.* v. *Carver* [1978] Q.B. 472, *R.* v. *Boyesen* [1982] A.C. 768).

Certainly, in both jurisdictions courts will seek to give uniform interpretation to fiscal legislation which applies throughout the United Kingdom.

Lord Advocate v. Earl of Moray's Trustees
(1905) 7 F.(H.L.) 116

The case concerned the interpretation of the Finance Act 1894, on a Scottish appeal.

LORD MACNAGHTEN: "I am not at all insensible to the grave difficulties which have been pointed out so forcibly by the learned Judges in Scotland. But I cannot think that those difficulties are insuperable. It must be borne in mind that the Act which your Lordships are now called upon to construe in its application to Scotland applies equally to the whole of the United Kingdom. It is a taxing Act. It must be presumed to have been the intention of Parliament to make the incidence of the taxation the same in Scotland as in England and Ireland, and to extend the same measure of relief, such as it is, to limited owners called upon to discharge a burthen on the inheritance wherever the property burthened may be situated.

Your Lordships may remember that much the same sort of question arose in *Lord Saltoun's* case (1860) 3 Macq. 659, which was referred to in this House not long ago in *Special Commissioners for Income-Tax* v. *Pemsel* [1891] A.C. 531. In *Lord Saltoun's* case the Succession-Duty Act, 1853, came under consideration, and it was held by this House, reversing the judgment of the Court of Session, that an extrinsic technicality—a technical rule of Scotch feudal conveyancing—must be disregarded when its effect would be to produce inequality."

[See also *Commissioners for General Purposes of Income Tax for City of London* v. *Gibbs* [1942] A.C. 402, 414; *Secretary of State for Employment and Productivity* v. *Clarke Chapman & Co. Ltd.* [1971] 1 W.L.R. 1094.]

III. JUDICIAL PRINCIPLES AND INTERPRETATION

In interpreting legislation judges may apply a variety of principles to the legislation unless the legislation expressly excludes them. So, when faced with a textual ambiguity in U.K. legislation, a court will adopt an interpretation which is in accord with international law in preference to one which is not (*e.g. Mortensen* v. *Peters* (1906) 8 F.(J.) 93), and will often give a strict construction to penal legislation (*e.g. H.M. Advocate* v. *R.M.*, 1969 J.C. 52). However, not all questions of interpretation concern textual ambiguity. A court may resolve such questions by applying principles which may affect the substance of the application of the legislation. Examples of the application of such principles are given below.

Sweet v. Parsley
[1970] A.C. 132

The Dangerous Drugs Act 1965, s. 5 provided:

"If a person—(*a*) being the occupier of any premises, permits those premises to be used for the purpose of smoking . . . cannabis resin . . . or (*b*) is concerned in the management of any premises used for such purpose as aforesaid; he shall be guilty of an offence . . . "

Miss Sweet let rooms in a farmhouse to tenants who, unbeknown to her, smoked cannabis. Cannabis was found in the farmhouse and she was charged and convicted under s. 5(*b*) of the 1965 Act. On appeal, one question before the court was whether a

s. 5(*b*) offence could be committed by a person without some blameworthy state of mind, mens rea.

LORD REID: "Our first duty is to consider the words of the Act; if they show a clear intention to create an absolute offence that is an end of the matter. But such cases are very rare. Sometimes the words of the section which creates a particular offence make it clear that mens rea is required in one form or another. Such cases are quite frequent. But in a very large number of cases there is no clear indication either way. In such cases there has for centuries been a presumption that Parliament did not intend to make criminals of persons who were in no way blameworthy in what they did. That means that whenever a section is silent as to mens rea there is a presumption that, in order to give effect to the will of Parliament, we must read in words appropriate to require mens rea."

[The presumption may be displaced by the subject matter of the statutory provision (see *Sherras* v. *De Rutzen* [1895] 1 Q.B. 918; *R.* v. *Bradish* [1990] 1 Q.B. 981 (possession of a weapon, a canister of CS gas); *Chichester D.C.* v. *Silvester* (D.C.), *The Times*, 6th May 1992 (organisation and management of an "acid house" party)) and may not be applicable where the statutory provision does not create a criminal offence (*Customs and Excise Commissioners* v. *Air Canada* [1991] 2 Q.B. 446).]

Malloch v. Aberdeen Corporation
1971 S.C. (H.L.) 85

LORD REID: "The right of a man to be heard in his own defence is the most elementary protection of all and, where a statutory form of protection would be less effective if it did not carry with it a right to be heard, I would not find it difficult to imply this right. Here it appears to me that there is a plain implication to that effect in the . . . Act. The terms of that Act have been altered by later legislation, but I can find nothing in any later Act which can reasonably be interpreted as taking away that elementary right."

Brown v. Magistrates of Edinburgh
1931 S.L.T. 456

LORD MACKAY: " . . . it is common ground that in [England] all statutes are enforceable, however antiquated, until repealed, and never fall into desuetude. It is also common that that is not true of the older Scots statutes, but it is true of all Acts passed for Scotland by the common Legislature after 1707. A few words are needed on what desuetude means and requires . . . I hold it clear in law that desuetude requires for its operation a very considerable period, not merely of neglect, but of contrary usage of such a character as practically to infer such completely established habit of the community as to set up a counter law or establish, a *quasi*-repeal . . . Erskine treats it as 'a posterior custom repealing or derogating from a statute'; and assigns his reason, 'for the contrary immemorial custom sufficiently presumes the will of the community to alter the law in all its clauses.' . . . My own disposition would be to think that very rarely, if ever, could a statute be judicially held by mere judicial knowledge to be in desuetude without averment of, and, if disputed, proof of, contrary custom."

The Statute Law Revision (Scotland) Acts 1906 and 1964 repealed many obsolete Acts of the Parliament of Scotland. There is a strong, but rebuttable, presumption that Scots Acts which remain in force are not in desuetude. See further, J.R. Philip, "Some reflections on desuetude" (1931) 43 J.R. 260; *D.B. Britton* v. *R. Johnstone* (O.H.), July 24th 1992 (unreported).

Kerr v. Marquis of Ailsa
(1854) 1 Macq. 736

LORD CRANWORTH L.C.: "My Lords, unless there be something in the language, context, or objects of an Act of Parliament showing a contrary intention, the duty and the practice of Courts of justice is to presume, in conformity with the adage of Lord Coke, that the legislature enacts prospectively and not retrospectively. There may, however, be enactments that are evidently on the face of them by their language and subject-matter intended to be retrospective; and when such is the case, the maxim of Lord Coke must give way."

[See also *Gardner* v. *Lucas* (1878) 5 R.(H.L.) 105.]

In *Wilson* v. *Wilson*, 1939 S.C. 102, it was held that the Divorce (Scotland) Act 1938, which introduced cruelty as a new ground for divorce, was retrospective to the extent that cruelty could be established by conduct which took place before the Act came into force. [See also *Santa Fe International Corp.* v. *Napier Shipping S.A.*, 1985 S.L.T. 481; *Forbes* v. *Forbes*, 1991 S.C.L.R. 389.]

IV. JUDICIAL RULES OF INTERPRETATION

The law of interpretation leaves considerable discretion to the judiciary. The attitude of judges to textual interpretation, as we have seen, depends to some extent on their perception of their constitutional rôle. The spectrum of attitudes has been traditionally characterised by the emphasis placed on various rules of interpretation. The principal rules are the literal rule, the golden rule and the mischief rule.

A. THE LITERAL RULE

R. v. Judge of the City of London Court
[1892] 1 Q.B. 273

LORD ESHER M.R.: "If the words of an Act are clear, you must follow them, even though they lead to a manifest absurdity. The Court has nothing to do with the question whether the legislature has committed an absurdity."

Black-Clawson International Ltd. v.
Papierwerke Waldhof-Aschaffenburg A.G.
[1975] A.C. 591

LORD DIPLOCK: "The acceptance of the rule of law as a constitutional principle requires that a citizen, before committing himself to any course of action, should be able to know in advance what are the legal consequences that will flow from it. Where those consequences are regulated by a statute the source of that knowledge is what the statute says. In construing it the court must give effect to what the words of the statute would be reasonably understood to mean by those whose conduct it regulates."

The literal rule, as expressed by Lord Esher and given a modern justification by Lord Diplock, emphasises the plain, ordinary or literal meaning of words. Perhaps, in practice, the literal rule creates a rebuttable presumption that words bear their most obvious meaning (see *Saul* v. *Norfolk C.C.* [1984] Q.B. 559). However, in some of the applications of the rule there is an assumption that words are unambiguous and this is not always so.

B. THE GOLDEN RULE

River Wear Commissioners v. Adamson
(1877) 2 App. Cas. 743

LORD BLACKBURN: " . . . we are able to take the whole statute together, and construe it all together, giving the words their ordinary signification, unless when so applied they produce an inconsistency, or an absurdity or inconvenience so great as to convince the Court that the intention could not have been to use them in their ordinary signification, and to justify the Court in putting on them some other significance, which, though less proper, is one which the Court thinks the words will bear."

[See also *Manson* v. *Duke of Westminster* [1981] Q.B. 323.]

The golden rule is, in reality, a gloss on the literal rule. It lays somewhat less emphasis on the plain meaning of words, but it offers no guidance on either identifying those inconsistencies, absurdities or inconveniences which permit a departure from a particular meaning of words, or on choosing an alternative meaning.

C. THE MISCHIEF RULE

Maunsell v. Olins
[1975] A.C. 373

LORD SIMON OF GLAISDALE: " . . . in construing an Act of Parliament, you identify the 'mischief' which the statute seeks to remedy (i.e., in modern parlance the statutory objective), and so construe the statute that it advances the remedy and suppresses the mischief (i.e., in modern parlance, in construing the statute you bear its objective in mind). It is, in other words, a positive and not a negative canon of construction; it enjoins a liberal, and not a restrictive, approach. For a court of construction to constrain statutory language which has a primary natural meaning appropriate in its context so as to give it an artificial meaning which is appropriate only to remedy the mischief which is conceived to have occasioned the statutory provision is to proceed unsupported by principle, inconsonant with authority and oblivious of the actual practice of parliamentary draftsmen."

The mischief rule, or purposive approach, may be traced to *Heydon's Case* (1584) 3 Co. Rep. 7a. Its modern use, and its limitations, are well described by Lord Simon. It places greater emphasis on the intention of the legislature and depends less on words having a plain meaning. However, the mischief rule offers little guidance as to when it is appropriate to depart from the legislative text and on how the intention of the legislature should be established.

V. INTERPRETATION IN PRACTICE

The three rules described in the last section have much in common. They all place a primary emphasis on the legislative text and recognise the possibility of legislative inconsistency or absurdity. This has led some commentators to suggest that there is only one rule of interpretation, which is a conflation of the three rules (see E.A. Driedger, *The Construction of Statutes*, 1974, p. 67). The argument may be presented in more utilitarian form, by suggesting that exclusive reliance on any of the three rules is of limited value. Judges frequently resort to all three in interpretation or, having formed a view by using one rule, resort to other rules to confirm their view.

Using any of the three rules in an absolute manner also has a limited utility, because each leaves a range of practical problems unresolved. The use made of them depends on the nature of the question before the court. Judges may resolve questions of interpretation by examining a statutory word or phrase in its linguistic, grammatical and legal context. In doing so, they may turn to dictionaries, legal dictionaries and other reference works. So, for example, in *Reed International Ltd.* v. *I.R.C.* [1976] A.C. 336, 359, Lord Wilberforce referred to Palgrave's *Dictionary of Political Economy* of 1896 to determine the meaning of "funded debt". And dictionaries have been consulted by the High Court of Justiciary for a definition of "prostitute" (*White* v. *Allan*, 1985 S.L.T. 396), by the Inner House for the meaning of "reciprocal" (*Nicoll (Liquidator of RDM (Contracts) Ltd.)* v. *Steelpress (Supplies) Ltd.*, 1992 S.C.L.R. 332), and by the Lands Tribunal for the meaning of "shopping mall" (*Sunblest Bakeries Ltd.* v. *Assessor for Strathclyde Region*, 1990 S.L.T. (Lands Tr.). 76). (See generally W.A. Wilson, *Introductory Essays on Scots Law* (2nd ed.), pp. 97–98.) Use may also be made of textbooks and of commentaries on the statute concerned (*e.g. Bastin* v. *Davies* [1950] 2 K.B. 579; *Allan* v. *Patterson*, 1980 J.C. 57; *Hardy* v. *Robinson*, 1985 S.L.T. (Sh.Ct.) 40).

In interpreting in linguistic, grammatical or legal context the courts may be seen to be adopting a literal approach to interpretation, albeit in a modified form. However, in many instances, interpretation in context also involves consideration of the purpose of the legislation, in effect using the mischief rule. Where interpretation in context fails to resolve an ambiguity, more reliance may then be placed on establishing the purpose of the legislation. In recent years there has been an increasing emphasis on the purposive approach to interpretation in U.K. courts. This may be a consequence of the many multi-national treaties which are now incorporated into domestic law by legislation, and also of membership of the European Communities. Certainly, the Court of Justice of the Communities places considerable emphasis on the purposive approach, and the same is true of courts in the United States and many European and Commonwealth countries.

A. LINGUISTIC CONTEXT

Maunsell v. Olins
[1975] A.C. 373

A landlord sought to recover possession of a farm cottage. The case turned on whether the farm fell within "premises" in the Rent Act 1968, s. 18(5).

LORD SIMON OF GLAISDALE: "Statutory language, like all language is capable of an almost infinite gradation of 'register'—i.e., it will be used at the semantic level appropriate to the subject matter and to the audience addressed (the man in the street, lawyers, merchants, etc.). It is the duty of a court of construction to tune in to such register and so to interpret the statutory language as to give to it the primary meaning which is appropriate in that register (unless it is clear that some other meaning must be given in order to carry out the statutory purpose or to avoid injustice, anomaly, absurdity or contradiction). In other words, statutory language must always be given presumptively the most natural and ordinary meaning which is appropriate in the circumstances . . .

The subject matter of the legislation under your Lordships' instance considered provides an example of what we mean by language having various 'registers.' In popular parlance 'landlord' can mean 'innkeeper'— indeed, even 'lessee from a brewery.' But in ordinary legal parlance, which is, we think, the appropriate register of language in legislation dealing with rent restriction and security of leasehold tenure, 'landlord' presumptively means 'lessor', and it would take a good deal to displace the presumption. Similarly, in popular parlance 'premises' can mean 'building.' But in ordinary legal parlance 'premises' means 'the subject matter of a letting.' Or, even higher in the register, if the Rent Act 1968 is considered as dealing with legal technicalities, 'premises' presumptively bears its most ordinary meaning as a term of art—namely, the subject matter of the habendum clause of the relevant lease."

Mills v. Cooper
[1967] 2 Q.B. 459

Section 127 of the Highways Act 1959 provided *inter alia*: "If, without lawful authority or excuse . . . (c) a hawker or other itinerant trader or a gipsy pitches a booth, a stall or stand, or encamps, on a highway, he shall be guilty of an offence . . . " The respondent was charged that, he, being a gipsy, did without lawful excuse or authority encamp on the highway contrary to section 127. The magistrates dismissed the charge on the ground that they were not satisfied that the respondent was a gipsy. On appeal the court had to consider the proper meaning to be given to the term "gipsy".

DIPLOCK L.J.: 'I agree that the word 'gipsy' as used in s. 127(c) the Highways Act, 1959, cannot bear its dictionary meaning of a member of a wandering race (by themselves called Romany) of Hindu origin. If it did, it would mean that Parliament in 1959 had amended the corresponding section of the Highway Act, 1835, (1) which referred to 'gipsy or other person' so as to discriminate against persons by reason of their racial origin alone. It would raise other difficulties too. How pure blooded a Romany must one be to fall into the definition? . . . As members of this race first appeared in England not later than the beginning of the sixteenth century, and have not in the intervening centuries been notorious for the abundance of their written records, it would be impossible to prove Romany origin even as far back as the sixteenth century, let alone through the earlier centuries of their peripatetic history from India to the shores of this island. The section, so far as it referred to 'gipsy', would be incapable in practice of having any application at all. Confronted by these difficulties, [counsel for the respondent] only faintly argues that the word 'gipsy' in the context of the section does not bear its popular meaning, which I would define as a person without fixed abode who leads nomadic life, dwelling in tents or other shelters, or in caravans or other vehicles. If this meaning is adopted, it follows that being a gipsy is not an unalterable status. it cannot be said 'once a gipsy always a gipsy'. By changing his way of life a modern Borrow may be a gipsy at one time and not a gipsy at another . . . ''

[See also *Blankley* v. *Godley* [1952] 1 All E.R. 436.]

Fisher v. Bell
[1961] 1 Q.B. 394

The defendant displayed a flick-knife, with a price-ticket, in his shop-window. He appealed against a conviction under the Restriction of Offensive Weapons Act 1959, s. 1(1), which provided that any person "who manufactures, sells or hires or offers for sale or hire, or gives to any person" a flick-knife, commits an offence.

LORD PARKER: "The sole question is whether the exhibition of that knife in the window with the ticket constituted an offer for sale within the statute. I confess that I think most lay people and, indeed, I myself when I first read the papers, would be inclined to the view that to say that if a knife was displayed in a window like that with a price attached to it was not offering it for sale was just nonsense. In ordinary language it is there inviting people to buy it, and it is for sale; but any statute must of course be looked at in the light of the general law of the country. Parliament in its wisdom in passing an Act must be taken to know the general law. It is perfectly clear that according to the ordinary law of contract the display of an article with a price on it in a shop window is merely an invitation to treat. It is in no sense an offer for sale the acceptance of which constitutes a contract. That is clearly the general law of the country. Not only is that so, but it is to be observed that in many statutes and orders which prohibit selling and offering for sale of goods it is very common when it is so desired to insert the words 'offering or exposing for sale', 'exposing for sale' being clearly words which would cover the display of goods in a shop window. Not only that, but it appears that under several statutes—we have been referred in particular to the Prices of Goods Act, 1939, and the Goods and Services (Price Control) Act, 1941—Parliament, when it desires to enlarge the ordinary meaning of those words, includes a definition section enlarging the ordinary meaning of "offer for sale" to cover other matters including, be it observed, exposure of goods for sale with the price attached.

In those circumstances I am driven to the conclusion, though I confess reluctantly, that no offence was here committed. At first sight it sounds absurd that knives of this sort cannot be manufactured, sold, hired, lent, or given, but apparently they can be displayed in shop windows; but even if this—and I am by no means saying it is—is a casus omissus it is not for this court to supply the omission."

Determining the linguistic context of a word or phrase has limitations as an aid to interpretation. By examining the linguistic context of the legislation, it was possible to prefer a non-technical meaning rather than a more precise technical meaning in *Mills* v. *Cooper*. However, as in *Fisher* v. *Bell*, the linguistic context does not help to decide between an ordinary meaning and a technical legal meaning.

Another limitation is that a word or phrase may change its meaning over time. Interpretation may change with the change of meaning. For instance, the interpretation of "family" in the Rents Acts has been extended to include, in some instances, unmarried couples who live together (see Chap. 14). However, in other cases, the courts have sought the meaning at the time of the enactment of legislation and applied that meaning in preference to a more modern meaning (*e.g. McKinlay* v. *McKinlay* (1851) 14 D. 162; *Scottish Cinema and Variety Theatres Ltd.* v. *Ritchie*, 1929 S.C. 350).

B. GRAMMATICAL CONTEXT

Judges may consider a word or phrase in its grammatical context as an aid to interpretation. In doing so, they can resort to a variety of maxims. So, they may apply the *ejusdem generis* rule: where general words follow more specific words with some common feature they will take their meaning from them. The maxim is often associated with the more general maxim *noscitur a sociis*, a thing is known from its associates. For example in construing the Offences Against the Person Act 1828, which made it a felony in England to shoot at or to "stab, cut or wound" any person, the word "wound" was held to be restricted by the preceding words to injuries inflicted by an instrument and not to include biting off a finger (*R.* v. *Harris* (1836) 7 C. & P. 446; *cf. Mortimer* v. *Samuel B. Allison Ltd.*, 1959 S.C. (H.L.) 1).

Another maxim which is frequently applied is *expressio unius est exclusio alterius*, to mention one or more things of a particular class can be regarded as excluding other things in the same class. Consequently, where the Poor Relief Act 1601 in England imposed a poor rate on the occupiers of "lands," houses, tithes and "coal mines," it was held that as coal mines were expressly mentioned, "land" did not include other types of mine (*R.* v. *Inhabitants of Sedgley* (1831) 2 B. & Ad. 65). The maxim will not be applied, however, where the court considers something has been inadvertently omitted from the legislation (*e.g. Stevenson* v. *Hunter* (1903) 5 F. 761); or where its application conflicts with the purpose of the legislation (*e.g. Dean* v. *Wiesengrund* [1955] 2 Q.B. 120). See further, J.M. Keyes, "Expressio Unius: the Expression that Proves the Rule" [1989] Stat. L.R. 1.

However, the purpose of the statute may prevail over the normal grammatical context of a word. For example, "shall" normally has a mandatory connotation, but it may be interpreted as merely directory (*e.g. H.M. Advocate* v. *Graham*, 1985 S.L.T. 498; *R.* v. *Sheer Metalcraft Ltd.* [1954] 1 Q.B. 586). Similarly, "must" is usually mandatory and "may" directory, but "may" is sometimes interpreted as mandatory (*e.g. Baron Inchyra* v. *Jennings (Inspector of Taxes)* [1965] 2 All E.R. 714, at p. 723 *per* Pennycuick J.). Again "and" is normally interpreted as conjunctive and "or" as disjunctive (*e.g. Docherty* v. *Stakis Hotels*, 1991 S.C.C.R. 6), but not where it conflicts with the purpose of the legislation (*e.g. John G. Stein & Co. Ltd.* v. *O'Hanlon* [1965] A.C. 890, at p. 904 *per* Lord Reid; *R.* v. *Oakes* [1959] 2 Q.B. 350).

C. LEGAL CONTEXT

The courts will interpret a word or phrase in its legal context. This may include considering the text of the legislation as a whole, other elements of the legislation and other legislation enacted both previously and subsequently.

1. THE WHOLE TEXT

Shepherd v. Pearson Engineering Services (Dundee) Ltd.
1980 S.C. 268

The pursuer sustained injuries while he was employed replacing lights on the superstructure of a ship. He sued his employers and argued that they had failed to comply with the Construction (Working Places) Regulations 1966. The argument depended on his work being "work of engineering construction" as defined in the Factories Act 1961 and in regulations made in 1960. The definition included work on "any steel or reinforced concrete structure." One question before the court was whether a ship could be a "steel . . . structure."

LORD CAMERON: "The 'steel structure' was a ship according to the pursuer's argument and this argument is crucial . . . Literally considered and even without reference to their context and the purposes the specific regulations are designed to serve, the words "steel structure' could or might be construed as the pursuer would wish . . .

But I do not think that this is a proper approach to the issue here. The question is not whether a ship can be properly described as a 'steel structure' in the abstract, but whether a ship is included within the meaning of 'work of engineering construction' as that is defined in the regulations founded upon and this required attention to be paid to the precise language of the relevant provisions as well as to the protective purposes of the legislation . . . Not only must the regulations founded upon be the lexicon from which the meaning of the words 'steel structure' is to be discovered but at the same time, as counsel for the defenders pointed out in the course of the debate, it is to be kept in view that the shipbuilding regulations of 1960 provide for the protection of workmen and place duties on employers of workmen in respect of access and plant in those circumstances in which it was reasonably to be expected that an employer could have some measure of control. Regulation 4 makes precise provision as to the various responsibilities of employers of workmen, dock operators, shipowners and shipmasters whose ships are under construction, repair or refit in dock or harbour as docks and harbours are defined in the Merchant Shipping Act. Here is a code of conduct and obligation precisely defining duties of inter alios such persons as the defenders, in respect of matters which form the subject of the present proceedings. It appears to me that there was force in the defenders' arguments to the extent that here is a statutory code specifi- cally referable to that type of operation which is in question, and that this fact is relevant when one has to consider the scope of definition in the regulation on which the pursuer founds. The definition of 'work of engineering construction' in s. 176(1) of the 1961 Act which contains no reference to 'steel structure' is detailed but certainly does not suggest that a ship under refit or repair would naturally fall within it unless it could be covered by regulations which so specified. When one turns to the regulation of 1960 and its Schedule—The Engineering Construction (Extension of Definition) Regulations 1960 (S.I. 1960 No. 421)—one finds it covered 'works to be included in the definition of the expression "work of engineering construction" ' and opens with the words 'The construction, structural alteration or repair (including re-pointing and re- painting) or the demolition of any of the following [other than in a defined factory or upon a railway or tramway]'. It goes on 'that is to say, any steel or reinforced concrete structure other than a building, any road, airfield, sea defence works or river works, and any other civil or constructional engineering works of a similar nature to any of the foregoing works.' In my opinion to deduce from this catalogue that ships are included sub silentio is an impossible task—the pursuer's argument to the contrary was only made plausible by ignoring the language of the Schedule itself and treating the words steel and structure as if the only structure covered by the Schedule were a steel structure. That however ignores the important words 'or reinforced concrete' which separate 'steel' from 'structure' in the Schedule. What therefore one has to interpret are the words 'steel or reinforced concrete structures' and not the simple words 'steel structure'. This in my view not only alters the sense, but gives a very clear indication of the meaning of the phrase and leads to the conclusion at which I arrive that a ship is not something which is buried within these words of extended definition of the phrase 'work of engineering construction'. I therefore reject the pursuer's construction of . . . the Construction (Working Places) Regulations 1966."

[See also *Parvin* v. *Morton Machine Co.* 1952 S.C. (H.L.) 9; *MacPhail* v. *Tayside Regional Council*, 1991 S.C.C.R. 370.]

The long title of a statute may be used as an aid to interpretation (*e.g. Ayr* v. *St. Andrew's Ambulance Association*, 1918 S.C. 158; *Black-Clawson International Ltd.* v. *Papierwerke Waldhof-Aschaffenburg A.G.* [1975] A.C. 591; *Manuel* v. *Att.-Gen.* [1983] Ch. 77; *cf. Re Boaler* [1915] 1 K.B. 21). The preamble may also be used as an aid to interpretation, although it cannot prevail over the legislative text (*e.g. Att.-Gen.* v. *Prince Ernest Augustus of Hanover* [1957] A.C. 436; *Andrew Oliver & Son Ltd.* v. *Douglas*, 1981 S.C. 193; *Manuel* v. *Att.-Gen.*, above). Similarly, the preamble of a Community regulation or directive may be used as an aid to interpretation (*e.g. H.P. Bulmer Ltd.* v. *J. Bollinger S.A.* [1974] 1 Ch. 401, Case No. 9/72, *Brunner* [1972] E.C.R. 961).

2. OTHER ELEMENTS OF THE LEGISLATION

D.P.P. v. Schildkamp
[1971] A.C. 1

LORD REID: "The question which has arisen in this case is whether and to what extent it is permissible to give weight to punctuation, cross-headings and side-notes to sections in the Act. Taking a strict view, one can say that these should be disregarded because they are not the product of anything done in Parliament. I have never heard of an attempt to move that any of them should be altered or amended, and between the introduction of a Bill and the Royal Assent they can be and often are altered by officials of Parliament acting in conjunction with the draftsman.

But it may be more realistic to accept the Act as printed as being the product of the whole legislative process, and to give due weight to everything found in the printed Act. I say more realistic because in very many cases the provision before the court was never even mentioned in debate in either House, and it may be that its wording was never closely scrutinised by any members of either House. In such a case it is not very meaningful to say that the words of the Act represent the intention of Parliament but that punctuation, cross-headings and side-notes do not.

So, if the authorities are equivocal and one is free to deal with the whole matter, I would not object to taking all these matters into account, provided that we realise that they cannot have equal weight with the words of the Act. Punctuation can be of some assistance in construction. A cross-heading ought to indicate the scope of the sections which follow it but there is a always a possibility that the scope of one of these sections may have been widened by amendment. But a side-note is a poor guide to the scope of a section, for it can do no more than indicate the main subject with which the section deals.

If we take these matters into consideration, then we are in effect searching for the intention of the draftsman rather than the intention of Parliament. And then it becomes very relevant to ask—could any competent draftsman have adopted this form of drafting if he had intended the result for which the appellant contends? If the answer is no, then there is such real doubt that it must be resolved in favour of the accused."

3. Previous Legislation

The courts may refer to previously enacted legislation, *in pari materia*, as an aid to interpretation.

Kiely v. Lunn
1982 S.C.C.R. 436

The appellant's son had failed to attend school because he had been in ill-health as a result of glue-sniffing. At the appellant's trial for having committed an offence under the Education (Scotland) Act 1980, s. 35, it was proved that the son's addiction could be treated with his co-operation, but the boy would not co-operate. The appellant was convicted and appealed by stated case to the High Court of Justiciary.

The Education (Scotland) Act 1980, s. 35, provides that where a child fails to attend school without reasonable excuse his parent shall be guilty of an offence. Section 42(1)(*b*) of the same Act provides that it is a "reasonable excuse" if "the child has been prevented by sickness from attending school".

The previous legislation, the Education (Scotland) Act 1945, contained a similar provision. However, in its original statutory form, the Education (Scotland) Act 1883, s. 11, the provision read "the child has been prevented from attending school by sickness *or any other unavoidable cause*" (italics added).

LORD JUSTICE-GENERAL (EMSLIE): "Looking at the terms of [the 1883 Act] it is perfectly clear from the words 'or any other unavoidable cause' that the word 'sickness' was not intended to include a state of mental or physical incapacity or disability induced or brought about by the deliberate actings of the person concerned. . . . Although the words 'or any unavoidable cause' were dropped from the legislation in and after 1945 it cannot be supposed that the word 'sickness' used in 1945, and in the Act of 1980, was intended to bear a different meaning from that which it had borne from 1883 to 1945. 'Sickness' accordingly, in the legislation from and after 1945, must be understood to mean an unavoidable cause of absence, at least in the sense that it cannot be construed to include a state of ill-health brought about by the deliberate actings of the child concerned."

Reference may be made, as above, to legislation no longer in force and, in the same way, to the previous common law position (*e.g. E.T.U.* v. *Tarlo* [1964] Ch. 720); courts may also refer to previously enacted legislation which is still in force (*e.g. Hamilton* v. *N.C.B.*, 1960 S.C. (H.L.) 1). In *Mackin* v. *Mackin*, 1990 S.C.L.R. 728 a statute was construed against the existing sheriff court procedure. *Kiely* v. *Lunn* is a somewhat vigorous use of previous legislation as an aid to interpretation; courts are usually more circumspect in its use: *e.g. R.* v. *Lawrence* [1982] A.C. 510, 522; *Gunning* v. *Mirror Group Newspapers Ltd.* [1986] 1 All E.R. 385.

Sometimes the use of previous legislation is quite unhelpful. In *Manson* v. *Duke of Westminster* [1981] Q.B. 323, it was necessary to determine the meaning of the undefined term "letting value" in the Leasehold Reform Act 1967 and the court was referred to a definition of "lettable value" in a 1944 statute. Stephenson L.J. (at p. 327) observed, "I derive no more help from the definition in the Act of 1944 than from the absence of any definition in the Act of 1967."

Previously enacted legislation will be used with caution to interpret legislation which codifies the law on a subject by subsuming and possibly amending statutory and common law rules (*e.g. Bank of England* v. *Vagliano Brothers* [1891] A.C. 107). It is also used cautiously in the interpretation of consolidation statutes.

R. v. Heron
[1982] 1 W.L.R. 451

LORD SCARMAN: "First, when construing a consolidating statute, it is particularly useful to have recourse to the legislative history if a real difficulty arises. Consolidation is, or is intended by Parliament to be, the re-enactment in a more convenient, lucid and economical form . . . of existing statute law. It is, in its 'pure' form neither amendment nor reform nor codification, but re-enactment. Strictly, as draftsmen have always recognised, a pure consolidation must incorporate the law as it stands, including its difficulties and ambiguities. The earlier statute law, therefore, and judicial decisions as to its meaning and purpose, are very relevant, if there be difficulty or ambiguity.

Second, I would not think it correct to distinguish between the various types of consolidation. There are now three and more may be added in the future. They are: (1) 'pure' consolidation, i.e. re-enactment; (2) consolidation with 'corrections and minor improvements'; (3) consolidation with Law Commission amendments. I have discussed the first. The second was made possible by the Consolidation of Enactments (Procedure) Act 1949 which confines permissible amendment to very minor matters. Certainly that Act in no way changes the essential character of consolidation, which is re-enactment. It cannot make any less legitimate a reference to the legislative history where there is difficulty or ambiguity.

The same observations apply to consolidation with Law Commission amendments. But here there is an added feature. The Law Commission publishes a report which specifies the particular mischief (or mischiefs) which its proposed amendments are intended to remove. It is, therefore, perfectly plain to what extent one may use legislative history in the interpretation of a Law Commission consolidation.

For those reasons I would not go further than Lord Wilberforce did in *Farrell* v. *Alexander* [1977] A.C. 59 at 73, where he said:

'. . . recourse should only be had [to antecedents] when there is a real and substantial difficulty or ambiguity which classical methods of construction cannot resolve.'

But, when there is such a difficulty, I believe the courts should not hesitate to refer to the legislative history. In some cases, as in the present, it will still doubt and resolve difficulty."

[*cf. Farrell* v. *Alexander* [1977] A.C. 59, at pp. 82–85 *per* Lord Simon of Glaisdale; *Prior* v. *Sovereign Chicken Ltd.* [1984] 1 W.L.R. 921, 928–929 *per* Lawton L.J.]

4. SUBSEQUENT LEGISLATION

Kirkness v. John Hudson & Co. Ltd.
[1955] A.C. 696

LORD REID: "[Unless the earlier statute is obscure or ambiguous] in construing a provision of an earlier Act, the provisions of a later Act cannot be taken into account . . . and . . . that rule applies although the later Act contains a provision that it is to be read as one with the earlier Act. Of course, that does not apply where the later Act amends the earlier Act or purports to declare its meaning; in such cases the later Act operates directly by its own force."

[See also *Payne* v. *Bradley* [1962] A.C. 343, at p. 357 *per* Lord Denning.]

Lord Reid refers to a later statute amending an earlier one. This may be done expressly or it may arise by implication. Where a later Act is inconsistent with an earlier one, but does not expressly amend or repeal it, the courts will normally apply the later Act. The earlier legislation is considered to have been impliedly amended or repealed by the later legislation (*e.g. Vauxhall Estates Ltd.* v. *Liverpool Corporation* [1932] 1 K.B. 733; *Ellen St. Estates Ltd.* v. *Minister of Health* [1934] 1 K.B. 590; *Manuel* v. *Att.-Gen.* [1983] Ch. 77). However this is subject to the maxim, *generalia specialibus non derogant*, general provisions do not derogate from particular ones. So, the Housing Act 1925 which empowered local authorities to appropriate any land vested in them for building purposes did not abrogate by implication the obligation imposed on the London County Council by the London Open Spaces Act 1893 to maintain Hackney Marshes as an open space (*R.* v. *Minister of Health, ex p. Villiers* [1936] 2 K.B. 29; *cf. Aberdeen Suburban Tramways Co.* v. *Aberdeen Magistrates*, 1927 S.C. 683). In such circumstances as these, reference will be made to subsequent legislation to resolve questions of the application, and possibly the interpretation, of an earlier Act.

In some cases a statute is interpreted by reference to delegated legislation made under it (*e.g. MacNeill* v. *Wilson*, 1981 J.C. 87; *Glasgow District Council* v. *Secretary of State for Scotland*, 1981 S.C. 188). This may be essential where delegated legislation may amend (*e.g.* International Conventions Act 1983, s. 8) or repeal (*e.g.* Transport Act 1985, s. 46) the enabling statute. In *Jackson* v. *Hall* [1980] A.C. 854, at pp. 889–890, Lord Fraser of Tullybelton suggested that this was only appropriate where the delegated legislation was subject to affirmative resolution (*cf. Hanlon* v. *Law Society* [1981] A.C. 124, at pp. 193–194 *per* Lord Lowry). See also *Pharmaceutical Society of Great Britain* v. *Storkwain Ltd.* [1986] 1 W.L.R. 903, 908–909 *per* Lord Goff of Chieveley; *British Amusement Catering Trades Association* v. *Westminster City Council* [1989] A.C. 147; *Drummond & Co., W.S.* v. *Scottish Legal Aid Board*, 1992 S.L.T. 337 (H.L.).

D. LEGISLATIVE PURPOSE

Faced with a legislative ambiguity, a court may try to establish the "mischief" which the legislation seeks to remedy. The process is also described as establishing the object or purpose of the legislation, or the intention of the legislator. This approach is adopted with primary (*e.g. Norris, Applicant* 1990 S.C.L.R. 628 (Sh.Ct.)) and secondary (*e.g. MacMillan* v. *Wimpey Offshore Engineers & Constructors*, 1991 S.L.T. 515) legislation. One important question is what material a court may appropriately consider to establish the purpose of U.K. legislation or the intention of the legislator.

1. LEGISLATION INCORPORATING TREATIES OR COMMUNITY LEGISLATION

Salomon v. Commissioners of Customs and Excise
[1967] 2 Q.B. 116

DIPLOCK L.J.: "Where, by a treaty, Her Majesty's Government undertakes either to introduce domestic legislation to achieve a specified result in the United Kingdom or to secure a specified result which can only be achieved by legislation, the treaty, since in . . . law it is not self-operating, remains irrelevant to any issue in the . . . courts until Her Majesty's Government has taken steps by way of legislation to fulfil its treaty obligations. Once the Government has legislated, which it may do in anticipation of the coming into effect of the treaty, as it did in this case, the court must in the first instance construe the legislation, for that is what the court has to apply. If the terms of the legislation are clear and unambiguous, they must be given effect to, whether or not they carry out Her Majesty's treaty obligations, for the sovereign power of the Queen in Parliament extends to breaking treaties . . . and any remedy for such a breach of an international obligation lies in a forum other than Her Majesty's own courts. But if the terms of the legislation are not clear but are reasonably capable of more than one meaning, the treaty itself becomes relevant, for there is a prima facie presumption that Parliament does not intend to act in breach of international law, including therein specific treaty obligations; and if one of the meanings which can reasonably be ascribed to the legislation is consonant with the treaty obligations and another or others are not, the meaning which is consonant is to be preferred. Thus, in case of lack of clarity in the words used in the legislation the terms of the treaty are relevant to enable the court to make its choice between the possible meaning of these words by applying this presumption.

It has been argued that the terms of an international convention cannot be consulted to resolve ambiguities or obscurities in a statute unless the statute itself contains either in the enacting part or the preamble an express reference to the international convention which it is the purpose of the statute to implement . . . I can see no reason in comity or common sense for imposing such a limitation upon the right and duty of the court to consult an international convention to resolve ambiguities and obscurities in a statutory enactment. If from extrinsic evidence it is plain that the enactment was intended to fulfil Her Majesty's Government's obligations under a particular convention, it matters not that there is no express reference to the convention in the statute. One must not presume that Parliament intends to break an international convention merely because it does not say expressly that it is intending to observe it. Of course the court must not merely guess that the statute was intended to give effect to a particular international convention. The extrinsic evidence of the connection must be cogent."

Diplock L.J. considered the interpretation of legislation which incorporated the provisions of a treaty, with or without express reference to it. Sometimes legislation incorporating treaty provisions may specifically require courts to refer to the Treaty (*e.g. James Buchanan & Co. Ltd.* v. *Babco Forwarding and Shipping (U.K.) Ltd.* [1978] A.C. 141; *Fothergill* v. *Monarch Airlines* [1981] A.C. 251).

In Scotland, it has been held that where a treaty has not been incorporated into domestic law, it may not be used as an aid to statutory interpretation (*e.g. Surjit Kaur* v. *Lord Advocate* [1980] 3 C.M.L.R. 79; *Moore* v. *Secretary of State for Scotland*, 1985 S.L.T. 38; *cf. Lord Advocate* v. *West End Construction*, 1990 S.C.L.R. 777 (Sh.Ct.); A.C. Evans, "Treaties and U.K. Legislation: the Scottish Dimension," 1984 J.R. 41). However, in England such treaties have been used in interpretation (*e.g. Waddington* v. *Miah* [1974] 2 All E.R. 377; *R.* v. *Home Secretary, ex p. Bhajan Singh* [1976] Q.B. 198; *Ahmad* v. *I.L.E.A.* [1978] 1 Q.B. 36; *Fothergill* v. *Monarch Airlines*, above; *cf. Malone* v. *Commissioner of Police for the Metropolis* [1979] Ch. 344), as have treaties to which the United Kingdom is not a party (*e.g. The Philippine Admiral* [1977] A.C. 373).

Where the provision of a treaty falls to be considered as an aid to statutory interpretation, it may itself be ambiguous and require interpretation. The court may then consider authoritative texts of the treaty in other languages (*e.g. Fothergill* v. *Monarch Airlines*, above), and they will certainly seek to interpret its provisions on broad principles of interpretation which are common to other states which are parties to the treaty rather than on narrower rules of statutory interpretation adopted in the United Kingdom (*e.g. Stag Line Ltd.* v. *Foscolo Mango & Co. Ltd.* [1932] A.C. 328; *James Buchanan & Co. Ltd.* v. *Babco Forwarding & Shipping (U.K.) Ltd.*, above; *Fothergill* v. *Monarch Airlines*, above; *ex p. Postlethwaite* [1988] A.C. 924). This may include resort to *travaux préparatoires*, including for example the records of a conference in which the treaty was drafted (*e.g. Gatoil International Inc.* v. *Arkwright-Boston Manufacturers Mutual Insurance Co.*, 1985 S.L.T. 68), the decisions of courts in other states on the interpretation of the treaty and academic commentaries on the treaty.

2. NON-GOVERNMENTAL MATERIAL

Exceptionally, legislation may empower the courts to consider certain non-governmental material as an aid to interpretation (*e.g.* Civil Jurisdiction and Judgments Act 1982, s. 3(3)). Otherwise, public reports on the subject of the legislation, by bodies which have a degree of independence from the Government may be examined to establish the purpose of the legislation and in some cases as aid to construction; see, for example, G. Maher, "Statutory Interpretation and Scottish Law Commission Reports," 1992 S.L.T. 277. The dangers of using such material, as perceived by the judiciary, were emphasised in *Assam Railways & Trading Co.* v. *I.R.C.* [1935] A.C. 445 and restated in *Davis* v. *Johnson*. It is conceivable that there may be some judicial reassessment following *Pepper (Inspector of Taxes)* v. *Hart* (see below).

Davis v. Johnson
[1979] A.C. 264

LORD DIPLOCK: "Where legislation follows on a published report of [the law commissions and committees or commissions appointed by government or by either House of Parliament to consider reforming particular branches of the law] the report may be used as an aid to identify the mischief which the legislation is intended to remedy, but not for the purpose of construing the enacting words in such a way as to conform with recommendations made in the report as to the form the remedy should take . . . This does not mean, of course, that one must shut one's eyes to the recommendations, for a suggestion as to a remedy may throw light on what the mischief itself is thought to be; but it does not follow that Parliament when it legislates to remedy the mischief has adopted in their entirety or, indeed, at all the remedies recommended in the report. This is well illustrated in the instant case. The report on which the Domestic Violence and Matrimonial Proceedings Act 1976 was undoubtedly based is the Report from the Select Committee of the House of Commons on Violence in Marriage published in July 1975. It deals almost exclusively with the plight of married women exposed to violence by their husbands and the resulting homelessness for themselves and their children. In the single paragraph referring to unmarried couples described (regrettably I think) as 'co-habitees' the members of the committee disclaim any particular knowledge of the problem, on which they had not taken evidence. Nevertheless they recommended that so far as the grant of injunctions against violence by their paramours was concerned mistresses should have the same procedural rights as married women. As regards homelessness of mistresses, however, all the committee recommended was that the Guardianship of Minors Acts should be amended to provide that, where there was a child of the illicit union of which paternity could be proved, the court should have power to make orders giving the mistress while she was caring for the children during their minority sole right of occupation of the premises which had been occupied by the unmarried couple as their home. Whatever s. 1(2) of the 1976 Act may do it does not do that."

[See also *Black-Clawson International Ltd.* v. *Papierwerke Waldhof-Aschaffenburg A.G.* [1975] A.C. 591; *Keith* v. *Texaco Ltd.*, 1977 S.L.T. (Lands Tr.) 16.]

3. GOVERNMENTAL MATERIAL

The general rule, as reflected in *Inglis* v. *British Airports Authority* below, is that courts will not consider material issued by the Government as an aid to construction, or to establish the purpose of legislation. The danger in using such material is that it may not reflect what is enacted and that it might come to be drafted with a view to influencing the interpretation of the legislation.

Inglis v. British Airports Authority
1978 S.L.T. (Lands Tr.) 30

W.A. ELLIOTT, Q.C.; WM. HALL, F.R.I.C.S.: "The respondents referred in their pleadings to para. 5 of the Scottish Development Department memorandum no. 85/1973 and at the hearing urged that the tribunal should be guided in construing the 1973 Act by this memorandum, a copy of which was lodged in process. It was explained by their solicitor that the respondent authority had relied on para. 5 in other cases as indicating that a person like the claimant should register his or her claim before selling; and that a notice of claim should be served before the actual sale of the interest in question. As the respondents' solicitor appeared surprised by our refusal to use this memorandum to guide our construction of the Act it is necessary to state why we decline to do so.

The memorandum is purely an administrative circular designed to give guidance to public authorities on the scope of the new enactment. It cannot provide a gloss on the actual words used by Parliament nor can it be used by a judicial tribunal as an aid to construing the wording of a statute or as a guide to the intentions of Parliament. To use a departmental memorandum in this way would indeed tend to undermine the rule of law as enacted by Parliament; and we cannot conceive that its use in judicial proceedings was ever contemplated by the department itself when it issued this circular for the help of public authorities."

There have been exceptions to the general rule. Government material, such as a White Paper, issued before enactment has been judicially considered to establish the legislative purpose (*Attorney-General's Reference (No. 1 of 1988)* [1989] A.C. 971. Government material issued after enactment, forms issued in respect of the administration of the Fugitive Offenders Act 1967, has been judicially considered (*Government of Canada* v. *Aronson* [1990] 1 A.C. 579; *cf. Jackson* v. *Hall* [1980] A.C. 854, 884 (Viscount Dilhorne)). A further exception to the general rule is technical matter to which the legislation makes express reference (*e.g. Lord Advocate* v. *Reliant Tool Co.* [1968] 1 W.L.R. 205; *cf. MacCormick* v. *Lord Advocate*, 1953 S.C. 396, 410–411 (*per* Lord President Cooper).

5. PARLIAMENTARY MATERIALS

Prior to the judgment of the House of Lords in the English appeal of *Pepper* v. *Hart*, in both England and Scotland there had been a general rule that reference to parliamentary material was not admitted either as an aid to statutory construction, or to establish the legislative purpose. The rule was sometimes ignored (*e.g. Re Aeronautics in Canada* [1932] A.C. 952, 971) but the danger of doing so was illustrated in *Hadmore Productions Ltd.* v. *Hamilton* [1983] A.C. 191. Sometimes it was avoided by judicial reference to articles and textbooks which contained quotations from parliamentary debates (*e.g. R.* v. *Local Commissioner for Administration for the North and East Area of England, ex p. Bradford Metropolitan City Council* [1979] Q.B. 287, 311 (Lord Denning)). However, *Pepper* v. *Hart* significantly relaxed the exclusionary rule, albeit cautiously. This caution appeared to be emphasised by the terms of the reported additions made on February 1st 1993 to the Practice Directions applicable to appeals to the House of Lords which read "supporting documents, *including extracts from Hansard*, will only be accepted in exceptional circumstances" ([1993] 1 W.L.R. 303; 1 All E.R. 573. However, both reports are incorrect in including the italicised words which were not included in the Practice Directions issued by the Judicial Office of the House of Lords.).

Pepper (Inspector of Taxes) v. Hart
[1992] 3 W.L.R. 1032

LORD BROWNE-WILKINSON: " . . . Under present law, there is a general rule that reference to Parliamentary material as an aid to statutory construction is not permissible ('the exclusionary rule'): *Davis* v. *Johnson* [1979] A.C. 264 and *Hadmor Productions Ltd.* v. *Hamilton* [1983] 1 A.C. 191. This rule did not always apply but was judge made. Thus, in *Ash* v. *Abdy* (1678) 3 Swans. 664 Lord Nottingham took judicial notice of his own experience when introducing the Bill in the House of Lords. The exclusionary rule was probably first stated by Willes J. in *Millar* v. *Taylor* (1769) 4 Burr. 2303, 2332. However, the case of *In re Mew and Thorne* (1862) 31 L.J.Bank. 87 shows that even in the middle of the last century the rule was not absolute: in that case Lord Westbury L.C. in construing an Act had regard to its Parliamentary history and drew an inference as to Parliament's intention in passing the legislation from the making of an amendment striking out certain words.

The exclusionary rule was later extended so as to prohibit the court from looking even at reports made by commissioners on which legislation was based: *Salkeld* v. *Johnson* (1848) 2 Exch. 256, 273. This rule has now been relaxed so as to permit reports of commissioners, including law commissioners, and white papers to be looked at for the purpose solely of ascertaining the mischief which the statute is intended to cure but not for the purpose of discovering the meaning of the words used by Parliament to effect such cure: *Eastman Photographic Materials Co. Ltd.* v. *Comptroller-General of Patents, Designs and Trademarks* [1898] A.C. 571 and *Assam Railways and Trading Co. Ltd.* v. *Commissioners of Inland Revenue* [1935] A.C. 445, 457–458. Indeed, in *Reg.* v. *Secretary of State for Transport, Ex parte Factortame Ltd.* [1990] 2 A.C. 85 your Lordships' House went further than this and had regard to a Law Commission report not only for the purpose of ascertaining the mischief but also for the purpose of drawing an inference as to Parliamentary intention from the fact that Parliament had not expressly implemented one of the Law Commission's recommendations.

Although the courts' attitude to reports leading to legislation has varied, until recently there was no modern case in which the court had looked at parliamentary debates as an aid to construction. However, in *Pickstone* v. *Freemans Plc.* [1989] A.C. 66 this House, in construing a statutory instrument, did have regard to what was said by the Minister who initiated the debate on the regulations. My noble and learned friend, Lord Keith of Kinkel, at p. 112B, after pointing out that the draft Regulations were not capable of being amended when presented to Parliament, said that it was 'entirely legitimate for the purpose of ascertaining the intention of Parliament to take into account the terms in which the draft was presented by the responsible minister and which formed the basis of its acceptance.' My noble and learned friend, Lord Templeman, at pp. 121–122, also referred to the minister's speech, although possibly only by way of support for a conclusion he had reached on other grounds. My noble and learned friends, Lord Brandon of Oakbrook and Lord Jauncey of Tullichettle, agreed with both those speeches. This case therefore represents a major inroad on the exclusionary rule: see also *Owens Bank Ltd.* v. *Bracco* [1992] 2 A.C. 443.

Mr. Lester, for the taxpayers, did not urge us to abandon the exclusionary rule completely. His submission was that where the words of a statute were ambiguous or obscure or were capable of giving rise to an absurd conclusion it should be legitimate to look at the Parliamentary history, including the debates in Parliament, for the purpose of identifying the intention of Parliament in using the words it did use. He accepted that the function of the court was to construe the actual words enacted by Parliament so that in no circumstances could the court attach to words a meaning that they were incapable of bearing. He further accepted that the court should only attach importance to clear statements showing the intention of the promoter of the Bill, whether a minister or private member: there could be no dredging through conflicting statements of intention with a view to discovering the true intention of Parliament in using the statutory words . . .

. . . [T]he reasons put forward for the present rule are first, that it preserves the constitutional proprieties leaving Parliament to legislate in words and the courts (not Parliamentary speakers), to construe the meaning of the words finally enacted; second, the practical difficulty of the expense of researching Parliamentary material which would arise if the material could be looked at; third, the need for the citizen to have access to a known defined text which regulates his legal rights, fourth, the improbability of finding helpful guidance from Hansard . . .

. . . I therefore reach the conclusion, subject to any question of Parliamentary privilege, that the exclusionary rule should be relaxed so as to permit reference to Parliamentary materials where (a) legislation is ambiguous or obscure, or leads to an absurdity; (b) the material relied upon consists of one or more statements by a minister or other promoter of the Bill together if necessary with such other Parliamentary material as is necessary to understand such statements and their effect; (c) the statements relied upon are clear.

Further than this, I would not at present go."

In *Pepper* v. *Hart* the use of parliamentary materials as an aid to statutory construction and to determine legislative intention was referred to an enlarged Appellate Committee of seven Lords of Appeal in Ordinary. Only Lord Mackay of Clashfern L.C. dissented from the Opinion of Lord Browne-Wilkinson and the dissent was primarily based on the increased costs of litigation which might flow from relaxing the previous exclusionary rule; *cf.* Lord Mackay of Clashfern, "Finishers, Refiners and Polishers: The Judicial Role in the Interpretation of Statutes [1989] Stat. L.R. 151 and the views expressed by various Law Lords in a parliamentary debate on the subject: 503 H.L. Deb., col. 278 January 18th 1989. Their Lordships were unanimous in holding that the relaxation of the exclusionary rule did not amount to questioning or impeaching proceedings in Parliament contrary to Article 9 of the Bill of Rights 1688 and no other parliamentary privilege was identified in the pleadings which would be breached by the relaxation of the rule. A statement in Parliament is "clear" and may be taken as an expression of parliamentary intention, for the purposes of *Pepper* v. *Hart*, if there is no subsequent inconsistent amendment to the Bill and the statement is not withdrawn or varied in Parliament (Lord Browne-Wilkinson at 1058 and 1063). There are, though, other aspects of the scope of the rule in *Pepper* v. *Hart* which may require refinement. So, for example, it is not entirely certain what is encompassed by "parliamentary materials," particularly to establish the context of a parliamentary statement; in *Pepper* v. *Hart*, Lord Browne-Wilkinson quoted from a press release in establishing the context of a Ministerial statement in Parliament. Certainly in the U.S.A. and in some Commonwealth jurisdictions, for example in Australia and New Zealand, the range of material admitted as an aid to construction is wider (*e.g. Marac Life*

Assurance Ltd. v. *Commissioner of Inland Revenue* [1986] 1 N.Z.L.R. 694). Again, although the rule in *Pepper* v. *Hart* admits parliamentary material to construe a statutory provision, Lord Roskill in *R.* v. *Warwickshire County Council, ex p. Johnson* [1993] 2 W.L.R. 1 appears to have considered such material to *confirm* a statutory construction. See further, T.St.J.N. Bates, "Parliamentary Material and Statutory Construction: Aspects of the Practical Application of Pepper v. Hart" [1993] Stat. L.R. 45; N. Walker, "Discovering the Intention of Parliament," 1993 S.L.T. (News) 121; T. St.J. N. Bates, "Judicial Application of *Pepper* v. *Hart*" (1993) 38 J.L.S. 251.

Finally, *Pepper* v. *Hart* again demonstrates that, in practice, the line between admitting material to establish the legislative purpose and as an aid to statutory construction is a fine one.

CHAPTER 14

CASE LAW AND THE DOCTRINE OF PRECEDENT

I. THE NATURE OF PRECEDENT

Twining and Miers, *How to do things with rules,* pp. 162–163
"In law, resort to precedent, that is to say the use of prior decisions to assist in the resolution of present disputes, has in general reached a considerable degree of refinement . . . [But] 'Precedent' and related notions are not unique to law. People who serve on committees, in administrative agencies and other decision-making bodies may often be faced with a problem which demands a solution but which, for instance, involves issues of conflicting values or competing interests in a borderline case. In such circumstances, in the process of reaching a decision, they may express their reluctance to resolve the conflict in one particular way in the phrase, 'Let's not create a precedent'. This phrase contains certain assumptions, about problem-solving both for the present and the future. Thus, it is implicit that future decision-makers have some kind of obligation to come to the same conclusion should a similar case arise; that others who observe or rely upon the decisions of the particular body may expect that similar cases in the future will be similarly decided and thus may base their conduct upon such expectations; that the decision-making process is not constituted simply by the *ad hoc* resolution of particular cases, but involves the rational development of general policies of principles through these cases; and that the individual decisions themselves have status as expressions of policy or principle. Such factors provide a basis for demands that precedents be treated as having force or weight, and should not be ignored upon a whim but departed from only on the basis of rational argument and distinction. These four notions, of obligation, expectation of future behaviour, interstitial growth of policy and principle, and the authority of decisions form the basis of the common law's treatment of precedent.

Systems of law may be unique in their development of rules which relate to the operation of precedents. Whatever those rules may prescribe, they are cumulatively and generally known by the expression, 'a doctrine of precedent'. In a sense, nearly all legal systems have a doctrine of precedent, though its requirements may vary from system to system. Even a legal system which explicitly prohibits the citation of prior cases in court can be said to have a doctrine of precedent in that it has a rule which regulates the use of precedent."

A. THE ORIGINS OF PRECEDENT

1. THE RATIONALE OF PRECEDENT

A number of justifications and explanations for the emergence of legal doctrines of precedent have been put forward.

Llewellyn, "Case Law", p. 249
"Toward its operative drive all those phases of human make-up which build habit in the individual and institutions in the group: laziness as to the reworking of a problem once solved, the time and energy saved by routine, especially under any pressure of business; the values of routine as a curb on arbitrariness and as a prop of weakness, inexperience and instability; the social venues of predictability; the power of whatever exists to produce expectations and the power of expectations to become normative. The force of precedent in the law is heightened by an additional factor: that curious, almost universal, sense of justice which urges that all men are properly to be treated alike in like circumstances. As the social system varies we meet infinite variations as to what men or treatments or circumstances are to be classed as 'like'; but the pressure to accept the views of the time and place remains."

In addition, precedent is said to provide or promote
(1) *Certainty* and *predictability* in the law, enabling citizens to conduct themselves and to arrange their affairs in the light of decided cases in the knowledge that future judges will normally uphold these decisions. In turn, certainty and predictability mini-mise unnecessary litigation and expense for citizens.
(2) *Guidance* to judges lower down in the legal hierarchy, legal officials and lawyers.
(3) *Uniformity* and *consistency* of judicial decisions, reducing judicial error, bias or idiosyncrasy and thus promoting public respect for the judiciary and the administration of justice.
(4) *Accountability*.

Lord Devlin, "The Judge and Case Law," p. 181
"[C]ase law, being made out of reasons which judges give in their judgments, necessarily contains the judiciary's account to the nation of the way in which they are using their vast powers. It makes possible criticism, amendment, or curtailment. It is more than an account; it is also, because of the doctrine of precedent, a broad description of the way in which, unless Parliament intervenes, the judges intend to continue using their powers. Respect for precedent is exacted, not only to keep the law in good shape, but primarily as a safeguard against arbitrary and autocratic decision-making."

2. The Emergence of Precedent in Scotland
The modern "strict" doctrine of precedent or *stare decisis* whereby a single decision in point can be binding on subsequent judges did not become established in Scotland or England before the nine-teenth century. In the preceding 200 years precedents in both countries were cited merely as evidence of what the common law

was or to prove the existence of an established policy or practice. Such precedents were not decisive of the point in question but more or less persuasive, depending in part on the rank and reputation of the judge(s) who decided them. The strict doctrine only took root once an established hierarchy of courts and appeals and an efficient system of law reporting came into existence. [For a useful historical account of the evolution of *stare decisis* in Scotland see G. Maher and T.B. Smith, "Judicial Precedent" in Vol. 22 of the *Stair Memorial Encyclopaedia: The Laws of Scotland*, pp. 92–98.]

Erskine, *An Institute of the Law of Scotland*, I, 1, 47
"Judgments ought not to be pronounced by examples or precedents. Decisions, therefore, though they bind the parties litigating create no obligation on the judges to follow in the same tract, if it shall appear to them contrary to law. It is, however, certain that they are frequently the occasion of establishing usages, which, after they have gathered force by a sufficient length of time, must, from the tacit assent of the state, make part of our unwritten law. What has been said of decisions of the Court of Session is also applicable to the judgments pronounced upon appeal by the House of Lords; for in these that august court acts as the character of judges, not of law givers; and consequently their judgments, though they are final as to the parties in the appeal cannot introduce any general rule which shall be binding either on themselves or inferior courts. Nevertheless, where a similar judgment is repeated in this court of the last resort, it ought to have the strongest influence on the determinations of inferior courts."

Smith, *The Doctrines of Judicial Precedent in Scots Law*, pp. 10–12
"It may be suggested that several causes concurred in developing doctrines of strict precedent in the Scottish judicial process. . . .
   The Court of Session was divided in 1808, and this, according to Lord Wark, was in part responsible for the growth of a strict doctrine of precedent, since it gave to the Senators of the College of Justice more time to formulate their opinions . . .
   It may be observed that soon after the court divided law reporting in Scotland was greatly improved and developed. One consequence of this was that it became no longer possible for the judges to disregard unwelcome decisions over which an official censorship was something exercised by excluding them from the reports. Thus Robertson, in the preface to his first volume of Scottish Appeals, notes that there had been occasions when the judgments of the Court of Session had been reversed in Parliament, yet the original decisions still remain as precedents in Scottish reports and works of authority. Nor were the judges of the Court of Session always anxious that a verbatim account of their opinions

should be noted by the reporter . . . When Mr Bell announced that he intended to report the opinions of the judges without any official appointment, his proposal was met with threats and obstruction, and it was some time before the publishing of full opinions was viewed favourably by the Bench. It is probable, therefore, that fuller and more accurate reporting from about 1825 gave an added incentive to the judges to prepare careful opinions which would bear close scrutiny. Associated with actual reporting, was the work devoted in the early years of the nineteenth century to compiling useful indexes to the decisions, so that they might be traced when required."

[Smith originally considered that the House of Lords (dominated as it was in the nineteenth century by English judges) was the single most important cause of a strict doctrine of precedent emerging in Scotland. However, he modified his position subsequently in his essay (co-authored with G. Maher) on Precedent in the *Stair Memorial Encyclopaedia of the Laws of Scotland*.]

Smith & Maher, "*Precedent in the Nineteenth Century*," para. 255
"255. The influence of the House of Lords in the nineteenth century. Various commentators have attributed much of the blame for the imposition of an alien doctrine of *stare decisis* into Scots law to the influence of the House of Lords as an appellate court. But it is necessary to make clear the ways in which the House of Lords could have, and did, influence Scottish courts on judicial precedent. Certainly after a period of hostility on the part of the Court of Session, decisions of the House came to be treated as binding precedents on the Court of Session, but this development can largely be explained by the idea of the role of appellate jurisdiction. Although it is arguable that decisions of the House of Lords in Scottish appeals imported into Scots law many doctrines of substantive law which were purely English in origin and inconsistent with Scottish legal principle, it is not so readily apparent how the House could have imposed the English approach to *stare decisis* on doctrines of precedent in the Court of Session. In any case, precedent in the nineteenth-century English legal system, although narrower than the Scottish conception of judicial practice, was itself in the process of developing towards *stare decisis*. This process was not finalised in the House of Lords until almost the beginning of the present century in the *London Tramways* case."

Some commentators have argued that historically Scots law has been deductive, rights oriented and based on principle whereas English law is said to have been primarily inductive, remedy oriented and based on precedent. Whatever may have been the truth in previous centuries scholars are now agreed that in modern times principles play a significant part in English law and that in Scotland a strict doctrine of precedent has evolved.

[See Lord Cooper, "The Common and the Civil Law," pp. 470–471; I.D. Willock, in J.P. Grant (ed.) *Independence and Devolution* (1976); *Pioneer Shipping Ltd.* v. *B.T.P. Tioxide Ltd.* [1982] A.C. 724 at p. 751 and *Lambert* v. *Lewis* [1982] A.C. 225 at p. 274. For a recent striking case in which three English Law Lords decided an appeal in the Lords on grounds of basic principle and the two Scots Law Lords dissented on pragmatic grounds, see *Woolwich Building Society* v. *IRC (No. 2)* [1992] 3 All E.R. 737.]

B. WHEN MUST A PRECEDENT BE APPLIED?

The doctrines of binding precedent in Scotland and England do not require every court to follow the earlier decisions of itself and other courts. The doctrines only require a court to follow a previous decision which is (a) "in point" and (b) binding. Even then, only part of the earlier decision need be followed. A case is in point if it decided the same issue of law as arises in the instant case and no material, *i.e.* legally relevant distinction exists between the facts of the two cases. This is always a question of interpretation and as we shall see the technique of distinguishing precedents on the grounds that they are not in point is one that is assiduously practised by judges who wish to retain their freedom for manoeuvre.

Precedents may be either binding or persuasive. While a case is either binding or it is not, there are varying degrees of persuasiveness. Sometimes, even though the judge in the instant case is not technically bound to follow an earlier decision it may be so strongly persuasive that he would find it difficult to justify not following the precedent. In other situations precedents even though in point may have little persuasive value. What determines whether a precedent is binding or merely persuasive (and if the latter, to what degree) is the level of the court which decided the case in the hierarchy of courts, the legal system from which the case emanated and the prestige of the judges who decided the case. The first of these, the place of the court in the hierarchy of courts, is the most significant factor.

THE HIERARCHY OF COURTS

The civil and criminal courts of Scotland (and England) each form separate hierarchies, which largely, though not entirely, coincide with their respective appeals structure.

Walker, *The Scottish Legal System,* pp. 370–371
"The general principle is that any court is bound by prior decisions in point pronounced by courts superior to it in its own vertical line of

authority, and that prior decisions in point of courts of equal or higher rank in other vertical lines of authority are persuasive in varying degree. Decisions of courts of lower rank in any vertical line of authority may be ignored but may sometimes be of persuasive value."

In the light of the 1966 Practice Statement on Precedent in the House of Lords (see p. 394 below) it is clear that the House when sitting as the final court of appeal in Scottish civil cases is not bound by earlier decisions of the House. Its decisions in Scottish appeals are binding on all civil courts in Scotland.

Dalgleish v. Glasgow Corporation
1976 S.C. 32

LORD JUSTICE-CLERK (Wheatley): "The question whether a decision of the House of Lords in an English case is binding on the courts in Scotland is not free from difficulty. In the seven Judge case of *Virtue* v. *Commissioners of Police of Alloa* (1874) 1 R. 285 the Judges were divided on the point as it arose in that case. Lord President Inglis, Lord Justice-Clerk Moncrieff, Lord Benholme and Lord Jerviswood thought that the English authority was binding, Lord Cowan, Lord Deas and Lord Neaves in varying degrees thought that it was not. Doubts were expressed by the minority Judges as to whether the legal point in issue in that case was the same as the legal point in the English case. Lord President Inglis said at p. 296: 'I think it is an error in constitutional law to represent the House of Lords as sitting at one time as a Scottish Court and at another time as an English Court. That House, I apprehend, sits always in one character, as the House of Lords of the United Kingdom, and as such the Imperial Court of Appeal for the whole three parts of the United Kingdom. It has occasion to administer at one time the law of Scotland, at another the law of England, and at another the law of Ireland. But in appeals coming from all three countries it has to deal with principles of law that are common to the whole three.' He went on to state that it was with such principles—the rules applicable to the construction of statutes of the Imperial legislature—that the House was dealing in the previous conflicting decisions of the House in appeals from the courts in Scotland and England. Lord Justice-Clerk Moncrieff said at p. 304 that he thought that the Scottish Courts were entitled to take as a precedent a House of Lords decision in an English case where on a question of general jurisprudence or of mercantile law the two systems concur. Lord Cowan on the other hand said at page 299: 'I cannot hold the judgment, even of the House of Lords—sitting as a Supreme Court of Appeal, and determining a purely English case under an English local statute—as a binding precedent on the courts of this country.'

In *Orr Ewing's Trustees* v. *Orr Ewing* (1886) 13 R. (H.L.) 1 Lord Chancellor Selborne said at p. 3: 'A decision of this House, in an English case, ought to be held conclusive in Scotland, as well as England, as to questions of English law and English jurisdiction which it determined. It cannot of course, conclude any question of Scottish law. So far as it may proceed upon principle of general jurisprudence, it ought to have weight in Scotland; as a similar judgment of this House on a Scottish appeal ought to have weight in England. If, however, it can be shown that by any positive law of Scotland, or according to authorities having the force of law in that country, a different view of the proper interpretation, extent or application of these principles prevails there, the opinions on those subjects, expressed by noble and learned Lords when giving judgment on an English appeal ought not to be held conclusive in Scotland.'

In *Glasgow Corporation* v. *Central Land Board*, 1956 S.C. (H.L.) 1 Lord Normand stated at pp. 16 and 17 that a decision in the House of Lords in an English case wherein no question of Scots law fell to be decided is not binding on the Scottish courts nor in the House of Lords sitting as a court of ultimate appeal in a Scottish case.

The difficulty is not just one of deciding which of the conflicting views our courts should adopt. It is one of finding an all-embracing and definitive formula to regulate the case where a decision of the House of Lords in an English case should be regarded as a binding precedent in our courts. Manifestly, in my view, a decision on a U.K. statute which has equal or similar applicability in both countries, is one such case. (I note in parenthesis that this does not apply to appeals in criminal cases in Scotland, where the ultimate court of Appeal is the High Court of Justiciary or the Court of Criminal Appeal, and decisions of the House of Lords in criminal cases in England are not binding on these Scottish courts even in relation to the interpretation of U.K. statutes applicable equally to both countries.) How far beyond that can the principle extend? Here I find myself inclined to resort to what might be regarded as an age-old cliché, but what is the practical answer to so many questions, namely, that each case must be determined on its own circumstances. I feel, however, that something more positive is required. Since we have in Scotland our own system of Law, then in my opinion no legal issue in Scots law should be held to be governed by a House of Lords decision in an English appeal, unless the point in issue is based on legislation which has equal applicability and force in both countries, or has been decided by an authoritative and binding court to be exactly the same and have the same legal significance in both countries."

In spite of Lord Wheatley's valiant attempt to clarify the position it is still unclear whether a House of Lords decision in an English appeal on a point of common law which is alleged to be general to both countries (sometimes called "a point of general jurisprudence") is binding on Scottish courts or only strongly persuasive. In practical terms it may not make much difference except in a few cases and in these the answer may well depend on whether it is English Law Lords or Scottish Senators of the College of Justice who are considering the point.

Normally, Divisions of the Inner House are regarded as bound by previous decisions of a Division. They are undoubtedly bound by decisions of seven or more judges of the Court of Session. Lords Ordinary are bound by decisions of seven or more judges or of the Divisions. One Lord Ordinary, however, does not bind another nor, probably, are his decisions binding in the sheriff court—though they may be persuasive. The decisions of a sheriff principal will normally be followed by sheriffs in his sheriffdom but it is not clear that this is an example of *stare decisis*. [Compare *Thomson's Trs.* v. *Harrison* (1958) 74 Sh. Ct. Rep. 77 and *MacKays* v. *James Deas & Son Ltd.*, 1977 S.L.T. (Sh. Ct.) 10.]

Smith, *The Doctrines of Judicial Precedent in Scots Law*, p. 105
"With regard to the criminal courts, the decisions of single judges are not binding on each other, but the practice has grown for a quorum of the High Court of Justiciary to follow the previous decisions of a like quorum unless a fuller court be convened to overrule the earlier case. And, of course, a single judge follows the law laid down by a bench of judges. There is no known precedent or reason which would restrict a full Court of Justiciary from reversing a precedent which it considered bad. The universal jurisdiction of the High Court of Justicary implies that it is to concern itself with all that pertains to the furtherance of justice in criminal matters. Certainty and finality can be no real substitutes for justice. However, in the interests of consistency, precedent normally is followed, subject to the safeguards of review of the doctrine by a larger court."

Until 1988 it was universally assumed that decisions of a single judge in the High Court of Justiciary did not bind a sheriff (there being no line of appeal between them). However, in a startling decision by the Lord Justice-General (Emslie) with the concurrence of Lords Grieve and Kincraig it was held in *Jessop* v. *Stevenson*, 1988 S.L.T. 223 that a "decision of a judge of the High Court of Justiciary is a decision of the High Court of Justiciary and unless it has been recalled on appeal, it is binding on all judges in the lower courts." This decision appears to be based on the principle that the High Court of Justiciary (like the Court of Session) is a collegiate court and single judges of the court exercise a delegated function on behalf of the whole court. While the historical logic of this argument seems beyond reproach it is very far from clear that it represented an accurate statement of the practice of the judiciary until that date. Yet precedent is not a set of legal rules. It is a set of normative practices, *i.e.* an amalgam of what the judges do and what they ought to do. As such, it is difficult to know what to make of the *Jessop* decision. It is clearly a statement of belief by eminent members of the High Court of Justiciary as to what they consider the normative practice of sheriffs and district justices ought to be. However, unlike the House of Lords Practice Statement in 1966 (see below pp. 394–5) it does not purport to be a statement on behalf of the whole of the court. In the end the impact of *Jessop* will depend on how it is viewed by the lower court judiciary. If it is adhered to, then irrespective of its correctness as a statement of the normative practice when it was decided, it will have become a self-fulfilling prophecy.

Jessop is also puzzling in that it offers no guidance as to whether a decision of one member of the High Court now binds any subsequent member of the Court sitting on his or her own. On the assumption that it does not, then which decision should the lower courts follow? Moreover, the same logic which underpins *Jessop* would also apply to Lords Ordinary in the Outer House binding sheriffs and sheriffs principal on civil cases. Until *Jessop* this was not the normative practice in civil cases. Since 1988 this question has arisen on several occasions. In *Cromarty Leasing Ltd.* v. *Turnbull*, 1988 S.L.T. (Sh. Ct.) 62 and *Johnstone* v. *Hardie*, 1990 S.C.L.R. 387 Sheriff Wilkinson and Sheriff Principal Ireland respectively, concluded that *Jessop* had changed the normative practice for sheriffs in civil cases as well as criminal cases. However, in a persuasive judgment Sheriff Stoddart determined in *Farrell* v. *Farrell*, 1990 S.C.L.R. 717 that despite *Jessop* he was not bound by the decisions of the Outer House—particularly since the issue at stake involved divorce where sheriffs and Lords Ordinary share a wide concurrent jurisdiction. The question will have to await the verdict of history but, in reality, it may not make much difference in practice since even if the traditional position is restored sheriffs will continue to regard the decisions of the Outer House as being highly persuasive, if not absolutely binding. [See further on *Jessop*, T.B. Smith, "Precedent in the Sheriff Court," 1988 S.L.T. (News) 137 and G. Maher, "Precedent, the Sheriff Court and Colleges of Justice," 1988 S.L.T. (News) 209.]

It is still unsettled (at least in the minds of some commentators) whether Divisions of the Inner House are always bound by the previous decisions of a Division and whether the whole court is bound by its own decisions or those of a seven judge court. At first sight it may appear somewhat curious that there is any doubt about such matters. Part of the answer lies in the fact that precedent is a set of normative practices. In the case of whole court decisions the doubt arises because whole courts are never convened now and even when they were, they were not often asked to reconsider decisions of seven or more judges. The celebrated case where the issue did arise, *Yuill's Trs.* v. *Thomson* (1902) 4 F. 815 is inconclusive because the judges split (largely on Divisional lines) over the question. The case is clear evidence that the judges in the Court of Session in 1902 had no settled practice on the matter and were heavily divided amongst themselves about what their practice ought to be. The issue was unresolved then and it remains so today.

On this analysis it may be asked why there is any doubt whether a Division is always bound by previous Divisional decisions. Surely situations must arise not infrequently when one Division has to consider a previous decision of the Inner House? In fact, in the bulk of reported cases where this has occurred the judges have regarded themselves as bound. But there have been a number of dissenting voices, particularly in older cases. This would seem to suggest that at one time (possibly even until as late as the 1930s) there was no settled practice on the question and no consensus amongst the judges. Nevertheless the practice of the judges for the last 50 years seems to have crystallised. Divisions nowadays do regard themselves as bound by previous Divisional decisions and a larger court is convened if it is felt that the earlier decision ought to be reconsidered. [See *e.g. Grainger* v. *City of Edinburgh District Licensing Board*, 1989 S.L.T. 633.]

These issues raise the larger question of whether courts ought to be bound by decisions of their own or of co-ordinate courts. Judges at the lower levels have always been free in this respect, even at the risk of producing conflicting decisions. [Compare, for example, *Macrae* v. *Macrae*, 1977 S.L.T. (Notes) 72; *McKay* v. *McKay*, 1978 S.L.T. (Notes) 36; *Craig* v. *Craig*, 1978 S.L.T. (Notes) 61; *Henderson* v. *Henderson*, 1981 S.L.T. (Notes) 25; *Lambert* v. *Lambert*, 1982 S.L.T. 144.] The House of Lords having resolved in 1966 that it should no longer be absolutely bound by its own decisions, the only courts that remain so bound are those at the intermediate level. The Divisions can resolve the problems by convening a larger court. The Court of Appeal in England, however, since it is not collegiate in origin cannot increase its powers by convening a larger court (see *Davis* v. *Johnson* [1979] A.C. 264). Lord Denning's solution was to assert that the Court of Appeal is and ought to be free to depart from its own decisions like Courts of Appeal in Australia and New Zealand. However, he signally failed to convince his colleagues that the court should change its practice in this way.

[For a much fuller account of the hierarchical rules of *stare decisis* in both civil and criminal cases see G. Maher and T.B. Smith, "Judicial Precedent".]

C. RATIO DECIDENDI

Even where a precedent is in point and binding, judges and commentators are agreed that only part of it, the *ratio decidendi*, must be followed by the later court. Unfortunately, here the consensus ends. Agreement over the definition of *ratio decidendi* or how it is to be ascertained in actual cases, is conspicuous by its absence. Some restrict its meaning to the proposition of law to be found in the judge's opinion, which forms a necessary part of his reasoning in disposing of the case. On this view (let us call it R_1.) every case has at least one *ratio* and that *ratio* does not vary although later judges may interpret it in different ways. Others argue that the *ratio* of a case is the proposition of law for which the case will be held to be authority by later courts (we shall call this R_2). From this standpoint the *ratio* of a case may well change over time. A third group asserts (correctly in our view) that *ratio decidendi* is used in both senses R_1 and R_2.

MacCormick, *Legal Reasoning*, p. 215

"Professor Rupert Cross, the leading English authority on judicial precedent in English law has put forward the following as a 'tolerably accurate description of what lawyers mean by "*ratio decidendi*" ': 'The *ratio decidendi* of a case is in any rule of law expressly or impliedly treated by a judge as a necessary step in reaching his conclusion, having regard to the line of reasoning adopted by him.'

By taking full account of the justificatory function and the general structure of the type of legal reasoning involved in judicial opinions, we can perhaps improve on that.

The *ratio decidendi* is the ruling expressly or impliedly given by a judge which is sufficient to settle a point of law put in issue by the parties' arguments in a case, being a point on which a ruling was necessary to his justification (or one of his alternative justifications) of the decision in the case. (The caveat must be repeated here that, on this view, by no means all cases—even 'leading' cases—have a single *ratio decidendi*.)"

Cross, *Precedent in English law*, pp. 76–7

"[It has been] suggested that the expression *ratio decidendi* is used in two senses: (i) 'The rule of law for which a case is binding authority', and (ii) 'The rule of law to be found in the actual opinion of the judge, forming the basis of his decision'. If our description of the *ratio decidendi* is correct, there is generally no distinction between these two senses of the phrase until a decision has been interpreted in subsequent cases. Up to that moment the rule of law for which the decision is binding authority is that which is to be found in the actual opinion of the judge, forming the basis of his decision. Very often there will continue to be no distinction

between the two suggested senses of the phrase *ratio decidendi* even after
the decision has been interpreted in subsequent cases."

Llewellyn, *The Bramble Bush*, p. 52
"There is a distinction between *ratio decidendi*, the court's own version of
the rule of the case, and the true rule of the case, to wit what it will be
made to stand for by another later court."

Twining and Miers, *How to do things with rules*, p. 176
"When we interpret cases we ask such questions as 'for what rule(s) of
law is this case an authority?' or 'for what proposition(s) of law can this
be made to stand?' Some have answered these questions by maintaining
that it is possible to extract from any case, one proposition of law and
that this constitutes its *ratio decidendi*. Although there are competing
versions of this view, we may characterize it as the 'buried treasure'
argument. In this view it is typically assumed (*a*) that every case had one
pre-determined *ratio decidendi* (at least for each question of law) and (*b*)
that the *ratio decidendi* can be *found*, by reading the case, without
referring to other cases; and (*c*) that the *ratio decidendi* does not, indeed
cannot, change over time. These assumptions do not accord with the
realities of the practice of handling precedents in our system. Talk of
finding the *ratio decidendi* of a case obscures the fact that the process of
interpreting cases is not like a hunt for buried treasure, but typically
involves an element of choice from a range of possibilities. How
unfettered is the choice and how wide the range of possibilities will
depend on a variety of factors. One such factor, of crucial importance,
relates to (*b*). In reasoning on a point of law we are typically confronted
not with a single isolated precedent, but a collection of potentially
relevant precedents. Each case has to be read in the context of all the
other potentially relevant cases and this is one factor which limits the
range of possible interpretations which can be put on it. Any test for
determining the *ratio decidendi*, which suggests, explicitly or implicitly,
that a case can be interpreted in isolation, without reference to other
cases, is unrealistic and misleading. As the courts hand down new
decisions, so the range of plausible interpretations of an earlier case may
change over time."

Harari, *Negligence in the Law of Torts*, pp. 16–17
"The *ratio decidendi* of a case is the proposition of law the case supports
when it is co-ordinated with all other cases. Once it is conceded that the
law is not static, but develops and changes, it must also be conceded that
the *rationes decidendi* of the cases change. If this is not generally
recognised it is only because the notion of a changing law is still a
relatively new one.

The concept *ratio decidendi* emerged at a time when it was seriously thought that the judges merely 'discover' the law, when there seemed to be a valid distinction between 'the law as such' and 'our conception of the law'. With *ratio decidendi* as a vague concept meaning 'the principle of law applied by the decision', and with a refusal to recognise that the judges were constantly making law, a distinction between 'the *ratio decidendi* of the case' and 'our conception of its *ratio decidendi*' was inevitable. A case would be regarded as establishing a certain rule of law, which would be modified when additional cases further 'clarified' the law: the *ratio decidendi* of the old case obviously was not what it appeared to be—that has been conclusively shown by the new decisions. Since the judges were not regarded as making or changing law it was quite logical to regard as the true *ratio decidendi* of the old case the rule of law which the new case seemed to imply.

To-day, when we no longer believe in 'the law as such', and when it is recognised that the law is not static, there is no room for the old concept of *ratio decidendi*. When looking for the *ratio decidendi* of a case we are not trying to discover the pre-existing rule of law which was applied in the case. What we are trying to determine is the *rule of law the decision will support when all other existing law-making decisions have been taken into account*. As new law-making decisions are given and taken into account, a given decision may no longer support a given rule . . . "

In most cases R_1 is clear enough—though not always (see "Multiple *ratios*," p. 410 below). In most cases also, as Cross argues, where R_1 is clear, it will coincide with R_2. Yet there are many cases where R_2 will differ from R_1. This is because ascertaining the *ratio* of a case is an art and judicial artists have a measure of licence in pursuing their art.

Glanville Williams, *Learning the Law*, pp. 66–67
"What is really involved in finding the *ratio decidendi* of a case is a process of abstraction. Abstraction is the mental operation of picking out certain qualities and relations from the facts of experience. Imagine a baby in whose household there is a terrier called Caesar. The baby will be taught to call this dog 'bow-wow,' because 'bow-wow' is easier to say than 'Caesar'. If he sees another dog he will guess or be told that this other dog is to be called 'bow-wow' as well. This is an example of one of the baby's earliest feats of abstraction. Abstraction comes through the perception of similarities between individual facts, and all language and all thinking depend upon it.

The next point to be noticed is that this process of abstraction may be carried to progressively higher flights. The individual dog Caesar is, at a low level of abstraction, a terrier; at a higher level he is a dog; higher still, a mammal; and then an animal and a living thing. In the same way a man might say that he was born at the Piccaninny Nursery Home; in

London; in England; in Europe. All these are 'facts,' but they are facts belonging to different levels of abstraction.

We are now in a better position to state the *ratio decidendi* of a case. The ascertainment of the *ratio decidendi* of a case depends upon a process of abstraction from the totality of facts that occurred in it. The higher the abstraction, the wider the *ratio decidendi* . . . How do we know when to stop with our abstraction? The answer is: primarily by reading what the judge says in his judgment, but partly also by our knowledge of the law in general, and by our common sense and our feeling for what the law ought to be."

Llewellyn, *The Bramble Bush*, pp. 42–43

"Our job [is] to crack the kernel from the nut, to find the true rule the case in fact decides: the *rule of the case* . . . Perhaps . . . we may find guidance in the facts the court assumes. Surely this much is certain: the actual dispute before the court is limited as straitly by the facts as by the form which the procedural issue has assumed. What is not in the facts cannot be present for decision. Rules which proceed an inch beyond the facts must be suspect.

But how far does that help us out? What are *the* facts? The plaintiff's name is Atkinson and the defendant's Walpole. The defendant, despite his name, is an Italian by extraction, but the plaintiff's ancestors came over with the Pilgrims. The defendant has a schnautzer-dog named Walter, red hair, and $30,000 worth of life assurance. All these are facts. The case, however, does not deal with life insurance. It is about an auto accident. The defendant's auto was a Buick painted pale magenta. He is married. His wife was in the back seat, an irritable, somewhat faded blonde. She was attempting back-seat driving when the accident occurred. He had turned round to make objection. In the process the car swerved and hit the plaintiff. The sun was shining; there was a rather lovely dappled sky low to the West. The time was late October on a Tuesday. The road was smooth, concrete. it had been put in by the McCarthy Road Work Company. How many of these facts are important to the decision? How many of these facts are, as we say, legally relevant? Is it relevant that the road was in the country or the city; that it was concrete or tarmac or of dirt; that it was a private or a public way? Is it relevant that the defendant was driving a Buick, or a motor car, or a vehicle? Is it important that he looked around as the car swerved? Is it crucial? Would it have been the same if he had been drunk, or had swerved for fun, to see how close he could run by the plaintiff, but had missed the guess?

Is it not obvious that as soon as you pick up this statement of the facts to find its legal bearings you must discard some of no interest whatsoever, discard others as dramatic but as legal nothings? And is it not clear, further, that when you pick up the facts which are left and which do seem relevant, you suddenly cease to deal with them in the concrete and deal with them instead in *categories* which you, for one reason or another, deem significant? It is not the road between Pottsville and Arlington; it is 'a highway'. It is not a particular pale magenta Buick eight, by number 732507, but 'a motor car', and perhaps even 'a vehicle'. It is not a turning around to look at Adorée Walpole, but a lapse from the supposedly proper procedure of careful drivers, with which you are concerned. Each concrete fact of the case arranges itself, I say, as the *representative* of a much wider abstract *category* of facts, and it is not in itself but as a member of the category that you attribute significance to it. But what is to tell you whether to make your category 'Buicks' or 'motor cars' or 'vehicles'? What is to tell you to make your category 'road' or 'public highway'? The court may tell you. But the precise point that you have up for study is how far it is safe to trust what the court says. The precise issue which you are attempting to solve is whether the court's language can be taken as it stands, or must be amplified, or must be whittled down.

This brings us at last to the case system. For the truth of the matter is a truth so obvious and trite that it is somewhat regularly overlooked by students. *That no case can have a meaning by itself!* Standing alone it gives you no guidance. It can give you no guidance as to how far it carries, as to how much of its language will hold water later. What counts, what gives you leads, what gives you sureness, *that is the background of the other cases* in relation to which you must read the one. They color the language, the technical terms used in the opinion. But above all they give you the wherewithal to find which of the facts are significant, and in what aspect they are significant, and how far the rules laid down are to be trusted."

It follows that every case contains not only (at least, in theory) an R_1 (or possibly more than one) but also a range of potential R_2s of increasing and decreasing levels of generality. Usually the later courts select an R_2 which coincides with or closely approximates to R_1. Yet if later judges feel that the R_1 of a case was too broadly stated, *i.e.* framed at too high a level of generality or abstraction, they can restrict it by reference to the facts of the case. This has been called "restrictive distinguishing" (see p. 401 below). If, on the other hand, they wish to apply the case analogically to a rather different set of facts they will frame R_2 more broadly than R_1. Although the R_2 of a case can continue to contract or expand over time as it is considered in later cases, in general the R_2 of a case will tend to crystallise after it has been interpreted on a number of occasions by later courts.

OBITER DICTA

Any proposition of law contained in the original judgment which does not form part of the *ratio decidendi* is termed an *obiter dictum*. Since it is defined by exclusion the concept of *obiter* is as hard to pin down as *ratio*. It is clear, however, the *obiter dicta* may be persuasive to a greater or lesser degree. In some situations, *e.g.* where there is a considered *dictum* of the House of Lords, the proposition may be so highly persuasive as to be binding in all but name. (*Hedley Byrne & Co.* v. *Heller* [1964] A.C. 465 is one such case.) On other occasions *dicta* may be little more than off-the-cuff speculations. Since the R_2 of a case may vary it follows that occasionally a proposition in the case which was initially considered to be *obiter* may subsequently become part of the *ratio* and vice versa.

Glanville Williams, *Learning the Law*, p. 72

"In contrast with the *ratio decidendi* is the *obiter dictum*. The latter is a mere saying by the way, a chance remark, which is not binding upon future courts, though it may be respected according to the reputation of the judge, the eminence of the court, and the circumstances in which it came to be pronounced. An example would be a rule of law stated merely by way of analogy or illustration, or a suggested rule upon which the decision is not finally rested. The reason for not regarding an *obiter dictum* as binding is that it was probably made without a full consideration of the cases on the point, and that, if very broad in its terms, it was probably made without a full consideration of all the consequences that may follow from it; or the judge may not have expressed a concluded opinion."

Saif Ali v. Sydney Mitchell & Co.
[1980] A.C. 198

LORD WILBERFORCE: "*Rondel* v. *Worsley* was concerned and only concerned with matters taking place in court which resulted in an outcome unfavourable to the client. But the speeches contain considered observations as to the extent of barristers' immunity for matters taking place outside court and in barristers' chambers. Since the case was not concerned with such matters, these observations have the status of obiter dicta. However, not all obiter dicta have the same weight, or lack of weight, in later cases. Of those then made in the House two things may be said. First, they were considered and deliberate observations after discussion of the same matters had taken place in the Court of Appeal and in the light of judgments in the Court of Appeal. It may be true that the counsel in the case did not present detailed arguments as to the position outside the courtroom—they had no interest in doing so—but I cannot agree that this invalidates or weakens judicial pronouncements. Judges are more than mere selectors between rival views; they are entitled to and do think for themselves. Secondly, it would have been impossible for their Lordships to have dealt with the extent of barristers' immunity for acts in court without relating this to their immunity for other acts. As I shall shortly show their Lordships attached the immunity to the conduct of litigation. But litigation takes some time to arrive in court for trial, so, unless they were prepared to confine the immunity to the part of litigation which occurs in the court room, it was not only appropriate but necessary to deal with such acts, in relation to litigation, as occur outside the courtroom. A statement of principle which stopped at the door of the court would have been truncated and irrational. These factors, in my opinion, tell in favour of giving considerably more weight to their Lordships' expressions than obiter dicta normally received. We may clarify them, but we should hesitate before disregarding them."

LORD SALMON: "When *Rondel* v. *Worsley* came to this House, this House faced a dilemma. The Law Lords did not agree with the majority of the Court of Appeal which had decided, obiter, that a barrister enjoyed a blanket immunity against any claim in negligence in respect of all paperwork. It was indubitably plain to this House that the obiter dictum of the majority of the Court of Appeal, although not binding, would carry great weight. Indeed it was extremely doubtful that any judge of first instance or any division of the Court of Appeal would depart from that obiter dictum unless this House disagreed with it. Accordingly, this House had no real choice but to deal with it. And this they did. By a majority of four to one the Law Lords rejected the proposition that the Bar enjoyed the blanket immunity proclaimed by the majority of the Court of Appeal."

[*Rondel* v. *Worsley* [1967] 1 Q.B. 443, C.A.; [1969] 1 A.C. 191, H.L.(E).]

D. THE DRAWBACKS OF PRECEDENT

The advantages conferred by a doctrine of precedent must be assessed in the light of that doctrine's attendant drawbacks. The doctrines of binding precedent which currently prevail in Scotland and England carry with them the risk that sometimes the certainty being pursued is the certainty of injustice. Justice demands not merely that like cases be treated alike but that different cases be treated differently. Where social conditions have greatly changed since the precedent was decided it may no longer be a "like" case. Similarly, uniformity and consistency may be purchased at the price of the perpetuation of error.

Lord Devlin, "Who is at fault when injustice occurs?," p. 71
"The object of a rule is to ensure that similar cases are similarly decided; if they were not, then there would not be justice at all . . . [yet] any rule, however well phrased, may occasionally interfere with judgment on the merits. Justice for all carries with it the possibility of something less than justice in the individual case."

Jackson, *The Struggle for Judicial Supremacy*, p. 295
"Stare decisis means that on the same point of law yesterday's decision shall govern today's decision. Like a coral reef, the common law becomes a structure of fossils. Precedents govern the conclusions and the reasoning of lawyers and judges . . . The judge who can take refuge in a precedent does not need to justify his decision by reason . . . He may reluctantly feel himself bound by a doctrine, supported by a respected historical name, that he would not be able to justify to contemporary opinion or under modern conditions."

Lord Devlin, "The Judge and Case Law," p. 184
"Case law has to be very skilfully made and maintained if its great asset, its elasticity, is to be properly used. The danger is that a precedent, once created, will be treated as if it was as impregnable to a judge as is statute law. It gets forgotten that a judge-made rule should always be designed to fit the circumstances. The circumstances are general and not special; the latter must be left for the trial judge. They are expected to last for some time, else there would be no place for a general rule, but they are not expected to last for ever."

II. THE JUDICIAL ROOM FOR MANOEUVRE

Any doctrine of precedent should permit the judiciary to draw a balance between the need for stability and the need for flexibility in the common law.

Lord Reid, "The Judge as Law Maker," p. 26
"People want two inconsistent things; that the law shall be certain, and that it shall be just and shall move with the times. It is our business to keep both objectives in view. Rigid adherence to precedent will not do. And paying lip service to precedent while admitting fine distinctions gives us the worst of both worlds. On the other hand too much flexibility leads to intolerable uncertainty."

Lord Edmund-Davies, "Judicial Activism," p. 13
"[W]hatever a judge does, he will surely have his critics. If, in an effort to do justice, he appears to make new law, there will be cries that he is overweening and that he has rendered uncertain what had long been regarded as established legal principles. On the other hand, if he sticks to the old legal rules, an equally vocal body will charge him with being a reactionary, a slave to precedent, and of failing to mould the law to changing social needs. He cannot win and, if he is wise, he will not worry, even though at times he may ruefully reflect that those who should know better seem to have little appreciation of the difficulties of his vocation."

In practice the judges have developed a number of techniques for handling precedents within the limits of choice permitted by the respective doctrines of binding precedent which currently prevail in Scotland and England.

A. OVERRULING

Courts higher up in a hierarchy have the power to overrule or not to follow the decisions of courts lower down in that hierarchy, and in certain instances, precedents of their own or co-ordinate courts. In the Court of Session an Inner House decision, which would normally be binding on a subsequent Division of the Inner House, may be overruled if a larger court is convened.

Even if a court considers that an earlier case was wrongly decided and it has the power to overrule it, it may hesitate to do so. This is in part because overruling a precedent involves the historical fiction that the precedent never represented the law— that is, overruling alters the law retrospectively. This is thought to be unfair to parties who have organised their affairs in the belief that the earlier case was good law.

For this reason some judges and commentators have called for the introduction of overruling with prospective effect only—a technique available in the Supreme Courts of India and the United States. See "Prospective Overruling" (below, p. 427).

Between 1898 and 1966 the House of Lords regarded itself as bound by its own decisions. However, in that year the Law Lords led by Lord Reid persuaded the Lord Chancellor (Lord Gardiner) to issue a Practice Statement on Precedent in the House of Lords announcing that the House would in future regard itself as free to depart from its own previous decisions. The choice of the phrase "depart from" rather than "overrule" undoubtedly reflected the Law Lords' awareness of the artificiality of the fiction that a previous decision never represented the law. The whole purpose of the Practice Statement was to permit them to change the development of the law openly rather than evading precedents by sleight of hand. Nevertheless, they did not embrace prospective overruling, retaining instead the traditional retrospective approach. This has led to continuing debates as to when the House should use its newly created power.

Practice Statement (Judicial Precedent)
[1966] 1 W.L.R. 1234

"Their Lordships regard the use of precedent as an indispensible foundation upon which to decide what is the law and its application to individual cases. It provides at least some degree of certainty upon which individuals can rely in the conduct of their affairs, as well as a basis for orderly development of legal rules.

Their Lordships nevertheless recognise that too rigid adherence to precedent may lead to injustice in a particular case and also unduly restrict the proper development of the law. They propose therefore to modify their present practice and, while treating former decisions of this House as normally binding, to depart from a previous decision when it appears right to do so.

In this connection they will bear in mind the danger of disturbing retrospectively the basis on which contracts, settlements of property and fiscal arrangements have been entered into and also the especial need for certainty as to the criminal law.

This announcement is not intended to affect the use of precedent elsewhere than in the House."

The statement was issued to the press with the following explanatory note:

"Since the House of Lords decided the English case of *London Street Tramways* v. *London County Council* in 1898, the House have considered themselves bound to follow their own decisions, except where a decision has been given per incuriam in disregard of a statutory provision or another decision binding on them.

The statement made is one of great importance, although it should not be supposed that there will frequently be cases in which the House thinks it right not to follow their own precedent. An example of a case in which the House might think it right to depart from a precedent is where they consider that the earlier decision was influenced by the existence of conditions which no longer prevail, and that in modern conditions the law ought to be different.

One consequence of this change is of major importance. The relaxation of the rule of judicial precedent will enable the House of Lords to pay greater attention to judicial decisions reached in the superior courts of the Commonwealth, where they differ from earlier decisions of the House of Lords. That could be of great help in the development of our law. The superior courts of many other countries are not rigidly bound by their own decisions and the change in the practice of the House of Lords will bring us more into line with them."

[*London Street Tramways Co. Ltd.* v. *L.C.C.* [1898] A.C. 375.]

Jones v. Secretary of State for Social Services
[1972] A.C. 944

LORD REID: "My understanding of the position when this resolution was adopted was and is that there were a comparatively small number of reported decisions of this House which were generally thought to be impeding the proper development of the law or to have led to results which were unjust or contrary to public policy and that such decisions should be reconsidered as opportunities arose. But this practice was not to be used to weaken existing certainty in the law. The old view was that any departure from rigid adherence to precedent would weaken that certainty. I did not and do not accept that view. It is notorious that where an existing decision is disapproved but cannot be overruled courts tend to distinguish it on inadequate grounds. I do not think that they act wrongly in so doing: they are adopting the less bad of the only alternatives open to them. But this is bound to lead to uncertainty for no one can say in advance whether in a particular case the court will or will not feel bound to follow the old unsatisfactory decision. On balance it seems to me that overruling such a decision will promote and not impair the certainty of the law

But that certainty will be impaired unless this practice is used sparingly. I would not seek to categorise cases in which it should or cases in which it should not be used. As time passes experience will supply some guide. But I would venture the opinion that the typical case for reconsidering an old decision is where some broad issue [of justice or public policy] is involved, and that it should only be in rare cases that we should reconsider questions of construction of statutes or other documents. In very many cases it cannot be said positively that one construction is right and the other wrong. Construction so often depends on weighing one consideration against another. Much may depend on one's approach."

Fitzleet Estates Ltd. v. Cherry
[1977] 1 W.L.R. 1345

The appellant company contended that a 3:2 decision of the House of Lords in 1966 on a point of statutory construction was wrongly decided.

LORD WILBERFORCE: "This contention means, when interpreted, that three or more of your Lordships ought to take the view which appealed then to the minority.

My Lords, in my firm opinion, the 1966 Practice Statement was never intended to allow and should not be considered to allow such a course. Nothing could be more undesirable, in fact, than to permit litigants, after a decision has been given by this House with all appearance of finality, to return to this House in the hope that a differently constituted committee might be persuaded to take the view which its predecessors rejected. True that the earlier decision was by majority: I say nothing as to its correctness or as to the validity of the reasoning by which it was supported. That there were two eminently possible views is shown by the support for each by at any rate two members of the House. But doubtful issues have to be resolved and the law knows no better way of resolving them than by the considered majority opinion of the ultimate tribunal. It requires much more than doubts as to the correctness of such opinion to justify departing from it."

Maher, "Statutory Interpretation and Overruling in the House of Lords," pp. 88–89

"In *Vestey* v. *I.R.C.* Lord Wilberforce spoke of the need to exercise discretion conferred by the 1966 Practice Statement 'sparingly and [to] try to keep it governed by stated principles.' The importance of the *Jones* case can be measured by the fact that the passage in Lord Reid's speech in that case concerning the general appropriateness of the use of the power has been cited in part or in full in a number of later cases, including *R.* v. *Knuller (Publishing etc.) Ltd., Fitzleet Estates Ltd.* v. *Cherry (Inspector of Taxes), R.* v. *Camplin,* and *Vestey* v. *I.R.C.,* and has also been referred to in a number of other cases by their Lordships and by counsel. Most of the cases where *Jones* has been cited are in the context of the general doctrine that the 1966 power is to be used sparingly, but the more specific point mentioned in *Jones* that matters of interpretation will rarely be suitable for use of the power to overrule has been expressly mentioned in *R.* v. *Knuller (Publishing, etc.) Ltd., Taylor* v. *Provan,* and *Vestey* v. *I.R.C.* . . . When we look at the cases involving the use of 1966 power, we find a whole range of standards, co-existing with and potentially conflicting with each other, that the House has regard to when contemplating use of the power to overrule. In those cases where the issue of statutory construction has been raised, three other principles have also been in issue, either competing with or adding support to that principle. These are the argument that the issue of injustice to the particular litigants is involved, that Parliament has approved the precedent in question, and that the age of the precedent and the reliance placed upon it precludes use of the 1966 power."

[*Vestey* v. *I.R.C.* [1980] A.C. 1148; *R.* v. *Knuller (Publishing, etc.) Ltd.* [1973] A.C. 435; *R.* v. *Camplin* [1978] A.C. 705; *Taylor* v. *Provan* [1975] A.C. 194.]

R. v. Cunningham
[1982] A.C. 566

LORD EDMUND-DAVIES: "The cases are probably rare where your Lordships' House would think it right to invoke the Practice Statement (Judicial Precedent) . . . notwithstanding the conclusion that a relevant earlier decision had been *correctly* arrived at. But that such a power exists is recognised in the Practice Statement itself, and *Miliangos* v. *George Frank (Textiles) Ltd.* [1976] A.C. 443 is an instance of this House, while not condemning as wrong a decision it had delivered 15 years earlier, declining to follow it on the ground that the instability which had meanwhile overtaken major currencies was such that, in the words of Lord Wilberforce, 'To change the rule would . . . avoid injustice in the present case' (at p. 467F).

Even where an earlier decision is *not* approved of, the Practice Statement stresses . . . 'the especial need for certainty as to the criminal law', and in *R.* v. *Knuller (Publishing, Printing and Promotions) Ltd.*

[1973] A.C. 435, 455 Lord Reid emphasised that ' . . . our change of practice in no longer regarding previous decisions of this House as absolutely binding does not mean that whenever we think that a previous decision was wrong we should reverse it.' "

Paterson, "Lord Reid's unnoticed legacy—A jurisprudence of Overruling," pp. 375–376, 380–382, 388–389

"Throughout his career in the Lords, Lord Reid endeavoured to spell out what he considered to be the limits of legitimate judicial lawmaking in the House. It was predictable, therefore, that once the Practice Statement had been made, Lord Reid's concern to demarcate between Parliament and the judiciary would lead him to formulate guidelines stipulating the typical situations in which the freedom asserted in the Statement should be exercised. This is precisely what occurred. Lord Reid, in a series of cases between 1966 and 1975 articulated at least seven criteria with respect to the new freedom. They were

1. The freedom granted by the 1966 Practice Statement ought to be exercised sparingly.
2. A decision ought not to be overruled if to do so would upset the legitimate expectations of people who have entered into contracts or settlements or otherwise regulated their affairs in reliance on the validity of that decision.
3. A decision concerning questions of construction of statutes or other documents ought not to be overruled except in rare and exceptional cases.
4. (*a*) A decision ought not to be overruled if it would be impracticable for the Lords to foresee the consequences of departing from it.
(*b*) A decision ought not to be overruled if to do so would involve a change that ought to be part of a comprehensive reform of the law. Such changes are best done 'by legislation following on a wide survey of the whole field.'
5. In the interests of certainty, a decision ought not to be overruled merely because the Law Lords consider that it was wrongly decided. There must be some additional reasons to justify such a step.
6. A decision ought to be overruled if it causes such great uncertainty in practice that the parties' advisers are unable to give any clear indication as to what the courts will hold the law to be.
7. A decision ought to be overruled if in relation to some broad issue or principle it is no longer considered just or in keeping with contemporary social conditions or modern conceptions of public policy.

In setting out these criteria Lord Reid showed that like Lord Wilberforce, his successor as senior Law Lord, he believed that the discretion asserted in the 1966 Practice Statement ought to be exercised according to set principles or guidelines. It is also clear that in the pronouncements on this matter, particularly his seminal excursus on the purpose and parameters of the Practice Statement in the *Jones* case, he was consciously seeking to influence his colleagues . . .

It is clear . . . that whether it is fair to attribute it to his influence or not, Lord Reid's criteria reflected very accurately the dominant consensus amongst his fellow Law Lords . . . at the time . . . of his retirement (January 1975). So accurately that apart from the criteria already mentioned, only one further criterion not suggested by him (though he probably accepted it) had received much support from his colleagues by the date of his retirement. This eighth criterion was the expectation that a decision in criminal law ought to be overruled only in exceptional circumstances, in view of the especial need for certainty in criminal law.

Lord Reid's success in providing a lead for his colleagues or in encapsulating their views was all the more noteworthy in that it was not (so far as I could ascertain) the result of formal or informal discussions. Moreover, there has been no shortage of alternative criteria suggested by his colleagues which have failed to achieve widespread support. An attempt by Lord Hailsham to introduce as a criterion for overruling a precedent, that it involved a 'logical impossibility' has been rejected more than once by his brethren. The Law Lords have also been divided as to the importance to be attached to the age of the precedent under review. Lord Dilhorne's reluctance to interfere with longstanding precedents (voiced in the *Jones* case) was shared by Lord Kilbrandon (and possibly Lords Diplock and Edmund-Davies) in *Dick* v. *Burgh of Falkirk* [1976 S.C. (H.L.) 1]. In *The Albazero* [1977] A.C. 774, Lord Diplock (Lords Dilhorne, Simon and Fraser concurring), concluded that 'the almost complete absence of reliance' by litigants on a House of Lords case for over 120 years did not provide 'a sufficient reason for abolishing it entirely'. On the other hand Lord Simon (with the express concern of Lords Wilberforce, Cross and Fraser on this point) held in *Miliangos* that the maxim *cessante ratione cessat ipsa lex* was a relevant consideration in deciding whether to override a previous decision of the House. To add to the confusion, Lord Dilhorne's suggestion that it is easier to depart from a recent case than one that has stood for a long time was rejected by Lord Pearson in his interview, by Lord Diplock in the *Jones* case and by Lord Reid in *Conway* v. *Rimmer* [[1968] A.C. 910]. Yet in *D.D.P.* v. *Nock* [[1978] A.C. 979] Lord Scarman (Lords Diplock, Edmund-Davies, Russell and Keith concurring) gave as a reason for not overruling a decision of the House, the fact that it was 'very recent'. In point of fact, none of the arguments relating to the age of the precedent in question seem as yet to have acquired particularly widespread support amongst the Law Lords except to the extent to which they are really a restatement of Lord Reid's second criterion.

The disagreements extended to other criteria. Some Law Lords considered arguments based on 'parliamentary inactivity' to be accepted in this area—others did not; some relied on a 'floodgate' argument to justify inaction—others did not. One appellate committee argued that judicial unanimity in a precedent was a reason for it not being overthrown. Yet, another appellate committee the year before had held that the converse was not true, *i.e.* that the lack of unanimity in a precedent was not a reason for it being overthrown. Acceptance of a precedent in other common law jurisdictions had been used to justify retaining it; yet the rejection of a precedent in other common law jurisdictions, has not proved a strong argument for overruling it here. Similarly, acceptance of a precedent by textbook writers has been used to justify its retention; yet overwhelming criticism of a precedent by academics and textbook writers has not proved a strong argument for overruling it here . . .

We saw earlier that in addition to the better established criteria, certain other criteria relating to the exercise of the Practice Statement have been put forward and rejected. This may suggest that the 'established' guidelines are nothing more than a convenient shorthand for the existing consensus amongst the Law Lords in this field. Alternatively, it might be argued that they reflect not just the Law Lords' views, not just their practice, but also their perceptions as to how they ought to act. The evidence from the Law Lords' interviews and from the decided cases . . . shows that the Law Lords perceive the established criteria as *prima facie* valid reason for justifications for, or as presumptions in relation to, the exercise of their new freedom. The guidelines are not simply rules of practice. In the Law Lords' eyes they clearly possess a normative content. But they are not rules of law either. What then is their status? They are, I believe, best described in terms of the social science framework or role analysis. Viewed from this perspective the guidelines are normative expectations which form part of the role of a Law Lord.

But the role expectations (the guidelines) are of a flexible nature. They may conflict with one another and they are not always determinitive of the outcome of a case. There are dissenting voices as to the scope and even the existence of some of the guidelines discussed in this article. The guidelines are open to different interpretations. In the words of Lord Scarman (with which Lord Reid would undoubtedly have agreed), 'Judicially indicated guidelines should not be treated as though they were a rule of law. They are to be followed unless the particular circumstances of a case . . . indicate that they would be inappropriate.''

[Since 1981 the House has been asked to invoke the 1966 Practice Statement in one to two cases each year, the most significant being *Pirelli General Cable* v. *Oscar Faber* [1983] 2 A.C. 1, *Khawaja* v. *Secretary of State for the Home Dept.* [1984] A.C. 74, *Paal Wilson & Co.* v. *Blumenthal* [1983] 1 A.C. 854, *President of India* v. *La Pintada Cia Navegacion S.A.* [1985] A.C. 104, *Food Corporation of India* v. *Antclizo Shipping Corporation* [1988] 2 All E.R. 513, *R.* v. *Shivpuri* [1987] A.C. 1, *R.* v. *Howe* [1987] A.C. 417 and *Murphy* v. *Brentwood District Council* [1991] 1 A.C. 398. Arguably, none of these cases involved a departure from the criteria articulated by Lord Reid. Indeed, *Pirelli*, *Khawaja*, *Paal Wilson* and *The Antclizo* contain positive endorsements of Lord Reid's criteria. In only four, *Khawaja*, *Shivpuri*, *Howe* and *Murphy* was the Practice Statement successfully invoked. While it is true that

two, *Khawaja* and *Shivpuri*, turned on points of statutory interpretation, in each case the House was able to argue, with some
conviction, that the precedents involved errors of interpretation of
constitutional or fundamental importance. Interestingly, both cases
involved departing from relatively recent decisions—a point which
seems to confirm the suggestion (see p. 399 above) that arguments
in relation to the age of the precedent are equivocal in the Law
Lords' ears when considering the Practice Statement.

Some commentators have argued that the practical importance
of the Practice Statement has been very limited. In fact, in the eyes
of the Law Lords, they exercised their new freedom in about nine
of the 36 cases between 1966 and 1983 in which the possibility of
invoking the Practice Statement was raised. The Law Lords saw
the Statement as a relaxation in their attitude to precedent, not a
revolution. But the change was psychologically important. The
commentators have been misled by the fact that the House (like
the U.S. Supreme Court) in the early years after 1966 was wary of
overturning decisions in explicit terms, preferring instead to distinguish them out of existence, even though they would not have
felt able to evade the precedents had the Practice Statement not
existed. In part, this could be attributed to understandable caution,
lest overt overrulings should encourage a flood of requests for
them to reverse earlier decisions. It was also due, however, to
divisions amongst the Law Lords as to the wisdom of overt as
opposed to covert, judicial law-making.

The power conferred by the Practice Statement has been used in
one Scottish appeal, *Dick* v. *Burgh of Falkirk*, 1976 S.C. (H.L.) 1.
See G. Maher, "Scots law and the 1966 Practice Statement," 1981
S.L.T. (News) 181. [See further on the House of Lords overruling
its own decisions, J.W. Harris, "Towards Principles of Overruling"
(1990) 10 Oxford Journal of Legal Studies 135.]

B. DISTINGUISHING

Any judge, irrespective of his or her location in the court hierarchy
may decline to follow a precedent which would otherwise be
binding on them provided they can establish some material distinction between the facts of the instance and those in the earlier
decisions which justifies them in departing from that decision.
Since no two cases are ever identical, if the precedent is one which
the later judges considers to be unjust or unsound, they may be
tempted to draw illogical or specious distinctions between the
cases.

Smith, *The Doctrines of Judicial Precedent in Scots Law*, p. 81

"The process of evaluating and comparing material facts may result in the rejection of an alleged precedent. The techniques of 'distinguishing', 'not following', 'doubting', and relegation for 'reconsideration' may in some cases be compared with diplomatic illness. They can provide opportunities—which the initiated understood—for evading undesirable results without undermining the corporate prestige of the Bench, or giving offence to particular judges. The practice of 'distinguishing' precedents is familiar in Scotland. The technique applies to two broad classes of case— the one where there is distinction with a substantial difference in material fact (which needs no further discussion); and the other where the distinction is without a substantial difference at all."

We saw earlier that the *ratio(s)* intended to be laid down by the judge(s) in a case may differ from that or those which subsequent courts will be prepared to hold the case to be authority for. As Professor Glanville Williams argues in *Learning the Law* at pp. 75–77:

"Courts do not accord to their predecessors an unlimited power of laying down wide rules. They are sometimes apt to say, in effect: 'Oh yes, we know that in that case the learned judge purported to lay down such and such a rule; but that rule was unnecessarily wide for the decision of the case before him because, you see, the rule makes no difference to fact A, which existed in the case, and which we regard as a material fact, and as a fact that ought to have been introduced into the *ratio decidendi*.' One circumstance that may induce a court to adopt this niggling attitude towards an earlier decision is the necessity of reconciling that decision with others. Or again, the court in the earlier case may have enunciated an unduly wide rule without considering all its possible consequences, some of which are unjust or inconvenient or otherwise objectionable. Yet another possibility is that the earlier decision is altogether unpalatable to the court in the later case, so that the latter court wishes to interpret it as narrowly as possible.

This process of cutting down the expressed *ratio decidendi* of a case is one kind of 'distinguishing.' It may be called 'restrictive' distinguishing, to differentiate it from the other kind, genuine or non-restrictive distinguishing. Non-restrictive distinguishing occurs where a court accepts the expressed *ratio decidendi* of the earlier case, and does not seek to curtail it, but finds that the case before it does not fall within this *ratio decidendi* because of some material difference of fact. Restrictive distinguishing cuts down the expressed *ratio decidendi* of the earlier case by treating as material to the earlier decision some fact, present in the earlier case, which the earlier court regarded as immaterial . . .

Some precedents are continually left on the shelf in this way, as a wag observed, they become very 'distinguished.' The limit of the process is reached when a judge says that the precedent is an authority only 'on its actual facts.' For most practical purposes this is equivalent to announcing that it will never be followed. It is not suggested that this extreme form of distinguishing is a common occurrence, for generally judges defer to the decisions of their predecessors both in the letter and in the spirit, even though they dislike them. But restrictive distinguishing does happen, and the possibility of its happening makes it of great importance to the lawyer."

Turner's Trustees v. Turner
1961 S.L.T. 319

The deceased left her house to her son in her will. In an addendum to the will (the codicil) she directed her trustees that in the event of her son predeceasing her daughter the house should go to the daughter and on her death to the deceased's grandson. The trustees sought guidance from the Inner House (by way of a Special Case) as to whether the codicil had restricted the son's interest in the house to living in it during his lifetime or whether it left him free to dispose of the house if he so wished.

LORD PRESIDENT (Clyde): "We were . . . referred to the case of *Jamieson's Trustees* v. *Jamieson* (1899) 2 F. 258, 7 S.L.T. 279, the facts in which it was contended were undistinguishable from the present and compelled us to reach an opposite conclusion to that which I have just indicated. But *Jamieson's Trustees* was decided on its own particular facts without reference in the opinions delivered by the Court to prior authorities, although these were quoted in the course of the argument. The case has, so far as I see, never been followed, it is not referred to in any of the text books and it is not a case that I would be prepared to follow unless the facts were completely identical. For it seems almost impossible to reconcile the case with principle, or with any of the other authorities. In my view, the facts in the present case although similar to those in *Jamieson's Trustees* are not the same. The basis as I understand it for the conclusion reached in *Jamieson's Trustees* was that stated by Lord McLaren, at page 263—'The conflict in the directions to the trustees which was to be found in the settlement and in the codicil were so direct as to constitute, in effect, a case of plain repugnancy between the two directions. If that be the *ratio decidendi* in *Jamieson's Trustees*, it does not conclude the present case. Here there is no such plain repugnancy at all. *Jamieson's Trustees*, therefore, is not a case which compels us to decide that the codicil cuts down the right of the second party to a liferent."

[For further examples of distinguishing see the cases set out on pp. 416–24 below and the treatment given to *Manners* v. *White-head* (1898) 1 F. 171 in *Ferguson* v. *Mackay*, 1985 S.L.T. 94.]

C. PER INCURIAM

Wesley-Smith, "The Per Incuriam Doctrine," pp. 58, 64
"For any judge impatient with the restrictions of *stare decisis* there is an

obvious temptation to overcome his difficulties by a liberal application of the *per incuriam* label. But there are dangers in doing so, and the courts have defined the doctrine very narrowly . . . In summary, it can be said that, as a general rule, a decision can properly be labelled *per incuriam* only when these conditions are satisfied: (1) there was a binding rule of law (contained in a statute, subordinate legislation or judicial decision) which, if taken into account, would have affected the result of the case; (2) the court was unaware of the binding rule of law when it made its decision; and (3) the court's decision was therefore manifestly wrong. A case is not *per incuriam* merely because counsel's argument before the court was weak or inexpert; or only one party was before the court; or only one side of the argument was considered; or the reasoning upon which the decision was based was faulty (for some other reason than ignoring a material, binding and contrary rule of law); or the court was not aware of practical or policy objections to the decision made, or of a rule of statutory interpretation; or the court adopted a conclusion not suggested by counsel; or the court appeared to misunderstand a binding rule of law to which it had been referred. It may be, however, that a case can properly be labelled *per incuriam* when ignorance of a binding authority arises from use of a misleading law report or where there is a clear error in the interpretation of a statute. A court may only apply the doctrine, and therefore decline to follow a precedent, in regard to the decisions of itself, a court of co-ordinate jurisdiction, or of a court lower in the hierarchy.

Per incuriam can be seen, not as an exception to, but as a necessary component of the *stare decisis* doctrine. All courts are under a duty to apply the law, and in so doing they must comply with the ground rules of the system; the most important of these are legislative supremacy and the binding effect of higher courts' decisions. A case decided in ignorance of and contrary to 'the law' (as represented by a statute or a binding judicial decision) is not 'the law' but a corruption of it, and the principle upon which the case proceeded cannot be considered authoritative. The notion that there are other circumstances in which *per incuriam* may arise has not proved fruitful, and it is difficult to imagine any situation which would justify departing from an otherwise binding judicial decision on the ground of want and care.''

Cassell & Co. Ltd. v. Broome
[1972] A.C. 1027

LORD HAILSHAM L.C.: '' . . . I am driven to the conclusion that when the Court of Appeal decided the decision in *Rookes* v. *Barnard* as decided 'per incuriam' or 'unworkable' they really only meant that they did not agree with it. But, in my view, even if this were not so, it is not open to the Court of Appeal to give gratuitous advice to judges of first instance to ignore decisions of the House of Lords in this way and, if it were open to the Court of Appeal to do so, it would be highly undesirable. The course taken would have put judges of first instance in an embarrassing position, as driving them to take sides in an unedifying dispute between the Court of Appeal or three members of it (for there is no guarantee that other Lords Justices would have followed them and no particular reason why they should) and the House of Lords. But, much worse than this, litigants would not have known where they stood. None could have reached finality short of the House of Lords, and, in the meantime, the task of their professional advisers of advising them either as to their rights, or as to the probable cost of obtaining or defending them, would have been, quite literally, impossible. Whatever the merits, chaos would have reigned until the dispute was settled, and, in legal matters, some degree of certainty is at least as valuable a part of justice as perfection.

The fact is, and I hope it will never be necessary to say so again, that, in the hierarchical system of courts which exists in this country, it is necessary for each lower tier, including the Court of Appeal, to accept loyally the decisions of the higher tiers."

The House of Lords made it clear that *per incuriam* cannot be used to avoid the binding decision of a higher court, for the reasons given in Lord Hailsham's speech. This cannot be an assertion of infallibility by the House but merely an indication that in the furtherance of judicial comity and discipline no court (other than the House itself) may declare that a House of Lords decision was made *per incuriam*, even if it was. [For a case where the House has described one of its own previous decisions as *per incuriam* see *Re Poh* [1983] 1 All E.R. 287.] Since higher courts do not need to offend lower courts by labelling their decisions as *per incuriam* it follows that the doctrine is only likely to be invoked by a court which is bound by its own decisions or those of a court of co-ordinate jurisdiction. In Scotland, only the Divisions of the Inner House are so bound, and they may convene a larger court. This may explain why *per incuriam* is rarely invoked in Scotland.

[For a fuller account of the doctrine see P. Wesley-Smith, "The Per Incuriam Doctrine" (1980) 15 J.S.P.T.L. 58. See also *Duke* v. *Reliance Systems Ltd.* [1987] 2 All E.R. 858.]

D. CESSANTE RATIONE CESSAT IPSA LEX

Maher, "Cessante Ratione Cessat Ipsa Lex," p. 162
"Two contrasting interpretations . . . can be given to cessante ratione. In the strong sense, which accords more readily with the literal translation of the phrase, the maxim is to the effect that where a rule has lost its underlying rationale then the rule itself is no longer a valid rule and no effect is to be given to it. In the weak sense, on the other hand, it simply means that a rule may have less weight as a result of changed circum-

stances and it may thus prove desirable to distinguish the rule or seek some way round it. Nonetheless, a rule it remains until repealed by a competent authority. The former approach has the quite radical consequence that no matter the origin of the rule in question, then any court irrespective of its position in the judicial hierarchy would be able to disregard it given the existence of changed circumstances."

In England the maxim is applied in the weak sense.

Miliangos v. George Frank (Textiles) Ltd.
[1976] A.C. 443

LORD SIMON: "To sum up . . . (1) the maxim in the form 'cessante ratione cessat ipsa lex' reflects one of the considerations which your Lordships will weigh in deciding whether to overrule, by virtue of the 1966 declaration, a previous decision of your Lordships' House; (2) in relation to courts bound by the rule of precedent the maxim 'cessante ratione cessat ipsa lex,' in its literal and widest sense, is misleading and erroneous; (3) specifically, courts which are bound by the rule of precedent are not free to disregard an otherwise binding precedent on the grounds that the reason which led to the formulation of the rule embodied in such precedent seems to the court to have lost cogency; (4) the maxim in reality reflects the process of legal reasoning whereby a previous authority is judicially distinguished or an exception is made to a principle legal rule; (5) an otherwise binding precedent or rule may, on proper analysis, be held to have been impliedly overruled by a subsequent decision of a higher court or impliedly abrogated by an Act of Parliament . . . This has nothing to do with the maxim 'cessante ratione': it arises from the legal rule of stare decisis together with the constitutional hierarchy of courts and the constitutional supremacy of Parliament over all courts."

In Scotland the scope of the maxim is a matter of academic debate.

Smith, *The Doctrines of Judicial Precedent in Scots Law*, pp. 100–101
"One does not need to go as far back as Morison's *Dictionary* before encountering decisions which any reasonable man would recognise as having now fallen into desuetude. There are many cases in Dunlop, Macpherson and Rettie which are so redolent of antiquated ideas that a Scottish court would, it is submitted, feel justified—as would a codifying commission—in ignoring them, even though it was impossible to distinguish them convincingly. If this is the correct view, then the maxim *cessante ratione legis cessat lex ipsa* can be invoked by a court in Scotland, not merely as in England to justify the overruling of obsolete decisions of inferior courts, but as warranty for refusing to follow the outmoded precedents of courts of equivalent jurisdiction. It is reasonably obvious,

of course, that antiquity is not *per se* an objection to a precedent. In some chapters of the law, as for example those concerned with heritable rights, the tendency is more towards conservatism than is the case where personal rights of negligence in relation to moveables have to be considered. Again, judges clearly may differ as to what decisions have been superseded by events . . . the personal factor cannot be eliminated from the judicial process.

In *Beith's Trustees*, 1950 S.C. 66 the Lord President, after quoting Lord Dunedin on precedent, continued, 'I propose to apply this authoritative guidance in considering the cases relied upon by the first parties, and to add this corollary that, if it is manifest that the *ratio decidendi* upon which a previous decision has rested has been superseded and invalidated by subsequent legislation or from other like cause, that *ratio decidendi* ceases to be binding'. In this case a wife's funds had been conveyed to marriage contract trustees for the wife in liferent, then for the issue of the marriage, whom failing for the wife's appointees or heirs in fee. The lady, having passed the age for child-bearing without issue, sought immediate payment of the fund to herself. When the case was argued before the First Division, counsel for the trustees cited three authorities, including a seven judge case decided in 1875, for the proposition that *stante matrimonio* the trust was irrevocable. These cases were swept aside by the Lord President with the concurrence of Lord Russell and Lord Carmont—the first two cases because in view of the diverse views expressed a *ratio* could not be spelled out without great difficulty; and the seven judge case because its *ratio* rested on the common law rules prevailing in 1875 as to the diminished capacity of a married woman—whereas the general law regarding the property and the rights of married women had been radically altered since that date. The Lord President observed, 'Nor do I see any need to convene a larger court for the purpose of reconsidering *Menzies* v. *Murray*. In 1875 and for some time after, the decision was unexceptionable and in harmony with the then existing general law. But the general law has passed *Menzies* v. *Murray* by, and under the fundamentally altered conditions which have prevailed for a generation the decision and its *rationale* have been as completely superseded as if they were based on a statute which has subsequently been repealed. There is no need to overrule *Menzies* v. *Murray* and no justification for so doing. The proper course is simply to cease to follow it.''

Maher, "Cessante Ratione Cessat Ipsa Lex," pp. 163–165

"The basis of Lord Cooper's approach in *Beith's Trs*. has often been characterised in terms of cessante ratione. If this is so, then it would be a case of applying the maxim in the strong sense, for Lord Cooper is evidently saying that due to changed circumstances one Division of the Court of Session can rightfully cease to follow a case decided by a court of seven judges, without there being any need to convene a larger court to reconsider *Menzies* v. *Murray*. But it is worthy of note that cessante ratione is used solely in commentators' accounts of *Beith's Trs.* and not in the case itself. And this is no doubt for the very good reason that *Beith's Trs.* has nothing at all to do with cessante ratione.

That this is so can easily be discovered if we look at what Lord Cooper actually said and did in *Beith's Trs.* For the relevant type of change which he held as justifying his course of action was not 'any substantial change in the social background' to *Menzies* v. *Murray* . . . or the changing social role or position of married women, but instead whatever alterations on the common law rules that had been brought about by statute. Lord Cooper was quite explicit about why he saw *Menzies* v. *Murray* as no longer constituting binding authority: 'We owe respect to previous decisions of superior or equal authority, but we also owe respect to Acts of Parliament; and if subsequent statutes have deprived a decision of its whole content, we have no duty to echo outmoded and superseded conceptions, (1950 S.L.T. at p. 73). Thus *Menzies* v. *Murray* could be simply ignored by the court in *Beith's Trs.*, not because of any rule about 'changed circumstances', but more straightforwardly by application of the standard doctrine of constitutional law that courts give effect to later statutes which abrogate previous common law rules. And such cases of repeal by statute, whether express or implied, as Lord Simon stressed in *Miliangos*, are only confusingly described in terms of cessante ratione . . .

In general, then, examination of actual practice does not bear out the traditional view, still urged by textbook writers, about the extent to which Scottish courts will disregard prior cases on the ground of substantial change in social or economic circumstances. In most cases the courts go no further than pursuing the necessary implications of statutory change. Admittedly, in England there is little scope for the application of cessante ratione, but at least the range of relevant 'changed circumstances' is fairly wide. In Scotland there must be countless cases in the reports where there has been some significant change in social and economic background (indeed many nineteenth century cases in areas of mercantile law, such as bankruptcy, are simply difficult to follow because of the different underlying commercial practices), yet these cases are still confidently cited as authoritative by practitioners and textbook writers alike."

Commerzbank Aktiengesellschaft v. Large
1977 S.C. 375

The pursuers were a bank incorporated, and carrying on business, in West Germany. The defender obtained a loan from the bank while he was stationed in West Germany on military service. The defender returned to Scotland and the pursuers raised an action against him for the repayment of the loan. The conclusion was in deutschmarks. The Lord Ordinary (Maxwell) reported to the Inner House as to the competency of a foreign pursuer seeking decree in the currency of a foreign country.

LORD PRESIDENT (Emslie): "We have no hesitation in holding that the . . . conclusion in this action is competent in our law. This was the course recommended to us by the Lord Ordinary. As his report discloses, the only decision which might be thought to preclude us from taking this course is *Hyslops* v. *Gordon* (1824) 2 Shaw's Appeals 451. This was an action raised in respect of a sum due on a transaction the money of account of which was American dollars. The sum sued for was expressed in sterling but the Court of Session, for a reason which is not obvious, pronounced decree for a sum expressed in dollars. When the case came before the House of Lords on appeal Lord Gifford said that the judgment ought to have been for the sterling equivalent converted at the date of raising the action. The arguments are not reported and no other conversion date appears to have been considered. In *Miliangos* v. *George Frank (Textiles) Ltd.* [1976] A.C. 443 Lord Fraser of Tullybelton at p. 502 had this to say about *Hyslops*—'the reason for that part of the decision was the difficulty of ascertaining the rate of exchange at the date when the action was raised, but that reason is not applicable today, at least where dollars or other important currencies are concerned . . . The case should, I think, be treated as one decided in accordance with a practice that existed in circumstances which were very different from those existing today and therefore as one not necessarily to be followed now.' We agree with these observations and in our opinion the case of *Hyslops*, decided as it was in the context of conditions which no longer apply, does not now bind this Court. We are accordingly free to consider, in the context of the age of floating currencies and rapidly fluctuating exchange rates, the true objectives of our law . . . In our opinion justice requires that a foreign creditor who is entitled to payment of a debt due in the currency of his own country or the currency of a particular foreign country should not be bound to accept payment of the debt in the money of his debtor's country if any prejudice would be caused to him thereby."

Commerzbank failed to convince the doubters. Maher sees it simply as relating to a rule of practice. Nor is he convinced by the case of *Todd* v. *H.M. Advocate*, 1984 S.L.T. 123 where a five judge High Court of Justiciary confirmed that the old common law rule that evidence adduced from a witness for one accused is not evidence against another accused where they have separate defences, had been abrogated by subsequent practice and by the impact of modern legislation. In support of Maher the Lords Ordinary in *Twomax* v. *Dickson, McFarlane and Robinson*, 1983 S.L.T. 98 at pp. 102–3 and *Weir* v. *J.M. Hodge & Son*, 1990 S.L.T. 266 at p. 270 concluded that the reported cases provided insufficient evidence for the existence of a strong doctrine of *cessante ratione* in Scots law.

Weir v. J.M. Hodge & Son, 1990 S.L.T. 266

LORD WEIR: "I do not consider that it is within my power to hold that the case of *Robertson* v. *Fleming* is no longer binding. In the case of *Beith's*

Trs., the supervening event was legislation and it is easy to see how this can deprive prior decisions of content. I am not clear what Lord President Cooper had in mind when he referred to such decisions being superseded by subsequent legislation 'or from other like cause'. In the case of *Commerzbank*, the full court was considering a rule of practice which had become outmoded by changing commercial and economic conditions. So far, no court has held that it is free to depart from a rule of the common law laid down by a higher court on account of subsequent developments in that branch of the common law. It may be thought desirable that in such circumstances a court should feel free to hold a decision, even of the House of Lords, to be no longer binding. On that question I express no opinion. However in the absence of clear authority that such a change of attitude towards the binding force of judicial precedent is permissible, I am not prepared to take this step."

[*Robertson* v. *Fleming* (1861) 4 Macq. 167; *Beith's Trs.* v. *Beith*, 1950 S.C. 66; *Commerzbank Atkiengesellschaft* v. *Large*, 1977 S.C. 375.]

However, in contradistinction it can be argued that *S.* v. *H.M. Advocate*, 1989 S.L.T. 469 in which the High Court abandoned the age old doctrine that a husband is legally incapable of raping his wife, is based on reasoning which is closely akin to the strong form of *cessante ratione*.

It seems, therefore, that the debate as to the status of the *cessante ratione* doctrine in Scots law today remains unresolved. Equally problematic is the question as to what the status of the doctrine ought to be in modern day Scotland. [For another critique of the Maher position see Willock, "Judges at Work," 1982 *J.Rev.* 237 at pp. 240–43. Maher provides a lengthy reaffirmation of his position and of his co-author's (T. B. Smith) disagreement with him in paras. 353–54 of Vol. 22 of the *Stair Memorial Encyclopaedia of the Laws of Scotland*.]

E. MULTIPLE RATIOS

Behrens v. Bertram Mills Circus
[1957] 2 Q.B. 1

DEVLIN J.: "It is well established that if a judge gives two reasons for his decision, both are binding. It is not permissible to pick out one as being supposedly the better reason and ignore the other one; nor does it matter for this purpose which comes first and which comes second. But the practice of making judicial observations *obiter* is also well established. A judge may often give additional reasons for his decision without wishing to make them part of the *ratio decidendi*; he may not be sufficiently convinced of their cogency as to want them to have the full authority of precedent, and yet may wish to state them so that those who later may have the duty of investigating the same point will start with some guidance. This is a matter which the judge himself is alone capable of deciding and any judge who comes after him must ascertain which course has been adopted from the language used and not by consulting his own preference."

[See also Lord Simonds, *Jacobs* v. *London County Council* [1950] A.C. 361 at p. 369.]

It does not follow, however, that each *ratio* is binding where in an appellate decision the judges have reached the same conclusion for different reasons, *i.e.* where each judge's opinion contains a different *ratio*. The *ratio* in an appellate decision is the highest common factor of the propositions which a majority of the court supports. If there is one or more dissent the *ratio* must be found in the majority opinions. Where the reasoning of a judge is so obscure that the *ratio* of his decision cannot be discerned, then his reasoning does not bind later judges. Similarly, if in an appellate decision there is no discernible majority support for any *ratio* then there is nothing to bind later courts except the decision of the specific facts of the earlier case. This leaves open the room for manoeuvre of later and lower courts. Thus, juggling with multiple *ratios* is one more technique which the wise judge acquires.

Aitken's Trustees v. Aitken
1927 S.C. 374

A testator, who professed to be one of the last of a family which had been connected with a burgh for several centuries, and who had twice by the votes of his fellow citizens acted as champion at the riding of the marches, expressed in his will the desire that a monument should be erected in memory of his family and himself. He conveyed his estate to trustees, and directed them to erect a massive equestrian bronze statue of artistic merit of himself as champion on a site in one of the main streets of the burgh then occupied by shops and dwelling-houses of which he was the proprietor. The trustees sought guidance as to the validity of the directions, by way of a special case.

LORD SANDS: "A testator's intentions may be reasonable, but may nevertheless fall to be disregarded if he has provided a means for carrying them out which will clearly be ineffectual. The object of the testator I take to be that the memory of his family should be held in honour in Musselburgh, that his own name and memory should likewise be held in honour, and that interest and pride in ancient civic customs should be

kept alive in his native town. Can the carrying out of the directions which
he has given be reasonably regarded as calculated to effect these objects
or any of them? . . . The municipality of Musselburgh, representative of
the community, are strongly opposed to the carrying out of the testator's
scheme, and they have passed a resolution to the effect that it is a
'fantastic proposition'. Eighteen years have been allowed to pass since the
testator's death without any steps having been taken by anybody to
stimulate the activity of the trustees. I conceive that, if there had been
any minority or other movement counter to the opinion of the Town
Council, it would have been the duty of the trustees to bring the matter
before us. The attitude of the trustees, in upholding in argument the
validity of the bequest, is correct, but it seemed clear in the course of the
discussion that, so far as they are concerned, there is no conviction
behind it.

These considerations all point in the direction that the purpose of the
testator would not be effected by the erection of the proposed statue, but
that, on the contrary, its erection would cause the memory of the testator
and his family to stink in the nostrils of the community of Musselburgh,
as associated with a monument which tended to make their town and
their ancient civic customs ridiculous.

The citizens of Edinburgh regard the Scott Monument with pride as an
imposing architectural memorial to a citizen whose name is held in
honour throughout the world. But, if that monument had been erected,
where it is and as it is, to the memory of an obscure tradesman who had
happened to be captain of the orange colours, with a massive statue of
the tradesman in the centre of it, would the citizens of Edinburgh have
regarded this monument with pride, would they have cherished the
memory of that tradesman with affection, would their hearts have glowed
with honest civic pride in the orange colours whenever their eyes rested
upon the stately pile? I think not. I think that they would have regarded
the monument and the statue with loathing as making the city ridiculous,
and that, despite the artistic merits of the edifice and sculpture, they
would have wished the monument and the statue and the orange colours
with the memory of the deceased tradesman all at the bottom of the
Forth.

One must not compare Musselburgh with Edinburgh, or High Street,
Fisherrow, with Princes Street. But Musselburgh people as well as
Edinburgh people may be credited with some local pride and sensitive-
ness, and with some sense of the ridiculous. It can hardly be suggested
that this equestrian statue can be of interest to anybody outside of
Musselburgh, except, perhaps, as a curious illustration of human vanity.
It is in Musselburgh that the memory is to be cherished and civic pride
stimulated. There is, in my view, every indication that the erection of this
statue would not effect these purposes, but would militate against them
. . . I am accordingly of opinion that the testamentary directions fail as
being an irrational, futile, and self-destructive scheme to carry out not
unreasonable purposes.''

LORD BLACKBURN: "In my opinion the directions in the present cases are . . . unreasonable, extravagant, and useless, and they merit fully the epithet of 'fantastic' applied to them in the resolution of the Town Council . . . They are . . . objectionable from a public point of view . . . in respect that they involve the destruction of a valuable rent-producing property in the middle of a burgh without any conceivable benefit to the inhabitants of the burgh . . . I do not think we are entitled to hold that the direction in this case is other than invalid as contrary to public policy."

LORD ASHMORE: "The adverse criticism of the Town Council seems to me to negative the suggestion of the testamentary trustees of the truster that the erection of the statue would be in the interest of the inhabitants of Musselburgh, or would confer a benefit of any kind on the community. Moreover, nothing is stated in the special case to show that the carrying out of the truster's directions would be helpful to the citizens of the burgh or beneficial in any way; nor was anything said to indicate that there is any desire on the part of the public, or any section of the public, for the erection of the statue . . . For the reasons which I have given, I am in favour of holding the truster's directions . . . invalid and ineffectual, in respect that if these directions were carried out they would confer no benefit or advantage of any kind on anyone."

[It is not clear what *ratio*, if any, can be derived from this case.]

For a case where a lower court has concluded that there is no discernible *ratio* in the majority opinions in a House of Lords decision, see *Harper* v. *National Coal Board* [1974] Q.B. 614. Because of the difficulties encountered in ascertaining the *ratio* of a decision in the House of Lords where there are several speeches, some judges and academics began to argue in the early 1970s that the House, particularly in criminal cases, should move towards the practice of the Privy Council of only issuing one majority judgment. Lord Reid was an inveterate opponent of single judgments in appellate courts except in special circumstances. His successors as presiding Law Lord (particularly Lord Diplock), however, seem to have been leading the House more in the direction of the Privy Council practice. (In 1975, when Lord Reid retired, 28% of decisions in the House consisted of single judgments. By 1983 the figure had reached 68 per cent. See Bradney, "The Changing Face of the House of Lords," 1985 J.R. 178 and Lord Diplock in the case of *Re Prestige* [1984] I.R.L.R. 166 quoted on p. 70 above.)

Cross, "The Ratio Decidendi and a Plurality of Speeches,"
pp. 379, 385
"A case with a clear *ratio decidendi* may sink to the level of being authority for no more than it actually decides on account of the impact of

subsequent decisions, but, when this lowly status has to be accorded to a case by the first court which considers it in a subsequent case, there has to some extent been a failure of judicial technique. This is because it is the function of courts to give judgment according to a principle or rule of law discernible to other courts. There are, however, several situations in which it is only too plain that this function has not been fulfilled. No reasons may be given for the judgment, something of a rarity these days, or, something of a rarity at any time, a judge may express himself so obscurely that it is impossible to say which facts he considered material and which immaterial; but the most frequent instances of cases which are only authority for what they actually decide are those in which five speeches are delivered in the House of Lords. There is of course no question of any want or obscurity of reasoning, there is simply nothing which can be described as the *ratio decidendi* of the House. The result is that the authority of the House of Lords as the body which finally declares what the law is is neither so extensive nor so coercive as is sometimes supposed, for, where there is no *ratio decidendi* of the House, lower courts are only bound by its decisions in cases in which the circumstances are not reasonably distinguishable from those which gave rise to the decisions. Everything said by any law lord in the course of his speech in any case is of course of great persuasive authority, but the persuasiveness loses much of its force when the observation is contradicted by that of another law lord in the same case; the result is that the lower courts have a wide choice in cases concerning matters on which there is a decision, but no *ratio decidendi*, of the House of Lords . . .

Provided it was liberally construed by the presiding judge, I would welcome a provision under which criminal appeals to the House of Lords were normally disposed of in a single speech. I think there is all the difference in the world between the functions of the House of Lords in civil and criminal cases. The assistance of the development of the law by the formulation of principles is so much more appropriate in the former. In criminal cases one particular certified point has to be clarified. The common law is a dynamic force in tort and contract in a way that it is not in the case of the criminal law.

Even if we cannot have the norm of single speeches in criminal appeals to the House of Lords, might we not have, in civil and criminal cases alike, a greater co-ordination of the speeches?"

Lord Reid, "The Judge as Law Maker," pp. 28, 29
"We are often told that there should only be one judgment instead of, it may be, five speeches in the House of Lords. At first sight that seems good sense: the law will then be clear and judges and others who have to apply it will know where they are. The trouble is that it won't work and experience has shown that. As you know, until recently there could only be one judgment in the Privy Council and now if there is a dissent there can only be one judgment on each side. If you compare the quality of

Privy Council judgments with speeches in the House of Lords for a long time back I think you will agree that from the point of view of developing the law Privy Council judgments have been much inferior. They are perfectly adequate to decide the particular case but not often of wide importance. Yet the same Law Lords have sat and they have taken just as much trouble. The reason is that a single judgment must get the agreement of at least all in the majority so it tends to be no more than the highest common factor in their views. So often in the House of Lords it is the second or third speech which now carries the greatest weight but we would not have had it at all if there had been only one judgment. Or take another example. For a time it was customary in the House of Lords to have only one speech in criminal appeals. But after the disaster of *Smith* v. *D.P.P.* we changed that: I don't believe that decision would have been so bad if there had been more than one speech. Differences would have been expressed which would have taken the edge off it.

The truth is that it is often not possible to reach a final solution of a difficult problem all at once. It is better to put up with some uncertainty—confusion if you like—for a time than to reach a final solution prematurely. The problem often looks rather different the second time you deal with it. Second thoughts are not always best but they generally are."

[*D.P.P.* v. *Smith* [1961] A.C. 290.]

Paterson, *The Law Lords*, pp. 184–185

"[Lord Reid commented], 'I take the view that when . . . you are breaking new ground, you don't know what your successors are going to do and you have got to leave a certain number of options open, and if you are going to try and define everything you'll do it wrong, it can't be done with one bite. You are far better, I think to put down your own views, having read the other man's . . . and then leave it to the next generation to pick out what they like best. The law develops very slowly you know, and we can't do it, not satisfactorily, by making a sort of final pronouncement on a new point. It would never do . . . and get us into far more trouble than the way we do it now.'

Even Lord Radcliffe who strongly disagreed with Lord Reid on the desirability of multiple opinions, was at one with him on this point. As he put it,

'I believe in the law as an inter-woven system and I do not believe in these great formative single decisions . . . It's the infinite number of cases which are influenced by a House of Lords case one way or the other that really makes the law'."

Cassell and Co. Ltd. v. Broome
[1972] A.C. 1027
LORD REID: "With the passage of time I have come more and more

firmly to the conclusion that it is never wise to have only one speech in this House dealing with an important question of law. My main reason is that experience has shown that those who have to apply the decision to other cases, and still more those who wish to criticise it, seem to find it difficult to avoid treating sentences and phrases in a single speech as if they were provisions in an act of Parliament. They do not seem to realise that it is not the function of noble and learned lords or indeed of any judge, to frame definitions or to lay down hard and fast rules. It is their function to enunciate principles and much that they say is intended to be illustrative and explanatory and not to be definitive. When there are two or more speeches they must be read together and then it is generally much easier to see what are the principles involved and what are merely illustrations of it."

F. PRACTISING PRECEDENT

The following cases on the meaning of "family" in the Rent Acts illustrate that the techniques for handling precedent set out above are frequently employed in combination.

Gammans v. Ekins
[1950] 2 K.B. 328

For some 20 years a man had lived with the tenant of a dwelling-house to which the Rent Restrictions Act applied. He had never married her, but he had adopted her name and posed as her husband. After her death in 1949 he remained in the house. In an action by the landlord for possession of the house, the defendant claimed the protection of the Rent Restrictions Acts on the ground that he was a "member of the tenant's family" within the meaning of the Acts.

ASQUITH L.J.: "It has been held that 'family' in the subsection should be given its popular meaning: see *Brock* v. *Wollams* [1949] 2 K.B. 388. Consanguinity is not a pre-requisite of membership of the same family. On the authorities not only are children members of their parents' family, but a husband is a member of his wife's family, an adopted child is a member of the adoptive parents' family, and a husband, on unusual facts, has been held to be a member of the same family as his wife's niece. Counsel for the landlord was right in saying that the material decisions limit membership of the same family to three relationships—first, that of children; secondly, those constituted by way of legitimate marriage between husband and wife, and, thirdly, relationships whereby one person becomes *in loco parentis* to another. Beyond that point the law has not gone. I do not think we should be justified in saying that the defendant was a member of Mrs. Smith's family. If the relations between them had been platonic I can see no principle on which one could say that they were members of the same family which would not require the court to predicate the same of two old cronies of the same sex innocently sharing a flat. If, on the other hand, the relationship involves sexual relations it seems to me anomalous that a person can acquire a 'status of irremovability' by having lived in sin, even if the liaison has been, not a mere casual encounter, but one protracted in time and conclusive in character. I would, however, decide the case on a simpler view. To say of two people masquerading, as these two were, as husband and wife—there being no children to complicate the picture—that they were members of the same family, seems to me an abuse of the English language . . . "

JENKINS L.J.: "The defendant was not, in my view, a member of Mrs. Smith's family in any reasonable sense whatever. The parties, for reasons of convenience, had chosen to live together, and the defendant had taken the name of Smith. The neighbours assumed that they were husband and wife and accepted them as such. I cannot regard this as giving the defendant the same claim to be considered a member of Mrs. Smith's family as if they had been lawfully man and wife."

SIR RAYMOND EVERSHED M.R.: "It may not be a bad thing that it is shown by this decision that in the Christian society in which we live one, at any rate, of the privileges which may be derived from marriage is not equally enjoyed by those who are not married."

Dyson Holdings Ltd. v. Fox
[1976] 1 Q.B. 503

The defendant and Mr. Wright lived together as man and wife for 40 years. She used his name but they were never married and they had no children. For the 21 years prior to his death in 1961 they lived in a house in which he was a statutory tenant. In 1973 the landlords discovered that the couple had never been married and sought to repossess the house on the grounds that the defendant was not "a member of the original tenant's family" within the meaning of the Rent Acts.

LORD DENNING: "In the present case the lady is protected if she was a 'member of the tenant's family'; but not otherwise . . . The word 'family' in the . . . Act is not used in any technical sense, but in a popular sense. It is not used in the sense in which it would be used by a studious and unworldly lawyer, but in the sense in which it would be used by . . . the ordinary man in the street . . .

Applying this test, there are two cases in this court which are near to the present. The first is *Gammans* v. *Ekins*. The other case is *Hawes* v. *Evenden* [1953] 2 All E.R. 737. A dwelling-house was let to a Mr Randall. He lived there with a Miss Evenden. For 12 years they occupied the same house as man and wife, though they were not married, and two children had been born of the association. She kept her own name—Evenden—but the children used the name Randall. He died. She claimed to be a member of the tenant's family. The county court judge held that she was. The court upheld his decision. Somervell L.J. said ' . . . there the evidence justifies a finding that they all lived together as a family, and so . . . I think that the [mother] is a member of the family . . . '

If both these cases were rightly decided, it seems to follow that an unmarried woman (who has lived with a man as his wife for many years) is a 'member of the tenant's family' if she has children by him; but she is not a member of his family if she has no children. That means this: if the couple had a baby 19 years ago which died when a few days old, or as a young child, the woman would be a 'member of the tenant's family'; but if the baby had been still-born, or if the woman had had a miscarriage 19 years ago, she would not be a member of his family. Yet for the last 19 years they had lived together as man and wife. That seems to me a ridiculous distinction. So ridiculous, indeed that it should be rejected by this court; and that we should hold that a couple who live together as man and wife for 20 years are members of the same family, whether they have children or not.

But, is this court at liberty to reject the distinction? Are we bound by *Gammans* v. *Ekins*? That case can be distinguished on narrow grounds, such as that the woman was the tenant and not the man, or that their relationship might perhaps have been platonic. But I dislike the device of distinguishing a case on narrow grounds. I prefer to say, as I have often said, that this court is not absolutely bound by a previous decision when it is seen that it can no longer be supported. At any rate, it is not so bound when, owing to the lapse of time, and the change in social conditions, the previous decision is not in accord with modern thinking.''

JAMES L.J.: "In *Gammans* v. *Ekins* . . . the strongly expressed view was that as at 1949, the relevant date, the popular meaning of family did not include the male consort of a female tenant whose relationship had all the incidents of a marriage short of the birth of a child and all the outward appearances of marriage. Between 1950 and 1975 there have been many changes in the law effected by statute and decisions of the courts. Many changes have their foundation in the changed needs and views of society. Such changes have occurred in the field of family law and equitable interests in property. The popular meaning given to the word 'family' is not fixed once and for all time. I have no doubt that with the passage of years it has changed. The cases reveal that it is not restricted to blood relationships and those created by the marriage ceremony. It can include de facto as well as de jure relationships. The popular meaning of 'family' in 1975 would, according to the answer of the ordinary man, include the appellant as a member of Mr Wright's family. This is not to say that every mistress should be so regarded. Relationships of a casual or intermittent character and those bearing indications of impermanence would not come within the popular concept of a family unit.

It is not easy to decide whether in 1961 the ordinary man would have regarded the appellant as a member of Mr Wright's family. The changes of attitude which have taken place cannot be ascribed to any particular year. Had we to consider the position as at 1955 I would not be satisfied that the attitude reflected in the words of Asquith L.J. in *Gammans* v. *Ekins* had changed. I am confident that by 1970 the changes had taken place. There is no magic in the date 1961. I think that, having regard to the radical change which has by 1975 taken place, it would be a harsh and somewhat ossified approach to the present case to hold that in 1961 the appellant was not in the popular sense a member of the family.

I turn to the issue whether there is any rule of law which precludes the appellant being a member of the family for the purpose of the Rent Acts. If there is, it is to be found only in the decision of this court in *Gammans* v. *Ekins*. I confess that I have been troubled in the course of argument as to how far the decision of this court in that case is conclusive of the present appeal. The court in *Gammans* v. *Ekins* reversed the trial judge. They could not have done so unless the issue was a question of law. It is not a decision which can be explained on the basis of a question of fact. The cases which are said to be inconsistent with the decision are in my judgment not shown to be inconsistent. They are based on the added fact of birth of a child or children to the illicit union. All the members of the court in *Gammans* v. *Ekins* left that situation open for future consideration. The distinction between the mistress who is childless and the mistress who has a child by the tenant all forming a family unit is to my mind a vital distinction, I find it impossible to say that the decision in *Gammans* v. *Ekins* was per incuriam; all the judgments were carefully directed to the precise point. On its facts the case is distinguished from the present case because the tenant was a female who had taken a man into her house and the man claimed the statutory tenancy. But that factual difference to my mind does not affect the general principle. I cannot take the view that *Gammans* v. *Ekins* was wrongly decided. The decision is binding on the court, but it is binding only on the meaning to be given to 'family' at that time. The point decided was that applying the popular meaning of the word 'family' as it was used and understood in 1949 the evidence of relationship could not support a finding that the defendant was a member of the tenant's family. The decision is not authority for the proposition that at some later time a person in a similar position to Mr Ekins could not in law be a member of the tenant's family within the meaning of the [Rent Acts]. The word 'family' must be given its popular meaning at the time relevant to the decision in the particular case.

To hold that *Gammans* v. *Ekins* precludes the appellant from bringing herself within the Act would be to apply a precedent slavishly in circumstances to which it is not appropriate having regard to reality."

BRIDGE L.J.: "It is clear . . . that *Gammans* v. *Ekins* . . . proceeded on the basis that the question who is a 'member of the tenant's family' is to be answered according to the understanding of the ordinary man, and this test has been consistently applied in all the other cases decided on this provision. It is, I think, not putting it too high to say that between 1950 and 1975 there has been a complete revolution in society's attitude to unmarried partnerships of the kind under consideration. Such unions are far commoner than they used to be. The social stigma that once attached to them has almost, if not entirely, disappeared. The inaccurate but expressive phrases 'common law wife' and 'common law husband' have come into general use to describe them. The ordinary man in 1975 would, in my opinion, certainly say that the parties to such a union, provided it had the appropriate degree of apparent permanence and stability, were members of a single family whether they had children or not."

Leaving aside the question whether a word used in a statute can change its meaning over time the difficulty facing the Court of Appeal in *Dyson* was how to evade the precedent of *Gammans* which they regarded as out of touch with modern conditions. For Lord Denning the answer was straightforward. He continued with his one-man crusade to free the Court of Appeal from the rule that it is bound by its own decisions. It is not clear what techniques the other judges in *Dyson* used to evade the decision in *Gammans*. In Scotland, of course, in a similar situation all that would have been required would have been a five judge sitting of the Inner House.

In *Joram Developments Ltd.* v. *Sharratt* [1979] 1 W.L.R. 3 the defendant, a young man, and the elderly childless widow of an English High Court judge (ironically one who many years previously had raised the question of what "family" meant in tenancy succession cases) had cohabited platonically together as "aunt" and "nephew" for 18 years. The widow was a statutory tenant of the flat in which they lived. Her family thoroughly approved of the relationship since the defendant looked after the widow and because he did so she did not have to enter a nursing home in her declining years. On her death the landlords sought to recover possession of the flat and the defendant claimed protection under the Rent Acts on the grounds that he was "a member of the original tenant's family." On appeal another division of the Court of Appeal distinguished *Dyson* on the grounds that no sexual cohabitation was involved, and applied *Gammans*.

The next case was *Helby* v. *Rafferty* [1979] 1 W.L.R. 13. Rafferty, the defendant, lived with a statutory tenant of a flat as her lover, for five years. The couple had no intention of getting married and did not hold themselves out to be married. The health of the tenant began to deteriorate and the defendant nursed her as a husband would have done. After the tenant's death the landlady sought to recover possession of the flat from the defendant. He claimed that he was "a member of the original tenant's family" and therefore protected under the Rent Acts. The case came before yet another division of the Court of Appeal. This time *Dyson* was acknowledged to be binding on the Court of Appeal but was distinguished once more on the facts because it was felt that in *Rafferty* the relationship was not of such permanence and stability that the ordinary man would say that the parties were "members of a single family." Then came *Watson* v. *Lucas*.

Watson v. Lucas
[1980] 1 W.L.R. 1493

The defendant's wife left him after the first year of their marriage. He subsequently went to live with a widow who was a protected tenant of a flat. The couple slept together but had no children. For the most part they continued to use their own surnames. The relationship lasted for 19 years until the widow's death. The owner sought to recover possession of the flat and the defendant claimed to be "a member of the original tenant's family."

STEPHENSON L.J.: "*Dyson Holdings Ltd.* v. *Fox* . . . [was] distinguished by this court in *Helby* v. *Rafferty* . . . because during their five years' cohabitation the parties never pretended to be married and the tenant wished to remain independent, so that their relationship lacked the permanence and stability necessary to create a family unit. All three members of this court in *Helby* v. *Rafferty* regarded *Dyson Holdings Ltd.* v. *Fox* as binding on them, and we must do the same. To go back to *Gammans* v. *Ekins* would be to introduce impermanence and instability into our own decision in this case. Only the House of Lords can reinstate *Gammans* v. *Ekins* and that they have so far declined to do . . . But can *Dyson Holdings Ltd.* v. *Fox* be distinguished? The county court judge thought it could . . . As I read his judgment he denied Mr Lucas the protection of the statute because (1) usually he and Mrs Sullivan kept their own names and so remained independent of each other and (2) Mr Lucas deliberately chose not to get a divorce from his legal wife and so get into a position to marry Mrs Sullivan. The county court judge seems to have regarded his married status as an absolute bar to his being in fact a member of her family. He was there accepting the argument of counsel for the plaintiff, . . . that a man cannot have two families; Mr Lucas had a family in Ireland and not having legally rid himself of his wife and children in Ireland he could not be a member of another family here.

That is, in my view, a plain error of law. The ordinary man often has two families, one by his first wife and another by his second, and often has, or at any rate knows, a man who has one by his wife and another by his mistress. I can see no legal impossibility in a man being a member of both families though he will have difficulty in fact in residing with more than one and it will be impossible in fact for him to reside with more than one, as required by the statute, if he is to succeed to a protected tenancy; and the question whether he is a member of his mistress' family cannot any longer be decided by any moral preference for the family to which his lawful wife belongs . . .

I agree with the judge that Mr Lucas's remaining married is an important factor, as may be the retention of the couple's own names. But not in this case. For both factors are of importance, in my judgment, only as indications of independence and instability. The retention of the woman's name may indicate both, as I think it did in *Helby* v. *Rafferty*, but, if it does not indicate either, it has little relevance to the right answer to the ordinary man's question. . . .

The ordinary man has to consider whether a man or a woman is a member of a family in the light of the facts, and whatever may have been held before *Dyson Holdings Ltd.* v. *Fox* I do not think a judge, putting himself in the place of the ordinary man, can consider an association which has every outward appearance of marriage, except the false pretence of being married, as not constituting a family. If it looks like a marriage in the old and perhaps obsolete sense of a lifelong union, with nothing casual or temporary about it, it is a family until the House of Lords declares . . . that *Dyson Holdings Ltd.* v. *Fox* was wrongly decided because the reasoning of the majority was wrong. The time has gone by when the courts can hold such a union not to be 'familial' simply because the parties to it do not pretend to be married in due form of law."

OLIVER L.J. (dissenting): "Essentially every case of this kind turns on its own facts and the impression that these facts make on the mind of the judge assuming for the purpose the mantle of the ordinary man. Speaking for myself I would regard the decision in the *Dyson* case as one which rested on its own peculiar facts and as standing at the very limit of an ordinarily accepted or acceptable definition of a family relationship. I would certainly not regard it as establishing a principle which is susceptible of further extension or which ought to be extended. The judge in the instant case had the difficult task of applying to the facts before him a test which, though neither an easy one nor a certain one, is certainly one which required him to consider all the available factors. The decision was essentially one which depended on the inferences to be drawn from all of the facts before him, which included the fact that the defendant was and remained by choice married to a lady who was living at the material time and who was the mother of his only child.

If and so far as the judge was of opinion that the continued existence of the defendant's marriage was, in itself, and by itself, an absolute answer in law to his claim. I respectfully disagree. I think, however, that it was one factor, and a not unimportant factor, to be taken into account, although I accept that a man may sometimes have two families. One possible inference to be drawn from it was that, however agreeable and convenient his relationship with Mrs Sullivan may have been, he was not prepared to make himself responsible for her maintenance and support indefinitely or to put himself in a position in which he might have become susceptible to convert the relationship into a permanent one by marrying her . . . I have concluded, not without hesitation, that I am not prepared to say that the judge, who saw and heard the witness, in making his assessment as a whole and in reaching the conclusion which he did reach on all the facts, was wrong to attribute weight to the factors which I have mentioned. They are, in my judgment, factors which do distinguish the instant case from the *Dyson* case, and I would dismiss the appeal."

SIR DAVID CAIRNS: "I do not find the test of Cohen L.J. as helpful in this case it was in *Brock* v. *Wollams* . . . To the question "Was Mr Lucas a member of Mrs Sullivan's family?', I have no idea what 'an ordinary man' would answer, Stephenson L.J. would answer Yes and Oliver L.J. would answer No.

I agree with both my brethren that we should proceed on the basis that *Dyson Holdings Ltd.* v. *Fox* . . . was rightly decided, though I respectfully share the doubts that have been expressed about that decision and I recognise the force of the reasoning of Oliver L.J. . . .

I have reached the conclusion that this case cannot sensibly be differentiated from *Dyson Holdings Ltd.* v. *Fox*. I attach little or no importance to the continued use by Mr Lucas and Mrs Sullivan of different surnames. It is the relations between the man and the woman that are relevant rather than the appearance that they present to the public. In this case the permanence of the relationship is not in doubt.

That Mr Lucas had a wife in Ireland is to my mind, having regard to the brevity of cohabitation, the long separation and the refusal of Mr Lucas of reconciliation, neither an absolute bar to his being considered a member of Mrs Sullivan's family nor a weighty reason for finding as a fact that he should not be so considered. Even if he could be regarded as a member of his wife's family (which I doubt) I agree with Stephenson L.J. that it is perfectly possible for a man to be a member of more than one family."

Appeal *allowed*.

These cases illustrate not merely the techniques used by judges for avoiding precedents they dislike but also the problems that can be encountered where judges operate at the limits of these techniques. Following *Joram* v. *Sharratt* and *Helby* v. *Rafferty* it began to look as if the Court of Appeal had embarked on a campaign to distinguish restrictively the *ratio* of *Dyson* v. *Fox* in an effort to return to the law as it was stated in *Gammans* v. *Ekins*. The majority in *Watson* v. *Lucas* may have interrupted this trend but the central issues in the debate have yet to be ruled on by the House of Lords.

The ratio of *Dyson* v. *Fox* was narrowed still further by the decision of the Court of Appeal in *Harrogate B.C.* v. *Simpson* [1985] R.V.R. 10 from which it appears that neither a homosexual nor a lesbian couple could count as "Family" for the purposes of the Rent Acts. However, *Dyson* received welcome support in *Chios Property Investment Co. Ltd.* v. *Lopez* [1987] *The Times*, 3rd November. In this case the Court of Appeal held that Ms

Lopez who had moved into her cohabitee's flat with the intention of marrying him when their financial circumstances permitted had become a member of his family for the purposes of the Rent Acts by the time of his death two years later. *Chios* is significant for the Court not only concluded that two years' cohabitation could constitute a sufficient state of permanence to establish a familial relationship, but also that children are not necessary for the constitution of a family and neither is a common surname (Ms Lopez had retained her maiden name).

If *Chios* marked a reversal in the gradual erosion of the ratio of *Dyson*, *Sefton Holdings Ltd.* v. *Cairns* [1987] *The Times*, 3rd November reaffirmed the limitation to *Dyson* which was laid down in the *Sharratt* case. In *Sefton Holdings* the defendant in 1941 went to live with her friend's family when aged 23. Her parents were dead and her boyfriend had just been killed in the war. She was effectively adopted by the family and treated as a daughter of the family. (Because of her age she could not legally be adopted.) Her friend succeeded to the tenancy on her parents' death but on her death the landlords served notice to quit on the defendant (now aged 70). The Court of Appeal held that although she had been a member of the household for 46 years, who was treated as a member of the family, she was not actually a member of the family. In the circumstances this seems a decision which accords neither with common sense, contemporary conceptions of "family", nor equity. It does, however, firmly underline that platonic relationships will not be considered by the courts as being capable of creating a familial nexus.

[See further on the *Chios* and *Sefton Holdings* cases, G. Howells, "Winners and Losers in the Family Circle," *Law Society's Gazette*, 18th May 1988 No.19 at p. 13.]

G. CAVEAT

In distinguishing at such length the judicial room for manoeuvre which exists—especially in the case of appellate judges—under the doctrines of binding precedent currently prevailing in Scotland and England, there is a risk of misleading the reader. Judicial law-making is inhibited by a number of factors quite apart from doctrines of precedent. A judge can only rule on points which are relevant to the cases brought before him. Thus even if the House of Lords is convinced that a particular case was wrongly decided, it may have to wait many years before the vagaries of litigation provide the court with the opportunity of reconsidering the case. Nor will Scottish courts normally rule on hypothetical or moot cases.

[See *Glasgow Navigation Co. Ltd.* v. *Iron Ore Co. Ltd.*, 1910 S.C. (H.L.) 63 and "Pronouncing on Hypothetical Questions" (1980) 48 SCOLAG 126.]

Moreover, appellate judges, particularly those in the House of Lords, while they have become more open in the past 20 years in discussing their law-making role, have been careful to stress the limits within which their creative powers can be exercised.

Lord Reid, "The Judge as Law maker," p. 22

"There was a time when it was thought almost indecent to suggest that judges make law—they only declare it. Those with a taste for fairy tales seem to have thought that in some Aladdin's cave there is hidden the Common Law in all its splendour and that on a judge's appointment there descends on him knowledge of the magic words. Open Sesame. Bad decisions are given when the judge has muddled the pass word and the wrong door opens. But we do not believe in fairy tales any more.

So we must accept the fact that for better or for worse judges do make law, and tackle the question how do they approach their task and how should they approach it."

Lord Devlin, *The Judge*, pp. 5, 9

"Let me repeat the distinction, since it may be one which I have freshly drawn, between activist and dynamic lawmaking. In activist lawmaking the idea is taken from the consensus and demands at most sympathy from the lawmaker. In dynamic lawmaking the idea is created outside the consensus and, before it is formulated, it has to be propagated. This needs more than sympathy: it needs enthusiasm. Enthusiasm is not and cannot be a judicial virtue. It means taking sides and, if a judge takes sides on such issues as homosexuality and capital punishment, he loses the appearance of impartiality and quite possibly impartiality itself . . . It is essential to the stability of society that those whom change hurts should be able to count on evenhanded justice calmly dispensed, not driven forward by the agents of change.

It is this even handedness which is the chief characteristic of the British judiciary and it is almost beyond price. If it has to be paid for in impersonality and remoteness, the bargain is still a good one . . . The reputation of the judiciary for independence and impartiality is a national asset of such richness that one government after another tries to plunder it. This is a danger about which the judiciary itself has been too easy going. To break up the asset so as to ease the parturition of a judicial creativity, an embryo with a doubtful future, would be a calamity. The asset which I would deny to governments I would deny also to social reformers.

I have now made it plain that I am firmly opposed to judicial creativity or dynamism as I have defined it, that is, of judicial operations in advance of the consensus. The limit of the consensus is not a line that is clearly marked, but I can make certain what would otherwise be uncertain by saying that a judge who is in any doubt about the support of the consensus should not advance at all. This however leaves open quite a large field for judicial activity. In determining its extent it is, I think, necessary to distinguish between common law and statute law. This is because the requirement of consensus affects differently the two types of law. The public is not interested in the common law as a whole. When it becomes interested in any particular section of it, it calls for a statute; the rest it leaves to the judges. The consensus is expressed in a greater warrant for judicial lawmaking. This warrant is an informal and rather negative one, amounting to a willingness to let the judges get on with their traditional work on two conditions—first, that they do it in the traditional way, *i.e.* in accordance with precedent, and second, that parliamentary interference should be regarded as unobjectionable. In relation to statute law, by contrast, there can be no general warrant authorising the judges to do anything except interpret and apply."

See also *D.D.P. for Northern Ireland* v. *Lynch* [1975] A.C. 653 at p. 700, *per* Lord Kilbrandon; *Miliangos* v. *George Frank (Textiles) Ltd.* [1976] A.C. 443 at pp. 481-482, *per* Lord Simon of Glaisdale; and A.A. Paterson, *The Law Lords*, pp.170-173. Despite these avowals of judicial restraint there have been several powerful (and controversial) examples of judicial activism in the High Court of Justiciary in recent years. These have included: *H.M. Advocate* v. *Wilson*, 1984 S.L.T. 117 (malicious mischief being held to cover pure economic loss caused by pressing the emergency stop button in a power station); *Khaliq* v. *H.M. Advocate*, 1984 S.L.T. 137 (supplying "glue sniffing kits" being held to be a crime known to Scots law) and *H.M. Advocate* v. *Paxton*, 1985 S.L.T. 96 (where it was held that a husband could be found guilty of raping his wife where the parties were living apart from each other); *Purcell Meats Ltd.* v. *McLeod*, 1987 S.L.T. 528 (in which it was held for the first time that a limited company could be guilty of a common law offence involving *mens rea*); *S.* v. *H.M. Advocate*, 1989 S.L.T. 469 (holding that a husband could rape his wife if they were still living together). These cases have provoked a not inconsiderable body of academic comment, see *e.g.* I. Willock, "The Declaratory Power; an Untenable Position" (1989) 157 SCOLAG 152; T. Jones, "Common Law and Criminal Law" (1990) C.L.R. 292; L. Farmer, "The Genius of our Law" (1992) Modern Law Review 25.]

III. REFORM

Proposals for the reform of precedent in Scotland in recent years have focused on two main points: introducing overruling with prospective effect and abolishing the doctrine of binding (as opposed to persuasive) precedent.

A. PROSPECTIVE OVERRULING

Lord Simon, "Some Judicial Processes in England," p. 17
"My own view is that there are two further desirable developments if the
House of Lords is to make the most effective use of its newly vouchsafed
power. First, I think that it should enjoy the power (already enjoyed by
the United States Supreme Court) to over-rule its previous decisions
prospectively only, with a discretion even whether to apply the new rule
to the parties before the court. This might well require legislation; since,
according to our existing doctrine of precedent, a decision only constitutes binding law in so far as it is necessary for the determination of the
issues before the court; and the decision I have envisaged would apply
only to future situations, not that before the court. But such a power of
prospective over-ruling would mean that desirable developments in the
law could be made without anxiety that existing rights were being
disturbed.

The second development that I venture to suggest is that, where the
court is uncertain as to the social repercussion of any decision, it should
be enabled to obtain from the Law Officers a balanced executive view.
The great difference between forensic and executive (or, for that matter,
legislative) decision-making is that it is only in the minor field of 'lawyers'
law' that courts can adequately envisage the repercussions of their
decisions, whereas, in an executive decision, repercussions in other fields
than those immediately in question (often entirely unlooked for) are
carefully assessed."

Tur, "Varieties of Overruling and Judicial Law-Making,"
pp. 33-34, 63-64
"Prospective overruling is a technique whereby courts can change the law
without upsetting the reasonable expectations of those who relied upon it
prior to the change. 'In the hands of skilled judicial craftsmen, acting
under well-reasoned guidelines, it can be an instrument of justice that
fosters public reason for law.' It is also a potential instrument of law
reform by the judiciary. Whenever a court is of the opinion that a well-
established precedent is 'bad law' (which might simply mean that the
social conditions have changed since the original decision) it may yet be
unwilling or reluctant to change the law because doing so will redound
not only upon the parties to the instant case, but also upon all parties to
unexhausted transactions based upon the law as then understood, all of
whom might reasonably be thought to have acted in reliance on the then
known law. If it is a necessary consequence of overruling a precedent that
a number of individuals are treated unfairly, judicial development of the
law will be limited. Prospective overruling seeks to provide a solution to
this predicament by insisting that there are no jurisprudential or constitutional obstacles to a court overruling for the future only, whilst deciding

the instant case according to the law in force at the time the transaction was entered into. Prospective overruling implies a clear admission that the courts do make new law, and the very raising of the question, 'Prospective or retrospective?' indicates an awareness of this. Thus prospective overruling is antithetical to the Blackstonian doctrine, still accorded lip-service, that the courts do not pronounce new law but merely maintain and expound the old . . .

What is clear, however, is that overruling in Scotland tends to proceed by way of a public-warning-before-disqualification process whereby the judiciary satisfies itself that an overruling is not upsetting legitimate expectations. Thus judicial changes are presaged by 'rumblings for Olympus.' The destructive work is cleanly done, albeit in two stages. First, doubt is expressed, a precedent is questioned; secondly, it is overruled, though the second stage may only follow the first after a 'sufficient' span of time. Nor should it be too readily assumed that any and every expression of doubt gives warning that overruling is in the offing. Thus the public-warning-before-disqualification functions more as a justification for the judiciary once it has decided to overrule rather than a criterion whereby the lawyer can anticipate overrulings. The Scottish position differs to a considerable degree from the English situation where doubtings, etc., issue less frequently in subsequent overrulings but more often in increasingly restrictive distinguishings.

An advocate of prospective overruling would urge that his technique achieves everything that the public-warning-before-disqualification system achieves *and*, as a further bonus, permits instant overrulings without thwarted expectations. It provides a facility for judicial reform without upsetting those who reasonably relied upon the law. It would seem that prospective overruling could quite happily be added to the armoury of the Court of Session."

Lord Devlin, "Judges and Lawmakers," p. 11

"Courts in the United States have begun to circumvent retroactivity by the device of deciding the case before them according to the old law while declaring that in future the new law will prevail: or they may determine with what measure of retroactivity a new rule is to be enforced. This device has attracted the cautious attention of the House of Lords. I do not like it. It crosses the Rubicon that divides the judicial and the legislative powers. It turns judges into undisguised legislators. It is facile to think that it is always better to throw off disguises. The need for disguise hampers activity and so restricts the power. Paddling across the Rubicon by individuals in disguise who will be sent back if they proclaim themselves is very different from the bridging of the river by an army in uniform and with bands playing. If judges can make law otherwise than by a decision in the case at Bar, why do they wait for a case? Prevention is better than cure, so why should they not, when they see a troublesome point looming up, meet and decide how best to deal with it? Judicial lawmaking is at present, as Professor Jaffe phrases it, 'a by-product of an *ad hoc* decision or process.' That this is so is of course in itself one of the objections to judicial lawmaking. Dependent as it is upon the willingness of individuals to litigate, it is casual and spasmodic. But to remove the tie with the *ad hoc* process would be to make a profound constitutional change with incalculable consequences. What is the business of a court of law? To make law or to do justice according to law? This question should be given a clean answer. If the law and justice of the case require the court to give a decision which its members think will not make good law for the future, I think that the court should give the just decision and refer the future to a lawmaking body."

Would Lord Devlin's objections apply equally to overruling by the House of Lords in pursuance of the 1966 Practice Statement? Do you think the case for experimenting with prospective overruling has been sufficiently made out?

[See, further on prospective overruling, R. Traynor, "Quo Vadis, Prospective Overruling: A Question of Judicial Responsibility," 1975, University of Birmingham, A. Nicol, "Prospective Overruling—a new Device for English Courts?" (1976) 39 M.L.R. 542 and Lord MacKay, "Can Judges change the Law," *The Times*, December 3, 1987.]

B. ABOLISHING BINDING PRECEDENT

Lord Cooper, "The Common and the Civil Law," pp. 206–207
"Everyone will freely admit that in judicial administration a very large measure of consistency must be secured in order that the law affecting any given situation may be reasonably predictable. The utmost respect will always be conceded to a tract of similar decisions, or the settled opinion of jurists of weight, or the accepted practice and understanding of the profession. But such principles are far from the superstitious fetish of ancestor worship which inspires the rigid rule of the individually binding precedent. For practical reasons, if for no other, the rule is bound to be abandoned soon, because the crushing weight of centuries of law reports, digests, and indices has become all but overwhelming, and it is fast increasing every year. But, practical considerations apart, is there any answer to the protest of Holmes that it is revolting to act in blind imitation of the past and to magnify consistency at the expense of common sense? Too often the imitation of the past is a 'blind' imitation, for the parallelism between cases is much less common than we lawyers pretend. Very slight differences in the facts—and these are not always recorded fully in the reports—may easily turn the scale; and even when the facts are to all appearances identical, the social, political, and economic background may be entirely different if the cases are separated, as often happens, by a long period of time . . . In the eyes of the civilian

the common lawyer has tried to make his professional life too easy by excessive reliance upon precedent and the ascription of infallibility to hierarchies of judges down the ages. The attempt has failed, and its abandonment will be joyfully received in Scotland by those who are ashamed to have to decide cases upon grounds with which they disagree simply because their remote ancestors have decided another case long ago upon a rationale which it is impossible to distinguish. All legal systems require a cement to bind them into a coherent whole; and the question which the common law system will . . . have to face is whether a better cement than rigid precedent cannot be found in more codification and in methodized reasoning from clear principles in accordance with the civilian tradition. The judge should not be the parties' oracle, but he must be something more than an animated index to the law reports."

Walker, "Reform Restatement and the Law Commissions," pp. 256–259
"The principle of *stare decisis* is a natural and, on the whole, valuable development, making for continuity, uniformity, reasonable certainty and predictability of law. But the rules have become so complicated, and the task of searching out the precedents so onerous that it is self-defeating. Above all, too frequently the question is not, what is the proper principle to apply, and what is the reasonable course or the fair and just decision? but: has the precise issue arisen before, and what was done then? Deference to the authority of precedent, frequently the opinion of a long-dead judge in a case arising in quite different social, political and economic circumstances, too frequently counts for more than the convincing of reason or the reference to some overriding principle.

It is thought that the most useful liberalisation of the principles, while not destroying the undoubted value of the system of judicial precedent, would be to provide by statute that from a stated date no court, tribunal, judge or arbiter should in any circumstances be bound to follow or apply the principle of the decision in any previous case merely because of the rank in the judicial hierarchy of the court pronouncing the precedent decision. In other words the doctrine of binding precedent should be abolished, leaving it quite open to a subsequent court to be influenced or persuaded by the *ratio* of, or *obiter dictum* in, any precedent case, having regard to such factors as the status of the court, the personal eminence and reputation of the judges, whether or not the precedent had been criticised in the journals, looked upon askance by the profession, or generally approved and acted upon, and regarded as embodying a sound statement of principle. Precedents, that is, should continue to be persuasive.

The only good ground for following precedent is that a particular precedent contains a statement of a legal principle or rule which satisfies the reason of the subsequent judge, as being just and fair and reasonable, consistent with settled and accepted principles in that general branch of law, and capable of generalisation and application to other similar instances without apparent absurdity or injustice. A precedent should commend itself to the reason and for its reason, not impose itself by any artificial rule of antiquity or authority. The modern doctrine of *stare decisis*, with its elaborate grading of courts in the judicial hierarchy, its deference in many cases to previous rulings of courts of equal authority, and casuistic distinctions when the court does not wish to be bound by a precedent, is as artificial as the Theodosian Law of Citations. It is also quite inconsistent with the older Scots law, and with the Romanistic tradition generally and the United States experience shows that some liberalisation is essential to avoid a breakdown.

Such a change would, it is thought, in fact have a valuable, but only marginal effect. The majority of precedents are accepted as sound and sensible and reasonable, but a few are not, and if pronounced by superior courts cannot easily, if at all, be circumvented . . .

It need not be thought that, if all precedents were reduced to merely persuasive authority, chaos would result. Precedents can be, and are, of different degrees of persuasiveness, and any court or judge will naturally treat a decision of a higher court or of more eminent judges or one long accepted and acted upon as much more highly persuasive than some other decisions. No doubt under a legal system in which no precedent is binding it would be open to a single judge to say that *Donoghue* v. *Stevenson*, 1932 S.C. (H.L.) 31, was bad law and that he would not follow or apply it, but in practice is it conceivable that any judge would do so? What is important and valuable is that such a single judge could, if he considered [a] decision unreasonable and the criticisms convincing, refuse to follow or apply [it]. A superior court may have power to reverse, but it does not necessarily have a monopoly of judicial wisdom, particularly in the light of more mature consideration, academic criticism and changed conditions.

The change would undoubtedly introduce a slightly greater measure of uncertainty into the law in permitting rules at present 'settled by authority' to be challenged, but in the first place such a challenge is likely to be successful only where the precedent is really questionable, which applies to only a minority of cases, and in the second place, the law is in fact much less fixed and certain than the layman thinks and any increased uncertainty seems likely to be negligible in relation to the whole corpus of the law. It is not in anyone's interest frivolously, or merely for the sake of the argument, to challenge precedents, but only if there do seem substantial grounds for doing so, and in such a case it is very much in the interests of justice that the precedent should be challenged and the point reconsidered. Certainty of law is a merit, but certainly can be of bad law and irrational and unjust rules."

MacCormick, "Can *stare decisis* be abolished?" p. 213
"In the path of those who would like to see an end of strict *stare decisis*, the obstacle is this: even if it ceases to be necessary to justify a decision

by reference to precedent, it may in effect remain sufficient to do so. Such is the warning of history. The needs for reasonable finality in litigation and for judicial impartiality tend also in the same direction. It is suggested with great diffidence that reform can only be meaningful if generally acceptable grounds for setting aside single precedents or even 'established usages' can be thoroughly worked out and perhaps actually included in the Act of Parliament envisaged."

While the words of Lord Cooper and Professors Walker and MacCormick have so far fallen on deaf ears, it remains to be seen what impact the advent of computerised legal information retrieval (and the greater accessibility to unreported cases which comes with this) will have on the Scots doctrine of precedent. In England the House of Lords acted swiftly in an attempt to forestall the excessive citation of unreported cases which it considered might follow from the arrival of legal databases. See 1983 S.L.T. (News) 56 and *Roberts Petroleum Ltd.* v. *Bernard Kenny Ltd.* [1983] 2 A.C. 192.

CHAPTER 15

AUTHORITATIVE WRITINGS, CUSTOM AND EQUITY

Three further formal sources of Scots law are recognised: Authoritative Writings, Custom and Equity. Nevertheless, though their theoretical status is secure, it is debatable whether in practice any of them now constitute a significant source of new or hitherto unrecognised rules in Scotland.

I. AUTHORITATIVE WRITINGS

Writings, like judicial precedents, are more or less persuasive in character. Some, referred to as "institutional writings" are, or have been, very highly persuasive indeed, while others are cited by counsel at their peril. The institutional writings include Craig's *Jus Feudale* (1655), Stair's *Institutions of the Law of Scotland* (1681), Bankton's *Institute of the Laws of Scotland* (1751–3), Erskine's *Institute of the Law of Scotland* (1773) and Bell's *Commentaries on the Laws of Scotland* (1804) and *Principles of the Law of Scotland* (1829). In the criminal sphere Mackenzie's *Laws and Customs of Scotland in Matters Criminal* (1678) and Hume's *Commentaries on the Law of Scotland Respecting Crimes* (1797) are accorded institutional status. Some of these institutional works were written, and possibly available to practitioners in manuscript, long before publication: Craig's *Jus Feudale* for example was written in 1603, but only published in 1655. For the standard editions in modern use see D.M. Walker, *The Scottish Legal System* (6th ed., 1992), pp. 481–2.

Like precedent, the authority of writings depends on the normative practice of the legal community. A century ago only institutional writings were regarded as authoritative sources of law. Other legal writings could usually not even be cited in court if their author was still alive. The practice of the legal community in the United Kingdom has now departed from this restrictive approach, although the House of Lords and English courts seem to be more receptive to the writings of living academics—particularly in the sphere of criminal law—than the Scottish judiciary.

Lord Reid, "The Judge as Law Maker," p. 22
"I think we are making some progress . . . In the House of Lords at least we turn a blind eye to the old rule that an academic writer is not an authority until he is dead, because then he can no longer change his mind."

433

Lord Diplock, "A.L.G.: A Judge's View," p. 459

"In contrast to the judicial attitude in my early days at the Bar, judges no longer think that the sources of judicial wisdom are confined to judgements in decided cases and, exceptionally, some pronouncement of the illustrious dead. In appellate courts, at any rate, when confronted with a doubtful point of law we want to know what living academic jurists have said about it, and we consider that counsel have not done their homework unless they come equipped to tell us about it."

Willock, "Scottish Criminal Law—Does it Exist?" p. 226

"[Gordon's *Criminal Law*] in a manner pioneered by the founder of Scottish Criminal Law, David Hume, in 1797, seeks to reconcile the decisions of judges, to show their underlying reasoning and their implications. Yet while still paying lip-service to Hume's genius, the judges have either studiously ignored Gordon's work (see e.g. *Cawthorne* 1968 J.C. 32, *Brennan* 1977 J.C. 38, *Watt* v. *Annan* 1978 S.L.T. 198, *Allan* v. *Patterson* 1980 S.L.T. 77) or brusquely rejected his views. Thus in *Smart* v. *H.M.A.* 1975 S.L.T. 65 they rejected his suggestion that consent is a defence to a charge of assault, though not of murder, as 'wrong' . . . Things are very different in England, where the role of writers in helping to put order into the law is well recognised, at least at the highest level. For instance in *Lynch* v. *D.P.P.* [1975] A.C. 653 the views of Glanville Williams and of Smith and Hogan in their works on Criminal Law were repeatedly canvassed by their Lordships in exploring the scope of the defence of duress. So too in *D.P.P.* v. *Majewski* [1977] A.C. 443—on self-induced intoxication as a defence.

The Scottish judges have preferred the terse snippets of Macdonald's *Practical Treatise on the Criminal Law*, the last edition of which is more than 30 years old. But Macdonald was a High Court judge and so was one of his last editors, who became Lord Walker."

The persuasiveness of writings varies with the prestige of the writer (thus institutional writings edited by a later hand lose some of their authority), the respect accorded to the work by the legal community and the age of the writings (either because they have been repeatedly relied on or because they have become severely dated). The normative practice of a substantial body of specialists over an extended period of time is rarely uniform in all respects. Hence, it is not surprising that there have been differing views, both over time and within the legal community at any given time, as to the authority of institutional and other writings and as to whether certain writings have or have not attained institutional status.

Blackie, "Stair's later reputation as a Jurist," pp. 209 *et seq.*

"The title Institutions or Institutes [was not in the late seventeenth and the eighteenth centuries] . . . evidence that there was a recognised category of 'institutional' writing forming an authoritative and binding source of law. The word 'authoritative' was used in connection with this class of writing, but it meant no more then that this was appropriate material for a court to take into account in coming to a decision. That a work should be entitled Institutions or Institute indicated to contemporaries nothing in itself, other than that the author was adopting a recognised method in the treatment of his subject, namely that of systematic, ordered exposition . . . Notwithstanding that certain writers, including Stair, were in fact accorded particular respect, this was always subject to the view that an opinion reported by a number of writers was more entitled to respect than a single opinion. This approach was the counterpart, as it were, of the recognition that a tract of decisions was of weight rather than an individual decision . . .

From the early years of the 19th century a different attitude to Stair and other writers emerges. By the 1840s it had become a matter of considerable moment that an 'institutional' opinion was not followed. This is associated with an express unwillingness to depart from written authority, with a tendency to distribute badges of ability amongst the writers, and a resulting special place being accorded to Stair . . .

Present day views of Stair are grounded in the 19th century understanding of his work, which was itself an elaboration on the earlier understanding. Why did this come about? The answer to this question goes deep into the way Scots lawyers have thought about the law, and only a tentative answer can be given. Four factors, however, stand out. Firstly, having neither a code nor a wealth of case law, the institutional writers and particularly Stair filled the gap . . . Secondly, the end of the critical technique of the enlightenment resulted in a changed attitude to the value of opinions. Thirdly, the creation of a system of judicial precedent had as its counterpart the need to create an equivalent with the works of writers. Finally, romantic nationalism as it affected the 19th century almost certainly played an important role."

[For a more detailed account of what is meant by the term "institutional writing", the role which such writings played in the development of the law of Scotland in the seventeenth and eighteenth centuries and their modern significance, see John W. Cairns, "Institutional Writings in Scotland Reconsidered" (1983) 4 J.L.H. 76. See also "Sources of Law", *Stair Memorial Encyclopaedia*, Vol. 22, paras. 433–441.]

Drew v. Drew
(1870) 9 M. 163

LORD BENHOLME: "When on any point of law I find Stair's opinion uncontradicted, I look upon that opinion as ascertaining the law of Scotland."

Lord Normand, "The Scottish Judicature and Legal Procedure," p. 40. "Stair, Erskine and Bell are cited daily in the courts, and the court will pay as much respect to them as to a judgment of the House of Lords, though it is bound to follow a judgment of the House of Lords whatever the institutional writers have said."

Smith, *A Short Commentary on the Law of Scotland*, p. 32
"The precise relative authority of an institutional opinion in comparison with a judicial decision is uncertain. An opinion from Stair, Erskine or Bell, for example, would never be rejected by a Scottish court without anxious consideration . . . The present writer would submit that the authority of an institutional writer is approximately equal to that of a decision by a Division of the Inner House of the Court of Session."

Walker, "Introduction to Stair's *Institutions*" (1981 ed.), p. 40
"In the literature of Scots law the *Institutions* has always held a pre-eminent place, as the most authoritative and respected general treaties, and one of the few institutional works, statements in which, save where and when clearly overruled or rendered obsolete by later law, have an authority similar to that of decisions of the Court of Session and which settle the law."

It might seem from the foregoing that in the absence of statutory or higher judicial authority a Division of the Inner House, a Lord Ordinary or a sheriff is now bound to follow an institutional writing on a point before them and that if the writing is not brought to their attention then their decisions may be said to be *per incuriam*. While institutional writings—particularly where they are unanimous on a point—are still considered to be very highly persuasive it is far from clear that the judiciary regard themselves as absolutely bound in this way. This is perhaps supported by the fact that the Scottish judiciary have never felt the need for an equivalent to the Roman Law of Citations (A.D. 426) to rank jurists in the event of a contradiction between them. For an instance of such a contradiction see *Fortington* v. *Kinnaird*, 1942 S.C. 239.

Irrespective of their present authority institutional writings are not now relied on in the courts with the frequency that they were in the 19th century.

Smith, *The Doctrines of Judicial Precedent in Scots Law*, p. 70
"Naturally in the course of the centuries many of the principles set out in the institutional writers . . . have been adopted by judicial reasoning and given additional warrant thereby. Moreover, citation from the institutional writers unsupported by other authority is now relatively rare. [It has been said that] during the present century there has been a noticeable trend from institutional law to case law. There have, however, been a

number of important decisions in recent years depending . . . on the institutional writers. The fact that they are few does not affect the fundamental position that such citations are treated with great respect."

[Such decisions include *Wills' Trs.* v. *Cairngorm etc. School Ltd.*, 1976 S.C. (H.L.) 30, *Sloans Dairies Ltd.* v. *Glasgow Corporation*, 1977 S.C. 223, *Spook Erection (Northern) Ltd.* v. *Kaye*, 1990 S.L.T. 676, *Spencer-Thomas of Buquhollie* v. *Newell*, 1992 S.L.T. 973 and *Stirling* v. *Bartlett*, 1993 S.L.T. 763.]

Black, "Review of Stair's *Institutions*" (1981 ed.), p. 284
"[Lord Cameron] in his foreword to the volume under review, [writes that Stair's] *Institutions* 'are still the daily resort of the practising lawyers and their authority is still accorded the highest respect'.
The reviewer respectfully and regretfully takes leave to doubt whether, in the past two decades at least, recourse to and citation of Stair by practitioners has been as frequent as these statements might suggest. Certainly during the present century practitioners have been in use to treat judicial decisions rather than institutional works as the first (and too often today, the only) source of authority to which resort will be made. Citation of the institutional writers, even in such areas as obligations, property and family law in which their authority would seem to be still most clearly of contemporary relevance, has become the exception and not the rule. The hunt is for decided cases with facts as similar as possible to those giving rise to the instant dispute rather than for an institutional statement of principle from which a solution to that dispute can be obtained by deduction."

II. CUSTOM

It seems curious to us now, but Stair considered custom to be the most important formal source of Scots law. Custom for Stair consisted not only of immemorial usages (which he sometimes termed "the common law or laws of the realm") but also recent custom (by which he principally meant judicial decisions). However, recent work by Scottish legal historians suggests that Stair's views on formal sources were not shared by the majority of institutional writers. In the mainstream of Scottish legal writing from the sixteenth century, written law (Acts of Parliament and Acts of Sederunt) was afforded primacy over unwritten or customary law. (A view which is epitomised in the writings of Sir George Mackenzie.) Moreover, precedent was not generally regarded as an authoritative source of law during the seventeenth and eighteenth centuries, although a uniform series of decisions could establish a usage which in time was accepted as part of the customary or unwritten law (Erskine, *Institute*, I, 1, 47).

Today custom is still recognised as a formal source—in at least three senses—but its significance has declined and it ranks behind statute and case law in authority.

A. ANCIENT AND IMMEMORIAL USAGE

Stair, *Institutions*, I. 1, 16

"Next unto equity [*i.e.* natural law], nations were ruled by consuetude [*i.e.* custom], which declareth equity and constituteth expediency . . . so that every nation, under the name of law, understand their ancient and uncontroverted customs time out of mind, as their fundamental law . . . In like manner we are ruled in the first place by our ancient and immemorial customs, which may be called our common law . . . By this law is our primogeniture, and all degrees of succession, our legitim portion of children, communion of goods between man and wife, and the division thereof at their death . . . which are anterior to any statute, and not comprehended in any, as being more solemn and sure than those are."

MacQueen, "Mackenzie's Institutions," p. 500

"Mackenzie's views were very different. He distinguished between the written and unwritten sources of law. Written law comprised statutes or Acts of Parliament, acts of sederunt and the books of *Regiam Majestatem* collected by Sir John Skene. Unwritten law was made up first of 'the constant tract of decisions past by the Lords of Session', second 'our ancient customs'. Roman law had 'great influence in Scotland, except where our own express laws or customs have receded from it', and, he went on, 'by the common law in our Acts of Parliament is meant the civil law'. For Mackenzie, it is clear, statute was the pre-eminent source of law. It is ranked first among the written sources and is used to justify the inclusion of the other examples of written law. So acts of sederunt are 'statutes made by the Lords of Session by virtue of a particular Act of Parliament', but 'are not properly laws, the legislative power being the King's prerogative'. Skene's collection, *Regiam Majestatem*, was 'called the old books of our law by many express acts of parliament'. Ancient custom was law because 'the tacite consent of king and people operates as much in these as their express concourse [i.e., in Parliament] does in making laws'; so adverse custom could have the effect of repealing a statute. But the decisions of the Lords of Session could only be 'considered as law' because the lords, although entitled to do so, seldom actually departed from them. And finally . . . Roman law was a source because it was described in statute as the common law of Scotland (Institutions I, i)."

Not all of the immemorial customs were derived from the usages of the indigenous community. W.D.H. Sellar has argued in the

Stair Tercentenary Studies (1981) that Stair's ancient customs, the common law of Scotland, were in great measure taken from the Anglo-Norman law of England. Other of our customs seem to have been derived from civil law. Nevertheless all of these immemorial customs have become part of our common law. As such they do not require to be proved in court. Custom used in this sense is no longer a source of new or unrecognised rules of law in Scotland.

B. PARTICULAR CUSTOMS

Since the 18th century particular customs whether local or general have not been recognised as rules of law unless it has been shown to the satisfaction of a court that the alleged customs possess certain identifying features. A custom must (1) be generally acquiesced in as having the force of law in the areas in which it is observed, for a substantial—though undefined—period of time. (2) It must be definite and certain and (3) fair and reasonable. (4) A custom cannot be inconsistent with legal principle. It will necessarily vary in some particular from the general rule of the common law—yet it must not conflict with a statutory provision or other fundamental rule of law. [*Walker Trs.* v. *Lord Advocate*, 1912 S.C. (H.L.) 12.] Clearly, custom used in this sense has a very limited potential as a source of new rules of law in modern times.

Erskine, *Institute*, I, 1, 44

"44. The most essential articles of our customary law are so interwoven with our constitution that they are notorious, and so require no evidence to prove them; . . . but where any later usage which has been gradually gathering strength is pleaded upon as law, the antiquity and universality of that usage must be proved to the judge as any other matter of fact; for all customary law is founded on long usage, which is fact. No precise time or number of facts is requisite for constituting custom; because some things require in their nature longer time, and a greater frequency of acts to establish them than others. Neither is it necessary for this purpose, as some writers have affirmed, that the custom be declared by the previous sentence of a judge; for no court of justice can constitute law; and therefore any sentence declaring the customary law is of itself a clear proof that the law was constituted before."

Bruce v. Smith
(1890) 17 R. 1000

LORD JUSTICE-CLERK (MacDonald): "The pursuer in this case is the proprietor of lands in Shetland, who raises an action against certain fishermen and others for his alleged claim on the value obtained for a school of caaing whales which were captured on the sea-shore next to the property. He founds his action upon an alleged custom having the force of law by which the heritor where whales of this description are captured in this way has right to a certain proportion of their value . . .

Before going into the facts it is desirable to see what is the legal principle on which the matter is to be dealt with. There is no doubt that the customs of particular districts, though merely local, may have the force of law. But must not the custom, to have such force, commend itself as reasonable? Must it not be according to sound legal principle? Must the custom not conform to good reason and to justice? It may no doubt arise from the consent of the community in the locality, and in that case there is every presumption in favour of its reasonableness, and therefore in favour of its being in accordance with sound principle and justice. If a law-abiding community acquiesces in such a usage, it is not to be supposed that it is against principle and justice.

On the other hand, the custom may be the result of compulsion; it may be forced on an unwilling community. I question whether the mere existence of a custom is sufficient to establish its legality without regard to the circumstances in which it is found existing. The nature of the custom, the relations of those who benefit by the custom and suffer from it respectively, the position of power of the one party to enforce and the position of feebleness of the other party effectually to resist, may all have a most important bearing on the question whether the custom is truly the outcome of a social *consensus*, or is, on the other hand, truly of the nature of an impost,—the result of a law made by one part of the community as against the other,—which the other could not effectively resist. My opinion is that no local custom can be proved to have the force of law merely by proof of its existence, unless it be either in itself consonant with the principles of justice, and demonstrably based on reasonable grounds, or be so plainly the outcome of the consent of the local community, as that there is an absolute presumption that, in the circumstances of the locality, it was a custom based on just principles.

In this case I think there can be no doubt that a custom is established. But nothing more is established. I find nothing in the evidence to shew that there is any basis of principle or of justice for the custom . . .

I cannot hold that such a custom is established as local law by its inherent reasonableness, and upon the facts I hold that it has not become local law by *consensus* of the community.''

LORD YOUNG: "I am not prepared to . . . admit a particular or local custom to govern outwith . . . those considerations of utility and expediency and also of good sense upon which all the local customs or admissions of them hitherto by our Court have rested.''

LORD RUTHERFORD CLARK: "That a custom may have the force of law is an obvious proposition . . . But it does not necessarily follow that every custom by the mere fact of its existence has legal force . . . [especially] where the custom is confined to a particular locality, and is different from, or it may be opposed to the general law . . . [W]e should not enforce a particular or local custom which consists neither with legal principle nor with reason, for if it do not it must be unjust."

[For a detailed consideration and critique of this case see "Sources of Law", *Stair Memorial Encyclopaedia*, Vol. 22, paras. 385–88.]

C. CUSTOM AS COMMUNITY PRACTICE

Today custom is most commonly relied on as a source of law in a third sense, namely taking account of the practice of a trade or profession. In this sense custom is only a secondary source of law since the recognition of the usage depends on other common law rules. Typically such usages are founded on for assistance in the interpretation of a contract between individuals engaged in a particular trade. In such cases it is alleged by one party that the usage is so universally accepted in that trade, that in the absence of express words in the contract to the contrary, the contract and the usage should be read as one. As with particular customs such usages need not be known to the other party but must meet certain criteria. Thus, they must be (1) universally or widely accepted within the trade; (2) definite and certain; (3) reasonable; and (4) not inconsistent with the terms of the contract.

Hogarth & Sons v. Leith Cotton Seed Oil Co.
1909 S.C. 955

The pursuers owned a ship which was carrying a mixed cargo from Bombay to Leith for delivery to a number of different consignees. On the ship's arrival at Leith the owners in order to save time and money delivered the cargo into shed rather than over the side to the individual consignees. The consignees refused to pay the extra charges necessitated by this mode of delivery. The shipowners then sued for the charges asserting that it was the custom of all ships discharging mixed cargoes at Leith to deliver them into shed.

LORD ARDWALL: "A custom of trade must have quite as much certainty as the written contract itself. The reason of this is evident; if the custom is not definite, it is not possible to say what is the term which is to be held to be incorporated in any individual contract. But in this case the uncertainty does not end with the description of the class of cargo to which the alleged custom is to apply. It also extends, according to the proof, to the amount or proportion of charges to be paid . . .

But in the second place, a usage or custom of trade will not be admitted to add to or explain a contract unless it can be shewn to be uniform and universal in the trade to which it relates, and so notorious that both parties to the contract must either have known or be held to have known of it. Now, I agree with the Lord Ordinary that this has not been made out by the pursuers with regard to the alleged custom . . . In the present case, it is noticeable that not a single Leith merchant is brought by the pursuers to say that he is aware of the alleged custom, while, on the other hand, the defenders adduce a number of well-known Leith merchants and manufacturers as witnesses who say that they never heard of the custom alleged by the pursuers . . .

Accordingly, I consider that on the evidence that has been led in this action it has not been proved that the practice alleged by the pursuer is either uniform, universal, or notorious.

In the third place, I am of opinion that the alleged custom is contrary to the contract between the parties, and therefore cannot be given effect to in the present case, even supposing it had been otherwise proved."

[The shipowners were unsuccessful in the action.]

Wilkie v. Scottish Aviation Ltd.
1956 S.C. 198

The pursuer, a chartered surveyor, was employed by the defenders under a contract which made no reference to his remuneration. His account was feed in accordance with the schedule of charges issued by his professional body but the defenders refused to pay for his services at these rates. The pursuer sued for his fees alleging that remuneration on the basis of the schedule was customary and should therefore be deemed to be an implied condition of the contract.

LORD PRESIDENT (Clyde): "To establish a custom . . . of this kind the evidence must show that it is reasonable, certain and notorious . . . To establish the custom it is not essential to prove that the defenders actually knew of it. It is enough if it was so well recognised that it ought to have been known to both parties . . . There is, after all, nothing inequitable in such a requirement. If a person employs a professional man to perform some service and makes no inquiry as to the basis upon which the professional man is to be remunerated for the service, it is not unreasonable that he should pay for the service on the usual and customary basis. It is not open to him to complain that he is unaware of it, if he has never even taken the trouble to ascertain it before engaging another to do work for him without specifying a precise fee."

In discussions of custom it is sometimes overlooked that the practice of a profession or a community can be taken account of in delict as well as contract. The standard of care required of a professional man in negligence cases is highly dependent on the practice of that profession provided it is generally followed, clear, reasonable and not illegal.

[For a more comprehensive and perhaps controversial account of legal custom in Scotland see T.J. Cameron, "Custom as a Source of Law in Scotland" (1964) 27 M.L.R. 306 and "Sources of Law", *Stair Memorial Encyclopaedia*, Vol. 22, paras. 355–93.

III. EQUITY

Equity as a legal term has several meanings. In Scottish legal writings it has been used to denote two different aspects of justice, "justice as equality" and "justice as fairness".

Stair, *Institutions*, I, 1, 6

"6. [The] law of nature is also called Equity, from that equality it keeps amongst all persons, from that general moral principle . . . whereby just persons in their deliberations and resolutions state themselves in the case of their adversaries, and so change the scales of the balance; which holds most in commutative justice. So parents in the duties of children ought to consider, as if their children were their parents, and what in that case they would do to them: and children in their obedience ought to yield all to their parents that they would demand, if they were their children. But equity is also taken for the law of rational nature . . . whereby the common interest of mankind is preferred to the interest of any part of men; whereas vicious self-love preferreth the interest of a part to the interest of the whole."

Walker, "Equity in Scots Law," pp. 105–106

"General rules of law take no account of the circumstances of individual cases where their generality may work injustice . . . Likewise human foresight cannot provide against all eventualities where a wrong may require a remedy, and in such cases it is sometimes necessary to go beyond the law or even contrary to the strict letter of the law, and to administer justice in accordance with the dictates of natural reason. So far as a tribunal can supplement or reject rules of law in special cases by admitting pleas founded on reason and justice it is a court of equity as opposed to a court of law and it is in this sense . . . that the Court of Session is a court of equity as well as of law."

Both these usages must be distinguished from the more specific use of the term in England to denote the body of legal rules and principles formerly administered by the Court of Chancery, as contrasted with the common law.

Gibson's Trs.
1933 S.C. 190

LORD PRESIDENT (Clyde): "Owing to its peculiar history the law of

Scotland has never known either distinction or conflict between common
law and the principles of equity. It is often said, and truly said, that in the
law of Scotland law is equity, and equity law; and when a Scots lawyer
uses the expression common law, he uses it in contradistinction to laws
made by Parliament."

[On the historical reasons why a separate equitable jurisdiction
never arose in Scotland, see D.M. Walker, "Equity in Scots Law",
1954 J.R. 103.]

Walker, "Equity in Scots Law," pp. 145–147
"There is overwhelming evidence that the Court of Session has always
been regarded as a court both of law and of equity. In numerous branches
of Scots law the basis or justification of the rule in observance has been
ascribed to 'equity,' 'natural justice,' 'substantial justice,' 'reason and
justice' and similar phrases, and . . . there are repeated acknowledge-
ments of this fact in judgments and the most authoritative text-writers.
There is not, and never has been, any separate jurisdiction in equity in
Scotland, and consequently equity and the equitable do not refer almost
exclusively, as in England, to the subjects which belonged to a particular
jurisdiction. On the other hand it is equally manifest that equity and the
equitable in Scottish practice do mean that which is fair, reasonable, and
naturally just . . . Numerous subjects . . . are equitable in their nature
and basis but are administered in and through and as part of the common
law.

Of the subjects falling within the ordinary equitable jurisdiction . . .
many have their roots in Roman law; one or two, such as the law of
trusts, have derived something from the equity of the Chancery; in many,
Chancery authority has been referred to with respect, and it is particularly noteworthy how many of the topics of Scottish equity have their
counterparts in Chancery equity. Substantially every topic dealt with in a
modern English textbook on equity not only has a Scottish counterpart,
albeit under a different name, but a counterpart which has been considered to be founded on equity and natural justice.

Examination of the subject today gives strong support to Kames's
contention that 'many actions, founded originally on equity, have, by
long practice, obtained an establishment so firm as to be reckoned
branches of the common law.' This is abundantly true today when every
branch . . . is applied in accordance with fairly settled rules and takes
account of precedent. The submergence of fundamentally equitable pleas
in common law actions has contributed to the neglect by Scottish judges
and text-writers of the existence of equity. So, too, many pleas, originally
reserved to the equitable powers of the Court of Session, have been
extended by statute to inferior courts.

With the increasing extent to which law is made and modified by
legislation and the extent to which doctrines of law and equity have
become settled, it rather appears that the creative function of equity in

Scots law is ended. No substantial new doctrine or change in common law seems now possible, save by statute."

As Walker's essay shows, equity as a source of law in Scotland is a testimony to the perceived importance of "justice as fairness" in the eyes of the Scottish legal profession over the centuries. For this very reason Walker's pessimistic assessment that equity is now past the age of childbearing in Scotland, seems unjustified. Judicial attempts to evade the binding chains of precedent (see Chapter 14 above) attest to the continuing force of equity today. Moreover, equity is an important secondary source of law, for in a number of fields judges are required by statute and the common law to pay heed to equitable considerations, or to pursue the lodestar of "just and equitable" or "fair and reasonable" solutions. [For an informed discussion of equity in Scots law see "Sources of Law", *Stair Memorial Encyclopaedia*, Vol. 22, paras. 394–425.]

THE NOBILE OFFICIUM

The precise historical relationship between the *nobile officium* of the Court of Session and the High Court of Justiciary and the ordinary equitable jurisdiction of the courts is obscure. Many of the matters referred to by Stair as pertaining to the *nobile officium* are now treated as part of the general equitable jurisdiction of the courts or of the common law. Some have even argued in the past that the two jurisdictions are not really separable. Nevertheless the modern view is that a clear distinction should be drawn between the special or extraordinary equitable jurisdiction of the Court of Session and the High Court of Justiciary (their *nobile officium*) and their general or ordinary equitable jurisdiction.

1. THE NOBILE OFFICIUM OF THE COURT OF SESSION

The Royal Bank of Scotland v. Gillies
1987 S.L.T. 54 at p. 55

LORD JUSTICE-CLERK (ROSS): "The *nobile officium* has been defined as an extraordinary equitable jurisdiction of the Court of Session inherent in it as a supreme court; it enables it to exercise jurisdiction in certain circumstances which would not be justified except by the necessity of intervening in the interests of justice. Although the court tends to limit the exercise of its jurisdiction under the nobile officium to cases in which the power has already been exercised, it is neither possible nor desirable to define exhaustively or comprehensively all the circumstances in which resort may be had to the nobile officium."

[See also Maxwell, *The Practice of the Court of Session*, (S.C.A.: 1980) at p. 127.]

London and Clydeside Estates v. Aberdeen D.C.
1980 S.C. (H.L.) 1

LORD KEITH: "It was suggested that recourse might be had to the nobile officium of the court. I regard that suggestion as entirely misplaced. The nobile officium does not exist to deal with matters of disputed right. Its chief object is to provide a means of rectifying obvious errors or omissions, principally of an administrative character, which cannot be dealt with in any other way."

The *nobile officium* has been exercised under three main heads:

1. Application by petitions not founded on statute, *e.g.* for the appointment of judicial factors or public officers *ad interim* where the incumbent official is ill or has died. New remedies where no other means are available can be granted under this head. Thus in *Solheim Petitioners*, 1947 S.C. 243 the widows of three Norwegian seamen who had been buried in Scotland during the Second World War successfully petitioned the court for authority under its *nobile officium* to disinter the bodies and to transport them to Norway for reinterment in the family burial grounds.

2. Equitable jurisdiction with relation to charitable trusts particularly their variation through cy-près schemes.

3. Rectifying omissions in statutes or deeds, or curing procedural deficiencies which have arisen through inadvertance, and for which the statute provides no remedy. (The Bankruptcy and the Licensing Acts seem to be the worst culprits under this head.) If the omission is thought to have been deliberate the court will not exercise its *nobile officium*.

Maxwell, *The Practice of the Court of Session*, p. 127

"With regard to statute, the following principles may be said to be settled. Where a matter depends entirely on the construction of the words of a statute, there cannot be any appeal to the *nobile officium*; and it cannot be used to extend or derogate from the provisions of a statute. It is, however, available to parties to meet a *casus improvisus* in a statute; and where the intention of a statute is clear, but the machinery required for carrying out that intention is lacking, the *nobile officium* can under special circumstances be invoked to provide the necessary machinery."

Roberts, Petitioner
(1901) 3 F. 779

The Bankruptcy (Scotland) Act 1856 required that before discharge a bankrupt should swear that he had made a full and fair disclosure and had not made any secret arrangements with his creditors. The petitioner having become of unsound mind was unable to make the declaration and without it the Act provided no other way for him to be discharged.

LORD PRESIDENT (Balfour): "This case is attended with some nicety, because it appears that the bankrupt has satisfied all the requirements of the statute, in so far as it is possible for a man mentally afflicted to do so. The sequestration was awarded as far back as 1894, and all the known estate has been got in and divided among the creditors, including certain estate which accrued to the bankrupt after the sequestration. In these circumstances the alternatives are either that the bankrupt shall never get his discharge, or that someone else shall make the declaration or oath required by . . . the Bankruptcy Act . . . in place of him, or that the Court should in the very special circumstances of the case dispense with that declaration or oath. It appears to me that the last-mentioned course is the proper one to follow."

[The court agreed to exercise its *nobile officium* to dispense with the oath.]

Ferguson, Petitioners
1965 S.C. 16

The petitioners discovered that their names had been taken off the register of persons entitled to vote because the registrar had been told they were dead. No remedy for the deletion was contained in the regulations. The court was persuaded to exercise its *nobile officium* by restoring the petitioners' names to the register.

[On the use of the *nobile officium* in Court of Session generally see McBryde and Dowie, *Petition Procedure in the Court of Session* (W. Green & Son: 1987), Chap. 18. and "Sources of Law," *Stair Memorial Encyclopaedia*, Vol. 22, paras. 426–431.]

2. THE NOBILE OFFICIUM OF THE HIGH COURT OF JUSTICIARY

While the Court of Session is reluctant to exercise its *nobile officium* except in situations where there is a precedent for it, the High Court of Justiciary until relatively recently has been reluctant to exercise its *nobile officium* at all.

Stoddart, "The Nobile Officium," p. 37

"Until recently the nobile officium of the High Court of Justiciary seems rarely to have been invoked since the time of the institutional writers . . .

Many of the circumstances enumerated by Hume and Alison in which the court exercised its nobile officium to fill gaps in the law have either been dealt with by statute or have vanished with the passage of time . . .

Hume was being over-optimistic when he envisaged that many other instances would occur with the development of the criminal law, for the power seems to have remained dormant for many years before Scottish criminal procedure became the creature of statute around the beginning of the present century. Even in modern times prior to 1966 only two cases on the nobile officium found their way into the law reports."

Anderson v. H.M. Advocate
1974 S.L.T. 239

LORD JUSTICE-GENERAL (Emslie): "As it is stated by Alison, *Criminal Law of Scotland*, Vol. II, in the well-known passage beginning on p. 23: 'Akin to the well-known nobile officium of the Court of Session, is a similar power enjoyed by the Justiciary Court, of providing a remedy for any extraordinary or unforeseen occurrence in the course of criminal business in any part of the country. This is an unusual remedy, not to be called into operation when any of the ordinary courts are adequate to the matter; but still abundantly established wherever no other means of extricating it appears . . . In short, the principle is, that wherever the interposition of some authority is necessary to the administration of justice, and there exists no other judicature by whom it can competently be exercised, or which has been in use to exercise it, the Court of Justiciary is empowered and bound to exert its powers, on the application of a proper party, for the furtherance of justice.' To the same effect is Moncrieff in *Review in Criminal Cases*, p. 264, who says 'In addition to its power of reviewing, the High Court of Justiciary as the Supreme Court in criminal matters has in respect of its nobile officium the power of interfering in extraordinary circumstances for the purpose of preventing injustice or oppression although there may not be any judgment, conviction or warrant brought under review.' These classical descriptions of the power have been accepted by this court as authoritative in all cases in which the scope of its power under the nobile officium has been called in question, and as the cases show, have been interpreted to mean that the power will only be exercised where the circumstances are extraordinary or unforeseen, and where no other remedy or procedure is provided by the law . . . We have only to add that the nobile officium of this court, and for that matter of the Court of Session, may never be invoked when to do so would conflict with statutory intention, express or clearly implied."

[See also *Macpherson, Petitioner*, 1989 S.C.C.R. 518 at p. 522.]

Wan Ping Nam v. Federal German Republic
1972 J.C. 43

The petitioner was accused of murder by the German government who sought his extradition under the provisions of the Extradition Act 1870. The Act provided the English remedy of habeas corpus where detention under the Act was challenged as illegal, but no Scottish remedy was provided.

OPINION OF THE COURT: "The answer to this question depends essentially upon the intention of the Act. In our opinion the intention that relief shall be available to all persons committed under s. 10 is plain. This we discover from the express reference to habeas corpus procedure in s. 11. In any event, we cannot decern in the statute any indication of an intention that persons committed by a sheriff in Scotland should be in any less advantageous position than those committed by a police magistrate in England. In these circumstances we are in no doubt that, the statute having disclosed the intention, this court has ample power to provide what the statute has omitted to provide, namely, the means of giving effect to that intention . . . In our opinion, the circumstances of this case to which we have drawn attention are, on any view, extraordinary and we are satisfied that in the exercise of the nobile officium this court may properly examine the allegation of injustice made by the petitioner."

The apparent similarily between the third head under which the civil *nobile officium* is exercised (see p. 000 above) and the criteria outlined in *Anderson* v. *H.M. Advocate* is misleading. Over 10% of the civil petitions to the *nobile officium* which are granted are the result of procedural errors or omissions on the part of solicitors (McBryde, 1978). The High Court of Justiciary takes a stricter approach to such cases.

Fenton, Petitioner
1982 S.L.T. 164

OPINION OF THE COURT: "The nobile officium . . . is the power of the High Court to redress all wrongs for which a particular remedy is not otherwise provided . . . The petitioner's complaint is not that the legislature has not provided a means whereby he could appeal against a refusal to grant interim liberation. His complaint is that the legislature has not provided him with a statutory remedy to appeal when he has failed to observe the strict time-limit which the legislature had imposed for the lodging of an appeal. In our view it is not for the court to exercise its power under the nobile officium simply because an accused or his legal advisers have been mindless of a statutory time-table. If it were otherwise the court could be flooded with petitions to the nobile officium. If the legislature intended that failure to obtemper a strict statutory time-table could be excused on cause shown, that could have been provided for in the statute, as is the case in other procedural matters. That was not done and there is no justification for considering that this was a casus omissus. A statutory procedure was enacted, and in the absence of any provision to excuse non-compliance, non-compliance is fatal. The exercise of the nobile officium should not be regarded as the kiss of life in such circumstances.

We are accordingly of the opinion that this attempt to invoke the nobile officium is not justified and we accordingly dismiss the petition."

MacLeod, Petitioner
High Court, September 1975, *unreported*

The petitioner had been convicted of two motoring offences. He appealed against sentence but due to an error on the part of his Edinburgh solicitors no appearance was made on his behalf when the case called and the appeal was dismissed. Although the solicitors accepted full responsibility for the error, the High Court of Justiciary refused to exercise the *nobile officium* to reopen the case.

[See also *Ferguson, Petitioner*, 1980 S.L.T. 21]

It seems that the High Court of Justiciary is prepared (in some cases) to exercise its *nobile officium* to correct judicial errors (see *H.M. Advocate* v. *Keegan*, 1981 S.L.T. (Notes) 35; *Rae, Petitioner*, 1981 S.C.C.R. 356 and *Ferguson* v. *P.*, 1989 S.L.T. 681) and sometimes also those of the prosecution (see *H.M. Advocate, Petitioner*, 1990 S.L.T. 798) but (unlike the Court of Session) not those of the petitioner's legal advisers. Such a policy runs the danger of not appearing to be reasonable or fair. However, for recent cases where an accused has benefitted from the *nobile officium* see *Campbell, Petitioner*, 1990 S.L.T. 875, *Welsh, Petitioner*, 1992 S.L.T. 903 and *Schiavone, Petitioner*, 1992 S.L.T. 1059.

INDEX

451